Collect and Record!

Collect and Record!

*Jewish Holocaust Documentation
in Early Postwar Europe*

LAURA JOCKUSCH

Oxford University Press is a department of the University of Oxford.
It furthers the University's objective of excellence in research,
scholarship, and education by publishing worldwide.

Oxford   New York
Auckland   Cape Town   Dar es Salaam   Hong Kong   Karachi
Kuala Lumpur   Madrid   Melbourne   Mexico City   Nairobi
New Delhi   Shanghai   Taipei   Toronto

With offices in
Argentina   Austria   Brazil   Chile   Czech Republic   France   Greece
Guatemala   Hungary   Italy   Japan   Poland   Portugal   Singapore
South Korea   Switzerland   Thailand   Turkey   Ukraine   Vietnam

Oxford is a registered trade mark of Oxford University Press in the UK and certain other countries.

Published in the United States of America by
Oxford University Press
198 Madison Avenue, New York, NY 10016

© Oxford University Press 2012

First issued as an Oxford University Press paperback, 2015.

All rights reserved. No part of this publication may be reproduced,
stored in a retrieval system, or transmitted, in any form or by any means, without
the prior permission in writing of Oxford University Press, or as expressly
permitted by law, by license, or under terms agreed with the appropriate
reproduction rights organization. Inquiries concerning reproduction outside the
scope of the above should be sent to the Rights Department, Oxford University Press,
at the address above.

You must not circulate this work in any other form
and you must impose this same condition on any acquirer.

Library of Congress Cataloging-in-Publication Data
Jockusch, Laura.
Collect and record! : Jewish Holocaust documentation in early postwar
Europe / Laura Jockusch.
p. cm.
Includes bibliographical references and index.
ISBN 978-0-19-976455-6 (hardback : alk. paper); 978-0-19-025932-7 (paperback : alk. paper)
1. Holocaust, Jewish (1939–1945)—Historiography.
2. Holocaust, Jewish (1939–1945)—Personal narratives—Europe—History and criticism.
3. Holocaust survivors—Europe—History. 4. World War, 1939–1945—Historiography.
5. Germany—History—1933–1945—Historiography. 6. Memorial books (Holocaust)
7. Collective memory—Europe. 8. Historiography—Europe—History—20th century. I. Title.
D804.348.J63   2012
940.53'18072—dc23   2012004841

Frontispiece: Poster, Central Historical Commission in Munich,
Spring 1947. Yad Vashem Archives M1P/689

To my mother, and in memory of my father.

CONTENTS

Acknowledgments ix
List of Abbreviations xiii
Note on Transliterations and Translations xv

Introduction: Early Chroniclers of the Holocaust: Jewish Historical Commissions and Documentation Centers in the Aftermath of the Second World War   3

1. *Khurbn-Forshung*: History Writing as a Jewish Response to Catastrophe   18

2. Writing French Judaism's "Book of Martyrdom": Holocaust Documentation in Liberated France   46

3. Writing Polish Jewry's "Greatest National Catastrophe": Holocaust Documentation in Communist Poland   84

4. Writing History while Sitting on Packed Suitcases: Holocaust Documentation in the Jewish Displaced Persons Camps of Germany, Austria, and Italy   121

5. Joining Forces to Comprehend the Jewish Catastrophe: The Attempt to Establish a European Community of Holocaust Researchers   160

Conclusion: History Writing as Reconstruction: The Beginnings of Holocaust Research from the Perspective of Its Victims   186

Appendix: Major Participants in the Jewish Historical Commissions and Documentation Centers   207
Notes   223
Bibliography   281
Index   309

ACKNOWLEDGMENTS

This book is the outcome of the fortuitous combination of two seminars I took as a graduate student at New York University: one on the historiography of the Holocaust, the other on Jewish Displaced Persons in postwar Germany. Laboring through the extensive reading list of scholarly works on the origins and implementation of the Nazi Final Solution, I was led to believe the conventional wisdom that systematic Holocaust research had begun only in the 1960s by professionally trained historians who were not survivors themselves. At the same time, a research paper for the course on Jewish Displaced Persons took me to the YIVO Institute for Jewish Research and its records on the institutions created by Holocaust survivors in Allied-occupied Germany. While getting my hands dusty in archival research, I discovered evidence that fundamentally contradicted the image conveyed by my reading list on Holocaust historiography. Namely, the records in YIVO's Displaced Persons collection suggested that just months after the liberation from Nazi rule, survivors organized grassroots initiatives to collectively document the catastrophe they had endured and witnessed. Not only did they gather extensive collections of perpetrator documents, they also set out to interrogate thousands of their fellow survivors on their diverse wartime experiences by using a broad array of complex questionnaires they had designed to comprehend this Europe-wide catastrophe. My wish to understand the contradiction I had encountered between the common historiographical narrative and archival evidence from occupied Germany, bolstered by the further realization that early Holocaust research by survivors had been a transnational phenomenon in postwar Europe, led me to this study.

This book would not have been possible without the support and assistance of numerous people. Above all I wish to thank David Engel, who taught both of the crucial seminars and served as my advisor on the doctoral thesis that was the genesis for this book. This study has benefited immensely from our challenging conversations and from his invaluable guidance on the craft of archival research and the techniques of historical interpretation. I thank him especially for the confidence he has shown in my work and in the importance of this topic. Sincere thanks also go to Hasia Diner, Marion Kaplan, and Atina Grossmann, who have been indefatigable mentors and generously offered constructive criticism, incisive editorial comments, and steady moral support. I am further obliged to Ron Zweig, who completed the dissertation committee and enriched my project with thoughtful questions and comments.

I owe special thanks to those who have supported me in Israel both as a graduate student and as a postdoctoral researcher: Yfaat Weiss, Hagit Lavsky, Dan Michman, Renée Poznanski, Gulie Neeman-Arad, Eli Lederhendler, Daniel Blatman, Dalia Ofer, and Hanna Yablonka. Beyond the United States and Israel, Annette Wieviorka, David Cesarani, Michael Berkowitz, Michael Brenner, and Dan Diner have provided valuable insights, critical questions, and encouragement.

Many colleagues read various sections of this book, but I would like to express my appreciation in particular to Elisabeth Gallas and Tamar Lewinsky for their astute comments on my manuscript. Many thanks also go to Natalia Aleksiun, Nicolas Berg, Boaz Cohen, Daniella Doron, Gali Drucker Bar-Am, Gabriel Finder, Alexandra Garbarini, Shirli Gilbert, Dana Herman, Klaus Kempter, Zeev Mankowitz, Joanna Michlic, Avinoam Patt, Simon Perego, Alan Rosen, Ada Schein, and David Weinberg for sharing their deep knowledge of the history of Holocaust survivors. Likewise, I am indebted to Lutz Fiedler, Helen Przibilla, Oded Davidovitch, Bärbel Buchelt, Henrik Langsdorf, Amy Lowenhaar, Beatrice Szameitat, and Alfred Kalmbacher for their continued assistance with the major and the minor questions related to this project.

The advantage of abundant historical records for the student of recent history is balanced by the drawback that many key documents have not yet found their way into the official catalogues of research institutions. Hence, I am infinitely grateful to Naomi Wulf and Annette Wieviorka for their help in paving the way to accessing the uncatalogued administrative records of the Centre de Documentation Juive Contemporaine in Paris and to Karen Taïeb for letting me use those resources. In addition, I want to thank the staffs of numerous other archives: the Center for Jewish History in New York, especially Diane Spielmann; the YIVO Institute for Jewish Research, New York; the American Jewish Historical Society, New York; Yad Vashem, Jerusalem; the Alliance Israélite Universelle, Paris; the Zentralarchiv zur Erforschung der Geschichte der Juden in Deutschland, Heidelberg, in particular Peter Honigmann; Stadtarchiv Göttingen; the Jewish Historical Institute in Warsaw; and the American Jewish Joint Distribution Committee Archives in Jerusalem and New York. I also thank Amir Feigenbaum and Shalom Eilati for allowing me to include their fathers' photographs in this book.

I am much obliged to those who helped me wrestle with the English language and with the editing of the manuscript: most heartfelt thanks go to Amy Hackett, who carefully and sensitively revised the text and provided invaluable assistance with the difficult metamorphosis of a dissertation into a book. I also owe thanks to those who assisted me with word choice and syntax at the dissertation stage, in particular Thomas McKean and Ben Kern. Małgorzata Maksymiak and Barbara Klein provided valuable help with translations.

At Oxford University Press, I wish to thank Nancy Toff for her determination to tackle this project. I am further indebted to Sonia Tycko, Rick Stinson, and Ben Sadock for navigating through the various stages from manuscript to book. I am particularly grateful for the erudite and perceptive comments I received from William G. Rosenberg and Francis X. Blouin Jr., the editors of the Oxford Series on History and Archives, as well as from the anonymous readers of the manuscript.

This study would not have been possible without generous financial support from the Graduate School of Arts and Science at New York University, the Memorial Foundation of Jewish Culture, the Center for Jewish History in New York, the Bucerius Institute for Research on Contemporary German History and Society at Haifa University, and the Vidal Sassoon International Center for the Study of Antisemitism at the Hebrew University of Jerusalem, the Kreitman Foundation at Ben-Gurion University of the Negev, the Minerva Foundation of the Max-Planck-Gesellschaft in Munich, as well as the Leo Baeck Institute in New York. My travel was made possible through the generosity of the Dorot Foundation and the Fondation pour la Mémoire de la Shoah in Paris.

Last but not least, I want to thank my mother, Vera Jockusch, to whom I owe far more than can be conveyed. I dedicate this book to her, and to the memory of my father, Peter Jockusch, whose inquisitive, unrelenting, and passionate love for research remains an inspiration. Finally, I thank my companion and husband, Omer Offen, for his unconditional support and true friendship.

LIST OF ABBREVIATIONS

AIU	Alliance Israélite Universelle
ACC	Archives of the Central Consistory during World War II, Maurice Moch Collection at the Alliance Israélite Universelle, Paris
ACDJC	Archives of the Centre de Documentation Juive Contemporaine in Paris
AJC	American Jewish Committee
AJDC	American Jewish Joint Distribution Committee
AJDCJ	Archives of the American Jewish Joint Distribution Committee in Jerusalem
AJDCNY	Archives of the American Jewish Joint Distribution Committee in New York
AJHS	American Jewish Historical Society
AYIVO	Archives of the YIVO Institute for Jewish Research in New York
AŻIH	Archives of the Jewish Historical Institute in Warsaw
BHTA	Archives of the Bialik House in Tel Aviv
CDJC	Centre de Documentation Juive Contemporaine (Center of Contemporary Jewish Documentation)
CKŻP	Centralny Komitet Żydów Polskich (Central Committee of Polish Jews)
CKŻP/KH	Archives of the Central Committee of Polish Jews, materials relating to the Central Jewish Historical Commission at the Jewish Historical Institute in Warsaw
CNRS	Centre National de la Recherche Scientifique
CRIF	Conseil Représentatif des Israélites de France, or Conseil Représentatif des Institutions Juives de France (Representative Council of the Israelites in France; Representative Counsel of Jewish Institutions in France)
CŻKH	Centralna Żydowska Komisja Historyczna (Central Jewish Historical Commission)
DPA	Displaced Persons Camps and Centers in Austria Collection at the YIVO Institute in New York

List of Abbreviations

DPG	Displaced Persons Camps and Centers in Germany Collection at the YIVO Institute in New York
DPI	Displaced Persons Camps and Centers in Italy Collection at the YIVO Institute in New York
ECC	European Coordination Committee (Comité Européen de Coordination)
FSJF	Fédération des Sociétés Juives de France (Federation of Jewish Societies in France)
HIAS	Hebrew Immigrant Aid Society
HICEM	Jewish emigration agency operated by HIAS in collaboration with the Jewish Colonization Association and Emigdirect
IMT	International Military Tribunal at Nuremberg
JA	Jewish Agency for Palestine
JHD	Jüdische Historische Dokumentation (Jewish Historical Documentation)
JHK	Jüdische Historische Kommission für Niedersachsen in Göttingen (Jewish Historical Commission for Lower Saxony in Göttingen)
JLC	Jewish Labor Committee
LBI	Leo Baeck Institute
MAG	Municipal Archives, Göttingen
MAGCO	Municipal Archives, Göttingen: Records of the Cultural Office
ORT	Organisation-Reconstruction-Travail (Professional Retraining and Reorientation Organization)
OSE	Œuvre de secours aux enfants (Children's Relief Agency)
PKWN	Polski Komitet Wyzwolenia Narodowego (Polish Committee of National Liberation)
PPR	Polska Partia Robotnicza (Polish Workers' Party)
TsHK	Central Historical Commission, Munich
UGIF	Union Général des Israélites de France (General Union of Israelites in France)
UNRRA	United Nations Relief and Rehabilitation Administration
WJC	World Jewish Congress
YIVO	Yidisher Visnshaftlekher Institut; YIVO Institute for Jewish Research
YV	Yad Vashem Holocaust Martyrs' and Heroes' Remembrance Authority
YVA	Yad Vashem Archives Jerusalem
ŻIH	Żydowski Instytut Historyczny (Jewish Historical Institute)
ZAH	Zentralarchiv zur Erforschung der Geschichte der Juden in Deutschland, Heidelberg (Central Archives for Research of the History of the Jews in Germany, Heidelberg).

NOTE ON TRANSLITERATIONS AND TRANSLATIONS

The transliteration of Yiddish words follows YIVO standards (unless Latin characters were used in the original). The transliteration of Hebrew words is based on the Library of Congress system. Geographical and political names are used according to contemporaneous usage and borders. Place names are used in the original language unless there is a common English usage, as with Warsaw rather than Warszawa. People are identified according to their most commonly used name at the time. All translations from the Yiddish, Hebrew, French, German, and Polish are my own.

Collect and Record!

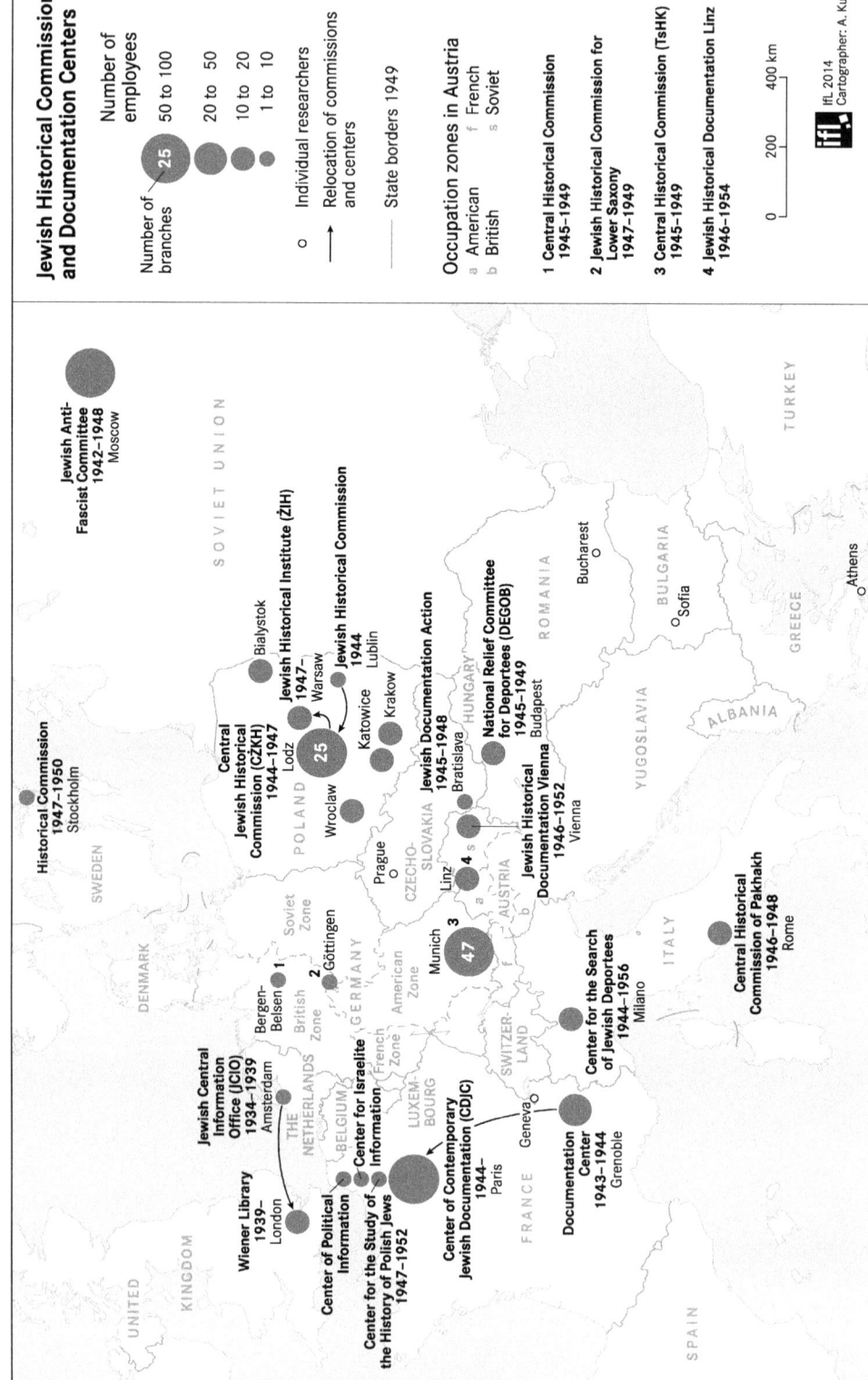

Introduction

Early Chroniclers of the Holocaust

Jewish Historical Commissions and Documentation Centers in the Aftermath of the Second World War

In December 1947 survivors of the Nazi genocide of European Jews gathered in Paris for the first European Jewish Holocaust conference.[1] Only two and a half years earlier, Nazi Germany had surrendered unconditionally, and it had been just over a year since the International Military Tribunal at Nuremberg had sentenced to death twelve central figures of the Third Reich's politically and military leadership. The Nuremberg court had established that among its innumerable and unprecedented crimes, Nazi Germany had murdered 5.7 million Jews, two-thirds of the Jewish population of Europe and one-third of Jews in the world. The thirty-two delegates from thirteen nations met under the auspices of the Center of Contemporary Jewish Documentation (Centre de Documentation Juive Contemporaine; CDJC), an institution created by French survivors to collect documents and prepare historical works on the cataclysm of their nation's Jews. The delegates represented various Jewish historical commissions and documentation centers which studied the fate of their own communities under German occupation. Their goal was to discuss how to comprehend and ultimately write the history of the traumatic events they had recently survived. Although these events are now widely known as the Holocaust, most of the survivors at the time used the Yiddish term *khurbn* (destruction) or referred to it as "the catastrophe" or "the cataclysm."[2]

Delegates came from Allied-occupied Germany and Austria, Sweden, France, Greece, and Italy. From across the divide that now separated Western and Eastern Europe, Poland, Romania, and Bulgaria also sent delegates, as did Great Britain, the United States, Palestine, and Algeria. Most delegates had personally experienced the Nazi genocide of European Jews, surviving only by the skin of their teeth. They had lost parents, siblings, spouses, children, and friends, and witnessed the destruction of their communities. After enduring rising levels of disfranchisement and discrimination, most of them had lived through ghettoization, deportation, internment in concentration and extermination camps, and forced labor. Others had joined armed resistance movements or survived in hiding or under a false identity.

"You were not only spectators of this terrible period: you lived it. You were not only present at the monstrous horrors committed by the Nazis: you suffered them." With this tribute Isaac Schneersohn, the charismatic founder and president of the Paris documentation center, greeted his guests when he opened the conference on the morning of December 1, 1947. "You are missionaries of the history of an epoch where mindlessness was the ally of barbarism, where the assaults of a different age provoked the magnificent rise of resistance, at first passive and then armed, in which many of us nobly participated. Delegates of the suffering of European Judaism, its combat, its superhuman moments of heroism, this is the title each of us deserves." Speaking directly to the occasion, Schneersohn lauded those gathered in Paris for assuming "the difficult . . . and onerous task of unmasking and decrying . . . the true face of the monster of Nazism" by collecting, preserving and organizing "materials of truth" as a testimony to the Jewish catastrophe.[3]

This first Holocaust conference truly embodied the urgent and indefatigable efforts by survivors across Europe to chronicle, witness, and testify. Immediately after their liberation from Nazi rule and with the end of combat, Jews in fourteen European countries founded historical commissions, documentation centers, and projects for the purpose of documenting and researching the recent annihilation of European Jews.[4] These initiatives of Jewish Holocaust documentation arose as grassroots movements impelled by the survivors' own will and with no government backing. Barely emerging from the compound trauma of the Holocaust, these survivors found themselves still living under materially and physically precarious conditions, and often on the move. Out of fear that the Nazis' efforts to destroy all evidence of their murderous crimes would condemn the Jewish cataclysm to oblivion before its full scope was even known to the world, activists in the documentation initiatives furiously collected every vestige of the past that they could get their hands on: thousands of documents and photographs left behind by the Nazis and their collaborating governments, along with diaries, letters, and other records from the Jewish victims, as well as artifacts and objects, songs, poems, and stories from an extinct Jewish world.[5]

These survivor documentarians also recorded the individual stories of other survivors in thousands of testimonies and questionnaires. In a war-torn Europe short of even such basic materials as pencils and paper, they often recorded these stories on unused stationary—emblazoned with Nazi emblems—abandoned by departing German military personnel and bureaucrats. Often of prewar vintage, this paper was superior in quality and durability to paper produced during and shortly after the war. The survivors' use of this paper symbolized the act of "turning the page" to a new era in which the survivors of genocide took revenge on their tormenters by registering the details of their crimes.

By collecting and recording traces of the lives and suffering of those who had been murdered, survivors mourned and commemorated their dead and created "substitute gravestones"[6]—to use anthropologists Jack Kugelmass and Jonathan

Boyarin's term—for those whose burial places, if any, were unmarked or unknown. In addition to preserving these materials in archival collections to nurture historical research in the near and distant future—and even as collecting continued— these documentation projects published numerous research guidelines, source editions, local and regional studies of ghettos and camps, memoirs, diaries, and historical periodicals featuring eyewitness testimony and the first synthetic works on the fate of the Jews in various town, regions, and camps. The conference in Paris was a united action by some of the main activists of the Jewish documentation initiatives to coordinate these efforts.

Among the conference participants was Dr. Joseph Kermisz, a Warsaw-trained historian who had survived the war in hiding in eastern Poland and in 1947 served as vice-director of the Jewish Historical Institute (Żydowski Instytut Historyczny; ŻIH) in Warsaw. The Institute had its origins in a historical commission formed in Lublin in August 1944, just five weeks after the city's liberation by the Red Army, when a handful of emaciated and traumatized survivors organized a historical commission for the purpose of chronicling the mass murder of three million Polish Jews. Several weeks later, the commission became the Central Jewish Historical Commission (Centralna Żydowska Komisja Historyczna; CŻKH), which in the spring of 1945 moved to Lodz and oversaw a countrywide network of local branches. By the fall of 1947, the CŻKH had collected more than three thousand survivor testimonies and several thousand pages of Nazi documents, along with diaries, memoirs, Jewish folklore, artifacts and photographs; the commission had also published thirty-nine scholarly works.[7]

Dr. Philip Friedman, an acclaimed historian of Polish Jews, had followed a different path to Paris from his former colleague in the Lodz commission. After losing his wife and daughter and surviving in hiding in his native Lvov, Friedman served as founder and first director of the CŻKH. However, in the summer of 1946 he left for the American Zone of occupied Germany in exasperation at the continued anti-Semitic climate and growing political pressure of the communist regime in Poland. He attended the conference in Paris in his capacity as the head of the Education and Culture Department of the American Jewish Joint Distribution Committee (AJDC) in Munich, where he lived as a Jewish Displaced Person (DP), waiting to immigrate to the United States. Friedman traveled to Paris in the company of his second wife, Dr. Ada Eber, who had also survived in hiding in Lvov and had been active in the historical commission in Lodz.[8]

Other former CŻKH affiliates at the conference represented historical commissions they had founded throughout Europe. Dr. Nella Rost, a journalist and scholar of literature and the daughter of a prominent rabbi and Zionist politician in the prewar Polish parliament, survived the Plaszów concentration camp and imprisonment in Krakow while losing her husband and teenage son. She became vice-director of the CŻKH's branch in Krakow, but in the spring of 1946 left Poland for Sweden, where she founded a historical commission in Stockholm under the auspices of the World Jewish Congress. Two of Rost's closest affiliates in Krakow were also present at the 1947 conference: the commission's director, the writer Michał Borwicz, who after escaping from the Janowska concentration camp in Lvov served as a commander of a socialist partisan unit; and its secretary, Joseph Wulf, a member of a Jewish fighting organization operating in the Krakow and Bochnia ghettos and a survivor of the Auschwitz-Birkenau extermination camp. Both men settled in Paris in 1947 and established a small research center on the history of Polish Jews. Moshe Yosef Feigenbaum, an accountant, worked for the CŻKH after surviving two ghettos in eastern Poland, escaping execution and deportation to Treblinka and hiding in a bunker in Biała Podlaska. Like Friedman, he left Poland for the American occupation zone of Germany, where in November 1945 he founded the Central Historical Commission in Munich. Feigenbaum, however, saw his time as a Jewish DP as a temporary transit stop on his way to a new life in Palestine. He traveled to Paris in the company of Menachem Marek Asz, a founding member and first secretary of the historical commission in Lublin and at that time the head of the Munich commission's branch in Frankfurt am Main.[9]

Delegates from Jewish DP groups in Austria included, most notably, the engineer Simon Wiesenthal, who headed the Jewish Historical Documentation in Linz beginning in early 1947. Born in Galicia in the Austro-Hungarian Empire, he had survived several camps and a period hiding in Poland before his liberation from Mauthausen by the U.S. Army. Towia Frydman, a survivor of the ghetto of his native Radom, escaped deportation and survived under false identity in Poland. In early 1946 he left for Austria, where he established a Jewish documentation center in the international zone of Allied-occupied Vienna. Both Wiesenthal and Frydman focused on collecting survivor evidence with the aim of hunting down former Nazis and bring them to justice with the help of the Allies.[10]

Other participants had escaped the Nazi orbit and begun documentation already during the war, most notably Dr. Alfred Wiener, the cofounder and director of the Jewish Central Information Office, or Wiener Library, in London. One of the leading repositories for Holocaust documentation, this collection had its roots in Amsterdam in 1934, where Wiener fled from the intensifying anti-Jewish policies of the Nazi regime. For Wiener, a German Jew who was an orientalist by training and a former high-ranking coworker of the German Jewish defense organization, the Central Association of German Citizens of the Jewish Faith, documenting Nazi anti-Semitic policies was an obvious countermeasure. After relocating his center to London in 1939, he spent the war as a refugee in Britain while gathering and disseminating information on the criminal nature of the Nazi regime.[11]

Other participants brought both geographic diversity and in some cases more particular interests to the conference. For example, Massimo-Adolfo Vitale, an Italian Jewish army colonel whose family had been deported, headed a tracing service in Rome which in the fall of 1944 had begun to compile information on Jewish deportees from Italy. The lawyer Dr. Asher Moissis headed the Council of

Jewish Communities of Greece in Athens; Dr. Mayer Halevy represented the Society for the Study of Romanian Jewry in Bucharest; and Elie Echkenazy served as director of the Jewish Scientific Institute, established in March 1947 under the auspices of the Central Jewish Consistory in Sofia, Bulgaria. Other foreign delegates were not survivors but Jews from Palestine or the United States representing the Jewish Agency for Palestine; the AJDC, which covered the costs for the meeting; and the American Military Tribunal at Nuremberg.[12]

Invitees from a number of organizations were thwarted by budgetary constraints or could not obtain valid documents to travel across a European continent still recovering from war and destruction that was now divided into a patchwork of occupation zones controlled by increasingly antagonistic forces. Among the missing were the Jewish Documentation Action in Bratislava, the documentation department of the Central Board of Hungarian Jews in Budapest, the Society of Jewish Historical Studies in Geneva, and the incipient Israeli memorial and archive Yad Vashem in Jerusalem. One invited guest, the Lithuanian-born writer and teacher Israel Kaplan, director of the Central Historical Commission in Munich, himself a survivor of the Kovno and Riga ghettos and a death march who had been liberated near Dachau by the U.S. Army, canceled his trip at short notice because he deemed the train ride to Paris unsafe at a time when France was experiencing violent workers' strikes and riots that had particularly affected trains, leaving dozens of dead.[13]

Not surprisingly, conference host CDJC—free from such concerns as travel expenses and visas—dominated the proceedings. Presiding over the event was CDJC director Isaac Schneersohn. Born in the Russian Empire, a descendent of the founder of Lubavitch Hasidism, he immigrated to France after World War I and become a successful entrepreneur. In 1943 Schneersohn founded a clandestine Jewish documentation center in Grenoble; however, the actual documentation work began only after liberation in 1944, when he reconstituted the center in Paris and became its director. By the conference's opening, the center had already published ten scholarly works on the Jewish cataclysm in France. Schneersohn was supported by his long-term collaborators, the French Jewish writer Henri Hertz and the Romanian-born lawyer and the center's secretary Marcel Livian, in addition to the Russian-born lawyer and journalist and the CDJC's research director Léon Poliakov, all of whom had survived the war in the south of France. Delegates from other French Jewish organizations included Léon Meiss, a renowned lawyer and president of the Consistoire Centrale, and Eugène Weil of the Alliance Israélite Universelle.[14]

The delegates who met in Paris, like the perhaps one to two thousand Jewish women and men who worked for the Jewish historical commissions and documentation centers throughout Europe, were dissimilar in their educations, nationalities, and class status, as well as in their wartime experiences.[15] Despite their various nationalities, most were Jews of eastern European, particularly Polish, origin. By and large untrained in the historical profession—Philip Friedman and Joseph Kermisz were two notable exceptions—these activists were lawyers, accountants, teachers, writers, journalists, and engineers who—as witnesses—sensed that they had a moral duty to document the past. They saw the fact of their survival as an obligation to bear witness for the sake of the dead and future generations and for their own posttraumatic recovery, since their historical research let activists "work through" the past and helped them separate the here and now from the traumatic events of the then and there.[16]

The Paris conference gave delegates an unprecedented opportunity to relate their wartime and postwar experiences and to hear about what Jews in other countries had endured in the recent war. They could also begin to assess ongoing documentation efforts and discuss crucial questions that arose in the course of collecting and recording the Jewish cataclysm, most basically: What distinguished the Holocaust from previous traumatic events in the history of the Jews—indeed, in the history of humankind? Was it the number of victims, the geographical scope of the onslaught, or the means of its execution? Which sources would provide the most reliable foundation for this recent history: documents created by the German murderers and their collaborators or by their victims? If the former, how should survivor historians deal with the Germans' use of euphemisms and codes to obfuscate their genocidal intent and their conscious effort to destroy any paper trail? The Nazis' efficiency in achieving their goal of erasing the traces of a people and its culture made the collection of Jewish sources even more daunting.

If survivors were to create their own records, what strategies would quickly assemble the largest and most representative collection of testimonies while inherently fallible memories were still vivid? And could a history of the Jewish cataclysm even be written so soon after the events? Or should the activists see themselves as archivists, urgently scooping up every scrap of paper left behind by the perpetrators and their victims and swiftly recording as many vivid memories as possible, while leaving the analysis of those materials to the longer perspective of future historians? Moreover, should the activists focus primarily on providing a foundation for systematic historical scholarship, whether sooner or later, or should their work serve more practical and immediate ends, such as the prosecution of war criminals or the fight against anti-Semitism and fascism? Finally, on the most practical level, where should the physical products of all this international labor ultimately reside—in a sovereign Jewish state in Palestine, whose creation had been approved by the United Nations at the eve of the conference, or in Europe, where the catastrophe had taken place and where most of its survivors currently lived?

While the conference delegates found no conclusive answers to these questions when they met in Paris, the significance of the early postwar Jewish efforts to document and research the mass murder of European Jews cannot be overestimated. This vibrant and widespread activity belies the supposed silence of Holocaust survivors about their traumatic experiences in the immediate wake of the catastrophe. Indeed, in the first five years after the war they demonstrated the energy, determination, and skills that enabled them to begin actually writing their history. In doing so they touched upon the major phenomenological and methodological problems that have preoccupied Holocaust researchers until the present day.

For the first time, these commissions and documentation centers raised questions regarding the origins and implementation of the Final Solution and the role of racist ideology and anti-Semitism in Nazi anti-Jewish policies. They considered the "singularity" of the Holocaust compared to both earlier catastrophes visited on the Jewish people and the effects of the Nazi regime on other national, ethnic, religious, and political groups. They already saw the need for comparative studies of Nazi policies in various countries, not only because the Holocaust had affected Jews across Europe but also because they understood the conundrum that although the Nazis pursued a global genocidal scheme, its implementation differed from country to country, as did the experiences of the Nazis' primary victims. From the outset, the Jewish historical commissions and documentation centers dedicated significant attention to the study of Jewish behavior in the face of Nazism. Their nuanced understanding of the concept of resistance went beyond the taking up of arms in order to consider those actions that aimed to save Jewish lives, perpetuate Jewish culture, and thwart German genocidal plans. At the same time, survivor documentarians examined the controversial roles of the Jewish leadership and the issue of collaboration. From a similar nuanced perspective, they addressed the ambivalent roles of non-Jewish bystanders, whom they described less as passive onlookers than as either collaborators with the Nazis or as helpers and rescuers of Jews (and sometimes both).

These documentation efforts maintained an intensely self-reflective discourse on the methodological challenges of representing the Holocaust in historical narrative. Internal debates raised problems of subjectivity, emotional preoccupation, and ideological bias, as well as questions about intended audience, reception, and the function of history writing in Jewish and non-Jewish society. The survivor documentarians introduced methodological innovations that would enter the academic study of the Holocaust only decades later, in the 1980s and 1990s. Most notably, they pioneered the development of a victim-focused Holocaust historiography that used both perpetrator as well as victim sources. While they clearly saw a problem in writing the history of the Nazis' victims exclusively on the basis of perpetrator sources, which altogether concealed or misrepresented the behavior and experiences of the victims, they introduced the use of various kinds of ego-documents from the Jewish victims, i.e., historical sources which intentionally or unintentionally reflect the life stories, experiences, and self-perceptions of their creators, as diaries, letters, autobiographies, and memoirs, along with testimony drawn from survivors' memories. The survivors active in the historical commissions and documentation centers were aware, however, that such sources had value for historical research only if collected in a critical mass; moreover, such testimonies must be matched and read against each other and further placed in context with perpetrator documents.

In compiling victim sources, the commissions and documentation centers applied social science–oriented research methods to prepare comprehensive questionnaires and careful instructions to guide interviews. But the commissions' concept of victim sources did not end with questionnaires and testimonies; rather, it also included "folklore"—poems, songs, legends, stories, jokes, and idiomatic expressions from ghettos and camps—sound recordings, images, artifacts, and material objects. From such materials the documentation initiatives sought to write the history of everyday life and death—or *Alltagsgeschichte avant la lettre*—of European Jews at the hands of the Germans and their collaborators, placing major emphasis on socioeconomic and cultural aspects. Not least, through their indefatigable efforts to retrieve any evidence pertaining to the persecution of European Jews left behind by the Germans and their collaborating governments, the documentation initiatives stockpiled extensive archival collections that formed the basis for the major Holocaust archives, museums, and research facilities in Europe and Israel that have provided an institutional structure for subsequent research.

At the Margins: Jewish Holocaust Documentation in Historiographical Perspective

The public attention large-scale testimony projects have received and the abundance of historical research and scholarly publishing on the Holocaust in later decades have ironically rendered these early postwar initiatives virtually invisible. In the 1970s and 1980s, as historian Annette Wieviorka has shown, the overall political climate and the emergence of social history created a general "craze for ethnological 'life stories'"[17] that brought with it both a willingness to listen to the persecuted, the excluded, and the voiceless and a democratization of the concept of historical actors and agents, giving rise to what Wieviorka called the "era of the witness."[18] Historians, scholars of literature and psychology, film makers, and artists—as well as a broader public—took a growing interest in survivors as "bearers of history," as they realized that the generation that had experienced and witnessed these events would soon disappear. With them would be lost what literary scholar Lawrence L. Langer termed "deep memory"[19]—recollections of traumatic experiences that only the survivors possessed and which could not be passed on to future generations.

This focus on victims and witnesses yielded several large-scale documentation projects aimed at recording "collectively endured history"[20] through audio and videotaped eyewitness testimonies relating the Holocaust from the vantage point of its victims. These projects included the Fortunoff Video Archive at Yale University, founded in 1981, the Shoah Visual History Foundation, launched in 1994 on the initiative of Steven Spielberg, the testimony collections of Yad Vashem in Jerusalem, and the United States Holocaust Memorial Museum in Washington, DC, along with many smaller interview programs by museums and memorials. That these projects took shape some four to five decades after the events appeared unavoidable, because, as historian Dominick LaCapra suggested, "testimonial witnessing typically takes place in a belated manner, often after the passage of many years."[21] Similarly, literary critic Geoffrey Hartman, cofounder and then project director of the Fortunoff Archive, described the processes leading to the inception of the project as the realization by those who were not survivors that the time had finally come "to allow survivors to speak for themselves,"[22] while the survivors, in this case primarily those who had relocated in North America, showed a readiness to communicate their experiences. Socially secure and mindful of their grandchildren, they realized that "now if ever was the time to talk."[23]

As scholars sought to capture survivors' voices, they saw the promise of a valuable new understanding of the Holocaust. They began to reconsider the hierarchy of sources dominant in Holocaust historiography since the 1960s, one that elevated "objective" sources created by and focusing on the perpetrators over the "subjective" voices of the victims. The use of survivor testimony to supplement perpetrator documentation put German actions into full perspective and allowed for a deeper understanding of victims' responses to unfolding events.[24] In questioning the dichotomy between history and memory—or historian and witness—scholars also began to understand that testimony could reveal how memory served to enable survivors to come to terms with the past. This, in turn, led to an ever-growing body of literature on testifying by Holocaust survivors and on the interpretation of their testimonies.[25] The historical development of memory and the representation of the past became major themes in historical analysis as exemplified by the journals *History and Memory* and *Representations*, as well as a wealth of monographs.[26] Moreover, survivors' accounts of the Holocaust became a prime reference for broader theoretical debates on language, literary theory, aesthetics, truth, trauma, representation, and interpretation, which gained increasing currency in history, literary theory, and trauma research in the 1990s.[27]

This augmented attention to memory toward the end of the twentieth century left earlier Holocaust testimony projects largely forgotten and created the misconception that *all* testimony was belated and that survivors had initially kept their experiences to themselves. Already on the occasion of the Paris conference in 1947, Philip Friedman remarked that "hundreds and hundreds of people who in their entire lives have never mustered any interest in historical research, now, out of an irresistible inner urge, grab a pen to write." Rather than being "isolated cases of some kind of graphomania," these writers represented "a mighty social phenomenon."[28] Indeed, by the end of the 1950s the Jewish historical commissions and documentation centers had already collected some eighteen thousand written survivor testimonies and approximately eight thousand questionnaires.[29]

By comparison, the Shoah Visual History Foundation collected 52,000 testimonies (48,361 from Jews) in sixteen years, while the Fortunoff Video Archive gathered 4,400 testimonies over twenty-nine years.[30] A bibliography of Yiddish books and brochures about the Holocaust, compiled by Philip Friedman and Joseph Gar and published in New York in 1962 as a joint venture of the YIVO Institute for Jewish Research and Yad Vashem, gives ample evidence of the plethora of works written and published by Jews during the war and in the first decade and a half afterward. Of its total of 1,900 biographical entries, it lists 619 documentary descriptions, testimonies, and memoirs published by individual authors or various kinds of Jewish organizations, 550 of them describing the destruction of Jewish communities, towns, and cities and sixty-eight addressing specific camps and prisons. It also registers 295 books of poetry, 184 fictional works, and thirty-six plays, as well as twenty musical works. Not least, it catalogues 163 scholarly periodicals and yearbooks, thirty-five historical monographs, and twenty-nine treatises on the methodological problems of Holocaust research published by Jewish research institutes—among them historical commissions and documentation centers.[31] These early postwar Jewish achievements are all the more impressive given the challenging conditions of their genesis: extreme material shortages in countries devastated by war and collectors of documents, interviewers, interviewees, as well as researchers, who were not only traumatized by their experiences and, in the latter half of the 1940s, also uncertain of their most basic needs such as food, housing, and physical safety.

Few scholars have noted, let alone studied, this vast documentation activity in the wake of the war. Geoffrey Hartman acknowledged that there had been an "initial outpouring of narratives"[32] immediately after the liberation. Similarly, Raul Hilberg identified "two peaks . . . in the gathering of oral history information" from Holocaust survivors, the first occurring already the years 1944–1948, the second only in the 1980s and 1990s.[33] Saul Friedländer suggested that a few years after the war survivors had given in to the public silence over the Holocaust and entered a "period of latency"[34] that lasted for at least two decades, in which they kept their traumas as a private matter, although he conceded that "silence did not exist *within* the survivor community."[35] Michael R. Marrus in his 1985 book *The Holocaust in History* claimed that Holocaust historiography had awaited the perspective afforded by time—and in particular the catalyst of the 1961 Eichmann trial in Jerusalem. Marrus did note two surveys in the early 1950s, one by French survivor and documentation activist Léon Poliakov, as well as the collection of materials and "the establishment of institutes to house and study them. Little of this information reached the wider public, however, and historians outside a small circle of survivors tended to ignore the issue."[36] However, an in-depth analysis of the incentive, spirit, and history of these "initial outpourings" of Holocaust narratives as well as the formation of archives and research institutes by survivors is long overdue. This book is a first step toward rescuing from oblivion the vibrant story of the Jewish historical commissions and documentation centers and their protagonists.

The American historian Lucy S. Dawidowicz was the first to discuss the historical works of survivors in her survey of Holocaust historiography.[37] In 1981, she published *The Holocaust and the Historians*, a general-interest book that dedicated a separate chapter to the "survivor as chronicler" and placed the documentation projects on a par with the works of nonsurvivor and non-Jewish researchers in Germany, Great Britain, Poland, the United States, and the Soviet Union. Dawidowicz (then known by her maiden name, Schildkret) had personally encountered the commissions and their researchers in 1946–1947 as a fieldworker for the AJDC in Germany.[38] In 1988 and 1990 Yad Vashem published two conference volumes, one on the history of Holocaust historiography, the other on the rehabilitation of Holocaust survivors in the immediate wake of the Second World War, which also gave some credit to the early Jewish documentation projects, although they nevertheless remained a marginal and underresearched topic.[39]

Over the past two decades, two main developments in the fields of post-1945 European history and post-Holocaust Jewish reconstruction prepared the ground for a critical reappraisal of the early Jewish documentation projects. First, the increasing interest of historians (and the wider public) in the postwar period led to an ever-growing literature on the rebuilding of European societies and the role played by patriotic wartime myths, memories, and commemoration in this reconstruction process, as exemplified by Tony Judt's eight-hundred-page book *Postwar*.[40] By exploring sensitive issues of anti-Semitism and Nazi collaboration, some of those works—such as those by Jan T. Gross for Poland, Jeffrey Burds for the Ukraine, Henry Rousso for France, and Pieter Lagrou for western Europe—created fierce public debate in the respective countries and beyond and thus brought historical topics directly into contemporary politics.[41]

Second, historiography on the "surviving remnant," the *She'erit Hapletah*, in postwar Europe has begun to use the survivors' own archival records in an effort to understand how they saw themselves.[42] Thus scholars concentrated on the survivors' agency—that is, the extent to which they acted on their own volition rather than serving the objectives of external powers such as military governments and relief agencies. This research has begun to show that the survivors were not a demoralized, defeated, passive, and monolithic mass dependent on the Allied armies and international aid agencies, but rather were active players who on their own initiatives rebuilt their communities, reestablished their political representation, and built up a rich organizational and cultural life. By examining the diverse political allegiances and the varied wartime experiences, memories, and group identities of the *She'erit Hapletah*, historians have also refuted the image of the survivors as a monolith that was wholly and unequivocally committed to Zionism. New studies have also begun to examine the role of cultural activity, family, reproduction, and gender in the processes of postwar reconstruction.[43]

Further, historians have pointed out that survivors broke their supposed silence well before the early 1960s. Thus Israeli historian Hanna Yablonka speaks of a "silence that never was," and American historian Hasia R. Diner refers to a "myth of silence" in her study of American Jewish responses to the Holocaust.[44] In the context of postwar France, French-Israeli historian Renée Poznanski applies the term "strange silence" to the silence immediately after the liberation not of the survivors but of their surrounding society.[45] Annette Wieviorka has made a powerful case that Jews had an urge to testify about their suffering during and after the Holocaust, yet it was several decades until the non-Jewish world was willing to listen and give survivors public attention. Likewise, Zoë Vania Waxman has shown—by looking at works published in English—that Jews created a multifaceted testimonial literature as the cataclysm was unfolding and continued with even greater vigor thereafter.[46] A 2012 volume edited by David Cesarani and Eric Sundquist provides a first synthesis of the great variety of new research questioning the postwar silence on the Holocaust in the Jewish world.[47] Recent research on survivor communities after the war—such as works by Atina Grossmann and Margarete Myers Feinstein—has demonstrated that already from the moment of their liberation, survivors actively confronted and publicly commemorated their pasts, making those pasts an essential marker of their cultural, political, and social lives and identities. This research also rejected the notions of generic "victim" and "survivor" by attending to gender, social background, nationality, and ideological outlook as factors diversifying the ways in which survivors experienced loss and survival and related to their wartime experiences after the liberation.[48]

In the context of these developments, the early Jewish attempts to document and research the Holocaust have received increasing attention. Zeev Mankowitz's *Life Between Memory and Hope* in 2002 was the first study of the political, social, and cultural activities of survivors in postwar Germany to include a full chapter on survivors' attempts to write Holocaust history.[49] Orna Kenan's and Boaz Cohen's studies on the history of Holocaust historiography in Israel also addressed the phenomenon of historical commissions in Europe as a precursor of Israeli Holocaust research.[50] In his 2010 book *The Wonder of Their Voices*, literary critic Alan Rosen discussed the commissions when setting the contemporary context in which the American Jewish psychiatrist David Boder carried out his interviews with Holocaust survivors in France, Germany, Italy, and Switzerland in 1946.[51] Especially in the past five years, when the present study was already underway, several articles and monographs have examined early Holocaust documentation and testimony projects in individual countries, paying particular attention to some of the personalities involved in these projects.[52] Scholars have also begun to edit and analyze portions of the early testimonies collected by the commissions and documentation centers.[53] In 2008, the volume *Holocaust Historiography in Context*, edited by David Bankier and Dan Michman, an outgrowth of a conference on the occasion of Yad Vashem's fiftieth anniversary in 2004, brought together articles on various Jewish and non-Jewish research centers in Europe, the United States, and Israel. The volume also shed light on the seminal role of survivors in early Holocaust historiography.[54]

From the Margins to the Center: A Transnational Comparative History of Jewish Historical Commissions and Documentation Centers

These important contributions notwithstanding, *Collect and Record!* fulfills the need for a study that places the phenomenon of the early Jewish documentation initiatives at its very center and that, utilizing previously unexplored archival materials, investigates the motivations, goals, and research techniques at work, while also moving beyond one particular national framework.

A comparative analysis—the distinctive venture of the present study—is an imperative in several respects. As Israeli historian Shulamit Volkov observed, "Jewish history, having as its subject matter a typically diasporic people, is inherently transnational."[55] This holds especially for the *She'erit Hapletah*. Although the majority of survivors in one way or another acknowledged their belonging to a Jewish *nation* centered in a homeland in Palestine/Israel, they nevertheless were a *transnational* group in the sense that they represented a number of countries of birth, prewar residence, and citizenship, and were separated by political borders but linked through culture, religion, language, ideology, or their diverse experiences of victimhood, loss, and survival. Moreover, in seeking to rebuild their lives, they also formed a community on the move, whose journey traversed many countries and whose cultural, political, and philanthropic networks crossed national political borders. The fact that Jews in fourteen European countries responded to the Holocaust by recording these events and their own experiences reveals early Jewish documentation as a supralocal or transnational phenomenon.[56] Only a comparative analysis can fully grasp both its multinational dimensions and its distinct manifestations in particular national contexts and place the phenomenon of postwar Jewish Holocaust documentation within the larger context of Jewish history writing in the twentieth century.[57]

Five countries—France, Poland, Germany, Austria, and Italy—stand at the center of this comparative analysis. In each, survivors successfully undertook collective efforts to document and research their recent pasts. Equally important, these countries, distributed through western, central, and eastern Europe, exhibited significant differences in the level of persecution and the reconstruction of their respective Jewish communities. At one extreme, Poland lost 90 percent of its Jewish population and experienced total destruction of all communal and cultural foundations of Jewish life, whereas in France 75 percent survived, and most Jewish communal institutions remained intact. Most of the postwar Jewish populations in Germany, Austria, and Italy consisted of large numbers of Displaced Persons, who before the war had not been citizens or residents of these countries, and their presence remained transient and provisional as they sought emigration overseas.[58]

The timeframe of this study spans the years 1943–1953, beginning with the establishment of the Jewish historical commission in wartime France and continuing to the establishment by the Israeli parliament, the Knesset, of Yad Vashem—the "Holocaust Martyrs' and Heroes' Remembrance Authority"—in Jerusalem. By then, many of the early Jewish documentation initiatives had disbanded and bequeathed their materials to this new central Holocaust memorial and research institution. Meanwhile, the commissions in France and Poland went on to establish two major European research centers dealing with the history of the Jews under Nazi occupation.

In accordance with the general historiographical trend to examine the *She'erit Hapletah* from an inside perspective through their own source material, this study uses records produced by the commissions and documentation centers themselves, some of which had not been open to the public previously: their administrative archives, minutes of meetings, work reports, and correspondence; the private papers and memoirs of their main actors; and the publications of the documentation initiatives. In addition it relies on the Jewish press, as well as on sources related to individuals and organizations not directly connected to the documentation initiatives but which observed their activity, such as the American Jewish Joint Distribution Committee, the YIVO Institute for Jewish Research, and Yad Vashem.

In the context of these sources, the book explores a variety of questions: Why did traumatized survivors in war-ravaged Europe take on the painful task of documenting the catastrophe they had survived and witnessed? Who were the Jewish women and men involved in these projects, and what motivations and goals guided their work? What function did history writing serve as they sought to come to terms with survival, loss, and destruction?

What kinds of material did they collect in compiling their archival collections? What research methods did they develop to study a European-wide genocide which had exceeded all previous incidents of collective violence against Jews in terms of numbers of victims, method, intent, and geographic scope? To what extent did the survivors active in the Jewish historical commissions and documentation centers perpetuate a historiographical genre that had developed prior to the Holocaust, under the impact of other incidents of anti-Jewish mass violence?

How did they interact with the surrounding Jewish and non-Jewish populations? What forms of interaction did the commissions and documentation centers develop, and to what extent did they manage to step beyond the national contexts in which they worked to research and document the Holocaust globally and in comparative perspective?

What historical works did they produce, and which narratives of the recent past did they transmit? In what ways did the distinct political, social, cultural, and material conditions they found in their respective countries shape the ways in which they researched and wrote about the Holocaust? What was the outcome and lasting legacy of the survivor documentarians' ambitious efforts, and why did it take six decades for historians to turn their scholarly attention to the history of those early documentation initiatives?

The story that emerges from the chapters that follow, intriguing, unduly overlooked, and long-forgotten as it is, demonstrates that neither silence nor clamor characterized survivors' postwar encounters with the catastrophe they had witnessed, endured, and narrowly survived; it reveals that some reconstituted their lives around the unrelenting mission of inscribing the tragedy that had engulfed humanity and claimed the lives of two-thirds of European Jewry into the world's historical consciousness. This book seeks to retrieve their remarkable efforts from oblivion and establish their rightful place as the foundation stone for later historical writing on the Holocaust.

1

Khurbn-Forshung

History Writing as a Jewish Response to Catastrophe

Early postwar Europe witnessed an outburst of historical activity among survivors. According to a contemporary observer, Jews set up historical commissions and documentation centers to collect and record the Holocaust "at the very same moment when they opened the first public soup kitchens to cook thin little soups."[1] As suggested in the introduction, the activists grappled with complex questions concerning the goals, methodology, and ultimate usage of their documentation work. Although the Third Reich's Final Solution exceeded all previous Jewish catastrophes in its death toll, geographic extent, technology, and dedicated state resources, a number of pogroms in eastern Europe earlier in the twentieth century inspired comparable Jewish documentation projects. These earlier victims and witnesses of anti-Jewish mass violence also gathered eyewitness accounts and established archival repositories for their collections. They disseminated their material in publications depicting the events "from below," from the perspective of the victims, while highlighting the behavior of perpetrators, bystanders, and authorities.

In their quest to collect and record Jewish suffering during times of mayhem and wanton violence, they faced fundamental issues similar to those of their postwar counterparts: Whose sources would provide the most reliable foundation for writing a historical account of the atrocities—documents created by the instigators and perpetrators or those of their victims? What strategies should Jews use to assemble large numbers of testimonies and other victim sources, and how could they construct an objective picture of events out of the subjective accounts of individual victims? What would be the ultimate purpose of documentation—collecting evidence to bring those responsible to justice and to fight for Jewish rights and against anti-Semitism, or creating an archival foundation for future historical scholarship? Was documentation of an event after the fact a valid form of Jewish self-defense, and did it serve to preserve the memory of the victims?

Beyond these parallels, the earlier documentation projects provided a frame of reference—indeed, a model for the postwar Jewish historical commissions and documentation centers. Throughout their history, moreover, Jews had responded to bondage, persecution, collective suffering, and destruction by creating a literature comprising hagiography, poetry, liturgy, and fiction. Jewish culture thus displays a vibrant array of literary figures, archetypes, and tropes through which to comprehend destruction, commemorate the dead, and conceptualize suffering within a theological paradigm of sin and punishment, oppression and salvation. Texts such as the book of Lamentations, the medieval Crusade chronicles, the numerous accounts of the Chmielnicki pogroms of 1648–1649—the most famous being Nathan Nata Hannover's *Yeven Metsulah* (The deep mire)—are prominent examples of what American literary scholar David Roskies termed the Jewish "literature of destruction."[2] Traditional literary tropes and renditions of Jewish suffering gained particular currency during and after the Second World War, also among those who chronicled and researched the Holocaust.[3]

Yet, more than these ancient literary traditions, a distinct "historiography of trauma," a genre of historical documentation which had developed under the impact of anti-Jewish violence in the early twentieth century, guided the survivors in their mission to document the mass murder of European Jewry in its immediate aftermath. Best termed *khurbn-forshung*, Yiddish for "destruction research,"[4] this historiographic genre departed from previous literary accounts of collective Jewish suffering in its documentary and nonfictional character, its secular motivations and functions aiming at legal, material, and moral redress. Unlike the traditional Jewish "literature of destruction," where, as Roskies observed, "what was remembered and recorded was not the factual data but the meaning of the destruction,"[5] *khurbn-forshung* took the facticity of the wrongs most seriously. Its main endeavor was to establish, understand, and publicize their facts before teaching their lessons. Tracing the development of *khurbn-forshung* before and during the Second World War therefore serves as an instructive template through which to better understand the motivations, goals, and methods that guided people and organizations after the war in collecting and recording the evidence of the Holocaust.[6]

In the Maelstrom of Violence: The Origins of *Khurbn-Forshung*

On April 6–7, 1903, a vicious pogrom occurred in Kishinev, the multiethnic capital of the Russian Empire's Bessarabia Province, sparked by a ritual murder accusation in the neighboring town of Dubossary.[7] In response to the onslaught on the Jewish population of Kishinev (which totaled some 50,000, or 46 percent of the city's inhabitants), a group of Jewish intellectuals in Odessa—including Russian Jewish historian Simon Dubnow, Zionist essayist and editor Asher Ginsberg (Ahad Haam), writers Sholem Yankev Abramovich (Mendele Moykher Sforim) and the young Hebrew poet Chaim Nachman Bialik, and future Tel Aviv mayor

Meir Dizengoff—launched a call for self-defense.[8] By self-defense they meant both taking up arms and gathering data at the crime site to form the basis for an accurate historical report on what had happened. Convinced that they could not count on the tsarist authorities to bring the truth to light and the perpetrators to justice, they planned to disseminate this account to Jewish communities in western Europe, who—the Odessa group hoped—would use it to persuade their governments to apply diplomatic pressure on the Russian government to stop anti-Jewish violence and to take in Jewish refugees.[9]

The group dispatched the thirty-year-old Bialik to Kishinev to gather various kinds of evidence on the atrocities. While the recording of eyewitness testimonies from the Jewish population was central to his mission, Bialik's mandate included the collection of other kinds of material evidence to document the course of the pogrom, the social backgrounds and ideological orientations of its instigators and perpetrators, and the behavior of local bystanders, the authorities, and the Jewish community. Photographs could provide visual proof of the four dozen dead and 586 wounded, the 1,350 Jewish homes and close to six hundred shops destroyed, as well as the piles of desecrated ceremonial objects. From hospital visits, he should compile a detailed list of the patients and gather information from nurses and doctors on injuries, disabilities, causes of death, and cases of rape. Further, Bialik's assignment included registering the physical and material damage suffered by the Jewish population and estimating the sums required from Jewish relief organizations to rehabilitate the community.[10]

As a guideline for recording the experiences of individual Jewish victims, the Odessa group provided Bialik with a battery of questions. Beginning with personal data—age, profession, and social status, as well as where and how long a witness had resided in the city—Bialik was to ask his interviewees about local Jewish-Christian relations before, during, and after the atrocities, both witnesses' own experiences and what they saw in their neighborhoods; the rumors that Jews might have heard from Christians before the pogrom; whether witnesses had received shelter or other help from their Christian neighbors; and whether Christians they knew had participated in the violence, and—in case they were instigators—their names, addresses, and social status. Several questions asked interviewees to chronicle the events, differentiating between details they had directly witnessed as opposed to hearsay. Other questions aimed to elicit information on the response of the Jewish community, including individual and collective attempts at self-defense and whether witnesses had received material relief. A last set of questions assessed personal and property damage, from the pogrom's impact on witnesses' overall material situation to their psychological state, including their thoughts about the future.[11]

The Kishinev events were not the first pogrom in the Russian Empire. An era of anti-Jewish violence had begun in 1881–1882, following the assassination of Tsar Alexander II, when pogroms in the southern and western regions of the empire killed approximately fifty Jews, caused property damage of more than 9 million rubles, and made 20,000 Jewish families homeless. These events and those that followed prompted Jews to rethink their hopes of assimilating into Russian society and nurtured the growth of various alternative political ideologies, such as Jewish nationalism.[12] Why, then, did such innovative practices as using the memory of individual witnesses to document an event and the gathering of data, photographs, and other material evidence not arise before the Kishinev pogrom?

One important explanation for the post-Kishinev innovations is the influence of Simon Dubnow, in particular the methodological foundation for collecting and historical documentation laid in his programmatic essay "On the Study of the History of Russian Jews and the Establishment of a Russian Jewish Historical Society."[13] Written in Odessa in spring 1891 and published that November in the Russian Jewish periodical *Voskhod* in St. Petersburg, the essay responded to growing state restrictions on Jews, including the recent expulsion of Jewish artisans from Moscow and lingering fears of an Easter pogrom. Dubnow lauded western European Jews for establishing historical scholarship that followed modern "scientific" standards but took his own Jewish compatriots to task for their lack of historical knowledge and their careless neglect of historical documents. "Only among us, the Jews of Poland and Russia," he lamented,

> has the passion not arisen to expose the mystery of our past, to know who we were, how we got to our country, and how our ancestors have lived here from the beginning of their settlement in Poland eight hundred years ago. Sometimes my heart lets me believe that we lack all historical consciousness, like negroes, like the wild people of the desert who have no history at all, like gypsies who live all their lives in the present and have no future and no past.[14]

Dubnow, for whom Jews constituted a nation rather than a religious or kinship group, attributed major importance to history, believing that "historical consciousness" was the main factor in preserving Jewish identity: "It is this historical consciousness which has been imbued in us and sealed in our hearts for thousands of years and which renders us the firstborn of history, eternal and immortal among the nations."[15] Consequently, he called upon the Jews of the Russian Empire to understand the political and cultural significance of historical knowledge and begin systematic inquiry into their past. To that end he envisioned the founding of a central archive which, under the auspices of a "historical society," would amass a great variety of Jewish sources drawn from both the community's elites as well as from its rank and file, ranging from official records of communal institutions and associations to such personal records as letters, diaries, and account books.

Dubnow even demanded the collection of "oral sources," by which he meant personal recollections by the older generation on the everyday life and customs of their communities. These materials of Jewish provenance would be complemented by non-Jewish documents in state and community archives. Dubnow enlisted communal leaders as well as interested individuals from the wider Jewish public (although he only addressed men) to compile the materials in what he envisioned as a collective—indeed, national—effort:

> I appeal to all of you, come and join the camp of the builders of history! Not everyone who can read and write can be a brilliant writer or the chronicler of events, but every one of you can be a collector of material, an aide to building the edifice of Jewish history. The construction of history is a national cause, and therefore we are obliged to participate in this work—all those in the nation who can write, all those who understand a book and appreciate history.... Let us work together, let us gather all the remote sources from scattered places, and let us arrange them and make them known to the public and use them for building the edifice of history. Let us search and research![16]

Even as Dubnow upheld western European Jews as an example, his endeavor to include Poland and Russia within the field of modern Jewish historiography departed from the "scientific" conceptual and methodological approach of the predominantly German Jewish scholars associated with the *Wissenschaft des Judentums*.[17] While this historical school understood Judaism in terms of a religious denomination, Dubnow viewed Jewish history as national history. Raising Jewish historical consciousness through historical research and compiling an archive of primary sources constituted a national cause that would underwrite a new kind of secular Jewish identity. As the history of the Jewish *people*, Jewish history would use source material drawn from all segments of the community— from the intellectual elites to the simple man—not just the urban intellectual elites favored by historians in the West. A highly educated autodidact, Dubnow did not address an audience of university-trained scholars. He knew that Jewish history must be developed as a scholarly discipline, yet, unlike the German Jewish scholars, he believed that it should be "close to the people," not confined to an academic setting (which in any case remained barred to most Jews in the Russian Empire). Therefore, Dubnow advocated Jewish historical studies that were both scholarly and popular: they should be accessible to a broad audience; connected to the social, communal, and political issues of the day; and built on the active support of wide segments of the Jewish community.[18]

Dubnow's appeal elicited immediate and fervent responses from both the urban Jewish intelligentsia and the Jewish population of the Pale of Settlement.[19] In St. Petersburg, most notably, a small circle of intellectuals led by the lawyer, publicist, and communal activist Maxim Vinaver established the Ethnographic Historical Commission in 1892 under the auspices of the Society for the Promotion of Culture among the Jews of Russia (OPE), an organization founded in 1863 to further the acculturation of Jews in the empire. Dubnow's vision of a centralized administrative body became a reality in 1908, when the Ethnographic Historical Commission ended its affiliation with OPE and became the Jewish Ethnographic Historical Society.[20] According to historian David Fishman, Dubnow's essay "became the credo of three generations of east European Jewish intellectuals,"[21] including, we should add, those Jews who became active in the postwar Jewish historical commissions and documentation centers. Under the impact of continued and amplifying anti-Jewish violence and persecution, the historical practices that Dubnow had blueprinted in 1891 shaped the genre of *khurbn-forshung* that stood its first practical test in Kishinev but that also informed later Jewish documentation projects.

Bialik arrived in Kishinev four weeks after the pogrom and stayed for almost two months, recording the information requested, often hastily, in dozens of small- to medium-sized notebooks while translating all interviews on the spot from Yiddish and Russian into Hebrew, which he sought to promote as the Jewish national language and a lingua franca connecting Jews East and West. Assisted by a number of educated Kishinev Jews, among them the Hebrew teacher and writer Pesach Auerbach, he also used material compiled by the local Jewish community on material damage and expenses incurred in helping victims.[22]

By disseminating the truth about the Kishinev massacre, the Odessa committee sought to inspire Jews in western Europe and the United States to lobby their governments on behalf of Russian Jews. The vehicle would be *Sefer Kishiniov*, a Hebrew-language anthology that incorporated Bialik's material under Dubnow's editorial direction. Dubnow envisioned a three-part publication: an introduction that placed Kishinev in the context of the Russian situation and previous pogroms; a synthetic overview of the violence based on Bialik's work; and an appendix with eyewitness accounts, documents, pictures, and statistics. Dubnow asked Bialik to write the second part; an editorial committee in St. Petersburg would write the introduction, as well as "finish organizing the material and filter the essence from the irrelevant."[23]

The Kishinev anthology never saw publication. Bialik turned his full attention to completing "In the City of Slaughter" (*Ba-ir ha-haregah*), a formidable and shocking poetic rendition of the disaster which gave Kishinev an iconic status in Jewish memory.[24] But other factors appear to have been more decisive. In addition to lack of financial support and tsarist censorship, pogroms continued over the next three years on a scale that made the 1903 atrocity seem like a minor incident.[25] As against the forty-nine Jews who died in Kishinev, some 3,100 perished in the pogroms of 1905 and 1906.[26] Bialik and his collaborators soon concluded that the escalating violence against the Jews of eastern Europe demanded a more ambitious and longer-term project of historical documentation, one that covered violent outbursts in a number of places, using a larger team of researchers and the platform of an international Jewish organization.[27]

Such a possibility arose when the Cologne-based World Zionist Organization (WZO), responding to the pogroms that accompanied the revolutionary upheavals of 1905, commissioned Leo Motzkin, a Russian Jewish mathematician, Zionist politician, and publicist, to investigate the ongoing anti-Jewish violence in the Russian Empire. Funded by the London-based Zionist Relief Fund, which the WZO had established for pogrom victims, Motzkin followed the model of the Odessa Committee in collecting eyewitness accounts from local Jews, but did so on a much larger scale than Bialik in Kishinev. Motzkin's team of forty researchers, assisted by local staff and hundreds of volunteers, visited more than eighty-five places in the Russian Empire between December 1905 and July 1906.[28] With the goal of reconstructing events on the basis of "multiple descriptions and manifold eyewitness accounts,"[29] the group used a detailed questionnaire to collect a large number of testimonies from Jewish witnesses. The survey inquired about demographic and cultural traits of the respective community, historical events preceding the pogrom, the course of the pogrom itself, the behavior of the Jews, and the responses of non-Jews, i.e., local and central authorities, neighbors, bystanders, and other non-Jewish ethnic minorities, in addition to asking about the economic and demographic effects of the violence.[30] Although eyewitness accounts of the Jewish victims stood at the center, the researchers also collected documents of non-Jewish provenance, such as material issued by local governments, press accounts, and protocols of the Duma, to the extent that they were accessible.[31] Even though they sought to avoid the impression that they wanted to "amass an enormous amount of accusatory material against Russian society,"[32] the researchers faced difficult working conditions: local authorities and the police in some cities tried to ban the printing of the questionnaire, confiscated completed forms, or tried to arrest researchers, and parts of the collection were lost in the mail.[33]

Motzkin's study did not appear until 1910, mainly because he had decided to look backward and include all pogroms since 1881. The two-volume, 950-page study came out in a German translation under the pseudonym "A. Linden." Although originally written in Russian, *Die Judenpogrome in Russland*—published by the Jüdischer Verlag, the WZO's press—targeted readers outside the Russian Empire. The first volume gave a general description of pogroms between 1881 and 1906; the second volume featured case studies of individual communities in the Russian Empire affected by the pogroms of 1903–1906.[34] As Motzkin emphasized in his introduction, this survey of the pogroms' social and political causes and effects did not pursue a Zionist agenda but rather supported a broader Jewish cause: the "bitter fight of eastern European Jewry for human rights."[35] By publishing the magnum opus in Germany, Motzkin and his collaborators tacitly acceded to Russian censorship, while still making clear that they would use the documentation they had so assiduously collected in the international diplomatic arena.

The destruction which the First Word War brought to Jewish life in eastern Europe gave new impetus to the idea that Jews needed to gather evidence of their suffering. More than four million Jews lived in areas devastated during the years 1914–1918 as the opposing forces of the German/Austro-Hungarian alliance and the Russian Empire fought over territorial control in a war of constantly shifting frontlines. While all civilian populations in these areas suffered the lethal effects of this first "modern war" in terms of its geographic scope and arms technology, Jews also experienced anti-Semitic violence. Alleging collective disloyalty and treason, the Russian army subjected the Jewish populations in its own territory and in those it conquered from the Austro-Hungarian Empire (Galicia and Bukovina in particular) to mass expulsion and deportation from areas near the front, hostage takings and executions, and plundering, marauding, random violence, and rape, perpetrated mainly by Cossack units. The exact number of victims remains unknown.[36]

Five months into the war, the Jewish ethnographer and writer S. An-ski (Shloyme Zaynvl Rapoport) and his close friends, the writers Isaac Leib Peretz and Jacob Dinesohn from Warsaw, launched an effort to document the experiences of the Jewish populations in the war zones. Before the war, S. An-ski had conducted ethnographic expeditions since 1912 under the auspices of the Jewish Ethnographic Historical Society to small towns in Volhynia and Podolia in the Pale of Settlement. An-ski and his helpers had recorded folksongs and stories, collected manuscripts and ritual objects, and taken photographs to preserve the remnants of Jewish folk culture threatened with obliteration by the growing impact of modernization, urbanization, secularization, and linguistic assimilation.

The world war added a new sense of urgency to the drive to preserve Jewish folk culture while also yielding a novel interest in recording Jewish daily life at times of war. In late December 1914 and early January 1915, An-ski, Peretz, and Dinesohn used the Warsaw-based Yiddish-language dailies *Haynt* and *Der Moment* to exhort fellow Jews to document their observations of events: "We turn to all members of our people, men and women, young and old, who live and suffer and see and hear, with the following appeal: Be your own historians! Don't depend on others [to tell your story]! Record, make notes, and collect [material]!"[37] The three intellectuals viewed the war as a historical moment of unprecedented significance which would sweep away existing borders and political systems. To obtain justice following the war's destruction and to secure equal rights in the new order, Jews must document both their wartime suffering and their contributions to the war efforts of the contending powers. Without the evidence to make a cogent case for Jewish rights, they would risk their history being falsified by others.

In direct response to the appeal, Siedlce resident Anne Kahan began a diary on December 31, 1914, with the words: "It's been five months since the outbreak of the war. Today an article in the *Moment* calling on everyone to mark down facts or events for history awakened in me the desire to record all my past and present experiences since the mobilization—not because I expect my writings to serve history, but, should we survive this terrible time, I'd like to have a record of all we went through."[38] Nevertheless the efforts of An-ski and his friends to compile a comprehensive documentation failed, largely because wartime censorship banned the Hebrew and Yiddish press and barred the sending of Hebrew characters in the mail.[39]

A number of Jewish institutions, some of them dedicated to relief work among Jewish war victims, collected eyewitness reports and other information on the atrocities in the war zones. These included widespread pogroms perpetrated by the Russian army, predominantly in the Vilna, Kovno, Minsk, and Volhynia Provinces and in Galicia and Bukovina in the years 1914–1917.[40] In St. Petersburg, the Jewish Historical Ethnographic Society set up a Bureau for War Relief, and the Political Bureau of EKOPO (Jewish Committee for the Relief of War Victims) established a "war archive," both of which gathered documents and eyewitness accounts in the hope that such evidence would help the Jewish populations of the collapsing Russian Empire claim equal civil rights after the war.[41] The influx of thousands of Jewish refugees from Russian-occupied Galicia and Bukovina into Vienna caused Zionists in that city to establish a "Jewish war archive" to collect and publish material on the wartime experiences of Habsburg Jews under Russian occupation. They sought to prove their loyalty to the homeland for which they were fighting, appealed for equal rights for Jews in the formerly Russian territories under Austrian occupation, and endeavored to turn public opinion in favor of accepting the tens of thousands of refugees pouring into Vienna, western Austria, Bohemia, and Moravia.[42]

In Vilna, a city which between 1914 and 1922 would come under seven different Russian, German, Lithuanian, or Polish governments, the Jewish community also documented its wartime history. Beginning in 1915, a group of Jewish intellectuals, writers, and communal activists of various backgrounds—Hebraist and Yiddishist, Zionist and non-Zionist, religious and secular—led by the journalist and communal activist Moyshe Shalit and the physician Zemach Shabad—collected material from individual Jews along with official pronouncements of the German army (which occupied the city from 1915 to 1918) in order to create a war chronicle that documented Jewish life in that city at a time of upheaval. The first volume of the *Vilne Zamlbikher* appeared in 1916, followed in the summer of 1917 by the foundation of a Historical Commission under Shalit's auspices.[43] "Now, in the time of destruction [*khurbn*]," the activists explained, "when so many rich national cultural treasures have been lost, many old books, manuscripts and communal records burnt, and when so many artifacts have been stolen, it would be the greatest sin to discontinue [our] work. It is a holy duty to save at least the remainder [*sheyris hapleyte*] with all our strength."[44]

With the help of *zamlers* (voluntary collectors) from among Vilna's Jewish population, the Historical Commission collected artifacts of the war years: publications (including newspapers and books, official proclamations, and advertisements by communal, educational, and cultural institutions and voluntary organizations), private documents (such as diaries, tax books, and letters), artistic works, folktales, songs, and even idiomatic expressions. On February 20, 1919, S. An-ski, who had moved to Vilna the previous fall, founded the Historical Ethnographic Society of Lithuania and White Russia, which replaced the Historical Commission, taking over its staff and collections. The society established six departments, among them a folklore section, which compiled poems, idiomatic expressions, sayings, and rhymes; a music section, which collected Jewish folk songs; and a historical section, headed by Moyshe Shalit, which now added material from previous centuries to its documents on the recent past. The founders hoped that this material would serve as "an invaluable treasure, an encyclopedia of materials, and an inexhaustible source for a poet, historian, musician, and artist."[45]

Thus the experience of the First World War generated a distinct Jewish historical consciousness, which expressed itself in documentation efforts that aimed both to defend Jewish rights in the changed international arena and to preserve Jewish culture threatened by growing modernization and damaged by the upheavals of war.[46]

These trends gained further momentum when a new wave of anti-Jewish violence devastated the 1.6 million Jews of the Ukraine in the years 1917–1921. Amid the political turmoil that followed the collapse of the Russian and Austrian Empires—the Russian Revolution and its subsequent civil war, several attempts at Ukrainian independence, the establishment of a Ukrainian Soviet Socialist Republic in March 1919, and its incorporation into the Soviet Union in December 1922—pogroms claimed between 50,000 and 100,000 Jewish lives. The perpetrators included various armies and armed groups—anti-Soviet White forces, the Red Army, anarchists, and freelance hoodlums. Troops loyal to the independent nationalist Ukrainian government (known as the "Directorate," headed by Symon Petliura) perpetrated some 40 percent of the pogroms, although this government briefly granted Jews national cultural autonomy.[47]

In response to the pogroms, several Jewish agencies in the Ukraine began documentation initiatives. In late May 1919, members of the Jewish National Council, the Central Committee for the Relief of Pogrom Victims, and the publishing house Folksfarlag formed the Editorial Committee for the Collection and Research of Material concerning the Pogroms in the Ukraine (*Redaktions-kolegye oyf zamlen un oysforshn di materialn vegn di pogromen in Ukraine*) in Kiev. Committee members included the historian Elias Tcherikower as secretary, the philologist Nokhem Shtif as editor-in-chief, and, among others, the journalist Ya'acov Ze'ev Wolf Latzky-Bertholdi and the literary critic Isidor Yisroel Eliashev ("Bal-Makhshoves"). In addition to Simon Dubnow, the project's supporters included Moyshe Zilberfarb, a politician of the Jewish Socialist Fareynikte party and the minister for Jewish affairs in the independent Ukrainian government; the sociologist and demographer Jacob Lestschinsky; and the writer and communal activist Nokhem Gergel.[48]

From the outset the Editorial Committee sought to prepare "a fundamentally objective work" that examined and documented the pogroms "without political biases and without the intention to evoke pity."[49] To this end, it aimed to collect large numbers of eyewitness testimonies from various segments of the Jewish community, especially refugees from the devastated areas who were pouring into Kiev. The Editorial Committee posted appeals in the local Jewish press, inviting people from diverse political, social, and ideological backgrounds, scholars and laypeople, to join the project and write personal accounts of events:

> Brothers! A curse of terrible pogroms is befalling Jewish villages and towns, and the world does not know, we ourselves do not know or know only very little about it. This must not be concealed! Everything must be told and written down. It is a duty for every Jew who has come or comes from the devastated Jewish towns to report everything that he has seen, for the news must not be lost. We request people to contact the commission for collecting and research at the following address: Mikhaylovski Street 11, apt. 1, telephone 88–12, open from 12 noon–3 PM except for Saturdays.[50]

The editors asked only that those willing to join the effort provide material "of a strictly documentary or purely memoir-like character, not tendentious or publicist writing."[51] In its quest for nuanced description of events, the Editorial Committee acknowledged that relying solely on victim testimony was in fact one-sided: as Nokhem Shtif warned in 1923, "We see and hear those who are being beaten but in general not those who are beating." While Shtif and his colleagues recognized that the incorporation of official documents on the condition of Ukrainian Jews would make possible a more comprehensive and "objective" description of the traumatic events, they lacked access to Soviet state offices and archives. In Shtif's own words: "That a Jewish editorial board will be able to obtain a word from the perpetrators about their reasoning and their deeds is almost unthinkable."[52] Thus forced to rely mainly on victim accounts, they nonetheless made sure that these represented a wide variety of perspectives.[53]

Their endeavor netted an archive of several thousand eyewitness accounts of the pogroms, memoranda, protocols, and correspondence of Jewish communal organizations; diaries and letters of individual Jews; and clippings from the Jewish press. It also gathered several hundred documents of non-Jewish provenance, including calls issued by pogrom instigators and government statements, along with hundreds of photographs depicting the devastation.[54] Rivka Tcherikower, Elias's wife, catalogued the material and created a card index of 1,350 pogroms in 750 places. She also assembled a "pogrom graveyard," a list of seventeen thousand victims of the pogroms, arranged by location. For fear that the material might be lost in the turmoil of civil war or that pogrom instigators and some political leaders might have an interest in its destruction, the Editorial Committee made three copies of every incoming document and kept them in different locations.[55]

In order to protect the collection from confiscation by Soviet authorities and to enable the publication of historical works in various languages that would inform both Jews and non-Jews in the West of the plight of Ukrainian Jews, the Editorial Committee transferred its holdings to Germany. In April 1921, after eight months of planning, and with the help of Lithuanian diplomats based in the Soviet capital, the collection reached Berlin via Moscow and Kovno.⁵⁶ The Hebrew and Yiddish essayist Hersh Dovid Nomberg commented on the transfer of the archives in the Warsaw daily *Der Moment* that while "all peoples in the world research . . . and write about the smallest details of their heroism and victories," Jews had "a different kind of idealization." Namely, he opined, "Like dogs do we lick our own blood! We collect, collect, and collect: blood, tears, and sorrows. Tons of written papers are our trophies." Hence he advised his readers: "Rejoice, five full boxes have joined our national treasure."⁵⁷

In Berlin, then the temporary home of many eastern European Jewish intellectuals and scholars and a center of Jewish publishing in Yiddish, Hebrew, and Russian, Tcherikower transformed the Editorial Committee into the Eastern Jewish Historical Archive (Mizrekh-Yidisher Historisher Arkhiv, or Ostjüdisches Historisches Archiv) under his auspices.⁵⁸ Although the archive continued to collect documents, its main focus now was editing and publishing the transferred holdings.

In spring 1922, Tcherikower and his colleagues began to prepare the publication of a seven-volume opus, *Di geshikhte fun der pogrom bavegung in Ukraine, 1917–1921* (History of the pogrom movement in Ukraine, 1917–1921). Evoking Nathan Nata Hannover's account of a seventeenth-century pogrom, Dubnow (who lived in Berlin between 1922 and 1933) described the project as a new "Yeven Metsulah," which would ascertain that "the rivers of Jewish blood and tears . . . will not disappear in the sea of the worlds' misfortunes."⁵⁹ Each volume would provide a summary description of events and feature original documents. The manuscripts were completed, but due to financial problems, only two volumes appeared: Tcherikower's account of the years 1917–1918, published in 1923 in Russian and Yiddish editions, and a Russian-language work by writer and Zionist politician Joseph Schechtman on the pogroms perpetrated by the anti-Bolshevist White Russian army of General Anton Denikin, which was not published until 1932.⁶⁰ Tcherikower edited a separate volume of documents on Jewish suffering during the Russian Revolution, published in 1924.⁶¹

Although Tcherikower's project received financial assistance from the American Joint Distribution Committee (AJDC), Ukrainian Jews in the United States, and the Jewish National Council in Warsaw, it seems to have aroused little initial support from the broader Jewish public in Europe.⁶² Disappointed, he noted that in the wake of the pogroms, few Jews could see beyond their material needs or realized that historical documentation had an even greater potential to serve the victims than did material relief. Writing to Baruch Zuckerman, a Russian-born American Labor Zionist and the executive director of the socialist People's Relief Committee in New York, Tcherikower complained that "the Jewish public and the Jewish communal organizations" showed no more interest in historical documentation than "in last year's snow." He continued: "We have never overcome the sentiment that what one needs to throw to someone hungry and devastated by pogroms is a little money or a package. We are not yet mature enough for a national historical work, creating an archive and publishing the material about our destruction."⁶³

A few years later, Tcherikower had the opportunity to prove the practical value of documentation, at least in a society that recognized the rule of law. On May 25, 1926, in Paris, a Ukrainian Jewish watchmaker and anarchist named Sholem Schwartzbard assassinated the Ukrainian nationalist politician Symon Petliura. Schwartzbard sought to avenge his relatives who had died in 1919 in pogroms perpetrated by armies under Petliura's command as head of the Directorate of the Ukrainian National Republic. The trial, in October 1927, aroused a sudden public interest in the history of the pogroms in general and Petliura's role in particular. Tcherikower—along with Dubnow—joined an international defense committee organized by Leo Motzkin, then head of the Paris-based international representative body of Jewish organizations, Comité des Délégations Juives, and served as an advisor for Schwartzbard's lawyer, the renowned French jurist Henri Torrès. With Motzkin's help, he transferred large sections of the Berlin archives to Paris for use in Schwartzbard's defense.[64] The documents enabled Torrès to focus the proceedings on their historical context, the Ukrainian atrocities that had motivated Schwartzbard, rather than on the deed itself, and the eight-day trial ended with Schwartzbard's acquittal.[65] The trial also turned the Ukrainian pogroms into a cause célèbre. Some of the resultant publications used materials from Tcherikower's archive—most notably a three-hundred-page collection of documents and testimonies, edited and published anonymously by Motzkin as an imprint of the Comité des Délégations Juives.[66]

Tcherikower and his collaborators thus made a significant contribution to establishing historical documentation as a fitting response to catastrophe. Placing a strong emphasis on comprehensiveness and "objectivity," they collected testimonies of people from various social, ideological, and educational backgrounds, including multiple perspectives on the same events. For the first time, documenting atrocities yielded a real and useable archive and the publication of collated documentary evidence in synthetic works. The Schwartzbard trial and subsequent publications made the archive's material known and available to a wider Jewish and non-Jewish audience in eastern and western Europe. This occurred with the help of the Comité des Délégations Juives, an umbrella organization of Zionist and non-Zionist Jewish organizations in Europe, the United States, and Palestine, which had come into being to represent Jewish interests at the Paris Peace Conference in 1919 and which remained a central organ of Jewish diplomacy in the interwar years. Through its activity the Comité cemented the idea that any effort to claim minority rights for Jews or to defend against violent onslaughts and anti-Semitism must draw from documentary evidence to gain credibility and political impact.[67]

In the two and a half decades between the pogrom in Kishinev and the Schwartzbard trial in Paris, Dubnow, Bialik, An-ski, Motzkin, Tcherikower, and their followers had worked to establish a culture of *khurbn* documentation as the basis for a history "from below" that would give voice to the victims of traumatic events by mobilizing a collective grassroots effort from within the Jewish community. While the impetus to record Jewish suffering derived from a fundamental distrust of the authorities, it also expressed a quest for self-defense, legal redress, and the commemoration of the dead and the wish to compile raw materials for historical research. These rationales and practices would be further refined and disseminated in the interwar years, fostered especially by a once more independent Poland. Emerging as the center of Jewish historical research, the new nation forged a Jewish cultural milieu that professed social activism and the importance of social history. This environment had a formative impact on several individuals who would later play leading roles in documenting the Holocaust.

Historical research became a vital factor in Polish Jewish life in the interwar years as Jews sought to position themselves inside the newly reconstituted Polish nation-state. In a climate of aggressive anti-Semitism, studies of the local economic and social history of the Jews provided a necessary tool in what historian Natalia Aleksiun called "setting the record straight" by bringing Jews' longstanding commitment and rootedness in Polish society to the awareness of the public.[68] Already beginning with the turn of the twentieth century, three academically trained Jewish historians of Galician origin—Moses Schorr, Ignacy Schiper, and Majer Bałaban—had pioneered in developing a distinct Polish Jewish historiography, which focused on the local history of Jewish communities but also studied the political, intellectual, and economic history of the Polish Jews as a crucial component of the history of the Polish lands. In 1928 Bałaban and Schorr opened the Institute for Jewish Studies in Warsaw, which provided training in Jewish history; seven years later, Bałaban became the first (and prior to World War II the only) professor of Jewish history at a Polish university.

That history writing found public interest within the Jewish community was due mainly to the indefatigable activities of a new generation of young university-trained Jewish historians, disciples of Schiper, Bałaban, and other preeminent Polish historians, such as Marceli Handelsman at Warsaw University. The most prominent of this generation were Emanuel Ringelblum and Raphael Mahler. Affiliated with the Left Poale Zion ("Workers of Zion," the Marxist wing of the Zionist labor party), they combined historical scholarship with political and social activism for the Jewish community. In 1923 the two men founded the Young Historians Circle (Yunger Historiker Krayz) as a forum for students of Jewish history to exchange ideas and discuss each other's work. Its members included Isaiah Trunk, Joseph Kermisz, Philip Friedman, and Artur Eisenbach—all of whom were later active in the Jewish historical commissions and documentation centers.

This circle functioned as an incubator for new ideas about Polish Jewish historiography, as well as for two periodicals, *Yunger Historiker* and *Bleter far Geshikhte*, founded in 1926 and 1934, respectively. Its members, Ringelblum and Mahler in particular, viewed the historian as "a fighter in a national struggle,"[69] in the words of historian Samuel Kassow. They believed in the social and political significance of history writing and its strength as a weapon in the fight against anti-Semitism and for equal rights.[70] Indeed, through history writing these young scholars sought to reveal the prolonged interactions and mutual influences between Jews and non-Jews in the Polish lands and to demonstrate that the Jewish nation was an integral part of Poland. Historical studies also provided ammunition against anti-Jewish stereotypes by helping to refine the mutual perceptions of Jews and non-Jews beyond rejection and hostility on the one hand and apologetics and idealization on the other. To this end the young generation of university-trained Polish Jewish historians studied the socioeconomic and cultural forces in the everyday life of "ordinary Jews," in the framework of local studies. They also aimed to raise the historical consciousness of Polish Jews through a broad outreach that would bring history to the people and unite scholars and laypeople in a joint endeavor to know their past, gather its sources, and even use recreational tours to learn about the cultural treasures of Polish Jews. The young historians also sought to foster a distinct Yiddish secular culture, which transcended political borders and in which history served a central role.[71]

The founding in 1925 of the YIVO Institute for Jewish Research in Berlin and Vilna proved a milestone in further establishing Yiddish-language scholarship. YIVO's founders were a diverse group of self-taught and academically trained scholars, among them Nokhem Shtif, Elias Tcherikower, Jacob Lestschinsky, Mark Wischnitzer, and Max Weinreich. Dubnow played a formative role as YIVO's founding member and "intellectual godfather."[72] The YIVO scholars venerated Dubnow as the creator of a historical scholarship which placed the history and culture of Diaspora Jewry in eastern Europe at its center.[73] They embraced his concept of the Jewish *people* as the key actor in and subject of its past, and they understood Jewish scholarship as a collective endeavor and a service to the community, as well as a national mission.[74] But they went beyond Dubnow in their focus on Yiddish philology and their interest in researching the cultural, socioeconomic, and political aspects of Jewish society in the past and the present. They pioneered in developing an interdisciplinary concept of Jewish scholarship that combined history, sociology, philology, demography, ethnography, economics, and pedagogy and that used methods from the social sciences such as interviews, questionnaires, autobiographies, and statistics.[75] The members of the Young Historians Circle, especially Emanuel Ringelblum, soon played a prominent role in YIVO's historical work. In 1926 Ringelblum established a Historical Commission, first in Vilna and then in Warsaw, which in 1934 became the Historical Commission for all of Poland. It also complemented YIVO's Historical Section, headed by Tcherikower, in Berlin and Paris. The interaction between the largely self-taught older generation of scholars from the former Russian Empire and the younger generation of university-trained Polish scholars led to continued tensions, especially between Tcherikower and Ringelblum, who respected each other's work but differed in their approaches.[76]

In the years 1925–1939, YIVO further developed the *zamler* tradition which Dubnow and An-ski had initiated, turning it, as David Fishman has noted, into "a virtual cult of documentary collection."[77] Rather than limiting research to academically trained scholars, YIVO also reached out to the wider Jewish community and recruited nonprofessional *zamlers*.[78] Thus in many ways Jewish historians in interwar Poland and beyond perpetuated, institutionalized, and refined scholarly traditions that Simon Dubnow had set in motion in 1891, while adding the methods of social science as new instruments for writing Jewish social, economic, and cultural history.[79] These approaches to studying Jewish society in the past and the present continued in the shadow of Nazi occupation.

Voices from the Abyss: Chronicling the Catastrophe during the Second World War

German persecution and extermination policies elicited widespread and multifaceted individual and collective Jewish documentation efforts across Europe. Countless individuals wrote down their experiences in diaries, notebooks, and letters, whether for personal use or as conscious record creation for posterity. Most, like their authors, did not survive the war.[80] The members of the *Sonderkommando* of Auschwitz-Birkenau—deportees selected and thus temporarily spared from death so they could move bodies from gas chambers to crematoria—documented their experiences in secret diaries, chronicles, and letters which they buried at the site of mass murder.[81] Likewise, prisoners in the Chełmno extermination camp recorded the horrors they witnessed in a collective notebook.[82] With these written testimonies, whose intended audiences were Jews abroad, generations to come, or future historians and tribunals, the victims sought to leave traces of their lives and deaths in the hope that these vestiges would survive and help to build a better future, keep alive the memory of the victims, avenge the dead, and bring the perpetrators to justice. Specifically, the evidence they left behind would—they hoped—subvert the Nazis' painstaking attempts to erase all traces of their crimes. As historian Alexandra Garbarini observed, knowing that the genocide would not succeed if future generations remembered its victims, Jews sought to "prevent their killers from controlling the knowledge of their deaths."[83]

Jewish historians played a central role in encouraging these efforts. Survivors reported that Simon Dubnow called upon Jews in the Riga ghetto to record all atrocities before he was murdered in December 1941.[84] Similarly, the Polish Jewish journalist and survivor Aleksander Donat recalled a conversation among inmates in the Majdanek camp in which Ignacy Schiper had argued that since history is usually written by the victor and posterity only knows as much about victims as the perpetrators "vaingloriously cared to say about them," everything depended on who would transmit European Jewry's "testament" to future generations. He feared that, should the Nazis be victorious, the murder of European Jews "will be presented as one of the most beautiful pages of world history, and future generations will pay tribute to them as dauntless crusaders. Their every word will be taken as gospel." Anxious that the Nazis might "wipe out our memory altogether, as if we had never existed, as if there had never been a Polish Jewry, a Ghetto in Warsaw, a Maidanek [sic]," Schiper called upon his fellow inmates to leave some trace in writing to counter the voices of the perpetrators. He anticipated that those who would survive and one day write the history of the Jewish tragedy would be met with disbelief; they would have "the thankless job of proving to a reluctant world that we are Abel, the murdered brother."[85]

In ghettos including Bialystok, Kovno, Lodz, Vilna, and Warsaw, Jews established secret archives in an effort to wrest the history of the destruction of Europe's Jews from the hands of the perpetrators and collect comprehensive evidence to convince the world of the truth of the atrocities. The most significant archive was in the Warsaw ghetto, directed by Emanuel Ringelblum, who before the war had led that city's YIVO-affiliated Historical Commission for all Poland.[86] Ringelblum strongly believed that Jewish historians had social and political responsibilities and a national mission that compelled them to encourage Polish Jews to fight for equal rights, improve Polish-Jewish relations, and demonstrate that Jews constituted a separate national group that was nevertheless deeply rooted in Poland. Documenting the onslaught that Polish Jews suffered under German occupation was not just a logical continuation of earlier activities but also a moral imperative.

Ringelblum established his secret archive—codenamed Oyneg Shabes (Yiddish for "joy of the Sabbath")—on November 22, 1940. Although he kept a diary and had been collecting material since the second month of the war, Ringelblum concluded that only a collective endeavor could capture the experiences of Polish Jews under German occupation. Oyneg Shabes used both fifty to sixty regular workers and occasional volunteers—many of them among the 130,000 refugees from the Warsaw District who descended on the city in the spring of 1941—who might contribute only a single description of events in their former hometowns. The core of the participants belonged to the intelligentsia affiliated with the political left; some had worked for YIVO. While they included some well-to-do businessmen and prewar communal leaders, the majority were teachers, writers, and economists, joined by a number of workers or craftsmen who discovered a talent for writing through their activities for the underground archives.[87]

Ringelblum defined the archive's two major principles as "objectivity" and "comprehensiveness" in conveying the full and unadorned truth about the Jewish tragedy, no matter how bitter it might be. Therefore Oyneg Shabes collected multiple eyewitness testimonies and reports on the same events to represent various social, political, and ideological viewpoints, as well as those of different age groups.[88] "By comparing various accounts," Ringelblum held, "the historian is able to arrive at the historical truth, the actual course of the events."[89] "Objectivity" also demanded that the archive's workers conceive of the material as serving a future purpose. This gave them the freedom to speak about contemporary Germans and Poles, and about the current Jewish leadership, without fear of negative consequences.[90]

To achieve a full picture of the Jewish situation in the ghettos of occupied Poland, Oyneg Shabes collected an array of documents illustrating the victim experience: publications of the clandestine Jewish press in Yiddish, Polish, and Hebrew; letters; diaries; material produced by underground Jewish political organizations; artifacts; photographs; folklore; even ephemera such as posters, candy wrappers, and tram tickets. The archive also included synthetic reports by Oyneg Shabes members on such aspects of ghetto life as the economy; education and culture; women, children, and youth; eyewitness accounts of important events in the history of the ghetto; and monographs and reports on towns and villages.[91] Archive workers also used questionnaires to gather information on the socioeconomic and cultural effects of German occupation.[92] As far as they were available, the archives also included Nazi documents, such as announcements and regulations.

In early 1942, Ringelblum and his closest coworkers decided to use their findings in a report, "Two and a Half Years," that would depict Jewish life in occupied Poland since the beginning of the war. It was to cover social, political, and economic developments in the Polish Jewish community and describe its cultural, educational, political, and religious institutions. The onset of mass deportations in July 1942 halted the project before its completion.[93]

Ringelblum's motives went well beyond his desire as a historian to preserve an accurate and comprehensive account of events. As he stated in a December 1942 report, trusting that the Germans would ultimately be defeated and that a remnant of Jews would survive the war, the archival material would be "of great significance for the future tribunal of the war, which will call the guilty to responsibility, be they among the Jews, the Poles, or the Germans."[94] Future generations, he predicted, would value the collection as highly as they did the acts of those who fought the Germans with weapons. In this spirit, Ringelblum described Oyneg Shabes as "a band of comrades, an order of brothers that inscribed on its banners: self-sacrifice, mutual loyalty, and service to the public." He and his coworkers had internalized a concept of writing and documenting as a form of resistance that promised justice and revenge when the truth was revealed in the "free Europe" that would surely come. Indeed, Ringelblum believed that Oyneg Shabes would be bestowed the "highest honors" in a society liberated from Nazism.[95]

The "band of comrades" increasingly realized that they would not be part of this future and that their only option was to leave traces of the historical truth for future generations. Between August 1942 and April 1943 they buried the underground archive in three caches in and near the ghetto.[96] Nineteen-year-old David Graber, who helped bury the first cache on August 3, 1942, wrote in his testament before confiding the precious documents to the earth:

> What we were unable to cry and shriek out to the world we buried in the ground. . . . I would love to see the moment in which the great treasure will be dug up and shriek to the world proclaiming the truth. So the world

may know all. So the ones who did not live ... may be glad, and we may feel like veterans with medals on our chests. We would be the fathers, the teachers and educators of the future.... But no, we shall certainly never live to see it, and therefore do I write my last will. May the treasure fall into good hands, may it last into better times, may it alarm and alert the world to what happened ... in the twentieth century.... We may die now in peace. We fulfilled our mission. May history attest for us.[97]

Historian David Engel argued that Oyneg Shabes epitomized a "unique Jewish cultural attribute" and scale of values in which "documentation work and armed action or entering harm's way in order to save lives or inflict injury upon the enemy" were morally equal.[98] Not only had these ideals and historical practices developed in the decades preceding the Holocaust as an integral component of the genre of *khurbn-forshung*; they also served as the intellectual and methodological underpinnings of the postwar documentation projects in liberated Europe.

Living with the Past: Documenting the Holocaust in its Immediate Aftermath

Many survivors of Nazi rule saw documenting the recent catastrophe as a moral imperative for the sake of the dead and the generations to come: survival had bequeathed on them an obligation to publicize the truth of the German genocide and to write the history of the Holocaust from the perspective of its victims. For many participants in postwar documentation initiatives, chronicling events became a primary concern and a way of coping with loss and survival. For example, Dr. Ada Eber, a native of Lvov and postwar documentation activist in Poland, recalled many years later that on May 8, 1945, when she learned that the war had ended and Adolf Hitler had committed suicide, "this tremendous news did not impress me at all. It left me absolutely cold."

> What really mattered for us survivors was the power of our recent terrible past that we shared and remembered.... Eyewitness reports, fresh records of inhumanity—this is what we, the survivors of the Holocaust, had in common. Our moral obligation was to put on paper what we remembered, for the sake of *documentation*, for bringing the culprits to justice, for preventing the evil to happen again, not only for the Jewish people but [also] for the good of all humankind.[99]

Eber also recounted that documenting recent events had helped her second husband, Philip Friedman, get on with his life in the aftermath of the war. When they met, shortly after the liberation of Lvov at the end of July 1944, Friedman was mourning the deaths of his wife, Marina, and thirteen year-old daughter,

Elinka, who had been murdered in 1942. However, in the same breath as mentioning this loss, he told Eber: "But ... I have found a way to get even with Hitler and his criminal regime.... I have already started to collect eyewitness reports."[100] By the end of that year, Friedman became the first director of the Central Jewish Historical Commission (Centralna Żydowska Komisja Historyczna; CŻKH) in Lublin.

The organizers and activists of the postwar historical commissions and documentation centers for the most part appear to have been familiar with the documentation projects that emerged as a response to earlier incidents of anti-Jewish mass violence and with the individual researchers that had brought them to life. CŻKH had direct connections with the Ringelblum archives because the only three survivors of the Oyneg Shabes affiliates became active in the commission and initiated the excavation of a portion of the ghetto archives in fall 1946. Ringelblum and Dubnow also became models for survivors active in other historical commissions and documentation centers who learned about their efforts to record life in the Jewish ghettos and the details of the Nazi onslaught.[101] American Jewish historian Koppel S. Pinson, who served as the director of the AJDC's Education and Culture Department in Munich in the years 1945–1946, claimed that the survivors active in the historical commissions in the DP camps in occupied Germany had internalized Dubnow's 1891 command: "Let us search and research."[102]

The activists were well aware of *khurbn-forshung*'s focus on writing the history of Jewish suffering from the grassroots-level perspective of victims; they were also versed in YIVO's *zamler* techniques and social-science-oriented research methods. Indeed, they saw their urgent task as perpetuating this kind of history writing broadly among the "surviving remnant," the *She'erit Hapletah*, of Polish Jewry. When, in October 1945, Joseph Kermisz, director of the historical commission's archive in Lodz, reflected on the rationale for documenting the Holocaust, he cited "the opinion of professor Dubnow, that Jewish history is the chain uniting the generations, and someone who does not know the past is not a Jew." Kermisz went on to accuse generations of Jews of ignoring their past, especially the persecution and tragedy, yet credited Motzkin, An-ski, and Tcherikower for their more recent efforts in writing the history of anti-Jewish violence.[103] In Kermisz' eyes, survivors now had the duty to research the events they had witnessed themselves—events that had eclipsed all previous tragedies suffered by the Jewish people in number of victims, brutality and effectiveness of methods, and geographic extent: "The latest catastrophe has an international character. It affected nine million Jews in twenty-one countries. Polish Jews suffered most. The creation of a historical commission is a proof that Polish Jewry has understood its historical task." Yet the archive still lacked the materials needed "for a complete history of our *khurbn*. We must be able to answer the question which history will pose to us: What happened to Polish Jewry? The Central Jewish Historical Commission endeavors to answer this question." Kermisz remained optimistic that

Michał Borwicz and other members of the Central Jewish Historical Commission in Lodz unearth the first cache of the Oyneg Shabes archive from the ruins of the Warsaw ghetto, September 18, 1946. Emanuel Ringelblum's documentation project served as a model and inspiration for survivors after the war. *Yad Vashem Photo Archives 1605/1031*

the world would someday recognize its work, and "maybe then the hatred among human beings will cease. To a great extent this will be the achievement of the *She'erit Hapletah* of Polish Jewry, which in the heat of the moment understood [the need] to seize documents and materials."[104]

Some survivors active in the documentation centers and historical commissions viewed the genre of *khurbn-forshung* as a cultural legacy unique to eastern European Jews, a view seemingly confirmed by the biographies of virtually all the founders and coworkers of the documentation initiatives. At times these activists expressed a feeling of superiority over western European Jews, whose supposed failure to establish their own historical commissions betrayed a culture deficient in its response to catastrophe. For example, Moshe Yosef Feigenbaum, secretary of a postwar historical commission in Munich, rebuked German Jewish survivors for neither founding their own commissions nor participating in those run by Jewish DPs of eastern European backgrounds in occupied Germany.[105]

Citing German Jews' apparent disdain for this kind of historical work and the absence in Germany of underground Jewish archives, Feigenbaum argued that German Jews lacked the "dynamics of the Jewish communities in eastern Europe." Moreover, "brought up in discipline," they remained "far from revolutionary and conspiratorial deeds,"[106] even of a scholarly nature. Although this analysis contains gross oversimplifications, survivors with eastern European backgrounds did generally initiate and staff the postwar documentation projects in Germany and other western European countries; western European survivors participated in relatively small numbers or acted as individual researchers, not engaging in collective grassroots level initiatives. The question is, of course—why?

Israeli historian Yehuda Bauer has suggested that, before the Holocaust, Jews east and west had developed differences in cultural heritage, modes of self-understanding, and relationships with their surrounding societies which later conditioned their responses to the Nazi regime. Eastern European Jews primarily defined themselves as an ethnic group with its own national identity. In a climate of hostility, rejection, discrimination, and periodic violence, they maintained a fundamental mistrust and distance from their surrounding non-Jewish environments, while creating autonomous networks of culture, welfare, self-help, and political activism. This tradition held even for those who had migrated to western European countries.

By contrast, western and central European Jews—both "natives" and "ancient immigrants" who had left their countries of origin decades ago and had acculturated to the societies where they had migrated—regarded themselves primarily as citizens of the states in which they lived and which they considered their homeland. They understood Judaism as a religious denomination and relegated it to the private sphere. Emancipation had taught them to cherish a strong belief in the political and legal systems of the *Rechtsstaat* (state of laws). Bauer suggests that these cultural trends, combined with the nature of German rule in each country in the Nazi orbit of power and the respective roles of local non-Jews, influenced the initial response of each Jewish community to the onset of persecution, although, evidently and tragically, the final outcome was beyond their control.[107]

Bauer's model helps to explain the dominant role of eastern European Jews in postwar Jewish Holocaust documentation insofar as *khurbn-forshung*—collective grassroots-level initiatives focused on capturing the voices of victims—had been one of their principal cultural responses to persecution beginning long before the Holocaust. This strategy arose from both the external conditions faced by eastern European Jews—namely, large-scale anti-Jewish violence and the lack of government protection—and a self-consciously Jewish cultural milieu committed to social activism, self-help, and self-defense, as well as to popular approaches to history writing that conditioned Jews to document their suffering. The genre of *khurbn-forshung* developed from certain trends, practices, and research techniques rooted in Jewish historiography in eastern Europe that were less common in western Europe. These included a focus on social, economic, and cultural, rather than intellectual, history and a distinct popular concept of Jewish history writing as a collective enterprise not limited to university-trained scholars but also open to large segments of the Jewish community.

By contrast, the virtual absence of large-scale anti-Semitic violence in western Europe in the century before the Nazi seizure of power might explain why Jews living in those countries, having no reason to engage in collective, grassroots documentation of Jewish suffering, did not develop an equivalent to *khurbn-forshung*.[108] Even though anti-Semitism constantly challenged their acceptance into the surrounding society, western Jews could generally rely on protection by the state and its laws. This fostered a tradition of self-protection that relied on the avenues of legal defense and petitioning within the systems provided by the Rechtsstaat. In Germany, for example, the largest defense organization, the Central Association of German Citizens of the Jewish Faith (Centralverein deutscher Staatsbürger jüdischen Glaubens; CV), gathered facts and evidence on anti-Semitic incidents in order to seek redress through the established legal system and the court of public opinion.[109] Jewish scholarship and historiography in Germany lay largely in the hands of university-trained historians who focused more on the remote past than on recent events. By providing historical evidence for Jews' longstanding presence in their countries, they sought to buttress the quest for civic equality and social acceptance, while also forging a distinct secular Jewish identity.[110]

The work of several Jewish individuals of western and central European background who did engage in Holocaust research belies any notion that documentation of the Holocaust was reserved for eastern Europeans. The Wiener Library offers the most prominent evidence of efforts by western European Jews to document the Jewish catastrophe during and immediately after the war. During the Weimar Republic, the German Jewish orientalist Alfred Wiener—as secretary (syndic) of the CV's Greater Berlin chapter between 1919 and 1923 and as national deputy secretary and secretary between 1923 and 1933—had upheld the liberal strategies of countering anti-Semitism through gathering information on its proponents, analyzing their propaganda, and disseminating counter information. Having fled Germany for Amsterdam shortly after the Nazi seizure of power, Wiener began to collect printed matter by and about the Nazi regime. On February 1, 1934, Wiener, along with David Cohen, a Dutch Jewish professor of ancient history at the University of Amsterdam, founded a Jewish Central Information Office (JCIO), which aimed to mobilize world public opinion against the Third Reich, by gathering and disseminating information on its ideology and criminal behavior, as well as on the plight of Jews in Germany and the threat Nazism posed to the entire world. Operating both openly and clandestinely, the JCIO monitored the daily press in Germany and scrutinized all printed matter pertaining to National Socialism. It also supplied documentation for the Swiss League of Jewish Communities' case against the distributors of the Protocols of the Elders of Zion in April 1935, and the trial in 1936–1937 of David Frankfurter, who had assassinated the Swiss National Socialist Wilhelm Gustloff.[111] Thus the JCIO continued the practices of information gathering, public opinion, and legal defense work in which the Centralverein had engaged for four decades.

In September 1939, the JCIO—rightly fearing a possible German invasion of the Netherlands—moved its collection of eight thousand books and pamphlets and a staff of nearly twenty to London. Because the move made its resources available to British government intelligence, until the end of the war the JCIO received subsidies from the BBC and British government agencies. After August 1940 Wiener himself worked on behalf of the British government in Washington, DC, and New York. In London, the JCIO established a remarkable record of publications. The JCIO rejected counterpropaganda in striving for neutrality and scholarliness in periodical series such as *The Nazis at War* and *Jewish News*, which reached subscribers across Europe and overseas. Other publications included edited documents and mimeographed reports on the legal, social, political, and economic situation of the Jews in Germany.[112] From his early work with the Centralverein, on through the JCIO and the Wiener Library, Wiener pursued scholarliness and objective analysis; his arguments on behalf of Jews revealed a belief in Enlightenment values and in the importance of the Rechtsstaat for their protection. Reflecting this understanding of scholarly objectivity, the JCIO initially focused its collection efforts on the Nazis rather than on Jewish sources, although it did collect more than 350 eyewitness testimonies from Jews who managed to leave Germany, mainly relating to the events of *Kristallnacht*. But the primary focus for the JCIO and the Wiener Library that succeeded it after the war was the German propaganda machinery. After the war the Wiener Library also dedicated itself to studying Jewish responses and the agency of Jews under the Nazi regime and focused on collecting eyewitness testimonies.[113]

It took a decade after the war until German Jewish émigré scholars and communal leaders established the Leo Baeck Institute (LBI), the main archival repository and research institute administering the cultural heritage and memory of German-speaking Jewry. Founded in Jerusalem in May 1955, with branches in London and New York City—the three centers of German Jewish emigration—the LBI dedicated itself to researching and commemorating the intellectual, cultural, and social history of German-speaking Jewry, while also seeking the preservation or, in the words of Israeli historian Guy Miron, the "resurrection of the German-Jewish tradition of Jewish Studies and historiography."[114] Although the Jewish catastrophe provided the precondition for the institute's founding, the LBI was by no means a Holocaust archive or research institution. Rather, its major focus lay on German-speaking Jewry from the "Age of Emancipation" to the eve of the Third Reich. Since several of the institute's founders had been members of the Jewish leadership during the Third Reich, the Jewish past in those years remained a sensitive issue, and until the mid-1960s it was relegated to the margins of the LBI's agenda. It took decades until a younger generation of German-born historians who had left Nazi Germany in their youth and received their academic training at Israeli universities would render the history and behavior of German Jewry under the Nazi regime a central issue.[115]

A small number of western and central European survivors and émigrés did see research on the Holocaust as an urgent responsibility, but most worked alone, with no institutional support. H. G. Adler, a German-speaking Jewish writer from

Prague who survived imprisonment at Theresienstadt and Auschwitz, recounted his personal experiences and reflections on the moral, ethical, philosophical, and cultural implications of the Nazi camp system in several meticulously researched and documented works, beginning in 1955 with his monumental 950-page study *Theresienstadt 1941–1945*. After a brief postwar involvement with the Jewish museum in Prague, which provided a repository of documentation for his work, Adler left for Great Britain in 1947.[116] In Germany, the sociologist Hans Lamm, who returned from exile in America in 1945, used historical documents and survivor testimonies in a pioneering dissertation on the internal developments of the German Jewish community under the Nazi regime, with a chapter on the postliberation years.[117] Other German Jewish re-migrants began to undertake meticulous research on their community's history beginning in the 1950s; most, however, bypassed the Nazi years to focus on the intellectual and political developments of German-speaking Jewry since the early modern period.[118]

In the Netherlands, a handful of survivors and re-migrants became active in research and publication related to the Dutch Jewish Holocaust—not, however, as a separate Jewish initiative but rather on the mandate of the Dutch government. Already during the war in March 1944, the Dutch government-in-exile in London called upon the Dutch people to record their experiences of German occupation. Hearing this message in her hiding place, fourteen-year-old Anne Frank noted in her diary on March 29, 1944: "Bolkestein, an M.P., was speaking on the Dutch news from London and he said that they ought to make a collection of diaries and letters after the war." With a hint of disbelief she added: "Just imagine, how interesting it would be if I were to publish a romance of the 'Secret Annex'.... But, seriously, it would seem quite funny ten years after the war if we Jews were to tell how we lived and what we ate and talked about here. Although I tell you a lot, ... you only know very little of our lives."[119]

Anne's apprehensions notwithstanding, on its return to Den Haag, the government established the State Institute for War Documentation (later the Netherlands Institute for War Documentation; NIOD) in October 1945 as a research institute dedicated to studying the history of the Netherlands under Nazi occupation. The government appointed the Dutch Jewish journalist Louis de Jong, who had survived the war in Britain, as the institute's first director.[120] De Jong and two other Dutch Jewish survivors on NIOD's staff, Abel Herzberg and Jacques de Presser, dedicated themselves to researching the mass murder of more than 100,000 Jews, three-quarters of the Dutch Jewish community, a task which, according to Dutch historian Conny Kristel, they considered to be a "question of honor."[121] Yet it is also a telling example for the behavior patterns Yehuda Bauer had identified for western European Jews that de Jong, Herzberg, and Presser, as members of a highly acculturated community, did not document the tragedy of Dutch Jewry by founding a Jewish historical commission or documentation center but rather as individual researchers within the framework of a government research institute dedicated to studying the history of the Dutch nation under

German occupation in which the Jewish minority had a place yet the Holocaust was not a separate or distinctly Jewish story.

Conclusion

In sum, the predominance of Holocaust survivors of eastern European backgrounds in the various postwar Jewish historical commissions and documentation centers can be partially explained by their familiarity—by way of cultural milieu—with Jewish documentation projects that emerged in response to anti-Jewish mass violence in eastern Europe in the decades before the Second World War. The practices of *khurbn-forshung* developed in these earlier attempts to collect evidence and record Jewish suffering continued to influence the research techniques of postwar initiatives—above all, their shared insistence on using the perspective of victims and witnesses to describe accurately the atrocities committed against Jews. Like their predecessors, the postwar documentarians relied on a broad array of unofficial sources—in particular, eyewitness testimonies and questionnaires, but also diaries, letters, literary creations, artifacts, material objects, photographs, and folklore (poems, songs, legends, stories, jokes, and idiomatic expressions) collected during or immediately after the events—in addition to materials generated by the instigators and perpetrators of violence, as far as such sources were available to Jews.

Both *khurbn-forshung* and the postwar documentation projects also sought to transform the raw evidence they assembled into historical publications that would inform a wider Jewish and non-Jewish public about atrocities against Jews. They showed further continuity in realizing the multiple functions of a process that could at once provide evidence for juridical, material, and moral redress of anti-Jewish violence, a documentary foundation for future history writing, and a platform for mourning and commemorating the dead. Moreover, while both the developers of *khurbn-forshung* and the postwar practitioners of Holocaust documentation included some trained historians, most were laypeople with diverse educational and social backgrounds who, as witnesses, believed that recording the reality of the recent tragedy would serve their material, social, psychological, political, and moral needs. Viewing this effort as a collective enterprise, they sought to enlist the larger Jewish community by using a rhetoric of duty that made bearing witness a moral imperative for every Jewish woman and man who had survived and witnessed the tragedy.

The Jewish cultural tradition of *khurbn-forshung* thus played a demonstrable role in animating survivors in postwar Europe to engage in Holocaust documentation. An additional influence may have been the initiatives undertaken by governments and armies during and after the Second World War to document enemy atrocities against their citizens. Largely strategic and propagandistic—and to some degree humanitarian—they did not aim to influence future historical research per se.¹²² From 1939 to 1941, for example, the Polish embassy in the Soviet Union collected some eighteen thousand testimonies from Polish citizens, Jews and non-Jews alike, who, having fled the Wehrmacht into Soviet-occupied areas of eastern Poland, had been deported as "enemy aliens" into the interior of the Soviet Union.¹²³

The Jewish documentation initiatives understandably drew encouragement and a sense of vindication from the decisions of a number of governments, following the end of hostilities, to document atrocities perpetrated by foreign military forces—in particular the Germans—against their respective populations.¹²⁴ The institutionalization of a new juridical framework for the prosecution of war crimes, crimes against peace, and crimes against humanity, begun with the International Military Tribunal (IMT) at Nuremberg, required extensive documentary evidence. Upon entering German-occupied territory and Germany proper, the Allies collected a vast number of documents which the Germans had not managed to destroy. These documents played a crucial role in the war crimes trials and the denazification process, as well as in tracing missing individuals.¹²⁵

The commanders of the advancing armies carefully secured these records, which by September 1945 had been collected in thirteen provisional archival

Two American GIs work in the document room of the International Military Tribunal at Nuremberg in 1946. Members of the Jewish historical commissions in France and Poland visited the tribunal to submit and acquire documents pertaining to crimes against Jews across Europe. *Yad Vashem Photo Archives 359/42*

depots throughout Germany and Austria.[126] A special U.S. military unit headed by the Texas lawyer Colonel Robert Storey gathered what eventually amounted to some 36,000 documents pertaining to German war crimes to support the American prosecution at the IMT and the subsequent Nuremberg Military Tribunal. Legal historian Lawrence Douglas estimates that the prosecutors of the four Allied nations examined over 100,000 German documents, using around 4,000 as evidence in their trial against the "major war criminals" at the IMT.[127] An additional 30 million files of captured Nazi documents, in particular membership records of the Nazi Party, the SA, and SS, were stored at the Berlin Document Center, established by U.S. military authorities in the west Berlin district of Zehlendorf in July 1945; they served in the denazification of Germany and later became a major archival repository for historical research.[128] Yet despite the willingness of the American prosecution at Nuremberg to share some documentation concerning the fate of European Jews, the survivor historians knew that they must ultimately depend on their own purely civilian, grassroots initiatives.[129]

The survivors who established the postwar historical commissions and documentation centers drew from common models. Yet the question remains: To what degree does the shared Jewish cultural tradition explain the phenomenon of early postwar Jewish Holocaust documentation? The following chapters will describe the independent origins of the most significant documentation initiatives and their differences in terms of motivations, methods, and historical narratives. They will also explore the reasons for these variations. How important, for example, were the significant differences in the local political, social, and cultural contexts in which survivors found themselves at their time of liberation? By examining the specific settings in which postwar documentation initiatives arose in France and Poland and in occupied Germany, Austria, and Italy, the following chapters address the overarching question: How did local conditions shape the ways in which survivors documented, researched, narrated, and wrote the history of the recent destruction?

2

Writing French Judaism's "Book of Martyrdom"

Holocaust Documentation in Liberated France

Liberation was still sixteen months away when a group of French Jews in Grenoble embarked on a collective effort to document their wartime suffering. Perhaps encouraged by the failure of the Wehrmacht's military advances at El Alamein and Stalingrad, in April 1943 they formed a Jewish documentation center as preparation for the postwar era. Its leaders included representatives of Jewish communal, political, and welfare organizations, immigrants as well as French-born Jews. Given the circumstances of war and persecution, the actual collection and documentation project began only after the liberation, when survivors established a lasting institution in Paris. To put their work in context, this chapter begins with a discussion of the impact of the Holocaust on French Jewry, with its distinctive history and culture.

The postwar effort to document and research the history of the Jewish cataclysm in France began at a time when the remnants of the Jewish community struggled to recover from years of compound trauma: the loss of civic rights and property; the destruction of family structures and communal institutions; and ultimately, incarceration, internment, deportation, and mass murder. France's Jewish population—numbering between 300,000 and 330,000 in the summer of 1939—suffered up to 80,000 deaths during the occupation. Nearly 76,000 Jews—two-thirds of whom had immigrated to France—were deported to death camps; only 2,560 returned.[1] Even so, with 200,000–250,000 Jews in 1945, France became home to the largest Jewish community in noncommunist Continental Europe and a haven for Jewish refugees from eastern Europe.[2] As historian David Weinberg observed, compared to other European Jewish communities French Jews were "in the unique position of having experienced the Holocaust yet having survived in large enough numbers to reassert themselves after the war."[3]

Still, aside from coping with the psychological, physical, and material repercussions of persecution, the remnants of French Jewry had to come to terms with the profound shock that France had violated the republican and egalitarian traditions that Jews had identified with for generations. Not only had these traditions allowed a Jew, Léon Blum, to become prime minister in the 1930s, but for a century and a half Jews had been able to rely on state protection, even at times of popular anti-Semitic fervor. Yet, through its collaboration with Nazi Germany, France had both betrayed these cherished traditions and failed to protect the rights and lives of its Jewish citizens and let them fall prey to Nazi extermination policies.

In rapid succession after the German invasion on May 10, 1940, France's sudden military defeat had forced the French Republic's transformation into an authoritarian regime, legitimized by the National Assembly, which granted Marshal Philippe Pétain full governing powers and voted to suspend the republican law. The new regime professed to save France's national interests and cherished conservative concepts of patriotism and nationalism, along with Catholic values, while replacing the revolutionary ideals of "liberty, equality, and fraternity" with "work, homeland, and family." On June 22, Pétain signed a humiliating armistice, which gave the new Vichy-based government temporary autonomy in the "unoccupied zone" in France's mostly rural south, while ceding to direct German control the larger and more industrialized "occupied zone" in the north—including Paris. Nevertheless, the French government, administration, and police remained formally in charge of the entire country, and unlike other German-occupied states, France maintained a high level of sovereignty even after German troops occupied the "unoccupied zone" in the fall of 1942.[4]

Although French anti-Semitism lacked the "exterminationist quality" of the Nazi variety, the prevalence and historical roots of anti-Jewish sentiments in France eased the way for implementation of the Final Solution. Whether motivated by genuine anti-Semitic inclinations to solve the "Jewish question" in France, to win German favor, or to salvage some degree of French unity and independence, Pétain and his entourage went beyond collaborating with the Germans to voluntarily and at times zealously implement Vichy's own anti-Jewish policies. Indeed, the Vichy government ensured that its anti-Jewish measures applied throughout the country, calculating that persecuting the Jews for the Germans would strengthen French sovereignty and earn greater autonomy in other matters.[5]

Before the systematic deportations to death camps began in the spring of 1942, both the Germans and the Vichy regime launched aggressive persecution campaigns in both zones, intensifying from legislative discrimination, social isolation, and the destruction of livelihood to expropriation and internment, deportation, and eventually mass murder. Vichy's first comprehensive anti-Jewish legislation, the *Statut des Juifs* of October 1940—valid in both zones and passed without German imposition—provided a racial definition of "Jews" and mandated their exclusion from the civil service, the military, and all professions with an impact on public opinion, i.e., the government, the educational sector, and the media, and introduced quotas for Jews in the free professions. The following

March, the Vichy regime founded a government agency for anti-Jewish affairs, the Commissariat Général aux Questions Juives (General Commissariat for Jewish Questions) under the authority of the radical anti-Semite and conservative politician Xavier Vallat, which passed four dozen laws and decrees against the Jewish population. Intensifying its "Aryanization" policies, in July 1941 the Vichy government confiscated some 42,000 Jewish-owned businesses and houses in order to keep these assets out of German hands. That November, at the behest of the Germans, the Vichy authorities created the Union Général des Israélites de France (UGIF), a country-wide Jewish council with separate branches in the two zones. Supposedly representing French Jewry, the council controlled and coordinated the activities of Jewish organizations, membership in which was compulsory. While these measures applied to all Jews in France, the Vichy government first targeted primarily foreign, stateless, and naturalized Jews. As of October 1940, they were confined to internment camps on French soil, most of which were under French administration. By the end of 1940, these camps held some 40,000 Jews, most of them noncitizens.[6]

In March 1942, with the consent of the French cabinet, the Germans began the systematic deportation of Jews to death camps in Poland. The French police cut a deal with the SS apparatus in France stipulating that the police would carry out the arrests and roundups in return for autonomy. To facilitate the deportations, in June the Germans ordered all Jews in their zone to wear the yellow star and stepped up the pace of mass arrests. In mid-July, the most infamous *rafle* (roundup) of 12,884 Jewish men, women, and children occurred in Paris and its suburbs; most of those arrested were detained for several days under devastating conditions in the Vélodrome d'Hiver sports stadium before being deported first to Drancy and then to Auschwitz.

Throughout the summer and fall of 1942, roundups and deportations took place in both zones. Although immigrant Jews were targeted first, the French authorities—eager to fulfill SS-mandated deportation quotas—gradually pursued French citizens. Of some 42,500 Jews sent to Poland in 1942, about one-third came from the unoccupied zone. Protests in communist and church circles grew, and in August 1943, Minister of State Pierre Laval—executed for treason after the war—refused the German request to facilitate the deportations by stripping Jews of their French citizenship. Nonetheless, deportation trains left France undisturbed until the liberation. Of the seventy-nine transports to death camps in Poland, mainly to Auschwitz-Birkenau, between March 1942 and August 1944, one-third of the Jewish deportees were French nationals. Nazi Germany clearly contrived the Final Solution, but it could not have worked in France without the consent and active cooperation of the French authorities.[7]

Nonetheless, survivors in liberated France found reason for optimism. Although the majority of the French population had acted as indifferent bystanders to the fate of the Jews under the occupation, the fact that some non-Jewish individuals and institutions had not only shown sympathy and publicly criticized anti-Jewish measures but had also helped large numbers of Jews by providing hiding places or false identities seemed to suggest that most French citizens did not share Vichy's virulent anti-Semitism.[8] This impression is consistent with the estimate that some 75 percent of French Jewry survived the war—making France the country in Nazi-occupied western Europe with the lowest percentage of Jewish victims. Moreover, the resumption of French republican traditions with the Fourth Republic seemed to suggest that the dark years of Vichy had been a temporary aberration, allowing Jews to retain their faith in French republicanism.[9] As historian Tony Judt described the mood of most French people after the war, "Vichy was an authoritarian parenthesis in the history of the French Republic. Vichy . . . was not 'France,' and thus France's public conscience was clear."[10]

After the liberation, survivors hoped, above all, to return to some kind of normalcy in the form of civic rights and equality, jobs and property, reintegration into French society, and the rebuilding of the Jewish community and its institutions. In the immediate postwar years, however, conflicting actions from the state and society impeded their readjustment. French authorities revoked Vichy's anti-Jewish legislation by reestablishing republican law on August 9, 1944, and on November 14 decreed the restitution of "Aryanized" Jewish property.[11] But republican legislation alone could not expunge popular prejudice against Jews or change the fact that a significant portion of France's population still perceived Jews to be "alien" and "harmful to France." Those who had purchased or stolen Jewish property had particular cause to be hostile. Gentile compatriots often advised Jews to show "discretion" and to refrain from voicing their particular demands at a time of widespread need, and indeed warned that claims to unique Jewish victimhood would provoke anti-Semitism. As for employment reinstatement, the state accorded political prisoners, resistance fighters, and forced labor conscripts priority over Jews.[12]

Still, as historian Renée Poznanski has recently argued, in the years following the war, many French Jews were not silent about their traumatic experiences, although they gradually adjusted to non-Jews' resistance to hearing stories of distinct Jewish persecution or to admitting some share of responsibility for the Jewish fate.[13] Many survivors increasingly kept a low public profile by changing Jewish-sounding family names and dissociating from their religious communities.[14] Some of this process may have been due less to their fear of anti-Semitism than to an ongoing process of secularization and integration into their French surroundings. In any event, French Jews developed a distinctly secular Jewish identity, undergoing, as Pierre Birnbaum put it, a "more inward-looking development" which enhanced the "collective character of Jewish civil society"[15] in postwar France. In sum, the persecution of the Vichy years did not lead French Jews to abandon their loyalty to the French state or to question the legitimacy of the emancipationist model of state-sponsored equality and integration of ethnic and religious minorities.[16]

France's non-Jewish citizens generally remained unwilling to admit any responsibility for the Vichy regime, not to mention its treatment of the Jews, a phenomenon which French historian Henry Rousso dubbed the "Vichy syndrome."[17]

After an initial violent, incomplete, and random purge of collaborators in the months before and after the liberation—totaling as many as 10,000 deaths in summary executions—the new Gaullist government fostered a myth of collective resistance and the self-liberation of France from German occupation.[18] Public discourse on the recent past focused on the *Résistance* and held a handful of traitors responsible for Vichy's crimes. For its part, the Vichy leadership claimed to have executed its anti-Jewish measures only under German pressure; moreover, by forging a compromise with the Nazis that singled out foreign Jews, it had both saved most Jews who were French nationals and salvaged France's autonomy.[19]

Public commemoration of the recent past venerated a broadly defined category of "deportees" who had been sent to German camps because of their political activity, not as victims of racial legislation.[20] Those deported as Jews did not receive attention, and a "conspiracy of silence" shrouded the specific nature of their fate. Beyond the new republican government's consistent and well-intentioned wish not to discriminate against its citizens due to their ethnic or religious backgrounds, this silence also expressed the larger public's indifference toward the Jews and their suffering, and even broadly held stereotypes of Jews as not belonging to the French nation.[21] Political prisoners also came to dominate the narrative because of their relative numbers in postwar France: 60 percent of the 63,000 political non-Jewish deportees returned, as against 3 percent of the 76,000 Jewish deportees.[22] The canonic image of Vichy as a temporary deviation from France's republican past, the creature of a cabal of traitors and collaborators, glossed over inconvenient truths and inhibited critical self-reflection about the recent past for the next two and a half decades.[23] Survivors established the Center of Contemporary Jewish Documentation (Centre de Documentation Juive Contemporaine; CDJC) in Paris in the fall of 1944, months after the liberation, as a continuation of the documentation initiative that began in Grenoble in 1943.[24] The CDJC's emergence amid the complex challenges that Jewish survivors faced after France's liberation raises a number of questions. Why did these survivors take on the painful and difficult task of researching the German genocide? What was the relationship of the CDJC activists to France, and how did they deal with the fact that the country whose republican traditions they identified with and where they sought to live their postwar lives had collaborated with the Nazi regime? How did they address the specificity of Jewish suffering at a time when the unity of victimhood dominated public discourse? What kind of documents did they collect and how did their historical narratives present French society's complicity with the Germans?

Grenoble 1943: Preparing for Peace in Time of War

The driving force behind French Jewish documentation—beginning even before the liberation—was Isaac Schneersohn, a rabbinically educated communal activist and descendant of the Lubavitch Hasidic dynasty. In 1921, at the age of forty-two, Schneersohn migrated from the Ukraine to France, where he became a successful entrepreneur. After France's defeat in June 1940, he escaped from Paris to the Vichy-controlled south, ending up in Grenoble, where the company that he served as the executive director of had several factories. Having lost control of these factories as a result of Vichy "Aryanization" policies, Schneersohn began to collect documents on the suffering of French Jewry in the fall of 1942, evidently on his own initiative.[25] Later he learned of similar efforts underway among the major Jewish organizations in France: the immigrant mutual-aid Fédération des Sociétés Juives de France (Federation of Jewish Societies in France; FSJF); the national association of Jewish congregations, the Consistoire Central; and the Union Générale des Israélites de France (UGIF), the official body created by the Vichy government at the behest of Germany in November 1941 to represent and administer the Jewish population. These groups kept archives during the war and surveyed the situation and morale of the Jews in both zones.[26] Schneersohn concluded that these separate efforts should be coordinated under the aegis of a central body dedicated solely to documentation.[27] The ensuing wartime documentation activities demonstrate that the CDJC's leadership, structure, and goals did not arise fully formed with the departure of German troops from France.[28]

Schneersohn was initially met with skepticism from the many Jews who deemed his documentation project a far lesser priority than saving lives.[29] Still, the fact that Italy rather than Germany occupied the eight departments east of the Rhône River from November 1942 through September 1943 provided a more favorable climate both for Jews generally and for Schneersohn's project. Jews in these areas benefited from the Italians' general lack of enthusiasm for implementing harsh anti-Semitic policies and from their efforts to assert sovereignty as military occupiers. Thus they opposed the implementation of Vichy's anti-Jewish laws and German demands for deportation and protected immigrant Jews by providing them with legal papers.[30]

In Grenoble, Schneersohn gained the support of three important communal leaders who represented both the French Jewish establishment and immigrant Jews: Léon Meiss, a well-known French-born lawyer and future vice president of the Consistoire; Dr. Aron Syngalowski, the Russian-born chairman of the vocational training organization World ORT Union; and Ruven Grinberg, a key figure in the Fédération des Sociétés Juives de France. Encouraged to seek a larger audience, on April 28 or 29, 1943, Schneersohn convened a meeting of forty representatives of French Jewish official and underground organizations in his apartment at 42, rue Bizanet.[31] The organizations encompassed varying political, social, and religious orientations, as well as French-born and immigrant Jews. In addition to Meiss and Grinberg, those present included Raymond-Raoul Lambert, the prominent French-born secretary-general of the UGIF in the Southern Zone; André Baur, a banker from a well-known Parisian Jewish family, and UGIF vice president in the Northern Zone; Rabbi René Hirschler, formerly chief rabbi of Strasbourg and now chief chaplain to Jews in internment camps in the Southern Zone; Léonce Bernheim, a lawyer and president of the French ORT; André Weill, treasurer of the Consistoire; Léo Glaeser, a lawyer born in Riga and, like Grinberg, a leading figure in the FSJF; the Ukrainian journalist Nahum Herman, representing both the FSJF and Keren Ha-Yesod (the Foundation Fund of the World Zionist Organization); and the Alsatian-born Zionist writer Henri Hertz.[32]

The agreement to establish a "documentation center" that would compile a record of the crimes committed against the Jews of France had a distinctly political goal, namely, to prepare French Jewish political leadership for the postwar era and assure that Jews would speak with one voice, equipped with evidence that buttressed their legal and material claims. In part, Schneersohn and his collaborators wanted to avoid a repetition of the political weakness and ideological divisions in the Jewish community after the First World War.[33] The organizers designated Schneersohn as the center's president and elected a six-member *comité directeur*: Meiss and André Weill for the Consistoire, Grinberg and Herman for the FSJF, Rabbi Hirschler for the rabbinate, and Bernheim for ORT.[34] The meeting resolved to coordinate the documentation work of other institutions, maintaining their autonomy but working out a "common program."[35] An undated document, probably composed the day of the meeting or soon after, outlines an ambitious agenda:

> Above all, we want to write the Great Book of the martyrdom of French Judaism. To that end, we need to compile an immense documentation of what is happening in the two zones, and study the new legislation and its effects in all their aspects: account for the stolen or Aryanized Jewish property; portray . . . the suffering of so many internees, deportees and Jewish hostages shot dead; illustrate the heroism of the Jewish fighters . . . record the attitude of governments, of the administration, of the different levels of public opinion; it is important to note the reactions of the intellectuals, the middle and working classes, the people representing the old and new parties—the various churches. . . . In short, we deem it necessary to bring to light—in a strictly objective manner—everything having a favorable or unfavorable effect on the Jewish world of France. Secondly, there is reason to prepare . . . a file of claims of the Jews in France, foreign Jews as well as French. Thus, the goal we propose is to work together to compile this vast documentation [and] draw conclusions from it.[36]

In the midst of war the documenters thus sought to prepare for the demands of the postwar era, specifically to foster the reintegration of Jews into French society and support their claims for justice and redress, in France and internationally. Although they were themselves the rare beneficiaries of a relatively mild occupation, they assumed that they were not alone: "There is no doubt that at this current moment our coreligionists in other countries are also compiling documentations concerning their respective countries." When assembled, this international documentation would "eventually allow the Jews to take concrete positions [and] formulate them before the League of Nations, which we hope will be more just and stronger this time." The leaders' abiding faith in the ultimate triumph of objective and accurate information strengthened their confidence that those who might "be called upon to speak in our name one day"[37] would use the archive to preserve the voice of those assembled in Grenoble, and also to fight for justice, preserve the memory of the war years, and influence future history.

To carry out this program, the Grenoble group appointed "commissions" to research nine major focus areas.[38] This structure, as well as the research fields, strikingly foreshadowed the CDJC's postwar action plan. The first commission dealt with German and Vichy legislation affecting Jews in Continental France and its colonies; the differences in treatment between French and foreign-born Jews, whether naturalized or not; and, by comparison, the legal situation of non-Jews in France.[39] The second commission was to compile statistics for determining the economic consequences of this legislation. The third commission would collect information on conditions for internees in both zones, as well as on deportations, hostage takings, shootings or other executions of Jews, and the situation of Jewish fugitives.[40] The fourth commission covered the activities of official Jewish and non-Jewish organizations, especially the Jewish council of France, the UGIF, and the Commissariat Général aux Questions Juives, the Vichy regime's main organ for coordinating its anti-Jewish policies. The fifth and largest commission focused on Jewish organizations operating underground; it included most of the leaders as well as the only woman visible in the Grenoble records—the wife of ORT leader Léonce Bernheim.[41]

To demonstrate Jewish devotion to republican France, the sixth commission documented *Israélites combattants* who had served in the "War of 1939–1940" and in the First World War, including noncitizen Jewish volunteers.[42] The seventh commission focused on French public opinion about the Jews, in particular the press in both zones and the views of writers, publicists, scholars, government officials at all levels, including the mass organization of veterans founded after the defeat of 1940, and the Milice, the Vichy regime's militia. It also sought to assess the attitudes of Catholics and Protestants, the various political parties, and different social classes, especially the middle classes and "the little people, the workers, the peasants," as well as those of militant anti-Semites.

The eighth commission investigated Jewish responses to France's defeat and to the persecution, including the morale and cultural life of the Jewish populations in both zones, with particular attention to variant responses and attitudes of French-born and foreign-born Jews and to the relations between these groups. Finally, the commission responsible for the "file on peace" focused on "legal claims (moral reparations of war damage, abrogation of the legislation)," that would become relevant after the war.[43]

Four of the commissions met periodically at Schneersohn's apartment to discuss legislation, camps, Jewish responses to persecution, and French public opinion.[44]

The documentation center received its first records from the FSJF in Marseille some time before the end of the war, and Schneersohn commissioned the Polish-born poet Joseph Milbauer to write a book on "the tragedy of the Jews and the tragedy of France," parts of which he is said to have written before he escaped to Palestine in 1944.[45]

In addition to his documentation activity, Schneersohn worked with the UGIF to establish, in July 1943, the Foyer Amicale, a soup kitchen for impoverished immigrant Jews. He may have believed that such activities would make his commitment to research more acceptable.[46] Samy Lattès, the Consistoire's delegate in Grenoble, was not alone among Jewish leaders in the Southern Zone in observing: "As interesting as chronicling our 'Martyrdom' may be, I am afraid that at the current hour there are too many tragic and urgent problems ... [for] the leisure of writing, given that it requires spending hours at a desk in silent contemplation."[47]

Conditions for the 30,000–50,000 Jews who had sought protection in the Italian-occupied parts of the Southern Zone rapidly worsened after September 1943, when the Wehrmacht replaced Italian troops as the German-Italian alliance began to disintegrate after the fall of Mussolini and the Italian surrender to British and American armies.[48] The documentation center discontinued its activities and searched for safe places to hide its materials from the Germans or the Vichy Milice. As Henri Hertz recalled, "Packages of precious papers were confided to friends, leaving it to their judgment to destroy the papers if they were under suspicion and threat."[49] Despite these efforts, and even help from the *Résistance*, which became an increasing counterforce to the German occupiers and the Vichy regime, three-quarters of the collection was lost.[50] In particular, the camp commission's records vanished after the Gestapo arrested its director, Chief Rabbi Hirschler, in December 1943 and deported him to Auschwitz two months later.[51] Under constant threat of death, the group's members dispersed and went into hiding.[52] Schneersohn, whose apartment had served as the documentation center, left Grenoble for the Dordogne countryside in December 1943, where he was hidden with his wife by non-Jewish farmers.[53] Most of his associates also survived in hiding in the rural south.[54] But the group lost several of its key figures, among them Hirschler, Lambert, Bernheim, Glaeser, and Hermann.[55] The wartime agenda for researching the Jewish catastrophe had to wait for France's liberation.

Holocaust Research Institutionalized: Realizing the Center of Contemporary Jewish Documentation in Paris

Following the liberation of Paris on August 25, 1944, and the subsequent surrender of German forces in France, Schneersohn and his surviving collaborators moved to Paris, the French capital and—with almost half of the nation's 250,000

Jews—the center of French Jewish life. Accordingly, the main prewar Jewish institutions, including the Consistoire Central, the FSJF, and philanthropic organizations such as the Alliance Israélite Universelle (AIU), reestablished themselves in the capital, to be joined by such new organizations as the Conseil Représentatif des Israélites de France (CRIF). Uniting Zionist, non-Zionist, and Bundist (Jewish socialist) factions, the CRIF served as the central representative body of French Jewish organizations in parallel with the central religious institution, the Consistoire Central.[56]

Schneersohn and some thirty colleagues resumed their documentation work in mid-December 1944. Most were Jews of eastern European origin, including such veteran researchers from the Grenoble days as Ruven Grinberg, the Russian-born communal activist Wladimir Schah and his son Eugène, the Russian-born lawyer Jacques Szeftel, the Romanian-born lawyer Marcel Livian, and the Polish-born chemical engineer Joseph Milner. Schneersohn also recruited a number of new collaborators, among them the Russian-born lawyer and journalist Léon Poliakov, who had been familiar with the Grenoble center but had apparently not associated with it previously;[57] the Russian-born writers and journalists David Knout, Jacques Ratner, Don Aminado, and Joseph Billig; and the Russian-born artist Philippe Hosiasson. Most of these *métèques*—Schneersohn's own term[58]—had come to France before or after the First World War, received academic training at French universities, become naturalized in the 1930s, and engaged in the social, political, cultural and philanthropic networks of Jewish immigrants, mainly the FSJF, but also the emigration aid organization HICEM, the vocational training organization ORT, and the children's relief agency OSE.[59] A number of prominent personalities from established French Jewish families affiliated with the central institutions of French Jewry also assisted in the documentation work, among them Schneersohn's collaborators in Grenoble, the lawyer Léon Meiss, the journalist and lawyer Pierre Paraf, the communal activist Gaston Kahn, and the writer Henri Hertz.

The documentation team began its work by reconstituting five of the Grenoble commissions, those researching camps, public opinion and the press, the behavior of the Jewish population during the occupation, the economic effects of Vichy's anti-Jewish policies, and anti-Jewish legislation.[60] Now that the cataclysm of French Jews lay in the past, the Paris documentation center would focus on historical research. "Our mission is to write the history of the Jewish tragedy in France under the occupation,"[61] Isaac Schneersohn declared at a meeting of the camp commission in February 1945. Jacques Ratner of OSE, a journalist who acted as that commission's general spokesman, concurred in outlining the center's procedure. It would first "collect all the documents concerning Jewish life in France under the occupation." Based on this documentary evidence, it would then publish "works describing the economic, social, [and] material . . . life of the Jews at that time."[62]

In March 1945, the documentation center officially became the Centre de Documentation Juive Contemporaine (CDJC), a name that emphasized its interest in "contemporary Jewish" research.[63] Livian and Hertz proposed this change to distinguish the center from other documentation efforts underway, in particular the government-sponsored historical committee to study the occupation and liberation of France (later Comité d'Histoire de la Deuxième Guerre Mondiale; Committee for the History of the Second World War), initiated by the newly elected government of Charles de Gaulle in October 1944. Headed by the non-Jewish historians Lucien Febvre and Henri Michel, this official committee focused primarily on the history of the *Résistance* and largely ignored the history of French Jews.[64]

The new center's board of directors, reconstituted in March 1945, incorporated representatives from several major Paris-based Jewish organizations, among them Léon Meiss, president of the Consistoire and of the CRIF; Gaston Kahn of the AJDC (which financed the center); Wladimir Schah (HICEM); Joseph Milner (OSE); Jacques Szeftel (ORT); Ruven Grinberg and Marc Jarblum (FSJF); and Robert Gamzon, the founder of the Jewish scouting organization Eclaireurs Israélites de France.[65] Schneersohn—a headstrong personality disinclined to subordinate himself to the will of others—painstakingly worked to maintain the center's independence from these larger Jewish communal organizations. As he explained to the board of directors on March 15, 1945, "Certain organizations would have wanted us to be integrated into one or the other; this was the case for the Federation [FSJF] and the CRIF, but given the neutral and apolitical nature of our documentary and scholarly work, we preferred to stay independent."[66] At this time Schneersohn, as well as his colleagues, still regarded the CDJC as a temporary institution, based on his estimation that it would take another six to eight months to complete the documentation project.[67] In the following months, they realized that only a permanent institution could support the collecting, research, and publication of the intensity and scope required to bring the Holocaust into public consciousness and educate the nation into which the survivors sought to reintegrate.

Breaking the Silence: The Jewish Tragedy's Place in French Wartime Suffering

It did not take long for the CDJC activists to realize that non-Jewish Frenchmen would not acknowledge that the particular fate suffered by Jews distinguished them from political deportees, POWs, or forced laborers. The inclusive concept of victimhood promoted by the new de Gaulle government glossed over differences between groups and overlooked those who had been deported and systematically murdered for "racial" reasons. This policy enabled non-Jewish Frenchmen to deny responsibility for the cataclysm suffered by Jewish citizens and residents in France.

The CDJC activists acknowledged that this silence was not specific to their nation; rather, the malaise was endemic in postwar Europe. At a session of the camp commission in February 1945, Jacques Ratner noted that both "public opinion and the leaders of certain countries prefer not to speak about the tragedy of the Jews during the war, nor about their present situation or about their future." In particular, he cited Allied policies that—rather than addressing the specificity of Nazi crimes against the Jews—considered "the Jewish problem as being one and the same as that of the other populations who suffered from German terror."[68]

But Ratner's particular concern was France, where "people do not like to address the Jewish question. It has almost completely disappeared from the newspapers and magazines." He attributed this avoidance to the government's fear of stirring up dormant anti-Semitism, and to the *honte refoulée*—repressed shame—caused by an awareness of France's role in the assault on its Jews: "France knows what it did to the Jews and to what extent the French administration was implicated in the persecution. . . . For that reason the Jewish question in France is regarded as a 'shameful disease.'"[69]

Thus the CDJC workers saw their main goal as breaking the French public's "blockade of silence"[70] regarding the Jewish tragedy. The meticulous documentary evidence they gathered would bring about a moral and political catharsis of French society. In Ratner's words to the camp commission:

> France must purify itself. There is no need for false shame, we simply have to admit that parts of the French administration consciously did wrong to the Jews. The free forces must begin their work of purification. Our documents and information will be used by the government to bring the criminals of Vichy to justice, and if this is successful, then . . . the documentation center will have served both the Jews and France.[71]

Ratner further insisted that the CDJC documentation would help the French public understand that the Jews who sustained Nazism's most violent onslaught would succeed in "overcoming the blow and turning the world's attention to the power that intended to destroy them."[72]

CDJC activists generally agreed on their mission to educate the French: by documenting the Holocaust, they would advance France's return to the democratic path. By contrast, they engaged in constant internal debates over strategy. Would criticizing France and addressing French responsibility for the genocide brand them as "unpatriotic," thus jeopardizing Jews' fragile reintegration into French society? How could they address specific Jewish suffering while also seeking the return to a civic equality that disregarded religious or ethnic bonds? CDJC affiliates agreed that their place was in France, and they strongly identified with the nation's republican traditions. Some, however, opted for direct confrontation with the French over their past, whereas others advocated a more diplomatic approach. These differences played out in discussions about such subjects as French anti-Semitism and collaboration, as well as Jews' behavior and resistance during the occupation.

In February 1945, the commission on public opinion and the press took up the issue of French anti-Semitism. While researchers generally agreed on the persistence of anti-Semitism in France's past and present, recalling the fierce xenophobic and anti-Semitic atmosphere of the interwar years, they divided over how to present their views to the public, in particular how to do so without promoting prejudice against Jews.[73] Some advocated relentless confrontation to show how historically rooted anti-Semitic traditions had enabled the German occupiers to carry out their anti-Jewish policies.[74]

David Knout—a Russian-born revisionist Zionist, in France since 1920—argued against blaming everything on "the Krauts [*boches*]. Anti-Semitism must be fought where it is."[75] Similarly, Joseph Milner, a Polish-born chemical engineer living in France since 1909, told his colleagues: "In order to demonstrate the foolishness of French anti-Semitism itself, you have to see the origins of organized French anti-Semitism after 1870.... You have to reckon with the fact that French anti-Semitism still exists and is deeply rooted."[76] Agreeing that the French should be forced to look in the mirror, Marcel Livian proposed a CDJC publication featuring texts by pre-Vichy anti-Semites but inoculating them with commentary showing how anti-Semitism had "poisoned France and how to prevent such texts from being written again."[77] Jacques Ratner agreed that such a strategy was "the only way. Maybe it is painful, . . . but once you apply the scalpel you must go as deep as possible, because if you leave a little bit of pus it will reappear one day or another."[78]

Others countered that publishing classic French anti-Semitic texts would just reinforce hostility against the Jews and support ethnic stereotypes.[79] "There are many things which a non-Jewish Frenchman will consider true," Schneersohn cautioned, "among them the insufficiency of [Jews'] assimilation."[80] But Ratner again defended the "duty" of Jews to expose French anti-Semitic diatribes "and show to what level of spiritual and moral decadence human beings can sink in following the enemy."[81]

In the end, the CDJC activists struck a compromise. They would openly critique anti-Semitism, but, rather than to expose its historical roots in France, they would use Nazi and Vichy documents to demonstrate the German influence on public opinion and the press in France during the occupation.[82] After all, Schneersohn reminded his colleagues, although "France has always been an anti-Semitic country," they should not forget the essential point: "We do not want to accuse the French people . . . our mission is to settle a score with Vichy and the Germans."[83] As the center's director, his word often wielded an outsized influence in such discussions.

CDJC workers tended to limit direct criticism of France to their internal discussions. In public they focused on the actions of the Germans and their French collaborators while declining to accuse the French collectively of collaboration. This was a matter of political calculation, since the wish to become part of their French surroundings outweighed the drive to merely expose the inconvenient truth. Thus the activists sought to show that, while a "few bad Frenchmen... had helped the Germans in their work,"[84] large segments of the population had behaved decently toward the Jews and had helped them to survive the Holocaust in France. Consequently, the CDJC's study of public opinion considered the help that numerous individuals in the churches, the French police, and the Interior Ministry had extended to Jews.[85] For example, at a meeting of the public opinion and press commission in May 1945, the lawyer Jacques Rabinovitch discussed his research for a study on public opinion during the Vichy years:

> In the year 1941 the relations between Germans and French were not clearly defined, and, in the interest of a complete documentation... it must be mentioned that there was some level of resistance among the members of the Interior Ministry and of the Préfecture de Police; the constant pressure of the Germans must also be shown. I would even speak of a certain level of resistance among the French administration. Beginning in 1943, resistance groups were created inside the Préfecture de Police which communicated with all the resistance groups in the Northern Zone.... Without the help of these groups in the Préfecture de Police, fewer Israelites would have been saved.[86]

Similarly, the legal expert Lucienne Scheid-Haas, who had been active both in the UGIF and the underground, noted "the involvement of large numbers of minor functionaries in Paris and in the country in not only destroying Jewish files but also in providing [Jews] with 'real' false papers."[87] In order to give a nuanced picture of events, she also emphasized the role of informants in the police force who worked directly for the French branch of Adolf Eichmann's IV B 4 "Jewish Affairs" department under the authority of SS-Hauptsturmführer Theodor Dannecker.[88] Ultimately, the activists chose to focus on a version of the past that was lenient toward the French people as a whole but highlighted the behavior of some collaborators, while showing the profound German influence on French public opinion during the years of occupation.[89]

The issue of specific Jewish suffering and the behavior of the Jewish victims, inherent in the CDJC's intent to "educate public opinion in France and in the world about the way of life and the sacrifices of the Jews in this country,"[90] aroused still more controversy. Seeking a conciliatory approach, in June 1945 Ratner explained in the CDJC bulletin that Jewish suffering, although disproportionate, was not disconnected from that experienced by non-Jews. Rather, he explained, Jews had "suffered twofold—as Frenchmen and as Jews—from the violence of the occupier."[91]

The debates within the camp commission show that CDJC affiliates sought to portray Jewish suffering and victimhood while also presenting these victims as favorably as possible, in particular as an active group who, even as internees, displayed communal solidarity and a spirit of resistance. They pointed to both the relief work provided by Jewish organizations and the cultural life created by internees. For example, Alexandre Kowarsky, himself a former leader in the Zionist resistance group Armée Juive, noted:

> There is something interesting that not everybody knows and which has always struck me: to see that a magnificent intellectual life continued in the camps despite the atmosphere of pain. I was astonished by the number of lectures held, by the groups of people learning Hebrew, of painters, [of those] who studied languages [and] philosophy. I think that, from a moral point of view, this aspect of camp life must be stressed.[92]

Beyond lauding the relief work of Jewish groups, Kowarsky and others stressed the important presence in the camps of non-Jewish organizations such as the Quaker American Friends Service Committee and the Nîmes Committee, a body organized by non-Jewish relief workers to assist Jews.[93]

The varying wartime experiences of French- and foreign-born Jews complicated the effort to present a positive and unified picture of the Jewish victims. Although foreign or stateless Jews had been the first victims of both the Germans and the Vichy regime and made up two-thirds of France's Jewish dead, CDJC activists tended to minimize antagonisms between the two groups in the interest of presenting a picture of united action.[94] It was mainly the foreign-born who emphasized this distinction, thus echoing the social, cultural, and ideological divisions that had engulfed immigrant and native Jews before and during the occupation and had prevented a more unified response in the face of the persecution. Thus controversy arose during the occupation over the policy of the UGIF's French Jewish leadership, which, while providing relief and rescue networks to immigrant Jews, tried to avoid direct confrontation with Vichy and German authorities in the hope that the French state would ultimately protect its Jewish citizens.[95] The CDJC worked out some of these issues in discussing a work on Jewish resistance activities, the commission's first publication on Jewish behavior during the occupation. Its lead researcher, the Russian-born David Knout, argued in April 1945 that "it is commonly known in this country of France that at that time of confusion and misfortune, there were two segments of humanity: French Jews and foreign Jews. To deny this would only diminish the authenticity of your testimony."[96]

Alsatian-born writer and communal activist Gaston Kahn disagreed, citing "raids in Marseille, [in which] the percentage of French Jews was at least as significant as that of foreign Jews."[97] His fellow Alsatian Henri Hertz tried a more conciliatory approach. French and foreign Jews' different experiences had been largely a matter of timing and had not undermined group solidarity: "The French Jews were tolerated a little bit longer, but it does not mean that this resulted in a schism.... This forbearance toward French Jews allowed them to help the foreign Jews."[98]

Most foreign-born coworkers, however, agreed with Knout that the Vichy regime had fundamentally discriminated between French and foreign Jews. Thus Jacques Polonski noted that "foreign Jews were the first to be deported," and Schneersohn recounted his request to Foreign Minister Georges Bonnet to intervene on behalf of 350 foreign Jews who were to be sent to a camp. Bonnet had responded by recalling his conversation with the minister of state: "[Pierre] 'Laval told me: at the expense of foreign Jews I will save the French ones.' It is Vichy who said this."[99] Joseph Milner, also Polish-born, stressed that the targeting of foreign Jews had given many French Jews a false sense of security, leading them to believe "that they will not be touched. . . . That day when Xavier Vallat was appointed commissioner for Jewish questions, some people said 'This does not concern us.'"[100] Milner attributed this naïveté both to French-born Jews' blind belief in the French state and to their social distance from immigrant Jews.

While agreeing with Knout in principle, Romanian-born lawyer Marcel Livian warned that addressing such internal matters in a work aimed at a predominantly non-Jewish mass audience could distort the image of Jewish resisters. Like uplifting depictions of camp life, the intended publication aimed to show "that Jews did other things than weeping, being shot, deported, and despoiled."[101] The issue of French versus foreign Jews, Livian concluded "is essentially a family quarrel . . ., too painful to be mixed with what ought to be a song of praise."[102] Polonski and Schneersohn agreed that such divisions did not belong in a study of Jewish resistance, although they thought it should be examined elsewhere.[103] In the end, the commission urged Knout to leave internal Jewish divisions out of his monograph.

The protracted discussions of Knout's work opened a wider window on the CDJC's integrationist strategy. Its focus on resistance—indeed, the adoption of the dominant postwar French discourse of collective resistance—is telling, since the commission's mandate was to study Jewish behavior in general.[104] The CDJC's multifaceted image of Jewish resistance acknowledged a French society which celebrated the *Résistance* and honored victims of political persecution while largely ignoring those persecuted as Jews. CDJC works that considered spiritual and armed, individual and collective resistance refuted the image of passive victimhood in order to give Jews a role in the liberation of France.[105] In this way, the CDJC presented its documentation of the Holocaust as a contribution to the *Résistance*.

For Knout, cofounder and commander of the Armée Juive, a Zionist resistance group in the Southern Zone, "Jewish resistance . . . was conducted under the blue and white flag."[106] Some of his colleagues, however, rejected such a selective focus. Jacques Szeftel, for example, argued against any emphasis that would downgrade the actions of any Jews who fought against the Nazi occupiers and the Vichy regime, including those in non-Jewish groups. Only by considering the broadest spectrum of resistance activities by Jews would the work contribute to the history both of Jewry and of France.[107] Joseph Bass, a Russian-born industrial engineer who had commanded Jewish maquis groups in the Southern Zone, offered a particularly sharp rejoinder to Knout: "In a country where we live among non-Jews, how can you separate the actions of Jews from those of non-Jews?"[108] Bass observed that many of the "Jewish resisters," while fighting in more inclusive groups, "did not forget their Jewish roots." Indeed, even those who belonged to "the specifically Jewish resistance, which means those who particularly cared about the masses of persecuted Jews, were not necessarily Zionists." And while many Jewish resisters had no specifically Jewish political agenda, they were driven by "one political goal: to act against the persecution of the Jews."[109] Ruven Grinberg, formerly president of the Comité général de défense, one of the umbrella organizations of Jewish resistance fighters in the Southern Zone, agreed. Whether the book concerned "the Jewish resistance or the resistance of Jews," it must include everything from the Armée Juive to Jewish communist groups.[110] Isaac Schneersohn also backed an inclusive approach, reminding his colleagues that the publication's practical goals included countering "numerous attacks against foreign Jews," and that it was therefore "necessary to show the extraordinary role they played in this clandestine fight."[111] When published in 1947, Knout's *Contribution à l'histoire de la Résistance Juive en France, 1940–1944* adopted an integrative concept of Jewish resistance.[112]

Jewish resistance emerged as a central theme for the CDJC in the early postwar years because it allowed the survivors to tell their individual stories of persecution yet at the same time to integrate their experiences with the dominant *Résistance* discourse.[113] Not just victims, French and foreign Jews had joined in the armed struggle to liberate France and thus deserved acceptance as equal citizens. Thus the CDJC increasingly advertised its documentation project as a Jewish contribution to the *Résistance*. As Schneersohn explained in January 1947, "Jews were represented in all groups of the 'maquis,' and among the 'maquis' they experienced a full merger, a brotherly blending of foreign and French Jews. . . . I am proud to say that our Documentation Center was part of the [maquis] and fought together with them."[114] That April, on the occasion of the CDJC's fourth anniversary, Marcel Livian, then the center's secretary, stated that "the CDJC cannot be detached from the *Résistance* movement in its goals, the dangers to which it exposed its members, [and] the profound inspiration which animated it."[115] On the occasion of the first European-wide conference of Jewish historical commissions and documentation centers hosted by the CDJC in December 1947, Henri Hertz informed an audience of international visitors that the Grenoble documentation center had itself been a cell of the French *Résistance*.[116] Five years later, on the tenth anniversary of the founding meeting in Grenoble, the lawyer, politician, and writer André Spire described its activists as "maquis documentaires."[117]

The CDJC workers knew, however, that their efforts to break the silence about the Holocaust and to raise public awareness of the role of Jews in the *Résistance* would only succeed if they were able to assemble a broad range of documentary evidence to underpin their assertions and deflect accusations of bias or sectarianism.

Accordingly, from the outset, the CDJC undertook a wide-ranging campaign to acquire archival collections.

In Pursuit of Justice: Collecting the Evidence of Crime

Since most of the documents collected in Grenoble had been lost or destroyed, the Paris center voraciously collected anything pertaining to the fate of Jews in France, whether of Jewish or non-Jewish provenance.[118] After the liberation several Jewish organizations, including the FSJF, OSE, and ORT, handed over their wartime collections to the CDJC, in some cases responding to appeals published in the Jewish press.[119] For example, in April 1945, the CDJC appealed to local and regional Jewish organizations, communities, educational institutions, and individual Jews in France: "Everyone can help by giving us any documents concerning the life of the Jews under the Occupation. Individuals or communities that have such material and cannot give it away should contact us so that we may copy this material. We call upon everyone and thank you in advance for your collaboration."[120]

The majority of the CDJC's archival holdings assembled in the first years after the war consisted of materials of non-Jewish provenance, mainly original documents left behind by the Germans or the Vichy regime. These were acquired thanks to Schneersohn's good relations with several prominent personalities from the *Résistance* or the anti-Pétain camp who now enjoyed public recognition and supported the center's work. The most significant of these friends was Justin Godart, a non-Jewish politician of the Radical Party, formerly senator of the Rhône Department and minister of labor in the Third Republic, who served as the center's honorary chairman.[121] With Godart's assistance, Léon Poliakov, a Russian-born lawyer and journalist who had joined the group as its research director in fall 1944, obtained a box containing parts of the archives of the SS administration in France.[122] The retrieval of other major German archival material followed, including the records of the Gestapo in Paris, partial archives of the Wehrmacht and SS in France, and the personal records of Alfred Rosenberg, Nazi Party ideologue, racial theorist, and Reich minister for the Occupied Eastern Territories. The CDJC also obtained records of key Vichy offices, notably the Institut d'Études des Questions Juives, founded in May 1941 as the major German-sponsored instrument of anti-Jewish propaganda and "research" in France, as well as the archive of one of its directors, the racist anthropologist Georges Montandon.

By January 1946, the CDJC archives had "213 German files, with authentic signatures of Otto Abetz, [Theodor] Dannecker, Dr. [Helmut] Knochen, [Carl-Theodor] Zeitschel, and other torturers . . . and the documents that we received from Toulouse on the regional branches of the Commissariat Général aux Questions Juives."[123] During the following year the CDJC copied the archives of the commissariat itself, Vichy's central agency for the planning and implementation

Staff members of the Centre de Documentation Juive Contemporaine work in the documentation center's library and archives, Paris, 1953. *CDJC Photo Archives MXXA_53_1*

of its anti-Jewish policies, and of the German General Staff in France, formerly headquartered at the Hotel Majestic in Paris.[124] The CDJC's prompt action to retrieve any and all documents relating to French Jews during the occupation proved especially prescient, since in December 1946 the French Ministry of the Interior—as part of its proactive quest to reestablish the equality of all its citizens and to right the wrongs of Vichy—ordered its administration to destroy all documents on Vichy's racial discrimination and persecution of the Jews.[125]

That same year, after supplying the French Delegation at the International Military Tribunal (IMT) at Nuremberg with documents from its archives, the CDJC assumed an advisory function on Jewish matters to the French Delegation to the IMT and to the Nuremberg Military Tribunal.[126] It also obtained authorization to examine the American archives at Nuremberg, and sent Joseph Billig and Léon Poliakov to recover documents relating to Jews.[127] Between 1947 and 1949, with the permission of General Telford Taylor, chief counsel for war crimes of the Nuremberg Military Tribunal, Billig and Poliakov photocopied and microfilmed all the tribunal's materials pertaining to European Jews in general. Accommodated in a hotel requisitioned by the occupying forces, they shared an office in the rooms of the IMT archives.[128] In total the CDJC archives received

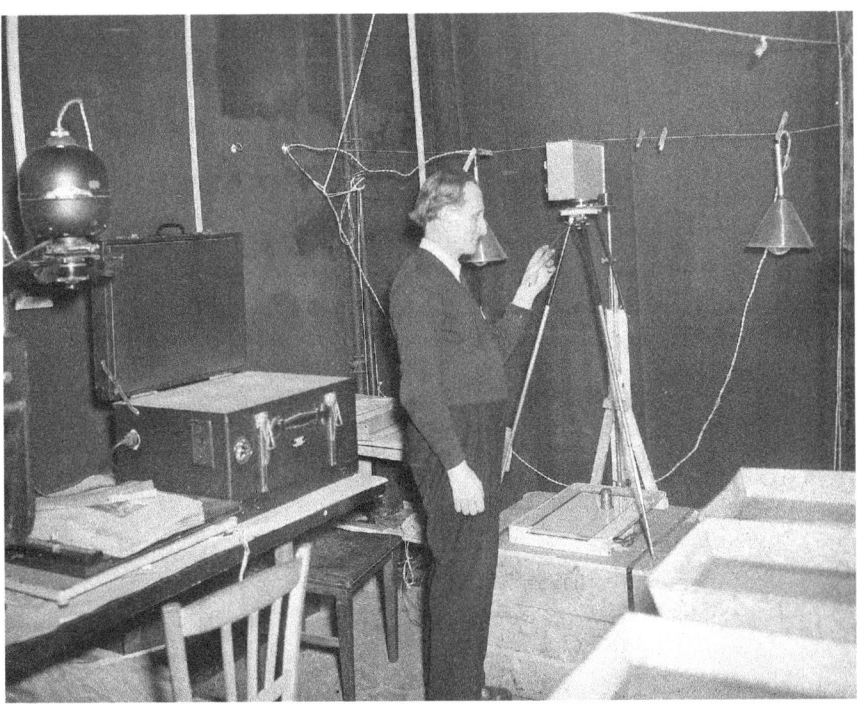

The photographic lab that the Centre de Documentation Juive Contemporaine in Paris acquired with the financial help of the American Jewish Joint Distribution Committee, 1953. *CDJC Photo Archives MXXA_53_132*

three tons of copied and filmed documents from the tribunal, as well as one hundred discs of sound recordings relevant to Jewish issues.[129] Further, and in the face of great technical and financial difficulties, they received 9,000 meters of film footage of German propaganda material and films made by the Allies when entering German camps.[130]

While the Nuremberg trials themselves did not allow for any "Jewish voice"—there was no official Jewish representation at the tribunal, and only a handful of Jewish witnesses testified—the presence of Billig and Poliakov, and the fact that the French and American delegations had consulted CDJC's archives, boosted the self-confidence of center activists at a time of uncertainty, both for their own material and physical security and concerning the inclusion of Jews in postwar French society.[131] Thus recognition by tribunal prosecutors and staff led Billig to think that "the high protection" that the center enjoyed in Nuremberg gave it "a semiofficial status."[132] Nonetheless, the CDJC's financial constraints caused him to return to Paris at the end of March 1949.[133]

Financial support from the American Joint Distribution Committee (AJDC/ Joint) enabled the CDJC to buy microfilm and Photostat equipment so that it could exchange documents with other institutions. The center also microfilmed its own archival holdings and placed the films in a bank vault to protect them against theft, loss, or damage by those who would like to see the evidence disappear.[134] This caution was warranted. In November 1945, the CDJC found numerous anonymous "leaflets, full of insults against the Jews and their monopolizing of flats" posted on its door at 6, rue Lelande. Schneersohn reasonably feared that "this band . . . will come one night . . . and take away our records."[135] With the Joint's help, the CDJC housed the card catalogue for its collection in a separate location and the actual archive at 19, rue de Teheran, where the Joint had its offices.[136] Yet this archive would serve the CDJC's goal of educating the French public about the fate of the Jews only if its holdings reached a broader audience.

"Sewage Workers" of Holocaust Historiography: Preparing and Publishing Studies of the Cataclysm

To carry out its public education mission, the CDJC designed an ambitious and multifaceted publication program that met high standards of accurate documentation and rigorous scholarship. The center's own publishing house brought out a monthly periodical and three series of books. These Éditions du Centre, financed with AJDC support, comprised a "legal series" (*série juridique*) featuring legal texts related to Jews in France and its colonies during the war; a series of "studies and monographs" (*études et monographies*) containing the first synthetic studies on different aspects of German and Vichy policies regarding the Jews of France as well as their responses to persecution; and a documents series with editions of original Nazi and Vichy records.

True to the CDJC's self-understanding as primarily a *documentation* center, and because its activists believed that the Nazis' own official words provided the most effective and objective picture of the Holocaust, the documents series made up half of the center's twenty books published between 1945 and 1954. The release of perpetrator documents both satisfied the wish to settle scores with the German occupiers and the Vichy regime and educated the French on the recent crimes against the Jews of France. The activists believed that these documents—unlike more problematic French anti-Semitic tracts—needed no embellishments to reveal the corruption and barbarity of the Nazi regime. As Don Aminado put it, "Some documents speak for themselves, better than any commentaries." In presenting the material in an unvarnished form, he explained, "we want to document and not create emotions. What we have is raw materials. Truly, our work is that of sewage workers."[137] The activists also believed that the focus on historical documents would help convince the French public of the center's high-minded objectivity. "We do not pursue . . . any political goal, we do not belong to any party, we do not make any propaganda,"[138] Schneersohn vowed in his preface to a CDJC publication in 1945.

Through its publications, the center sought to reach two different audiences simultaneously. Its primary audience was non-Jews, in particular the French political elites, and its language of publication was French. Yet Schneersohn also hoped to reach a non-Jewish audience beyond France.[139] Its secondary audience was Jews in and outside France. The publications served different purposes for each audience. For French gentiles they explained the fate of the Jews at the hands of the Germans and the Vichy regime and demonstrated the survivors' worthiness to be accepted as equal citizens. At the same time, they served commemorative needs for survivors, who—in Schneersohn's words—"were charged with an obligation to the martyrs, the victims of oppression or murder by the enemy, after having fought until the end against this monstrous wave of violence."[140] From this perspective, publishing the narrative of the Jewish cataclysm was a moral imperative. The survivors were equally obliged to future generations, and the CDJC's publications provided a means of passing on the narrative of the destruction to those who could not themselves be witnesses: "We . . . want our sons and the sons of all those who, like us, survived these years of hell to know, understand, and one day judge and act on the basis of exact knowledge of the monstrous events to which their fathers and so many of ours had succumbed."[141] Schneersohn also hoped that the CDJC's publications would serve as a model for Jews elsewhere in Europe when confronting their respective governments with the wrongs done to their Jewish populations in the recent past.[142]

Beginning in April 1945, the CDJC's monthly *Bulletin du Centre de Documentation Juive Contemporaine*, edited by David Knout, reflected current events in the Jewish and non-Jewish worlds, including news of the CDJC's work and a bibliography of literature on the recent past. A column entitled "The Enemy Speaks to You" presented German documents from the center's collection—in Knout's words: "a kind of intimate diary of notes taken by the Germans, terribly accusatory for them."[143] Unlike the CDJC's monographs, which addressed the political elites, the monthly aimed at a broad readership of Jews and non-Jews in France and to a lesser degree abroad.[144]

"The Passover of Liberation," an editorial by Schneersohn in the *Bulletin*'s first issue, described its mission as "a work of testimony" and stressed its quest for objectivity: "We conduct this work without any political goal, without any ulterior motive whether apologetic or propagandist in nature, with our only ambition to be impartial witnesses taking an oath to the truth on countless graves."[145] The editorial appealed to multiple audiences on several levels. Schneersohn even sought to reach Germans, in particular a young generation whose consciences might let them "realize what their fathers and brothers did and what they have to atone for." For his French readers Schneersohn invoked the situation of Jewish survivors who found themselves "in the country of the declaration of human rights and the Revolution, in the country of Pascal, Rénan, Montaigne," yet whose "Passover of the deliverance" in 1945 mourned "so many voids around the . . . holiday table at which every family counts its losses." The *Bulletin* would publish the survivors' testimonies and documents, thus letting future generations "know and understand the monstrous truth." Their publication would also provide "nutrition . . . for those who judge and govern. Our work will serve as an appeal to the conscience of the world."[146] The *Bulletin* was renamed *Le Monde Juif* (The Jewish World) in August 1946.[147]

The CDJC's most ambitious undertaking was the publication of three series of books, the fruits of its research commissions' work. Already in 1945 the juridical commission compiled—and the CDJC published—three volumes in its legal series on "the racial laws in economic and juridical perspective," edited by the jurists Raymond Sarraute, Jacques Rabinovitch, Joseph Lubetzki, and Paul (Pavel) Tager. They embodied the CDJC's conviction that publishing these legal texts was a vital tool in the struggle to return to a normal life in France.[148]

The Studies and Monographs series began in 1946 with three titles. Jacques Polonski's *Press, Propaganda, and Public Opinion in Occupied France*, a product of the public opinion and press commission, aimed explicitly at a non-Jewish audience, specifically political figures in the new Republic. Five of its six chapters discussed the collaborationist press, offering analyses of images and statistics as instruments of propaganda that aimed to turn public opinion against the Jews, paying particular attention to schools and universities; the sixth chapter concerned the underground press.[149] *On the History of Internment Camps in Anti-France*—a term indicating that these camps were not part of the true France—was based on work by the camp commission and written by Dr. Joseph Weill, a physician renowned for his humanitarian work in the French internment camps. Focusing on the camps at Gurs in the Southern Zone and Drancy in the Occupied Zone, his book discussed internment policies as an example of French collaboration with the Germans, the suffering of inmates, and efforts to provide humanitarian assistance. Weill's work largely drew from official government records and those of camp administrations and relief organizations. By contrast, George Wellers, a prominent Russian-born naturalized French scientist, described his personal ordeal of deportation, internment, and camp survival in the memoir *From Drancy to Auschwitz*.[150]

In 1947 the series published three complementary monographs on Jewish resistance produced by the commission on Jewish behavior during the occupation. *The Activity of Jewish Organizations in Occupied France* intended to acquaint readers with "the silent and fierce passive resistance of the Jewish associations and organizations,"[151] including the AJDC, the Consistoire, UGIF, OSE, ORT, and others. Knout's *Contribution to the History of Jewish Resistance in France, 1940–1944* set out to illuminate "active and aggressive resistance, which increasingly made use of arms and which was passionately undertaken by the elite of the Jewish youth."[152] He discussed a great variety of resistance movements, whose ideological outlooks ranged from distinctly Jewish and Zionist, to nonpolitical immigrant formations, to communist. Complementing these two document-based volumes was *Jews in Combat: Testimony on the Activity of a Resistance Movement*, the memoir of Jacques

Lazarus (nom de guerre "Capitaine Jaquel"), a commander of the Zionist Armée Juive and later the Jewish Combat Organization (which was formed in 1944 from the merger of the Armée Juive and the Jewish scouting organization EIF), with a preface by Henri Hertz.[153] In its focus on various forms of resistance, armed and unarmed, individual and collective, the CDJC adopted a stance that predated historiographic debates which entered academic Holocaust historiography beginning in the 1980s.[154]

The Documents series began in 1946 with a French translation of the "Stroop Report," a propagandist account of the Warsaw ghetto uprising and its subsequent vanquishing by SS officer Jürgen Stroop. Aside from Knout's introduction, *The Battle of the Warsaw Ghetto from the Perspective of the Germans* lacked any commentary. Since some of the CDJC activists feared that readers might take at face value this effort to discredit and belittle Jewish resistance, subsequent volumes in the series included critical commentaries.[155] These annotated volumes included two works by Léon Poliakov: *French Jews under Italian Occupation* (1946) and *The Yellow Star* (1949), a monograph covering the history of the yellow badge from the Middle Ages to Nazi-occupied Europe, with consideration of the responses of Jews and non-Jews.[156]

In 1947 the Documents series published a volume on the theft of Jewish cultural treasures, *The German Pillage of Works of Art and Libraries in the Possession of French Jews*, edited by the non-Jewish writer, poet, art critic, and former *Résistance* member Jean Cassou of the Musée d'Art Moderne in Paris; it included an introduction by Jacques Sabile (nom de plume of the Russian-born artist and future CDJC secretary Philippe Hosiasson) titled "National Socialist Aesthetics and the Organization of Fine Arts under the Third Reich." In the same year, the CDJC released a volume of documents on Nazi persecution of Jews throughout Europe, based on materials collected during the Nuremberg trials. *The Persecution of the Jews in France and other Western Countries as presented by France at Nuremberg* covered France, Denmark, and the Benelux and Baltic countries. Its editor was Henri Monneray, a lawyer of German Jewish émigré background and an assistant French prosecutor at the IMT. A preface by René Cassin, a prominent French Jewish lawyer, human rights activist, and vice president of the French Council of State, and an introduction by Edgar Faure, the French deputy prosecutor at the IMT, provided further credentials. The CDJC regarded this publication as vital in bringing the persecution and murder of Jews to public attention. Despite the widespread interest in—and numerous publications on—the Allied war crime trials, this volume was the first to shed light on the role of the Holocaust at Nuremberg.[157] Two years later, in 1949, a successor volume—*The Persecution of the Jews in the Countries of the East as Presented at Nuremberg*—also edited by Monneray, covered Poland, Romania, Hungary, Czechoslovakia, Bulgaria, Greece, Yugoslavia, and Russia. Like the earlier volume, it gained authority through its association with prominent names: in addition to the introduction by Cassin (who by then had played a central role in drafting the 1948 United

Nations' Universal Declaration of Human Rights), there was a laudatory preface by General Telford Taylor, chief prosecutor in the twelve American Nuremberg successor trials.[158]

Hoping to reach a broader audience, the CDJC increasingly supplemented its documentary volumes with commentary and synthesis that moved beyond the French context to provide an overview of Nazi policies against European Jews. In 1949, for example, the center published the lectures from a conference of Jewish documentation centers and historical commissions that it had sponsored in Paris in December 1947. In 1950, the CDJC published Michel Ansky's *The Jews in Algeria*, a study of the situation of the Jews in North Africa under the Vichy regime, and Joseph Billig's pioneering study, *Germany and the Genocide: Nazi Plans and Implementations*, which examined the German doctrine of "genocide" and compared its implementation in regard to Jews, Sinti and Roma, and Slavs.[159]

Acknowledging the CDJC's limited audience, in 1951 Poliakov turned to the commercial publishing house Calmann-Lévy to bring out his book *Harvest of Hate*, the first-ever overall study of the political history of the Third Reich's persecution and mass murder of European Jews. In addition to considering the responses of the Jewish victims, Poliakov's work also discussed the Holocaust in the wider context of the Nazis' treatment of other groups they deemed inferior.[160] Schneersohn objected that his colleague had spurned the CDJC's imprint, and the situation eventually led to a break between the two, as Poliakov described in his autobiography:

> President Schneersohn showed an extreme possessiveness regarding the CDJC's archives, which became obvious in his refusal to let anything be published outside of the Éditions du Centre. I found this policy absurd, and above all uncivil, because the works published in this manner only reached the hands of two or three hundred subscribers, almost all of whom were Jews and strongly committed. No bookstore sold these works and no critic could refer to them. The more I thought about the subject matter, which I got to know through collecting documents, the idea came to my mind to write a complete history of the genocide for a broad audience. Only a successful publisher could properly distribute such a work. I knew that Schneersohn would never be part of this project.[161]

In the wake of this dispute, Poliakov left the CDJC altogether. In fact, he had correctly assessed the potential audience of the center's publications. Their distribution fell short of expectations, and they went largely unnoticed by the wider public who regarded Jewish history as "exogenous."[162] Marginal in influence, these works left little imprint on the general French historiography of the period, which tended to ignore the Jewish fate. The Jews remained the *grand absent* for the next decades, during which Jewish and non-Jewish historiography on the Second World War in France followed parallel lines without convergence.[163]

Nevertheless, the CDJC can claim credit for its pioneer role in opening the historiography of Vichy's treatment of the Jews and for breaking the silence about the Holocaust in France, even if the circle of non-Jews willing to listen remained small.[164]

Counting on the Jewish Street: The Mobilization of Resources and Awareness in France and Beyond

In March 1945 Marcel Livian optimistically announced in a meeting of the CDJC board of directors that the documentation center "begins to count on the 'Jewish street' (yiddische gasse)."[165] Nonetheless, over the following two years, the activists were increasingly troubled by French Jews' lack of enthusiasm for either the center's work or its publications.[166] As noted earlier, continuing confrontations with anti-Semitism and non-Jews' unwillingness to listen to survivors' stories eventually caused many Jews to fall silent about their experiences as Jews during the years of occupation and to keep a low profile as Jews in public. By contrast, the CDJC sought to put the specific fate of the Jews on public display.[167] As a consequence, the center faced growing difficulties in reaching the Jewish community. Not only did its historical works and document collections apparently fail to interest larger segments of that community, in focusing on its mission on educating non-Jews, the CDJC had neglected its Jewish audience. Its documentation, for example, focused mainly on the perpetrators' words and actions against the Jews and how the organized Jewish community had responded, while giving limited attention to personal stories of individual Jews.

In 1947, the CDJC launched a campaign to increase its popularity within the French Jewish community. Léon Meiss, president of the Consistoire Central and the CRIF, reprimanded the CDJC for not trying hard enough to win the support of French Jews and for closing its eyes to the fact that "an important part of the Jewish population completely ignores the existence of the Center."[168] At his suggestion, in June 1947 the CDJC established a "commission for sales and distribution" that would devise a plan to "better reach Jewish and non-Jewish circles and sell our works."[169] Previously, the center had distributed its publications by subscription: for a fixed monthly sum interested readers received the latest publications. The new plan aimed to increase the number of subscribers throughout France from 600 to at least 2,000; at 150 francs per subscription, this would yield a projected monthly income of 300,000 francs.[170] Using the slogan "Every Jew must have the ten books of the CDJC in his library," the fundraising campaign aimed to market the center's publications as an essential component of Jewish identity in postwar France.[171] CDJC letters and appeals targeted Jewish communal and national organizations, trade unions and professional associations with large Jewish memberships—such as those of the tailors, furriers, hatters, diamond and leather merchants, lawyers, and bankers—and Jewish immigrant societies.[172] In addition, activists toured the country to promote the center through public lectures. They also created a network of Comités des Amis du Centre de Documentation Juive Contemporaine all over France; these societies of friends aimed to raise funds and advertise the center's work beyond Paris.[173] Although these efforts raised awareness of the CDJC within the French Jewish community, its main financial support continued to come from outside of France.[174]

The center's agenda of collecting and copying documents and publishing historical works would have been an expensive undertaking in any circumstance. Faced with a chronic lack of housing, a shortage of heating and electricity, especially in the winter of 1944–1945, and the continuous rise in living expenses and social security taxes, the CDJC existed on the verge of bankruptcy.[175] The French Jewish community itself still needed the help of international (mainly American) Jewish relief organizations in order to recover from the economic discrimination, disruption, and despoliation it had suffered. The AJDC alone invested $14.3 million in France in the years 1945–1948.[176] It was also the center's major source of income, providing a stable monthly endowment, which from March 1945 to 1949 gradually rose from 100,000 to 500,000 francs.[177] In addition, the Joint provided several onetime loans; for example, 1.5 million francs in November 1946 to support CDJC publications, and 1.2 million francs the following May for acquisition of an eight-room office at 19, avenue Foch. It also provided forty care packages when the CDJC could not pay its employees the thirteenth-month wage bonus customary in France.[178] At the end of 1947, the Joint announced repeatedly that it would end its financial support because it needed to give priority to the Middle East. Schneersohn fought bitterly for a continuation of the subsidies, at the risk of making himself a persona non grata with his obstinate petitioning for prolonged and higher funding.[179] Although Schneersohn said he felt "alone, struggling like a fish without water,"[180] the AJDC continued its subsidies.

Beginning in April 1947, the CDJC instituted an intensive fundraising campaign in the United States by establishing a "Friends of the CDJC Committee" in New York. Under the auspices of the Russian-born scientist Boris Pregel and the journalist Aron Alperin, vice-editor of the Yiddish daily *Der Tog*, it was to raise funds, inform the American Jewish public about the CDJC, and enlist subscribers for its publications.[181] Center delegates made periodic visits to New York—Isaac Schneersohn in April 1947, Justin Godart in June 1948, and Dr. Alexandre Safran, chief rabbi of Geneva, in June 1949. These visits gave the three men the opportunity to negotiate for support not just with the Joint but also with the American Jewish Committee, B'nai B'rith, the World Jewish Congress, the Jewish Labor Committee, and the Workmen's Circle, as well as with representatives of the American Jewish press, including *Der Tog*, *Forverts*, and *Aufbau*.[182]

In trying to raise funds in the United States, the CDJC faced a hard sell: convincing American Jews to finance a documentation center in France that published historical works in a language that most American Jews did not read, at a time when Jews in Europe and Palestine/Israel required major humanitarian relief.[183] Thus, in the growing cold-war atmosphere, the CDJC presented itself as the only independent Jewish Holocaust research institution in Europe fighting for democracy and interfaith tolerance and against racism, anti-Semitism, totalitarianism, and the rise of neo-Nazism. Unlike historical commissions and documentation centers "behind the iron curtain, which falsify history,"[184] the CDJC served "the Jewish cause, as well as all of free humankind" by opposing "every enterprise of lies and slander with the historic truth, based on authentic and unquestionable documentation."[185] As a "non-sectarian" organization, the center extended its help to all those "representing the democratic points of view," and its archives nurtured the work of "historians, authors, journalists and researchers who are fighting anti-Semitism and racism."[186] Not least, the CDJC committed itself to keeping alive the memory of "the six million Jews who died in horrible suffering" and to "let[ting] future generations know the wrongdoing of the Nazis, not only against Jews but also their genocide against the entire world."[187]

The CDJC's trans-Atlantic fundraising campaign yielded donations that saved the organization from bankruptcy and made American Jewish organizations its most vital financial resource. Considerable grants amounting to over three million francs in the years 1947–1950 came from the American Jewish Committee (AJC),[188] the Hebrew Immigrant Aid Society,[189] the American Jewish Labor Committee,[190] and the Workmen's Circle.[191]

Encouraged by the success of its American outreach, but still financially insecure, the CDJC also targeted Jews in Switzerland and Great Britain. Already in December 1946 it had established a friends committee in Geneva, under the auspices of Dr. Aron Syngalowski, a supporter of the initiative in Grenoble; the sociologist Dr. Liebmann Hersch; and Jacques Bloch of OSE in Geneva. Fundraising campaigns in May 1948 and July 1951 yielded 1.7 million francs.[192] In April 1948 the center established a friends committee in London, under the auspices of the Russian-born attorney Dr. John Machover, executive secretary of the Federation of Jewish Relief Organisations to Assist Jewish Victims of War and Persecution; Joseph Berman of the Zionist Federation of Great Britain and Ireland; and the journalist Joseph Leftwich, director of the Federation of Jewish Relief Organisations. Although the CDJC sought to draw the attention of British Jews to its work by emphasizing the Europe-wide scope of its Holocaust research,[193] the British campaign ran into two major obstacles: it not only competed with British Jewish fundraising for the *Yishuv* (the Jewish community in Palestine) but also with the London-based Wiener Library, as another institution dedicated to Holocaust research.[194] Most of the potential donors to the CDJC made their contributions contingent on preventing any harm to the Wiener Library, and the center ultimately had to share all the funds it raised equally.[195] As of July 1951, after three years of fundraising, proceeds from the British campaign amounted to 1.5 million francs; two-thirds of this sum came from the Jewish Colonization Association, a philanthropic organization based in Great Britain.[196]

Despite its outreach efforts, the CDJC's finances continued to deteriorate. By the summer of 1948, it had a deficit of 1.8 million francs, growing to 2.2 million francs by the following April.[197] By May 1952—even with continued AJDC grants[198]—the center's debts reached 3.8 million francs, almost half of which were social security taxes owed to the state.[199] Disappointed, exhausted, and in constant fear that financial troubles would force the center to discontinue its work, in January 1951 Schneersohn wrote to the Hebrew and Yiddish poet and novelist Zalman Shneour, a core supporter in New York: "Our center resembles an old asthmatic woman suffering from frequent attacks that hinder her breathing; it seems to be the end, but then she gets some air and breathes again and is saved until the next crisis."[200] Although the ultimate crisis never came, the fundraising efforts in France and abroad had shown that the center needed to remodel itself in a way that would attract more reliable financial support from the Jewish public than annotated documents and thoroughly researched historical studies did. At the same time, it would have to help the CDJC fulfill its mission of breaking the silence about the particular fate of the Jews during the occupation, while also bringing into public consciousness their contribution to the liberation of France and their roots in the French nation.

A Jewish *Arc de Triomphe*: From Documentation Center to World Memorial

In 1950, Isaac Schneersohn proposed the transformation of the CDJC from an archival research institute into a Holocaust memorial, which promised to reach a broader audience. His plan foresaw the addition to the existing documentation center of a new memorial and a museum, located at a prominent site in the heart of Paris. A crypt housing ashes from the extermination camps and a memorial book with the names of victims would form the commemorative site, while the museum would use the CDJC's collections to present the chronology and scope of the Jewish cataclysm. Schneersohn saw the proposed memorial, which would commemorate not only the destruction of the Jews of France but of European Jewry at large as more than an attempt to mend the CDJC's financial problems. Writing to Adolph Held of the Workmen's Circle in New York in fall 1949, when he first began to consider the issue, he asserted: "The *khurbn* that we have endured— the affliction and humiliation, the 6,000,000 dead—strongly imposes upon us a duty to establish a monument reminding everyone of the suffering of the Jews, which had been unknown in our [previous] martyrdoms."[201] Schneersohn's idea also responded to numerous smaller postliberation initiatives by French Jews to remember their dead through local memorials and commemorative ceremonies.[202]

Schneersohn presented his idea of a *mémorial du supplicié juif inconnu* (memorial to the unknown Jewish victim of torture) at a board of directors' meeting on November 8, 1950. His vision of "a crypt, in the middle of which the ashes will be kept, and a museum gathering the vestiges of the Jewish tragedy along with archives dedicated to its history" met with initial skepticism from some of his coworkers.[203] Isaïe Schwartz, chief rabbi of France, raised halakhic objections to the use of human ashes; he further deemed their transport to Paris from the death camps in Poland highly problematic.[204] Ruven Grinberg of the FSJF also opposed the plan, warning about "a danger of desecration."[205] Others expressed concern about location. Jacques Szeftel, for example, argued that Israel, rather than France—much less Paris—would be a more appropriate site.[206] Gaston Kahn was among the CDJC activists who gave their enthusiastic support to the project. He invoked the plight of a young Jewish orphan girl "who, lacking a better option, returns to the house from which her parents were deported to honor their memory."[207] The argument that French Jews needed a national commemorative site ultimately prevailed, even if it challenged traditional forms of Jewish burial and mourning.

The memorial also promised to fulfill the CDJC's initial goal, namely to bring the Holocaust into public consciousness and integrate the survivors into their surrounding society. While local survivor-initiated memorials had commemorated the fate of French Jews as *deportés*, *résistants*, or *fusillés* in the relatively closed context of local synagogues, Schneersohn's centralized project would provide a framework for telling a specific story of Jewish suffering in a way that France's non-Jewish citizens would understand and recognize. By honoring their rightful place in French society's commemoration of the recent past, the memorial would—for the first time—include France's Jews in the national discussion of wartime suffering. Schneersohn's project was promising because he chose to memorialize the specific story of Jewish suffering in a quintessentially French republican form of commemoration. The Tombeau du Martyr Juif Inconnu (tomb of the unknown Jewish martyr), as the project was officially named in 1951, would be a Jewish equivalent to the Arc de Triomphe, with its tomb for France's unknown war dead.[208] These memorials, which had dominated France's memorializing of its fallen soldiers since the *Grande Guerre*, gained new popularity in the wake of the Second World War.[209]

In July 1951 the municipal council of Paris approved the use of a prime 400-square-meter site for the Jewish memorial at the intersection of rue Grenier sur l'Eau and rue Geoffroy l'Asnier in the Fourth Arrondissement, in the vicinity of the Hôtel de Ville.[210] With this success in hand, the CDJC began to publicize the project among its potential supporters—and not just in France. Thus an English-language pamphlet explained:

> The sacred ashes of the victims taken [from] the death-camps will be laid down in this symbolic Tomb. If the Tomb of the Unknown Soldier is, in each country, a sacred place for those who have lost their dear ones, the Tomb of the Unknown Jewish Martyr will be a sacred place not only for the Jews but for the whole world, as it is a symbol of the suffering

undergone by the Jews—victims of racism and dictatorship to which we have paid a large tribute. If, in Paris and in other capitals, parents and children are coming on Sundays to pray and drop a tear at the *Tomb of the Unknown Soldier*, Jews who come to Paris will all pray and weep for their lost and dear ones at the *Tomb of the Unknown Jewish Martyr*.[211]

Even more pointedly, Schneersohn stated that "the Tomb of the Unknown Jewish Martyr will be a monument of respect, a symbol that may be compared to the Tomb of the Unknown Soldier under the Arch of Triumph."[212]

Beyond their invocation of the Arc de Triomphe, the CDJC activists took great care to emphasize that the memorial was "non-sectarian." Although commemorating distinct Jewish suffering, the tomb had universal significance. Against the backdrop of intensifying cold-war antagonisms, the center stressed the role of Holocaust commemoration in the defense of democratic values against (by implication) the common evils of anti-Semitism, racism, fascism, and totalitarianism. Thus the memorial would teach the world a lesson on "what anti-Semitism and racism can lead to,"[213] in addition to safeguarding the memory of the "martyred victims of racial hatred." Even more broadly, the memorial embodied the "abhorrence of these barbarian crimes on the part of every human being committed to freedom and justice without distinction of nationality and religion."[214] The memorial complex would include a museum and the documentation center with its archives and library, whose educational facilities would provide "information to scholarly and educational organizations and institutions, the press, the courts, and all individuals dedicated to the defense of humanitarian principles," rendering the project "a powerful bastion in the fight against racist ideology."[215]

Beyond these universalistic messages, the CDJC activists advertised the memorial as an expression of their deep connection and loyalty to France. That nation, not Israel or eastern Europe, was the proper location for the memorial, because France more than other countries represented humanitarian and democratic ideals: France was, after all, the first country to give Jews equal rights. And despite enduring "three German aggressions," France was the "one country in the world least inclined to forget the crimes of the barbaric Teuton," ensuring that it would always remain "faithful to the humanitarian and democratic ideal."[216] Not least, the memorial *must* be built in Paris—the "capital of human liberties"[217] and "the spiritual capital of the civilization of the free world,"[218] where the "emancipation of the Jews had been announced and where once again . . . light had triumphed over the shadows of Barbarianism."[219]

To advertise the memorial's importance for Jews worldwide, the CDJC stressed its role as a "symbolic tomb" for all the murdered, but unburied, Jews of Europe. The crypt containing urns with ashes from extermination camps would display the names of victims' home countries and cities, so that survivors would be able to mourn their own dead.[220] The memorial would thus function as a surrogate common grave, fulfilling "the hope of so many people that the six million souls will find a place to rest."[221] In its quest to unify European Jews as a "community of victims," the CDJC would collect names of the murdered to be inscribed in the walls of the "memorial hall" and in a "memorial book" to commemorate the "six million . . . who should never fade from the memory of future generations." Every country and community, including "each Eastern Community razed to the ground," would "have its history" within the memorial. While the "memorial book" echoed a medieval Ashkenazic commemorative custom, the overall concept reflected a new, secularized kind of worship where "people and delegations will come and pray before the sacred ashes."[222] Schneersohn himself denied any intention to import a secular republican European memorial culture into a Jewish context. As he explained to Jacob Kaplan, chief rabbi of Paris, in November 1950, although the memorial resembled in some ways the monuments to the fallen in every French city and village, the proposed project would introduce something new to Jewish spiritual life, "a *tombeau-Panthéon* to the unknown Jewish Martyr . . . [as] a place for prayer and contemplation."[223]

Nonetheless, Schneersohn faced a barrage of criticism from within the Paris Jewish community. Not surprisingly, Parisian Zionist groups argued that such a memorial belonged in Israel, while voices favoring acculturation and integration of Jews into their French surroundings expressed concern that singling out and drawing attention to Jewish suffering would hinder Jews' integration into French society and undermine the promise of the French state to grant full equality to its citizens regardless of ethnic or religious background. Some dismissed the memorial's location because France was not the country where millions of Jews had met their deaths. Still others complained that the proposed memorial lacked Jewish content or broke with traditional Jewish forms of mourning and memory.[224]

Similarly, some of the American Jews working for the AJDC in France complained about the memorial's cost and its divergence from Jewish tradition. Judah J. Shapiro, director of the Joint's Education and Culture Department in Paris, admitted to its secretary Herbert Katzki that he was personally ill-disposed toward the project because "the name as well as the concept is a distorted one and not at all in keeping with a Jewish sense of respect for martyrdom."[225] The Joint's country director for France, Laura Margolis Jarblum, complained to Dr. Moses Beckelman, the organization's director for overseas operations: "If Mr. S. stuck to his Centre work and didn't launch out into this 'grotesque' Tomb du Martyr, he could pay his Social Security. The publicity alone on the Tomb which is bang-spread all over costs a fortune."[226]

Yet even some supporters of the project accused Schneersohn of promoting the memorial as a way to solve the center's financial problems. This critique was not unfounded. Schneersohn did hope that the combined research institution, memorial, and museum would attract a broad audience and eventually achieve financial stability. He was therefore obliged to make certain that funds raised for the memorial would be used exclusively for that purpose.[227] Exasperated with the struggle for French Jews' support of the memorial, Schneersohn referred to himself as a "martyr connu" (known martyr).[228]

France's Ministry of Education, the National Center for Scientific Research (CNRS), and the Paris municipal council together contributed an initial grant to the memorial of 1.25 million francs in the years 1950–1951.[229] But it soon became clear that the rest of the estimated 200 million francs in costs would have to be sought outside of France, from international Jewish sources.[230]

In January 1951 the CDJC organized a World Committee to Erect a Tomb for the Unknown Jewish Martyr. With loyal non-Jewish supporter Justin Godart as president, the committee was tasked with promoting the project and coordinating fundraising campaigns in various countries. In the following two years the committee recruited as patrons a number of international Jewish and non-Jewish dignitaries, including gentile politicians such as French president Vincent Auriol, French foreign minister Robert Schuman, British foreign minister and deputy prime minister Sir Anthony Eden, Prime Minister Winston Churchill, and former American First Lady and human rights activist Eleanor Roosevelt, along with such European royals as Princess Wilhelmina of Holland, Queen Elisabeth of Belgium, and Prince Jean of Luxembourg. Prominent Jewish patrons included Israeli prime minister David Ben-Gurion and Israeli president Chaim Weizmann; U.S. senator Herbert Lehman (New York) and former treasury secretary Henry Morgenthau Jr.; Albert Einstein; Rabbi Leo Baeck; Oxford historian Cecil Roth; jurist René Cassin, president of the Alliance Israélite Universelle; Baron Guy de Rothschild, president of the Consistoire Central; Isaïe Schwartz, the chief rabbi of France; AJDC chairman Edward Warburg; and Jacob Blaustein, president of the American Jewish Labor Committee.

Under the auspices of the World Committee, beginning in spring 1951, individual activists and national committees—including the friends committees established earlier—raised funds on behalf of the memorial among the Jewish populations in Belgium, Denmark, Germany, Great Britain, Luxemburg, the Netherlands, North Africa, Norway, Switzerland, and the United States.[231] In each country fundraisers stressed the benefits of supporting the memorial to the local Jewish community, as well as the memorial's universal significance in the fight for freedom, equality, and democracy and against anti-Semitism, racism, and totalitarianism.

While still in the midst of its fundraising campaign, the CDJC began planning a ceremonial laying of the memorial's cornerstone. Center activists, like their supporters abroad, believed that such a concrete sign that the project was underway would encourage contributions in France and abroad. The date chosen was May 17, 1953, the tenth anniversary of the end of the Warsaw ghetto uprising.[232] The ceremony took place in "an atmosphere of solemn piety and profound emotion,"[233] in the presence of members of the French political elite—among them President Vincent Auriol and representatives of the National Assembly, the Senate, and the Council of the Republic—as well as foreign diplomats, representatives of French Catholic, Protestant, and Jewish communities, a detachment of the French Guards of Honor, and representatives of associations of former political prisoners and resistance fighters.[234]

An orphaned Jewish girl lays down flowers shortly before the unveiling of the foundation stone for the Tomb of the Unknown Jewish Martyr in Paris, May 17, 1953. The stone reads "On this site, donated by the city of Paris, will be erected the Tomb of the Unknown Jewish Martyr, dedicated to the memory of all the dead without a grave, to the victims of Nazi barbarism." *CDJC Photo Archives MXXA 53_65*

The ceremony combined elements of republican rites to honor the fallen in the two world wars with traditional Jewish modes of commemoration and new forms of mourning. This syncretism epitomized the CDJC's larger integrative quest, which in itself provided the driving force behind the memorial. The Jewish religious content consisted of the reciting of the Kaddish. Orphans of Jewish *déportés* served as the ceremony's main celebrants. As Schneersohn described the ceremony a few days later, a Jewish orphan girl unveiled the memorial stone, after which "fifty-five orphans of deportees carrying a large poster, 'Orphans of deportees,' marched past throwing flowers; the synagogue choir sang the March of the Ghetto Partisans, accompanied by the singing of thousands of Jews; the regiment honored [the dead], and the military orchestra played the 'Chant à mort.' This was a distressing moment."[235] According to Justin Godart's report, "The emotion reached its culmination when the Chief Rabbi, assisted by an orphan boy, said the Kaddish accompanied by the Great Synagogue's choir. Many of the audience, Jews and non-Jews, could not keep back their tears."[236]

Apart from the memorial stele, a large Star of David adorned the wall of a house adjacent to the site, several meters above the audience, covered on one side with the French flag, on the other with a black veil.[237] An estimated seven

The audience gathers at the ceremony to unveil the foundation stone for the Tomb of the Unknown Jewish Martyr, at the intersection of rue Grenier sur l'Eau and rue Geoffroy l'Asnier in the Fourth Arrondissement of Paris. An iron Star of David with a black veil and the French tricolor symbolizes both mourning the victims of the Holocaust and patriotic commitment to France. *CDJC Photo Archives MXXA 53_7*

thousand people attended the ceremony, some following it via loudspeakers in the adjacent streets.[238] In the following days, Schneersohn reported in a letter to André Meyer, a French-born Jewish businessman in New York, that crowds "passed by in tens of thousands"; "women and children wept and kissed the stone and it became a truly holy place." Even "old Parisians" who were present admitted that "never have the Jews here had such a splendid and grand ceremony." To Schneersohn's satisfaction, the event received full national and international press, radio, and television coverage.[239]

The memorial site opened its doors three and a half years later, on October 30, 1956. Ashes from death camps in Poland were placed in the crypt four months later, on February 24, 1957.[240] A major step toward the project's realization was an allocation from the Conference on Material Claims against Germany in 1954 and 1955 totaling $300,000, even through the memorial continued to face opposition from elements of the French Jewish community. Subsequently, the conference allocated another $240,000 for the CDJC's research and documentation activities.[241] The continuing disorganization of the center's administrative archive makes it impossible to answer one obvious and important question: How much money did the center receive from all its fundraising activities in France and abroad? In any case, the allocations from the Claims Conference brought the project to realization.

The Claims Conference's payments were part of an agreement between the CDJC and the Israeli Holocaust memorial Yad Vashem. The publicity and international fundraising activity on behalf of the French memorial had triggered action by the Israeli government to build a central Holocaust memorial in Jerusalem in order to guarantee the hegemony of the Jewish state over projects in the Diaspora. On August 19, 1953, the Israeli parliament passed a law proclaiming the official founding of Israel's "Holocaust Martyrs' and Heroes' Remembrance Authority," Yad Vashem. That December—less than a year after the CDJC established its New York fundraising committee—Ben-Zion Dinur, the Israeli minister for education and culture, and Isaac Schneersohn signed an accord which set clear boundaries between the institutions and regulated their coexistence: as of May 1954, the Conference on Material Claims against Germany would finance the Paris memorial on the condition that the CDJC refrain from mobilizing American and European Jewish communities for support of its project and forfeit its claim to being world memorial.[242] Still, for Schneersohn, the agreement provided a unique opportunity to implement his vision and secure the center's financial security for the near future.

Conclusion

Immediately after their liberation, a number of Jews in France—aware that their specific fate distinguished them from other groups of war victims—established the Center of Contemporary Jewish Documentation as a means to counter the silence or hostility from the surrounding society that greeted their stories. CDJC activists developed strategies for making the Jewish tragedy known, while garbing it in the hegemonic language of postliberation France. In the late 1940s they universalized the narrative and pointed out the larger implications of their genocide: the bitter consequences of the betrayal of democratic values and the ideals of equality and human rights. With the Tomb of the Unknown Jewish Martyr, the CDJC presented an understanding of the Jewish tragedy in which Jews not only appeared as the "first victims" of a German mass murder plan which ultimately targeted all humanity; they also became "martyrs" in a universal fight for liberal and democratic antitotalitarian ideals. By emphasizing universal lessons of the

Jewish cataclysm and by invoking a secular republican memory cult in the tradition of the grave of the Unknown Soldier, the CDJC succeeded in claiming a public space for memorializing victims of the Holocaust.

The CDJC's story also illustrates the processes of acculturation and integration of Jews in an essentially liberal society. The impetus to document the recent cataclysm came from Jews of eastern European backgrounds, who constituted the majority of CDJC activists. A shared heritage of communal activism and ethnic identity stemming from their eastern European Jewish and immigrant milieus might explain why they established the documentation center as part of a popular effort to rebuild the Jewish community. Although the CDJC did not rely on the social-science-oriented research techniques with which historical commissions and documentation centers in other countries gathered survivor testimonies and other victim sources, some of its collaborators nevertheless seem to have been familiar with the goals and techniques of *khurbn-forshung* (destruction research); they also appear to have acted out of an impulse for self-defense and grassroots-level activism similar to that in other Jewish documentation projects. Moreover, their quest for reintegration into postwar French society seems to have been a major factor. By documenting the Holocaust, they sought to strengthen the Republic that had once accepted them, and which they had never ceased to see as the true France. Yet the targeting of foreign-born Jews during the occupation had taught them not to take equality and liberalism for granted; rather, they must fight for it by proving yet again that they were "at home" in France. For French-born Jews, the CDJC responded to their profound shock that their generations-long loyalty to France had not protected them from racial persecution by the state. Together they sought to strengthen the republican order by educating non-Jewish Frenchmen on the dire consequences of the "historical error" of Vichy and by showing that Jews merited inclusion. Further, by emphasizing the Jews' contribution to anti-Nazi resistance and the liberation of France, they adjusted to the myth of the *Résistance* that dominated public discourse on the recent past.

In its first decade the CDJC assumed a pioneer role in documenting the history of French Jews under Vichy and the German occupation. From its origins in 1943 as a small underground archive, it grew to become a prominent public memorial and research institute in the heart of Paris, with an agenda that extended beyond France to researching and commemorating the destruction of the Jews of Europe. By erecting a memorial that universalized the Jewish tragedy and embodied a secularized and republican cult of commemoration, the CDJC began to integrate the memory of the Holocaust into the topography of the French memory of the Second World War.

Compared to France, the Jewish community in Poland suffered higher losses in terms of numbers of victims and the destruction of Jewish culture and social, political, and communal life. Moreover, Polish Jews tended to define themselves as a national minority rather than as a religious group, and political instability, anti-Semitic violence, and growing political restrictions posed severe challenges to rebuilding Jewish life after the Second World War. Nor did Polish history offer the kind of stirring national history full of liberal promises that was available to French Jews. How, then, did these distinct circumstances affect the quest by Jewish survivors in Poland to write the history of the recent Jewish catastrophe?

3

Writing Polish Jewry's "Greatest National Catastrophe"

Holocaust Documentation in Communist Poland

Five weeks after Lublin's liberation by the Soviet Army on July 24, 1944, a handful of Holocaust survivors established a historical commission and began to collect testimonies from survivors in and around the city, which by then had become the temporary capital of the liberated areas of Poland under Soviet control. Their goal was to chronicle the cataclysm of Polish Jewry for future generations and to help rebuild Jewish life in Poland—a nation that had experienced not only the near total destruction of its Jewish population and culture but the devastation of the entire country wrought by the German occupation.

The Nazis used Polish territory as their central extermination site for all of European Jewry. Half of the Jews the Nazis murdered were Polish citizens—90 percent of a Jewish community which, at 3.3 million in 1939, had been the largest in prewar Europe. Of a surviving remnant estimated at 350,000 Polish Jews, some 30,000–50,000 found themselves in Polish territory upon liberation. Of these, an estimated 5,000–20,000 kept their false wartime identities and did not identify themselves publicly as Jews. In addition, of the 70,000–80,000 Polish Jews liberated from camps in Germany and Austria, 40,000 returned to Poland after the war had ended, as did 180,000 of the 230,000 Polish Jews who had survived in the Soviet Union.[1] In the first years after the liberation, the Jewish population in Poland was in constant flux, due to remigration and emigration. Large numbers of Jews returned in the hope of finding surviving relatives and friends and rebuilding their lives where their families had lived for generations. Back in Poland, they encountered levels of destruction that turned their former home into one gigantic graveyard. Despairing of any hope for the future or even the likelihood of making a living, many left the country for good.[2] Historian David Engel estimates that a total of 266,000–281,000 Jews sojourned on Polish territory at some point between July 1944 and July 1946, although the majority eventually chose to live outside of Poland.[3]

Beyond the Jewish cataclysm, Poland as a whole experienced a unique scale of devastation under Nazi occupation. Materially, the total cost of German looting in Poland ran as high as $18.2 billion. In addition to six years of warfare and the exploitation of material and human resources, including Polish slave labor, the German occupiers systematically eliminated the country's social, military, and intellectual elites: 50 percent of its lawyers, 40 percent of its medical doctors, and one-third of its university professors and clergy. Poland also lost one-third of its urban population.[4] In what historian Jan T. Gross has called a "demographic catastrophe without precedent,"[5] the Nazis murdered twenty percent of Poland's total prewar population. Three million of these 4.5 to 5 million Polish citizens were Jews.[6] As a consequence of genocide, the westward shift of borders, and the flight or expulsion of some eight million ethnic Germans, the multiethnic Poland of the interwar years was transformed into the first ethnically homogenous nation state in Poland's long history.[7]

In yet another partition, the Soviet Union, with the agreement of the United States and Britain, annexed Poland's eastern borderland, nearly half of its prewar territory. In return, it gained land in the west and north—the former German territories of Lower Silesia, Pomerania, and Posen—giving Poland a Baltic seacoast, better farmland, and more industrialized areas. However, these border changes reduced Poland by one-sixth of its prewar size and made the country's security dependent on the Soviet guarantee of its western borders.[8]

Liberation by the Soviet Army also brought about critical changes in Poland's political landscape. In the first three and a half years after the war, the ultimately successful attempts by Polish communists and their Soviet allies to transform Poland into a Soviet-sponsored communist state plunged the country into a civil-war-like state of political instability and violence. The political struggle between a communist minority and a noncommunist majority dated back to before the occupation. During the war, broad segments of Polish society had built a complex underground resistance movement loyal to the Polish government-in-exile in London. It included an underground combat force, the "Home Army" (Armia Krajowa; AK), and an "underground state," which comprised a network of clandestine organizations replicating prewar political parties and a quasi-governmental body that encompassed four major conservative and liberal political parties.[9] The prewar Polish Communist Party had been a minor force due to its affiliation with one of the country's historic enemies, which challenged Polish national independence. In 1942 Polish communists built their own parallel underground loyal to Moscow. Foreseeing liberation by the Soviet Union, it encompassed a new Polish Worker's Party (PPR) and as of December 1943 a provisional legislative body, the National Council for the Homeland, which only became a significant force when liberation was imminent. Once the Soviet Army entered the Polish territories, Polish communists who had spent the war in Moscow took administrative control of the liberated areas and established Lublin as the interim Polish capital, using as a vehicle the Polish Committee of National Liberation (Polski Komitet Wyzwolenia

Narodowego; PKWN), established in July 1944 as a quasi-governmental body under Soviet patronage.[10] Segments of Polish society—especially the intelligentsia, as well as the peasant and working classes—shared a basic sympathy for the agenda of political change, as well as for social and economic reform, which the new government promised would lead Poland into a better future after they had vanquished Nazi barbarism. Yet communism itself did not enjoy broad support. It remained an extrinsic system that could only set down roots because the outcome of the war had led to a Soviet military presence in the country.[11]

The Soviets had their own interest in subjugating liberated Poland, namely, imposing their hegemony and installing their communist protégés in positions of political power. The Nazis' decimation of the country's elites had weakened the potential for opposition, and the Soviet military presence and direct control over security and police agencies facilitated the establishment of a regime of intimidation, terror, and violence against political opponents, especially members of the AK and the underground state. After a short democratic interlude that involved the participation of the London-affiliated Polish Peasant Party and an attempt to hold free elections—a concession to the British and the Americans—by December 1948 all political parties but the communists had been terrorized, purged, and forced out of existence.[12]

Under these difficult conditions, survivors undertook to rebuild their communities, hoping to return them to their prewar form even if not their size and spirit. Lublin—the first city liberated and the temporary capital—became the initial provisional center of postwar Polish Jewish life, sheltering some three thousand of the eight thousand Jews in the surrounding liberated territories. These survivors had fled there or emerged from hiding; some had endured the camps or partisan combat.[13] On August 10, 1944, they organized a Jewish committee, which in late October 1944 became the Provisional Central Committee of Polish Jews. Under the auspices of Zionist leader and interwar parliamentarian Emil Sommerstein, it oversaw nutrition, housing, education, employment, medical care, and cultural activities for Jews in all the liberated areas, facilitated by a network of regional and local committees. In February 1945, after the complete liberation of Polish territory, the committee dropped its provisional status and moved to Warsaw as the Central Committee of Polish Jews (Centralny Komitet Żydów Polskich; CKŻP, or Central Committee).[14] As the principal body representing the Jewish population to the government, its executive board included various Zionist parties, the socialist Bund, Jewish youth movements and defense organizations, and representatives of the Jewish faction in the PPR. Seeking to integrate the Jewish population into the Polish economy, the committee ran vocational training schools, an employment agency, and loan banks, and supervised the settlement of Jewish repatriates from the Soviet Union in formerly German towns in Lower Silesia.[15] It also subsidized various cultural institutions that had become active by the end of 1944: the historical commission; the Union of Jewish Writers, Journalists, and Artists; a Jewish press agency; two Yiddish theatres; a

Yiddish-language radio program; and over twenty Jewish newspapers in Yiddish, Hebrew, and Polish, of which the CKŻP organ, *Dos Naye Lebn* (New life), was the largest, with a circulation of seven thousand copies per issue. In addition, the government allowed a nationwide body of Jewish religious congregations to administer all religious matters.[16]

During the first two years after the liberation, the new Polish government initially extended moral and financial support to Jewish institutions—less from a genuine interest in rebuilding Jewish life than out of strategic considerations. Given the dearth of popular support, winning over the Jewish minority might prove useful in itself, in addition to possibly securing the goodwill and financial support of Western powers and Jewish organizations.[17] Upon taking administrative control of the liberated Polish territories in July 1944, the PKWN issued the "July 21st Manifesto," which proclaimed Poland's independence from the Germans. It also acknowledged the brutal murder of Jews by the German occupiers, announced the return to equal rights, and promised survivors the rebuilding of their communities. A month later, the PKWN set up an "Office of Aid to the Jewish Population" to provide material support to Jews in the liberated areas. The new government also became the CKŻP's major financing body.[18]

Despite the government's apparent support, the Jewish population experienced widespread hostility and violence at the hands of ethnic Poles, escalating in some cases to pogroms, most infamously in Kielce, where mobs killed forty-two Jews in July 1946. In the years 1944–1947, between 600 and 1,500 Jews lost their lives in violent attacks, perpetrated mainly by opponents of the communist regime.[19] The factors inciting this violence included traditional modes of religious and economic anti-Semitism, as well as persistent stereotypes of Jews as "aliens," "spoilers," and "enemies of Poland." The notion of Żydokomuna (Judeobolshevism) gained new currency in the postwar years, not only associating Jews with communism but also blaming them for the new regime and Soviet influence.[20] Also, the survivors' mere presence led some ethnic Poles who had looted Jewish property to fear the loss of wartime gains. Indeed, Jan T. Gross has suggested that some ethnic Poles sought to eradicate reminders of their collaboration—either by forcing Jews to leave or even murdering them—not only as a way to assert ownership over formerly Jewish property but also to avoid confrontation with the moral failure of much of Polish society under Nazi occupation.[21]

Paralleling the situation in France, postwar Polish public discourse focused mainly on the victimization of non-Jewish Poles by the German occupiers, while either ignoring the distinct fate of the Jewish population or subordinating it to general national narratives of wartime suffering. The large loss of life among non-Jewish Poles sustained this view, as well as the related notion that once the Nazis had exterminated the Jews, ethnic Poles and other Slavs would have been next on the genocidal agenda. This perception blurred meaningful distinctions in Nazi racial policy and hence conflated the wartime situations of Poles and Jews under German occupation. For the most part, the Nazis deemed Poles and other Slavic peoples to be racially inferior, and they effectively created a vast racist colony that ruthlessly exploited Polish land and labor in the name of serving Germany's quest for *Lebensraum*, at the cost of tens of thousands of lives and the destruction of the Polish state. By contrast, Nazi genocidal policies aimed to physically eradicate every Jew in Europe.[22] Since—apart from the Polish elites—ethnic Poles were not targeted for large-scale Nazi murder, most of them became passive—and largely indifferent—onlookers to the Jewish cataclysm. A considerable minority of Poles, however, risked their lives and those of their families to save Jews, while others assisted the Germans in their crimes by denouncing, looting, and even murdering Jews.[23]

From the postwar perspective of most ethnic Poles, the wartime experiences of Poles and Jews remained two separate stories, and hence a fundamental "division of memory" separated both groups.[24] Many Poles further believed that Jewish survivors of German genocide were in a privileged position under the new regime. They found proof of the government's favoritism, for example, in Nathan Rapaport's sculpture memorializing the Warsaw ghetto uprising, unveiled in May 1948, which became part of the state-sponsored memory cult that venerated the antifascist struggle. By contrast, there was no official recognition of the Warsaw uprising of August 1944, when the Polish underground attempted to shake off the German occupiers—hoping in vain for support from the approaching Soviet troops.[25]

For many Jews, however, the new government appeared to be the only possible political ally. The anticommunist opposition was not only anti-Soviet but also anti-Semitic, and it fought for a Polish nation-state that was both independent from Soviet influence and devoid of ethnic minorities. The communist government, however, promised equal rights and opportunities as well as protection in a hostile environment.[26] Even if most Jews eventually left the country after they realized that the government did not live up to its promises, the material support for the Jewish community and the official condemnation of anti-Semitism temporarily nurtured the hope that the renewal of Jewish life in Poland was indeed possible.[27]

The Polish Jewish historical commission operated during a brief yet important interval between the early days of the liberation from Nazi occupation and the consolidation of Soviet-sponsored communist rule which ended autonomous Jewish life in Poland and marked the closing of the commission in fall 1947. Against the backdrop of the fragile, ambiguous, and contested position of the Jews in communist Poland, the commission's vibrant historical activity between 1944 and 1947 raises a number of crucial questions. What did the survivors active in the historical commission hope to gain from the systematic documentation of the almost total destruction of the Polish Jewish community? How did they believe these efforts would advance the rebuilding of Jewish life in the new Poland, an endeavor which proved to be a temporary and futile mission for most survivors? What kinds of materials did the historical commission collect, and what methods did it develop for its research? How did the commission address the specific fate of the Jewish minority at a time when non-Jewish Poles focused on their own victimization and when Poland was becoming an ethnically homogeneous nation state? How did the growing politicization, state repression, and emigration affect the historical commission?[28]

Recording in Extremis: The Establishment of the Central Jewish Historical Commission in Lublin

On August 29, 1944, the survivors Marek Bitter, Menachem Marek Asz, Jehuda Elberg, Mieczysław Szpecht, and Ada Lichtman met in newly liberated Lublin to form a historical commission (historishe komisye) that would use eyewitness testimonies as the basis for a detailed description of Jewish suffering in German-occupied Poland. Although Bitter, the commission's chairman, feared that the project "might appear unimportant" given the dire circumstances, he emphasized that "if we see the bigger picture, we will understand how necessary it is for our future."[29] To guide the collection of testimonies, which had already begun days before the first meeting of the commission and which became more systematic thereafter, the activists drafted a questionnaire that covered the experiences of diverse segments of the city's survivor population: former ghetto and camp inmates, partisans, escapees, deportees to the Soviet Union, and Jews who had lived in hiding. After registering an interviewee's personal data, the interviewer would elicit responses to an extensive series of questions on three main areas, beginning with German anti-Jewish policies in the witness's city or town: curfews, arrests, "humiliating markings" (such as arm bands, yellow badges, and tattoos), tribute payments, expulsions, the confiscation of property and restriction of economic activity, and conscription for forced labor and ghettoization, continuing on to deportation and murder. Second, the questionnaire solicited descriptions regarding how the Jews experienced and responded to these measures, such as by escaping to the Soviet-occupied parts of Poland or to the Soviet Union or by coping with daily life in ghettos and labor camps. It also asked about relations between the Jewish leadership and the Jewish population, as well as about cultural and social activities in ghettos and camps and manifestations of Jewish resistance. Third, the questionnaire examined relationships between Jews and non-Jews, from casual contact to instances of non-Jews providing assistance or even hiding places. Finally, the interviewer asked the survivor to describe the experience of liberation.[30]

The commission soon grew to a body of twelve coworkers.[31] The members agreed that they should collect only material "from an exclusively Jewish point of view in order to get exact knowledge of what the Jewish cataclysm looked like."[32] But they disagreed on methodology. Some wanted to interview only Jews whose experiences they deemed more important, such as partisans, ghetto fighters, and survivors of the death camps or the Warsaw ghetto uprising. Although himself a survivor of the Warsaw ghetto and Majdanek, as well as a former partisan, Marek Bitter argued for "collecting testimonies from every Jew, not only those who have survived these cruel camps. Every Jewish survival, wherever it endured the German occupation, is a historical document," an idea which would become key to the commission's approach to survivor testimony. Bitter's model was the YIVO Institute in interwar Poland, which gathered up "every shred of paper having to do with Jewish folklore," regardless of whether its precise historical value was obvious at the time. The full scope of the Jewish tragedy could only be drawn from large numbers of testimonies and documents from "ordinary people."[33]

Commission workers took testimonies in private homes and temporary shelters, then catalogued and stored them in a cupboard in the commission's "office," a desk in a dark corner of a room it shared with the Jewish committee, whose monthly subsidy for the project of up to 4,000 zloty supported a handful of full-time *zamlers* (collectors).[34] To adopt an official appearance, the commission acquired a Yiddish typewriter and designed a bilingual stamp proclaiming itself the "Zaml komisye far yidishe geshikhte Lublin—Komisja dla Historii Żydów Lublin" (Collection Commission for Jewish History Lublin). The activists planned to publish the testimonies when they reached the goal of gathering one hundred, in order to inform Jews in Poland, the United States, Canada, and Palestine about the fate of Polish Jewry.[35] They also sought to provide the new Polish government with detailed reports on Treblinka, Majdanek, and Sobibór and to serve as experts in government investigations into these death camps—embodiments of the distinct Jewish suffering on Polish soil. The commission publicized its project to the Jewish public through circulars to Jewish committees and "historical literary evenings" where testimonies were read out aloud to encourage other survivors to follow suit. But, hampered by financial constraints and insufficient personnel, the documentation work proceeded slowly and unsystematically.[36]

The liberation of more Polish territory west of the Vistula River and the westward shift of the country's eastern border accelerated the rate of change for all Jewish organizations. The historical commission attracted new collaborators, including professional historians—notably Philip Friedman, who held a doctorate from the University of Vienna and who in the interwar years had mingled with the cohort of young Polish Jewish historians around Emanuel Ringelblum. On his own, after emerging from hiding, Friedman had begun to collect material on the Jewish community in his native Lvov.[37] He arrived in Lublin in mid-November 1944, amid a migration of hundreds of survivors with Polish citizenship who had left formerly Polish borderlands now under Soviet control. Upon his arrival, the new Provisional Central Committee asked Friedman to reorganize the historical commission into a nationwide institution.

The founding meeting of the Central Jewish Historical Commission (Centralna Żydowska Komisja Historyczna; CŻKH) took place in Lublin on December 28, 1944. Those present included Friedman, as director; six of the previous activists;

and a number of new collaborators, among them the journalist Ruven Feldschuh-Safrin (Ben-Shem); Leon Bauminger, a graduate of Warsaw University, who became the commission's first secretary; the historian Joseph Kermisz—also a graduate of Warsaw University—who had returned from the Soviet Union; the teachers Mejlech Bakalczuk and Noe Grüss, also returning from the USSR; and the Hebrew poet and partisan leader Abba Kovner, from Vilna.[38] Three weeks after its founding, the CŻKH publicly advertised its mission in the triweekly Yiddish bulletin of the Jewish Press Agency as "researching and illuminating the German murder campaign committed against the Jews in Poland" based on documents and eyewitness testimonies, while also "popularizing the results of the research and making them available to . . . Jewish and non-Jewish circles in and beyond Poland."[39] In the following weeks more collaborators joined the commission: writer and partisan commander Michał Borwicz (Maksymilian Boruchowicz); Auschwitz survivor Joseph Wulf; Ada Eber, a former high school teacher with a doctorate in history from the University of Lvov; Nella Rost, a Ph.D. in literature from Krakow University; and Nachman Blumental, a graduate in literature from Warsaw University. Two coworkers who would become active in the commission in the spring of 1945, writer Rachel Auerbach and lawyer Hersh Wasser, were (along with Wasser's wife Bluma) the sole survivors of the inner circle of Emanuel Ringelblum's Oyneg Shabes.[40] Isaiah Trunk and Artur Eisenbach, two close affiliates of Ringelblum's, would join the commission several months later, after their repatriation from the Soviet Union in the first half of 1946. Both had been students of history in Warsaw and participants in Ringelblum's Young Historians Circle.

In March 1945, the CŻKH moved its headquarters to Lodz, which—with Warsaw in ruins—served as the unofficial capital and Jewish center of postwar Poland.[41] By the end of that year, the Jewish population in Lodz had grown from 1,160 at the city's liberation in January 1945 to over 38,000.[42] In the following weeks the commission established a national network of more than twenty branches. By mid-1945, despite poverty, housing shortages, and the transient Jewish population, it had established five—at least rudimentary—District Jewish Historical Commissions (Wojwódska Żydowska Komisja Historyczna) in Krakow, Wrocław, Warsaw, Bialystok, and Katowice,[43] which in turn oversaw twenty-one local historical commissions, each of which employed *zamlers* to collect historical documents and eyewitness testimonies in their own cities and regions.[44]

Friedman and his collaborators developed a long-term plan to create a professional and permanent framework for documentation work by transforming the CŻKH into a "Scholarly Institute."[45] In the meantime, a "Scholarly Council" staffed by a cadre of academically trained researchers—Friedman as director, Kermisz as secretary, and Wasser as head of the archives, along with Auerbach, Blumental, Borwicz, Grüss, Rost, and Wulf—supervised the commission's work by formulating research guidelines, giving methodological and practical advice, cataloguing material, and editing it for publication.[46] An advisory board, responsible for

The employees of the Central Jewish Historical Commission assemble for their second scholarly conference on September 19 and 20, 1945, in Lodz: Nachman Blumental seated by the door, Philip Friedman at the head of the table, next to Noe Grüss taking notes. To Grüss's right are Joseph Kermisz in uniform and Rachel Auerbach. The poster on the wall advertises the commission's work in Yiddish and Polish with the slogan: "The Historical Truth is the Grave of Fascism!" *Yad Vashem Photo Archives 1427/224*

financial matters, included representatives of the CŻKH, the Writers' Union, and the Jewish Central Committee.[47] Itself funded by the Polish government, and with supplies from the American Jewish Joint Distribution Committee (AJDC/Joint), the Central Committee provided the commission's primary financial support: monthly subsidies of 200,000–300,000 zloty, plus additional support for publications.[48]

The CŻKH and its regional and local branches employed on average about one hundred workers who received monthly salaries ranging from 5,000 to 10,000 zloty (depending on the position), health care, and—for those located in Lodz—free lunches in the commission's kitchen.[49] While it is difficult to determine the educational and class backgrounds of most employees, not to mention their personal stories or how long and for what reason they served the commission, it appears that—in stark contrast to France—women constituted the majority of collaborators. In November 1945, the central branch in Lodz had thirty coworkers, two-thirds of them women. The regional and local branches had about fifty employees, divided equally between men and women.[50] Women held prominent positions in some district commissions, such as Dr. Nella Rost, the vice-director in

Krakow, and Dr. Rita Sobol-Masłowska as director and Franciszka Modrzew as secretary in Katowice.

The CŻKH workers acted out of a sense of moral obligation that reflected multiple motivations. For one, they sought to fulfill "the task with which history has entrusted us: to immortalize the last path of our martyrs, to engrave in our chronicle with golden letters the heroic fight which our heroes fought against death." By "once again go[ing] through events day by day, hour by hour, collecting documents, testimonies, photographs and everything else which can help . . . to uncover the entire tragedy of the Jewish community in Poland," they hoped to assure that "all the lakes and seas of innocent Jewish blood . . . [would] not be cast into the chaos of present events" and that "no tear, no drop of blood [was] spilled in vain."[51] The entire documentation project would thus function as a symbolic "memorial to millions of dead, which shall be a lighthouse for future generations."[52]

In the perception of commission activists, Jews had suffered a unique fate. The mass murder of European Jews constituted "the greatest national catastrophe of the Jewish people,"[53] a crime like no other in the long and dolorous history of the Jews, indeed in the history of humankind. It exceeded all previous cataclysms in terms of "its quantity and character . . . scope, criminality, and the premeditated plan to murder millions of human beings irrespective of age and sex."[54] The novelty also lay in "the sophisticated and sadistic methods . . . applied for the first time in world history,"[55] as well as in combining the almost complete physical extermination of human beings with the destruction of their cultural heritage.[56] Since Polish Jews suffered disproportionate loss and all Nazi extermination camps had operated on Polish soil, the CŻKH activists also saw the Jewish cataclysm as an integral part of the history of Poland under German occupation, and thus the CŻKH documentation project contributed to writing Polish history.[57] Moreover, they linked their past to that of Poland because they understood themselves as remnants of a national minority with centuries-long ties to Poland.

The activists also found a call to documentation in the indifference to the Jewish tragedy within the surrounding Polish society and among what Philip Friedman in September 1945 described as the "non-Jewish part of society abroad and in the Anglo-Saxon countries." During the war, news of the German mass murder of European Jews had met with disbelief or was dismissed as "atrocity propaganda." The western Allies had discovered the truth when they liberated the camps, but still, Friedman maintained, "they do not want to hear about it, they want to forget the war and its atrocities." Only "certain scholarly circles of jurists, economists, historians, politicians, publicists show an interest in the history of the occupation from a scholarly or political viewpoint, and [it is] for them in particular that we must prepare documentary and not just sensational material."[58]

Not least, the commission workers derived a sense of duty from their identity as remnants of what had once been Europe's largest and culturally most vibrant Jewish community, one which had spread "religious scholarship and worship, national Jewish creativity and energy into the entire Jewish world,"[59] and one which,

Friedman believed, still possessed "great moral authority"[60] among Jews throughout the world. As such, they saw it as their duty to "weav[e] the uninterrupted thread of our centuries-old history."[61] By perpetuating the "golden chain" of Jewish history and culture in Poland, they would avenge the dead and fulfill a moral obligation toward future generations.[62]

Khurbn-Forshung Revisited: Survivor Historians Research the Holocaust

The teacher Noe Grüss aptly described the CŻKH's initial dilemma when he noted: "Neither we nor anyone else in the world had any experience in the research of . . . the theory and practice of German fascism with regard to the Jews." Thus, he admitted, "in the course of our work we educated ourselves."[63] The crux of the problem for commission workers was whether their dual identity as survivors *and* historians, witnesses *and* researchers allowed them to be "objective" or "scholarly."[64] Accepted standards of historical research required that, in Friedman's words, "the relation of the researcher to the events must not be sentimental or emotional under any circumstances," but rather must follow "sharp and thorough analysis."[65] He admitted, however, that survivors could not chronicle six years of German occupation with "purely scholarly goals in mind," since "emotional factors, feelings, individual experiences, and personal loss"[66] inevitably affected their views. Grüss put the dilemma in more graphic language: survivors writing about the recent past did not "look at the matter . . . like a professor approaches a body in a morgue. Our historical materials are the dead bodies of our children and parents, . . . the bodies of our dishonored wives and sisters . . ., the memories of partisans and ghetto fighters, . . . the courageous hearts and burning love for [our] people and the disdain for our tormentors."[67] Apart from the emotional baggage carried by each survivor, the research in itself imposed an almost unbearable emotional burden on the researchers:

> Every document is a tragedy, every file is a murder—tragedies of individuals and families, murders of entire generations. You look at photographs of people hanged or of those who were candidates for the ovens; you read reports on the amount of fuel used to burn people. There are no words that can possibly describe the state of mind in which we work—'graveyard atmosphere,' 'mood of the grave'—all these do not express the experiences and thoughts evoked by our work.[68]

Nonetheless, the CŻKH activists felt that they could not postpone their undertaking until they achieved a greater temporal and emotional distance. As Friedman explained, there was no time "to shed tears, to tear our clothes [and] to pour ashes over our orphaned heads. . . . We, the survivors, carry the responsibility on our shoulders and the great duty toward our murdered martyrs and also ... toward the coming generations."[69] They also agreed that the unprecedented nature of the destruction rendered previous methods of historical research, and even its terminology, insufficient.

Nella Rost, a scholar of literature, invoked the inadequacy of language to describe the German crimes when reflecting on her experiences leading CŻKH's Krakow branch: "Intellect and emotions can find no words to express such suffering and crimes. Any ordinary expression is insipid." Perhaps, she suggested, only psychologists could invent the terms that might adequately begin to describe what Jews had experienced during the Nazi onslaught:

> Who would be able to describe the feelings of a mother ... hearing the screams of her children being buried alive, or the feelings of fear and threat of thousands of people incarcerated in a narrow and dark gas chamber, aware of their agonizing deaths, whose shrill screams are heard well beyond the factory of death? Who can reproduce the fear and pain of human beings locked in burning synagogues and burnt alive? The feelings of the youths tortured ... in concentration camps, humiliated, ... emaciated ... and frozen?

Confronting such experiences, Rost (whose only son was shot by the Germans in the Montelupich Prison in Krakow at the age of fourteen)[70] concluded that "the apparatus of human reason and of human language are insufficient." Until the development of a "new system for a new historiosophy of the massive crime of the German spirit," the commission workers must continue to investigate and establish the facts of the destruction, despite the inadequacy of available language to describe "German brutality that exceeds the limits of human cognition."[71]

Developing methods for studying the mass murder of Polish Jews remained a central CŻKH endeavor, exemplified by its return to research methods developed by YIVO before the war, but adapted to the new context of Holocaust historiography—in Friedman's terminology, *khurbn-forshung* (destruction research).[72] Many of the activists had worked with YIVO, and a few had a direct link to the Young Historians Circle, including Rachel Auerbach and Hersh Wasser from Ringelblum's Oyneg Shabes staff. While placing victims' experiences at the center, the commission used tools of social history such as questionnaires, interviews, and statistics to investigate the social, cultural, and economic effects of German occupation and persecution on Jewish society.[73] According to Friedman, the Holocaust defied historians' usual focus on official administrative records because such German documents "are not capable of portraying the most difficult, saddest chapters of our martyrdom ... in a true and thorough manner." For example, they rarely revealed the horror of mass roundups, shootings, or extermination camps; indeed, Nazi documents "tried to cover up these horrors through the camouflaging jargon of criminals."[74] Thus, Holocaust research must also use source material from the victims, such as survivor testimonies, memoirs, diaries, photographs, literary creations from ghettos and camps, and artifacts and memorial objects.[75] Commission workers held such documents, particularly eyewitness accounts, to have the greatest potential for the accurate reconstruction of everyday life and death of the Jews of Poland under the occupation, provided that the number and diversity of testimonies reflected a broad variety of experiences and viewpoints of men, women, and children from various social strata.

As early as summer 1945, the CŻKH published Polish- and Yiddish-language versions of a comprehensive questionnaire with guidelines for nonprofessional "collectors of historical material," in this case interviews with survivors on their personal experiences during the occupation.[76] After inquiring about the personal, social, and educational backgrounds of the witness, the questionnaire asked for information on his or her residence on the eve of war, and how this changed under the German occupation.[77] Like its prototype from Lublin, the complex new questionnaire paid close attention to perpetrator behavior, responses of the Jewish population, and relations between Jews and non-Jews. Its 209 questions and subquestions covered a broad range of historical and sociological issues, such as witnesses' experiences of German anti-Jewish policies, like forced labor and confiscation of property, the establishment of ghettos and liquidation *Aktionen*, and the impact of these policies on the socioeconomic makeup, class structure, and social cohesion of Jewish society.[78]

Jewish responses to persecution, including everyday life and death in ghettos, camps and prisons, constituted another continuing focus, but now witnesses were asked to draw maps and other images to illustrate their testimonies.[79] Apart from soliciting details about such practices as forced labor, punishments, and "medical" experiments on Jewish prisoners, the questionnaire investigated social relations within the Jewish population, in particular the behavior and functioning of the Jewish councils and ghetto police, mutual aid, social mobility among the ghetto population, as well as mortality rates and causes of death,[80] clandestine political and cultural activities,[81] as well as forms of resistance and revolt, including the refusal to comply with orders.[82] The questionnaire also inquired into the psychological condition of the Jewish populations in ghettos and camps,[83] as well as spiritual life, religious ritual, and changes in gender relations under the occupation.[84]

Social relations between Jews and non-Jews under German occupation were another area of inquiry, particularly the interviewee's experiences with gentiles while seeking to supply ghettos with food or to survive in hiding or under false identity.[85] The questionnaire's final, multipart section ranged from exceptional German cruelties and famous Jews who were murdered to the destruction of Jewish cultural treasures, such as libraries and manuscripts.[86] The questionnaire's scope reflected the CŻKH's quest for a scholarly and balanced approach to the past, as well as its wish to reach the largest possible number of survivors in order to obtain a thorough, comprehensive, and nuanced description of Polish Jews' experiences during the occupation.[87]

In addition to the general questionnaire, the teachers Noe Grüss and Genia Silkes in 1945 developed an instrument for interviewing children up to the age of sixteen.[88] Its ten sections and 136 questions and subquestions elicited personal data on the child and his or her family as well as information on changes in the family's life in the early months of the occupation; life in the ghettos; *Aktionen*; life in camps and prisons, and in hiding, both in the forest and on the "Aryan side." A final section covered the child's most difficult experiences, hopes and dreams, and whether he or she had kept a diary or possessed pictures and other objects from the past.[89] This research stood in the tradition of YIVO's *yugnt-forshung* (youth research), which had developed in the 1930s with autobiographical essay competitions.[90] It also reflected a widespread notion in survivor society that children represented survival, reconstruction, and resilience, even as they also symbolized, in their vulnerability and innocence, the victimization of the entire Jewish people.[91]

The CŻKH believed that a clearer picture of children's wartime experiences would not only serve historical research but also help teachers, social workers, staff in Jewish orphanages, and foster families and parents improve the situation of Jewish youth.[92] Because Grüss and Silkes attributed a greater moral weight to child survivors,[93] the interviews would constitute so potent an "indictment of fascism" that it would "convince the world that fascism must be ruthlessly eliminated."[94] Since the children's very survival "in some way foiled the Hitlerite plans," the interviews would also demonstrate children's "power of resistance and heroic deeds."[95] So that the children did not feel like research animals, this questionnaire—unlike the one for adults—was meant only to serve as a general reference for the interviewer, who would also monitor and take notes on a child's moods, expressions, and social behavior and make sure the sessions were short but frequent, since bored children were less cooperative. Interviewers were counseled to take the children and their responses seriously and to convey the impression that their experiences and memories mattered.[96]

A third questionnaire, also published in 1945, addressed collectors of "ethnographic materials"—popular literature, poetry, plays, songs, idiomatic expressions, jokes, and riddles—that Jews had created during the occupation.[97] YIVO had earlier collected such materials as sources for the study of Jewish society. The CŻKH deemed them particularly appropriate to the recent past because, as Grüss observed, they allowed researchers "to penetrate the psychological situation in the ghettos, bunkers, and forest settlements."[98] According to Nachman Blumental, the editor of the questionnaire and its instructions, popular texts from the war years had developed as "living words ... passed from mouth to mouth," and their creators functioned as "street singers telling about current issues of Jewish life while also criticizing it."[99] Such texts revealed their creators' wish to leave a record of the traumatic times, register the German crimes, and also seek symbolic revenge. Blumental's instructions for *zamlers* stressed that folklore material could be collected "at any time in the street" by talking and listening to people, their songs, stories, and anecdotes. In addition to songs—a main interest—the *zamler* would inquire about idiomatic expressions, jokes, swear words, superstitious beliefs, wonder tales, and the use of gematria (calculation of the numerical equivalent of letters, words, and phrases) in Jewish texts to predict the end of the war.[100]

The CŻKH used nonprofessional *zamlers* to conduct interviews and collect other data on the basis of the questionnaires. While it is difficult to establish their gender, class, or social and educational backgrounds, the instructions they received provide a clear notion of the responsibility expected of them. In general, interviewers and interviewees came from the same geographic area. Although this helped to avoid factual errors in the testimony, the interviewer was cautioned against allowing personal biases and knowledge of events to influence the witness's testimony. The guidelines encouraged "an individual approach" that adjusted the interview's pace to the witness's intellectual level and willingness to talk. Articulate and intelligent witnesses should be left to talk freely and could even write their own testimonies in the *zamler*'s presence. Passive and introverted witnesses, on the other hand, must be questioned carefully and in detail in order to elicit as much information as possible. The interviewer should specify when testimony was firsthand. Witnesses who related hearsay should give detailed descriptions of the source and its reliability.[101] Despite the cautions against excessive intrusion, in some cases, *zamlers* were expected to help "refresh certain memories":

> We have to be prepared that after so many . . . occupation experiences, memory has become weakened, and with the distance of several years, some facts . . . will come out vague and not without mistakes. The *zamler* will do well not just to help the witness with questions but also to provide him with facts that he [the interviewer] already knows from other sources (that is, an associative method), [or by] reading aloud the testimony of another witness on a similar or the same topic.[102]

Interviewers transcribed the testimonies and provided brief descriptions of the witnesses, their manner of speaking, body language, and intelligence, as well as an overall assessment of the value of the testimony. The instructions prohibited *zamlers* from altering the testimony unless it proved incomprehensible, in which case they might adjust formulations for clarification, but could not change the content. An interviewer who disagreed with a witness on matters of fact should explain the problem on a separate piece of paper. By signing the protocol, a witness accepted "moral responsibility for the document."[103] The testimony's quality and how much of the questionnaire was actually covered depended greatly on the competence of individual interviewers, who by selecting the questions and putting the answers into writing played a powerful role. With the help of its *zamlers*, the CŻKH collected over three thousand testimonies by late 1947.[104]

Archives of Destruction: Collecting the Traces of a Lost Jewish World in Lodz

Convinced that a complex and accurate picture of the past required the voices of both victims and perpetrators, the CŻKH set out to gather a great variety of documents of both German and Jewish provenance. From the outset, it collected the records of official and underground Jewish institutions, such as the Jewish councils and self-help organizations, as well as underground political and cultural associations.[105] But its first windfall came when the German occupiers fled western Poland as the Red Army advanced in the spring of 1945, leaving behind a paper trail of their crimes.[106] The abandoned documents came from German civil and military authorities, as well as from the Gestapo and the SS, in almost every Polish city that formerly had a large Jewish community.[107] The Germans also left materials relating to the concentration and extermination camps on Polish territory.[108] When the commission relocated to Lodz in March 1945, it acquired numerous documents pertaining to that city's ghetto as well as to other ghettos located in the Wartheland (part of western Poland that Germany had incorporated into the Reich). In their haste to flee Lodz, the Germans had not destroyed the ghetto, their paper records, or those of the Jewish council. The CŻKH seized as many as 2,700 documents of the German ghetto administration, including its correspondence with the Jewish council, reports on the conscripted ghetto labor force, and lists of confiscated Jewish property. The CŻKH also obtained partial records from the Lodz Jewish council, including internal and external correspondence, as well as information on its workshops, the ghetto's food supplies, and deportations from the ghetto. By the end of 1945, the CŻKH archives included documents on ninety cities and towns in Poland.[109]

Apart from the Lodz ghetto material, the CŻKH's prize acquisition was portions of the Ringelblum archives. The commission had sought from the outset to recover the archives from the ghetto's rubble, but financial problems held up excavation until the fall of 1946. Ringelblum's former secretary Hersh Wasser knew that some of the archive had been buried in the cellar of 68 Nowolipki Street, but even identifying the building's ruins proved difficult, and the commission feared that delay would result in further damage or destruction of the material.[110] Now head of the Warsaw district commission, Wasser took lead responsibility for the excavation. Based on engineers' assessments of the volume of debris that would have to be removed, the cost of retrieving the archive was estimated at 250,000 zloty.[111] Because the Central Committee lacked sufficient funds, the CŻKH turned to Jews abroad. The American Jewish Labor Committee offered 200,000 zloty, and YIVO, which would receive copies of any documents uncovered, promised to cover the rest.[112] The dig proceeded and on September 18, 1946, uncovered the first of what turned out to be ten tin boxes with documents buried in the first week of August 1942. Humidity and mold had so damaged the material that

Joseph Kermisz and Artur Eisenbach (seated at right) and five of their colleagues work in the archive of the Central Jewish Historical Commission in Lodz, August 1946. Wall, door, and tile stove in the back display historical documents and a German map of the Lodz ghetto. *Yad Vashem Photo Archives 7732/12*

conservation experts from the Polish National Library in Warsaw had to be called on before the CŻKH could catalogue and prepare them for publication.[113]

In October 1946, commission members in Lodz under Kermisz's guidance and with the help of Nachman Zonabend, a former inmate of that city's ghetto, retrieved parts of another buried cache: the so-called Rumkowski archives from the semiofficial archival department of the local Jewish council. This material, discovered in a well on the site of a building used by ghetto firefighters, included reports on life in the ghetto, personal diaries, literary works, and museum objects, as well as a secret ghetto chronicle from January 1941 through July 1944.[114] Menachem Turek (Tamir), head of the Bialystok district commission, in 1946 recovered material from the underground archives of the Bialystok ghetto, collected by the Dror youth movement leaders Mordechai Tennenbaum and Tsvi Mersik between November 1942 and March 1943 and buried in three tin boxes outside the ghetto in the spring of 1943.[115]

The CŻKH also collected printed matter: journals and periodicals published during or after the war; anti-Semitic literature in German and Polish; maps, plans, statistics, and graphic illustrations related to ghettos, camps and hiding places; and artwork.[116] Indeed, the miscellany of relics and objects collected from the occupation period encompassed

> something made of wood to eat one's soup with in the Stutthof camp, shoes adorned with strands of women's hair [and] with a sole from the parchment of the Jewish Holy Book with Hebrew words of the Jewish liturgy, pieces of soap produced by a firm in Danzig, made from human fat with the inscription R.I.F. (Rein jüdisches Fett), a letter of transport proving that once in Brünlitz, Czechoslovakia, a sealed railway car arrived which had not been opened for a long time, and when the car was opened with blowtorches several dozens of corpses fell out and the rest of the people were close to death.[117]

The CŻKH also acquired several thousand photographs and reels of film footage taken by the Germans during their *Aktionen* and deportations.[118] By late 1947, the commission's photograph and film collections included as many as four thousand items.[119]

The CŻKH received most of its documents of German origin, such as materials of the Nazi ghetto administration and the Jewish council, as a loan from the city of Lodz. When, in early 1947, the commission decided to consolidate its archival holdings in Warsaw, the municipal authorities objected to these documents' removal from the Lodz municipal archives on grounds of archival integrity. They opposed organizing a separate archive for an individual historical event; the transfer of material from the ghetto administration to an archive on the "Jewish question at the time of the occupation" would make no more sense than one "on the Swedish Wars" (the seventeenth-century conflict between Sweden and Poland).[120] Underlying this critique was the Lodz authorities' unwillingness to acknowledge that Jews had experienced a specific kind of persecution at the hands of the Nazis. A separate archive in a central location might draw unwarranted public attention to Jewish suffering as against that of the Polish people. The issue was only resolved in fall 1947, with the founding of the Jewish Historical

Institute (Żydowski Instytut Historyczny; ŻIH) in Warsaw, discussed later in this chapter, which was able to centralize archival records under its roof with the support of the Polish government.[121] In the meantime the CŻKH used its own trove of materials to publish a number of historical works.

Depicting the Atrocities: The Commission's Publication Activities

The CŻKH intended its publications, which described the anti-Jewish policies of the German occupiers and the multifaceted responses of the Jewish victims, to serve as "an eternal admonition against fascism and reaction."[122] From the outset, the publications targeted both Jewish and non-Jewish audiences in Poland and abroad. In order to educate both gentile Poles and Polish-language readers worldwide, only six out of thirty-nine CŻKH publications between 1945 and 1947 appeared in Yiddish; in these cases, either their authors understood themselves as Yiddish writers or the works dealt with Yiddish literature. By publishing primarily in the Polish language, the commission members, all of whom were multilingual, hoped to expand their audience and potential influence and to avoid accusations of Jewish particularism and separatism.[123]

The CŻKH publication list, encompassing a wide range of subjects and categories, constitutes a pioneering editorial feat, accomplished under trying circumstances over a period of only two years, with financial assistance from the American Jewish Joint Distribution Committee.[124] The CŻKH began by publishing its various instructions on methodology and questionnaires for *zamlers* of adult and child testimonies and folklore materials.[125]

The second category of publications comprised monographs on labor, concentration, and extermination camps in Poland. The CŻKH's predecessor organization in Lublin had already undertaken research on some death camps in order to provide information to government investigators, and camps continued to be a major concern for the commission's research, collection, and publication activities.[126] In 1945, Philip Friedman published *This is Auschwitz!*, the first history of the Auschwitz-Birkenau camp based on documents and survivor testimonies. In the following year, the commission published works on the Janowska internment camp in Lvov and on the Bełżec extermination camp. The former, written by Michał Borwicz, head of the Krakow district commission and a former Janowska internee, described its operations, its brigades, the suffering of the inmates, and their involvement in the armed underground, to which he paid special attention. In 1947, Rachel Auerbach published a Yiddish-language report on Treblinka which was partly based on her visit to the camp in November 1945 as a member of a governmental delegation. It was also inspired by the fact that in September 1942 when working for Emanuel Ringelblum in the Warsaw ghetto, Auerbach had recorded the testimony of a Treblinka escapee.[127]

Local studies on the history of Jewish communities under German occupation constituted the third category of CŻKH publications. Some of these works covered the destruction of the Jewish population and its resistance, while others focused on particular uprisings. The series began in 1945 with Philip Friedman's thirty-eight-page work on the destruction of Lvov's Jewish community, which was based on documents and on his own experiences. Other monographs documented the last days of the communities in Sosnowiec, Żółkiew, and Vilna, while a demographic study examined the Jewish populations of Lodz, Krakow, and Lublin during the occupation.[128] Several of the local studies, including one by Joseph Kermisz, focused on the Warsaw ghetto and its uprising. Studies on revolts in other ghettos followed, based on district commissions' research and collections, including two on the Bialystok ghetto.[129]

Annotated editions of primary documents covered a broad range of topics, including German policies toward the local Jewish populations, material on ghettos and camps, Jewish responses to German policies, Jews in hiding on the "Aryan side," life in partisan units, Jewish cultural and artistic activity under Nazi occupation, and Jewish children. Again, revolt and resistance became a major focus. In 1945, the heads of the Krakow district commission, Michał Borwicz, Nella Rost, and Joseph Wulf, edited a two-hundred-page compendium, *Documents of Crime and Martyrdom*. The following year brought a volume of materials and documents on the underground movement in the ghettos and camps, edited by Betti Ajzensztajn, as well as a three-volume edition of documents and materials on the German occupation in Poland, focusing on camps, *Aktionen* and deportations, and the Lodz ghetto.[130]

To provide the Jewish and non-Jewish public with raw material from the occupation years, the CŻKH published diaries and memoirs that revealed the lives of those in ghettos and camps and in the resistance movement, as well as the fate of Jewish children.[131] Most notable among these was the 1947 volume of children's memoirs edited by Maria Hochberg-Mariańska and Noe Grüss, *Dzieci oskarżają* (Children accuse). It included the testimonies collected by CŻKH *zamlers* of fifty-four children and sixteen adults relating to children under the occupation. The book focused on ghettos; camps; life "on the Aryan side," in hiding, and in prison; and on the resistance movements.[132]

CŻKH editions of literature and folklore written by Jews under German occupation included several volumes of poetry and prose written in the ghettos and camps. Nachman Blumental, a university-educated literary scholar, edited a dictionary of ghetto and camp language, which presented new idioms such as "death brigade" and "Muselman" and explained their meaning based on the commission's collections.[133]

In addition to its primary publications, in 1946 the CŻKH brought out an album of annotated photographs taken from its collections on Jewish communities, ghettos, and camps in Poland.[134] That same year, Philip Friedman published a pioneering synthesis titled "The Destruction of Polish Jewry, 1939–1945." It appeared in the inaugural volume of the journal of the High Commission for the Investigation of German Crimes in Poland (Główna Komisja Badania Zbrodni Niemieckich w Polsce), a government body formed to investigate and prosecute German war crimes on Polish soil. Friedman's study used detailed statistical evidence to relate the particular suffering of Poland's Jews through the stages of Nazi persecution and extermination. At the same time, he acknowledged the recent ordeals of non-Jewish Poles, who—like other Slavs—"as ethnic elements posing a threat to German expansion in the east, were the next candidates for mass extinction."[135]

Available data do not allow an estimate of how many CŻKH publications were sold or any sense of their readers. AJDC and Central Committee subsidies covered printing costs, and the CŻKH did not try to recover expenses through sales, since the overriding goal was to publicize the fate of Polish Jews to the world. The commission sent its publications gratis to diplomatic missions and to Jewish and non-Jewish research institutions outside of Poland. Any financial gains from its publications were secondary.[136] The commission received requests from Polish Jews in the United States, South America, and various European countries.[137] The photo album was especially popular among survivors, many of whom had no pictures from the occupation years.[138]

History Writing as a Collective Endeavor: Promoting Holocaust Research among Survivors in and outside Poland

The CŻKH's focus on survivor testimonies and its reliance on nonprofessional *zamlers* presupposed interaction with the local Jewish populations. Survivors seem to have visited the various branches of the commission on their own. Nella Rost described "thousands of victims who had been miraculously saved" who came to the commission office in Krakow: "single women whose children and families had been murdered before their eyes, men . . . saved from sinister death camps, . . . the remnants of heroic Jewish partisans, . . . small and tiny children accompanied by accidental or well-paid caretakers and older children who managed to save themselves . . . through their own devices." Commission employees interviewed these visitors in one large room, recording their accounts "and compar[ing] reports on the same camps, cities, and time periods, to clarify dates and facts." In this way "the archive filled with thousands of eyewitness accounts on small and large cities, on hundreds of concentration camps, with reports by people from prisons and hiding places, from the resistance movement, with reports by children and Jews with falsified Aryan papers who, in the face of death, successfully played their role until the very end." [139]

To attract witnesses, the CŻKH used repeated appeals in the Jewish press, as well as flyers and posters urging survivors to join in the documentation project.

Recurring themes included the moral duty of every survivor to bear witness.¹⁴⁰ For example, the commission exhorted the survivor public in Poland: "The blood of our martyrs, our relatives, is still fresh. It screams to us and calls upon us not to forget!" Whether they had "spent the German occupation in ghettos, camps, on the Aryan side, hidden in the woods, [or] fighting in partisan units," every surviving Jewish woman or man should provide the historical commission with a full account of their personal experiences during these years: "Everything that can be reported of these events will, without doubt, serve as precious material on our bloody history, and therefore all details must be carefully collected and immortalized. The brutal and horrific measures of violence perpetrated by the Germans and their collaborators will be eternalized, as will the struggle of the Jews against their bloody enemy." In addition to their stories, the commission sought "pictures, documents, community registers, diaries and other items.... *This is a duty for every single individual*. We hope that everyone will understand the importance of this and will fulfill this duty toward the Jewish past."¹⁴¹ In stressing survivors' obligation to share their knowledge about the historical truth, the commission implied that wartime memories and documents were communal goods, not private property. Elaborating on this theme, the CŻKH appealed to the "sense of civic duty of everyone in Poland, and especially to the conscience of those Jews who possess diaries: do not keep them to yourselves! Help to uncover the historical truth of the bloody German Hitler regime!"¹⁴² The commission promised to return these journals with a small material reward after consulting, copying, and perhaps publishing them.

The documentation project, being intrinsically collective in nature, could not "be made by a single person, or even by a couple of people. This must become a societal matter."¹⁴³ Hence, the CŻKH urged:

> In order to preserve and respect this blood-soaked historical treasure, we call upon the entire Jewish population of Poland to deliver immediately all materials which are in private hands to the archives of the Central Jewish Historical Commission.... Brothers and sisters! Every surviving Jew is a piece of history, and everyone has experienced the horrific life of martyrdom, whether in the ghettos, on the "Aryan side," or in the various concentration and death camps, or in the ranks of the heroic partisan groups. In a word, every Jew is obliged to record his experiences because every survivor . . . has experienced the events in a different way.¹⁴⁴

Another prevalent theme advertised the documentation work as both a weapon against forgetting and a means to commemorate the dead. For example, when calling upon survivors to join its *Yizker-leksikon* project by submitting written portraits of Jewish writers, artists, and communal leaders, the CŻKH exhorted:

> Brothers, do not believe your survival was accidental. Who, if not you, should be the writers, the contributors to this eternal gravestone, which must be established for your dear ones? The work must be done immediately, while the details are still engraved in memory; later it will be forgotten. The *Yizker-leksikon* . . . will also be a gravestone for millions of murdered martyrs, . . . an eternal warning to the murderers that we the survivors will never forget nor forgive or pardon anything![145]

In preserving these memories, survivors would thus foil the perpetrators who had tried to erase all traces of their crimes, so that "it would be forgotten that these human beings once lived in this world."[146]

The commission also advertised its project as a contribution to postwar justice. In the fall of 1945—as the Nuremberg trials began—the CŻKH issued a call in Yiddish and Polish, "To all Jews in Poland!":

> We must collect all documents of the human bestiality, horrifying barbarism, sadism and bloodthirstiness which the 'cultured' German people showed in these years; we must collect all the documents demonstrating how the educated of the German people used their education, science, methods, and technical and medical achievements to murder millions of innocent Jews. . . . Brothers and sisters! These documents, written with the innocent blood of millions of our brothers and sisters, fathers and mothers, children, friends, and comrades, will be the greatest accusation against the 'cultured,' 'educated' German people. These documents will be the best propaganda material against fascism, Hitlerism, and all other dark forces of the world. At this moment, when a series of trials is being opened against the German criminals, our tragedy must not be concealed; we must mobilize all our forces in order to compile a complete indictment for the world's public.[147]

Among its other strategies for promoting its historical mission, the CŻKH designed curricula for Jewish schools, asked Jewish teachers to collect children's testimonies, and promoted autobiographical essay contests.[148] In addition, ten-minute Polish-language radio broadcasts by commission workers informed Jewish and gentile audiences about its work. Topics included events during the occupation, such as the Warsaw ghetto uprising or the actions of Hans Biebow, head of the German administration of the Lodz ghetto, and their impact on the ghetto population.[149] In one of these broadcasts, on May 23, 1945, a gentile journalist described a visit to the CŻKH office and her emotional encounter with the vestiges of the Jewish tragedy. Her report began with a mysterious rocket casing serving as a "provisional urn," within which she hears a "soft sound," but is loath to look inside:

> Let the bones of the murdered of Majdanek rest, let us not look at the photographs which we are shown by the secretary of CŻKH and which

are so dreadful in their authenticity.... Our commemoration of the murdered shall not be accompanied by screams, not even if the screams concern the greatest crime and anger against the murderers. Let us ask ourselves how and why this group of people . . . works here. There are historians and lawyers, psychologists and Jewish publicists—an intellectual elite that gathered not long ago around one task: collecting . . . all documents regarding the Hitlerite crimes against the Jews and the publication of this work.... The large room ... cannot hold all these files, piling up on shelves from floor to ceiling, in heaps on the floor, and still more are being sent from the charnel houses of the Lodz ghetto, from cities, towns, and villages all over Poland.... On shelves and in closets we see files and documents of the German government, archival documents of the Jewish communities and other Jewish communal institutions. Files of the Jewish police and of the councils, documents of the antifascist fighting organizations, protocols of oral testimonies, diaries, Jewish and Polish folklore, creations of Jewish poets, writers and painters . . . photographs of Jewish life in the ghetto, of resettlement actions and of most dreadful "Aktionen" with which the Germans immortalized themselves. We see official and illegal underground press, items from the ghetto era, topographical maps of ghettos and camps, and many more documents. The material is enormous because the number of victims was enormous. In Poland alone, over 3,200,000 Polish Jews and ca. 3 million from other European countries were murdered. So far only 40,000 people survived in Poland. In Soviet Russia . . . another 200,000.... 40 percent of the Jewish people [in the world] were murdered. Which other people in history suffered so much in just five years? None and never! ... In the entire history of humankind, people have never been murdered with such cold systemization, with such unlimited cynicism and in such great numbers. No human being could have done that!—it erupts from us when we leave these tragic archives. No wonder that those who remained lost any belief in humankind, progress, and justice, and what words of comfort can . . . convince them that . . . humankind will overcome . . . its own base instincts? Or that . . . democracy will educate the new man? . . . Perhaps we should not go on talking . . . let us commemorate in silence those who perished and the commitment of those who are willing to rebuild new life atop the rubble.[150]

In order to build "a bridge between the commission and the broad public," in September 1945 in Lodz, the CŻKH founded a friends society.[151] This effort was needed because, as observed at the inaugural meeting, "the commission workers are fanatics, and they are only few. Society as a whole must assist in uncovering the truth." And, as Friedman noted, "many people who possess valuable documents do not understand their duty to give these materials to our archives."[152] In the following months, the CŻKH established local groups in other Polish cities and in the first half of 1946 in London, Paris, and Prague.[153] Like similar YIVO groups in interwar Poland, these societies' mission included promoting amateur historical work among the general Jewish and non-Jewish publics, distributing the commission's publications, raising funds, and recruiting *zamlers*.

It is difficult to estimate how many survivors volunteered as CŻKH *zamlers*, but commission correspondence offers a glimpse of recruitment strategies and the significance attributed to the *zamlers'* work. Most recruits apparently responded to the commission's public appeals or publications. In May 1946, for example, a Mr. Ayges, head of the Jewish committee in Chojnów in Lower Silesia, wrote: "I want to establish contact with you and work ... for your commission. Here and in the vicinity there is much of historical value. Before the war, there used to be a Jewish community of German Jews. ... Send me a work plan and some general instructions on your requirements."[154] Several months later, a Mr. Gotlieb turned to the CŻKH for help in unearthing archival material he had buried during the war.[155] After reading in the newspaper that the CŻKH and the Central Committee planned to compile a list of Jewish mass graves in Poland,[156] Gesja Grynwald, who had survived on "Aryan papers" with her two children, wrote in July 1946:

> I can point out many places, where thousands of victims are buried. ... I am very pleased that finally there is an organization which wants to know where our brothers and sisters lie scattered ... in the woods and the fields. ... In those tragic days, I often thought ... if I survive, I will do much for those who have tragically perished. But unfortunately, ... I am simply ashamed in front of the dead ... that we, the survivors, have forgotten so quickly. ... When I read [about your project] ... I cried with joy because finally people are beginning to take an interest.[157]

She herself had documented her survival in a diary written "just as well as I could,"[158] which she offered as a historical source.

Zelig Pacanowski, a thirty-eight-year-old native of Lodz and a manufacturer of gaiters, was recruited as a *zamler*. He had survived the Lodz ghetto and the Birkenau extermination camp, where he had lost his wife and child, then was transferred to several camps in Lower Silesia before his liberation on May 10, 1945. A year later, while recuperating in a hospital in Gerbersdorf in Lower Silesia, Pacanowski wrote to the commission: "When Mrs. [Pola] Hirsz visited us in the hospital she invited me to work for the Jewish historical commission. This invitation is the most beautiful present I have received these days. This work will give my life a purpose. I take up a broad project, because in Lower Silesia there used to be a network of camps."[159] This man became an active *zamler* for CŻKH in that region.[160]

Although the commission equipped *zamlers* with its questionnaires and instructions, the material received did not always meet its standards. In such cases,

CŻKH workers confirmed receipt of documents with thank-you letters or, if appropriate, offered gentle criticism in order not to discourage the *zamler*. For example, in July 1946, Friedman and Kermisz thanked a *zamler* for the precious material he had sent, but cautioned him against interviewing only Zionists; the commission needed testimonies from people with differing social and professional backgrounds and political orientations.[161]

Although many *zamlers* hoped to receive some compensation, the CŻKH only paid if contributions were outstanding and collectors had proven their abilities on a regular basis. Otherwise—in addition to being acknowledged on lists of donors—the *zamlers* received CŻKH publications, copies of the material they collected, or other documents or photographs they requested.[162]

Because of its proximity to the sites of the catastrophe, for many Jews who had left Poland, the CŻKH served as a bridge to the past and a link to those murdered on Polish soil. The commission enjoyed considerable renown among such Jews worldwide, who after learning about the documentation work through the Yiddish-language press, turned to it for information on missing relatives and friends. The vast majority of such queries came from internees in DP camps in Germany, or from émigrés to the Americas. For example, Rózka Borusztajn, a DP in the U.S. Zone of Germany, approached the commission looking for her mother and three brothers, who had been in the Lodz ghetto at the time of its liquidation.[163] Mr. H. Bresler in New York City, who had obtained the CŻKH's address from the editors of the New York Yiddish daily *Der Tog*, hoped to find his wife, two daughters, brother and sister-in-law, nephew, and niece, as well as several friends and their children, "because of your good work in helping to find survivors in Poland. I hope you will not deny my request, for you know even better yourselves, the situation is very sad and one does not stop looking for names in the hope that maybe they are still . . . !"[164] Similarly, Isaac Bondar from Buenos Aires, who had emigrated before the war, explained in a letter of November 1946 that he had learned about the commission's "great and holy work" through Jacob Pat, secretary of the American Jewish Labor Committee in New York. He was writing to inquire about his brother, who had survived the war, but with whom he had lost contact after the Kielce pogrom four months earlier.[165]

Survivors seeking information on relatives were extremely eager to receive pictures of loved ones as tangible reminders. For example, Efraim Grünbaum wrote from the DP camp Belsen in the British Zone of Germany in December 1946: "I have a great request for you . . . since I am the only survivor of my large family; I have not been able to find anyone. How sad this is you will understand. . . . You will understand that I dearly wished to have a bit of consolation in my life [and] that [I am asking] you to send me some photographs of my family which would give me a small cure for my misery."[166] From another camp in the U.S. Zone, forty-two-year-old Abraham Szmuel Ejdelman, a survivor of the Lodz ghetto and concentration camps, wrote in the belief that the commission had records of the ghetto's employment office, which photographed many inmates. He provided ghetto addresses for his wife and his father, as well as their workplaces, hoping that the CŻKH could find pictures of his lost family so he could "have at least a small reminder of them." Unfortunately, the archive staff could not meet his request.[167] Survivors also asked CŻKH for copies of documents relevant to their new lives, such as proof of ghetto employment, high school diplomas, or marriage certificates—records needed to apply for work in the DP camps, register for higher education, or request overseas immigration visas.[168]

Landsmanshaftn—mutual aid societies of immigrants from the same place of origin—turned to the CŻKH for historical documents for *yizker-bikher*, memorial books, for their destroyed Jewish communities. The United Dubienker Relief Committee in New York, for example, which had been founded in June 1939, asked about archival material on the shtetl Dubenke in the Lublin District, which had "been completely destroyed by the Germans. We mean the Jewish population and its property. As we have heard from individual survivors, the population was brought to the Sobibór death camp." The relief committee planned to "publish a book which portrays the life and work of our old town and its tragic destruction."[169] Some landsmanshaftn and other Polish Jewish associations overseas asked for "memorial objects," most often books and pictures, but the Jewish community council in Montevideo inquired about "some ashes or a piece of soap" for a planned memorial for the murdered Jews of Poland. The CŻKH sent them some ashes.[170]

Universalizing the Jewish Experience: The Quest for a Jewish Voice in the Polish Chorus

As much as the CŻKH provided solace to Jews in Poland and abroad, its staff worked in an unwelcoming environment. Thus, in addition to telling their own story of the national catastrophe of the Jewish people, they sought to link this story to the Polish experience. The extermination camps and uncounted other atrocities against the Jews were intrinsic to the history of Poland under German occupation. Moreover, commission activists hoped to rebuild their postwar lives as a national minority in a multiethnic Poland like the one they had known before the occupation. They also subscribed to the new government's promise to right the wrongs of fascism by building a better society in which social inequality, political reaction, and anti-Semitism had no place.

Yet the Nazi genocide, shifting postwar borders, and mass expulsion of ethnic Germans had profound demographic and cultural consequences for Poland, which became a monoethnic, largely Roman Catholic nation state. Widely perceived as "alien" in this new state, Jews often encountered everyday hostility and violence, and occasionally even pogroms. The majority of ethnic Poles tended to focus on their own wartime victimization, martyrdom, and resistance while ignoring the cataclysm suffered by their Jewish neighbors. Moreover, Poland's transition to a one-party state sent out conflicting messages; initial government support, followed by growing state suppression, raised questions about the possibility of independent scholarly research on the Jewish tragedy. Under these circumstances, the CŻKH increasingly emphasized the universal lessons of Jewish suffering in the hope of helping to build a society that rejected fascist reaction and anti-Semitism.

Seeking a message that might integrate the particular Jewish story into a broader national narrative of wartime suffering, the CŻKH focused on Nazi ideology and its consequences to counter the widespread perception that Jews had no connection to Poland and to reassert their rightful presence in the new Polish state. While still presenting the *khurbn* as singular in its geographic extent and tactics, the commission emphasized that Nazi Germany had targeted "all humanity." Jews were the first victims of "Hitlerite" ideology, but only the Nazi regime's collapse had spared the Poles from becoming the next target for annihilation. At a CŻKH press conference in March 1945, which attracted non-Jewish journalists from major Polish papers, Philip Friedman explained the CŻKH's goal as "carrying out research on the German occupation, which . . . ended with a catastrophe for the Jewish nation." Yet despite the unprecedented nature of Nazi atrocities in the long and terrible history of Jewish suffering, it was no longer possible "to discuss the Jewish problem in isolation; in the present case it is closely connected with the . . . existence of other nations, because fascism aimed at the destruction of all the nations of Europe."[171] Thus Friedman recognized the Jews as a nation in their own right, but insisted on their connection with other victims of the Nazi regime. He also carefully used Marxist terminology in asserting the CŻKH's choice of "historical materialism" over "historical idealism." Rather than limiting its work to the "task of recording history, which would be a compilation of facts and a reflection on the epoch," the commission aimed to write history that would yield "the moral annihilation of fascism and Hitlerism."[172]

From the outset, the CŻKH universalized the Jewish experience by stressing Jews' contribution to Poland's resistance against the German occupation. In particular, it sought to correct the stereotype of Jews as passive victims subservient to the enemy and unfit to be allies in Poland's fight against the German occupiers, a prejudice that remained widespread after the war.[173] As early as April 1945, the commission identified research on the "heroic fight and death of our heroes" as a central endeavor, with special attention to "the contribution of Jews on the battlefields in east and west" and the "heroic struggles of the Warsaw, Bialystok, Vilna, and Czestochowa ghettos, in Treblinka, Sobibór, and other places."[174] Similarly, it sought to "convince the world that the Jews did not just die like sheep but also like heroes."[175]

By September 1945, the study of resistance in all its manifestations had become an integral part of the commission's research agenda, encompassing armed resistance in separate Jewish fighting organizations and in non-Jewish partisan units in Poland and the Soviet Union, as well as unarmed or "passive" resistance, such as the refusal to follow orders or cultural activities in the Jewish underground. The commission also studied German disinformation strategies meant to disorient the Jews and mislead them about the true nature of their situation; German countermeasures against Jewish resistance; Jews' psychological state and their awareness of their predicament; and the complex relations between Jews and local gentiles.[176] Jewish resistance became a theme in all the CŻKH's local studies of ghettos and in its research on children and youth, whom the activists understood as symbols of Jewish victimization and resistance. In this way, they hoped to legitimize the presence of the Jewish minority in Poland and thus reduce their social and political isolation.

A dominant motif in the commission's public presentation as well as in its internal self-understanding was the view of its research project as a service to Poland's continuing struggle against fascism and reaction. For example, in September 1945, Friedman reminded his colleagues that the historical narrative of the destruction of Poland's Jewish community would serve as "an eternal . . . warning against fascism . . . which shall awaken the conscience of the peoples and mobilize them for the fight against reaction."[177] On another occasion, he remarked that since the catastrophe was caused not by nature but rather "by 'human beings' who must be punished," the commission's task was "giv[ing] proof of the Hitlerite murders" and "gather[ing] material that charges the perpetrators." Such a "weapon against fascism and anti-Semitism" served not only Jews, but "the entire world."[178] In this spirit, the commission advertised its work with a bilingual Yiddish-Polish poster featuring the slogan: "May historical truth bury and vanquish fascism!" In a Polish-language brochure summarizing the CŻKH's first year in the spring of 1946, Noe Grüss asserted that the commission followed the universal goal of "unmasking and fighting against Hitlerism, racism, and anti-Semitism," while also working toward the "just punishment of the crimes"[179] the Nazis had committed on Polish territory.

Positioning the Jewish fate in the wider context of wartime suffering and antifascism had practical relevance when the CŻKH began to cooperate with the High Commission for the Investigation of German Crimes in Poland. Established on March 29, 1945, by the Polish Ministry of Justice, the High Commission investigated and prosecuted German war crimes on Polish soil. The CŻKH and the High Commission exchanged documents, and commission workers joined delegations investigating the sites of the extermination camps Auschwitz-Birkenau, Chełmno, Treblinka, Sobibór, and Majdanek. Friedman served in the High Commission's Lodz branch and as advisor in its preparatory work for the Polish delegation to the Nuremberg trials.[180] Encouraged by the public prosecutor of the Polish Supreme National Tribunal (Najwyższy Trybunał Narodowy; NTN), Stefan Kurowski, the CŻKH supplied the Polish delegation with evidence and prepared a German-language affidavit, "Deutsche Verbrechen gegen die jüdische Bevölkerung in Polen, 1939–1945" (German crimes against the Jewish population in Poland, 1939–1945).[181] CŻKH representatives appeared as experts in five of the

Nachman Blumental (center) and Joseph Kermisz (right, in uniform) take notes while listening to a Polish eyewitness (left) during a government-sponsored expedition to the site of the Chełmno extermination camp, May 1945. *Yad Vashem Photo Archives 1427/358*

seven trials against forty-nine German war criminals for war crimes and crimes against humanity perpetrated on Polish soil held at the NTN, as well as in several trials at local Polish courts in the years 1946–1948.[182]

Participation in these trials represented a degree of public recognition for the CŻKH on the part of the new government and its judicial institutions. Yet internal discussions about the trials reveal apprehensions, insecurities, and divisions among the commission's core of scholars about publicly presenting their analysis of the Jewish cataclysm.

A heated discussion ensued when Artur Eisenbach was invited to give expert testimony in the district court in Lodz at the trial of Hans Biebow, the chief German administrator of that city's ghetto. At an internal meeting on March 17, 1947, five weeks before the trial began, the activists debated whether the Germans had followed a premeditated murder plan in the ghetto or whether they had initially considered keeping Jews alive for the sake of their economic exploitation—a question that in many ways anticipated later historiographic debates about Nazi extermination policies.[183] Eisenbach argued that German policy exhibited two conflicting tendencies: an "economic" strand that exploited Jewish labor and a "political" one that sought their extermination outright. Economic considerations had prevailed "as long as the technical possibility of mass murder did not exist."[184] As evidence for the "economic tendency," Isaiah Trunk noted that the Lodz ghetto was the last to be liquidated.[185] Other coworkers, most notably journalist Abraham Wolf Jasny, rejected any notion that the Germans had ever had "such liberal views as keeping the Jews alive to exploit their work force";[186] rather, their only goal had been extermination. Another colleague noted that the Germans had for a time stealthily hidden their real goal.[187]

Debate also arose as to whether, given the prevailing anti-Semitism, expert testimony should mention the fact that the Lodz Jews had manufactured uniforms for the Wehrmacht, even if they had done so in order to secure food for the population of the ghetto and slow the pace of deaths and deportations. Kermisz argued that gentile Poles could interpret this as Jewish collaboration with the enemy.[188] Jasny disagreed, on the grounds that the ghetto economy provided evidence against anti-Semitic charges of Jews' lack of economic productivity. Also, the fact that Jews were murdered when they were "most productive"[189] showed that German extermination policies were independent of economic considerations.

Whether to accuse Biebow as an individual perpetrator or as a symbol of the entire Nazi regime provoked further contention. Kermisz argued that the "loss of Jewish material and spiritual culture" was an indictment of fascism itself.[190] Eisenbach concurred in supporting "a trial against the entire German policy and all levels of authority," beginning with the Nazi party program.[191] Others wanted to focus on "Biebow and his perfidy."[192] Leon Szeftel, in particular, argued that not focusing the trial on Biebow would exonerate him for having followed "higher authorities."[193] In the end, CŻKH testimony portrayed Biebow's individual actions as a mirror of the larger criminality of the fascist regime.[194]

Similar debates occurred in the context of the even more significant trial against Rudolf Höss, the commander of Auschwitz-Birkenau, held at the NTN in Warsaw from March 11 to March 29, 1947. The Polish prosecutor commissioned Nachman Blumental, then the head of the CŻKH, to present expert testimony on Germany's genocidal policy toward Jews, both generally and in regard to Auschwitz-Birkenau. Blumental was aware of the publicity surrounding the trial, which coincided with the meeting of the Four Power Council of Foreign Ministers in Moscow, when he previewed his testimony before colleagues and Central Committee representatives on March 21, 1947. Höss as an individual perpetrator mattered relatively little to Blumental, who saw the trial as an indictment "against the entire fascist system." Many other Nazi officials could have stood in the dock in his stead.[195] Blumental's three- to four-hour-long testimony focused on the overall ideological background of the genocide, without addressing the specific accusations against Höss. He explained that the concept of *Lebensraum*, as the core of German policy, demanded territorial conquest and the annihilation of existing populations. The Nazis' selection of Jews as the first victims, a consequence of their anti-Semitism, fulfilled several useful functions: it diverted German public attention away from domestic problems; it mobilized the population for a war that the majority of Germans did not want; and—in stripping Jews of their property and eventually annihilating them—it served the economic purpose of enriching the German people and the state. In addition, the Jews made an easy test case. No state would interfere on their behalf, as would not have been the case with other national groups. Thus, "the extermination of the Jews was a preparation for the annihilation of other peoples." Blumental explained that the Nazis had considered Jews "inert objects," not human beings, as reflected in their language and methods of annihilation.[196] He further noted that no piece of legislation had specifically authorized mass murder; instead, German laws and regulations aimed to disorient the Jews and lull them into believing that they still lived under a rule of law, while disguising the actual goal of German policy. Indeed, he went beyond the Nazi regime to observe that "the entire [German] people were involved in the anti-Jewish action." Such efficient mass murder had required "all institutions and technical devices ... such as railroad cars, automobiles, crematoria," all of them "built by great engineers. Poisoning the Jews required a well-educated SS man."[197] German firms even used the hair and clothing of the dead for economic profit.[198]

While Blumental's colleagues generally accepted his approach, some demanded that he highlight the *specificity* of Jewish suffering with regard to that of other groups. An interviewer and *zamler* identified as B. Mosiężnik reminded "the expert" that he personally would be present at the trial "as an accuser in the name of all the Jews killed" in the Holocaust. Although the Nuremberg trials had prosecuted a broad category of "crimes against humanity," this testimony should highlight the murder of the Jews as a distinct "case of genocide," and also "distinguish between the situation of the Jews and that of inmates of other nationalities in the camp." Another coworker, Michał Rajak, reminded Blumental "that he appears as the accuser in the name of six million. The testimony has two goals: firstly, to prove to the world the entire ugliness of Hitlerism; secondly, to become part of Jewish history."[199]

In presenting himself as a representative of "the six million," Michał Rajak ignored Blumental's accounting of the number of deaths at Auschwitz-Birkenau, which—to the surprise of his listeners—he had inserted in the midst of his testimony. Namely, his own thorough study had shown that 1.5 million Jews had been killed in Auschwitz-Birkenau, not four million as initially assumed.[200] The journalist Michał Mirski, secretary of the Central Committee, directly addressed Blumental's calculations while critiquing his testimony overall. "For scholarly purposes accuracy is necessary. However, this trial pursues political goals," especially given the international political context:

> This trial should be a demonstration before the Council of the Four Powers convening in Moscow. It is unimportant whether 1.5 or 3 million Jews perished in Auschwitz. We need to see Auschwitz as a system, as a symbol of fascist power. In standing up against Auschwitz we also stand up against all camps, against the Hitlerite system itself.... For the

one million Jews who died in the ghettos, Auschwitz must be held responsible as well. It is true that Jews were only the first victims; that was only a preparatory laboratory. The legal argumentation of German politics is also irrelevant.... The deeds as carried out must be taken into consideration. The accusation should draw from *Mein Kampf*.[201]

Blumental had his defenders. Leon Szeftel and Abraham Rozenberg advocated accuracy and caution when it came to numbers, and Rozenberg even asserted that a political emphasis would weaken the appearance of expertise.[202] In his own defense, Blumental argued that he appeared not "as an accuser but as an expert," who must treat this topic "objectively." This meant, in particular, downplaying "the difference between the status of Polish and Jewish inmates." At this moment, it was "the common enemy that should be combated."[203] And this was the position taken in Blumental's expert testimony at the Höss trial. It found a positive echo in the non-Jewish press, precisely because the argument about German *Lebensraum*—which Blumental at the trial described as a *Todesraum* (death space) for all non-German people—linked the victimization of Jews and non-Jews.[204]

A Polish woman serves coffee and baked goods to the members of the government-sponsored inquiry commission at the site of the Chełmno extermination camp, May 1945. Philip Friedman (in overcoat) at the center helps himself to the food, with Joseph Kermisz and Nachman Blumental to his left. *Yad Vashem Photo Archives 1427/344*

Between the Fronts: Historical Research and Political Agendas on the Eve of Poland's Stalinization

As much as two years before the consolidation of communist control annulled autonomous Jewish life in Poland, the CŻKH faced pressure from the Jewish Central Committee—itself increasingly dominated by members of the communist Polish Workers Party (PPR)—to abandon collection and research in favor of political agitation. For Friedman and his colleagues, fighting fascism was an integral part of educating the public about the Jewish cataclysm. If they occasionally resorted to politically correct jargon, they nonetheless upheld a firm commitment to rigorous scholarship that was not compromised by political concerns.[205]

To exert pressure, the Central Committee cut its funding and prevented the CŻKH from independently seeking financial support from Jewish organizations abroad.[206] In March 1946 Friedman resigned from his post as director over the issue, but the committee refused to accept his decision and signaled willingness to compromise. Subsequently, the commission received occasional subsidies from the AJDC, the American Jewish Labor Committee, YIVO in New York, and the friends societies in London and Paris. However, the dispute extinguished any hope of launching more systematic and full-fledged fundraising campaigns abroad.[207] Likewise, the committee became increasingly intolerant of CŻKH efforts to maintain contacts with Jewish researchers and other Holocaust documentation projects in the West, or to seek the help of foreign publishers to disseminate its publications beyond Poland.[208] Fed up with budgetary disputes and sensing that independent scholarly research would become increasingly difficult, Friedman left Poland in July 1946.[209] Over the following four years, most of the CŻKH's founding members also emigrated, depriving Jewish Holocaust research in Poland of its scholarly core and intellectual backbone.

Initially, the communist victory in the elections of January 19, 1947—which rendered the "Democratic Bloc" (a coalition of the communist PPR, socialist PPS, and two smaller left-wing parties) the strongest political faction—had seemed auspicious for the commission's work. Yet the defeat of the PPR's conservative rival, the Peasant Party, put it in a dominant position and in the long run consolidated Poland's metamorphosis into a one-party state.[210] In the meantime, it brought nominal fulfillment of the CŻKH's original goal of becoming a permanent scholarly institute. On January 27, 1947, Nachman Blumental—Friedman's successor as director—and the new secretary-general, Joseph Kermisz, proposed turning the commission into a permanent Jewish Scholarly Institute with centralized Jewish archives in Warsaw, modeled on the interwar YIVO. They found open ears among the PPR representatives in the Central Committee, especially Szymon Zachariasz, head of the party's caucus. Because the institute served the PPR agenda of bringing more Jews to the party by influencing Jewish cultural life, it mobilized government support.[211]

In the summer of 1947, after receiving Central Committee approval, the CŻKH moved from Lodz to Warsaw. By then all but seven of the regional and local commissions had been closed down.[212] On October 1 of that year, with no official fanfare, the Jewish Historical Institute (ŻIH) formally replaced the CŻKH, with Nachman Blumental as director and Joseph Kermisz as vice-director. The new secretary-general was the sociologist and PPR member Rafał Gerber, a recent returnee from the Soviet Union, where he had been a functionary in the Union of Polish Patriots. Other coworkers who had formerly been active in the commission were Eisenbach and Trunk.[213] Ironically, by the time the CŻKH achieved its original goal of a permanent institute, independent Holocaust research effectively came to an end.

In 1948, with communist rule firmly established and in an atmosphere of growing Stalinization, the government began to systematically limit the diversity and number of Jewish organizations and curtailed the autonomy of those that remained. While this was part of a general political shift toward abrogating the autonomy of non-Party groups and placing institutions and society under state control, in its policies against the Jewish community the Polish government followed its Soviet patron, which increasingly took a restrictive course against its own Jewish population and turned against the young Israeli state.[214] On June 1, 1948, the authorities forced Jewish religious congregations to merge with the Central Committee as the only official body of Polish Jews. Following a purge of the Socialist Party, its remaining members were forced to dissolve the PPS and join the newly named Polish United Workers' Party (Polska Zjednoczona Partia Robotnicza; PZPR), which had formed in December 1948. Its members' assumption of top positions in Jewish institutions and communities exacerbated the rift between communists and Zionists until the communists seized control of the Central Committee in April 1949.[215]

Later that year, Zionist parties and organizations were abolished, and Jewish relief agencies, most notably the AJDC, were forced to close their offices and to leave the country. In the first three years after the war, the AJDC had invested close to $18 million in the rehabilitation of the Polish Jewish community.[216] The Jewish Labor Bund dissolved itself in January 1949 and its members either merged with the PZPR or emigrated.[217] In July 1949 the Central Committee replaced the ŻIH directorate—Blumental and Kermisz—with party members less concerned with scholarship but possessing the necessary party credentials. The new director as of September 1, 1949, was Bernard Mark, a veteran communist who had spent the war in Moscow.[218] As part of the government effort to restrict Jewish institutions, by January 1950 the Central Committee lost its authority over Jewish educational facilities, hospitals, orphanages, and cooperatives, which now came under state control, and the use of Yiddish in schools was relegated to religious instruction.[219] In late October 1950, the government liquidated the Central Committee altogether and appointed a new communist-controlled body, the Social and Cultural Association of Jews in Poland (Towarzystwo Społeczno-Kulturalne Żydów w Polsce; TSKŻ), as the sole official Jewish organization dedicated to welfare and culture.[220]

The Jewish Historical Institute remained the only other legal Jewish institution in Poland. While it profited from the centralization of Jewish archival collections and the creation of a museum of Jewish history and culture under its auspices, the ŻIH enjoyed the government's tolerance only on condition that it followed the party line. Hence the institute adjusted to the approved narrative of the Holocaust as a consequence of German capitalism and imperialism.[221] It joined the official chorus celebrating communist resistance, while it minimized the influence of Zionist and Bundist opposition. Similarly, the institute idealized Polish-Jewish relations during the German occupation, lauding the help that non-Jewish Poles had extended to their Jewish neighbors.[222] The ŻIH had no choice but to adhere to the increasingly anti-Semitic and anti-Israeli positions of the Polish government and the Soviet regime, as well as to their reluctance to see the Holocaust as a historical event worthy of special attention. Thus the institute expanded the scope of its research to cover the millennium-long Jewish presence in Poland, although its focus remained on the years 1939–1945.[223] Beyond these ideological adjustments, the institute's "ghettoization" through a narrow scope of activities and limited Jewish audience, as well as the interest of the government to prove to the West that there was in fact a vibrant Jewish life in Poland, might explain its survival throughout the communist years as the only Jewish research institute in the Soviet bloc.[224]

Conclusion

Holocaust research in Poland began at a brief moment when survivors—despite devastating human and cultural loss—had reason to believe in the possibility of rebuilding organized Jewish life on the prewar model. The founders and coworkers of the CŻKH acted out of a deep sense of obligation toward the dead as well as toward future generations, and with a commitment to perpetuate the cultural traditions of what had been Europe's largest and most vibrant Jewish community. Hopeful that Nazi barbarism had been vanquished and that the new regime was truly committed to fighting reaction in order to create a better society, the activists saw their own efforts to educate the public as a contribution to this struggle, one that would buttress connections with their Polish surroundings.

Most commission workers believed that rigorous scholarship, free of political considerations, best served these goals. Yet the CŻKH struggled against widespread reluctance among gentile Poles—given their own suffering under the occupation—to recognize the Jewish cataclysm as deserving of special consideration. While the commission took great care to document the enormous scale and particularity of Jewish suffering, they also adapted to the political climate by linking the fate of the Jews to that of the majority population. Much like their French colleagues, they emphasized the universal lessons of the recent past: the persecution of Jews exemplified the crimes of fascism; Auschwitz-Birkenau symbolized a crime that began with the Jews but targeted all humanity; the Jews, despite their specific victimization, had been active resisters and allies in Poland's fight against the fascist occupiers.

The CŻKH's history illustrates cultural continuity as survivors sought to perpetuate prewar traditions of researching the Jewish past. More than other Jewish documentation initiatives, the Polish case—in particular due to close personal ties with YIVO and Ringelblum—followed in the tradition of *khurbn-forshung*. Despite clear lines of continuity in terms of using the methods of social history, *zamlen*, and the idea of historical scholarship as a service to the community, the CŻKH creatively adapted these methods to the unprecedented magnitude of the recent tragedy, thereby providing a model for other Jewish documentation initiatives in postwar Europe and beyond.

The CŻKH story also reveals the ultimately futile quest of Polish survivors for reintegration into the surroundings they had once known, and in which they had their cultural roots. Unlike their counterparts in France, when outside pressures threatened to compromise their scholarly standards, most documentation activists felt they had no choice but to leave their home country, thus abandoning the vision of a Jewish future in Poland. Sooner or later the activists came to the painful realization that the now monoethnic Polish state had no room for the Jewish minority, nor did the political climate allow for independent historical scholarship on its tragedy. The government upheld its promise to support Jewish life only so long as it was opportune and tolerated by its Soviet patron. Old stereotypes of Jews as "foreign" and "hostile elements" survived the Holocaust and received increased impetus from the popular perception that ethnic Poles now were being victimized by the Żydokomuna, whom they held responsible for the new order—even after the majority of Jewish survivors had left Poland precisely *because* of the regime.

Most of the CŻKH's founders and staff members had already emigrated before 1951, when the Polish state stopped granting emigration permits to Jews. The first large emigration wave occurred between July and October 1945, when 40,000–50,000 Jews left Poland. An additional 100,000 followed between May and September 1946, among them Philip Friedman and his wife, Ada Eber; Noe Grüss; Michał Borwicz; Nella Rost; and Joseph Wulf. For many of these émigrés, the Kielce pogrom in July 1946 was the turning point, when they abandoned any hope of permanently and securely reestablishing themselves in Poland. Another 30,000 departed in the two years following the establishment of the State of Israel in May 1948, including Nachman Blumental, Rachel Auerbach, Joseph Kermisz, Isaiah Trunk, Hersh Wasser, and Genia Silkes.[225] Many of the CŻKH workers found a way station in the DP camps of Germany, Austria, and Italy until they were able to make their permanent homes in Israel, the United States, or elsewhere. They took their experience in *khurbn-forshung* with them and continued their work as Jewish DPs. In what ways did those Polish survivors inspire the creation and influence the work of the historical commissions that operated in the temporary and transitional space of the DP camps?

4

Writing History while Sitting on Packed Suitcases

Holocaust Documentation in the Jewish Displaced Persons Camps of Germany, Austria, and Italy

The Jewish Displaced Persons camps in Allied-occupied Germany, Austria, and Italy emerged as centers of Jewish Holocaust documentation during the years 1945–1949. The founders and activists of the historical commissions in these countries were survivors of eastern European backgrounds who either had been liberated from concentration and labor camps in Germany and Austria or, after surviving the war in eastern Europe, had fled westward in search of Allied protection and care. Unlike their colleagues in France and Poland, for the most part they were neither citizens nor prewar residents of these countries. As so-called Displaced Persons (DPs)—a category created by the Allies to describe foreign nationals who by accident of war found themselves outside the prewar borders of their countries of origin[1]—they saw their sojourn as a transitory inconvenience on the way to new lives overseas. Camps in the U.S. Zone of Germany held the majority of the roughly 250,000–330,000 Jews living as DPs in Germany, Austria, and Italy at some point during the four years after the war.[2] Because this zone also had the largest network of historical commissions, it is the primary focus of this chapter, which also compares documentation activities among Jewish DPs in the British Zone of Germany and in Austria and Italy.

Of the twenty million people on the move in war-torn Europe in May 1945, eight million found themselves displaced from their homelands into the territories of Germany and Austria. They included forced and voluntary foreign laborers, POWs, concentration and labor camp inmates, and survivors of the notorious death marches by which the Germans had "evacuated" the surviving prisoners of their labor, concentration, and extermination camps in the east from the advancing Soviet army.[3] Those liberated included 50,000–80,000 Jews in Germany and 20,000–30,000 in Austria.[4] The Allied armies, in collaboration with the United Nations Relief and Rehabilitation Administration (UNRRA), set up provisional assembly centers in former concentration and labor camps, army barracks, and administrative and communal buildings or requisitioned private homes or hotels, where they provided food, clothing, and care, as well as family-reunification services.[5] Following a policy of fast and indiscriminate repatriation, between May and September 1945 the Allies returned six million DPs to their countries of origin.[6] However, by January 1946 the western Allies had identified approximately one million "unrepatriable" DPs who remained in the western zones of Germany and required the extended care of the occupying forces.[7] In addition to 200,000 lost, abandoned, and orphaned children and youth, they included 400,000–500,000 non-Jewish Poles and Ukrainians and 175,000–200,000 Balts, as well as Hungarians, Romanians, Bulgarians, and those of other nationalities who were either unwilling to return to the Soviet sphere of control or who wanted to avoid punishment at home for collaboration with the Germans. Another 100,000–200,000 of these DPs were Jews, mainly eastern European, who refused to go back to the places of the Jewish cataclysm.[8]

While all DPs suffered with primitive and overcrowded housing, as well as insufficient nutrition and clothing, Allied policies that accommodated them according to their prewar nationalities meant that Jews often suffered from anti-Semitic mockery or even violence from compatriots, some of whom had collaborated with the Nazis. Reports by American service personnel and American Jewish Joint Distribution Committee (AJDC/Joint) workers on poor conditions for the survivor population under American authority in July 1945 led President Truman to commission University of Pennsylvania Law School dean Earl G. Harrison to investigate, with particular attention to Jewish survivors. Harrison's report, submitted to Truman at the end of August, was a devastating indictment: "We appear to be treating the Jews as the Nazis treated them except that we do not exterminate them. They are in concentration camps in large numbers under military guard, instead of the S.S. troops. One is led to wonder whether the German people seeing this, are not supposing that we are following or at least condoning Nazi policy."[9] Harrison demanded that the military authorities ensure a general improvement of the survivors' material conditions as well as their recognition as a separate national entity, one that had suffered a particular fate under the Nazi regime: "Jews as Jews (not as members of their nationality groups) have been more severely victimized than the non-Jewish members of the same or other nationalities. . . . Refusal to recognize the Jews as such has the effect, in this situation, of closing one's eyes to their former and more barbaric persecution, which has already made them a separate group with greater needs."[10] Harrison recommended not only separate camps but that the British Mandatory powers issue 100,000 entry visas to Palestine—the first time an American governmental document recognized the Jews as a separate national entity with a homeland in Palestine. By linking the DP problem with Jewish statehood in Palestine, it placed both of these issues on the international agenda.[11]

Harrison's report and Truman's order pushed the American military governments in Germany and in Austria to appoint a special advisor on Jewish affairs, establish separate Jewish camps, and increase the aid provided to survivors in its zone. The British refused to open the gates to Palestine, but in December 1945 they moved their Jewish DP population to separate camps and in the spring of 1946 also appointed an advisor on Jewish affairs.[12]

Of 184 Jewish DP camps and assembly centers in Germany, 150 were located in the American Zone, twenty-three in the British Zone, and eleven in the French Zone.[13] Among the seventy-three Jewish DP camps in Austria, fifty-three were in the American Zone, twelve in the British, and eight in the French Zone.[14] In Italy, half of the Jewish DPs lived in seventy-three *hachsharot* (agricultural training farms); the other half resided in seventeen mixed-population camps formally under Italian supervision but cared for by UNRRA and the AJDC.[15]

In the years 1946 and 1947, the Jewish DP population in these three countries constantly rose as growing numbers of Polish, Czechoslovakian, Romanian, and Hungarian Jews moved westward in search of protection by the western Allies. In addition to hoping to escape hostility and violent assault, they sought better living conditions and a way to leave Europe for Palestine, the Americas, and other destinations.[16] Most of these refugees had help from the semiclandestine Zionist organization Brichah (Hebrew for "flight"), which aided legal and illegal immigration to Palestine. Organized by survivors themselves and supported by the Joint, the Jewish Brigade (Palestinian Jews who had fought in the British army) and the Jewish Agency, the Brichah moved thousands of refugees west and south under the eyes of the occupying armies, in particular the Americans, in whose zone most refugees concentrated.[17]

Between February and July 1946, the Jewish DP population in the western zones of Germany grew from roughly 70,000 to 106,000. From the Kielce pogrom that July until the fall of 1947, approximately 100,000 Jews left Poland. Consequently, the number of Jewish DPs in Germany peaked in summer 1947 at 184,000, of whom 157,000 were concentrated in the U.S. Zone, due to the relatively liberal policies of the American occupying forces.[18] In Austria, a total of 95,000 Polish Jews and 14,000 Hungarian Jews had arrived by the end of 1946, although 75,000 of them went on to Germany and 5,500 to Italy, leaving only 30,000 at the end of 1946.[19] The Jewish DP population in Italy, approximately 14,000 at the end of 1945, was 15,000 in February 1946. These relatively stable numbers disguise the highly transient nature of this population.[20]

The political and social conditions in the three countries—and in their various occupation zones—differed considerably. Although all three countries found themselves under military occupation, they enjoyed different degrees of sovereignty. As the main aggressor and the perpetrator of unprecedented war crimes and genocide, Germany came under strict Four Power military occupation, with no sovereign national government until 1949, when rising cold-war tensions led to the formation of two German states: the western Zones forming the Federal

Republic of Germany and the Soviet Zone becoming the German Democratic Republic under Soviet tutelage. Full sovereignty followed in 1955, although allied troops remained stationed for the next three and a half decades.[21] Germany, due to its size and central geographic location, housed by far the largest number of Jewish survivors, although they remained a minority among DPs of all nationalities. At the same time, Jewish DPs were the majority of Jews in Germany in the early postwar years. Germany's own Jewish community, numbering about 500,000 in 1933, had been reduced to approximately 27,000–29,000 individuals, most of whom had survived thanks to marriages with non-Jews or a non-Jewish parent; others had returned from exile to rebuild their communities and resettle in Germany permanently.[22]

Austria, with its ambiguous status as both ally and victim of Nazi Germany and formally under Four Power military occupation, established its own democratic quasi-sovereign government in April 1945 but gained full sovereignty only in 1955.[23] The Jewish DP population, despite its highly transient nature, constituted the majority of the Jewish population, since Austria's native Jews numbered around 5,000–7,000 shortly after the war.[24]

Italy had yet a different status due to the early liberation and Allied occupation of its southern regions, while central and northern Italy remained under Fascist rule and German control or occupation until April 1945. By June of that year, liberated Italy was practically ruled by an independent democratic government, although formally under the auspices of the Anglo-American Allied Control Council until the Paris peace treaty of February 1947.[25] The 50,000 foreign Jews who passed through Italy in the years 1945–1948 outnumbered the surviving Italian Jewish community of 28,000.[26] Unlike the German and Austrian cases, the Italian government controlled the country's borders and established its own refugee policy, which in the case of Jews amounted to turning a blind eye.[27] Despite British protests about "infiltrees," Italy's Mediterranean ports made it the preferred destination for DPs seeking illegal immigration to Mandatory Palestine: 21,000 Jews made the transit prior to the foundation of the State of Israel in May 1948.[28]

Despite these differences, the experiences of Jewish DPs in Germany, Austria, and Italy shared a number of characteristics. Most notably, DPs understood their status as such as a transition between the catastrophe and a new life overseas. The DP population steadily decreased after Israel's founding and the enactment of the DP Acts by the U.S. Congress in 1948 and 1950.[29] Between April and September 1948, the number of Jewish DPs in the western zones of Germany dropped from 165,000 to 30,000; by 1953, fewer than 15,000 were left behind. Only four DP camps in these zones remained open by 1950, and the last one closed in 1957.[30] In Austria, only 5,000 Jewish DPs remained by the end of 1951; three years later, when there were 1,000, the last DP camp closed. By the summer of 1950 only 2,000 Jewish DPs remained in Italy.[31]

Lack of understanding, callousness, and anti-Semitic stereotypes among occupying forces and relief organizations often made for difficult interactions with survivors. The military government staff, army personnel, and UNRRA's multinational workforce—especially those who had not been present at the liberation of the camps but arrived at the European theater later—tended to prefer stereotypically "clean and well-behaved" German or Austrian civilians over the emaciated and traumatized survivors, who often appeared demanding, obstinate, recalcitrant, and disobedient to authority and order, and whose behavior seemed alien and unpredictable to people with little understanding for what the survivors had been through.[32] Under these circumstances, American Jewish army chaplains and Jewish GIs served as crucial mediators between the survivors and military forces by showing sensitivity to the DPs' psychological and spiritual needs.[33] Although the AJDC only arrived in the DP camps in late summer 1945—leading survivors to think that American Jews had abandoned them like the rest of the world—the Joint nevertheless served as the single most important relief organization for Jewish DPs, providing some $20.6 million to rehabilitate Jewish cultural, educational, and religious life in Germany and Austria and another $6.6 million for Italy in the years 1945–1948.[34]

In Germany and Austria, tensions between Jewish DPs and the local non-Jewish populations were persistent. Because most camps were in rural areas outside the destroyed cities, the influx of DPs brought major demographic changes; indeed, some of the towns had never had Jewish communities.[35] The non-Jewish populations largely responded with rejection and anti-Semitic stereotypes that criminalized the Jewish DPs as black-marketers and profiteers, whose activities brought them privileged treatment by the occupying forces.[36] These views had their roots in prewar anti-Semitism and Nazi propaganda but were also nurtured from the self-perception of most Germans and Austrians as victims. German victim narratives drew from Allied bombings, mass sexual assault on German women by Soviet soldiers, territorial loss and expulsions of ethnic Germans from eastern Europe, extended captivity of German soldiers in Soviet POW camps, and from Allied occupation after decisive military defeat.[37] Austrian victim narratives centered on Austria's annexation by Nazi Germany, which was widely interpreted as having both exempted Austrians from any responsibility for the regime's crimes against the Jews and rendered the Allied occupation unjustified.[38] The survivors, on the other hand, reacted with outrage to Germans' and Austrians' unwillingness to bear responsibility for the crimes against the Jews, as well as to their better health, nutrition, and housing. Nonetheless, as historian Atina Grossmann has shown, daily interactions occurred between Jews and Germans. For example, Germans found employment as cleaning and medical personnel in the camps; German doctors and midwives assisted Jewish mothers in the baby boom among the *She'erit Hapletah* ("surviving remnant") in Germany, and Jewish men and German women frequently maintained romantic relations.[39]

Anti-Semitism played a negligible role in the everyday experience of Jewish DPs in Italy, who generally maintained friendly relations with the local population. A widespread Italian self-perception blamed the crimes of Fascism on Italy's alliance with Nazi Germany, since anti-Semitism was widely viewed as "un-Italian."[40] Although partisan fighting against German occupation was only the experience of a minority of Italians in the north, it became the quintessential wartime memory of the entire nation and the founding myth of the Italian republic. Not unlike the French postwar perception of Vichy, historian Claudio Fogu observed that in the immediate postwar period, Fascism became a "parenthesis in Italian history and an external virus that had penetrated its healthy historical body," while twenty years of aggressive foreign policy, anti-Semitism, and racism were actively forgotten.[41] The survival of 83 percent of Italian Jews seemed to confirm Italians' innate humanism.[42]

In all three countries, the *She'erit Hapletah* came from territories throughout central and eastern Europe; overcoming their diverse wartime experiences, they were bound together by survival, loss, and traumatization and by their self-understanding as a community in transit on the verge of a new historical epoch. As they awaited the visas that would take them beyond Europe, the survivors built a wide variety of political, religious, social, and cultural institutions. Modeled upon traditional eastern European Jewish communal organizations, these institutions helped to express the DPs' agency over their lives and to forge the self-perception of the *She'erit Hapletah* as constituents of a Jewish *nation*.

Just days after the liberation from concentration camps, Jewish survivors organized local camp committees for the purpose of self-representation; regional and zonal committees soon followed. Recognized by the occupying forces as official bodies of Jewish self-government, they administered the distribution of material aid provided by the UNRRA (after 1947 the International Refugee Organization) and Jewish relief organizations, searched for remaining relatives, and spoke out against repatriation and for separate Jewish camps and the right of emigration. In the British zone of Germany a provisional Committee of Liberated Jews formed in Bergen-Belsen on April 25, 1945. It became the Central Committee of Liberated Jews in the British Zone at a congress of survivors held that September.[43] In the American sector, survivors meeting in the Bavarian town of Feldafing on July 1, 1945, proclaimed themselves the Central Committee of Liberated Jews in Bavaria. The following day this committee set up its headquarters in the building of the Deutsches Museum in Munich, which became a new Jewish center. On July 25, the committee legitimated itself at a conference held at the former St. Ottilien monastery, which had become a sanatorium for former camp inmates. Ninety-four delegates from the American, British, and French occupation zones—joined by guests from Austria—elected members of a Central Committee of Liberated Jews in Bavaria, later expanded to the entire American Zone.[44] While a united representative body for all occupation zones never came into being, each of the central committees held zone-wide congresses between 1945 and 1948, two in the British Zone and three in the American.

Austrian delegates returning from the St. Ottilien conference set up their own representation to address the difficulty of interzonal cooperation. Like Berlin,

Vienna was geographically in the Soviet sector but, as Austria's capital, was itself under joint Four Power control. Survivors met there in August 1945 to found the International Committee for Jewish Concentration Camp Inmates and Refugees in Transit (Internationales Hilfskomitee für durchreisende jüdische KZler und Flüchtlinge), headquartered in the Rothschildspital, a Viennese Jewish hospital serving as the largest and most significant DP camp in Austria. In the U.S. Zone, survivors set up a Jewish Central Committee in October 1945 in Linz.[45] In the following month, a conference of Jewish DPs established the Organization of Jewish Refugees in Italy (Irgun ha-plitim be-Italia), based in Rome, with regional committees in Milan, Florence, and Bari.[46]

In addition to these DP organizations, survivors who were citizens of Germany, Austria, and Italy maintained their own communal organizations. The Allies initially classified these survivors as "enemy aliens" and excluded them from the special assistance allocated to Jewish DPs; this situation changed after the Harrison report. Native and foreign survivors generally maintained a degree of social distance due to cultural and language differences.[47] However, cooperation became necessity as DP populations shrank and the surrounding communities absorbed the remaining Jews of foreign origin.[48]

Zionism and the idea of a sovereign Jewish state in Palestine emerged as the most attractive political position for Jewish DPs, regardless of where they might ultimately end up living. As Atina Grossmann has argued, Zionism both as a utopian idea and as a practical political agenda had a "therapeutic" quality for traumatized survivors who had lost their families and communities. They now spurned their countries of prewar residence in search of a better alternative to the diaspora that had led to the destruction of two-thirds of Europe's Jewish population. Unlike such political models as Bundism (Jewish socialism), communism, and liberal integrationism, Zionism promised hope and pride and a future independent of the goodwill and protection of other nations.[49] Zionist consciousness found systematic encouragement from emissaries of the *Yishuv* (the Jewish community in Palestine). They included soldiers of the Jewish Brigade, who arrived in the DP camps in Germany and Austria in June 1945, and Zionist leaders such as David Ben-Gurion, head of the Jewish Agency for Palestine, who visited several times beginning in October 1945. These delegations engaged in cultural, educational, and political activity and prepared the survivors for a future life in *hachsharot* and kibbutzim (collective settlements).[50]

Although the society of Jewish DPs underwent increasing politicization, especially after the founding of an Israeli state, Jewish DP life included more than political activism. The camps offered extensive kindergartens, schools, and vocational training facilities, as well as theatres, orchestras, movie halls, sports clubs, and services to help survivors locate dead and surviving relatives.[51] The camps' own police maintained order, and their courts prosecuted violations in the camps, mostly theft and physical assault, though they also tried cases of Jews accused by fellow survivors of having collaborated with the Nazis.[52] The DPs also built up a vibrant Yiddish press and publishing industry, financed with the Joint's support and featuring over 150 periodicals in Germany.⁵³

Historical commissions assumed a prominent place among the camps' cultural institutions. A contemporary observer of Jewish DPs in Germany, the American Jewish historian Koppel S. Pinson, remarked in 1947 that the DPs were "preoccupied almost to the point of morbidity" with the past and showed "a heightened historical sense that is responsible for almost passionate devotion . . . to the collection of historical material [and] data on ghetto and *kotzet* [concentration camp] life and death." Pinson, who had headed the AJDC Education and Culture Department in the U.S. Zone in 1945 and 1946, concluded: "Every DP is a private document center and every DP camp has an historical commission."⁵⁴

Why did Jewish DPs—who were liberated but not free to settle where they desired—take on the documentation of the recent past while they waited to rebuild their lives overseas? And what use did collecting and recording serve for their lives in transit? What kinds of documents did they gather and what methods did they apply in their research? Given the multinational origins of Jewish DPs—predominantly eastern European but with diverse wartime experiences—what "past" stood at the center of their documentation work? And, finally, how did the survivors active in the historical commission position themselves in regard to the Zionist project of a sovereign Jewish state in Palestine?

The U.S. Zone in Germany, which housed by far the largest number of DPs, has understandably been the primary focus for historians interested in the post-Holocaust experience of European Jews. From the perspective of historical documentation by survivors, however, Austria, Italy, and the British Zone in Germany offer useful comparisons.⁵⁵

Part One: The U.S. Zone of Germany
Recording the Jewish Tragedy in the Land of the Perpetrators: The Establishment of the Central Historical Commission in Munich

On November 28, 1945, a dozen survivors established a historical commission (*historishe komisye*) in Munich, the center of postwar Jewish life in the American Zone. The initiative came from Israel Kaplan, the commission's future director, and Moshe Yosef Feigenbaum, its future secretary. A former journalist, Yiddish writer, and history teacher in Kovno, Kaplan had survived the Kovno and Riga ghettos and the Kaiserswald and Dachau-Kaufering concentration camps, before being liberated by the Americans during a death march to Tyrol.⁵⁶ Feigenbaum, an accountant, had survived the war in hiding in his native Biała Podlaska, near Brest; he was briefly affiliated with the Central Jewish Historical Commission (Centralna Żydowska Komisja Historyczna; CŻKH) in Lublin and Lodz before leaving Poland in the fall of 1945.⁵⁷ Shmuel Glube, another commission cofounder and its future archivist and

Writing History while Sitting on Packed Suitcases

The Central Historical Commission at Möhlstrasse 12a in Munich suffered from a chronic lack of space for its archives in 1946. Moshe Yosef Feigenbaum (right), Israel Kaplan (center), and Shmuel Glube look through some of their archival treasures. The administrative records of the Dachau concentration camp outside Munich, acquired in 1946, remained in the sacks piled at left for two years because the commission lacked shelves. *Ghetto Fighters' House Archives 565000, courtesy of Shalom Eilati*

librarian, was a Polish-born bookkeeper and librarian who, like Feigenbaum, had briefly worked for the CŻKH.[58] Other founding members included the writer Levi Shalitan, founder and editor of *Undzer Veg* (Our Path), the main organ of the Central Committee of Liberated Jews in the American Zone, and its affiliates the Zionists Marian Pucyz, Yitzkhok Ratner, Chaim Kagan, and Joseph Leibowitz.

The activists defined the commission's goal as gathering documents and testimonies on the Jewish cataclysm that would "enable the future historian to fathom the reason why liberalism turned into Hitlerism in Germany." Once placed at the disposal of the Jewish Agency, this material would also serve political ends, namely "the fight for our rights in the international arena." While sources pertaining to the victims' experiences—eyewitness accounts and also "folk songs, folk creations . . . [and] folk humor"—stood at the center of the commission's focus, it also looked for German documents from government bodies and institutions, as well as from individual perpetrators or other Germans.[59] Three days after its founding, the Munich commission established its first subcommission in the nearby St. Ottilien DP hospital.[60] Over the following months a network of subcommissions covered the U.S. Zone, particularly in large camps such as Feldafing, Neu-Freimann, Landsberg, Föhrenwald, Waldstadt-Pocking, Leipheim, and Bad Reichenhall, each of which at the time held between 3,000 and 6,000 DPs.

In many respects the commission followed the CŻKH model. Structurally, each had a central commission that supervised a number of regional commissions, which in turn oversaw a network of local commissions. In September 1946, the Munich body named itself the Central Historical Commission (Tsentrale Historishe Komisye; TsHK) and began to supervise regional commissions in Bamberg, Frankfurt, Stuttgart, and Regensburg.[61] Together with the Munich center, they supervised between forty-two and sixty local branches throughout the U.S. Zone (including the American Sector of West Berlin) between the summer of 1946 and winter of 1948. Due to the fluctuation of commission staff, many branches only operated for a few weeks or months and often had as few as one or two coworkers.[62]

While exact statistics on the total number of commission workers are lacking, an estimated 80–160 people worked for the TsHK and its branches until its dissolution in January 1949. According to Feigenbaum, the commission's coworkers came exclusively from among the DP population; the relatively few German Jews were busy rebuilding their own communities.[63] Next to Feigenbaum and Glube, other former affiliates of the CŻKH also joined the Munich commission's ranks: Menachem Marek Asz, a founding member of the historical commission in Lublin who now headed TsHK's Frankfurt branch; Betti Ajzenstajn, who had already edited a volume of sources on Jewish resistance in ghettos and camps for the commission in Lodz in 1946; and Leon Weliczker, who in the same year, at age twenty-one had published with the help of Rachel Auerbach a wartime diary relating his horrendous experiences in the Janowska camp and the Sonderkommando 1005, which exhumed and cremated thousands of bodies in eastern Galicia in 1943.[64] In general, the commission workers, like the DPs themselves, were a heterogeneous group of people with varied educational backgrounds, from all social strata and age groups, including women as well as men. In May 1947, the commission's publication *Fun Letstn Khurbn* (From the Latest Destruction) lauded "the participation of women who are particularly active"[65] among its staff. While it did not tally the exact number of female employees, some women assumed prominent positions—such as Ajzensztajn, Mina Levitas, and Shoshana Fabritz as members of the Munich commission and S. Alitzka as head of the local commission in Eschwege. Most workers were untrained in history.[66] Yet, as Feigenbaum noted, they acted out of a sense of "duty to bring to daylight as quickly as possible various archives that were hidden in the ghettos, and also to find . . . the documents which the Nazis had hidden before they escaped."[67]

The survivors' sense that they had an obligation to fulfill a "holy duty" to the dead and the generations to come and that documenting the past was "holy work" appears to have been a major motivation for commission workers. They also understood the documentation project as a symbolic "gravestone," "memorial," or "monument" to those who had been murdered and had not received a proper burial. Thus the TsHK appealed to the *She'erit Hapletah* in the U.S. Zone: "Do not forget that every document, picture, song, legend is the only gravestone which we can place on the unknown graves of our murdered parents, siblings, and children!"[68] On another occasion, Feigenbaum explained to his colleagues that working for the commission meant "lay[ing] the bricks for the great historical folk monument, which must eternalize the memory of our murdered sisters and brothers and embody the suffering, anguish, and heroism of the Jews under the Nazi regime."[69]

The activists also sought to influence what future historians would write about the Jewish catastrophe. Keenly aware that the Nazis had intended to deny and distort the fate of the Jews, the activists hoped to create a historical foundation that would avert the falsification of the past. They harbored a deep distrust of non-Jews—not only perpetrators but also members of the Allied occupying forces—who might have an interest in denying the historical truth, distorting the facts, or barring Jewish historians from access to the evidence. Only by establishing their own archives could survivors guarantee a truthful portrayal of historical events and ensure that Jews would have unrestricted access to the historical evidence of their suffering, without depending on the forbearance of other nations. As Feigenbaum explained to the readers of *Fun Letstn Khurbn* in August 1946: "We, the *She'erit Hapletah*, the surviving witnesses, must create the basis . . . for the historian, through which he will be able to get a clear picture of what happened to us and amongst us." He further reckoned that "the Jews themselves must document this bloody epoch—[and] for that, historical commissions are necessary."[70] This attitude reveals the agency of the survivors and their commitment to self-government in the realm of history writing, as elsewhere. It also indicates the general affinity of the commission's key actors with the Zionist project. Even as Zionists demanded political sovereignty because the survivors could not depend on other nations, so Jews needed sovereignty over the historical records of their recent tragedy.

Other, more practical calls to action resulted from the DPs' involuntary presence in the land of the murderers. On the one hand, the activists sought to endow their sojourn with meaning and to fulfil their "duty of honor to use the waiting time in Germany for the work of eternalizing the Jewish holiness and heroism during the latest destruction."[71] By documenting German crimes in a defeated and occupied Germany, the survivors achieved a symbolic form of revenge, affirming the failure of the Nazi project to create a *judenrein* Germany and Europe by wiping out Jewish existence in actuality and in memory and thereby eliminating all traces of the crime. On the other hand, the activists saw the temporary concentration of large numbers of survivors in the limbo of DP camps as a unique resource for their historical project. "It is clear that the Jewish settlement in Germany will sooner or later be liquidated," Feigenbaum admitted in May 1947,

> and the people who will come to the end of their journey will have to throw themselves with all their senses into the fight for existence. Then one will not get a testimony out of them. Apart from that, the important details of their difficult experiences will blur in their memory. The current

sad situation of the *She'erit Hapletah* in Germany, life in the camps, being excluded from the economy of the country, nevertheless provides a splendid opportunity for our work."[72]

Feigenbaum took this inevitability as a call to immediate action: "If we do not manage to seize this material, it will be almost entirely lost."[73] Understandably, the commission workers also feared that time would diminish the clarity of survivors' recollections. As a work report of one of the commission's regional branches remarked, "Our work is urgent and must be completed rapidly—simply for one reason: people forget, or want to forget. Maybe this is a healthy symptom for a people—but we must chronicle all the experiences of the Jews to prevent them from being lost from our history."[74] Thus the commission saw its task as recording large numbers of survivor accounts while memory was still vivid and the survivors found themselves in a liminal stage that was both an epilogue to their former lives and a preface to their future existence.

Excavating Memory: The Commission's Research Methods

The Central Historical Commission—like its Polish and French forerunners—worked under the premise that an account of the Jewish tragedy should not draw solely from perpetrator sources, which deliberately presented a one-sided picture

Two members of the historical commission in Feldafing study the inmate registry of the DP camp in search of potential interviewees. *Yad Vashem Photo Archives 1486/316*

and neither revealed Jewish responses to events nor described the vitality of prewar Jewish life. A truthful account of the recent past must make use of materials by both perpetrators *and* victims.[75] Yet because the Nazis had largely succeeded in obliterating evidence of their victims' fate—indeed, in the absence of conventional and academically accepted institutional, administrative or communal records—the survivors' "only possession in this respect is their memory, the testimonies that they can give."[76]

An ambitious effort to gather testimonies assumed a central position in the TsHK agenda, although its instructions to interviewers lacked the sophistication of those formulated by the CŻKH. Kaplan and Feigenbaum believed that every survivor, including children and adolescents, was capable of writing and that every testimony revealed a precious piece of the past—as long as the testifiers obeyed the basic rule: write what they had experienced with no fictional adornment.[77] They merely asked *zamlers* (collectors) to make sure that their interviewees' "descriptions contain large amounts of facts, episodes, names of Germans, dates of *Aktionen* and the like. When taking testimonies regarding the ghettos, try to cover the entirety of Jewish life, the cultural, political, sanitary, social, resistance movements, as well as relations within the Jewish population."[78] They also asked local and regional branches to pay "particular attention to taking testimonies on Jewish heroism and resistance against the Nazis."[79] Further, *zamlers* were to verify dates and to make "the greatest effort that testimonies shall be given without internal conflicts and contradictions, that the numbers given in the testimony are indeed correct."[80] In addition, survivors should be encouraged to supplement their accounts with drawings and maps of ghettos and camps.[81] Witnesses either wrote their testimonies down themselves in the presence of commission workers or dictated and then validated them with a signature in the presence of commission personnel and, at times, one to two other witnesses.

The commission also used nine questionnaires (eight in Yiddish, one in German) to gather information from survivors. Three of them were modeled on the methodological instructions published by the CŻKH in 1945, with one difference: whereas in Poland the questionnaires served as guidelines for interviewers, in Germany there were printed forms to be completed by survivors or commission workers. The "statistical questionnaire," drawn up at the commission's founding meeting, followed the first section of the CŻKH's questionnaire for collectors of historical material. Focusing on an individual survivor, it requested personal data, educational background, occupation before and after the war, and knowledge of languages and nationality, and also inquired about the individual's suffering: loss of family members, deprivation of property, forms and conditions of forced labor for German firms, injuries, corporal punishments, "medical" experiments, and resultant physical disabilities. The questionnaire also solicited data on current physical and social conditions and morale of the survivor population. Before concluding with a question about the survivor's thoughts about the future, it

The members of the historical commission in Leipheim record the testimony of a female survivor. Witnesses giving their testimonies faced an audience of commission employees and other witnesses. *Yad Vashem Archives 1486/297*

asked him or her to identify individual perpetrators and firms that might be brought to justice.[82]

A "historical questionnaire" circulated in the U.S. Zone after April 1947, also following a CŻKH model, sought information on the history of Jewish communities in cities and villages under German occupation.[83] In addition to asking for details on the demography of the respective Jewish populations; the major social, cultural, and educational institutions; important personalities; and the community's cultural treasures, it inquired about the acts of perpetrators, the experiences and responses of Jewish victims, and relations between Jews and non-Jews.[84]

The third questionnaire modeled on a CŻKH prototype concerned the collection of ethnographic materials, which Kaplan deemed a particularly valuable source for Jewish responses to persecution.[85] It asked survivors to collect popular poetic creations, idiomatic expressions, proverbs, jokes, legends, and folk songs from concentration camps, ghettos, and partisans units; these materials might concern the Jewish leadership, the Germans, or Jewish heroism and resistance, as well as Jewish suffering.[86]

Particularly noteworthy among the six questionnaires the Central Historical Commission did not base on an outside model was a German-language survey directed not at survivors but rather at German officials. Indeed, this questionnaire was unique among all those produced by Jewish historical commissions in Europe.

It asked mayors (*Oberbürgermeister*) and district administrators (*Landräte*) about the fate of the Jewish populations in their towns and districts; the number, distribution, and history of the camps; their personnel; and the lives and deaths of their inmates.[87] Rather than establishing the individual guilt of officials by interrogating their personal roles and activities under the Nazis—which was, after all, the purpose of the Allies' denazification process—the survey sought to gather information on "how many concentration camps existed in Germany, their origin, their commanders, the life of the Jews in them, and also to get some figures on the annihilation of German Jewry."[88] The idea of interrogating Germans initially stirred debate among commission workers as to the morality of such "collaboration." At the commission's second meeting on December 3, 1945, one worker rejected the idea on the ground that "we do not deal with murderers"; he suggested instead turning "to all peoples of Europe." To which another worker countered: "The 'peoples of Europe' is not an address"; moreover, since the commission's goal was "to receive material and documents necessary for Jewish history . . . it is no crime to turn to the Germans."[89] This latter view eventually prevailed. Beginning in April 1946, the TsHK distributed the questionnaire first in the U.S. Zone and in the following months in the British and French zones as well. The Soviet authorities refused a request to cooperate in their zone.[90]

The approximately five hundred German officials addressed generally proved forthcoming on the matter. Their answers provided precise information on the number of Jews, or rather, in the categories recorded, "full-Jews" and "half-Jews" in their respective districts or towns during the years 1933–1939, as well as what happened to the major Jewish institutions.[91] It turned out that the officials knew precisely when and where the Jewish residents had emigrated,[92] how many had committed suicide or been deported ("sent east"), as well as how many had been brought in for slave labor from German-occupied territories.[93] They also had precise knowledge of how many Jews lived in their districts after the war, whether they were former residents or newcomers, and how many of them were in mixed marriages.[94] Only rarely did their answers hint at a personal opinion. For example, the mayor of Augsburg, reporting on a group of five hundred Hungarian Jewish women brought there in 1944 to work in the local industry, commented: "The sight of these people, dressed in sacks with their hair shaven, was horrible."[95]

Many officials distanced themselves from local events. Responsibility for the Aryanization of Jewish property and forced emigration and incarceration of Jewish citizens lay with those who had been in the administration "back then," or with the SS, the SA, the Gestapo, and the Nazi Party, which no longer existed and therefore could not answer for their acts. For example, the mayor of the Bavarian town of Ansbach, reporting on a local work camp (a subunit of Flossenbürg), claimed that the guards had been members of the SS and Wehrmacht, and that the local police force—which still existed as before and with some of the same personnel—had no responsibility. The number of Jewish inmates, he claimed, was unknown and indeterminable.[96] It is likely that officials' readiness to give information stemmed from their hope that cooperation with the commission could favorably influence their fate in the denazification process. Especially in larger communities, Social Democrats—many of whom had themselves suffered persecution as political opponents—had replaced known Nazi officials. Moreover, special commissioners appointed by the American military government to deal with the claims of German citizens who had suffered political, religious, or racial persecution (Beauftragte für politisch, religiös und rassisch Verfolgte) were often the ones who filled in the questionnaires.

The commission in Munich also independently developed a "questionnaire on postwar experiences" that asked survivors about their lives as DPs. At the commission's founding meeting, Kaplan and Feigenbaum, among others, expressed the importance of capturing this extraordinary, transitional, and—as they believed—historically significant phase of Jewish life in occupied Germany.[97] Beyond documenting the life of the *She'erit Hapletah*, they hoped to raise the historical consciousness of the survivors and encourage them to write their own history in the "land of the enemy."[98] Distributed in the U.S. Zone in spring 1948, the questionnaire inquired about survivors' living and working conditions, recent developments in their camps, and the Jewish and non-Jewish administrations under which they lived as DPs, as well as about interactions among the DPs, with the German population, and with the Allied forces, and about how DPs viewed their future.[99] Many of the completed questionnaires revealed problematic encounters between DPs and the German public, as well as anti-Semitic acts committed against the survivors by Germans.[100] Along with the completed questionnaires, the commission collected all printed matter published by the survivors throughout Germany.[101]

The TsHK also developed four smaller questionnaires directed at specific groups of survivors. One addressed former members of drama groups in order to document the destruction of Jewish culture in the performing arts. It asked about the histories and repertoires of specific theatres, companies, and performers before and during the war and asked survivors to submit posters, scripts of plays, and press clippings they might improbably have salvaged.[102] Another questionnaire asked former partisans to recall their experiences in such groups, as well as to assess the relationship of Jewish partisans to non-Jewish fighters. It also asked for details of major partisan actions, relations between Jews and gentiles, the involvement of Jewish women and children in the units, and individuals' injuries and decorations, as well as for biographical data about comrades killed in battle.[103] Other questionnaires targeted former residents of Lvov[104] and members of the more than three dozen kibbutzim run by various Jewish youth movements in the U.S. Zone.[105]

Despite the German commission's borrowing of research tools, there were distinct institutional differences between it and the CŻKH. While the commission in Lodz employed untrained *zamlers* in its branches, its core staff included a high percentage of academically trained scholars. The commission in Munich lacked a similar level of professionalism. Feigenbaum and Kaplan (who held a degree in history from the University of Kovno and had taught history in a Jewish school in

Kovno before the German occupation) clearly saw themselves as the commission's intellectual backbone, but they understood their primary task as gathering sources for future historical work that would begin once the DP phase was over, preferably in the context of a sovereign Jewish state in Palestine. Thus they viewed themselves first and foremost as *zamlers*, maintaining a popular approach that allowed every survivor to write his or her history, often without critical reflection on the potential problems of individual memory.

These differences became evident when Philip Friedman moved to the U.S. Zone as head of the AJDC's Education and Culture Department in 1946–1947. Feigenbaum and Kaplan had hoped to recruit him as an active member of the commission.[106] Instead, he mainly focused on his own research and limited his support of Kaplan and Feigenbaum to constructive criticism, in particular demanding a more critical approach to testimony and awareness of its selectivity, emotionality, and bias.[107]

At a zone-wide meeting of TsHK employees in Munich in May 1947, attended by one hundred commission workers as well as by representatives of the AJDC and the Jewish Agency, Friedman demanded that the commission become more "professional" by raising its standards and employing academically trained scholars.[108] Objecting that "we are only simple people and not scholars," Dovid Graysdorf, head of the regional commission in Stuttgart, rejected Friedman's criticism. He also suggested sending the material collected in Germany to YIVO in New York or to Jews in Palestine working to found a central Holocaust memorial to be called Yad Vashem in Jerusalem.[109] The latter suggestion resonated with other attendees, who saw their historical work in Germany as preparation for a monumental "folk memorial" in an independent Jewish state.

Kaplan himself admitted that the task of the *She'erit Hapletah* in the DP camps was mainly to chronicle events. Systematic analysis would follow later, since it was impossible "when the entire people, as the history writers themselves, are sitting on packed suitcases." Indeed, he added, "history might be made sitting on suitcases in corridors, but it cannot be written."[110] Similarly, Feigenbaum expressed his wish that commission members could soon end their work "on soil [of] the murderers of our people" and proceed to their task of "help[ing to] build our historical people's memorial as free Jews in a liberated Land of Israel."[111] While in the DP camps Kaplan and Feigenbaum viewed their historical project less as a scholarly endeavor than as a collective effort to gather large amounts of perpetrator documents and survivor testimonies.

Memorial for a Murdered People without Graves: Archival Collections and Publications in the DP Camps

The Central Historical Commission used its uncomfortable presence in "the land of the murderers" to compile an archive for future research. The urgency of this task was due not only to the temporary nature of their sojourn in Germany but also to the fact that by the time the survivors had begun their collection work, the German archives were already "in the hands of the Allies,"[112] who were scouring them for evidence of war crimes. Meanwhile, the Germans had had time to hide or destroy crucial documents.[113]

In an effort to urge German civilians to turn over documents pertaining to the Jews, in late December 1945 the commission sent an appeal to DANA, the German General News Agency, which, under Allied control, was the sole source of information for all press in the western zones.[114] More profitably, the TsHK scrutinized the holdings of several major German institutions and archives in the American sector. Thanks to its formal affiliation with the Central Committee of Liberated Jews in the U.S. Zone, which was officially recognized by the military government, and the support the commission itself enjoyed from the AJDC, whose relief workers wore U.S. army uniforms and held the rank of sergeant, the commission received access to archives and government offices.[115]

In the municipality of Munich, the commission found documents on the city's Jewish educational system in the interwar period, on Nazi anti-Jewish policies and their implementation, and on formerly Jewish-owned private property.[116] Subsequently extending its investigations to other municipal archives, including those of Ansbach, Coburg, Eltmann, Frankfurt, Garmisch, Gauting, and Landsberg, the TsHK added to its collection such valuable finds as the archives of the Dachau concentration camp and some twenty thousand documents on the Aryanization of Jewish property in Bavaria, which the branch commission in Bamberg retrieved between the fall of 1947 and spring of 1948.[117] In late 1946 and early 1947, the commission had access to the archives of the International Military Tribunal in Nuremberg and the Polish Mission in Augsburg, including permission to copy, photograph, Photostat, or film most of the documents.[118] In addition, the U.S. military government provided some original documents. In other cases, commission employees copied documents by hand, which the head of the archive or the magistrate of the respective city then notarized.[119]

While the TsHK initially intended to concentrate on documenting the Jewish past from the Nazi seizure of power in 1933 to the postwar present, it soon widened its scope, because *zamlers* found Jewish ritual objects and historically relevant materials from earlier centuries that they also sought to salvage.[120] The archives of German Jewish congregations in the American Zone, so far as they had survived, netted about seven hundred items for the collection in Munich.[121] By December 1948, the Central Historical Commission held close to two hundred items just from the pre-Nazi era in Germany, including archival material from ten synagogues in the German district of Franconia, some dating back to the seventeenth century.[122]

Jewish folklore material comprised yet another essential part of the collection. As a Yiddish writer, Israel Kaplan, in particular, dedicated himself to collecting folk literature and songs, as well as material related to humor and language used in ghettos and concentration camps. Accompanied by a composer who transcribed the melodies, Kaplan visited DP camps in the U.S. Zone and asked people to sing their songs.¹²³ In summer 1946, the TsHK issued an appeal: "Those who can sing songs from ghettos and camps are invited to visit the historical commission to have them recorded on gramophone records." Because many DPs were reluctant to spend time dwelling on the past rather than on the present and future, the announcement noted: "To make one record takes seven minutes."¹²⁴ The names and backgrounds of most of the many individuals who seem to have responded are unknown, but well-known artists made some recordings. For example, the Yiddish poet and partisan Shmerke Kaczerginski in November 1947 undertook a field trip to the DP camps in the U.S. Zone, after he had left Poland and settled down in Paris.¹²⁵

Not least, the TsHK's collection included artifacts and Jewish cultural objects testifying to Jewish suffering in ghettos and camps and to the destruction of Jewish culture throughout Europe.¹²⁶ It listed "camp clothing, an urn with burnt human bones from Dachau, earth from the extermination camp Treblinka, a container of Zyklon gas, a piece of Torah written on deer skin . . ., a piece of 'R.I.F.' soap, which is said to be of human fat," and "a copy of a siddur [prayer book], which a Polish Jew wrote in hiding, thinking that there will not be any siddurim in Poland. On every couple of pages there is a Yizkor [prayer for the dead] for his murdered family members."¹²⁷

The collection also contained many photographs of Jewish life and death in Germany, Poland, Lithuania, Hungary, Byelorussia, and the Ukraine—close to one thousand items by the end of 1946—and film footage taken by the Nazis in Poland and Germany.¹²⁸ Finally, the commission collected books, mostly with anti-Semitic content, and any kind of printed matter produced by the survivors in Germany; these items totaled 1,095 by the end of 1946.¹²⁹

In February 1946, Kaplan and Feigenbaum began to prepare a Yiddish-language historical journal chronicling the crimes against European Jews. The first volume of *Fun Letstn Khurbn*, edited by Kaplan, appeared in August of that year.¹³⁰ Printing in Hebrew characters posed a challenge due to the scarcity of Hebrew type sets.¹³¹ In January 1947, the commission bought 150 kilograms of Hebrew characters for its own manual typesetting machine, which was then used in a German print shop.¹³² Seven months later, AJDC worker Lucy Schildkret—later the acclaimed historian Lucy S. Dawidowicz—who supervised the licensing of DP publications, obtained the use of a linotype machine owned by *Die Neue Zeitung* in Munich, a triweekly newspaper founded and published by the U.S. military government for the German population in Bavaria.¹³³ This change not only accelerated the printing process but represented a particular triumph, since the facility had formerly printed the *Völkischer Beobachter*, the official Nazi party organ.¹³⁴

Fun Letstn Khurbn appeared in ten issues, which together came to a total of more than one thousand pages; it had a circulation of 1,000 to 8,000 copies per issue and sold for four marks a copy. The paper featured eyewitness testimonies and reports on the history of specific geographic areas, places, towns, ghettos, camps, and institutions. The editor, Israel Kaplan, a former teacher and a father who was reunited with his surviving teenage son in Munich, paid particular attention to children's testimonies, which received a separate series.[135] The journal also offered a regular column on ghetto language and anecdotes, along with folklore material and original German documents and photographs. The journal's target audience was Yiddish-reading eastern European Jews in Europe, Palestine, and the Americas, but in particular the *She'erit Hapletah* in Germany.

Kaplan and Feigenbaum conceived *Fun Letstn Khurbn* as a "folk journal produced by the masses," which would encourage survivors to write their own histories.[136] The journal published a large number of testimonies by men, women, adolescents, and children from various regions in eastern Europe, especially Lithuania, Byelorussia, Galicia, and the Ukraine, reflecting a broadly eastern European Jewish experience of Nazi occupation. These testimonies advanced an agenda that sought to unite survivors of different geographic and national backgrounds and with diverse wartime experiences by focusing on a canon of Holocaust experiences—ghetto; concentration, labor, and death camps; hiding; partisan units; bunkers; and survival "on the Aryan side." Kaplan's ideal collective admitted only those Jews—like the founders of the historical commission and the leadership elites in the camps—who had survived in Nazi-occupied eastern Europe. For this reason, *Fun Letstn Khurbn* excluded the experiences of Jewish communities in western Europe and, more significantly, those of Polish Jews who had survived outside of Nazi-occupied territory in the Soviet Union—a group that happened to constitute the majority of the DP population in Germany by the beginning of 1947. The journal did, however, take on the task of educating this group about the experiences of those who had survived Nazi occupation.[137]

Given its dedication to chronicling Jewish life in German-occupied eastern Europe, *Fun Letstn Khurbn* also sought to curb the influence of landsmanshaft organizations in the camps, one of whose activities was writing histories of their own communities in the form of *yizker-bikher*, memorial books. Kaplan deemed these publications to be nonfactual and sentimental, smudging any clear demarcation between fiction and fact. Moreover, he sought to secure a monopoly on history writing and publication for the historical commission. This proved to be a losing battle.[138] In addition to fierce competition from periodicals published by landsmanshaftn, professional organizations, and political parties, *Fun Letstn Khurbn*'s comprehensive treatment of the past did not resonate with a readership affiliated with Zionist parties and youth movements and eager for laudatory works on ghetto uprisings and resistance movements.[139]

Kaplan exercised a strong hand as an editor. According to his own account, he had to choose from among hundreds of testimonies, submitted "in the form of bare facts and in a disfigured state"; he then worked "whole days and nights" to bring them to a "form that is adequate for publication."[140] Philip Friedman praised *Fun Letstn Khurbn* as the "most beautiful Yiddish publication in Germany," one that should "serve as a model for others." Yet he criticized the "Kaplan-izing" (*kaplanizirn*) of testimonies, which decreased the publication's value from a scholarly perspective.[141]

"Grab a Pen!": Committing Survivors to Document Their Past

The DP camps provided fertile soil for the activists of the Central Historical Commission, not only because they made large numbers of survivors easily accessible, but also because, in Kaplan's words, "today history lies on the tip of everyone's tongue ..., fills every wrinkle of our memory," so that commission workers merely needed to "lend an ear, ... collect it [and] save it."[142] Similarly, Lucy Schildkret recalled survivors' "compulsion to talk" about the past, which helped them to "expiate the guilt feelings that tormented them" and to preserve "their experiences ... for history and posterity."[143]

Nevertheless, the commission in Munich often found it difficult to motivate survivors to testify or to provide other documentation. One observer suggested that they did "not sufficiently appreciate the importance of the historical commission,"[144] nor did they grasp the significance of methodical documentation. Others diagnosed a "timidity complex"[145] that inhibited survivors from subjecting their personal experiences to interrogation and recording by commission workers. Survivors' guilt and the fear of exposing embarrassing and painful personal details of their survival also played a role.[146] TsHK activists knew that confrontation with the past was an unpleasant experience for survivors, and also that they competed for attention with political parties, educational programs, and entertainment, not to mention the urge of many survivors to concentrate on the future by starting families.[147]

Like its Polish counterpart, the commission in Munich had to rely on moral pressure to persuade reluctant witnesses to testify. It therefore began a systematic public relations campaign to win the *She'erit Hapletah* for the historical project. Workers throughout the U.S. Zone were told not to "sit in their office and wait until someone passes by to deliver a testimony or document"; instead they should "visit [camp] inhabitants in their homes and establish contacts with them."[148] With a car borrowed from the AJDC, it dispatched its employees to tell survivors in face-to-face meetings about the necessity of historical documentation and, with the help of sample documents and testimonies, to educate them about the contributions they could make.[149] Jewish holiday celebrations, commemorative meetings, and congresses held in the DP camps proved especially vital for promoting the commission's work.[150] At the First Congress of the *She'erit Hapletah* in the American Zone, held on January 27, 1946, in Munich, and at the Third Congress in Bad Reichenhall from March 30 to April 2, 1948, the commission promoted its work by exhibiting pieces from its collections.[151] TsHK members visited Jewish schools and vocational training facilities, asking teachers to assign students to write essays on the theme "My Experiences of the Nazi Occupation."[152] Local commissions also held writing contests for children and adolescents on topics related to their "war experiences in general or particular important events of Jewish life under the Nazi regime, in ghettos and camps, with the partisans, or on the Aryan side." The commission did not want "literary piece[s]" but rather "matter-of-fact description[s] of the events," written "clearly on one side of the paper with a broad margin," in any language, but "preferably in Yiddish and Hebrew."[153]

In addition, the Yiddish-language press served as a vehicle for informing the Jewish DPs about the commission's work and for encouraging survivors—mainly by launching appeals or publishing sample testimonies—to "grab a pen and describe their wartime experiences."[154] For example, in April 1946, the *Landsberger Lager Cajtung* informed local camp inhabitants of a new local historical commission which had the "purpose of collecting all documents, pictures, testimonies, folklore, and other materials pertaining to our life in the ghettos, the concentration camps, with the partisan movement, and elsewhere during these dreadful years of Hitler's rule." Documenting the past was "an extremely important communal work," since "the memory of our millions of martyrs and our own interest demand that every single one of us make sure not to let anything of the terrible Nazi crimes against us Jews vanish."[155]

The Central Historical Commission also reached the camp population with leaflets and posters—mostly handwritten, but sometimes printed. They typically asked survivors from specific villages, cities, regions, ghettos, or camps, as well as people with knowledge of particular war criminals to give their testimonies; some also described types of documents the commission was seeking.[156] Above all, historical documentation was a way for survivors to fulfill their moral duty to the dead whose memory it perpetuated. An undated appeal urged the survivor population in the U.S. Zone to think of their contributions to history as "the only gravestone which we are able to place on the unknown graves of our murdered fathers, mothers, brothers, sisters, and children!"

> Therefore, help the historical commission in its work! Describe the economic, social, and cultural life of the destroyed Jewish community from which you come. Describe the activity of the society or organization you used to be a member of before the war. Eternalize how the Jews have lived, fought, and were murdered during the Nazi regime. Eternalize all expressions, legends, and stories of the bygone tragic days. Write down the songs sung in ghettos, camps, and among the partisans during the Nazi era. Hand the material over to the historical commission, which is collecting and preserving this material for the generations to come! Do not refuse your help when the historical commission turns to you![157]

The appeals often verbalized a duty to educate future generations about the Jewish catastrophe. The local commission in Leipheim urged survivors to visit its office to "eternalize"—in writing or orally—their "experiences in ghettos,

Writing History while Sitting on Packed Suitcases 143

A poster of the historical commission in the Pocking DP Camp near Passau in Lower Bavaria implores inmates to testify and "Remember what Amalek did to You! Remember and Do Not Forget!" *Yad Vashem Photo Archives 1486/701*

camps, bunkers, woods, hiding places, and partisan units." Because the Nazis had made it virtually impossible for Jews to record events as they unfolded, there was a "danger that the coming generations [would] have no idea what the Nazis, the beasts in human form, did to our children, of the torture and agony which our sisters and brothers endured, of the anguish and suffering of our mothers and fathers," unless survivors fulfilled their duty to record the events now.[158]

Two official TsHK posters, printed in color, adorned the offices of historical commissions and survivor institutions throughout the U.S. Zone.[159] These were the top two winners of a public competition organized by the commission in spring 1947.[160] First place, and an award of three thousand marks, went to Pinkhes Shvarts, whose poster (see frontispiece) showed a dead *katsetler* (concentration camp inmate) in front of barbed wire; on his chest lay an otherwise empty scroll that depicted the opening verse of the book of Esther, "And so it happened in those days . . ." in calligraphic Hebrew letters. A quill pen in an inkpot above the Yiddish slogan "Help to write the history of the latest destruction!" invited those who saw it to become chroniclers themselves and fill the scroll with their own histories.¹⁶¹ The second-place poster, which earned two thousand marks for P. Shuldenreyn, quoted Deuteronomy 25:17—"Remember what Amalek did to you!"—and displayed a clock on whose face were scenes from past Jewish catastrophes, biblical and historical, in place of the hours. Beneath each episode was a reference to the relevant Jewish text: for example, slavery in Egypt was paired with the Passover Haggadah and the pogroms in the Ukraine of 1648–1649 with Nathan Nata Hannover's *Yeven Metsulah* (The deep mire).¹⁶² The hour hand pointed to the Yiddish-language invocation "Collect and record!"¹⁶³ Both posters represented the Jewish past as a timeless cycle of atrocities that linked the Amalekites' smiting of the Jewish people to the Holocaust—the last link in a long chain of Jewish suffering. Yet by suggesting that Jews had always overcome collective suffering by recording the events, the posters exhorted survivors to fulfill their duty with respect to the most recent catastrophe.

It is difficult to determine the direct impact of the commission's multifaceted efforts to draw the larger public of Jewish DPs to its work. Feigenbaum claimed that *Fun Letstn Khurbn* inspired both "the simple Jew to describe his wartime experiences" and "the Jewish intelligentsia [to] visit the Central Historical Commission to get to know its work," thereby increasing its collections.¹⁶⁴ Between December 1945 and December 1948, the TsHK collected as many as 2,550 testimonies, of which nearly three hundred came from children and adolescents under the age of sixteen, in addition to over six thousand completed questionnaires.¹⁶⁵ According to the TsHK's own statistics, one in twenty survivors in the U.S. Zone either testified or filled out a questionnaire.¹⁶⁶ The pace of testimonies slowed over time—from 1,500 collected in the first eleven months (December 1945–November 1946) to a little less than 1,000 in the period up to the end of 1948. This might suggest a waning of survivors' readiness to testify, but there are two other possibilities. First, the influx of survivors from Poland from the latter half of 1946 through the first half of 1947 came to constitute over 80 percent of Jewish DPs by fall 1947.¹⁶⁷ They included Jews repatriated from the Soviet Union, who made up two-thirds of the entire Jewish DP population.¹⁶⁸ Neither the TsHK's questionnaires nor the pages of *Fun Letstn Khurbn* reflected their experiences in Soviet Central Asia, where the Soviet authorities had deported most Jewish refugees. Their divergence from what Kaplan and his colleagues and many other Jewish DPs saw as the paradigmatic survivor experience might explain why this group was not addressed in the questionnaires and was less likely to cooperate with the commission. Moreover, the growing number of survivors who emigrated in the course of 1948 both reduced the population to be interviewed and affected TsHK staffing.¹⁶⁹

While they enjoyed considerable recognition among the survivor public, commission activists constantly felt that the DP leadership, most notably the Central Committee of Liberated Jews, on whose financial support the documentation depended, failed to adequately appreciate the significance of the historical work.¹⁷⁰ Indeed, as the activists saw things, the Central Committee regarded the TsHK as a "miserable nuisance,"¹⁷¹ ignoring the fact that its efforts were "most necessary

A color poster advertising the work of the Central Historical Commission in Munich in 1947 urges survivors, "Remember what Amalek did to You!" and invites them to "collect and record" historical documents of the Holocaust. This poster was distributed across the U.S. Zone and displayed in DP camp offices and on billboards. *Yad Vashem Photo Archives M1P/685*

for our history and our current fight for the existence of the nation."[172] The Jewish Central Committee even used bureaucratic strategies to hinder the TsHK's work, such as trying to reduce its paper supplies and delaying the allocation of secure archival space in Munich.[173] Aware that their German sojourn must end and impatient to leave the "earth of the murderers of our people and . . . help build our historical folk monument as free Jews in a liberated Land of Israel,"[174] in the spring of 1947 the TsHK established contacts with the *Yishuv* to negotiate transfer of its collections.

From the Land of Amalek to the Land of Israel: Creating the Basis for Future Holocaust Research in Jerusalem

In accordance with the resolutions of the Third Congress of the *She'erit Hapletah* of the American Zone in Bad Reichenhall, March 30–April 2, 1948, Feigenbaum and Kaplan began to take concrete steps to terminate their work in Germany and move their collections to Palestine.[175] A year earlier, they had established contact with a group of Palestinian Jews working with Mordechai Shenhavi to build Yad Vashem as a central Holocaust memorial in the *Yishuv*.[176] In the spring of 1947, Moshe Mark Prager, an affiliate of the initiative, visited the commission in Munich to assess its holdings. Kaplan and Feigenbaum were invited to a conference on Holocaust documentation held that July by the Yad Vashem group at the Hebrew University of Jerusalem. As DPs, they could not get visas to enter Palestine. The conference nonetheless passed a resolution requesting all documentation centers in Europe to transfer their collections to the proposed memorial,[177] and in September 1948, Shenhavi visited Munich to negotiate the transfer of the TsHK's holdings.[178] From November 1948 to the spring of 1949, the archival collection—28,000 Nazi documents, 1,081 photographs, 1,074 anti-Semitic publications, and close to three hundred folklore items—were shipped to Israel in nearly fifty boxes, sent via Marseille through the Immigration Department of the Jewish Agency.[179]

The DP population in Germany dwindled rapidly after the foundation of the State of Israel. Of the 165,000 Jewish DPs in Germany in April 1948, fewer than half remained in September of that year. Their number dwindled further to 44,000 by the end of 1949.[180] Responding to the same forces, the number of commission workers fell from forty-seven in June 1948 to four in October of that year.[181] *Fun Letstn Khurbn* ceased publication in December 1948; the Central Historical Commission in Munich was officially dissolved in January 1949; and Feigenbaum and Kaplan immigrated to Israel in the following months, hoping to continue their documentation work under the auspices of Yad Vashem.

While the Yad Vashem foundation accepted the commission's archival holdings, it had neither the means nor the interest to provide employment for its two founders.[182] Each reverted to his prewar profession, Kaplan as a teacher and Feigenbaum as a bookkeeper, relegating any historical endeavors to their private lives. Their disappointment was all the more keen, given their ardent support for a central memorial in Jerusalem, built with the help of the historical commissions in the Diaspora.[183] "After I, in the course of three years, have worked so devotedly to collect a vast body of material in Germany," Feigenbaum wrote from Tel Aviv to Isaac Schneersohn in Paris in September 1949, "my heart aches when I see what becomes of it here in Israel. It will become rotten and moldy." He believed that his experiences in Israel were "quite symptomatic" for the "indifference prevailing in the Jewish world regarding *khurbn-forshung*": people lost their interest in the recent past "as if such a dreadful cataclysm had never occurred in Jewish life."[184]

The inability of Kaplan and Feigenbaum, like other colleagues of theirs from Munich, to secure employment at Yad Vashem resulted from their lack of professional credentials as historians. The early leaders of Yad Vashem, in particular its first director, the historian Ben-Zion Dinur, pursued an elitist agenda that aimed to establish an academic research institution staffed with academically trained historians with no personal experiences of the Nazi regime.[185] The archival collection that the commission in Munich had assembled did not, however, rot and molder in oblivion. Rather, it constituted the core of Yad Vashem's archives when the new institution opened its doors in 1954 as the government-sponsored "Holocaust Martyrs' and Heroes' Remembrance Authority." Thus the commission archivists ultimately succeeded in their endeavor to help build a "historical folk monument" in Israel.

Part Two: The British Zone of Germany, Austria and Italy

Collecting the Vestiges of the Past: The Jewish Historical Commissions in the British Zone of Germany

While the British Zone initially was home to half of the 50,000–80,000 Jews liberated in Germany, its Jewish population declined due to death and repatriation and to restrictive official policies that did not allow further refugees into the zone. At the end of 1946 its Jewish DP population numbered 16,000, with over half of them concentrated in the DP camp Belsen.[186] Nonetheless, two historical commissions operated in the years 1945–1949, if on a much smaller scale than their counterpart in the American Zone. Thus their workers numbered fewer than one dozen. They did not use questionnaires or systematic interviews, nor did their publications have the breadth and variety of those published in the U.S. Zone. Because the administrative archives of both commissions seem to have been lost, any account of their composition and activities remains fragmentary.

On October 10, 1945, the Polish-born journalists and editors of *Undzer Shtime* (the official organ of the *She'erit Hapletah* in the British Zone)—Paul Trepman, Dovid Rosental, and Rafael Olewski—founded an "archive of the time of the extermination of Jewry."[187] In the belief that gathering "every fact of Jewish life under German occupation, at the time of the ghettos, concentration camps, and crematoria" constituted a "holy task," it would collect "pictures, photographs, publications of all kinds (newspapers, announcements, circular letters, posters . . .), songs and stories in all languages, clothing and uniforms, urns of the deceased and burnt, lists of people resettled, killed, testimonies of prisoners, books and Torah scrolls—everything . . . relating to the Hitler era."[188] Unlike the sometimes contentious relations between the historical commission and the Central Committee of Liberated Jews in the U.S. Zone, the archive's founders in the British Zone also headed the newly founded cultural office of its equivalent Central Committee. Indeed, in the spring of 1947 the archive became the Central Historical Commission of the Central Committee in the British Zone. In addition to a few *zamlers* in Celle and Bremen, it supervised a subcommission in the university town of Göttingen, the Jewish Historical Commission for Lower Saxony (Jüdische Historische Kommission für Niedersachsen), which began its work in May 1947.

The commissions in Belsen and Göttingen asked survivors in the British Zone to collect all manner of "materials and cultural treasures which give a picture of the life and [cultural] creations of the annihilated communities."[189] They sought to encourage cooperation by the camp population by distributing posters with images of oppression and destruction, such as barbed wire and devastated landscapes.

Far more than their counterparts in the U.S. Zone, the commissions in Belsen and Göttingen emphasized the displays of objects in their collections, such as a small exhibit with the title "Our Way to Freedom" in the DP camp Belsen on the occasion of the Second Congress of the *She'erit Hapletah* in the British Zone in July 1947.[190] The intent was to give "a picture of our fight for justice and liberation during the last two years,"[191] and to address "all realms of our life after the liberation and our struggle for a new life in the Land of Israel."[192] The Göttingen commission had its own section at the exhibit, with documents from that city's municipal archives relating to the long history of the local Jewish community.[193] While the commission in the U.S. Zone also attempted to uncover artifacts from Jewish life in Germany, its focus was almost exclusively on preserving the history of eastern European Jews as embodied in the memories of its remnants.

Much of the impetus behind this unusual interest in German Jewish history, in particular of Göttingen's six-hundred-year-old Jewish community, came from the head of that city's historical commission, Cwi Horowic, a Polish-born jack-of-all-trades and sometime writer with Zionist socialist leanings. Unfortunately, many of Horowic's daring projects—some of them overly ambitious given economic constraints and a distinct lack of interest among Göttingen's conservative political leadership—bore no fruit. His first run-in with the authorities was a futile attempt to mount an exhibit on the local Jewish community in the city's municipal museum, which failed when its director, insulted because Horowic had printed invitations before he had given his consent, claimed that the museum lacked space for the exhibit.[194] The museum subsequently denied a request from the Belsen commission for a loan of Judaica artifacts.[195] Horowic responded angrily, demanding that the museum reopen its Judaica room, closed since the Nazi period, so that "the Jewish items stored in boxes" would "at last [be] displayed at a worthy place in the museum, as this was the idea of their donors, instead of letting them rot."[196] The museum's administration failed to acknowledge this request.[197]

Horowic's efforts provide useful insights on how some municipal authorities in postwar Germany dealt with the recent past. Whereas officials in the U.S. Zone had willingly filled out that commission's questionnaires, the Göttingen authorities balked at more visible memorials. They deemed the projects insufficiently important and moreover doubted Horowic's motives, assuming that he had created the historical commission "for reasons of personal advantage," since he sought to profit from the fact that "nobody dares to criticize and make an energetic appearance against him because he is a Jew."[198] Still, conscious of the "political side of the matter," namely that refusing any concessions might mean "serious trouble" from the occupation authorities, and also reluctant to risk the international reputation of their university town, the municipal officials assured Horowic of their goodwill—but found technical and other reasons to thwart his demands,[199] especially when Horowic and a coworker requested the use of Nazi documents from Göttingen's municipal archives in May 1947. The city officials ignored his request for four months before finally letting him see the documents.[200]

The final straw was Horowic's suggestion in September 1947 that the municipality build a memorial on the site of a former synagogue so that the ninth anniversary of *Kristallnacht* could be commemorated there on November 9, 1947. The site—now covered by a large bunker—was owned by a real estate company. The city's office of urban planning cited a number of legal, construction, and labor issues and "recommended settling the legal matters first."[201] They further rejected Horowic's suggestion to rename the site "Synagogue Square"; after all, the synagogue had been located at the intersection of two streets, not on a square.[202] In November 1947, city authorities also refused the historical commission's request to reinstall memorial plaques, removed during the Nazi period, that marked houses where prominent Jews had lived. The city did not deem the matter sufficiently important.[203] Although thwarted, Horowic's projects are a unique instance of DP interest in memorializing the history and fate of German Jews.

The commissions in Belsen and Göttingen discontinued their work in the fall of 1949. Virtually no evidence remains on the size and content of DP collections in Belsen and Göttingen. The commissions' publications were few in the context of the otherwise prolific publication activity in the British Zone.[204] Their founders intended from the outset that the archives would ultimately leave Germany.[205] In the end, so far as can be determined, the archive's holdings were divided among the YIVO Institute, the World Jewish Congress, and the AJDC in New York, as well as several institutions in Israel.[206]

Bringing the Perpetrators to Trial: The Jewish Documentation Centers in Austria

Two historical commissions operated in Austria, one in the U.S. Zone and the other in the international zone of Vienna. With fewer than two dozen workers, they differed from both the U.S. and British zones in Germany in their primary dedication to collecting evidence to help prosecute perpetrators of the Holocaust. By the same token, they paid relatively little attention to historical research.

In the U.S. Zone, the teacher and former CŻKH affiliate Mejlech Bakalczuk established a Jewish Historical Commission (Jüdische Historische Kommission) in the Bindermichl DP camp near Linz in early 1946, with four full-time employees, including his wife, Neche Tabachowicz.[207] That summer, the Jewish Central Committee for the American Zone in Linz incorporated the historical commission into its cultural office and placed it under the auspices of Bakalczuk and the Galician-born architect Simon Wiesenthal. Since his liberation from the Mauthausen concentration camp in May 1945—which he had reached after a death march from the Gross-Rosen concentration camp in southern Poland in January that year—Wiesenthal had been active in the Central Committee while also working as an interrogator of suspected war criminals for the American occupying forces, thus aiding in the arrest of Nazi camp personnel.[208]

In early January 1947, Wiesenthal renamed the commission the Jewish Historical Documentation (Jüdische Historische Dokumentation; JHD). Its statutes directed the JHD to collect "documents on Jewish history in Austria, especially from the time of occupation, and testimonies of the destruction of the Jews in other occupied countries." It would also "publish a scholarly journal," which welcomed contributions from anyone previously engaged in "Jewish scholarly work."[209] Nonetheless, the commission made legal redress for Nazi crimes against Jews its primary goal.[210]

In internationalized Vienna, Polish-born Towia Frydman initiated a parallel undertaking in July 1946.[211] Like Wiesenthal, he focused on gathering evidence against war criminals.[212] After enduring the Radom ghetto, Frydman had escaped from the city's Szkolna Street labor camp and fled to the woods, where he posed as the Polish gentile Tadek Jasinski. In this identity, by February 1945 Frydman had arrested and interrogated suspected German war criminals for the Polish Ministry of Public Security in Gdańsk. At the end of 1945, he returned to his Jewish identity and decided to leave Poland for Palestine. Assisted by the Brichah, he reached Vienna via Prague and Bratislava in early 1946.[213] His desire to bring the Nazi culprits to justice had not flagged. In Vienna he enjoyed the support of Arthur Piernikarz (also known as "Arthur" and Asher Ben-Natan), head of the Brichah in Austria, who provided him with a preliminary list of war criminals compiled by the Jewish Agency during the war.[214] By spring 1947, the two Austrian commissions collaborated closely and established a network of correspondents in the DP camps in the American and British zones. Frydman recruited his coworkers from among the Jewish student community in Vienna, many of whom belonged to the newly formed Union of Jewish Students of Austria (Verband Jüdischer Hochschüler Österreichs), which included both Austrian and eastern European Jews.[215]

Several factors had led Frydman, Wiesenthal, and their collaborators to work toward the prosecution of Nazi war criminals. First, the increasing leniency of Allied authorities toward Nazi criminals in light of the nascent cold war led the activists to believe that survivors must help bring perpetrators to trial. They had experienced this problem in their face-to-face postwar encounters with Austrian civilians whom they had earlier known as camp guards.[216] Second, the transitory nature of their situation as DPs in Austria lent urgency to the quest to obtain and present evidence to the military government or the Austrian police. Not least, they also endeavored in this way to bring the full extent of the Jewish tragedy to public consciousness by lifting the "mantel of silence" and "cloak of oblivion"[217] with which the non-Jewish public obscured the Jewish fate, while urging survivors not "to scrounge off the pity of the world," but rather to "draw a line under what happened."[218]

The focus of survivors in Austria on war criminals reflected in part their dissatisfaction with the justice system's lax approach to crimes against Jews, especially in the absence of a more rigorous denazification program such as occupation authorities imposed on Germany. However, commission activists' animus against Austria—which was, after all, the birthplace of Adolf Hitler—was strikingly visceral. Wiesenthal's own highly ambivalent relation with Austria included a sense of commitment to that country, although he was a Polish citizen before the war. Born in Buczacz in Galicia when it belonged to the Austro-Hungarian Empire, he was the son of a German-speaking mother. During World War I his father fell fighting in the Austro-Hungarian army, and Wiesenthal spent his elementary school years in Vienna. Following the Second World War, Wiesenthal came to believe that his fight for justice and against anti-Semitism could counter the many postwar myths with which Austrians tended to embellish their wartime behavior.[219]

While the new republic constructed a self-image of Austria as Germany's "first victim," the survivors tended to judge the nation's guilt for the Final Solution as at least equal to that of the Germans.[220] With some justification, they based this judgment on the belief that post-*Anschluss* Austria had produced a disproportionate number of Nazi perpetrators—as reflected in the many war criminals harbored in postwar Austria.[221] In a hyperbolic manner, Towia Frydman estimated that 70 percent of all war criminals involved in the Final Solution were Austrians,[222] while Wiesenthal stated that if the Austrian population had approved of "only one point of the Nazi program, it was the mass murder of the Jews." This meant that virtually no family in Austria was "free of guilt toward the Jews," since in one way or another, everyone had "an SS, SA, or Gestapo man or Aryanizer in its ranks."[223] Commission workers' day-to-day experiences as DPs led them to believe that Austrian society—steeped in centuries-old anti-Semitism—had provided fertile soil for seven years of Nazi indoctrination and helped facilitate the implementation of the Nazis' racist program.[224] Uncritical portrayal of the recent past in the Austrian press, the seemingly unbroken traditions of Christian anti-Semitism, and the anonymous threats often sent to the commissions, some with clippings from *Der Stürmer*, led Wiesenthal to conclude that in some parts of Austria, especially in the Tyrol, "anti-Semitism had survived the Jews."[225]

The commissions in Linz and Vienna proceeded to gather large quantities of eyewitness testimony from survivors in Austria to prevent the release of suspected war criminals already under arrest and to aid in the capture of others still going free. Unlike their counterparts in Germany and Poland, their primary purpose was not to document survivors' experiences during the German occupation but rather to interrogate them about the crimes of specific individuals. JHD posters in DP camps and messages in the Jewish press called upon anyone with such knowledge—usually after a perpetrator's arrest by the Allied occupying forces—to submit testimony in the commission's office. A typical appeal would read:

> Attention, former concentration camp inmates of KZ Mauthausen! All persons who know something about the behavior and deeds of Josef Giett, pictured below, born December 12, 1906, . . . guard in Mauthausen between September 1, 1944, and March 30, 1945, are requested to report to the Jewish Historical Documentation, Linz, Goethestrasse 63, in writing or orally.[226]

If possible, an appeal included a photograph of the perpetrator, because survivors rarely knew the names of their tormentors, but they knew their faces all too well.[227]

As in Germany, over time commission workers faced difficulties in collecting testimonies. In February 1948, Helen Fuchsman from the Linz commission noticed that many survivors refused to respond to the appeals, because they had developed "a certain passivity, an indifference," and diminished "feelings of revenge . . . toward their tormentors and murderers." She attributed these changes to the lenient nature of Austrian justice, which led survivors to sense that "the murderer will be acquitted anyway or will just go free after a few months."[228] She also complained that the historical commission's posters and appeals were almost immediately covered over by announcements of cultural events or notices from political parties. Fuchsman persuaded the camp carpenter to design a special commission notice board, but the responses did not improve. She even made home visits, but the survivors said they had better things to do—whether work or entertainment—than reliving their past.[229]

The activists became so frustrated by the apathy of some survivors that the Vienna commission threatened to publish the names of the recalcitrant in the Jewish press.[230] It even tried to convince the AJDC to discontinue its material support for such Jews on the grounds that their behavior amounted to an act of "sabotage," insofar as it "worked against the interest of the Jewish community" and helped perpetrators to remain at large.[231] The AJDC refused, and the activists resigned themselves to the use of moral suasion. Thus the Linz commission followed in the path of its counterparts elsewhere: "In the name of the dozens, hundreds, and millions of victims who were shot, hanged, burnt alive, and gassed; in the name of our children ..., our women, brothers and sisters, fathers and mothers who perished in martyrdom, *we fulfill our holiest duty*: we testify—we remind the world and demand justice of humankind, of all peoples!" Promising not to rest "until the last criminal is handed over to the democratic justice of humanity," the commission summoned "former camp inmates" to "remember the names [of the torturers], identify and help find the murderers! Give information, testimonies, and other documents to the Jewish Historical Documentation in Linz."[232] Beginning in September 1947, the commissions in Linz and Vienna distributed a special badge to testifiers. Designed by Wiesenthal and bearing the slogan "I exposed a murderer," the badges were awarded along with a "diploma" that bore the witness's name and the message: "Thanks to whose testimony it was possible to bring ... [name of the perpetrator], criminal against the Jews, in ... [name of the place or camp] to justice, Mr. ... [name of the witness] is entitled to wear our special 'I exposed a murderer' badge."[233]

To organize their information on war criminals, the commissions developed a comprehensive card-indexing system that categorized material by concentration camp, work camp, and some thousand other sites in the territories under Nazi control, and matched these locations to the names of individuals who could provide relevant information. Two additional card indexes contained the names of criminals, one for those who were still wanted, the other for those under arrest but for whose prosecution more evidence was needed.[234] The lists primarily contained perpetrators against whom survivors could testify because of direct contact, namely the lower rank and file of the SS and the SD, Gestapo and police officers, Wehrmacht lieutenants, German civil officials such as mayors and civilian district administrators, factory heads, foremen of factories and workshops, heads of employment offices, camp administrators and guards, Ukrainian militia, and wives of German military and civilian officials.[235] They rarely mentioned higher-echelon Nazis from the heart of the Third Reich.

This began to change when, with news of the Nuremberg trials and information and persuasion from *Yishuv* emissaries, the commission leaders came to understand the full scope of the destruction and directed some of their attention toward higher-ranking Nazi officials—most notably Adolf Eichmann. The effort to capture him was instigated by Arthur Piernikarz, who persuaded Frydman and Wiesenthal that Eichmann was a key perpetrator and therefore a primary JHD target.[236] Gradually, they came to comprehend Eichmann's significance in the machinery of the Third Reich. They even "managed to get hold of a photo of him which all the Allies have tried [but failed to get] up to now." In November 1947, Wiesenthal called the Nazi bureaucrat whom he and Frydman would pursue for the next decade and a half a "man ... who should be called enemy number one for us Jews."[237]

Some perpetrators whose arrests were a cause célèbre among survivors at the time would later—despite the degree of their culpability—occupy relatively minor positions in the larger picture. Such was the case with Franz Murer, a native of Austria who, as deputy district commissar in Vilna, was responsible for the murder of approximately 60,000 Vilna Jews.[238] In the summer of 1947, a group of survivors notified Wiesenthal that Murer was working as a farmer in the Steiermark region of Austria.[239] In August the British authorities arrested him in Graz, but he was eventually transferred to a prison in the U.S. Zone.[240] The JHD used connections with survivors from Vilna living in Europe, Palestine/Israel, and the United States to collect evidence, ensuring that wherever Murer was prosecuted, he would be tried as "one of the greatest war criminals and criminals against humanity, who is responsible for organizing and carrying out the mass murder of hundreds of thousands of civilians in Vilna and vicinity in the years 1941–1944."[241] The JHD activists wanted Murer tried at the scene of his crimes, convinced that Polish, Lithuanian, or Soviet courts would impose harsher punishments.[242] In March 1948, he was extradited to the Soviet military government, which in September tried Murer in Vilna and sentenced him to twenty-five years of hard labor. In 1955, however, the Soviets released Murer in accord with the State Treaty that restored Austrian sovereignty, whereupon the Austrian government set him free.[243]

The commissions also compiled evidence against Austrian policemen responsible for mass shootings in Lodz and in the Galician towns of Stryj, Kołomyja, and Stanisławów, many of whom were still in active service.[244] Between 1945 and 1947, sixty-four of these suspects were arrested, extradited to the Soviet authorities, and sent to Siberia; fifty of them returned to Austria in 1955.[245]

It is difficult to assess how many testimonies the commissions in Linz and Vienna collected or how many perpetrators they helped bring to trial, since Wiesenthal and Frydman did not stint on self-praise, as a result of their heightened sense of mission. Wiesenthal claimed that the commissions' work led to as many as five hundred arrests of war criminals in Austria during 1947.[246] But these arrests did not necessarily lead to further legal prosecution or convictions. A list of war criminals compiled by Frydman indicates that by the end of 1947, the Vienna commission's testimonies had figured in only fifty-three arrests; investigations of thirty-eight criminals in Allied and Austrian prisons continued because of new evidence against them.[247] In addition, Austrian courts turned over forty-two criminals to Allied authorities as a result of additional evidence provided by the JHD in Vienna.[248]

Widespread reluctance to admit any Austrian responsibility for the destruction of European Jews or support for the Nazi regime led to growing exasperation among commission activists, especially because public sympathies, combined with the mountainous terrain, made it easy for the criminals to hide.[249] In 1947, the Austrian government passed a law stipulating a "Lesser Incrimination Amnesty" that covered 90 percent of the half million Austrian citizens affected by the country's denazification process. From 1948 on, war crime trials in Austria declined by 50 percent each year. The Allies granted Austria sovereignty to deal with denazification trials in its own courts. These events occurred in the context of the cold war, as the western Allies sought to win Austria as an ally.[250] In November 1947 Frydman cited mild sentences for war criminals to claim that Austrian authorities were trying to hide evidence "in order to be able to declare that there were no Austrian war criminals."[251] Wiesenthal accused the Austrian courts of deliberately delaying the trials of war criminals in their custody until all the Jewish DPs who could testify had left the country.[252] Historical commission members, Wiesenthal in particular believed that this situation could be changed only with letters and newspaper articles that put moral pressure on Austrians, direct interventions against anti-Semitic attitudes, and lobbying public opinion abroad.

The Austrian commissions first began to pay attention to historical research and publishing only in the late 1940s. This "turn to history" was a reaction to growing impatience with the Allied and Austrian authorities.[253] In the spring of 1948, Frydman's coworkers Otto Suschny, a chemistry student, and Kurt Weigel, a medical student and the commission's secretary, began to prepare a history of the Jews of Austria in the period 1938–1945, with due attention to the German occupation, Austrian involvement in Nazi policies, and the roots of Austrian anti-Semitic and pan-German ideas.[254] The commissions also prepared a series of studies on the fate of the Jews of Galicia under German occupation, which focused on Kołomyja, Stryj, and Stanisławów. The studies used the commission's testimonies in order to encourage the arrest of members of police battalions active in those regions, many of whom were still serving in Austria.[255] After Frydman had settled in Haifa in 1952, an abridged version of the larger history, as well as the monographs, was finally published in Israel, with the help of the World Jewish Congress.[256]

Like their counterparts in Germany, the commission activists in Austria largely saw their time in DP camps as temporary. Gathering evidence against perpetrators endowed their prolonged sojourn with meaning. As Wiesenthal remarked in November 1947, the JHD in Linz had been created "in order to make use of the time spent here in the Austrian waiting room," while "further[ing] the fight of the Jews for equality in the world, and the fight for expiation of the crimes of the war years, as well as to secure historical material for the coming generations."[257]

Upon leaving Austria for Israel in 1952, Towia Frydman closed the Vienna commission and transferred his archives to Yad Vashem. Two years later, he worked as that institution's representative in northern Israel, compiling a database of Holocaust victims' names. When Yad Vashem terminated Frydman's employment in 1957, he opened the small Documentation Center for Nazi War Criminals in Haifa, which received minimal funding from the World Jewish Congress and otherwise depended on the income of Frydman's ophthalmologist wife, Anna.[258]

The JHD in Linz closed its doors in 1954, and in 1956, Wiesenthal, a committed Zionist who nevertheless did not consider living in Israel, sold his archives to Yad Vashem for $2,000. Wiesenthal, who had become an Austrian citizen, worked for the Austrian branches of AJDC and ORT and served as vice president of the Linz Jewish community. In 1961, after having earned considerable public recognition for his contribution to capturing Adolf Eichmann in Buenos Aires and putting him on trial in Jerusalem, Wiesenthal returned to being a full-time "Nazi hunter" and opened a Jewish Documentation Center in Vienna.[259]

Eternalizing the Memory of Jewish Partisans: The Jewish Historical Commissions in Italy

The Jewish DP experience in Italy differed from those in Germany and Austria in three primary respects: the absence of occupation zones; the small number of survivors and the brevity of their time as DPs; and the dominance of partisans in DP historical commissions.[260]

The Pakhakh movement played a lead role in the establishment of historical documentation by survivors in Italy. (Its name was an acronym for the Yiddish Partizaner, Khayalim, un Khalutsim—partisans, soldiers, and pioneers.) The movement had originated in Poland in early 1945, when some five thousand former Jewish partisans and ghetto fighters in Lublin, Lodz, Bytom, and Krakow developed organizational structures to provide mutual aid and to prepare for immigration to Palestine.[261] Meanwhile, in Lodz, in May 1945, "a small bunch of enthusiasts" had begun to collect "autobiographical narrations and documents of surviving partisans, their comrades in battle, their way of life in the woods and steppes, their fighting and means of combat against the Nazis."[262]

Pakhakh members who left Poland regarded Italy as "the last stopover on our way to our homeland,"[263] primarily because of the relatively easy transit from its ports to Palestine/Israel. In November 1945, on the initiative of the Lithuanian-born journalist Moshe Kaganovitch, a group of Pakhakh members established historical commissions in Milan and Rome, eventually becoming Pakhakh's Central Historical Commission (Tsentrale Historishe Komisye bay Pakhakh),[264] headquartered in Rome, with Kaganovitch as director and Yitskhok Kvintman as secretary.[265] Pakhakh also established small historical commissions in the Leipheim DP camp in the U.S. Zone of Germany, and in Graz and Linz in the British and U.S. Zones in Austria.[266]

The Pakhakh commissions focused specifically on documenting the history of Jewish partisans and other fighters. By Kvintman's account, the partisans followed in the spirit of Simon Dubnow: "As soon as they saw the first ray of liberation, the partisans began to fulfill the last will of the well-known Jewish historian Professor Dubnow, who shouted on his final way: 'Brothers write, record, and report this to the coming generations.' . . . When they were still in the woods, a number of partisans felt the need . . . to record certain episodes, events, facts, and names." By gathering testimonies and data on battles of Jewish partisans against the Nazi regime, the former partisans sought to "build a monument to the unknown Jewish partisan and ghetto fighter." Their historical work would thus immortalize this heroic chapter of Jewish resistance. It was therefore "the duty of the surviving Jewish partisans to cherish the last will of thousands of their comrades who fell in the fight with the Hitler beasts on the steppes of eastern Europe."[267]

This connection to future generations was not just inspirational. As Kvintman observed in November 1947, no doubt looking toward their future life in Israel: "The Jewish partisans recorded this bloody epoch for coming generations, who will have a model for learning how to fight and to defend Jewish honor with a rifle."[268] By documenting their achievements, they also sought to secure for themselves an honorable position in their future home.

In its effort to document a positive story of Jewish resistance and heroism, the commission in Rome collected both testimonies from former partisans on their own exploits and their memories of fallen fighters. Commission coworkers complained that the partisans did not always follow the commission's appeal for rigorous documentation. Indeed, Pakhakh members' praise for the partisans and ghetto fighters, which they saw as "one of the most beautiful and heroic episodes of Jewish life and struggle in the bloody years of the Nazi hell,"[269] often rose to the level of self-aggrandizement.

Farn Folk (For the people), the central Pakhakh newspaper, was the commission's main vehicle for encouraging former partisans to document their experiences.[270] In addition to invoking historical documentation as a symbolic memorial, it appealed to the partisans' moral duty to testify. Pakhakh also planned to publish a *yizker-bukh* or "partizaner almanakh" based on the testimonies as a "gigantic printed memorial to the fight of our Jewish partisans."[271] The commission promoted the book as "documentary proof of Jewish participation in the fight against fascism. The publication will silence all our enemies who are trying to say that the Jews did not defend themselves against the German occupier and were not represented among the resistance."[272]

To guide interviews, the commission used a basic twenty-question survey on the partisan interviewee's prewar education and occupation, life in the ghetto, membership and function in ghetto underground organizations and in partisan units, operations, weapons used, and injuries suffered.[273] Instructions specified that "all details given must be in accordance with truth, or else the material will not be used—therefore refrain from coloring and exaggerating, because we . . . must transmit only the pure truth of the heroism of the Jewish partisans."[274] When an interview ended, the person testifying had to sign a statement attesting to the honesty and correctness of his or her answers.[275]

Some former partisans showed indifference to the commission's work, especially due to "psychological difficulties"[276] and the passage of time. Kvintman observed in 1948 that the best time to have captured details was "immediately after the liberation . . . when everything was still fresh in memory and there had been an inclination to record and . . . recount among the partisans. But the driving force of the *Ha'apalah* [illegal immigration to Palestine] made it impossible to carry out this work." Although the DP camps provided structure and a semblance of normalcy that aided collection work, Kvintman admitted that "the will of many to give their personal experiences and memories to society waned, and the motivation to write and narrate generally diminished."[277]

In order to popularize its work, the historical commission in Rome published some of its collected testimonies in *Farn Folk*, beginning in August 1946. It also pursued but did not complete the publication of a study of Jewish partisans in specific regions of eastern Europe, the fighting units under certain commanders—such as Tuvia Bielski, survivors from whose group were DPs in Aqua Santa, Italy—and Jews who had hidden in forests in so-called family camps.[278] It also planned two larger publications: a work on "the history of the national Jewish partisan units, . . . their genesis, their provisioning, arming, struggle, and actions, and their desperate attempts to save the Jews"; and a *yizker-bukh* of fallen Jewish partisans in Byelorussia and the Ukraine.[279] Although printing problems and a chronic lack of funds prevented their publication, they were incorporated into a four-hundred-page book on Jewish partisans in the Soviet Union, which in 1948 was published in Rome by Moshe Kaganovitch, with the help of a donation from the New York-based Zionist Labor Committee.[280]

The Central Historical Commission in Rome understood its work as a preparation for further documentation of the Jewish partisan movement, to be continued in Israel. The commission dissolved in late 1948. The following year, Kaganovitch, along with the collection, left for Israel; there the collection became part of Yad Vashem.[281]

Conclusion

The survivors who documented the past in the DP camps of Germany, Austria, and Italy, like their counterparts in France and Poland, acted out of a deep sense of obligation toward both the dead and future generations. Yet gathering evidence of Nazi crimes also endowed their "waiting time" in camps on the "blood-soaked soil" of Europe with meaning.

Unlike the historical commissions in France and Poland, the DP camp commissions did not focus on the destruction of the Jews of one particular country. Although they tended to view the Jewish people as a distinct national entity, their primary mission was documenting the eastern European Jewish experience of Nazi persecution, in keeping with these survivors' primarily eastern European background. The Central Historical Commission in Munich, the largest institution of its kind in Germany, pursued this direction in its own broad-based research. The smaller commissions in Austria and Italy had distinct focuses: respectively, the collecting of evidence against war criminals and the history of Jewish partisans in eastern Europe. The history of German and Austrian Jews largely remained a marginal concern of the commissions. Survivors' extended presence in the "land of the perpetrators" triggered their documentation of the crimes as an affirmation of "*mir zaynen do*"—of having prevailed in spite of everything—and as a form of symbolic revenge, most directly in the Austrian commissions' pursuit of war criminals. They also profited from proximity to official documents unavailable in eastern Europe—and in the case of Austria to some of the perpetrators. In their populist research techniques of employing voluntary *zamlers* and subscribing to the idea that every survivor had a story worth recording, the DP camp commissions largely continued prewar traditions of *khurbn-forshung* (destruction research).

Although commitment to Zionism was not the primary motivation for the DPs' documentation work, most commission activists strongly subscribed to the idea of a Jewish national home in Palestine. They also applied the Zionist conviction that Jews needed a sovereign homeland for writing their history. In documenting the Holocaust and assembling their own archival collections, the survivors sought to ensure that Jews would control their own story. And in transferring these collections to Jerusalem, they sought to help build a sovereign Jewish state. The central memorial and research institution they envisioned would safeguard their materials against those who denied and distorted Jewish suffering and allow it to serve the transgenerational commemoration of the destruction of Diaspora Jewry. Meanwhile, the transitional and extraterritorial arena of the DP camps allowed commission activists to cope with the traumatic past and prepare for a new life abroad. They were motivated by their conviction that historical documentation was itself a kind of gravestone for those whose final resting place was unknown or far away from the DP camps. Yet survivors could take this "portable" monument with them wherever they continued their postwar lives. While most commission workers chose to leave Europe for Israel or the United States, Simon Wiesenthal, as the exception to the rule, believed that his work of bringing the perpetrators to justice was most needed in Austria.

Having explored the separate stories of the Jewish Holocaust documentation projects in five different national contexts, one fundamental question remains: namely, in what ways did the survivors active in parallel efforts cooperate across national borders, and to what degree did their respective documentation initiatives cross-fertilize each other?

5

Joining Forces to Comprehend the Jewish Catastrophe

The Attempt to Establish a European Community of Holocaust Researchers

Each of the Jewish documentation initiatives that arose throughout postwar Europe operated under unique conditions, responding to such factors as the ethnic and religious composition of the surrounding society, its history and political institutions, and its recent experience of war and occupation. Nonetheless, the cataclysm that had decimated Jewish communities in twenty-one countries under the control of Nazi Germany or its allies impelled cooperation among the activists and their institutions across national borders. The westward migration of Polish activists in itself led to an exchange of documentation experience. One of the most notable of these migrants, Philip Friedman, observed in October 1947 that only a "collective of scholars" could manage "a deeper, critical, and analytical treatment, and a synthesized coverage of all the complicated economic, social, cultural, and demographic problems and events" of the Holocaust.[1] That December, representatives of Jewish historical commissions and documentation centers in thirteen countries gathered in Paris for a ten-day conference, in order to discuss their work and shared concerns, compare wartime experiences, and confer on documentation methods. In the end, the conference prompted them to explore the common ground they shared, and also to understand what separated them from each other.

Rival Visions: Europe or Palestine as the Center of Holocaust Research

In May 1945, the Central Jewish Historical Commission (Centralna Żydowska Komisja Historyczna; CŻKH) in Lodz first raised the idea of a conference of Jewish historical commissions to coordinate research and publication on the recent cataclysm in its correspondence with Jewish organizations in the United States and with academic and political bodies in Palestine.² Despite initial support from the Central Committee of Polish Jews, plans for an international conference, to be held in Lodz in September 1946, fell apart due to increasing uneasiness among Polish Jews after the Kielce pogrom, which resulted in a massive exodus from Poland; the sharpening of government restrictions on Jewish life; and the Central Committee's growing wariness of international contacts.³

As head of the AJDC's Education and Culture Department in the U.S. Zone of Germany, in May 1947 Philip Friedman encouraged the Central Historical Commission in Munich to organize a European conference that would coordinate historical research, organize an executive organ to continue institutional collaboration, found a historical journal, and prepare for a congress of Jewish historians that would meet periodically.⁴ Because of visa difficulties for international delegates seeking entry to occupied Germany, Paris was seen as a more suitable location. Friedman turned to his employer for funding, and the Joint's prior sponsorship of the Center of Contemporary Jewish Documentation (Centre de Documentation Juive Contemporaine; CDJC) in Paris made it the most likely conference organizer. Although Herbert Katzki, secretary of the American Jewish Joint Distribution Committee (AJDC/Joint) in Paris, was favorable, Friedman's proposal led nowhere.⁵

Meanwhile, Isaac Schneersohn—apparently unaware of Friedman's proposal—had begun to develop his own idea for a European conference in Paris. During a visit to the United States in March 1947—a trip organized in large part to seek funds to shore up the CDJC's own desperate financial state⁶—Schneersohn mentioned the idea to Max Weinreich, the director of YIVO, and to jurist and Zionist politician Zorah Warhaftig of the Institute for Jewish Affairs, the research department of the World Jewish Congress in New York. Both expressed skepticism, though for different reasons. As a scholar, Weinreich advised waiting: "It would be better if the institutions involved stuck to their work for now and kept in touch with each other by correspondence before an ill-prepared conference is convened which might leave many people disappointed."⁷ Moreover, while YIVO remained the greatest supporter of the historical commissions, Weinreich's organization had to conserve its resources and could not attend a Paris meeting.

Warhaftig suggested instead a closed meeting of commission activists who would focus on the technicalities of documentation. As a member of the executive committee in charge of planning Yad Vashem as the central site for Holocaust commemoration, he was understandably concerned that Schneersohn's conference might lead to calls for a central Jewish memorial or research institution in Europe.⁸ In June 1947 a Yad Vashem supporter, the Polish-born ultra-Orthodox journalist and historian Moshe Mark Prager, who had been visiting historical commissions and documentation centers in Europe, informed the committee of the CDJC's ambitions for European leadership, and added that "if there is no immediate large-scale action from Yad Vashem, the initiative is in danger of being taken from our hands."⁹ The memorial committee responded by announcing its own conference on Holocaust documentation in Jerusalem, to be held on July 13–14, 1947, in collaboration with the Hebrew University.¹⁰ In addition to gaining a clearer picture of the institutions and personalities involved in the European documentation efforts and of the extent of their collections, the conference planning committee headed by Hebrew University historian Ben-Zion Dinur (Yad Vashem's future director) aimed to promote the idea of Yad Vashem as *the* central memorial and world documentation center. To that end, Dinur hoped to negotiate the transfer of archival material from the Diaspora to Palestine and to discuss the methods and organization of research on the recent catastrophe.¹¹

Although the Yad Vashem conference organizers invited the heads of most of the European commissions and documentation centers, visa problems kept a number of European activists away. The British Mandatory power denied entry to DPs Moshe Yosef Feigenbaum, Israel Kaplan, Simon Wiesenthal, Towia Frydman, and Philip Friedman. Jacques Fink, editor of *Le Monde Juif*, attended, representing the CDJC, joined by Nachman Blumental, representing the CŻKH. Most of the 165 participants represented various local institutions, among them the Jewish Agency, the Jewish National Council, the Historical Society of Israel, the Hebrew University, the Central Zionist Archives, and a number of publishing houses, as well as various landsmanshaftn and other immigrant organizations.¹²

Not surprisingly, the conference passed a resolution that declared *Eretz Yisrael* (the Land of Israel) to be the most appropriate site for Holocaust commemoration; it also stipulated the founding of a World Documentation Center as part of the larger project to erect a central memorial in Jerusalem. Since this new center would house all documentary evidence on the destruction of European Jews, all European Jewish institutions were asked to transfer their archival holdings.¹³ This request met with vocal opposition from Fink, who spoke for Paris' central role among the "surviving remnant," the *She'erit Hapletah*, in Europe. While stressing the desirability of collaboration between Jerusalem and Paris, he made it clear that the CDJC wanted to keep its material in France.¹⁴ In any case, the resolution had little immediate significance. Most of the European documentation initiatives were simply preoccupied by trying to collect all the documentary evidence available to them.

The Yad Vashem activists realized that a resolution alone could not curb the autonomous European efforts. Not only was the documentation material physically located in the Diaspora, the memorial committee lacked the wherewithal to influence the European centers by financing their collection work. In anticipation of the proposed conference in Paris, internal discussions oscillated between threatened boycott and offers of cooperation in the hope that the European centers would voluntarily subscribe to building the World Documentation Center in Jerusalem. In the end, cooperation prevailed, leavened by rhetoric that emphasized *Eretz Yisrael* as the only proper site for a central memorial to the Holocaust.¹⁵

Setting the Agenda: Planning a European Conference of Holocaust Documentation

Ignoring the contretemps in Jerusalem, planning for the first European conference of Jewish historical commissions and documentation centers proceeded smoothly. In late May 1947, the CDJC invited colleagues in Poland, Germany, Hungary, Romania, the Soviet Union, Sweden, Switzerland, Bulgaria, Great Britain, and Greece to participate in a "conference of experts who deal with Jewish problems." Participants were to provide an overview of the techniques and results of their research; the type, origin, preservation and organization of their archival collections; and the potential of their materials for courtroom use, as well as the possibilities for document exchanges among the various commissions.[16]

Although the CDJC received positive responses from a number of countries, working out a detailed agenda proved difficult. The organizers had a clear idea that the Holocaust had affected the Jews of Europe as a whole, but they were still struggling to grasp the complexity of recent events, and their knowledge was often limited to their own survival experiences and a general idea of what had occurred in their own country. Thus they generalized from the French experience with Nazi control: a central institution, such as the Commissariat Général aux Questions Juives, passing anti-Jewish laws and coordinating the Aryanization of Jewish property, and an officially mandated Jewish council, such as the Union Général des Israélites de France, representing the Jewish population vis-à-vis the authorities. The conference would be a first step toward gaining a comparative perspective on these institutions, as well as on anti-Jewish legal and economic measures, and ultimately on Nazi extermination policies.[17] Since ghettos were not part of the French Jewish experience, their role in the Holocaust would be addressed by Polish delegates.[18]

Schneersohn identified a number of issues that the reports of all delegates should address. These included an overview of "the Jewish problem during the occupation," touching on racial legislation; government organizations dealing with the Jews and the official Jewish leadership; internment camps; the behavior of the non-Jewish population; and "the problem of the restitution of despoiled property (in particular the situation of vacant or heirless property)." In addition, each delegate was to address "the state of research and the importance of the existing archives" in the respective country and to specify the "work carried out before and after the liberation" as well as the "exploitation of the collected documentation."[19]

Some of Schneersohn's coworkers immediately cautioned that the attempt to discuss both historical events and documentation techniques in the various countries would yield massive tomes on the recent history of European Jews but would ignore "the technical problems [of coordination] that constituted the main purpose of this conference."[20] The lawyer and CDJC affiliate Henri Monneray suggested two different kinds of lectures, one on the general situation of the respective Jewish communities and the other on questions of research methodology. Although Schneersohn himself deemed methodological questions to be slightly less important than informing delegates about the fate of Jews in the various countries under German occupation,[21] the organizing committee heeded Monneray's concerns and announced that participants could focus on either historical events or issues of historical research.[22]

For the CDJC's leaders, particularly for Schneersohn, the conference had the additional goal of establishing the organization's primacy among Jewish documentation initiatives in Europe, as evidenced by "a European Documentation Center [in Paris] dedicated to the four years of occupation."[23] Nonetheless, he cautioned that putting the CDJC's ambitions on the conference agenda would "risk inciting protests and discontent among the foreign guests"; instead, the idea of a Paris documentation center should "result from the debates as a whole," preferably suggested by a non-French delegate. "If it came from us it would immediately become a political question."[24] CDJC affiliate Samy Lattès proposed that his friend the Italian delegate Colonel Massimo-Adolfo Vitale be asked in advance to suggest the creation of a joint European Jewish documentation center. Once the issue was on the table, Lattès argued, "it would only be most natural if this center were in Paris, given that the French Jews constitute the largest group of occidental Jews [in Europe]."[25]

Vitale agreed to speak for the documentation center, and it remained the conference's key issue for Schneersohn and some of his coworkers.[26] To counter those activists who wanted the center's leadership role at the top of the agenda, Marcel Livian attempted to broker a compromise: rather than including the Paris center as part of the formal agenda, it could be brought to the delegates' attention "in a diplomatic tone, without any imperative. . . . It must be left to the guests to take the initiative on coordination."[27] Schneersohn continued to insist on the "delicacy of the question," warning against "hurting the legitimate feeling of autonomy among the delegates. . . . At no price should we give the impression of wanting to impose some sort of unification over which the Documentation Center of Paris would take the lead. It would be better if the initiative came from the foreign delegates."[28] As he often did, Schneersohn prevailed, and the official agenda omitted any mention of CDJC leadership.

Eventually, the CDJC decided to shift the conference's focus from the centralization of documents to their exchange, along with an emphasis on the future of materials collected in the Displaced Persons camps of Germany and Austria, which were in danger of being lost when the camps were dissolved and the DP population dispersed.[29] Besides being a legitimate and somewhat urgent issue, the disposition of the DP archives offered an opportunity for the CDJC to step into the breach and offer its facilities as a depository. Since the French delegates would constitute a majority, the conference would afford disproportionate attention to the French Jewish experience, thereby promoting a leading role for the CDJC among the various documentation projects.

This Francocentric focus had its detractors even among Jews residing in France. Barely four weeks before the conference, Michał Borwicz, a former CŻKH worker who earlier that year had settled in Paris, where he organized the Center for the Study of the History of Polish Jews (Centre d'Étude d'Histoire des Juifs Polonais), harshly criticized the agenda for underrepresenting the experiences of eastern European Jews.[30] He took particular issue with what he saw as a reductive emphasis on ghettos, which were "only one part, and not even the main part, of the Jewish problem during the occupation." The conference should not ignore the equally important issues of "the camps, the Aryan [identity] papers, the suffering of children, the cultural work, the Jewish partisans, the Jewish resistance fighters, the activity of the Jewish fighting organizations in the ghettos, the Jewish activity in the Polish resistance movement, etc." Borwicz further demanded that this first Europe-wide meeting of Jews engaged in documenting the recent past "must not be dominated by historical events already treated in various publications [e.g., the ghettos]."[31] Rather its focus should be on "scholarly questions, and the analysis of current events."[32] While these complaints did not result in changes to the conference program, they anticipated a rift between the delegates of Polish background and their French hosts that would characterize the conference as well as the subsequent history of Holocaust documentation.

Paris, December 1947: A Representative Assembly of European Jewish Documentation Projects

The First European Conference of Jewish Historical Commissions and Documentation Centers convened on November 30, 1947—a day after the U.N. General Assembly's decision to establish separate Jewish and Palestinian states—and continued through December 9, 1947. With generous support from the AJDC, thirty-two delegates represented Jewish historical commissions, documentation centers, and communal organizations in thirteen countries, not limited to Europe: Algeria, Austria, Bulgaria, France, Germany, Great Britain, Greece, Italy, Palestine, Poland, Romania, Sweden, and the United States. Visa or financial problems kept away a number of the more than fifty invitees, including those from Hungary, Switzerland, Czechoslovakia, the Soviet Union, Belgium, and the Netherlands.[33]

Twelve Jewish documentation initiatives sent delegates to the conference: the Jewish Central Information Office in London; the CŻKH/ŻIH in Warsaw; the Jewish Historical Documentation Centers of Vienna and Linz; the Central Historical Commission in Munich and its regional branch in Frankfurt am Main; the Historiska Kommissionen in Stockholm; the Committee for the Search of Jewish Deportees in Rome; Borwicz's Center for the Study of the History of Polish

Jews; and three French organizations: the Center for Political Information (Centre d'Information Politique), the Center for Israelite Information (Centre d'Information Israélite), and, of course, the CDJC.

Half of the delegates represented non-documentation-related national and international Jewish organizations, some of whose members nevertheless engaged in collecting materials on the recent past. These included religious or communal organizations such as the Central Consistory of the Jews in France,[34] as well as Jewish scholarly institutions including the Jewish Scientific Institute of Sofia and the Society for Jewish Studies in Romania. Although interested in the documentation efforts, they were neither founded by survivors nor focused only on the Holocaust. Other delegates represented groups as diverse as the Union of Sephardic Israelites of France, the Israelite Consistory of Paris, the Federation of Jewish Societies in France, and the Union of Jewish Intellectuals of France. The Office of Chief of Counsel for the U.S. Military Tribunal in Nuremberg sent a delegate, as did the Jewish Agency for Palestine, the AJDC, and the Alliance Israélite Universelle. The Yad Vashem executive committee intended to send two delegates but had to make do with a telegram[35] that nonetheless clearly conveyed its message:

> We hope that your reunion at the historical hour of the establishment of the Jewish state will proclaim its approbation of the resolutions of Yad Vashem in order to place in Jerusalem the World Conference of documentation as well as its consent to concentrate the documentation of Jewish martyrdom and heroism at Yad Vashem. [This will involve] close collaboration with the documentation center and all other historical commissions of the European countries.[36]

As a venue, the organizers chose the Salle des Centraux, at 8, rue Jean-Goujon in the Eighth Arrondissement, a city mansion owned by the alumni society of the École Centrale Paris, now most famous as the site in 1945 of Jean-Paul Sartre's public lecture "L'existentialisme est un humanisme." The location—in close proximity to the Elysée Palace and the major embassies—suited the CDJC's self-image as a central institution of postwar France and Europe and its wish to appeal to non-Jewish political circles. The CDJC sent an invitation to the president of the Republic of France, Vincent Auriol, who neither attended nor sent a representative. Other invited but nonattending political figures included former prime minister Léon Blum, Conseil d'État president Robert Schuman, Finance Minister René Meyer, and Minister of Interior Jules Moch, all of whom, except Schumann (a Christian), were Jewish.[37] Justin Godart, the CDJC's most vigorous non-Jewish supporter, was the only representative of the French political elite; indeed, he gave a keynote address.

The conference opened on the evening of Sunday, November 30, 1947, with the singing of "Hatikvah," followed by "The Marseillaise." The U.N. decision a day earlier had heightened the euphoric spirit. The first session the following morning began on a more somber note with a religious service commemorating the "martyrs of German barbarism and hatred"[38] and a sermon by France's chief rabbi, Isaïe Schwartz.[39] Godart's keynote address emphasized that the conference was being held to honor the memory of the victims, prevent the tragic events from falling into oblivion, and allow future generations to draw their lessons from the past. In conclusion, he forcefully argued that the documentation effort—by demonstrating "to the world that anti-Semitism was the herald . . . of Nazism"—not only possessed "tremendous universal significance" but offered lessons for the future: "If tomorrow anti-Semitism rises again," Godart warned, "it is because . . . ideas of hatred, conquest, destruction still exist, whose consequences will affect not only the Jews but humanity as a whole."[40]

The conference planners chose to emphasize that the delegates represented countries as much as they did organizations; indeed, many delegates saw themselves as representatives of both their nations and their Jewish communities. Thus they tried to present a positive image not only of their respective countries but also of the attitudes of gentiles toward the Jews since the end of the war. Elie Echkenazy from Bulgaria emphasized that the Bulgarian people had both "opposed the deportation of Bulgarian Jews" and treated the Jews well after the war.[41] Asher Moissis observed that, while there had been many Greek collaborators, ordinary Greeks and the Orthodox Church had helped save more than ten thousand Jews; moreover, the postwar Greek government had been among the first to deal with the issue of intestate property.[42] Romanian delegate Mayer Halevy praised all the newly established people's democracies for their advanced policies on the return of stolen Jewish property and the revocation of anti-Jewish legislation.[43] No one admitted to pessimism regarding the situation of the Jews in his country or criticized the hostility of the local population.

As for the French delegates, they took every possible opportunity to laud the *grande nation* they called their own. Indeed, the fate of France's Jewish community received unparalleled attention simply by dint of the fact that France provided fourteen of the thirty-two delegates—bolstered by CDJC's extensive documentation. The topics covered included the Aryanization of Jewish property, Jewish youth movements, Jewish involvement in the resistance, French public opinion toward the Jews, the role of the church regarding the Jews, the search for Jewish deportees, and the activity of major Jewish religious institutions during the occupation, as well as the CDJC and its history and various other French documentary archives.[44] The French delegates intended the ardent portrayal of their nation and of the significant role of the Jewish community in France to support the CDJC's leadership in Europe.

While the various national reports dominated the conference, its sessions touched on a number of overarching issues. For example, Fred Herz, representing General Telford Taylor, chief prosecutor for war crimes of the U.S. Military Tribunal at Nuremberg, spoke about the necessity of providing evidence for these trials, especially once the Allied prosecutors had discontinued their work.[45] The physician Eugène Minkowski addressed the impact of Nazi persecution of Jewish children and youth, and Dr. Léon Kurland spoke about the responsibility of the German medical profession in conceiving and implementing the Final Solution.[46] Joseph Kermisz addressed the commemoration and visual representation of the past, citing the exhibition at Auschwitz-Birkenau which had opened in July 1947 on the initiative of the Polish government, and suggesting that site as a Jewish documentation center.[47]

Reports on the activities of international Jewish organizations during the Nazi period and the actions of Jews outside the German sphere of influence provided another angle on the recent past. In an address during the conference's first session, Schneersohn insisted on the need for such reports. It was not enough to speak of the occupation, its tribulations, and the ultimate triumph of its survivors. "We must also consider what our brothers in then-unoccupied countries have done, the Jews of America, Palestine, etc. Judaism is one; its fight is one. European Judaism had, and continues to have, powerful 'rearguards' to support it and help it get back on its feet."[48] In this spirit, Georges Garel described the social welfare activities of the OSE; Dr. Walter Beckelman, head of the AJDC's European Division in Paris, outlined the Joint's activities in Europe during the occupation; Dr. Joel Wolfsohn of the American Jewish Committee described the AJC's fight against anti-Semitism; and Isaïe Klimoff reported on the Jewish Agency's efforts to rescue European Jews.[49]

Only a small number of reports addressed the histories and activities of the Jewish historical commissions and documentation centers per se. Fewer still dealt with methodological questions, and in all of these the focus was on France. Two reports addressed the history and holdings of the CDJC: Henri Hertz lectured on the organization's history, and Edmond-Maurice Lévy discussed preservation and the use of the CDJC's cache of documents.[50] In addition, there were reports on other French Jewish organizations that collected documents for use as evidence of anti-Semitism in legal proceedings.[51] No other commission or documentation center had the opportunity to describe its holdings in such great detail. Other countries' historical commissions presented their work, but there was only one report per country, even for those that had more than one commission. Thus Joseph Kermisz, one of the few members of the original CŻKH staff remaining in Poland, recounted the history of both the CŻKH and the newly founded Jewish Historical Institute, ŻIH, of which he was vice-director. Moshe Yosef Feigenbaum reported on the Central Historical Commission in Munich, while Simon Wiesenthal spoke for both commissions in Austria (Towia Frydman arrived late due to travel complications and missed the opportunity to report on his work in Vienna). Nella Rost described the historical commission in Stockholm, which had been set up by the World Jewish Congress, and Alfred Wiener reported on the work of the Jewish Central Information Office in London.[52]

Envisioning a Historical Synthesis: Strategies for Creating a Common Methodological Framework

All five delegates who dominated the conference debates about Holocaust-documentation methodology had eastern European backgrounds: Léon Poliakov, head of the CDJC's research department; Philip Friedman, director of the AJDC's Education and Culture Department in Munich; Mayer Halevy, president of the Society for Jewish Studies in Romania and also representing the Romanian Jewish Historical Institute; Michał Borwicz, director of the Center for the Study of the History of Polish Jews; and Moshe Yosef Feigenbaum, secretary of the Central Historical Commission in Munich. (Friedman, Borwicz, and Feigenbaum also shared an earlier affiliation with the CŻKH.) Although they were a small minority of the delegates, and their pleas for close attention to methodological questions remained unheard, the conference for the first time provided them with a unique platform for exchanging their diverse views on these issues.

While agreeing on the unprecedented nature of the recent catastrophe, the five men differed on what had made it unique in the long history of Jewish suffering. For Halevy, it was the sheer scale of Jewish loss, while Poliakov emphasized the Nazis' extensive planning and coordination in a "gigantic scheme" that differed fundamentally from previous forms of mass violence against Jews.[53] Friedman cited the geographic extent and totality of the violence as marking the catastrophic years 1939–1945 as fundamentally unique. The Nazi assault not only targeted men, women, children, and the aged, it achieved the "almost complete destruction of the creative resources of the life of the Jewish nation in Europe, resources from which world Jewry—Palestine and the United States included—also drew its revitalizing vigor and renewing forces. The reservoir of forces in eastern Europe no longer exists."[54] More boldly, Friedman argued that the Holocaust's "significance for universal history [was] in no way inferior to its significance for [Jews'] national history." Because of its "international character" the Jewish tragedy intersected with "the workings of general history," and its study thus requires taking "the larger international context" into account.[55]

Friedman concurred with Borwicz's call for a "new Jewish historiography,"[56] since the unprecedented nature of the disaster had rendered conventional tools of historical research obsolete. This new field, which Friedman named *khurbn-forshung* (destruction research), had to be interdisciplinary because "the analysis and interpretation of its sources are more informed by the methods belonging to sociology than by [those of] the historical disciplines. Purely historical methods . . . do not suffice. A new method must be elaborated and implemented, one that is much more complex and eclectic, embracing the most diverse aspects of the problem." The synthesis of historical and sociological methods, Friedman claimed, would give rise to several subdisciplines, among them what he termed "the study of the 'camp universe' in the form of 'campography' and 'campology'; [and] the study of the guerrilla warfare of the partisans, its sociological analysis, and the strategic aspects of this fight, which so far have been neglected."[57]

Poliakov, Friedman, and Borwicz agreed that researchers already had an exceptional abundance of sources on the catastrophe, despite—or because of—its historical proximity. Poliakov cited Simon Dubnow's complaint about the dearth of medieval Jewish records: "It is on foreign sources that we have to rely to know the ordeals that our fathers suffered." Future historians, he observed, "will not reproach our generation for that."[58] Indeed, survivor historians had to apply "judicious selection," since they "risk at times being overwhelmed with the magnitude of the documentation."[59] Similarly, Friedman cautioned against "uncontrolled pseudo-historic and even false writing" and "hasty and erroneous conclusions," as well as "poetic and artistic visions contrary to the truth,"[60] while Feigenbaum warned about a "psychosis of publicity" among many survivors.[61]

The delegates agreed that the new research field must utilize both sources created by victims and those left behind by perpetrators. They disagreed, however, on their relative value. For Poliakov, the Nazi mass murder of European Jews had been a conspiracy, a grand scheme that could only be understood through the "confessions of the perpetrators," including Germany's collaborators.[62] Surviving German documents would reveal "the substructure of this world scheme for which we have been chosen as the first victim." Such documents would provide "invaluable information on the anti-Semites' methods, motives, and mentalities" and allow researchers "to penetrate the laboratory where the Nazi venom was distilled."[63]

In contrast, Borwicz warned that relying on the "accidental selection" of documents left behind by the Germans might lead to an entirely false historical narrative. His own experiences had shown him that "all German documents are false, not in terms of their authenticity but in terms of their content. First of all, they are full of pseudonyms or euphemisms. Murder per se is never indicated, cremation is never called by its name." Indeed, the entire "German system was based . . . on a double accounting of the murders in inverse proportion to the[ir] actual importance. . . . Very few traces were left of the most dreadful acts, while on the less significant issues there is extensive communication."[64] Thus one must always compare German records to Jewish sources. In the end, this disagreement was more theoretical than real, although Holocaust historiography in some ways recapitulates these discussions. Poliakov admitted that in certain—unspecified—areas, German sources might provide "the frame," but survivor testimonies alone could provide "the tissue of which the history of the martyrdom of our people is made."[65] Feigenbaum and Friedman also subscribed to the belief that both kinds of sources were needed for a complete picture of the Jewish catastrophe.

The realities of wartime destruction also informed a debate about the relative value of different kinds of Jewish sources. Borwicz trusted sources created during the occupation more than he did postwar testimonies written from hindsight. To prove his point, he cited the Ringelblum archives, in particular copies of "the Jewish underground press, the detailed reports on sanitary conditions, on cultural life and other realms, the photographs, pamphlets, testimonies, etc." Only such sources—not just "figures, dates, or definitions"—could provide real insights into the Jewish experience of Nazi persecution. "Psychological and moral problems are equally and maybe even more important. In this respect, these personal diaries teach the most profound truth about human beings."[66] Feigenbaum noted the very real problem that "the Jewish historian stands before archives emptied by the Nazis," but stressed that when using postwar documents, "what matters most is that we get the testimonies of the simple people, the man in the street"[67] in order to obtain a record of Jewish society as a whole.

Unwilling to assign a hierarchy of value to Jewish and German sources, Friedman cautioned *khurbn-forshers* to maintain a scholarly perspective and base their histories on a broad array of sources.[68] In practice, even Poliakov—the strongest proponent of the value perpetrator documents—encouraged the use of a broad range of sources: in addition to official statistics and records, archives should collect testimonies and questionnaires, as well as such physical vestiges of the past as "yellow stars, arm bands of the ghetto police, pajamas of the camp inmates, posters, and announcements."[69]

The possibility of objectivity on the part of researchers who had themselves survived the Holocaust understandably sparked discussion. For Feigenbaum, this was less of an issue: because of his lack of academic credentials, he viewed himself simply as a survivor who was "creating a reservoir [of sources] for future historians to work with."[70] As both a survivor and a professional historian, Friedman took on this problem at some length, beginning with the presupposition that "every historian gathers and interprets historical materials according to his particular point of view. . . . There is no such thing as uncolored historiography." Nonetheless, the historian must remain "loyal to the documentary sources," and not let "passionate, political, or personal considerations influence him in his analysis and interpretation."[71] In the case of *khurbn-forshung*, objectivity meant resisting the "accusatory tendency" that survivors and historians might encounter in themselves, as well as among their intended audiences, especially around such issues as "the Jewish police, the members of the 'Jewish Councils,' the collaborators in the ghettos and camps," or the "moral degradation visited on us from our deadly enemy, the dissolution of the holy institutions of family, matrimony, nation, and religion, in the corrosive atmosphere of the diabolic tortures of ghettos, camps, [and] roundups."[72] Friedman also acknowledged the challenge to objectivity posed by the admirable moments of resistance and heroism. And his experience in postwar Poland had shown him the pitfalls of discussing the role of non-Jewish bystanders among whom Jews might still live; further, researchers might be subject to "political influences" and should be "cautious about any inconsiderate generalization."[73]

However tempting accusation might be, Friedman explained that it jeopardized the goal of constructing a historical record: "It goes without saying that historical scholarship does not address itself exclusively to reason, but also to the heart." Nonetheless, it was not poetry. "Classical historiography is always most influential if it is a sober, simple, and realistic presentation of condensed facts." Ultimately Friedman believed that "a researcher with a shrewd eye, learned in the finer points of dialectical thinking, will know how to differentiate in the chaos ... between good and evil, strength and weakness, nobility of soul and vulgarity, [and will see] the dialectic unity of ... a time which has seen the most rapid evolution from life into death, rise into fall, that the history of humankind has ever seen." Historical research would reveal the truth of the Jewish tragedy to the world, but only if researchers refrained from "bombastic phraseology and exaggerated pathos," since an obviously "tendentious, emotional, or pathetic presentation undermines the trust of the reader [and] destroys the plausibility of the historical work."[74] The historian must first identify obstacles in order to become aware of them and then attempt to deal with them, through trial and error and open methodological discussion.

Finally, Friedman anticipated the criticisms of professional historians who were not themselves survivors. "Some say," he observed, "the memories are too fresh; we lack the detachment that is indispensable for every historian deserving to be called such; the materials have not been assembled completely. It would be better to wait, collect more in order to get a more complete insight into the events. ... Moreover, the historian is too intimately tied to this recent past to be able to judge with objectivity."[75] He rejected these arguments on three counts. First, the subject matter of the *khurbn* was already identifiable; moreover, it constituted a particular epoch in Jewish history with a clear periodization—1933 to 1945—although a study of the factors that led to this era should begin in 1870 or 1918.[76] Second, unlike earlier but recognized historical phenomena, the *khurbn* was extremely well documented, and survivors as well as the larger public needed to understand what "really" happened.[77] Third, the commissions and documentation initiatives provided a therapeutic outlet for survivors eager to express their experiences in writing, ensuring that their sometimes overly emotional responses did not distort the historical truth.[78] The comments of other delegates focused on the urgency of the situation: memories must be captured while they were still fresh and historical documents collected before they disappeared.[79]

The topic of methodology exhausted, the delegates considered their future direction. They agreed on the need to begin working toward a "grand synthesis," which would require all historical commissions and documentation centers to collaborate closely, standardize their research methods, and—as a form of quality control—set general guidelines for the publication of historical works.[80] Feigenbaum recommended that researchers assemble a catalogue to inform individual centers and commissions about the holdings of partner organizations.[81] He also proposed a periodical that would link the historical commissions and "the great mass of the people."[82] Friedman, on the other hand, wanted a more scholarly journal that would advance and intensify the discussion among the historical commissions begun in Paris.[83]

As a foundation for the suggested work of synthesis, Mayer Halevy recommended an encyclopedia of vanished Jewish communities—a "new 'memorbuch,' which contemporary historiography must write."[84] This "encyclopedia of martyrdom,"[85] or "lexicographic bibliography and geography of the European *khurbn*,"[86] would cover "the entire geographic map of tormented Israel, the map of all European and extra-European countries subjected to the ordeal of fascist and anti-Semitic contamination."[87] Such a tome would both assist future synthesizers and serve "as a blueprint for a monument to the memory and glory of the vanished communities."[88]

While based on documentation that the respective projects had assembled so far, the Paris conference envisioned a new stage of history writing that would transcend the collection of materials. Indeed, Borwicz warned that, rather than making documentation an "end in itself," activists should think of their archives as "the foundation for historical research."[89] Friedman similarly urged the *khurbn-forshers* to move beyond "simple documentation collections with analytical introductions and critical notes" and look to synthesizing the "enormous mass of handwritten and printed materials. . . . The difficulties . . . are technical rather than conceptual in nature." A particular problem was the sheer volume of literature, some "only published in the daily or periodical press in countries in many different parts of the world." As a solution, Friedman proposed "the creation of an international bibliography [and] the publication of archival catalogues and accurate indexes."[90] Along the same lines, Poliakov envisioned uniform guidelines that would enable each historical commission to condense the results of its research in a single work—an international Jewish body would then coordinate the work, supervise its standards, and synthesize the results.[91] Friedman conceded that the synthetic work he envisioned would "certainly not represent the last word in Jewish historical scholarship on this subject, but it must constitute a beginning." He hoped that the conference would establish "a general plan for collective *khurbn* research," which would move the effort closer to the goals he had outlined. "Our conference today constitutes a great step forward in establishing a permanent exchange of ideas, an indispensable network of contacts, and the elaboration of a common language."[92]

Some of the delegates most engaged in this discussion expressed dissatisfaction that the conference agenda had not given a more prominent place to methodology and spent even less time on organizational issues.[93] In Borwicz's words, "the essential questions concerning methodology were drowned in episodic or descriptive reports."[94] The French hosts, on the other hand, seemed to think there had been quite enough discussion of "technical issues."[95] These disagreements as to the relative importance of methodology reverberated underlying tensions related to the delegates' respective national backgrounds as well as to their understanding of the purpose of their various documentation projects.

Fissures in the Unity: Was there a Shared Holocaust Experience, and What is the Purpose of Holocaust Research?

In his welcoming address, Isaac Schneersohn emphasized that the delegates were united in their shared endeavor of collecting, recording, and preserving for the future "stories of the atrocities and miseries"[96] of European Jewry's cataclysm, and thus fighting for "the will for peace, [for] a unification of the world, so that the horror of the war will not repeat itself."[97] Léon Poliakov echoed this theme: "We represent here a dozen different countries, but we are facing a historical phenomenon which is indivisible. The history of the destruction of Judaism is a whole bound together."[98]

Yet over the course of the conference, the sense of unity based on shared experiences and similar goals gave way to differences and conflicts between delegates of various national backgrounds. The French hosts themselves admitted that not all survival experiences were alike. Thus, in his keynote address, Justin Godart recognized that some delegates came from countries that had suffered more than France,[99] and in opening the first session, Schneersohn specifically addressed the Polish delegates, in whose country "most of the crimes were methodically and scientifically perpetrated; on your soil the last sojourn of almost all the deportees of Europe [was] prepared."[100] The conference agenda did not, however, set aside any particular space for the experiences of Polish Jews. Discussions about ghettos and death camps were virtually absent, perhaps in part because Nachman Blumental, who had been invited to speak about ghettos, could not attend.[101] As noted earlier, the experiences of French Jews received disproportionate consideration in several lectures, while other countries were generally allotted one lecture each. Borwicz reflected a more general tension when, in criticizing the conference's Francocentric perspective, he reminded the delegates that the "entire Jewish catastrophe occurred in eastern Europe, where the Jewish masses lived in their great majority: this aspect . . . always has to be taken into consideration."[102] In line with his earlier request that conference organizers not limit the experiences of Polish Jews to the issue of ghettos, he now criticized them for ignoring their survival in various kinds of camps, in hiding, and under false identity—experiences central to the history of the cataclysm and consequently to the work of the commissions. In sum, the conference simply did not reflect the eastern European Jewish experience under the Nazi onslaught.[103]

Language—in particular the predominance of French—proved to be another source of disunity. While the conference was officially bilingual—French and Yiddish—the only French delegates who understood Yiddish were immigrants from eastern Europe. Yiddish was also foreign to the Algerian, Italian, and Bulgarian delegates, while a significant number of the other delegates did not know French. Postal delays had prevented the translation and distribution of written versions of the reports prior to the conference, and the full agenda only allowed for rough paraphrasing of the reports and proceedings, rather than actual translations, which angered some of the foreign delegates.[104] Borwicz declared that, although he "admire[d] the French culture and language," Yiddish was the native language of most of the Jews who had been murdered: "It is in Yiddish that one ought to talk about things Jewish."[105] The implication was that the audience for the new historical works would be Yiddish-literate—in particular eastern European—Jews in Europe, Palestine, and the Americas. The conference hosts, on the other hand, primarily intended a non-Jewish Francophone audience.

Even more fundamental divides opened when delegates discussed the larger purpose of documentation: Was it the foundation for historical scholarship or did it serve political ends? The majority of delegates had no intrinsic interest in historiography. Rather, they saw documentation as a means by which survivors could fight for justice and restitution and combat anti-Semitism. In this vein Simon Wiesenthal advised delegates that "the most urgent and practical problem, which is in no way inferior to purely scholarly research, is the problem of war criminals."[106] From his perspective, historians did not have the right to seclude themselves in their archives; rather, their obligation was to gather evidence against Nazis who remained on the loose.[107] Fred Herz used this opening to alert delegates that the Nuremberg Military Tribunal would soon end its responsibility for the prosecution of war criminals, although the process was far from complete. "Your role," he told them, "is to make sure that all war crimes are brought to justice so that those responsible will be prosecuted." They could not continue to depend on the Allies to prosecute those war criminals not yet sentenced. "You must work in cooperation with other European countries, with all sorts of organizations, trade unions, and the press—and not only with Jewish organizations."[108]

Borwicz acknowledged the value of scholarship for assisting the pursuit of war criminals, but Jews had to do more than collect legal evidence. Namely, they must formulate their "own charges in the name of our dignity, in the name of everything that is dear." For example, the Nuremberg trials did not consider the urgent issue of restitution. Thus Jews themselves should compile "an inventory of confiscated Jewish property," in order both to gain compensation and to make known the extent of the problem.[109] Greek delegate Asher Moissis even argued that the commissions' primary task should be collecting evidence to resolve issues of contested Jewish property.[110]

Many delegates saw historical documentation as a means to combat anti-Semitism. In the words of Massimo-Adolfo Vitale, "Scholarship is a great and beautiful endeavor, but it must also serve to cure an illness."[111] Borwicz also saw the writing of history in this light, though he urged researchers to abandon their old-fashioned "apologetic" methods in favor of "a positive method based on solid and indisputable documentation."[112] Wiesenthal and Bulgarian delegate Elie Echkenazy warned of another danger—the likelihood that the impending cold war would lead to another world war, which would take the heaviest toll on the Jews of eastern Europe.[113]

A number of delegates remained skeptical about the mixing of scholarship and politics. Not surprisingly, Philip Friedman urged the strict exclusion of the pursuit of political and legal aims from historical scholarship: historians should provide the evidence on which others make judgments, not make judgments themselves. No doubt aware of the propaganda uses of the Treaty of Versailles, Justin Godart cautioned that the mingling of scholarly and political considerations could harm the fight against anti-Semitism itself, since questionable evidence could cost the Jewish cause its credibility. The survivors must ensure that "the Germany of tomorrow will not be able to say that the sentences [imposed on the perpetrators] have been hasty and not supported by evidence. The truth alone must stand against the crimes committed, with no room for any possible objection."[114] Another French delegate, Léon Meiss, argued that writing history demanded "a certain distance, and if we try to make history through a conference we risk committing errors."[115] CDJC secretary-general Marcel Livian agreed that the conference was not the venue for issues of "Jewish politics": "It does not suit historians to take sides; this should be left to politicians."[116]

With all of these issues unresolved on the conference's last day, Henri Monneray—who was himself involved in research on war crimes and had been part of in the French delegation at the International Military Tribunal at Nuremberg— sought to bridge the divides, reminding the delegates that they shared "the same commitment to truth in order to condemn what happened and the [same] hope that the documents of historical research will serve a purpose." Yet he thought it understandable that discussions had strayed from theoretical considerations of Jewish historical commissions and documentation centers and that the conference had assumed "a political appearance, in the best sense of the word." Of course, delegates considered how documents could assist in the prosecution of war criminals or provide tools to combat anti-Semitism, issues that "constitute the psychological motivation for our work."[117]

The one issue on which delegates found common ground was Jewish resistance to Nazi persecution, a subject whose emotional appeal Friedman had warned them about. Not surprisingly, the role of Jews in the *Résistance* in France received ample attention, with reports by Henri Hertz and David Knout that encompassed activities from armed resistance to underground welfare work.[118] Knout's slightly idealized discussion suggested that the diverse constituencies of France's Jewish community—whether established or newcomers, secular or religious—had been united under the banner of resistance.[119] Fayvel Schrager, a Polish-born Bundist who had come to France in 1927, now the president of the Association of Foreign Jewish Volunteers in the Second World War, stressed the "glorious role" of foreign Jews in the French armed forces.[120]

Even more than the partisans, the Warsaw ghetto uprising represented the epitome of Jewish resistance and heroism for delegates from both France and

Poland. On behalf of all the delegates, Marcel Livian paid tribute to the insurgents, whom he called not only "the greatest heroes since antiquity, symbols of the Jewish armed resistance of all countries,"[121] but "the embodiment of Jewish resistance as such." Because of its symbolic importance, he noted, the CDJC's publication on the uprising was the only one that did not concern French Jews.[122] Yet Livian also stressed the importance of all Jewish resistance, in particular in combating anti-Semitic accusations of Jewish passivity.[123]

Delegates even used Jewish resistance as a raison d'être for the historical commissions. Thus Mayer Halevy argued that their work "in itself constitutes an attempt at moral reparation in memory of the martyrs and heroes of the resistance."[124] And Joseph Kermisz, in reporting on resistance among Jewish prisoners in Auschwitz-Birkenau, emphasized the role it would have in the exhibition planned for the memorial site at the camp.[125] Jewish resistance also provided a common denominator that bridged the different experiences of the catastrophe from country to country and allowed delegates to connect recent events to a glorious past. Resistance and valor thus partially counterbalanced the thread of persecution and suffering that ran through the Jewish past, making it easier for survivors to cope with their tragic experiences and to communicate them to the outside world.

Bridging the Divides: The Outlines of a European Jewish Documentation Center in Paris

The Paris conference presented its organizers with a challenge: promoting a central European documentation center under CDJC leadership while avoiding the impression that the organization sought a position of dominance. While CDJC leaders graciously proposed that other commissions and centers assume guardianship of the DP collections before the camps were dissolved,[126] Schneersohn touted the advantages of centralizing French materials in a main Jewish archive in Paris—"the great political and cultural center of Europe"—thus making it available to a large audience of researchers and writers. The implication was that other document collections might similarly profit from this location. As a modest first step, he proposed "a little center in Paris, which, in collaboration with all historical commissions that are present here, will create a library with documents, books, testimonies, archival collections, and publications, so that Jewish and non-Jewish historians and writers will be able to consult these items, which will facilitate the writing of the history of the martyrdom that we have suffered during these four terrible years."[127]

The French delegates resolutely presented a France that had purified itself of the Vichy "aberrations" and returned to the enlightened republican values that made it the leading state in western Europe. Dramatically, the fragility of this picture became apparent during the trial of Xavier Vallat, the Vichy regime's commissioner general for Jewish questions, which proceeded concurrently with the conference.[128] Two CDJC affiliates, Gaston Kahn and an attorney by the name of Braun, were witnesses at the trial, and the CDJC had provided evidence against Vallat, who was sentenced to ten years in prison on December 10, 1947 (although he would be released two years later).[129] At the conference, they, as well as other CDJC delegates, freely admitted their exasperation with the trial, at the same time revealing their self-understanding as French Jews. Vallat used the trial to freely express his anti-Semitic views before jurors and a demonstrably sympathetic courtroom audience. Testimony by the few Jewish witnesses was limited; the Jewish community and the victims had no chance to speak, nor did any representative body speak on their behalf.[130] Indeed, Léon Meiss, president of the CRIF, an the umbrella organization of French Jewish organizations, advised against any organized Jewish action on the grounds that "it is not up to the Jews to defend the Jews in this trial, ... it is up to France to defend the Jews in accusing Xavier Vallat. Consequently ... if France does not find a spokesman against the accused, it is hopeless for France."[131] Moreover, Meiss feared that a press campaign or other intervention "would achieve the exact opposite of the goal that ought to be reached. It is a matter of showing moderation and tact in the matter."[132] Similarly, Braun warned against any action that might be seen as seeking vengeance.[133]

It was left to Italian delegate Massimo-Adolfo Vitale—identified by the CDJC as a reliable ally—to draw the desired conclusion from the regrettable Vallat trial. Reaching back to the Dreyfus affair, he recalled that once upon a time "there were men and money to save one man; today when it is a matter of avenging 6,500,000 victims we should be able to find the necessary means and people to defend the spiritual, if not physical, lives of millions of people in Europe and the world." For him, the Vallat trial argued for a central Jewish documentation center in Paris, which could not only provide evidence for trials but also publish a periodical to articulate the Jewish position.[134] And beyond Schneersohn's modest proposal, other CDJC affiliates spoke more forthrightly. Thus the lawyer Joseph Lubetzki used the issue of material compensation for confiscated Jewish property to claim that all European institutions would benefit from a CDJC-administered "World Documentation Center, bringing together everything pertaining to the life of the Jewish Diaspora."[135] And Joseph Gottfarstein—with support from Simon Wiesenthal—argued that centralization would provide a strong foundation for real scholarly research.[136]

From his perspective of the Nuremberg proceedings, Fred Herz strongly advocated the creation of a central organization—location unspecified—that could pursue and prosecute war criminals after the imminent end to Allied prosecutions: the matter was so urgent that the delegates should "abandon all questions that are secondary or matters of nuance, and deal with this primary important task."[137] Delegates agreed on the value of a central repository for these and other documents, and several delegates advised storing multiple copies of documents in different countries as a precaution against theft or destruction, with Jerusalem, New York, and Paris being the most likely sites.[138] However, Joseph Kermisz's suggestion of a repository at the newly opened memorial at Auschwitz provoked outraged rejection from Moshe Yosef Feigenbaum, in the name of delegates who had recently fled Poland: "No one can or should expect us to place our holiest relics in a country where since the war the newly erected Jewish memorials for the memory of the annihilation are systematically destroyed. Absolutely no." Rather, he insisted, such a memorial should be built "in the country of our hopes and our future . . . [where] we will be free and impartial enough to shed light on the complete disgrace of the twentieth century."[139] He proceeded to make a case for transferring the collections to Yad Vashem, on the grounds that the European *She'erit Hapletah* had a duty to help Jews in Palestine establish a central memorial and research institution.[140] In the end, the delegates seemed to favor centralizing the material, most likely in Paris, with copies in other centers. The final decision was left to a central administrative body, to be created at the end of the conference.[141]

United Action Suspended: Shattered Hopes for a Collaborative History of the Holocaust

As the organizers tried to sum up the conference's achievements and look toward future collaboration, a number of delegates—most of them recently from eastern Europe—raised complaints regarding the lack of discussion time and insufficient attention to methodological issues. Friedman and Borwicz repeated their earlier critiques,[142] while Feigenbaum noted that the commission reports were too few and superficial. In addition to insisting that any future central administrative body be comprised of individuals actually engaged in documentation work, he called for "a real conference of historical commissions and documentation centers that will focus exclusively on questions relevant to historical research."[143] Friedman concurred, stressing that such a conference should be "dedicated entirely to the discussion of methods."[144]

The French hosts responded defensively to these criticisms. Schneersohn emphasized that the conference had achieved its goals of assessing existing document collections and promoting the coordination of research.[145] Livian noted the conference's "historical importance" as "the first gathering of the greatest number of documentation centers and historical commissions since the liberation of Europe." He also reminded the delegates of their common goals: first, "instructing this generation, and certainly the generations to come, on the suffering of the Jews, so that we know how to prevent such a thing in the future," and second, assembling comprehensive records of the survivors.[146] Many delegates, Livian reported, had told him that the conference had been a revelation about the wartime fate of the Jews of other countries: "We came here believing that we knew everything. . . . Well, here we became aware that our country has been insufficiently informed, and this conference certainly allowed all of us to become aware of the vastness of the task, of our ignorance as far as the coordination of our documentation is concerned, and if only for establishing contact with [other] delegates, . . . this conference will not have been in vain."[147] For Livian himself, the conference had affirmed European Jewry as "the people of the Bible and the people of the book; this is a tribute we can still pay ourselves without shame."[148]

Because many delegates expressed a desire for future periodic conferences, Livian closed the proceedings with a riff on the Passover parting "Next year in Jerusalem!": "Next year again in Paris for the Second European Conference of Jewish Historical Commissions and Documentation Centers."[149] It was not to happen.

On the first day of the conference, the delegates had elected a Resolution Commission—heavily weighted toward France—to formulate a statement for the delegates to vote on at their final assembly.[150] Three subcommissions, respectively, would address the practical, financial, and legal aspects of future institutional cooperation; develop related scholarly methods and techniques; and oversee collaboration regarding the collection of evidence for the prosecution of war criminals.[151]

The resulting resolutions provoked a lively discussion at the final session on December 9. As lawyer and journalist Léon Czertok observed in an ironic allusion to Livian's tribute, "Our people are the people of the Bible, the book . . . [and] also of discussions and debates."[152] Eventually the delegates agreed on the following statement:

> Insofar as Jewish suffering under the fascist occupation is one and indivisible, the study of this suffering must be inspired by this tragic unity of the historical facts;
>
> Insofar as coordination of the means, the methods, and the results is necessary so that the facts of the past be analyzed, known, and propagated to the full extent they deserve, and that they may also serve as a lesson;
>
> Insofar as cooperation is equally required in order to contribute effectively to the fight against anti-Semitism, to the search for and identification of the victims of persecution, and to the moral and material compensation owed to the survivors;
>
> The first European Conference of Jewish Historical Commissions and Documentation Centers adopts the following resolution:
>
> A Coordination Committee of Jewish Historical Commissions and Documentation Centers is to be created. The Coordination Committee has the goal of enabling the European Jewish Historical Commissions and Documentation Centers to coordinate their work and activities and to guarantee efficient cooperation among them.[153]

To this end the delegates mandated the Coordination Committee (later the Comité Européen de Coordination—European Coordination Committee; ECC) to standardize research methods and centralize files, indexes, and lists of war criminals, as well as to facilitate the exchange of documents, the collection of all publications concerning the European catastrophe, and the compilation of all materials relating to material compensation claims. It would also encourage the publication of historical studies, translations, and a journal in French and Yiddish, and also utilize the press, radio, and films to promote historical work. The delegates further resolved that the committee should organize periodic conferences to discuss its ongoing work and its results and methodologies. The committee would be located in Paris, and all historical commissions and documentation centers adhering to its criteria could become affiliates.[154]

The subcommission on scholarly research further proposed the development of common terminology related to the cataclysm and a standard classification and filing system for all documentation. Accordingly, the ECC's responsibilities included: overseeing all the catalogues produced by member institutions; preserving copies or microfilms of their holdings; maintaining contacts and exchanges with Jewish and non-Jewish institutions engaged in relevant historical research or documentation; preparing the publication of a periodical and establishing operational guidelines for the commissions.[155] It also recommended the creation of a Scholarly Committee to coordinate affiliates' work and research topics. The proposed publications included a journal dedicated to methodological issues, reviews of other publications, and a bulletin that featured a current bibliography, minutes of meetings and work reports, and a chronology of scholarly and organizational activities.

The third subcommission's resolution charged the ECC with centralizing information and documentation useful in war crimes trials, as well as with collaborating with relevant authorities to facilitate the prosecution of war criminals.[156]

The delegates agreed that the ECC would consist of three organs: a General (or Plenary) Assembly, a Council of Directors, and a General Secretariat. The General Assembly would convene yearly to appoint members of the other two bodies. Given the absence of delegates from several potentially eligible countries, all eligible historical commissions could assign representatives until the next conference was able to determine membership.[157]

The proposed Council of Directors (or Conseil d'Administration; Conseil de Direction) would consist of a president, two vice presidents, and one representative of each country represented in the General Assembly, except that the ECC's host country would have four delegates. Responding to complaints about France's disproportionate representation, Henri Monneray noted the need for day-to-day decisions, while also stressing that the ECC and its constituent bodies had no intention of "establishing a hierarchy of centers"; rather, the goal was "true cooperation" through sharing experiences, methods, and information."[158] Despite concerns raised by delegates from smaller organizations,[159] the conference settled on a country-based structure, except that, for administrative reasons, France would have four Paris-based members. The Council of Directors would, however, answer to the General Assembly, where all member organizations would be represented.[160] Delegates elected Isaac Schneersohn as president of the new council and as vice presidents Léon Meiss (CRIF) and Philip Friedman (who planned to move to Paris while waiting for a U.S. visa).[161] Notable council members included Moshe Yosef Feigenbaum (Germany), Simon Wiesenthal (Austria), Alfred Wiener (Great Britain), Joseph Kermisz (Poland), and—the only woman—Nella Rost (Sweden).[162] Finally, delegates elected three CDJC members to the General Secretariat: Marcel Livian, Léon Czertok, and Philippe Hosiasson.[163]

Responding to concerns about inadequate attention to methodology—and anticipating the recommendation of the second subcommission—Kermisz suggested that the General Assembly elect a Scholarly Committee (Comité Scientifique), to be headed by a respected Jewish historian.[164] Despite arguments that historians on the Council of Directors made such a body superfluous, Friedman's insistence on the need for a separate scholarly body prevailed.[165] The assembly selected Friedman as president representing France, Mayer Halevy as president for other countries, and Joseph Gottfarstein (CDJC) as secretary. Other members included Michał Borwicz, Jacques Fink, Joseph Kermisz, Maurice Vanikoff, and Alfred Wiener.[166] They were to direct scholarly publications and historical research; formulate a detailed research plan; establish bibliographical and historiographical directories on the recent past; and elaborate and propose to the Council of Directors a detailed study and research agenda to be carried out collaboratively.[167]

The Scholarly Committee held its first meeting on December 11, two days after the conference ended. As its first task, the committee set out to collate and publish the conference lectures, which the CDJC published in 1949 as *Les Juifs en Europe (1939–1945)*. It would then develop a periodical journal and begin its lexicographic work. The committee also aimed to explore ways to consolidate all available documentation on the Jewish councils, the persecution of Jewish children, Jewish resistance, and anti-Semitism. Its ambitious agenda further included the collection of all the questionnaires and catalogues used by ECC member organizations in order to standardize cataloguing and archiving methods, using as models the systems developed by the CŻKH. Finally, it would invite a number of historians to take on supervisory functions.[168] Those members living in Paris were to meet monthly, while all would gather once or twice yearly in plenary session.

Despite these auspicious beginnings, the ECC's sole achievement was *From the Cataclysm to a New Life*, a permanent exhibition on the fate of European Jews, organized under CDJC auspices and mounted in Paris in August 1949. As described by Schneersohn, the exhibition's purpose was to educate in order to combat the surrounding society's tendency to ignore European Jews' fate during the war. In addition, it served the survivors' wish to commemorate the dead and to celebrate Jewish resistance against the Nazis in all its manifestations—moral, passive, and armed.[169] The CDJC took on the task because the ECC lacked the technical skills for such an ambitious project.[170] Most affiliate organizations did, however, contribute materials from their collections to illustrate the histories of their own Jewish communities, each of which had a separate display area.

As conceived by the ECC, the exhibition covered three major aspects of the recent past: Jewish responses to Nazi persecution; the behavior of non-Jews inside Nazi Europe; and the assistance that Jews outside the Nazi orbit had extended to European Jews. In regard to the first theme, the exhibition sought to demonstrate "the vitality and resistance of the Jewish people against the general background of Nazi persecution," promoting an understanding of resistance that encompassed "the solidarity and safeguarding of cultural and religious traditions and values," as well as armed partisans. For its second theme the exhibition showed and paid tribute to "the manifold ways in which gentile elements in Europe assisted Jews during the persecutions." While not denying the reality of collaboration, it offered a more nuanced picture, including non-Jewish resistance that "helped the Jews either to escape terror or fight the oppressor." Finally, the exhibition aimed to present "an impressive picture of the part played by Jewish communities and organizations of Allied and neutral countries in assisting their brothers who were victims of the German Holocaust, as well as of the work of reconstruction undertaken by these groups after liberation."[171]

Apart from this exhibition, whose attendance and publicity remains unclear, the ECC achieved none of its larger goals. The primary reason lay in its constant lack of funds. Schneersohn raised this issue as early as the second meeting of the Council of Directors, by suggesting a focus on low-cost projects, such as centralizing bibliographies and lists of war criminals.[172] However, the inability to subsidize travel expenses for geographically far-flung activists inhibited scholarly exchange.[173]

Moreover, because of the instability of some ECC-affiliated institutions, in particular those in the DP camps or in communist Eastern Europe, the documentation work largely fell to a handful of individuals, several of whom were constantly on the move—not only within Europe but between continents. In addition to Friedman's departure for the United States in the fall of 1948, Feigenbaum immigrated to Israel in the spring of 1949, followed by Kermisz a year later; Nella Rost settled in Uruguay in 1951, while in the mid-1950s Wiesenthal decided to stay in Austria.

Individual conflicts rooted in power struggles, personal vanities, and various ideological and national tensions further hindered interaction, even among activists in the same place. In the aftermath of the conference, for example, Michał Borwicz and Joseph Wulf again challenged the CDJC's hegemony in a letter that disparaged the conference for having been "conducted in a tendentious manner with all decisions made beforehand." Moreover, they alleged, the CDJC had squelched discussions and left unclarified theoretical issues critical to collaboration. The gravest charge was that the conference had not accorded due attention to the suffering of the Jews of eastern Europe. As evidence, they cited CDJC machinations to prevent researchers in this area—i.e., their Center for the Study of the History of Polish Jews—"from exerting any influence." Affronted, Borwicz and Wulf withdrew their formal support from the committee, while—in the interest of history—allowing the center's workers to participate in ECC activities as individuals.[174] Although CDJC leaders subsequently took Borwicz even less seriously, the tension continued throughout the exhibition's planning.[175] Meanwhile, the CDJC's fundraising activities in the United Kingdom damaged its relationship with Alfred Wiener, whose library could have been a stable partner for the CDJC in Western Europe.[176]

Conclusion

In retrospect, the 1947 European conference of Jewish historical commissions and documentation centers is notable as the first attempt to fully comprehend the Jewish catastrophe—its scope and its challenges to researchers and historians. At the same time, neither the conference nor the ECC produced more than minimal tangible achievements, and the conference revealed divisions that had previously been largely submerged.

While the delegates generally agreed that Holocaust research should become a collective endeavor based on a comparative perspective, their primary concerns remained recent events in their own countries, the details of which the survivors still struggled to fully understand and document. The conference structure encouraged this tension, beginning with the antagonisms generated by the dominance of French Jewish organizations. Most delegates reported only on their own national experiences. Indeed, since they themselves still grappled with understanding those events, they did not attempt to—or were unable to—raise the kinds of broader comparative questions sought by some of the delegates. Thus there were no real discussions about such questions as the similarities and differences in the behavior of the Nazis and their collaborating governments toward the Jews in the countries and territories under their control or about the response of Jews in these various situations. By contrast, the 1949 exhibition stands out as the first attempt to present a common narrative of the catastrophe of European Jewry that highlighted Jewish resistance and the assistance given to victims by Jews and non-Jews.

After 1949, financial constraints, changing political circumstances, and personal differences and power struggles among the activists thwarted the development of a fully comparative approach to documenting and understanding the destruction of European Jews. From the CDJC's perspective, however, the ECC had successfully established the center's de facto leadership position among European Jewish historical commissions. Other issues were of secondary importance. With the dissolution of the DP commissions in Germany and Austria and the ŻIH's isolation behind the Iron Curtain, the CDJC's leadership role was virtually unchallenged in Europe. Its position was further cemented in the early 1950s when the Tomb of the Unknown Jewish Martyr—for which the exhibition had been a kind of rehearsal—attracted considerable public attention to the CDJC within and beyond France, and even more so when the Claims Conference supplied the necessary funds for its publications and the acquisition of additional archival material.

Conclusion

History Writing as Reconstruction

The Beginnings of Holocaust Research from the Perspective of Its Victims

The Holocaust survivors who founded historical commissions and documentation centers in postwar France, Poland, Germany, Austria, and Italy shared a conviction that their survival bequeathed to them a duty to bear witness for the dead and an obligation to future generations. To some extent this perceived injunction to write the history of the Jewish cataclysm involved an effort by survivors active in the documentation projects to rationalize their own relative fortune compared to that of loved ones and millions of others had perished. The belief that they had been spared not by accident but in order to bear witness surely helped them cope with loss and feelings of guilt. However, these survivors' claim to historical significance rests with their overt agenda as activists seeking to commemorate the dead; gain legal retribution, material restitution, and moral redress for survivors; promote political education to combat anti-Semitism and fascism and foster democratic values; and prepare a foundation for further historical scholarship.

Wherever they found themselves after the war, most commission workers shared an eastern European background; apart from a few leaders with academic degrees, all were lay historians. The experience of survival, commitment to the cause of documentation, and will to act in the present counted more than professional training. The rank and file included both women and men; indeed, in Poland and in the Displaced Persons (DP) camps, women may have been the majority of those active in documentation, which is especially remarkable since they had survived in smaller numbers. Women's relatively high level of representation reflected the commissions' popular approach to historical research as well as the chaotic, improvised, and provisional postwar conditions that undermined established gender roles. Nonetheless, men filled most positions at the top, while women served predominantly as *zamlers* (collectors of historical material), interviewers, archivists, and secretaries.

Activists built the documentation initiatives on their shared belief in an intrinsic connection between history and memory. They understood, however, that history and memory stood in conflict: while history was rational, analytical, methodical, and evidence-based, memory was selective, individual, emotional, and unreliable, because it changed and faded over time. Yet the recent loss and destruction of historical sources often compelled those who wrote the history of the Jewish catastrophe to rely on the memories of individual survivors. Thus they devised a number of techniques to control for the fallibilities of memory and make it useful for their projects. For example, they sought out survivors' memories while they were still fresh, and before the survivors had adjusted to their postwar lives. Where possible, they compared the memories of different survivors who had experienced the same event and weighed them against documentary sources—often official German ones. The activities of the historical commissions show that memory of the recent past was an integral part of survivors' daily lives, something both physical and palpable in nature and often connected to "transitional objects" mediating between the survivors and their traumatic experiences, as well as vestiges of their dead, such as ashes, bones, soil from the death camps, camp uniforms, urns, and pieces of soap which survivors (falsely) believed to have been made from the bodies of Jewish victims. On a more abstract level, the commission workers viewed their accumulated documents and chronicles of the past as "memorials" or "gravestones" for their dead.

The different documentation initiatives also shared a reliance on the tradition of *khurbn-forshung* (destruction research) that had developed among Jews in eastern Europe since the early twentieth century. Like these earlier efforts to chronicle anti-Semitic atrocities, the postwar historical commissions and documentation centers understood their work as a form of post factum resistance or self-defense. As communal projects for revealing the truth about recent crimes, their work would support the legal defense of the victims and the prosecution of perpetrators, as well as claims for compensation for material and physical damage. The documentation projects also demonstrated continuity in the idea that in times of raw and pervasive violence, Jews *themselves* must control the gathering of documentary evidence to support the writing of their own history. Only a case that embraced the perspective of victims would be sufficient to bring the perpetrators to justice, both in a moral and juridical sense. Like the earlier documentation initiatives, the commissions largely employed interdisciplinary social science-oriented research methods and sought an eclectic array of sources which reflected or embodied the victims' experiences.

The postwar commissions did, however, develop methods that were more refined, focused, and professional than those their predecessors used, thereby helping to establish *khurbn-forshung* as a separate field of research. The earlier documentation projects were carried out by a relatively small circle of Jewish intellectuals and communal activists who sought to win the attention of the common people through appeals to their moral duty to testify. In the wake of the Holocaust, which had directly affected Jews in twenty-one countries, *khurbn* documentation spread beyond small groups of intellectuals to reach a broader Jewish audience, and indeed became a Europe-wide phenomenon.

For all their common goals and shared cultural heritage, the documentation initiatives in the countries examined for this book exhibited significant differences. For some, historical scholarship predominated, whereas others focused on legal and political concerns, areas that were always affected by the personal priorities and ideological commitments of the key actors. The institution initially most committed to scholarly study of the Holocaust, the Central Jewish Historical Commission (Centralna Żydowska Komisja Historyczna; CŻKH), was increasingly subjected to political pressure as Polish society came under communist control and commission workers dedicated to independent scholarship left the country. In France, although the activists of the Center of Contemporary Jewish Documentation (Centre de Documentation Juive Contemporaine; CDJC) had at first declared that their primary aim was to fight for justice, equality, and the redress of grievances, their postliberation work concentrated on historical scholarship. In part this was due to the influence of key activists whose major interest was historical research (most importantly Léon Poliakov). In addition, CDJC activists who saw themselves as French citizens sought to bring Jewish suffering to the awareness of the non-Jewish public, which they believed could only occur through scrupulous research and abundant documentary evidence. By comparison, the activists in the DP camps saw their audience as exclusively Jewish, harboring few expectations for the surrounding gentile populations. The historical commissions in Germany and Italy, which were at once helped and hindered by the DP camp structure, viewed their documentary work as a means either to prepare the ground for future historians or to perpetuate the memory of Jewish partisans in an independent Jewish state. The commissions in Austria focused primarily on the fight for justice, limiting documentation largely to collecting evidence against perpetrators whom the activists encountered during their detention there as DPs.

The commissions also differed in their levels of professionalism and erudition. The highest levels of scholarship were reached in the Polish commission, because of the comparatively large numbers of academically trained coworkers and their connections with the field of Jewish historical study as it had developed during the interwar years. Many French activists had a university education, but in law rather than history. In Germany, Austria, and Italy, most commission workers were (as far as their backgrounds are known) autodidacts, Philip Friedman and, to a lesser degree, Israel Kaplan being notable exceptions.

The third major difference among the commissions was that the activists in France and Poland for the most part operated within a national framework, whereas in the DP camps in Germany, Austria, and Italy the commission workers were refugees largely disconnected from the countries of their temporary sojourn, and had also severed their ties with their countries of origin. Indeed, most DPs looked toward a life beyond the lands of the perpetrators; for many, this meant emigration to a sovereign Jewish state in Palestine/Israel. The researchers among the DP population thought of themselves as belonging to a multinational group, unified only by their mostly eastern European descent, their common experiences as survivors and DPs, and the commitment of many activists to the Zionist project.

In contrast, the activists in France and Poland tried to integrate Jewish suffering during the recent war into the history of their respective countries. This became most evident in France, where the activists saw themselves first as French citizens and then as Jews, and believed the "martyrdom of French Judaism" to be an important symbol of Germany's occupation. Jewish participation in the *Résistance* became a dominant theme in the CDJC's work, and this emphasis on the Jews' contribution to France's "self-liberation" showed how closely connected these Jews felt to France. In Poland, the commission workers tended to regard themselves as part of a separate Jewish nation whose recent history was unique. Not only had the Jews as a people been singled out by the Nazis for extermination, but Polish Jews had suffered higher losses than those of any other country. At the same time, they saw their history as deeply rooted in the history of German-occupied Poland and thus inextricably part of Polish history. For commission activists in the DP camps, the particular national contexts of their various countries of origin, which they had left either by force or choice, mattered less than their experience of iconic Jewish suffering in German-occupied eastern Europe—whether in Poland, the Baltic states, or Soviet territories. Although many activists initially focused their research on their towns and regions of origin, the DP commissions' questionnaires generally addressed experiences shared by virtually all eastern European Jews who had survived under Nazi occupation. These commissions therefore came closest to constructing a common eastern European Jewish past that crossed national borders.

Depending on whether their orientation was national or transnational, the commissions addressed different audiences. Those working within a national context made great efforts to reach a non-Jewish audience in the hopes of bringing the Holocaust to public consciousness, (re)integrating the Jewish populations into the predominantly non-Jewish society, and demonstrating the interconnections between the wartime memories and experiences of Jews and non-Jews. Therefore they published in the language of their respective countries. The Polish commission, however, also aimed at Polish-speaking Jews in and outside Poland. The DP commissions, on the other hand, published primarily in Yiddish for an eastern European but multinational audience of Jews in DP camps, Palestine/Israel, and the Americas.

The commissions also differed in their proximity to the surrounding Jewish community. The CŻKH had the backing of the Jewish community that remained in Poland and even of Polish Jews who had left. This connection was due to the commission's reliance for its historical work—in particular for its YIVO-style *zaml-arbet* (collection work)—on broad communal cooperation among a Jewish population which tended to be sympathetic to a kind of Jewish research they had known before the war. Under different circumstances, the DP camp commissions existed in the closest proximity to Jewish populations, and they were among the camps' central institutions. This did not, however, assure the support of the general population of Jewish DPs, many of whom focused their attention on the present and the future, not the painful past. In France, the CDJC tended to operate at a remove from the larger Jewish community. Because its work focused more on studying the Jewish fate through perpetrator sources than on survivor testimony, it did not depend on the cooperation of the larger French Jewish community.

Not surprisingly, the commissions operating in countries where their activists had been residents and citizens before the war tended to be more integrated into their respective national societies, as a consequence of which their work received at least limited acknowledgement and minimal support from their countries' new postwar governments. Commission employees gave expert testimonies at some of the major war crimes trials in Poland and France and supplied documentation to their respective delegations at the trials held under Allied military authority in Nuremberg. The DP camp commissions were not directly involved in any of the Nuremberg trials; however, the Austrian commissions initially collaborated with the American military government and the Austrian police in tracking down war criminals.

The documentation initiatives also varied in the relative importance they gave to perpetrator and victim sources, and in whether they aimed to provide an internal or external perspective on Jewish suffering. The French activists largely focused on how the Germans, and, to a lesser degree, the Vichy regime and French society, perceived and treated the Jews of France during the occupation, while the responses of French Jews received secondary attention. Moreover, as if to assure their reliability, activists derived these responses primarily from administrative records of recognized Jewish bodies and the wartime recollections of a small number of prominent individuals, not through the testimonies of rank-and-file survivors. The commissions in Poland, occupied Germany, and Italy, however, concerned themselves almost entirely with the ways in which Jews had experienced and responded to persecution. They sought to capture this information through assembling large numbers of testimonies from a critical mass of survivors who offered diverse social and educational backgrounds as well as varied wartime experiences. Although the Austrian commissions focused on the deeds of the perpetrators while their Italian counterpart concentrated on Jewish partisans, their common perspective was that of individual victims.

These differences, as well as the commissions' lack of success in European-wide collaboration, showed the practical limits of both their shared tradition of history writing in response to catastrophe and their largely identical motivations and aims. The different postwar contexts in which each initiative operated—including, of course, the political forces unleashed by the war and its aftermath—ultimately proved to be more formative and divisive than their common prewar cultural roots and shared postwar goals.

Postwar Jewish Holocaust Documentation and the "Myth of Silence"

In general, the record established by Jewish historical commissions and documentation centers in postwar Europe shows that a significant group of Holocaust survivors belied the myth of their silence by zealously working to chronicle and publicize their traumatic experiences, even to the extent that it tried the understanding of some contemporaries. Historical documentation imposed a distinct psychological burden on its advocates. Not surprisingly, the majority of survivors did not engage in documentation but chose alternative paths to achieve "normality" and to "work through" their traumatic experiences. Some may have avoided documentation work out of a sense of guilt for having survived when family and friends had not. Moreover, survivors often experienced hostile receptions from former neighbors who begrudged or even aggressively opposed their claims to rights, jobs, apartments, and property. Such experiences, exacerbated in the case of Poland with anti-Semitic violence, often led Jews to conceal their Jewishness in public, as well as to keep their memories of the recent past private. Even survivors who chose to document their pasts showed a notable decline in their historical activity by 1950, largely reflecting the surrounding societies' indifference to the survivors' experiences.

Thus the "strange silence" about the Jewish tragedy that commission activists in all countries sensed after the liberation came mainly from non-Jews. In response, the commissions made breaking the silence one of their primary tasks. They quickly realized, however, that the indifference to their work on the part of many gentiles—indeed, their impatience when Jews insisted on their distinct fate of racial extermination—led the larger survivor population to turn inward and keep their stories to themselves.

Postwar governments also tended to turn a blind eye to the specifically racist nature of Germany's genocidal persecution of the Jews—regardless of whether the country had been occupied by, or was allied with, Nazi Germany and no matter the level of complicity of its authorities and citizens in implementing the mass murder of European Jews. Moreover, Holocaust survivors suffered marginalization due to the far greater visibility of the victims of political persecution, most of whom—unlike the Jewish deportees who had suffered systematic extermination as a result of Nazi racist aspirations of creating a world devoid of the "Jewish race"—returned from German slave labor or concentration camps after the war. Those who suffered or died for their political convictions rather than their racial origins, in particular those who committed heroic acts of anti-Nazi resistance, stood at the center of public discourse and commemoration.

With more than enough wartime aggression, suffering, and crimes to rightly blame on the Germans—acts laid out in great detail by the international tribunal in Nuremberg—most non-Jewish Europeans could conveniently place responsibility for the deaths of their Jewish compatriots on the Germans and a handful of local collaborators. There was no need to draw wider circles of responsibility, or even to question their own behavior. Given a past that included military defeat, collaboration, and acts of violence against ethnic and religious minorities committed by local populations, many Europeans chose to concentrate on their *own* victimization—the material hardship, deprivation, loss, and displacement they had suffered because of German aggression in gigantic bloody war zones. Under these circumstances, many Europeans clung to uplifting and heroic national "resistance myths," which provided moral entitlement and psychological compensation, served to rebuild social cohesion and order, and legitimated new postwar governments.[1]

The general absence of Jews from these myths was not just a matter of repressed guilt and shame on the part of many non-Jews in Europe. Anti-Semitic stereotypes had survived the war; indeed, they flourished thanks to new postwar opportunities to brand Jews as alien and hostile elements, to blame them for the war itself or for the rise of communism in its wake, and to stoke widespread fears among non-Jews that they would have to relinquish the Jewish property with which they had enriched themselves. Yet for the most part, the absence of the Jews was met with indifference, callousness, and lack of compassion. For most non-Jews, as Tony Judt rightly observes, the Second World War had simply not been about Jews. Focused on healing the wounds of their own wartime suffering and victimization, they remained indifferent toward Jews, whose distinct fate—extermination—they had not shared and often could not even imagine to be true. Thus, in Judt's words, "post-war Europe was built upon deliberate *mis*memory—upon forgetting as a way of life."[2] For most non-Jewish Europeans in the mid- to late 1940s, the fate of the Jews could not be turned into a "usable past" and was therefore ignored.

The growing cold-war atmosphere further stifled the will to acknowledge distinct Jewish suffering. Crude narratives that subsumed European Jews into an indiscriminate category of victims of "fascism," "Hitlerism," "dictatorship," or "totalitarianism" obscured the ethnic and religious origins of a large portion of the dead and blocked critical investigation of the wartime behavior of non-Jews toward their Jewish neighbors. Survivors who wanted to bring their traumatic experiences to the attention of a broader public beyond their own communities and family circles had to tailor their narratives to fit these broad paradigms of victimhood. The Jewish documentation initiatives responded to these challenges in different ways. In Poland and France, they shifted from efforts to solely promote the notion of a specific Jewish tragedy to incorporating the mass murder of European Jews within a larger narrative of wartime suffering, resistance, and heroism, strengthening the universal implications of commemorating the Jewish catastrophe. This strategy proved successful to a degree.

Yet in general the commissions and documentation centers were ahead of their time in their quest to break the public silence about the specific nature of the Nazi persecution of European Jews, as well as in shining a light on the supporting roles of local governments and citizens. It would take several decades before European societies began to recognize the centrality of the Holocaust and publicly debate their roles in helping the Germans to carry it out, thus in some measure acknowledging their own historic responsibilities. In Western Europe, beginning with the 1960s, a long and twisted process of self-critical reflection and public debate was set in motion by factors that included several trials of Holocaust perpetrators, troubling questions raised by the younger generation, and disturbing truths exposed by historians and captured on screen by filmmakers.

Nevertheless, only in the 1990s would this development yield a broader public recognition of the Holocaust's significance for the respective pasts of the nations of Europe. In Eastern Europe, a Soviet myth of heroic antifascism suppressed painfully entangled memories of wartime and postwar aggression and of the victimization of different national groups. The fall of communism in 1989 lifted the lid that had contained discussion of the suffering inflicted by the Soviets on the Eastern Bloc. It also sparked a secondary discourse on how these nations had treated their Jewish populations during the war, although the focus largely avoided issues of historic responsibilities in order to gauge the "competitive suffering" of Jews versus non-Jews and of Hitler's victims as against those of Stalin.[3]

Not until the first decade of the twenty-first century, as a result of these complex processes in the east and west, did the Holocaust (too often reduced to "Auschwitz" as the quintessence of the event) enter public consciousness as *the* central element of the Nazi regime and *the* seminal event of the Second World War—indeed, to use Omer Bartov's expression, as the "leitmotif of the twentieth century."[4] This delay helps explain why the documentation projects, despite their ambitious, daring, and indefatigable activity so soon after the war, attracted little attention from their surrounding societies. Thus marginalized, the projects and their accomplishments fell into oblivion long before the wider public even began to recognize their potential.

From Margins to Mainstream: The Survivor Documentarians' Long Journey to Historical Recognition

So why did it take more than fifty years for historians to turn their attention to the proliferation of early postwar Jewish research on the Holocaust? One explanation is the short-lived and transitional nature of most of these initiatives, due in some cases to their inability to attain financial stability. For the most part the rank and file of survivors active in documentation work were often on the move. Once they relocated permanently and established "normal" lives, their day-to-day obligations, in many cases to sustain their newly founded families, often precluded full-time research. By the mid-1950s, only a handful of individuals continued their research on a professional basis, explicitly turning away from documentation of events and toward historical analysis: at Yad Vashem, Joseph Kermisz, Nachman Blumental, and Rachel Auerbach; in New York City, Isaiah Trunk at the YIVO Institute and Philip Friedman at Columbia University; in Paris, Joseph Billig at the CDJC and Léon Poliakov at the CNRS; in Warsaw, Artur Eisenbach at the Jewish Historical Institute; in London, Alfred Wiener; and in West Germany, Joseph Wulf as an independent scholar. Simon Wiesenthal in Austria and Towia Frydman in Israel dedicated themselves more to hunting down Nazi war criminals than to historical research. These individuals were among the few who, through great effort, developed the necessary standing to gain the attention of historians beyond the *She'erit Hapletah*.

A second explanation for the belated recognition of the Jewish historical commissions and documentation centers is the limited attention that contemporaries in the historical profession paid to their activities. Not survivors themselves, they took exception to the projects' popular and predominantly nonacademic structure, their largely amateur workforce, and the suspiciously personal motivation of the documentarians. Most commission activists saw their personal experiences as victims of Nazi persecution as both a source of obligation and a qualification for their work. Professional historians such as Philip Friedman were more likely to question whether survivors could be "objective" about the Holocaust. Thus Friedman insisted on the imperative to scrupulously monitor the quality of testimonies and questionnaires in order to avoid distortions of the historical truth in a flood of emotionally tainted accounts.[5] When he surveyed the postwar documentation activities for an international conference on the Second World War at the Netherlands Institute of War Documentation in Amsterdam in September 1950 (at which the prominent British historian Arnold J. Toynbee also participated), Friedman classified research on the Jewish catastrophe as "still in a prescientific stage."[6]

This would change only when the process of assembling comprehensive documentation had been concluded and the materials were made available to researchers through catalogues and accessible archives. While Friedman hoped that more professional historians would join the efforts to research the Jewish tragedy, he thought that survivors would still have leading roles to play once Holocaust research entered its "scientific stage." Other historians in the United States, Germany, and Israel passed harsher judgments. They appreciated survivors' efforts to collect materials and to record and chronicle recent events, but doubted that ordinary commission workers could reach the more abstract and analytical perspective that distinguished historiography from documentation.

Notably, Salo W. Baron, founding father of the academic study of Jewish history in the United States, harbored some skepticism regarding the historical objectivity of the survivor initiatives, even though he maintained contact with, and was generally sympathetic to, these efforts. In addition to testifying at the Eichmann trial in 1961, Baron demonstrated his professional concern for the European Jewish catastrophe as one of the founders of the Conference on Jewish Relations and as the editor of its periodical *Jewish Social Studies*, which became a primary forum for the publication of Holocaust-related research in English.[7] He also played a seminal role in the postwar restitution of Jewish cultural treasures as the chairman of Jewish Cultural Reconstruction Inc.[8] Baron valued historical inquiry into and the teaching of the catastrophe of European Jews, even if—in choosing other topics as his own areas of research—he left this task to others. Of particular relevance, Baron was instrumental in bringing Philip Friedman, his former student at the Jewish Teachers' Seminary in Vienna, to New York in 1948 and providing him with a position as adjunct professor at Columbia University to teach Jewish history courses that included the Holocaust.[9] In an introduction to a posthumous collection of Friedman's essays, published in 1980, Baron credited Friedman as "the chief founder of a new discipline in Jewish studies."[10]

Nonetheless, twenty years earlier—in a preface to the first bibliographical survey of writings about the Holocaust, edited by Friedman and the Lithuanian-born international lawyer Jacob Robinson—Baron had suggested that despite the glut of works chronicling the Holocaust, it might be premature to begin in-depth analysis of the event: "Does historical research benefit more from direct observation interlaced with much hearsay by contemporaries or from proper historical perspective, which is possible only after a passage of time?" This "perennial and never fully resolved" question, Baron observed, had particular relevance to early postwar writing on the Holocaust: "We have the record of an overwhelming plethora of eyewitness accounts, documentary evidence from archival collections, and observations by well-informed contemporaries. On the other hand, these more or less reliable records have to contend with an even larger mass of ill-informed, purely emotional outpourings, often reflecting personal biases rather than facts."[11] Baron recognized Friedman and Robinson's "deep-rooted desire for historic objectivity," especially given Friedman's personal experiences as a survivor and Robinson's arduous escape from Lithuania to the United States in 1940 via the Soviet Union, Romania, Yugoslavia, France, and Portugal. Indeed, Baron credited Friedman's scholarly credentials for the editors' success in treating "these tragic events, the most sanguinary in the many bloodstained annals of the Jewish people, with sufficient scholarly impartiality to lay the ground for all future detailed historical researches." But Baron could not say the same for the documentation endeavors as a whole. The time was not yet ripe for historical objectivity on the recent European catastrophe: "Generally speaking, fifteen years are not long enough to secure the necessary detachment and sense of proportion. Moreover, a generation that has gone through that extraordinary traumatic experience cannot completely divorce itself from its own painful recollections and look upon the Holocaust from an Archimedean standpoint outside of its own turbulent arena."[12]

Lucy S. Dawidowicz, who herself had observed and even worked with members of the historical commission in Munich, had similar misgivings. In her 1981 book *The Holocaust and the Historians*, she acknowledged that survivors had "lived through experiences beyond the conception of most men and women, and those extraordinary experiences have deepened their understanding and broadened the range of their vision." Still, she thought that

> survivor chroniclers can seldom transmit more than their individual circumscribed experiences, however harrowing, however extraordinary; they can seldom transcend their own suffering and bereavement. For few survivors had an overview of the events beyond their immediate experience. . . . Survivor-chroniclers, caught up in the whirlwind of history, were so buffeted by its winds that they could not chart the storm's course, measure its velocity, assess the damage it wrought.[13]

For this reason, she argued, survivors who try to write history—rather than a chronicle of their experiences—must, "despite the authority of their own experience, have recourse to documents, and they must subject these documents, even their own accounts, to the rigors of critical historical method." Unlike a chronicle, history "demands a distance that only the remove of time or space can provide." Because the history of the Holocaust presented such extreme demands, Dawidowicz thought that only a few survivors might be able to achieve the necessary distance "by an act of will, by the imposition of discipline over self."[14]

Not surprisingly, perhaps, non-Jewish historians in the Federal Republic of Germany failed to appreciate the act of collecting and documenting by survivors, let alone their ability to research the events they had endured. Although all Jewish historical commissions in Germany had dissolved in 1949 and their researchers had subsequently left, Joseph Wulf, who returned to Germany as an immigrant and settled in West Berlin in 1952, carried on their legacy as the only Jewish historian. While he had no formal training in history, Wulf researched and wrote as a historian rather than as a survivor. He took meticulous care never to use his personal experiences or to present himself to his audience as a witness. Indeed he adopted a document-based approach as the most neutral and unbiased way to present the crimes of the Nazi regime.[15] Nonetheless, many of the first generation of German historians to research the recent German past sharply criticized Wulf as "unscholarly." As historian Nicolas Berg recently observed, "The unchallenged logic that dominated the German discourse in the late 1950s and early 1960s held that Jews who survived the Holocaust were a priori unable to adopt an objective line."[16] Thus, Hans-Guenther Seraphim, in reviewing Poliakov and Wulf's 1955 study *Das Dritte Reich und die Juden*, claimed that it would take "super-human objectivity" for a "Jew to write the history of this persecution of the Jews."[17]

The Institute for Contemporary History (Institut für Zeitgeschichte), founded in 1949 in Munich, was largely responsible for making West Germany a center of academic research on the Third Reich by the early 1950s. Most of the historians who began their careers after the war and were influenced by the institute, among them Martin Broszat, Thilo Vogelsang, and Andreas Hillgruber, had grown up in Nazi Germany and served in the German army. Ironically, they criticized Wulf's work on the grounds that he had participated in the events he sought to analyze, while never applying their criteria for historical impartiality to themselves. Further, the fact that Wulf's works demonstrated the involvement in the Nazi regime of individuals from all levels of German society—many of whom held positions in the new Federal Republic—was widely seen as evidence that the Jewish historian wanted to settle scores with the Germans.[18]

In a further irony, even survivors who immigrated to Israel encountered mistrust from those who began Holocaust research as part of Yad Vashem in the mid-1950s. Historian Ben-Zion Dinur, Yad Vashem's first director (1953–1959), viewed the Holocaust, although unprecedented in its magnitude, as the outcome of a dialectical historical pattern that had characterized the Jewish nation's millennia-long struggle for existence in exile: successive periods of thriving and consolidation for the Jewish Diaspora communities, each ended by periods of destruction and violence caused by non-Jews' archetypical antipathy to Jews—a pattern that ultimately doomed any attempt to establish a prolonged Jewish existence among non-Jews.[19] Just as this struggle could only be ended by Jewish sovereignty, the State of Israel was the only place, according to Dinur, where Jews were independent and distanced enough from the Holocaust to objectively study and commemorate the event. Thus Dinur aspired to make Holocaust research in Israel an academic field under the auspices of the Hebrew University, to be carried out by his students, not by the survivor historians who had recently arrived in Israel. For the most part devoted amateurs, they had oriented their projects toward eastern European models of Jewish scholarship. Dinur, by contrast, was trained in German academic methods, even though he was Ukrainian-born and never received a doctorate. German-style *Wissenschaft* was not only the standard for Dinur, but it also dominated the Hebrew University at the time, since virtually all of its founders shared this academic background.[20]

Thus while the documentation initiatives in Europe provided invaluable resources for Yad Vashem's still nascent archives, their activists generally did not continue their work within the institution's framework. Dinur and the Yad Vashem directorate believed that the witnesses' emotional ties to the Holocaust and, in most cases, their lack of professional training in historical research made them unsuited for scholarly work on this subject. Only the most prominent CŻKH affiliates who immigrated to Israel found employment at Yad Vashem: Joseph Kermisz as director of the archives, Nachman Blumental as researcher and editor, and Rachel Auerbach as head of the Testimony Division established in Tel Aviv in 1954.[21] Yet Dinur and his colleges tended to leave actual research on the Holocaust to young professionals who had not themselves been witnesses and harbored skepticism about the value of survivor testimony, which hardly counted in

Yad Vashem's research.²² This led to acrimony between the memorial's leadership and the survivors among its staff, who enjoyed the support of parts of the broader Israeli public, provoking public confrontations in the late 1950s. Agitation by Auerbach, Kermisz, and Blumental, joined by landsmanshaftn and survivors' organizations, began in the spring of 1958, culminating in Dinur's resignation as director in March 1959. Thereafter, the survivors had a stronger position in the institution's decision-making processes.²³

Under the impact of the Eichmann trial in 1961, which raised public awareness of both the role of the witness and the effectiveness of oral testimony in presenting the history of the Holocaust, academic historians in Israel began to value oral documentation. After the trial, the Hebrew University's work on the history of the Jewish labor movement and the Jewish community in prestate Israel reflected this recognition of oral testimony as a vehicle for understanding past events.²⁴ In the long run, what Israeli historian Dan Michman has termed an "Israeli school" of Holocaust research developed, which studied Jewish communities under Nazi rule and the Jewish responses to persecution from an internal perspective, based on both Jewish testimony and perpetrator documentation.²⁵ Thus Israeli Holocaust research adopted a perspective on the Holocaust that was similar to that of the postwar commissions in its focus on a Jewish perspective on the persecutions, on Jewish responses, and particularly on Jewish resistance, while not ignoring the actions and ideology of the perpetrators. Yet this change was due less to any continuity in the work of former commission workers in Israel and their connections with historians trained at Israeli universities than it was a product of developments in Israeli society in the 1960s and 1970s.²⁶

These examples show that the skepticism with which professional historians greeted the documentation projects of the early postwar years should be understood in part as a conflict over who "owned" the history of the Holocaust as it would be written: those with firsthand experiences but without professional skills or those with academic training in the historical profession but no direct experiences of the historical events.

A third factor to be considered in understanding historians' belated reception of the postwar Jewish documentation initiatives lies mainly with the dynamics and overall development of the academic field of Holocaust studies. The Jewish historical commissions and documentation centers, as this book has shown, used research techniques, approaches, and perspectives that were anathema to professional historians of the day. Indeed, they would enter the mainstream of academic Holocaust research only decades later. Not only did the postwar activists study a past too contemporary to be "historicized," but they also wrote the history of the mass murder of European Jews "from below" and from the periphery of the Third Reich. By focusing primarily on local manifestations and on the actions of perpetrators at the periphery of the Nazi regime, they sought to understand the power structure, ideology, and policies at its center. Concentrating on the victim experience, they drew on a broad array of Jewish sources, most importantly eyewitness testimony, which they contextualized using perpetrator sources. Thus they advocated the use of testimony as a way to focus on the experiences of "ordinary" Jews, as well as the integration of memory with the historical narrative at a time when these ideas were far from accepted in historical scholarship. They were also prescient in their openness to social history and interdisciplinarity, as well as in their use of innovative sources, which allowed them to write what later historians would call *Alltagsgeschichte*, the history of everyday Jewish life and death under the Nazi regime. Thus the survivor historians anticipated many still-current debates regarding such issues as the relative value for scholars of victim testimony and of individual memory versus "objective" administrative sources left behind by the perpetrators, the overall place of the Holocaust in Jewish history and in history more generally, and the universal or specifically Jewish implications of that cataclysm.

Yet for several decades after its publication in 1961, Raul Hilberg's foundational 1,300-page masterpiece *The Destruction of the European Jews* set the standard for Holocaust historiography in North America and Europe. Hilberg's study differed from the commissions' endeavors in three decisive ways. First, in Hilberg's own words, it took a "top-down approach,"[27] focusing on the regime's center and its organizational structures as they determined its policies toward the Jews of Europe. Second, Hilberg (who was trained as a political scientist) explicitly saw his work as within the fields of German and European history, not as a contribution to Jewish history, just as his book—despite its title—was not about the Jews but about their murderers. He placed the perpetrators at the center and used German sources assembled by the Allies in support of the Nuremberg trials of German war criminals. Perpetrator documents, not victim testimony, provided the lens through which Hilberg explored Jewish suffering.[28] Third, Hilberg had some difficulty convincing his advisor at Columbia University, Franz Neumann—himself the author of the first structural analysis of the Third Reich[29]—that the Final Solution was a topic worthy of research and that it would not ruin his academic career. After its publication—preceded by rejections from several prestigious academic presses in the United States, as well as from Yad Vashem—Hilberg's monumental study began the gradual emergence of Holocaust studies as a highly respected *academic* field of interdisciplinary research and teaching.[30]

Before he began his research, Raul Hilberg (who escaped the German occupation of Austria to the United States at age thirteen) had read Léon Poliakov's pioneering 1951 *Bréviaire de la haine* (published in English in 1954 as *Harvest of Hate*). The fact that this book—alone among the numerous commission publications—received significant attention beyond the survivors' own circles was surely due to its deviation from the usual local focus and "bottom-up approach." Instead, Poliakov outlined the Nazi regime's policies toward the European Jews and proposed the Nazis' hatred of Jews as a general explanation for the genocide. He also cited German sources from the archives of the International Military Tribunal at

Nuremberg, but hardly any victim testimony. Although in many respects Poliakov's work introduced the perspectives that would come to dominate the academic study of the Holocaust, Hilberg rejected its explanation: the bureaucratic mentality of thousands of German officials, not hatred, had produced the Final Solution.[31]

Before the publication of his pathbreaking work, Hilberg had become acquainted with Philip Friedman, who in January 1955 had replaced Salo Baron on his dissertation defense committee. Forty years later, when Hilberg wrote his autobiography, his only description of Friedman was: "A survivor, marginally employed as a lecturer in history by the university. He was interested in the Jewish scene in Poland and hoped to write a book about ghettos. It did not come to that because he died early, before undertaking the project."[32] This passage suggests at least a lack of either knowledge or interest regarding both Friedman's pre- and postwar work and the achievements of the historical commissions. One can surmise that the reason Hilberg gave some credit to Poliakov's work but ignored Friedman's publications was that *La Bréviaire de la haine* was the first synthesized overview of the development of the Final Solution. Although their conclusions differed, both Poliakov and Hilberg based their studies of Jewish suffering almost entirely on German sources. Until recently, this focus on the perpetrators, the use of German documents, and the categorizing of the Holocaust as part of German or European rather than as Jewish history remained the dominant trends in German and Anglo-American historiography on the Third Reich and the Holocaust.

It is certainly not surprising that the academic study of the Third Reich's mass murder of the Jews began by analyzing the regime's central figures and institutions—as did the Allied war crime trials held at Nuremberg between 1945 and 1949, which set the stage for a perpetrator-focused historiography. Such a perspective was a crucial prerequisite to understanding the connections between the regime's inner workings, power structures, and means of communications, and the deaths of millions of human beings. The activists of the Jewish documentation initiatives themselves knew that they would have to go beyond the experiences of the victims on the regime's periphery in order to fully understand the Nazi machinery of persecution and mass murder. Therefore they indefatigably collected—and tried to match—both perpetrator documentation and victim testimony. Yet from today's perspective it is surprising that for so long subsequent generations of academic historians who laid out in detail the Nazi regime's policies toward the Jews and the actions, motivations, and ideological backgrounds of the perpetrators did so almost entirely *at the expense* of the voices of the Nazis' victims.

Not until the last decade of the twentieth century did historians begin to write scholarly accounts of the Nazi mass murder of European Jews which considered both perpetrator and victim perspectives, describing Nazi policies "from above" *and* Jewish experiences and responses "from below." A critical event precipitating this turn—apart from the broader movement toward writing social history, microhistory, and *Alltagsgeschichte* within the historical profession in the 1970s and 1980s—was a historiographic debate in 1987–1988 between Martin Broszat and Saul Friedländer over the Third Reich and the Holocaust.[33] Broszat had sparked the controversy by juxtaposing the "mythical memory" of the victims and their families against "rational" German historical scholarship.[34] Friedländer returned to this issue in 1997 in the introduction to the first volume of his monumental study *Nazi Germany and the Jews*: "It is too often forgotten that Nazi attitudes and policies cannot be fully assessed without knowledge of the lives and indeed feelings of the Jewish men, women, and children themselves." Accordingly, in this work Friedländer approached the Holocaust with what he termed an "integrated framework" that wove together the perspective of the perpetrators, the attitudes of the surrounding societies, and the experiences of the Jews to create a comprehensive narrative. In the author's own explanation, "At each stage in the description of the evolving Nazi policies and the attitudes of German and European societies as they impinge on the evolution of those policies, the fate, the attitudes, and sometimes the initiatives of the victims are given major importance." For Friedländer, the anti-Jewish policies implemented from the top could not be understood without the words of victims on the ground. "For it is their voices that reveal what was known and what *could* be known; theirs were the only voices that conveyed both the clarity of insight and the total blindness of human beings confronted with an entirely new and utterly horrifying reality. The constant presence of the victims in this book, while historically essential in itself, is also meant to put the Nazis' actions into full perspective."[35] In the second volume, published in 2007, Friedländer continued to insist that the "history of the Holocaust should be both an integrative and an integrated history."[36]

Friedländer's approach resonated with the works of historians such as Renée Poznanski and Marion Kaplan who arrived at similar conclusions at about the same time.[37] Since then, Jewish responses to Nazi persecution—as illuminated by a great variety of sources created by Jews during and after the war—has emerged as a central topic of Holocaust research.[38] Several Holocaust historians who previously had focused on *perpetrator* history—for example, Christopher Browning, Omer Bartov, and the late Hilberg himself—have turned their attention to the victims' perspectives, subjecting their testimony to the same rigorous source criticism as they would perpetrator documents.[39] Moreover, some of the early postwar testimony collected by the Jewish historical commissions has guided historians to new aspects of Holocaust research. This is how Jan T. Gross discovered the July 1941 mass murder by ethnic Polish inhabitants of Jedwabne of their Jewish neighbors. Gross's monograph *Neighbors* thus opened up for research and fierce public debate the topic of interethnic violence in the shadow of the German occupation.[40]

The growing interest in victims does not mean that historians have realized the full potential of survivors as a historical source. Omer Bartov, for example, has recently called for a more extensive use of "testimony" in the reconstruction of the Holocaust. Under this category he includes such varied evidence as personal accounts and diaries, whether contemporaneous or retrospective; postwar interviews; written, oral, audio, and videotaped testimonies; courtroom witness transcripts; and memoirs by victims, perpetrators, and those usually referred to as bystanders. Such materials "bring into history events that would otherwise remain completely unknown," given their absence from the largely perpetrator-created documents usually found in archives. More specifically, they offer both a "factual correction to official accounts" and an alternate vantage point on events known from conventional documentation. Not least, according to Bartov, they provide insights into the "lives and minds of men, women, and children who experienced the events and, thus, tell us much more than any official document about the mental landscape of the period, the psychology of the protagonists, and the views and perceptions of others."

Although Bartov expects historians to treat survivor documents "with the same care and suspicion as any other piece of evidence pulled out of an archive," they also deserve "the same respect as yet another more or less important piece in the puzzle of the past." Indeed, Bartov seems to suggest that historians have a certain moral obligation to the historical actors who left behind evidence with the intent "that what they experienced and saw and remembered would not be forgotten. Historians have largely betrayed these witnesses. By now the vast majority of them are dead. But their recorded accounts can and should still be used, not merely in order to respect those who left them behind, but to set the historical record straight."[41]

Bartov's words echo the perspectives and practices formulated six decades earlier by the Jewish documentation initiatives. Does this suggest that Holocaust historiography has come full circle and that we can now welcome the postwar efforts of the survivor historians into the academic mainstream? Clearly the works compiled by the commission activists should not be equated with the scholarship of later historians who have dedicated decades of their lives to studying the Holocaust with the advantages of their own and others' extensive research, guided by the perspective and wisdom of hindsight. Nonetheless, the survivor documentarians laid out a remarkable long-term agenda for historians to follow, one that encompasses the questions to be asked, the themes to be covered, the issues to be addressed, and the source materials most relevant to understanding the Holocaust.

The Enduring Vision: Archives of a Lost Jewish World and Its Surviving Remnant

The most palpable and enduring legacy of survivors' efforts to document a horrific chapter in human history was an "archive of the Holocaust" that constitutes the core of the major Holocaust research institutions in Europe and Israel: the Center of Contemporary Jewish Documentation which is part of the Mémorial de la

Shoah in Paris, the Jewish Historical Institute in Warsaw, the Wiener Library in London, and Yad Vashem in Jerusalem. In the United States the YIVO Institute in New York houses important collections from the DP camps as well as the personal papers of some of the activists who left Poland for the United States, including Philip Friedman, Isaiah Trunk, and others. By providing raw material for later historians and other scholars, this archive has significantly shaped their ever deeper knowledge and understanding, and that of the wider public, of the catastrophe from which it emerged. This, after all, was the survivor documentarians' hope and intent.

Given the circumstances of its creation, the postwar "Holocaust archive" inevitably falls short of current archival standards, which, for example, expect control of the provenance and original order of documents and strive for coherent organization and completeness.[42] Beginning almost at the moment of liberation, these highly improvised Jewish initiatives were undertaken in extremis by traumatized survivors facing severe material want and unstable and insecure living conditions, troubled by anxieties over their past, present, and future. Moreover, while the documentation activists certainly sought to establish archival repositories that would provide an evidential foundation for future historical research, they also sought to commemorate the dead, educate future generations, combat anti-Semitism, secure Jewish rights, bring the perpetrators to justice, and register Jews' contribution to anti-Nazi resistance. Finally, while a few of the survivors possessed a trained historian's familiarity with archives, none were professional archivists. Intensely aware of both the destruction wrought by the war and the evanescence of the postwar moment—and with no sophisticated acquisition guidelines—they urgently collected every scrap of paper and material object relating to the Jewish catastrophe that they could get their hands on. By the same token, they viewed *every* Jew to emerge alive, regardless of how he or she had survived, as a "piece of history," a living document and a repository of memory whose story merited recording.

Indeed, with extraordinary foresight and audacity, the survivor documentarians believed that any vestige of the past could be relevant to later researchers who sought to comprehend in all its dimensions the gigantic and unprecedented catastrophe that had annihilated two-thirds of European Jewry. Jewish historical commissions and documentation centers thus *succeeded* in compiling a comprehensive and diverse collection of documents pertaining to the actions of the perpetrators and their collaborators, the experiences and responses of the victims, and the behavior of bystanders. Some of these sources, generated in the course of events, were not intended for future generations—indeed, many Nazi records were slated for destruction—but they were more or less accidentally spared. Other sources were created with an enduring purpose, such as to transmit to posterity the truth about horrific events as they were unfolding, to record a memory, or to commemorate the recently dead, most of whom lacked gravestones. The commissions' archival endeavors transcended traditional notions of "documents" as the records of bureaucratic institutions and public figures. Such personal artifacts as diaries, memoirs, letters, questionnaires, and testimonies—from "ordinary" women and men, children and youth, not just from communal leaders—could provide valuable insights into the minds, emotions, and actions of individuals who experienced firsthand the horrendous events. Thus the amateur archivists collected literary and poetic creations and music—even sound recordings of survivors singing ghetto and camp songs from memory—in anticipation that these materials would illuminate not only a ghastly historical reality but also how individuals and groups confronting those events had responded. Their interest in language as documentary evidence also led them to compile annotated glossaries of words and expressions that originated in ghettos and camps, so that future generations of historians as well as others who had not personally endured the Holocaust might understand this peculiar patois of horror and the historical reality it reflected. Photographs—mainly taken by perpetrators, but also by victims and bystanders—captured a visual record of a now destroyed Jewish world, in addition to providing evidence of unspeakable crimes.

The largely self-conscious nature of the Jewish documentation efforts came to the fore first and foremost in such activities as the solicitation of postwar testimonies, the creation and distribution of survivor questionnaires, and the collecting of prewar or wartime songs written down and sometimes performed for recording. Most in charge of collection initiatives rejected the notion that one type of documentation was intrinsically more authoritative than another, although they realized that German documents could not be taken at face value. While they believed that at times of extreme violence they were more likely to find truth in the voices of the victims than in those of the instigators and perpetrators of that violence, they knew that survivor stories could contain many inaccuracies. Indeed, they seem to have anticipated the concerns regarding the limits of postwar testimony, which Raul Hilberg would voice five decades later: namely, that those who had survived the catastrophe were no random sample of the entire Jewish collective that the Nazis had destroyed, that the faction of survivors who testified were not representative of the *She'erit Hapletah* as a whole, and that their accounts might be a random sample of all their experiences.[43] Ultimately the survivor historians hoped to find the closest approximation of the truth about an event by gathering the accounts of a critical mass of witnesses on a great variety of experiences and then comparing them, both among themselves and against perpetrator sources.

The documentation initiatives demonstrated an understanding of the European, transnational dimension of the Holocaust in December 1947 when representatives from thirteen nations gathered in Paris to frame the future direction of their work. Nonetheless, most of the initiatives themselves operated within distinctly national frameworks and territorial boundaries. For Poland and France this meant a dual focus on the crimes of the German occupiers and their collaborators as well as on the Jewish tragedy within the territory of the respective countries, and on the fate of Jewish citizens and residents who had been deported or displaced elsewhere. In each case, the documentation activity occurred in the same territory where the anti-Jewish policies were made or carried out. Thus it is not surprising that products of the French and Polish documentation efforts ended up in archives in those countries, where their collections on the Jewish tragedy could become part of the French or Polish national narrative.

The initiatives operating within the zones of occupied Germany were an exception to this rule. First, the Allied authorities were already addressing the crimes of the perpetrators and their collaborators through trials and denazification procedures. Moreover, the DP initiatives focused almost entirely on survivors from various eastern European countries who found themselves on German soil by force of circumstance; their stories related primarily to events that had occurred in their countries of origin or in the camps where they had been transported. Similarly, the Austrian commissions focused especially on interviewing survivor DPs who had suffered crimes committed in eastern Europe by Austrian nationals. Italy figured hardly at all in the partisan-run initiatives that sprang up there. The attenuated bonds between the DP initiatives and their accidental place of sojourn in occupied Germany facilitated the eventual removal of their materials to Israel, a new nation that consciously rejected any connection with the site of the Jewish cataclysm. In Israel, these materials would serve the study of traumatic events that happened "there," in Europe, in the Diaspora.

Even if the Jewish historical commissions and documentation centers together managed to assemble impressive, focused yet wide-ranging archival collections, their multifarious activities did not result in what we might call a complete archive. The survivor documentarians themselves were acutely aware that many aspects of the Holocaust would never be known. As an event characterized by destruction and annihilation, the Holocaust could by its very nature not be fully documented. Or rather, the incompleteness of the record was itself ample evidence of the void it had created. The majority of victims were murdered without leaving a trace, much less a paper trail. The destruction of entire families and communities left no one to remember them and write down their stories. To this extent the Nazis were successful in their genocidal ambition to erase all evidence of the Jewish people's existence.[44] Even a collective effort to mine the memories of the small minority of European Jews who survived could produce only an incomplete record of the victims. Perpetrator sources were incomplete for reasons that went beyond the Germans' often successful efforts to destroy the evidence of their crimes. In particular, the intentional use of coded terminology and euphemistic language meant that German documents often obscured historical reality. Under these circumstances, the Jewish documentarians sought to gather every piece of perpetrator evidence they could lay their hands on.

Scholars' use of the abundant materials collected by postwar Jewish documentarians has so far been selective, focusing largely on perpetrator documents and the collections compiled by DP camp commissions on the lives of the surviving remnant in the postwar period. The thousands of survivor testimonies and questionnaires still await their use by historians and other scholars. Captured at a unique moment in time when survivors' memories of the recent past were still vivid, raw, immediate, and unmediated, these testimonies have the potential to greatly enrich the narratives of the Holocaust and its immediate aftermath. In particular, these records would provide an invaluable supplement to the now familiar voices of survivors that have come to us many years later through published memoirs or recorded testimony projects. At a time when the generation of survivors is dwindling in numbers, it is all the more important that scholars and the wider public acknowledge and fully use the records that the postwar documentarians so carefully assembled under extreme conditions soon after the catastrophe.

Appendix

MAJOR PARTICIPANTS IN THE JEWISH HISTORICAL COMMISSIONS AND DOCUMENTATION CENTERS

This list of short biographies includes a majority of the most prominent individuals active in the Jewish historical commissions in France, Poland, Germany, Austria, and Italy. The biographies are necessarily fragmentary because of a paucity of information. Few of these activists appear in bibliographical references. Academic Holocaust studies did not recognize their work, nor did they hold public office in Europe, the United States, or Israel. Information is especially scarce for the many female commission workers. Even basic dates or births and deaths are missing for some, and often the details of wartime survival in particular remain unclear.[1]

Aminado, Don (Aminad Petrovich, Aminadov Peisakhovitch Shpoliansky) (1888–1957): Russian Jewish poet and satirist, born in Elizavetgrad in the Kherson Province of the Russian Empire to a lower-middle-class family. Trained in law at the University of Odessa, he came to France in 1920 and contributed as a journalist to the *Tribune Juive* in Paris (1920–1924). In the 1920s and 1930s he became a popular figure in the Russian (Jewish) émigré community and beyond and was awarded the Légion d'honneur in 1935 for his cultural activities. After surviving the Second World War in Montpellier and Aix-les-Bains, he joined the CDJC staff in Paris in 1945.

Asz, Menachem (Marek): Founding member and first secretary of the Jewish historical commission in Lublin in the summer of 1944 and a communist member of the Central Committee of Polish Jews. In 1946 he left Poland for the DP camps in the U.S. Zone of Germany, where he was active in the Frankfurt branch of the Central Historical Commission in Munich.

Auerbach, Rachel (1903–1976): Born in Łanowce, Galicia, then in the Austro-Hungarian Empire, today in Ukraine; family moved to Lvov, where Auerbach studied psychology and philosophy and became active as a journalist and editor of the

Yiddish literary journal *Tsushtayer* in Lvov. In 1933 she moved to Warsaw, where she published in the Yiddish and Polish press on literary and educational topics. In September 1939, Emanuel Ringelblum invited her to help organize soup kitchens in Warsaw; in 1941 he recruited her for his secret Oyneg Shabes archive, where she contributed a study on soup kitchens and the fight against hunger in the ghetto and recorded the testimony of a Treblinka escapee in 1942. In March 1943 she fled the Warsaw ghetto and survived on the "Aryan side" under a false identity. While working as a courier for the Jewish underground, she recorded her experiences in essays and a diary. After the liberation, Auerbach was active in the Central Jewish Historical Commission in Poland. She immigrated to Israel in 1950 and in 1954 became head of Yad Vashem's oral history department. She was instrumental in choosing the Jewish witnesses for the Eichmann trial and appeared as a witness herself.

Bakalczuk (Felin), Mejlech (1896–1960): Born in Sernik, Polesia, then in the Russian Empire, today in Belarus. Bakalczuk studied at the University of Kiev and prior to the Second World War worked as a teacher at Hebrew and Yiddish schools in Bogoduchov, Dombrovitz and Pinsk and as an author of literary and pedagogic texts. He survived the war as a partisan in Soviet Union and began collecting documents on his own. Briefly settling in Lvov after the war, Bakalczuk soon moved to Poland, where he was a founding member of the Central Jewish Historical Commission in Lublin. He also contributed to *Dos Naye Lebn* in Lodz. In late 1945 he left Poland for the U.S. Zone of Austria. In the Bindermichl DP camp near Linz, he founded a historical commission and a school for DP children; he also was the editor of *Ojfgang*. In October 1947, Bakalczuk left for Palestine, donating his collection to Yad Vashem. In 1948 he immigrated to South Africa, where he died in Johannesburg.

Bakalczuk, Neche, née Tabachowicz (1908–1953): Born in Kaltinėnai, then in the Russian Empire, now in Lithuania; teacher and Poale Zion activist. After surviving the Stutthof concentration camp, she briefly stayed in Lodz, before leaving for the DP camps in the U.S. Zone of Austria in 1946. In the Bindermichl DP camp she married Mejlech Bakalczuk and became the secretary of the historical commission as well as the editorial secretary of *Ojfgang*. She was also active in building Jewish schools in the camp. With her husband, she left for Palestine in 1947 and the following year immigrated to South Africa, where she died in Johannesburg.

Bauer, André (1904–1943): Born in Paris to a respected family of rabbis and communal leaders; trained as a rabbi and banker. In the 1930s he was the president of the Rue Copernic reform community in Paris. Bauer played a formative role in the establishment in 1941 of the Union Générale des Israélites de France (UGIF), whose vice president he served as, in the hope that a central representative body would be able to mitigate the anti-Jewish actions of the Vichy government. In July

1943 the Gestapo arrested him; that December he was deported to Auschwitz and murdered, together with his wife and four children.

Bauminger, Leon (Arie) (1913–2002): Born in Krakow; earned a doctorate from the University of Warsaw. Bauminger was a founding member of the Central Jewish Historical Commission in Lublin and its first secretary. In 1947 he immigrated to Palestine, where he worked as a high school teacher and was active in Holocaust education and commemoration. After 1949 he worked for the Israeli Ministry of Education and Culture and in 1960 became administrative director of Yad Vashem.

Bernheim, Léonce (1886–1944): Born in France; a lawyer and director of the French ORT prior to the Second World War. A Zionist, Bernheim served as honorary president of the Zionist Youth Movement (MJS) and was a founding member of CDJC in Grenoble. He died at Auschwitz in December 1944.

Billig, Joseph (Ossip) (1901–1994): Born in St. Petersburg; after fleeing the Russian Revolution for Germany in 1917, he received a doctorate in philosophy from the University of Berlin in 1929. With the Nazi rise to power, he left Germany for France, where he fought as a volunteer in the French Army. Captured by the Germans in June 1940, Billig spent five years in a POW camp in Danzig, where he was liberated by Soviet troops in April 1945. As a researcher at the CDJC and its representative at the Nuremberg trials, he copied several thousand documents relating to the Jews of France from the archives of the International Military Tribunal and the American Military Tribunal in 1946–1949.

Bitter, Marek (1902–1965): Survivor of the Warsaw ghetto and the Majdanek extermination camp and founder and first director of the historical commission in Lublin. As a communist politician, Bitter also served as secretary-general of the Central Committee of Polish Jews.

Blumental, Nachman (1905–1983): Born in Borszczów, Galicia, then in the Austro-Hungarian Empire, now in Ukraine; earned a master's degree in literature from the University of Warsaw; a teacher in Lublin until the outbreak of the Second World War. Blumental survived the war in hiding in Poland. He joined the Central Jewish Historical Commission in Lublin and became the first director of the Jewish Historical Institute in the years 1947–1948. In 1950 he left for Israel, where he was affiliated with the Ghetto Fighters House and editor of its periodical *Dapim le-Heker ha-Shoah ve-ha-Mered*, as well as a researcher at Yad Vashem and editor of *Yediot Yad Vashem*.

Borwicz (Borochowicz), Michał Maksymilian (1911–1987): Born in Krakow; studied Polish literature at the University of Krakow; a writer and journalist;

affiliated with the Poale Zion movement. After the German invasion he escaped to Soviet-controlled eastern Poland and settled in Lvov. Following the German occupation of Lvov at the end of June 1941, Borwicz was interned in the Janowska camp. In 1943 he escaped and commanded Polish socialist partisan units in the Jewish underground in Krakow. After the liberation he became the director of the Krakow branch of the Central Jewish Historical Commission. In 1947 Borwicz left for France, where he was director of the Centre d'Étude d'Histoire des Juifs Polonais in Paris between 1947 and 1952. In 1954 he received a doctorate in sociology from the Sorbonne.

Eber, Ada Adolfina (also Obler or Friedman): Born in Lvov, Galicia, now in Ukraine; received a doctorate in history from the University of Lvov. Eber survived in hiding in Lvov, where she had worked as a high school teacher. After the war she was active in the Central Jewish Historical Commission and married Philip Friedman. In 1946, with her husband, she left Poland and immigrated to the United States via the U.S. Zone of Germany and France in 1948.

Eisenbach, Artur (Ahron) (1906–1992): Born in Nowy Sącz, Galicia, then in the Austro-Hungarian Empire, today in Poland; studied at the Academy of Commerce in Krakow, the Jewish Teachers' Seminary in Vilna, and the Universities of Krakow and Warsaw (German and history). In 1935 he became a YIVO *aspirant* (trainee). At the University of Warsaw he was part of a young generation of Jewish historians around Meier Bałaban and Marceli Handelsman and part of the Yunger Historiker Krayz led by Raphael Mahler and Emanuel Ringelblum (whose sister he married). After surviving the war in the Soviet Union (while his wife and child were murdered by the Germans in Buczacz in 1942), he returned to Poland in May 1946 and became a member of the Warsaw branch of the Central Jewish Historical Commission. He remained in Poland and was affiliated with the Jewish Historical Institute in Warsaw, as head of the archives and as a researcher, as well as institute director in the years 1966–1968. He immigrated to Israel one year before his death.

Elberg, Jehuda (1912–2003): Born in Zgierz (near Lodz), then in the Russian Empire, today in Poland; trained as a rabbi, he also studied textile engineering and became a master weaver in Lodz. As part of the Jewish Fighting Organization, Elberg survived the Warsaw ghetto. After the liberation he was among the founders of the historical commission. A cofounder of the Jewish Writers' Union, Elberg was also a member of the Central Committee and the editorial board of *Dos Naye Lebn*, where he served as editorial secretary in 1944–1945. In 1946 he left for France, serving there as editorial secretary of *Kiyoum*. In 1948 Elberg immigrated to the United States, where he worked as a writer, social worker, and labor activist.

Feigenbaum, Moshe Yosef (Mojżesz Józef Fajgenbaum, Moyshe Yosef Faygenboym) (1908–1986): Born in Biała Podlaska, then in the Russian Empire, today in Poland; trained as an accountant. During the Second World War he survived the ghettos of Biała Podlaska and Międzyrzec Podlaski, escaped execution in 1942, and one year later escaped from a transport to Treblinka. For the rest of the war Feigenbaum hid in a bunker in Biała, where he began to write about the life of Jews under the Nazi regime. After the liberation he was affiliated with the historical commission in Lublin. In the fall of 1945 he left Poland for the U.S. Zone of Germany and cofounded the Central Historical Commission in Munich. In 1949 he immigrated to Israel.

Feldschuh-Safrin, Ruven (Ben-Shem) (1900–1980): Born in Buczacz, Galicia, then in the Austro-Hungarian Empire, today in Ukraine; earned a doctorate in philosophy and psychology from the University of Vienna. Affiliated with Hashomer Hatsair and later with Revisionism, Feldschuh-Safrin went to Palestine in 1919, where he was a member of the Jewish National Council. In the 1920s he returned to Europe, where he worked as a journalist. After surviving the war in Warsaw, he was active in the historical commission and the Jewish Writers' Union in Lublin. In 1945 he left for Palestine.

Fink, Jacques (Jacob-Israel Finkelstein) (1894–1955): Born in Novgorod-Seversk, then in the Russian Empire, today in Ukraine; journalist and engineer. He left for France in 1918 and was naturalized in 1930. Fink was active in the Poale Zion movement and in the immigrant organization Fédération des Sociétés Juives en Frace; he was also the president of the Association des Journalistes et Écrivains Juifs de France. After the liberation he became affiliated with the CDJC and was the editor of *Le Monde Juif*.

Friedman, Philip (1901–1960): Born in Lvov, Galicia, then in the Austro-Hungarian Empire, today in Ukraine. Friedman studied modern history at the University of Vienna, where in 1925 he received a doctoral degree for his dissertation, "The Struggle of the Galician Jews for their Equality, 1848–1868." From 1925 to 1939 he taught history in the high school of the Association of Jewish Schools in Lodz, and in 1938–1939 he also lectured at the Institute for Jewish Studies in Warsaw on the economic and social history of Polish Jews in the nineteenth century. After the German invasion of Poland he returned to Soviet-occupied Lvov. In 1940–1941 he was a senior researcher at the Ukrainian Academy of Sciences and headed the department of industry in the Institute of Economics. After the German occupation of Lvov in late June 1941 and the establishment of the ghetto there in December, Friedman and his wife and thirteen-year-old daughter moved in with Friedman's parents. After Friedman's wife and daughter were murdered in 1942, he went into hiding on the "Aryan side" until the liberation of the city by the Red Army in July 1944. In November 1944, as part of the repatriation of Polish citizens from the formerly Polish territories annexed by the Soviet Union, Friedman went to Lublin. In December 1944 he founded the Central Jewish Historical Commission in Lublin, serving as its first director. In the summer of 1946 he left

Poland for a brief sojourn in Paris, where he collaborated with the CDJC, then went to the U.S. Zone of Germany, where in September 1946 he became head of the American Jewish Joint Distribution Committee's Education and Culture Department in Munich. In 1948, after another brief stay in Paris, where he was affiliated with the CDJC, Friedman left Germany for the United States, where he became a lecturer in Jewish history at Columbia University and head of the Jewish Teachers' Institute in New York City. He was also affiliated with YIVO in New York and directed the compilation of a bibliography of Holocaust writings.

Frydman, Towia (Tuviah Friedman, Tobias Friedmann) (1922–2010): Born in Radom, Poland, to a middle-class family. He survived the city's ghetto and the Szkolna Street labor camp, which he escaped from in 1944. Posing as a gentile, he survived in the woods until the liberation in mid-January 1945. In the following months, Frydman arrested and interrogated suspected German war criminals for the Polish Ministry of Public Security in Gdańsk. In early 1946 he left Poland for Austria, where he directed a documentation center in Vienna. In 1952 he immigrated to Israel, where he continued to collect testimonies and briefly worked for Yad Vashem. In 1957 Frydman opened the Documentation Center for Nazi War Criminals in Haifa.

Fuchsman, Helen (née Radoszycka) (?–1993): Born in Warsaw; received a secular high school education and worked in her mother's business until she married in 1935. Fuchsman survived the Vilna ghetto, and after its liquidation she lived under a false identity together with her husband and young son. In 1945 she left Poland for the U.S. Zone of Austria, where she was active in the Jewish historical commission in Linz. In 1948 she immigrated to the United States.

Glaeser, Léo (1887–1944): Born in Riga; immigrated to France in 1907; trained as a lawyer. A key Fédération des Sociétés Juives de France (FSJF) activist since before the war, Glaeser worked with the Comité rue Amelot in Paris, which coordinated Jewish relief work in the face of the occupation. After escaping to the Southern Zone, in 1943 he became secretary-general of the FSJF and of the Comité général de défense. Glaeser was a founding member of the CDJC in Grenoble. In June 1944, he was arrested and shot by the Milice in Lyon.

Glube, Shmuel: Born in Turek, then in the Russian Empire, today in Poland; bookkeeper by training; communal activist before the war. Glube survived the Lodz ghetto and several camps in Poland. After his liberation near Lodz in January 1945, he worked with the Central Jewish Historical Commission, but left Poland in September 1945 for the U.S. Zone of Germany, where he was a founder and key activist of the Central Historical Commission in Munich. Glube immigrated to the United States in February 1948.

Godart, Justin (1871–1956): Born in Lyon and trained as a lawyer. During the Third Republic, Godart, a leader in the Radical Socialist Party, served as mayor of Lyon, senator of the Rhône Department, minister of labor, and minister of public health. Although not Jewish, Godart was sympathetic to the ideas of Zionism and founded the Franco-Palestine Committee in the interwar years. During the war he extended his help to Jewish resistance fighters, as well as to individual Jews. After the war he became a strong supporter of the CDJC and served as its honorary chairman. Godart also played a seminal role in the CDJC's campaign for the memorial.

Gottfarstein, Joseph (1902–1980): Born in Pren (Prienai), then in the Russian Empire, today in Lithuania; after attending the Jewish Teachers' Seminary in Kovno, studied philosophy at the University of Berlin. In 1926 Gottfarstein left for Paris, where he became active in the FSJF and worked as a writer and journalist. After surviving the war in Switzerland, he returned to Paris, where he was affiliated with the CDJC.

Grinberg, Ruven: In 1943, he became, together with Leo Glaeser, a co-leader of the FSJF. Grinberg was also president of the Comité général de défense, an umbrella organization of Jewish resistance fighters in the Southern Zone. He was a founding member of the CDJC.

Grüss (also Gris), Noe-Shloyme (1902–1985): Born in Kiełków, Galicia, then in the Austro-Hungarian Empire, today in Poland; teacher training at the University of Krakow; history teacher at secular Zionist Tarbut schools in Lida, Grodno, and Rovno; Yiddish journalist and editor. Grüss survived the war in exile in the Soviet Union and returned to Poland in 1945. He left Poland for Israel in 1947, but in 1952 he moved to Paris, where he worked as a teacher and as head of the Hebrew and Yiddish section of the National Library.

Hermann, Nahum (1899–1944): Born in Shargorod, then in the Russian Empire, today in Ukraine; journalist. An active Zionist, Hermann was a key figure of the Zionist Foundation Fund (Keren ha-Yesod) in France, as well as a founding member of the Grenoble documentation center. In January 1944 he was arrested in Limoges and murdered.

Hirschler, René (1905–1944): Born in Marseille; chief rabbi of Strasbourg and a prominent communal leader of Alsatian Jews before the war. Hirschler played an instrumental role in establishing two social welfare groups: in October 1940, the Commission Centrale des Organisations Juives d'Assistance (CCOJA), an umbrella organization for numerous Jewish welfare organizations, and in early 1942, the Aumônerie Général Israélite, which cared for Jews in French internment camps in the Southern Zone. He was an early supporter of the CDJC in Grenoble.

Arrested on December 22, 1943, Hirschler, along with his wife, was deported to Auschwitz and murdered in February 1944.

Hertz, Henri (1875–1966): Born to a family of Alsatian Jews in Nogent-sur-Seine; writer, poet, political journalist, and Zionist. He survived the war in the Southern Zone and was affiliated with the *Résistance* and the CDJC.

Hochberg-Mariańska, Maria (Miriam Hochberg-Peleg): Born on a farm near Krakow. Before the war, Hochberg-Mariańska—who had been too poor for university study—wrote children's stories and edited the children's supplement of a Krakow daily. She belonged to the Polish Socialist youth movement. During the German occupation she joined the Polish underground, first in the Krakow ghetto, then outside under a false identity. She also worked for Żegota, the Council for Aid to the Jews. After the war Hochberg-Mariańska worked with the Central Jewish Historical Commission, for which she collected children's testimonies. She immigrated to Israel in 1949 and worked for Yad Vashem.

Horowic, Cwi (1899–?): Born in Krakow; after a traditional Jewish education, he learned a succession of trades, from the fur trade to plumbing, but practiced none, instead living as an obscure writer. In the 1920s, as an adherent of the Poale Zion movement, Horowic immigrated to Palestine, where he helped establish the Socialist Party (Mifleget Poalim Sotsiyalistim; MPS). The British Mandatory powers soon forced him to leave the country (probably because of the party's communist connections). He returned to Poland via Turkey, Romania, and Germany (where he briefly studied at the Akademie für die Wissenschaft des Judentums in Berlin). For unknown reasons he served an extended prison sentence in Stanisławów. Horowic survived the war in the Soviet Union, where he fought in the Red Army. After returning to Poland, in 1947 he left for the British Zone of Germany, where he founded a historical commission in Göttingen. In 1949 he immigrated to Israel.

Hosiasson, Philippe (pseudonym Jacques Sabille) (1898–1978): Born in Odessa; studied art history and law at the University of Odessa and in Rome; painter and artist. After working as a designer for the Russian ballet in Berlin, Hossiason settled in Paris in 1924. He joined the CDJC after the war.

Kaganovitch (also Kahanovitch), Moshe (1909–?): Born in Ivye, then in the Russian Empire, now in Belarus; journalist for the *Tsayt* and *Vilner Tog* and the Warsaw-based *Der Moment* and *Undzer Vort*, among other papers. In 1943 he escaped from the Ivye ghetto and became a partisan. Between 1945 and 1949 Kaganowicz lived in Rome as a DP. In 1949 he left for Israel.

Kahn, Gaston (1889–?): Born in Wingersheim in Alsace; communal leader and writer, active in Jewish welfare. Kahn became general director of the Refugee Aid

Committee (CAR) in 1936, and then succeeded Raymond-Raoul Lambert as head of the UGIF. After surviving the war in hiding, Kahn joined the staff of the CDJC. He was also president of B'nai B'rith France.

Kaplan, Israel (1902–2003): Born in Volozhin, then in the Russian Empire, today in Belarus; master's degree in history from the University of Kovno, where he also worked as a Hebrew school teacher and a journalist. After surviving the war in the ghettos of Kovno and Riga and the concentration camps Kaiserwald (near Riga) and Dachau, he was liberated by American troops in southern Germany on a death march to Tyrol. Remaining in the U.S. Zone, Kaplan cofounded both the Central Historical Commission in Munich, serving as its director, and the biweekly Yiddish newspaper *Undzer Veg*. As a journalist he wrote for the DP newspapers and was the editor of *Fun Letstn Khurbn*. He lost his wife and daughter in the Holocaust but was reunited with his teenage son after the war. In 1949 Kaplan immigrated to Israel, where he worked as an author and teacher.

Kermisz, Joseph (Józef) (1907–2005): Born in Złotniki, Galicia, then in the Austro-Hungarian Empire, today in Ukraine; in 1937 earned a doctorate in history from the University of Warsaw, under the guidance of Meier Bałaban, with a thesis on the history of Lublin. He was also an affiliate of YIVO's Warsaw branch. In September 1939 Kermisz escaped to Soviet-occupied eastern Poland, where he worked as a history teacher. After surviving the war in hiding, in June 1944 he joined the Polish army, where he held the rank of captain. Kermisz was among the founders of the Central Jewish Historical Commission in Lublin in December 1944, and as of 1945 served as the commission's secretary-general and director of archives. Subsequently the first vice-director of the Jewish Historical Institute in Warsaw (1947), he left Poland for Israel in 1950. Three years later he became director of Yad Vashem's archives.

Knout, David (also Dovid Knut; pseudonyms David Miranovitch Fishman, Fichman, or Fixman) (1900–1955): Born to a merchant family in the Bessarabian town of Orgeyev (then in the Russian Empire, today in Moldova), he grew up in Kishinev. In 1920 Knout left for France, where he studied chemical engineering in Caen. Active in the Russian Jewish émigré community in Paris, including its press, he also contributed to the French Jewish press and wrote his own poetry. A committed Revisionist Zionist, he visited Palestine in 1937. Drafted into the French Army in 1939, Knout escaped to the Southern Zone after France's defeat and settled in Toulouse, where he was active in Jewish armed resistance groups, most notably the Armée Juive after January 1942. After escaping to Switzerland in December 1942, he returned to Paris in the fall of 1944 and became active in the CDJC. In August 1946 Knout became editor of *Le Monde Juif*. In 1949 he immigrated to Israel.

Lambert, Raymond-Raoul (1894–1943): Born in Montmorency, France. As a prominent Jewish public figure and editor of a major French Jewish newspaper, *L'Univers Israelite*, during the 1930s Lambert worked with the Refugee Aid Committee (CAR) to provide relief for German Jewish refugees. Under the German occupation he was secretary general of the UGIF in charge of the Southern Zone, where he pursued a strategy of negotiation and petitioning with the Vichy authorities to secure autonomy for Jewish welfare organizations. Because of his protests against the confiscation of Jewish property in August 1943, Lambert was interned in Drancy together with his family and four months later deported to Auschwitz, where they were murdered. He was one of the founding members of the documentation center in Grenoble.

Lichtman, Ada (1920–?): Born in Wieliczka, Poland; studied at the University of Krakow. Lichtman, who survived the Sobibór death camp, was among the founding members of the historical commission in Lublin. In the late 1940s, she left Poland for Israel, where she appeared as a witness in the Eichmann trial.

Livian, Marcel (1901–1988): Born in Braila, Romania; immigrated to France in his youth and studied law at the universities of Paris and Bucharest. As a committed member of the Socialist Party of France, Livian was active in the FSJF. In 1940 he volunteered for the French army and later joined the socialist underground in the Southern Zone. Livian was an early member of the CDJC and its secretary-general after the war. He was naturalized in 1946.

Meiss, Léon (1896–1966): Born in Sarrebourg, France; studied law at the University of Strasbourg. A well-known lawyer, Meiss was active in Jewish communal affairs in Strasbourg and Paris, especially in the Consistoire Central. After France's defeat he went to the Southern Zone and reorganized the Consistoire in Lyon, initially as its vice president and after October 1943 as president. Meiss was influential in the founding of the Conseil Représentatif des Israélites de France and became its honorary president in 1950. He was also active in French ORT Union and the Children's Relief Agency (OSE), as well as the CDJC.

Milbauer, Joseph (1898–1968): Born in Warsaw; grew up in Brussels. In 1921 Milbauer went to Paris, where he wrote poetry and translated Yiddish and Hebrew works into French. During the 1930s he served as editor of *L'Univers Israélite*, a position he resigned from because of his growing Zionist convictions. Milbauer also headed the French branch of the Keren Ha-Yesod. An early collaborator of the documentation center in Grenoble, he escaped to Palestine in 1944.

Milner, Joseph (1887–1963): Born in Chełm, then in the Russian Empire, now in Poland; emigrated in 1905 to study at the University of Bern, then went to Palestine. In 1909 Milner settled in France, where he studied chemical engineering at the University of Toulouse. In the interwar years he worked for the OSE, while also researching the history of the Jews of France and writing as a journalist for the Polish Jewish press (*Der Moment*). During the Second World War he went to the Southern Zone and engaged in underground relief work for the OSE. After the liberation, he continued to work for that organization in Paris, as well as for the CDJC.

Monneray, Henri (Heinrich Meierhof) (1914–?): Born in Erfurt, Germany. After the Nazi rise to power, Monneray fled to France, studied law at the University of Paris, and was naturalized in 1936. After the German occupation, he first escaped to the Southern Zone, and then fled via Spain to Algeria. He returned to France with Gaullist troops in 1944. After the war Monneray worked in the French Ministry of Justice's war crimes office (Service de recherche des crimes de guerre enemis) and served with the French delegation to the International Military Tribunal at Nuremberg. He also was affiliated with the CDJC.

Olewski, Rafael Gerszon (1914–1981): Born in Osięciny, then in the Russian Empire, today in Poland; teacher and journalist. A committed Zionist, Olewski was active in the Keren Kayemet as a member of the General Zionist Party. In the Belsen DP Camp, he cofounded and edited *Undzer Shtime*; he also headed the historical commission and the culture department of the Central Committee of Liberated Jews in the British Zone. In 1949 he immigrated to Israel.

Paraf, Pierre (1893–1989): Born in Paris; trained as a lawyer. Paraf had a career in journalism, writing, and radio broadcasting. In 1927 he cofounded the Ligue Internationale Contre le Racisme et l'Antisémitisme. Between 1930 and 1939 Paraf was the literary editor of the Paris-based daily *La République* and later of the left-wing daily *Combat* and the monthly *L'Europe*. During the war he affiliated with the UGIF in the Southern Zone and was active in the *Résistance*. Paraf was also closely affiliated with the CDJC, both during and after the war.

Poliakov, Léon (1910–1997): Born in St. Petersburg; went to France in 1924. Trained as a lawyer, Poliakov worked until 1939 as a journalist for the *Pariser Tageblatt*, a German-language anti-Nazi paper. With the outbreak of war, he joined the French Army, then after its demobilization survived the war in the Southern Zone. In 1945 Poliakov became head of the CDJC research department. In 1952 he was appointed a fellow at the Centre National de la Recherche Scientifique, and in 1954 he joined the École Pratique des Hautes Études.

Rosental, Dovid (1919–?): Born in Warsaw; journalist and committed Labor Zionist. After surviving Auschwitz, Rosental ended up in the Belsen DP camp, where he was a director of the cultural office of the Central Committee of Liberated Jews in the British Zone. He was also active in the Belsen historical commission and as a member of the editorial board of *Undzer Shtime*. At the end of the 1940s, Rosental immigrated to the United States.

Rost, Nella (née Thon; also Rost-Hollander or Thon-Rost): Born in 1902 in Krakow, the daughter of Dr. Jehoshua (Osias) Thon, a prominent rabbi, cultural Zionist, political leader, and member of the Polish Parliament. Thon-Rost studied literature at the University of Krakow and worked as a journalist. She survived forced labor, the Krakow ghetto, the Krakow-Plaszów concentration camp, and incarceration and torture at the Montelupich prison in Krakow. With the help of the Jewish underground she was freed from Montelupich in the summer of 1944 and survived in the forests around Warsaw until the liberation of those areas in January 1945. She returned to Krakow, where served as vice-director of the Krakow branch of the Central Jewish Historical Commission in Lodz. In April 1946 she left for Sweden, where she led a historical commission in Stockholm that collected testimonies on behalf of the World Jewish Congress. In February 1951 she immigrated to Uruguay.

Schah, Wladimir: Born in Russia; immigrated to France. Active with the HICEM emigration organization, he headed the HICEM-affiliated Sixth Direction of the Union Générale des Israélites de France in the Southern Zone. Although he found the Union's cooperation with the Germans and the Vichy regime problematic, he hoped to smuggle Jews out of France. Schah's son Eugène, a worker for ORT, was also active with the UGIF in the Southern Zone. Both survived the war and continued their work with these organizations, as well as with the CDJC.

Schneersohn, Isaac (1879–1969): Born in Kamenets-Podolski (then in the Russian Empire, today in Ukraine), to the Schneersohn family of Lubavitch Hasidic rebbes; educated as a rabbi and involved in Jewish social work. Schneersohn belonged to the moderate liberal Russian party, the Cadets. From 1916 to 1918, he held municipal offices in Ryazan. In 1920 Schneersohn left for France, where he became an industrialist, while remaining involved in social work. During the occupation he escaped to the Southern Zone and survived in hiding. After the war in Paris, Schneersohn reconstituted the documentation center which he had founded in Grenoble, serving as its director until his death.

Silkes, Genia (1914–1984): Born in Brest-Litovsk, then in the Russian Empire, today in Belarus; trained at the Jewish Teachers' Seminary in Vilna. A teacher in Warsaw before the German occupation, Silkes helped set up a network of underground schools in the ghetto. She also contributed to the Oyneg Shabes archives. Silkes participated in the Warsaw ghetto uprising but escaped deportation, hiding in the forests and living on the "Aryan side" in Warsaw. In 1945 she became a member of the Central Jewish Historical Commission and worked to reestablish Jewish schools in postwar Poland. In 1949 she left Poland for Paris, where she worked as a teacher and as an affiliate of the Society of the Friends of YIVO in Paris. In 1956 she left for the United States, where she worked for YIVO.

Syngalowski, Aron (1890–1956): Born in the vicinity of Baranovichi, then in the Russian Empire, today in Belarus; attorney. Syngalowski went to Germany shortly before the First World War as a representative of the Russian ORT. He studied philosophy and law in Germany and Switzerland. In 1921 he became vice-chairman of the executive committee of World ORT in Berlin, but he fled to France after the Nazi takeover. An early supporter of Schneersohn's documentation initiative, he escaped to Switzerland in early 1943. After the war Syngalowski played a formative role in rebuilding the ORT network in Europe.

Szeftel, Jacques (also Scheftel or Cheftel) (1882–?): Born in Zhitomir, then in the Russian Empire, today in Ukraine; graduated from the law school at the University of St. Petersburg. In 1922, Szeftel immigrated to France, where in the mid-1920s he worked as counselor at the Court of Appeals in Paris. During the war he engaged in relief work with immigrant Jews interned in the Southern Zone. In 1945, he became the secretary-general of ORT in France and a close collaborator of the CDJC.

Szeftel, Leon (Arie) (1905–1980): Born in Vilna, then in the Russian Empire, now in Lithuania; Hebrew teacher. Szeftel was active in the Poale Zion prior to the German occupation. He survived the Vilna ghetto and a labor camp in Estonia. Returning to Poland after the war, Szeftel helped rebuild the Poale Zion movement and worked with the Central Jewish Historical Commission in Lodz. He immigrated to Israel in the late 1940s and became a communal politician in Rishon LeZion.

Trepman, Paul Pinchas (1916–1987): Born in Warsaw; teacher; active in the Revisionist Zionist movement. During the German occupation he survived under false identity and was interned in seven concentration camps. After a death march to Bergen-Belsen, Trepman was liberated by the British. He was a member of the Central Committee of Liberated Jews in the British Zone and served in the cultural office and on the editorial board of *Undzer Shtime*. He was also active in the historical commission and in building up a network of Jewish schools in Belsen. He immigrated to Canada in the late 1940s.

Trunk, Isaiah (1905–1981): Born in Kutno, then in the Russian Empire, now in Poland; studied history at the University of Warsaw with Meir Bałaban, earning a master's degree in 1929. Until the war Trunk taught history at the schools of the Central Yiddish School Organization in Bialystok and Warsaw. He belonged to the the Yunger Historiker Krayz led by Emanuel Ringelblum and Raphael Mahler, was a member of YIVO, and was affiliated with the Institute for Jewish Studies in

Warsaw, where he came to know Philip Friedman. At the beginning of the German occupation, he escaped to Bialystok and later deeper into the Soviet Union, where he spent the rest of the war. After returning to Poland in the summer of 1946, he was active in the historical commission in Warsaw until 1950. From 1951 to 1953, Trunk lived in Israel, where he worked for the Ghetto Fighters' House. In 1953 he left for Canada and a year later settled in the United States. In 1954 he joined the staff of YIVO in New York, where he was a member of the board of directors, chairman of the research and planning commission, and chief archivist.

Wasser, Hersh (Hersz) (1912–1980): Born in Suwałki, then in the Russian Empire, now in Poland; earned a master's degree from the University of Warsaw. An active member of the Left Poale Zion party, after December 1939 Wasser became involved in relief work for Jewish refugees arriving in Warsaw. He was the secretary of the Ringelblum archive and a member of the archives committee of the Jewish Fighting Organization in the Warsaw ghetto. After the war he was director of the District Jewish Historical Commission in Warsaw. He immigrated to Israel in 1950.

Weliczker, Leon (also Leon Wells) (1925–): Born in Stojanów near Lvov, then in Poland, now in Ukraine. He survived the war in Lvov, where was an inmate of the Janowska camp and a member of Sonderkommando 1005, which had the task of exhuming and burning bodies from mass graves in eastern Galicia. In November 1943 he escaped and went into hiding. After the liberation of Lvov he became acquainted with Philip Friedman. In July 1945 Weliczker left Lvov and began to study at the Politechnic Institute in Gliwice, Silesia while also working for the historical commission in Lodz, which published his wartime diary in 1946. In February 1946 he left for the U.S. Zone of Germany. Weliczker studied engineering and mathematics at the Technische Hochschule in Munich, and until January 1947 he also worked for the Central Historical Commission in Munich. In 1949, after getting his doctorate in engineering, he immigrated to the United States. He testified at the Eichmann trial in 1961.

Wiener, Alfred (1885–1965): Born in Potsdam; trained as an Orientalist. After the First World War, Wiener became active in the Jewish defense organization CV (Central Association of German Citizens of the Jewish Faith), as secretary of the CV's Greater Berlin chapter between 1919 and 1923 and as national deputy secretary and secretary between 1923 and 1933. In 1933 he escaped to Amsterdam and with Dr. David Cohen founded the Jewish Central Information Office in 1934. In 1939 the center moved to London, where it became known as the Wiener Library after the war. Wiener served as its director until his death.

Wiesenthal, Simon (1908–2005): Born in Buczacz, Galicia, the in the Austro-Hungarian Empire, today in Ukraine; studied architecture at the Universities of

Prague and Lvov. He endured the Lvov ghetto, went into hiding but was denounced and arrested, and survived several concentration camps, including Janowska, Plaszów, Buchenwald, and Mauthausen, where he was liberated by the U.S. Army in 1945. He was active in the Central Committee of Jews in Austria and in various organizations of former camp inmates, in addition to briefly serving as an interrogator for the American occupying forces. In 1947 he assumed leadership of the historical commission in Linz, which operated until 1954. In 1961 he opened a documentation center in Vienna, where he lived until his death in 2005.

Wulf, Joseph (Józef) (1912–1974): Born in Chemnitz, Germany, to affluent Polish Jewish parents, he grew up in Krakow, and he received rabbinical training at the Mir Yeshiva. Under German occupation he was active in a Jewish fighting organization operating in the Krakow and Bochnia ghettos. In 1943 he was arrested and deported to Auschwitz-Birkenau. He escaped from a death march in January 1945 and returned to Krakow, where in March/April that year he participated in the founding of a historical commission (whose secretary he became in May 1945 and deputy director a year later) as the local branch of the Central Jewish Historical Commission in Lodz. Wulf left Poland in 1947 for political reasons. After brief sojourns in Sweden, Denmark, and Finland, he settled in Paris, where (together with Michał Borwicz) he headed a research center for the history of Polish Jews; he also served as secretary-general of the Federation of Polish Jews in France. In 1952 Wulf moved to West Berlin, where he continued his Holocaust research. He committed suicide in 1974.

NOTES

Introduction

1. Although I am mindful of the non-Jewish victims of the Nazi regime, this study's use of the term "survivors" specifically relates to Jews, while Jewishness is understood rather broadly, in terms of both the religion and self-identity of the individuals as well as the racial definition imposed on them by their persecutors. For reasons of practicality, the term functions as the collective name denoting a highly diverse group whose members were dissimilar in age, gender, class, social status, education, ideology, nationality, language, and wartime experiences.

2. *Khurbn* (or *hurban* in Hebrew)—initially applied to the destruction of the First Temple in 586 BCE—was subsequently used more generally for catastrophic events in Jewish history, such as the major pogroms in eastern Europe in the late nineteenth and early twentieth centuries. Survivors continued to use *khurbn* or variations thereof even though the Nazi mass murder of European Jews far exceeded previous incidents of violence against Jews in totality of intent, global reach, method, and number of victims. Such elaborations as *letster khurbn* (the latest destruction), *hurban bet shlishi* (the destruction of the Third Temple), or specific location, e.g., *khurbn Tomashov*, indicate that the survivors tended to place their own experiences in the generations-long chain of Jewish persecution and suffering. See Niborski and Vaisbrot, *Dictionnaire Yiddish-Français*, 277.

    Alternative Yiddish terms for the Holocaust among survivors in the immediate postwar period included: *kataklizm* (cataclysm), *umkum* (death), *shkhite* (slaughter, massacre), *tragedye* (tragedy), *martirer veg funem yidishn folk* (path of martyrdom of the Jewish people), *martirologye* (martyrdom), *yidn oysrotung* (extermination of the Jews), *fartilikung funem yidishn folk* (annihilation of the Jewish people), *redifes oyf yidn* (persecution of the Jews), *di oysrotungs tkufe* (period of extermination), *di yorn fun redifes* (years of persecution), and *kidesh-hashem funem yidishn folk* (martyrdom of the Jewish people).

    Common French and English words included: *le cataclisme*/cataclysm and *le martyr*/martyrdom. The Hebrew term *Shoah* (destruction), which is used in Israel and beyond, was first used in 1940 when the United Aid Committee for the Jews of Poland in Palestine published the booklet *Sho'at yehude Polin* with documents and eyewitness accounts on persecution of the Jews of Poland after the German occupation. The term came into common use in the Hebrew language only with the Israeli parliament's passing of the laws for a national Holocaust Remembrance Day (1951) and for the establishment of the Yad Vashem memorial site (1953). The English-language term Holocaust (initially in lowercase) was used in the 1940s to describe the mass murder of European Jews as well as for crimes against other populations during the Second World War. Derived from the Greek *holokauston* (burnt offering), Holocaust is the translation of the Hebrew word *'olah*, relating to a burnt offering to God in 1 Samuel 7:9.

    The related term "genocide"—coined in 1944 by Polish Jewish refugee lawyer Raphael Lemkin—entered the English lexicon through its use in the International Military Tribunal's prosecution of German war criminals and in the UN Genocide Convention of 1948.

Although first coined to describe the Nazi persecution of Jews, the term is now broadly used for attempts to destroy, eliminate, or murder any national, ethnic, or religious group. See for example, Hasia R. Diner, *We Remember with Reverence and Love*, 21–22; Ofer, "The Strength of Remembrance"; Rabinbach, "The Challenge of the Unprecedented"; Tal, "Holocaust," 681.

3. CDJC, *Les Juifs en Europe*, 23.
4. These countries were Austria, Bulgaria, Czechoslovakia, France, Great Britain, Greece, Germany, Hungary, Italy, Poland, Romania, Sweden, Switzerland, and the Soviet Union.
5. This book uses the term "documentation" in the sense of establishing the facts of a historical event, understanding its nature and chronology, and publicizing and teaching its implications. As James E. Young rightly observed:

> In addition to establishing evidence, the term "document" retains echoes of both its Latin origin *documentum*—a lesson—and its French root *docere*—to teach. As a result, documenting an event suggests both establishing it as a fact and teaching about it. The very figures of witness, testimony, and documentary thus point respectively to having seen events, having been part of events, finding significance in events, and then teaching about and finding meaning through the transmission of events.
> —Young, *Writing and Rewriting the Holocaust*, 19.

This was precisely the case with the survivors engaging in the historical commissions and documentation centers after the war. The terms "collect" and "record" are borrowed from a poster with which the Central Historical Commission in Munich urged the survivor public to join its ranks in 1947 (discussed in chapter 4). "Collecting" implies the act of gathering the vestiges of the past, while "recording" signifies a more subjective and individualized act of writing about past events either from memory or on the basis of evidence gathered; both acts are essential components of postwar Jewish Holocaust documentation.

6. Jack Kugelmass and Jonathan Boyarin used this term in reference to the memorial books edited by Holocaust survivors to commemorate their destroyed communities through a collective act of writing. See Kugelmass and Boyarin, *From a Ruined Garden*, 34. Similarly, James E. Young spoke of the "missing gravestone syndrome" in reference to these books. See Young, *The Texture of Memory*, 7.
7. On Joseph Kermisz, see Niger and Shatsky, *Leksikon*, 8:237–238. On the Central Jewish Historical Commission's testimony collections, see Żydowski Instytut Historyczny, *Holocaust Survivors Testimony Catalogue*, vol. 3.
8. On Friedman, see Orenstein, *Dos lebn un shafn fun Dr. Filip Fridman*, 13–14.
9. For Nella Rost's biography, see her report "Verfolgungsvorgang," ZAH B.2/1, Zg. 00/03, no. 73; on Borwicz, see Niger and Shatsky, *Leksikon*, 1:245–246; on Wulf see ibid., 3:276–277; on Feigenbaum, see ibid., 7:342.
10. On Wiesenthal and Frydman see Segev, *Simon Wiesenthal*, and Frydman, *The Hunter*.
11. On Wiener, see Ben Barkow, *Alfred Wiener*.
12. On Vitale, see Nidam-Orvieto, "Fighting Oblivion." On the personalities and institutions represented at the 1947 conference, see CDJC, *Les Juifs en Europe*, and chapter 5 of this book.
13. On Kaplan, see Niger and Shatsky, *Leksikon*, 8:93–94. See also Moshe Yosef Feigenbaum's report on the conference, "Di ershte eyrop. konferents fun di historishe komisyes," *Undzer Veg* 152 (January 16, 1948), 6.
14. On Schneersohn and Poliakov, see Niger and Shatsky, *Leksikon*, 8:755, and Poliakov, *Mémoires*. For all the names mentioned in this section see also the appendix to this book.
15. It is most difficult to ascertain the exact number of the commission workers because of the high fluctuation in personnel and the lack of statistics. If we take into account that some workers remained for months and even years, while others stayed for only a few weeks, we can assume that the core of more permanent coworkers in France, Poland, Germany, Austria, and Italy in the years 1944–1949 amounted to 500–800 people, with an average of 80–100 coworkers in Poland and the U.S. Zone of Germany, between twenty and fifty in France and Austria, and less than twenty in Italy and the British Zone of Germany. If we

take into account that some voluntary helpers did not even register with the commissions and documentation centers, the total number of coworkers must have been considerably higher, perhaps between one and two thousand all across Europe. Given that the documentation initiatives collected some eighteen thousand testimonies and eight thousand questionnaires, the survivors who at some point in the first postwar decade and a half made a onetime contribution to the documentation initiatives in the form of a testimony or questionnaire (or both) must have numbered in the tens of thousands.

16. "Working through" is used here, following Dominick LaCapra, as an analytical process in which a traumatized individual gains a critical distance to traumatic events in the past and is able to distinguish between now and then without avoidance, harmonization, forgetting, or submergence. See LaCapra, *Writing History*, 143–145.
17. Wieviorka, *The Era of the Witness*, 97.
18. On the "discovery" of the witnesses of the Holocaust in public discourse, see ibid., 96–149, and Wieviorka, "From Survivor to Witness." The first to address the use of testimonies and memoirs as historical sources was Des Pres, *The Survivor*.
19. On this concept see Langer, *Holocaust Testimonies*, 1–38.
20. Hartman, *The Longest Shadow*, 137.
21. LaCapra, *History and Memory after Auschwitz*, 11.
22. Hartman, *The Longest Shadow*, 133.
23. Ibid., 143.
24. Ibid., 134, 136; Friedländer, "Trauma, Transference and 'Working Through,'" 50–53; Young, "Between History and Memory," 55. Most notably, Saul Friedländer has called for the writing of "integrated history" which would weave together the perspectives of the perpetrators, victims, and bystanders; see his *Nazi Germany and the Jews*, 1:1–2, 5–6. See the conclusion of this book for a discussion of Friedländer's concept.
25. For a general discussion of the issues of history, memory, and trauma in the framework of Holocaust testimonies and their interpretation, see, for example, Auerhahn and Laub, "Holocaust Testimony"; Ballinger, "The Culture of Survivors"; Caruth, *Trauma*, 13–75, 200–220; Felman and Laub, *Testimony*; Friedländer, *Memory, History, and the Extermination of the Jews of Europe*; Greenspan, *On Listening to Holocaust Survivors*; Hartman, *Holocaust Remembrance*; Jacobson, *Embattled Selves*; LaCapra, "Holocaust Testimonies," 209–223; LaCapra, *History and Memory after Auschwitz*; Langer, *Holocaust Testimonies*; Niewyk, *Fresh Wounds*; Waxman, *Writing the Holocaust*; Young, *Writing and Rewriting the Holocaust*. See also the special issue of *Poetics Today*, "The Humanities of Testimony" (vol. 27, no. 2, Summer 2006), edited by Geoffrey Hartman.
26. See, inter alia, Nora, *Rethinking France*; Winter, *Remembering War*; Assmann, *Der lange Schatten der Vergangenheit*; and seminal works specifically addressing Jewish memory: Yerushalmi, *Zakhor*, and Zerubavel, *Recovered Roots*.
27. See, for example, Friedländer, *Probing the Limits of Representation*; Bartov, "Intellectuals on Auschwitz"; Bartov, *Murder in Our Midst*; Lang, *Post-Holocaust*; Rothberg, *Traumatic Realism*; Weissman, *Fantasies of Witnessing*.
28. Philip Friedman, "Die Probleme der wissenschaftlichen Erforschung unserer letzten Katastrophe," ACDJC, box 13, p. 5.
29. The reference for eighteen thousand testimonies comes from Raul Hilberg, referring to Philip Friedman, the Polish Jewish survivor, historian, and first director of the Central Jewish Historical Commission in Poland. Cf. Hilberg "I Was Not There," 18. The total number of testimonies appears to be larger than Friedman's estimate.

Although these testimonies were written instead of recorded, there was nevertheless a strong oral component in their genesis, and we might even call them "written oral testimonies." If they were written down by the witnesses themselves, this generally happened in the presence of commission workers who posed questions and talked with the witnesses. It was also a common practice for witnesses to dictate their reports to commission workers who wrote them down in their presence. While the use of voice recorders would have been possible (and was carried out by the American Jewish psychiatrist David Boder in his 1946

Holocaust interviews), the Jewish historical commissions and documentation centers neither had the technical and financial means to do so, nor did they deem recorded testimonies to be of higher value than those on paper.

The most common terms used for "testimony" at the time was the Yiddish *gvies-eydes*, derived from the Hebrew *gviat-edut*. The Biblical word *edut* has multilayered legal and theological connotations such as "witness," "testimony," and "evidence" (for example, in Exodus 25:16, 21–22, the Torah is referred to as a "testimony" of God's deeds). In the immediate postwar context, the act of "collecting testimonies" was referred to as *zamlen gvies-eydes*, whereas "testifying" was *zogn eydes* ("to give testimony"). Alternative terms for testimony were also the Yiddish *iberlebungen*, the Polish *świadectwo*, the French *témoignage*, or the German *Zeugenbericht* or *Überlebnsbericht*. A survivor who testified was commonly called "witness," *eydes* (sing. and pl.) in Yiddish, *ed* in Hebrew, *świadek* in Polish, *témoin* in French, or *Zeuge* in German. On the history and significance of the term *edut* see Young, *Writing and Rewriting the Holocaust*, 18–22.

30. For these numbers see the websites of the institutions: http://college.usc.edu/vhi/aboutus and http://www.library.yale.edu/testimonies/index.html.
31. See Friedman and Gar, *Bibliografye fun yidishe bikher vegn khurbn un gvure*; other early bibliographies are Friedman, *Bibliografyah shel ha-sefarim ha-ivriyim 'al ha-shoah ve-'al ha-gevurah*; Friedman and Robinson, *Guide to Research in Jewish History, 1933–1945*; Friedman and Robinson, *Guide to Jewish History Under Nazi Impact*; and Gar, *Bibliografye fun artiklen vegn khurbn un gvure in yidishe periodike*.
32. Hartman, *The Longest Shadow*, 141.
33. Hilberg, *Sources of Holocaust Research*, 47.
34. Friedländer, "Trauma, Transference and 'Working Through,'" 43.
35. Ibid., 47–48. Emphasis in original.
36. Marrus, *The Holocaust in History*, 4. In 2003, Moishe Postone and Eric Santner still maintained that Holocaust research had begun in earnest only after the Eichmann trial; see Postone and Santner, *Catastrophe and Meaning*, 3.
37. In the late 1940s and 1950s, a few articles on Jewish Holocaust research written by activists and their contemporaries addressed a public of scholars and interested laypeople in Europe, the United States, and Israel. These include Berenstein, "Documents in the Archives of Poland"; CDJC, *Les Juifs en Europe*; Dawidowicz, "Khronikes fun khurbn"; Feigenbaum, "Peulot shel ha-va'adah ha-historit be-minkhen"; Philip Friedman, "A fertl-yorhundert khurbn-literatur"; Philip Friedman, "American Jewish Research and Literature on the Jewish Catastrophe"; Philip Friedman, "Dos gedrukte vort bay der sheyres-haple̊yte in daytshland"; Philip Friedman, "The European Jewish Research on the Recent Jewish Catastrophe"; Philip Friedman, "Holocaust Research and Literature in America"; Philip Friedman, "Preliminary and Methodological Problems of the Research on the Jewish Catastrophe in the Nazi Period"; Philip Friedman, "Problems of Research on the Jewish Catastrophe"; and Philip Friedman, "Research and Literature on the Recent Jewish Tragedy" (some of these papers were later published in English translation in Philip Friedman, *Roads to Extinction*); Kermish, "La-matsav ba-heker ha-sho'ah," 8–10; Poliakov, "Le Centre de Documentation Juive, ses archives ses publications"; and Schneersohn, "Der yidisher dokumentatsye-tsenter in Frankraykh."
38. Dawidowicz, *The Holocaust and the Historians*, 125–146. On Dawidowicz's encounter with the survivor historians in Allied-occupied Germany, see her memoir, *From that Place and Time*; see also Nancy Sinkoff's introduction to the 2008 Rutgers University Press edition of the memoir, "*Yidishkayt* and the Making of Lucy S. Dawidowicz."
39. Gutman and Greif, *The Historiography of the Holocaust Period*; Gutman and Saf, *She'erit Hapletah, 1944–1948*, esp. the contribution by Krakowski, "Memorial Projects and Memorial Institutions," 388–398.
40. Further examples are: Bardgett et al., *Survivors of Nazi Persecution*; Bardgett et al., *Justice, Politics and Memory*; Bessel and Schumann, *Life after Death*; Biess and Moeller, *Histories of the Aftermath*; Fulbrook, *Europe since 1945*; Hitchcock, *Liberation*; Lebow, Kansteiner, and Fogu, *The Politics of Memory*; Müller, *Memory and Power*; Levy and Roseman, *Three Postwar Eras*; Mazower, Reinisch, and Feldman, "Post-War Reconstruction in Europe"; Shephard, *The Long Road Home*; Stafford, *Endgame 1945*; Wegs and Ladrech, *Europe since 1945*.

41. Gross, *Neighbors*; Gross, *Fear*; Burds, *The Early Cold War*; Rousso, *The Vichy Syndrome*; Rousso, *The Haunting Past*; Conan and Rousso, *Vichy*; Lagrou, *The Legacy of Nazi Occupation*.
42. This term is of biblical origin (e.g., Genesis 32:9; 2 Kings, 19:30–31; Jeremiah 31:7). As of 1943 Jews in the *Yishuv*, the Jewish community in Palestine, began to use it to identify those who would survive the persecutions in Europe. The survivors themselves subsequently used this term to express their separate group identity. See, for example, Mankowitz, *Life between Memory and Hope*, 1–2.

    According to Dan Michman, the term *She'erit Hapletah* (or, in its Yiddish variant, *Sheyres Hapleyte*) can refer to:

    > (1) the entire Jewish world, because it had survived the Nazi assault on its national existence; (2) direct survivors of Nazi atrocities, plus refugees who had fled when German armies approached their original domiciles and returned to European soil immediately after their liberation; (3) Holocaust survivors in DP camps only; (4) Holocaust survivors who were still in Europe but had decided to settle outside the continent, mainly in Eretz Israel.
    > —See Michman, *Holocaust Historiography*, 330.

    Following Michman's second definition, this work uses the term to refer to the Jews who found themselves in Europe at the end of the war. It is important to note that while survivors tended to use the term *She'erit Hapletah* as a collective self-description, they also referred to themselves with the Yiddish terms *lebngeblibene yidn* (Jews who stayed alive) or *amolike katsetler* (former concentration camp inmates). The victims of the Final Solution were *di toyte* (the dead), *di derhargete* (the murdered), or *di kdoyshim* (the martyrs).
43. For examples of these research trends, see Bankier, *The Jews Are Coming Back*, and Patt and Berkowitz, *We Are Here*.
44. Yablonka, "The Myth of Holocaust Survivors' Silence," 210; as early as 1996 Dalia Ofer challenged the idea of Israeli silence about the Holocaust by showing that the Holocaust played a central role in Israeli public discourse already in the late 1940s, thanks in part to the roles of survivors arriving in the newly founded state: Ofer, "Israel," and Ofer, "The Strength of Remembrance." Hasia R. Diner, "Post-World-War-II American Jewry and the Confrontation with Catastrophe"; Hasia R. Diner, *We Remember with Reverence and Love*. Diner rejects Peter Novick's claim that the Holocaust was entirely absent in public discourse in the United Sates until after 1967 (Novick, *The Holocaust in American Life*).
45. See Poznanski, *Propagandes et persécutions*, 561–592.
46. See Wieviorka, *The Era of the Witness*, and her earlier work on postwar France, *Déportation et génocide*, 412–431, and also Waxman, *Writing the Holocaust*.
47. Cesarani and Sundquist, *After the Holocaust*; esp. 1–38 and 202–216.
48. Grossmann, *Jews, Germans, and Allies*; Feinstein, *Holocaust Survivors in Postwar Germany*. A number of recent studies have taken a broader perspective on survivors of Nazi terror, analyzing the experiences of Jews and non-Jews in context; see, for example, Holian, *Between National Socialism and Soviet Communism*; Bardgett et al., *Survivors of Nazi Persecution*; and Bardgett et al., *Justice, Politics and Memory*.
49. Mankowitz, *Life between Memory and Hope*, 192–225.
50. See Kenan, *Between Memory and History*, 19–41; Boaz Cohen, *Ha-dorot ha-ba'im*, chap. 2; Boaz Cohen, "The Birth Pangs of the Holocaust Research in Israel"; and Boaz Cohen, "Setting the Agenda of Holocaust Research."
51. Rosen, *The Wonder of Their Voices*, 10–12. See also Rosen, "Evidence of Trauma."
52. On some of the individuals involved in the historical commissions: Barkow, *Alfred Wiener*; Berg, "Ein Aussenseiter der Holocaustforschung"; Berg, "Joseph Wulf"; Boaz Cohen, "Rachel Auerbach"; Segev, *Simon Wiesenthal*; Stauber, "Philip Friedman and the Beginning of Holocaust Studies"; Stauber, *Laying the Foundations*. On historical commissions more generally: Aleksiun, "The Central Jewish Historical Commission"; Aleksiun, "Polish Historiography of the Holocaust"; Bensoussan, "The Jewish Contemporary Documentation Center"; Fredj, "Le Centre de Documentation Juive Contemporaine"; Horn, "Visnshaftlekhe un editorishe tetikeyt fun tsentraler yidisher historisher komisye"; Horn, "Żydowski Instytut Historyczny

w Polsce w latach 1944–1949"; Horváth, "A Jewish Historical Commission in Budapest"; Horváth, "Jews in Hungary after the Holocaust"; Jockusch, *"Khurbn-Forshung"*; Jockusch, "Jüdische Geschichtsforschung im Lande Amaleks"; Jockusch, "A Folk Monument"; Nidam-Orvieto, "Fighting Oblivion"; Poznanski, "La création du Centre de Documentation Juive Contemporaine," 57–59; Poznanski, "Hakamat ha-merkaz le-ti'ud yahadut zmanenu"; Schein, "Everyone Can Hold a Pen"; Stach, "Geschichtsschreibung und politische Vereinnahmungen"; Stach, *Das Jüdische Historische Institut*; Stach, "Praktische Geschichte"; Szurek, "Être témoin sous le stalinisme"; Tych, "The Emergence of Holocaust Research"; Wein, "The Jewish Historical Institute"; Wieviorka, *Déportation et génocide*, 412–431; Wieviorka, "Du CDJC au Mémorial de la Shoah".

53. Boaz Cohen, "And I Was Only a Child"; Boaz Cohen, "The Children's Voice"; Greenspan, *The Awakening of Memory*; Kenkmann and Kohlhaas, "Die Hitlerzeit hat die Seele des jüdischen Kindes zutiefst verändert"; Michlic, "The Raw Memory of War"; Ofer, "The Community and the Individual"; Tych et al., *Kinder über den Holocaust*.
54. Bankier and Michman, *Holocaust Historiography*; see esp. the contributions by Georges Benssoussan, Nicolas Berg, Boaz Cohen, Ido de Haan, Rita Horváth, Conny Kristel, Iael Nidam Orvieto, Dalia Ofer, Ada Schein, Roni Stauber, and Feliks Tych.
55. Volkov, "Jewish History," 190.
56. Moshe Rosman has recently called upon historians to move beyond studying the Jewish historical experience within distinct national borders and to return to supralocal, transgeographical, and transnational conceptions of the Jewish past. He argues that a transnational perspective exploring the "links between Jews in different countries, the characteristics they shared, their conjoint supralocal experience and the common denominators of their local experience" was vital in understanding the "cultural geography of Jewish history that transcends national political boundaries." See Rosman, "Jewish History across Borders," 28. This book seeks to provide such a transnational perspective on the phenomenon of Jewish Holocaust documentation.
57. This approach adopts neither a "generalizing comparison" (which emphasizes commonalities and general trends while underplaying the differences) nor an "individualizing comparison" (which emphasizes differences in historical developments among compared cases while deemphasizing similarities). Instead, it undertakes a "synthesizing comparison" that seeks to establish both similarities and differences between or among the cases being compared. For this typology of historical comparisons, see Kaelble, *Der historische Vergleich*, 26–30; Kocka, "Comparative Historical Research"; and Kocka, *Geschichte und Aufklärung*, 21–28.
58. On the death rates of Jews in the countries in question, see, for example, Benz, *Dimension des Völkermords*, 105–135, 411–497.

Chapter 1

1. Pat, *Ash un fayer*, 77.
2. See Roskies, *The Literature of Destruction*, esp. 1–12.
3. See Roskies, *Against the Apocalypse*, esp. 197–310, and Roskies, *The Jewish Search for a Usable Past*; Mintz, *Hurban*, esp. 157–269. See also Ezrahi, *By Words Alone*, and Rosenfeld, *A Double Dying*.
4. The Polish Jewish historian Philip Friedman created this term in 1947 both to describe the survivors' postwar documentation and writing and to draw parallels to earlier Jewish catastrophes; see Friedman, "Die grundsätzlichen Probleme unserer Churbnforschung," ACDJC, box 1, p. 1.
5. Roskies, *Against the Apocalypse*, 35.
6. There are, of course, instances of non-Jews responding to violence by chronicling the events that are in many ways comparable to the Jewish tradition of *khurbn-forshung*. However, it is doubtful that the protagonists of *khurbn-forshung* were aware of these non-Jewish initiatives, which is why they are not dealt with extensively here. One obvious example is the oral and literary tradition of slave narratives in the United States. Whether written by former

slaves who had become literate or transcribed by others, these narratives became a widespread literary genre that served as political tools for the abolitionists who published and promoted them. In the 1920s and 1930s, a number of social scientists—predominantly African Americans—undertook research projects using the recollections of ex-slaves. As against the moralistic character of the earlier narratives, these later efforts sought to present a comprehensive picture of slavery. Parallel to the Jewish researchers, these scholars were motivated by the declining population of those who had personally known slavery and by the wish, at a time of widespread racism, to contest the popular view of slaves as passive, submissive, and inferior. In both cases, the social sciences provided tools for and interest in the research. The Roosevelt administration's effort to fight the Great Depression fostered a great expansion of this effort through the Federal Writer's Project (FWP), which paid unemployed writers and artists to record the life stories of slaves, as well as to write local histories, record songs, and collect folklore. The wealth of information thus available ultimately influenced the development of "oral history" and the writing of black history in the United States. See for example: Cade, "Out of the Mouths of Ex-Slaves"; Egypt, *Unwritten History of Slavery*; Rawick, *The American Slave*; Yetman, "The Background of the Slave Narrative Collection"; Yetman, "Ex-Slave Interviews and the Historiography of Slavery."

The Turkish genocide of the Armenians during the First World War, though instructive, provides fewer parallels with *khurbn-forshung*. In 1915–1916 Ottoman soldiers and gendarmes along with Turkish and Kurdish troops and local tribal leaders, in concert with the ruling faction in the Ottoman government, murdered 1–1.5 million Armenians, one-half of the Ottoman Empire's Armenian population, and deported the remainder to desert areas in today's Iraq and Syria, where they suffered further atrocities. Eyewitness accounts of the events were written immediately. Some of them appeared in print with the help of British diplomats, in particular Sir James Bryce. Assisted by the young historian Arnold Toynbee, Bryce gathered data on the atrocities, transcribed eyewitness testimonies, and in 1916 published a seven-hundred-page documentary study under government imprint. Rather than using the accounts of Armenian eyewitnesses, he relied on those he deemed "objective observers," such as Western Christian missionaries, travelers, merchants, and Red Cross workers in the region. The British acted out of two primary motives: sympathy for a Christian minority in a Muslim empire and British interest in the geopolitical map following the anticipated collapse of the Ottoman Empire. The Armenian victims and survivors—mostly women and orphans—developed a predominantly private memory culture based on oral and literary forms such as poems, laments, novels, and folklore, often referring back to suffering in Armenian history. See: Alishan, "Crucifixion without 'The Cross'"; Beledian, "Die Erfahrung der Katastrophe"; Bloxham, *The Great Game of Genocide*, 1–4, 212; Dabag, "Der Genozid an den Armeniern"; Miller and Miller, *Survivors*; Toynbee, *The Treatment of Armenians*, esp. xxi–xxvii.

In its origins in racist ideology, the Nazi genocide of the Gypsies presents obvious similarities with the Jewish experience. Out of a population of approximately one million Sinti and Roma living in Nazi-controlled areas, the Germans murdered between 90,000 and 220,000. In this case, however, the Nazi regime did not pursue an explicit policy of total racial extermination, especially in the occupied territories. Sinti and Roma were, however, disproportionately represented among victims of sterilization and medical experiments, and they experienced deportation, internment, ghettoization, forced labor, and mass murder. Three decades elapsed before the survivors of this genocide, for which some scholars use the term *Porrajmos*—"devouring" in the Romani language—began to write about their experiences. In the oral culture of Sinti and Roma, enhanced by a rich musical and poetic tradition, rituals commemorating or memorializing the dead do not exceed a certain period of mourning and written documentation or historical chronicles are therefore mostly absent. And like other groups trying to survive in generally hostile environments, Sinti and Roma tried to adopt a low profile and keep to themselves. It was mainly due to the initiative of the Sinti and Roma elites and in response to their growing assimilation into their surrounding societies that autobiographies or fiction on their persecution first became common in the 1970s. See Bauer, *Rethinking the Holocaust*, 60–66; Browning, *The Origins of the Final Solution*, 178–184;

Eder-Jordan "Die nationalsozialistische Rassen- und Vernichtungspolitik"; Demir, "Literarische Antworten"; Hancock, "Responses to the Porrajmos," 39–64; Kapralski, "The Voices of a Mute Memory," 93–111; Lewy, *The Nazi Persecution of the Gypsies*.

7. For details about the pogrom, in which 1,500–2,000 rioters killed forty-nine Jews in two days of lawlessness, see Judge, *Easter in Kishinev*, and Klier and Lambroza, *Pogroms*, 195–247.
8. See Dubnow, *Mein Leben*, 137–139, and the newly edited German translation of Dubnow's Russian memoirs, *Buch des Lebens*, 1:410–415. For an English translation of the group's call for self-defense, see Roskies, *The Literature of Destruction*, 156–159.
9. David Engel argues that Dubnow and his collaborators pursued a concept of "popular self-help," comprising emigration from Russia, physical self-defense, political activism, and documentation of atrocities to improve the lot of the Jews in the Russian Empire. See Engel, "Writing History as a National Mission," 127–128.
10. Chaim Nachman Bialik's first notebook, sections "Ha-tekufa she-lifnei ha-pogrom" and "Ha-pogrom," "Bet holim," "Tmunot fotografiyot," and question 9 in "Sipurei nizokim ve-'edei re'iyah: Reshimat ha-she'elot," BHTA.
11. Ibid., section "Sipurei nizokim ve-'edei re'iyah: Reshimat ha-she'elot."
12. See, for example, Frankel, "The Crisis of 1881–82." On the impact of the pogroms see the essays by I. Michael Aronson, Moshe Mishkinsky, Erich Haberer, and Hans Rogger in Klier and Lambroza, *Pogroms*.
13. Dubnow, "Iz izucheniia istorii russkikh evreev." A Hebrew version appeared in spring 1892 in the Odessa-based literary anthology *Ha-Pardes*: Dubnow, "Nahpesa ve-nahkora." On the circumstances in which he wrote this essay, see Dubnow, *Mein Leben*, 93–96, and , "Introductory Remarks," 344–345.
14. Dubnow, "Nahpesah ve-nahkorah," 226.
15. Ibid., 223.
16. Ibid., 242.
17. On the conception and history of *Wissenschaft* scholarship, see, inter alia, Schorsch, *From Text to Context*; Roemer, *Jewish Scholarship and Culture*, and Brenner, *Propheten des Vergangenen*, chaps. 1 and 2. Dubnow's approach also went against the common practice of his contemporaries in the Russian Empire, whose primary concern was with legal documents relating to the Jews. See Nathans, "On Russian Jewish Historiography," 413.
18. Dubnov-Erlich, *The Life and Work of S. M. Dubnov*, 103, and Hilbrenner, *Diaspora-Nationalismus*, 148–152.
19. See Dubnow, *Buch des Lebens*, 1:308–309.
20. On the founding of the Jewish Ethnographic Historical Committee as a direct response to Dubnow's call, see Pinson, "Simon Dubnow," 17–18, Kuznitz, "The Origins of Yiddish Scholarship," 4, and Armborst, "Wegbereiter der Geschichtsforschung," 425. See also Dubnow, *Buch des Lebens*, 1:287, and Dubnow, *Mein Leben*, 99–101.
21. Fishman, *The Rise of Modern Yiddish Culture*, 141.
22. Dubnow explicitly asked Bialik to convey a witness' style and language in his translation. See the first notebook, section "Sipurei nizokim ve-'ede re'iyah: Reshimat ha-she'elot," BHTA. See also Goren, '*Eduyot nifge'e Kishinov*, 48, and Dubnow, *Dos bukh fun mayn lebn*, 1:380. After Bialik returned to Odessa, Auerbach worked on a statistical report on the victims and the damage. See Bialik's letters to Auerbach in Lachower, *Igrot*, 1:174, 178ff.
23. Simon Dubnow to Ch. N. Bialik, July 24, 1903, BHTA. See also Dubnow, *Dos bukh fun mayn lebn*, 1:380.
24. Before leaving for Kishinev, Bialik received 25 rubles for his poetry from the editor of *Hazman*, so he may have viewed the mission primarily as a way to finance his literary endeavors. On the evolution of Bialik's Kishinev-related poems, see Dan Miron's introduction to "Ba-ir ha-haregah" in Bialik, *Shire H. N. Bialik*, 162.
25. Dr. Mochnik, head of the Committee for Relief of Pogrom Victims and a public figure in the Kishinev Jewish community, promised 500 rubles to support Bialik's documentation work. When he had received only half of that sum, Bialik complained to Shlomo Dubinski of the relief committee on October 24, 1903: "Now, when very important material has been

collected and half of it has been edited, there is no money to continue the project...." See Lachower, *Igrot*, 180–181. For more on financial troubles, see Bialik to Auerbach, September 1903; October 1903 (during the *Sukkoth* holiday); October 17, 1903; *Tevet* 11 (January 1904), in ibid., 176, 178, 180, 191. Prior to publication, state censor Israel Landau advised Bialik to make several changes in his poem, notably to disguise its reference to recent events by linking its title to the seventeenth-century Chmielnicki pogroms. The censored version, "Masa Nemirov," appeared in the anthology *Ha-Zman*, vol. 3, in the month of Kislev 5664 (December 1903); its subtitle was the date of the memorial day for the earlier pogrom: Sivan 20, 5408 (June 10, 1648). Bialik's experience, along with Dubnow's difficulties in publishing his 1903 essay "A Historic Moment," which called for mass emigration and self-defense, might have discouraged the group from trying to publish eyewitness accounts in the Russian Empire. Dubnow, *Dos bukh fun mayn lebn*, 1:381; Goren, *'Eduyot nifge'e Kishinov*, 39; Miron, introduction to "Ba-ir ha-haregah" in Bialik, *Shire H. N. Bialik*, 163, 167.
26. See Lambroza, "The Pogroms of 1903–1906," 231. On Kishinev see Judge, *Easter in Kishinev*, 72.
27. When a pogrom broke out in Gomel in September 1903, Bialik suggested to Auerbach that it would be worth collecting new documents for a "second volume." See Lachower, *Igrot*, 175–176.
28. Motzkin, *Die Judenpogrome*, 1:vi.
29. Ibid., 1:5.
30. Ibid., 1:6–10.
31. Ibid., 1:vii–viii.
32. Ibid., 1:5.
33. Ibid., 1:ix.
34. On the work's genesis, see Bein, *Sefer Motzkin*, 73–78. When government archives were briefly accessible to researchers after the 1917 revolution, Dubnow and Grigorii Iakovlevich Krasnyi-Admoni published a two-volume Russian-language study on pogroms since 1881, based on government documents rather than on eyewitness testimonies. Dubnow and Krasnyi-Admoni, *Materialy*.
35. Motzkin, *Die Judenpogrome*, 1:v.
36. See Baron, *The Russian Jew under Tsar and Soviets*, 187–200; Engel, "World War I"; Levine, "Frontiers of Genocide."
37. *Der Moment*, December 31, 1914, 3.
38. Kahan, "The Diary of Anne Kahan," 141. An-ski's four-volume wartime diary chronicling the suffering of the Jews of eastern Europe, "Khurbn Galitsye," was published in English as *The Enemy at His Pleasure*. The Yiddish writer Sholem Asch recorded his wartime impressions in *Dos bukh fun tsar*; they inspired one of his major literary creations, *Kidesh ha-shem*, a historical novel on Jewish martyrdom.
39. Roskies, *The Jewish Search for a Usable Past*, 18–19, and Roskies, *Against the Apocalypse*, 135–139. In his autobiography, Dubnow describes how war censorship destroyed the Yiddish-language press in the Russian Empire and also affected Jewish Russian-language periodicals. See Dubnow, *Dos bukh fun mayn lebn*, 2:181.
40. On these pogroms see, for example, Lohr, "1915 and the War Pogrom Paradigm in the Russian Empire," 41–51, esp. 42, and Holquist, "The Role of Personality in the First (1914–1915) Russian Occupation of Galicia and Bukovina."
41. Dubnov-Erlich, *The Life and Work of S. M. Dubnov*, 165; Dubnow, *Dos bukh fun mayn lebn*, 2:180–181.
42. These materials appeared in an eight-volume periodical *Jüdisches Archiv: Mitteilungen des Kommittees "Jüdisches Kriegsarchiv,"* edited by the Austrian Zionist Robert Stricker, 1915–1918. See Lappin, "Zwischen den Fronten."
43. Kassow, *Who Will Write Our History?*, 10–11; Kuznitz, "An-sky's Legacy," 321–328; Shabad and Shalit, *Vilner zamlbukh*, 2:254.
44. Lunsky, "Di yidishe historish-etnografishe gezelshaft in Vilne," 47.
45. Ibid. See also Lunsky, "Di yidishe historish-etnografishe gezelshaft," 861–862. On the history of the Society, see Gottesman, *Defining the Yiddish Nation*, 75–108.

46. Kuznitz, "The Origins of Yiddish Scholarship," 28–30. See also Gottesman, *Defining the Yiddish Nation*, esp. xi–xxiii. Apart from a widespread commitment to folklore and "zamlung," this new history-mindedness found expression in a range of diaries and autobiographies written during the war and published in the interwar period. See, for example, Shatsky, "Idishe memuarn literatur." For a discussion of autobiographical writing after the First World War, see Roskies, *Against the Apocalypse*, 132–162.
47. Estimates of the numbers of Jewish victims vary: David Engel estimates 50,000–60,000 Jewish dead; see Engel, "Being Lawful in a Lawless World," 83. Cf. Abramson, *A Prayer for the Government*, 110, which speaks of "tens and even hundreds of thousand" victims. Other sources count up to 200,000 dead, or "about 10 percent of Ukrainian Jewry." Kenez, "Pogroms and White Ideology," 302. Kenez seems to follow Baron, *The Russian Jew under Tsar and Soviets*, 221. Similarly, Piotr Wróbel estimates 30,000–200,000 Jewish victims of violence in Wróbel, "The Kaddish Years," 219. See Abramson, *A Prayer for the Government* for a thorough overview on Ukrainian Jewish history in the years 1917–1920.
48. Tcherikower, *Antisemitizm un pogromen*, 1–2; Szajkowski, "Di geshikhte," 333, 335; see also Kuznitz, "Origins of Yiddish Scholarship," 47. On Tcherikower's role as a historian see also Karlip, "Between Martyrology and Historiography."
49. Tcherikower, *Antisemitizm un pogromen*, 2.
50. AYIVO RG 80, MK470.55, folder 664, frame 57221.
51. Tcherikower, *In der tkufe fun revolutsye*, 1:viii.
52. Shtif, *Pogromen in Ukraine*, 12.
53. Szajkowski, "Di geshikhte," 336–337.
54. Tcherikower, *Antisemitizm un pogromen*, 3; Szajkowski, "Di geshikhte," 347, n 37. The archive received material from other Jewish institutions in the pogrom regions: the Central Relief Committee for Pogrom Victims and the Jewish National Secretariat. Later it received the archives of the Jewish Ministry in Ukraine, of the Moscow-based EKOPO, and of a number of Jewish communities and other Jewish organizations.
55. Szajkowski, "Di geshikhte," 338. Other Jewish archives also faced the threat of confiscation. For example, in April 1918 the Bolshevik Commissariat for Jewish Affairs seized the archives of the Jewish Historical-Ethnographic Society. Dubnow, *Dos bukh fun mayn lebn*, 2:252–253. On his concern with moving his personal archives out of the Soviet Union, see Dubnow, *Buch des Lebens*, 2:359–361.
56. Szajkowski, "Di geshikhte," 335, 337, 339. Tcherikower, *Antisemitizm un pogromen*, 4–5.
57. Hersh Dovid Nomberg, "Finf kufers yidishe tsores," *Der Moment*, April 28, 1921.
58. Kuznitz, "Origins of Yiddish Scholarship," 48–52. In addition, Tcherikower created an office in Warsaw that would collect documents from refugees of the Ukrainian pogroms who had fled to Poland. Szajkowski, "Di geshikhte," 339–340. On Berlin as temporary center of eastern European Jewish culture, see, for example, Estraikh, "Vilna on the Spree."
59. Dubnow to Tcherikower, May 19, 1922, quoted in Szajkowski, "Di geshikhte," 341.
60. Tcherikower, *Antisemitizm un pogromen*, with an article by Dubnow on the third Haidamak massacre. The Russian version appeared as *Antisemitizm i pogromy na Ukrainie*. Schechtman, *Pogromy Dobrovolcheskoi armii na Ukraine*. The still unpublished volumes were a Yiddish translation of Joseph Schechtman's monograph *Di pogromen fun Denikins armey*; Shtif, *Di pogromen fun di Povstantses*; Lestschinsky, *Di resultatn fun di pogromen*; Gergel, *Kurtse bashraybungen fun ale faregistrirte pogromen*; and Gergel, *Materialn tsu der geshikhte fun zelbshuts*. See Szajkowski, "Di geshikhte," 342–344. Parts of the manuscripts can be found in the Tcherikower Collection, AYIVO RG 80 MK 470.56, folders 674 and 680. In 1965, the YIVO Institute in New York finally published an additional volume prepared in Berlin: Elias Tcherikower, *Di Ukrainer pogromen in yor 1919*.
61. Tcherikower, *In der tkufe fun revolutsye*.
62. Tcherikower, *Antisemitizm un pogromen*, 5.
63. Tcherikower to Zuckerman, May 25, 1923, quoted in Szajkowski, "Di geshikhte," 343.
64. Ibid., 344. See also Elias Tcherikower, "The Eastern Jewish Historical Archive in Berlin on the Role of Petliura in the Jewish Pogroms," AYIVO RG 80, MK 470, folder 481, frames 39265–39284.

65. On the trial and its wider implications, see Engel, "Being Lawful in a Lawless World," 83–97. See also Torrès, *Le procès des pogromes*.
66. Comité des Délégations Juives, *Les pogromes en Ukraine sous les gouvernements ukrainiens*. A contemporaneous publication that used documents from the Tcherikower archive was Schechtman, *Ver iz farantvortlekh far di pogromen in Ukraine?*
67. On the committee's interwar political advocacy defending Jewish minority rights and opposing anti-Semitism, see Graf, *Die Bernheim-Petition 1933*. On Motzkin's involvement as head of the defense committee, see Bein, *Sefer Motzkin*, 98–99.
68. Aleksiun, "Setting the Record Straight."
69. Kassow, *Who Will Write Our History?*, 60.
70. Engel, "Writing History as a National Mission," 136–138.
71. On the crystallization of this kind of historiography, see Kassow, *Who Will Write Our History?*, 49–89, esp. 58–78; Aleksiun, *Ammunition in the Struggle for National Rights*; Aleksiun, "Setting the Record Straight"; Aleksiun, "Polish Jewish Historians before 1918"; Eisenbach, "Jewish Historiography in Interwar Poland"; and Friedman, "Polish Jewish Historiography."
72. Friedman, "Polish Jewish Historiography," 375. On Dubnow's relation to the YIVO Institute, see Hilbrenner, "Simon Dubnow als eine Art intellektueller Pate."
73. Web, "Dubnov and Jewish Archives," 87.
74. Kassow, *Who Will Write Our History?*, 51–52.
75. For a general history of YIVO from its founding until the Second World War, see Kuznitz, "Origins of Yiddish Scholarship."
76. Kassow, *Who Will Write Our History?*, 78–89; Fishman, *The Rise of Modern Yiddish Culture*, 93–97.
77. Fishman, *The Rise of Modern Yiddish Culture*, 141.
78. Kuznitz, "Origins of Yiddish Scholarship," 96–102. See also Brenner, *Propheten des Vergangenen*, chap. 3, esp. 150–151.
79. Dobroszycki, "YIVO in Interwar Poland," 494–518.
80. For an analysis of Jewish wartime memoirs, see Garbarini, *Numbered Days*; Shapiro, *Holocaust Chronicles*; Waxman, *Writing the Holocaust*; and Zapruder, *Salvaged Pages*.
81. See, for example, Nathan Cohen, "The Diaries of the Sonderkommando"; Waxman, *Writing the Holocaust*, 81–87, and Graif, *We Wept without Tears*.
82. Krakowski and Altman, "The Testament of the Last Prisoners."
83. Garbarini, *Numbered Days*, 2.
84. According to Dubnow's daughter, he said: "'People, do not forget. Speak of this, people; record it all.' Of those who could have heard those words hardly one is alive today. Only the legend lives, no less truthful than the life itself." See Dubnov-Ehrlich, *The Life and Work of S. M. Dubnov*, 247. See also Dawidowicz, *The Holocaust and the Historians*, 125, Krakowski, "Memorial Projects," 388, and Pinson, "Simon Dubnow," 39. For a critical examination of the evidence on Dubnow's death, see Berg and Hilbrenner, "Der Tod Simon Dubnows."
85. Donat, *The Holocaust Kingdom*, 211, emphasis in original.
86. On Bialystok, see Bender, "Arkhiyon ha-mahteret be-Bialistok," and Klibanski, "The Underground Archives of the Bialystok Ghetto"; on Lodz, see Unger, "Ha-ti'ud ha-yehudi mi-geto Lodz," and Dobroszycki, *The Chronicle of the Lodz Ghetto*, ix–lxviii; on Vilna, see Arad, "Ha-arkhiyon ha-mehtarti shel geto Vilna," and Fishman, *The Rise of Modern Yiddish Culture*, chap. 10. On Warsaw, see the articles Raya Cohen, "Emmanuel Ringelblum," and Sakowska, "Two Forms of Resistance in the Warsaw Ghetto"; the meticulously researched study Kassow, *Who Will Write Our History?*; and Gutman, *Emanuel Ringelblum*.
87. Ringelblum, *Ksovim fun geto*, 2:82–83. For biographical information on the diverse personalities in Oyneg Shabes, see Kassow, *Who Will Write Our History?*, 145–208.
88. Ringelblum, *Ksovim fun geto*, 84–85.
89. Ibid., 86.
90. Ibid.
91. Kassow, *Who Will Write Our History?*, 239–283.
92. See a sample Oyneg Shabes questionnaire in Kermish, *To Live with Honor and Die with Honor*, 25–31.

93. Kassow, *Who Will Write Our History?*, 226–230.
94. Ringelblum, *Ksovim fun geto*, 86.
95. Ibid., 102.
96. Ringelblum was caught by the Germans in April 1943 and brought to the Trawniki labor camp, from which he escaped in August. He returned to Warsaw and went into hiding in an underground bunker in the home of a Christian family with his wife and son and over thirty other Jews. There he wrote on Polish-Jewish relations until the Germans discovered the bunker on March 7, 1944, and murdered all its inhabitants several days later. See Kassow, *Who Will Write Our History?*, 383–385.
97. Kermish, *To Live with Honor and to Die with Honor*, 66.
98. Engel, "Writing History as a National Mission," 120, 118.
99. Note by Dr. Ada Friedman (Eber), no date, AYIVO RG 1258, folder 982, box 59, p. 4, English; emphasis in original.
100. Ibid. Despite his commitment to collecting other survivors' testimonies, Friedman never testified on his own wartime experiences.
101. See for example: Yitskhok Kvintman, "A denkmol dem umbakantn yidishn partizan un geto-kemfer," *Farn Folk*, October 12, 1948, 10; report by Cwi Horowic on the activities of the Jewish historical commission in Göttingen [1947], MAG Cultural Office No. 475, German; Michel Mazor, "Historique du CDJC," *Le Monde Juif* 34–35 (1963), 43–44.
102. Pinson, "Simon Dubnow," 18.
103. Protocol of the inaugural meeting of the Society of the Friends of the Central Jewish Historical Commission in Lodz, September 10, 1945, AŻIH/CŻKH/303/XX, folder 405, p. 6, Yiddish.
104. Ibid, 6–7.
105. "Barikhtn tetikeyt," *Fun Letstn Khurbn* 10 (December 1948), 169.
106. Ibid., 163.
107. See Bauer, "Teguvotehen shel kibutsim yehudiyim," 109–128.
108. Some scholars argue that in western Europe—particularly in Germany—periodic anti-Jewish violence also constituted a central component in the Jewish experience from the early nineteenth century to the Holocaust (see, for example, Rohrbacher, *Gewalt im Biedermeier*, and Hoffmann, Bergmann, and Smith, *Exclusionary Violence*). Nevertheless, these outbursts were not comparable in geographic scale or numbers of victims to those in eastern Europe, and at least in principle, the Rechtsstaat provided protection to western Jews before the Nazi rise to power.

    That west European Jews did not engage in historical documentation of their suffering as did their east European counterparts does not mean, however, that the experience of persecution did not elicit a vibrant discourse about the Jewish past or that they lacked historical consciousness. The recent comparative analysis by Guy Miron has shown that Jews in Germany, France, and Hungary in the 1930s and 1940s responded to the experience of exclusion and persecution by debating and reimagining their history in search of a usable past that would help them bear their troubled present; see Miron, *The Waning of Emancipation*.
109. Prominent members of the liberal assimilated Jewish intelligentsia founded the CV in 1893. The Verein zur Abwehr des Antisemitismus (Association for the Defense against Antisemitism), founded in March 1891 on the initiative of both Jewish and non-Jewish middle-class notables, also fought discrimination. These mass-membership organizations gathered and publicized information on anti-Semites and their activities, petitioned government agencies, and lobbied against the election of anti-Semitic politicians. The CV in particular—with a peak membership of 40,000 by 1914—used German penal law concepts such as "instigation of class hatred" and "insult of a religious community" to bring civil lawsuits against anti-Jewish acts. Both organizations appealed to liberal segments of German society who agreed that anti-Semitism impeded progress; thus banning anti-Semitic activity was in the interest of all Germans. In addition to bringing anti-Semitic acts and their perpetrators to public attention, they produced materials proving Jews' loyalty and commitment to their fatherland. On similar groups in Austria, see Meyer, *German-Jewish History in Modern Times*, 3: chap. 8. In general, see Schorsch, *Jewish Reactions to German Anti-Semitism*; Barkai, *Wehr dich!*

110. For example, when in 1885—during a period of growing anti-Semitism—the Jewish historian Harry Bresslau established a historical commission in Berlin to show the national rootedness of German Jews, its main focus was the Middle Ages. See Meisel, "Ha-va'ada ha-historit"; Pawliczek, "Zwischen Anerkennung und Ressentiment."
111. For a general overview of Alfred Wiener's biography and the history of the JCIO, see Barkow, *Alfred Wiener*; on the Frankfurter trial, see 65–83. See also JCIO, *The Jewish Central Information Office*.
112. Periodical series were *Reports of the Jewish Central Information Office* (from July 1934), *The Nazis at War* (October 1939–April 1945), and *Jewish News* (January 1942-September 1945). Among the document collections were: *Wirtschaftsboykott*; *Der Kirchenstreit in Deutschland: Bibel und Rasse*; and *Dokumentensammlung über die Entrechtung, Ächtung und Vernichtung der Juden in Deutschland seit der Regierung Adolf Hitler. Abgeschlossen am 15. Oktober 1936*. For a detailed list of the library's mimeographed reports, see Barkow, *Alfred Wiener*, 197–203.
113. See Barkow, *Alfred Wiener*, 104–125. See also the critical edition of those testimonies, Barkow, Gross, and Lenarz, *Novemberpogrom 1938*.
114. Miron, "The Leo Baeck Institute and German-Jewish Historiography on the Holocaust," 306.
115. Ibid. On the history of the LBI see also Nattermann, *Deutsch-jüdische Geschichtsschreibung*, and Hoffmann, *Preserving the Legacy of German Jewry*. The only studies on the Nazi period that the LBI published before the Holocaust entered the center of its focus were Simon, *Aufbau und Untergang* (1959), and Freeden, *Jüdisches Theater in Nazideutschland* (1964), in addition to isolated articles in the institute's yearbook.
116. H. G. Adler, *Theresienstadt 1941–1945*; H. G. Adler, *Die verheimlichte Wahrheit; Theresienstädter Dokumente*; H. G. Adler, *Der verwaltete Mensch*. On Adler see Hocheneder, *H. G. Adler*.
117. Lamm, "Über die innere und äußere Entwicklung." Ten years later, the social worker and sociologist Harry Maor completed a dissertation on the reconstruction of Jewish communities in postwar Germany: Maor, "Über den Wiederaufbau."
118. Brenner, "Vergessene Historiker." I wish to thank Michael Brenner for allowing me to read this unpublished manuscript. A prominent example of German Jewish intellectuals whose historical interest was not the recent past but centuries of German Jewish culture is Heinz Mosche Graupe, who in 1961 published a 380-page intellectual history of German Jewry from 1650 through 1942. Graupe dedicated five pages to the Jewish community in Nazi Germany, focusing mainly on cultural and spiritual activity as well as emigration in response to persecution. Graupe, *Die Entstehung des modernen Judentums*. Another example is the rabbi and archivist Bernhard Brilling, a Breslau native who left Israel for Germany in 1955, who focused primarily on Jews in early modern Germany. In the late 1950s he sought to establish a central repository for German Jewish communal and institutional records under the auspices of the Central Council of Jews in Germany. However, the council eventually opted to locate the materials in Israel. On Brilling, see Honigmann, "Das Projekt von Rabbiner Dr. Bernhard Brilling."
119. Barnouw and van der Stroom, *The Diary of Anne Frank*, 578.
120. De Haan, "The Paradoxes of Dutch History," 356.
121. Kristel, "Survivors and Historians," 208. See Herzberg, *Amor Fati*; Herzberg; *Kroniek*; and Herzberg's camp diary, *Tweestromenland*; Presser, *Ondergang*; and de Jong, *Het Koninkrijk der Nederlanden*.
122. Engel, "Writing History as a National Mission," 119–120.
123. These testimonies are now part of the Anders Collection in the Hoover Institution Archives at Stanford University. In addition, the Polish intellectual Zygmunt Łakociński collected testimonies from five hundred Polish refugees in Sweden in the years 1939–1946. See Dahl, "'. . . this is material arousing interest in common history.'"
124. Such government-sponsored research institutes included, for example, the High Commission for the Investigation of German Crimes in Poland, the French Committee for the History of the Second World War, the Institute of Contemporary History in Munich, and the Netherlands Institute for War Documentation. Frei, *Transnationale Vergangenheitspolitik*,

provides a comparative perspective on how various European states dealt with Nazi crimes in the early postwar years and the role played by documentation in the prosecution of German crimes. On the Institute of Contemporary History in Munich, see Berg, *Der Holocaust*; Moeller, *War Stories*, 51–87; and Möller and Wengst, *50 Jahre Institut für Zeitgeschichte*.
125. The need to trace missing, incarcerated, deported, and displaced individuals led the Allied Forces Headquarters to create a Tracing Bureau within the framework of the British Red Cross in London as early as 1943. Administered by the Supreme Headquarters Allied Expeditionary Forces starting the following year, the tracing service moved to Versailles and with the occupation of Germany to Frankfurt am Main and later to Bad Arolsen, a small town at the center of all Allied occupation zones. With the end of warfare, the tracing bureau was placed under the auspices of the United Nations Relief and Rehabilitation Administration (UNRRA) and, as of July 1947, the International Refugee Organization (IRO). The International Tracing Service (ITS), as it was named in 1948, assembled 26,000 meters of documents on Nazi Germany's victims and perpetrators, including over 50 million reference cards for more than 17.5 million people. The collection became open to the public only in 2007. See http://www.its-arolsen.org/en/homepage/index.html.
126. On these documentation efforts in general, see United States Holocaust Memorial Museum, *In Pursuit of Justice*, esp. 31.
127. See Douglas, *The Memory of Judgment*, 12. Raul Hilberg describes the U.S. Army's transfer of the documents (28,000 linear feet) to the U.S. War Documentation Project, housed in a former torpedo-tube factory in Alexandria, Virginia. See Hilberg, *The Politics of Memory*, 71, and Hilberg, "The Development of Holocaust Research," 26.
128. See "Documentation Centers," in Gutman, *Encyclopedia of the Holocaust*, 1:390–392.
129. See, for example, Moshe Yosef Feigenbaum, "Tsu vos historishe komisyes?," *Fun Letstn Khurbn* 1 (August 1946): 2.

Chapter 2

1. Some 190,000–200,000 of these 300,000–330,000 Jews were French citizens (55,000 naturalized in the interwar period); 140,000 were foreign nationals or stateless (an estimated 30,000—10 percent of all Jews in 1939 France—were recent refugees from Germany, Austria, and Czechoslovakia. Of the 75,721 Jews deported to death camps, 70,000 went to Auschwitz-Birkenau, the remainder to Majdanek and Sobibór. Roughly 55,000 of the deportees were foreign nationals or stateless; 24,500 were French nationals. In addition, some 4,000 Jews died in French internment camps or were executed in France. See Jackson, *France*, 362; Kaspi, *Les Juifs pendant l'Occupation*, 20; Klarsfeld, *Vichy-Auschwitz*, 2: 179–180; Marrus and Paxton, *Vichy France*, 343.
2. Paula Hyman, *The Jews of Modern France*, 185; David Weinberg estimates that there were 180,000 Jews in liberated France (160,000 former residents and 20,000 foreign Jews) in addition to 35,000–40,000 Jewish DPs who arrived in France between 1945 and 1948; see Weinberg, "The Reconstruction of the French Jewish Community," 169; and Wieviorka, *Déportation et génocide*, 337, who estimates from 150,000 to 200,000 Jews in France right after the war.
3. Weinberg, "Between America and Israel," 97.
4. On the Vichy regime in general, see, for example, Jackson, *France*, and Paxton, *Vichy France*.
5. See Jackson, *France*, 355–360, and Marrus and Paxton, *Vichy France*, 24–71.
6. On racial laws and Aryanization policies, see, for example, Kaspi, *Les Juifs pendant l'Occupation*, 53–86, 112–129; Marrus and Paxton, *Vichy France*, 152–160; Poznanski, *Jews in France*, 105–135; and Zuccotti, *The Holocaust*, 51–64. On the Commissariat General see, for example, Billig, *Le Commissariat general aux questions juives*, and Marrus and Paxton, *Vichy France*, 123–152, 283–310. On the UGIF see Jacques Adler, *The Jews of Paris*, and Richard Cohen, *The Burden of Conscience*; Kaspi, *Les Juifs pendant l'Occupation*, 324–339. On internment camps, see Marrus and Paxton, *Vichy France*, 165–176, and Zuccotti, *The Holocaust*, 65–80.

7. On the mass arrests and roundups of summer 1942 see Kaspi, *Les Juifs pendant l'Occupation*, 211–284; Marrus and Paxton, *Vichy France*, 250–269; Zuccotti, *The Holocaust*, 103–137; and Poznanski, *The Jews in France*, 256–292. On French public opinion see Marrus and Paxton, *Vichy France*, 270–280, 321–329; Poznanski, *The Jews in France*, 292–302; and Zuccotti, *The Holocaust*, 138–156. On the deportations from France to Poland see Klarsfeld, *Vichy-Auschwitz*, and Klarsfeld, *Le Mémorial de la Déportation*.
8. In fact, the survival of three-quarters of France's Jewish community was largely due to the complexity of French-German relations, including French leaders' quest for autonomy, rather than to any humanitarian concerns; see Weinberg, "France," 12. However, the rootedness of Jews in French society also played a significant role. See Poznanski, *Jews in France*, 474–483, 488–491, and Marrus and Paxton, *Vichy France*, 343–372.
9. For a general overview of the history of Jews in France and the development of a distinct and deeply republican French Jewish culture and identity, see Berkovitz, *The Shaping of Jewish Identity*, Birnbaum, "Beween Social and Political Assimilation," Birnbaum, *The Jews of the Republic*, Paula Hyman, *The Jews of Modern France*, and Paula Hyman, *From Dreyfus to Vichy*; see also Leff, *Sacred Bonds of Solidarity*.
10. Judt, *Postwar*, 818.
11. The return of property proved a slow and difficult endeavor. See Mandel, *In the Aftermath of Genocide*, 54–55, 64–76.
12. Poznanski, "French Apprehensions, Jewish Expectations," 45–52; Poznanski, *Jews in France*, 462–473; Mandel, *In the Aftermath of Genocide*, 57–61; Weinberg, "The Reconstruction of the French Jewish Community," 176; and Lagrou, "Victims of Genocide," 182, 190–192.
13. Poznanski, *Propagandes et persécutions*, 578–592; Poznanski, "French Apprehensions, Jewish Expectations," 57.
14. Paula Hyman pointed out that 85 percent of the name changes of French Jews over the period 1803 to 1957 took place in the years 1945–1957; see Paula Hyman, *The Jews of Modern France*, 190. See also Benbassa, *The Jews of France*, 182–183; Mandel, *In the Aftermath of Genocide*, 162–165; Wieviorka, *Déportation et génocide*, 361–368.
15. Birnbaum, "Between Social and Political Assimilation," 127. Weinberg, "The Reconstruction of the French Jewish Community," 173–175, makes a similar point. See also Grynberg, "Après la tourmente," 249–286.
16. Mandel, *In the Aftermath of Genocide*, 110–111, 203, and Paula Hyman, *The Jews of Modern France*, 190. Pierre Birnbaum remarked that "to one degree or another, all French Jews, even those who shunned careers in government and chose instead to contribute to the growth of the economy or toil in a variety of professions, remained *fous de la République*, or zealots of the Republic." See Birnbaum, *Jewish Destinies*, 4.
17. See his famous monograph *The Vichy Syndrome*; as well as *The Haunting Past*.
18. On the purges see, for example, Jackson, *France*, 577–590. On the "resistance myth," some form of which arose in all formerly German-occupied or German-allied countries, see Judt, "The Past is Another Country," 162–169, and Rousso, *The Vichy Syndrome*, 15–59.
19. On the long afterlife of arguments downplaying Vichy's responsibility in the persecution of French Jews, see Judt, *Postwar*, 815–820.
20. See Judt, "The Past Is Another Country," 179.
21. See Mandel, *In the Aftermath of Genocide*, 53–55, Poznanski, *Propagandes et persécutions*, 561–578; de Haan, "Paths of Normalization," 89–90.
22. Lagrou, "Victims of Genocide," 187–190.
23. This began to change only in the 1970s and 1980s, in part due to a new generation, and also to the works of English-language historians on French society's encounter with Vichy and the Holocaust in France; see Fabréguet, "Frankreichs Historiker"; Goslan, "The Legacy of World War II in France," 72–101; Jackson, *France*, 6–20; and Rousso, *The Vichy Syndrome*, 98–167.
24. Several scholars provided valuable groundwork for this chapter: Bensoussan, "The Jewish Contemporary Documentation Center"; Jacques Fredj, "Le Centre de Documentation Juive Contemporaine"; Poznanski, "La création du Centre de Documentation Juive Contemporaine,"

Poznanski, "Hakamat ha-merkaz le-ti'ud yahadut zmanenu"; Wieviorka, *Déportation et génocide*, 412–431, Wieviorka, "Du Centre de documentation juive contemporaine au Mémorial de la Shoah," and Wieviorka, *Il y a 50 ans*.

25. See Pougatch, *Figures Juives*, 133–136, and Isaac Schneersohn's autobiography of his early years, *Lebn un kamf in tsaristishn rusland*.
26. Poznanski, "La création du Centre de Documentation Juive Contemporaine," 57–59.
27. Report on the history of the CDJC [Febraury 1946], ACDJC, box 16, p. 8, French (hereafter CDJC Report, February 1946). Because the CDJC's administrative archives are uncatalogued, the designation of boxes reflects the order in which they have been studied, not any official call numbers.
28. The only surviving documentation from the Grenoble initiative consists of a few records in the archives of the Consistoire Central discovered by Renée Poznanski. See Poznanski, "La création du Centre de Documentation Juive Contemporaine," 57–59, and Poznanski, "Hakamat ha-merkaz le-ti'ud yahadut zmanenu."
29. Isaac Schneersohn, "La Création du Centre de Documentation Juive Contemporaine," *Le Monde Juif Le Monde Juif* 63–64 (March–April, 1953): 3.
30. On the Italian occupation, see Marrus and Paxton, *Vichy France and the Jews*, 315–321, and Poznanski, *Jews in France*, 386–390. See also Carpi, *Between Mussolini and Hitler*, 79–192.
31. CDJC Report, February 1946, p. 9.
32. Poznanski, "La création du Centre de Documentation Juive Contemporaine," 56; Schneersohn, "La Création," 4.
33. Lambert, *Carnet d'un témoin*, 220–221. See also Bensoussan, "The Jewish Contemporary Documentation Center," 248. Faced with growing anti-Semitism, xenophobia, and racism, the interwar Jewish community was split among native and immigrant Jews, secular and religious groups, and integrationist or Zionist perspectives.
34. Poznanski, "La création du Centre de Documentation Juive Contemporaine," 56, and Schneersohn, "La Création," 5.
35. "La réunion décide," no date, ACC, reel 1, folder 4. See also Henri Hertz, "Historique du CDJC," ACDJC, DCCXIV.
36. "Voici quelques mots en ce que nous voulons," ACC, reel 1, folder 4.
37. Ibid.
38. "Ordre du Jour," no date, ACC, reel 1, folder 4.
39. See list of names attached to the outline of the nine research fields, ACC, reel 1, folder 4, French. This description of the nine commissions is based on this document.
40. It was headed by Chief Rabbi Hirschler and Rabbi René Kapel, who did relief work in the camps with the help of Jewish aid agencies.
41. These organizations included the Jewish immigration organization HICEM, the Consistoire, ORT, OSE, the Jewish scouting organization Eclaireurs Israélites de France, FSJF, the AJDC, and relief organizations including Comité d'Assistance aux Réfugiés, Entraide française israélite, and Commission Centrale des Organisations Juives d'Assistance. The other members were Schneersohn, Szeftel, Glaeser, Grinberg, Hermann, rabbis Hirschler and Kapel, Lambert, Livian, Lubetzki, Meiss, Hertz, Schah and his son Eugène, Joseph Milbauer, Joseph Milner, and Pierre Paraf.
42. An estimated 60,000 Jews served in the French army in 1940; thus Jewish conscripts made up 20 percent of the Jewish population, while non-Jewish soldiers comprised only 15 percent of the gentile population. See Kaspi, *Les Juifs pendant l'Occupation*, 21.
43. "Centre de Documentation," ACC, reel 1, folder 4.
44. CDJC Report, February 1946, p. 10.
45. Ibid., 9. Henri Hertz, "Les débuts du CDJC," *Le Monde Juif* 63–64 (March–April 1953): 2 and 24. See also "26 Avril 1947, Allocution de M. Léon Meiss" (hereafter "Meiss's speech"), ACDJC, box 10, p. 4. Schneersohn mentioned a study of the history of the Consistoire Central in his letter to Meiss in Lyon, June 25, 1943, ACC, reel 1, folder 4, French.
46. Schneersohn to Meiss, August 4, 1943, ACC, reel 1, folder 4, French, and Isaac Schneersohn, "Le Centre de Documentation Juive Contemporaine" [1947–1948] (hereafter "CDJC 1947–1948"), ACDJC, box 10, p. 1.

47. Report by Samy Lattès, August 4, 1943, ACC, reel 2, folder 5, French. See also the report by Albert Manuel, secretary-general of the Consistoire in Grenoble, "Œuvres du CDJC," Lyon, May 7 1943, ACC, reel 1, folder 4, pp. 7–8.
48. Marrus and Paxton, *Vichy France and the Jews*, 319.
49. Hertz, "Les débuts du CDJC," 2.
50. CDJC Report, February 1946, p. 10; report on the history of the CDJC, January 31, 1946 (hereafter CDJC Report, January 31, 1946), ACDJC, box 10, French, p. 1. The reports on *Résistance* involvement may be a postwar fabrication, but it is not unlikely that their contacts were sought to preserve the material.
51. CDJC Report, February 1946, p. 11.
52. Schneersohn, "CDJC 1947–1948," 1.
53. See Rayski, *The Choice of the Jews*, 167.
54. "Note," March 31, 1949, ACDJC, box 10, French.
55. CDJC, *The Jewish Contemporary Documentation Centre*, 1. As Renée Poznanski pointed out, after the war the CDJC activists commemorated these dead as if they had died as a consequence of their activity as *résistants*, not because they were persecuted as Jews. Poznanski, "La création du Centre de Documentation Juive Contemporaine," 52.
56. CRIF was originally founded in January 1944 as Conseil représentatif des israélites de France to coordinate resistance activities of various Jewish factions. See Kaspi, *Les Juifs pendant l'Occupation*, 377–380.
57. Poliakov's memoirs, written after his break with the CDJC, provide a somewhat dismissive account of Schneersohn's efforts: "I remember that, first, he [Schneerson] had established an office in Grenoble, rue Bizanet, where a half-dozen typists were charged with excerpting the Journal Officiel [record of government acts and laws] to compile the endless list of 'Aryanized' Jewish businesses, which I found utterly ridiculous, not realizing that for everything there is a need of a beginning. Back in Paris after the Liberation, Isaac Schneerson could at least boast of having created the Contemporary Jewish Documentation Center 'during the night of the Occupation.'" Poliakov, *Mémoires*, 184–185.
58. Schneersohn, "La Création," 4.
59. Between 1905 and 1939, an estimated 80,000 Russian/Soviet, Polish, Hungarian, Romanian, and Baltic Jews immigrated to France. Of the 300,000–330,000 Jews in France in summer 1939, 200,000 were foreign-born. An estimated 50,000 had become French citizens between 1927 and 1940. Although the immigrants embarked on a path of acculturating to their surroundings, they still maintained a stronger ethnic consciousness than their French-born coreligionists and formed their own associations, religious communities, loan societies, mutual aid organizations, press, and trade unions. See Kaspi, *Les Juifs pendant l'Occupation*, 28, and Poznanski, *Jews in France*, 7. On the social and cultural networks of eastern European Jewish immigrants in France see Caron, *Uneasy Asylum*, Paula Hyman, *From Dreyfus to Vichy*, chaps. 3–5; Malinovich, *French and Jewish*, 108–115; Weinberg, *A Community on Trial*.
60. "Réunion de la Commission des Camps," December 13, 1944, ACDJC, box 10, p. 4; "Nos activités," *Bulletin du Centre de Documentation Juive Contemporaine* 1 (April 1945): 10.
61. "Procès-verbal de la Réunion de la Commission des Camps" (hereafter Protocol, Camp Commission), February 22, 1945, ACDJC, box 10, p. 7.
62. Ibid., 2–3.
63. Other Jewish documentation initiatives included the Centre de Documentation Politique, created in 1944 under the auspices of the AIU, and the Centre Israélite d'Information, founded in 1945 by the CRIF.
64. "Procès-verbal de la Réunion de la Commission de Presse" (hereafter Protocol, Press Commission), March 8, 1945, ACDJC, box 10, p. 2. In fact, the Comité and the CDJC both sought to bring the recent past to public consciousness through collecting and research. On the history of the committee, see Jackson, *France*, 6–8, and Douzou, *La Résistance française*, 59–62 and 80–82. Renée Poznanski noted the close contacts among Henri Michel, Poliakov, and Schneersohn. (Initially both institutes were located on the same street.) In an interview, Michel told Poznanski that he donated any documents he found pertaining to Jews to the CDJC archives. Thus for Michel the history of the *Résistance* and the history of the Jews

of France were two entirely separate issues. I wish to thank Renée Poznanski for sharing this information.
65. "Procès-verbal de la Séance du Comité Directeur," March 15, 1945 (hereafter Protocol, Board of Directors, March 15, 1945), ACDJC, box 10, p. 1.
66. Ibid.
67. Ibid.
68. Protocol, Camp Commission, February 22, 1945, 3. This was a widespread impression among survivors in various countries. Scholars investigating British and American reactions to information on the mass murder of European Jews have reached similar conclusions; see, for example, Kushner, *The Holocaust and the Liberal Imagination*, chap. 7.
69. Protocol, Camp Commission, February 22, 1945, p. 3. This silence was also noted by prominent intellectuals of the time, most notably by Jean-Paul Sartre. In his famous essay "Réflexions sur la question juive," written in October 1944, Sartre criticized the lack of public discourse, indeed silence, with which non-Jews in liberated France responded to the cataclysm that the Jews had suffered during the war. See Sartre, *Anti-Semite and Jew*, 71–72.
70. Protocol, Camp Commission, February 22, 1945, p. 3.
71. Ibid., 7.
72. Ibid.
73. In 1934 the movements of the extreme right in France had more members than the Nazi Party in Germany at the time; Weinberg, "France," 8. See also Sternhell, "The Roots of Popular Anti-Semitism."
74. Protocol, Press Commission, February 26, 1945, ACDJC, box 10, p. 5.
75. Ibid.
76. Ibid. The Franco-Prussian War of 1870–1871 ended with the humiliating defeat of Louis Napoleon, the loss of Alsace-Lorraine, and the consolidation of the German Empire, as well as the restoration of the French republic.
77. Ibid., 2.
78. Ibid., 4. Others taking this position were Jacques Polonski and the Russian-born Jewish poet Don Aminado.
79. Ibid., 2ff.
80. Ibid., 3.
81. Ibid., 4.
82. Ibid., 1–6.
83. "Procès-verbal de la Réunion de la 5e Commission," March 22, 1945, ACDJC, box 10, p. 3.
84. Jacques Ratner, "Les travaux de la Commission des Camps: Contre la Conspiration du Silence," *Bulletin du Centre de Documentation Juive Contemporaine* 3 (June 1945): 2.
85. Protocol, Press Commission, April 26, 1945, ACDJC, box 10, pp. 1ff.
86. Protocol, Press Commission, May 31, 1945, ACDJC, box 10, p. 2.
87. Ibid., 3. Scheid-Haas was one of the very few women affiliated with the CDJC.
88. Ibid.
89. In a review of Jacques Polonski's *La presse, la propagande et l'opinion publique*, Zosa Szajkowski, who had escaped France during the war and settled in the United States, praised the book for its rich material but criticized the author's failure to both uncover the French roots of anti-Semitism and address voluntary engagement in the anti-Semitic propaganda encouraged by the Germans; see Szajkowski, "Antisemitishe propagande in Frankraykh 1940–1944," *YIVO Bleter* 27, no. 1 (Spring 1946): 183–185.
90. Ratner, "Les travaux de la Commission des Camps," 2.
91. Ibid.
92. "Procès-verbal de la Réunion de la Commission de la Lecture" (hereafter Protocol, Reading Commission), November 16, 1945, ACDJC, box 10, p. 3.
93. Ibid.
94. Ibid., 4.
95. The occupation-era divisions separated native Jewish leaders active in the UGIF from Jews of immigrant backgrounds. The former—unwilling to abandon their trust in the French

state and in its leaders' adherence to democratic and humanistic principles—believed that a policy of cooperating with Vichy authorities and reliance on law would improve the situation of the Jewish population or at least preserve the status quo. The latter, many of whom were familiar with anti-Jewish violence and lack of government protection, advocated self-defense and resistance. Neither strategy proved effective against the Nazi Final Solution, leaving both French and immigrant Jews helpless and vulnerable. See Jacques Adler, *The Jews of Paris*, and Richard Cohen, *The Burden of Conscience*.
96. Protocol, Reading Commission, November 16, 1945, p. 4.
97. Protocol, Press Commission, April 26, 1945, p. 3ff. Kahn apparently referred to the roundups lasting from January 22 through January 27, 1943, in Marseille, a reprisal action in which the Germans destroyed the old port of Marseille and arrested 5,956 "undesirables" of various kinds (of whom 3,000 were later released). Assisted by the French police, they also sent eight hundred Jews to Compiègne, from which they were transferred in March to Drancy and deported to Sobibór and Majdanek. Susan Zuccotti describes this group as consisting of 211 born in France, 254 born in North Africa, 120 naturalized citizens, and 215 foreigners. Zuccotti, *The Holocaust, the French and the Jews*, 173.
98. Protocol, Press Commission, April 26, 1945, p. 6.
99. Ibid., 5.
100. Ibid., 4.
101. Ibid., 4.
102. Ibid.
103. Ibid., 5ff.
104. Similarly, David Weinberg observed that many Jews adopted the resistance myth that dominated French society after the liberation, in the hope of building a better society after triumphing over Nazi barbarism; see Weinberg, "Between America and Israel," 97.
105. Protocol, Reading Commission, November 16, 1945, p. 3.
106. Protocol, Press Commission, June 7, 1945, ACDJC, box 10, p. 3.
107. Ibid., 2.
108. Ibid., 3.
109. Ibid., 1ff.
110. Ibid., 2.
111. Ibid., 4.
112. This debate again echoes wartime debates over whether the resistance of Jews should focus on Jewish self-interest in the struggle against Nazism or should join in general anti-German resistance that would also serve the Jewish population. See Poznanski, *Jews in France*, 449–457; Jackson, *France*, 367–370.
113. On the *Résistance* as the hegemonic discourse in France and the construction of positive national narratives and patriotic memories, see Rousso, *The Vichy Syndrome*, 15–59; Jackson, *France*, 6–9, 570–612; and Lagrou, "Victims of Genocide," 194–205. On Jewish communal leaders' emphasis on Jewish participation in the *Résistance*, see Weinberg, "The Reconstruction of the French Jewish Community," 176.
114. Schneersohn, "Der yidisher dokumentatsye-tsenter in Frankraykh," *YIVO Bleter* 30, no. 2 (Winter 1947): 249–257, 250.
115. "Le Centre de Documentation Contemporaine a Quatre Ans," *Le Monde Juif* 9–10 (May–June 1947): 20.
116. Hertz, "Historique du CDJC," 59.
117. André Spire, "Méssage," *Le Monde Juif* 63–64 (March–April 1953): 25.
118. One report claimed that three-quarters of the material collected before the liberation had been lost, but did not specify the extent and content of the collections. CDJC Report, January 31, 1946, p. 1, French.
119. Protocol, Camp Commission, February 22, 1945, p. 2; Protocol, Board of Directors, March 15, 1945, p. 1.
120. "Appel aux Organisations," *Bulletin du Centre de Documentation Juive Contemporaine* 1 (April 1945): 6.

121. On Godart and the CDJC, see Wieviorka, "Le combat de Justin Godart," 125–135.
122. Poliakov, *Mémoires*, 186ff.
123. CDJC Report, January 31, 1946, p. 2.
124. Schneersohn, "Der yidisher dokumentatsye-tsenter," 251ff.
125. While the order was rescinded a month later, the destruction of the archives took place in 1948. See Conan and Rousso, *Vichy*, 46–73.
126. For example, in July and August 1946, Henri Monneray, assistant prosecutor of the French delegation requested that Schneersohn supply documents concerning the SS-Einsatzgruppen reports. See correspondence between Schneersohn and Monneray, July–August 1946, ACDJC, box 5, French. See also, Faure, *Mémoires*, 33, and Moisel, "Résistance und Repressalien," 258–259.
127. "Séance du Comité Direction," June 5, 1947, ACDJC, box 10, p. 1 (hereafter Board of Directors Meeting, June 5, 1947). See also Poliakov, *Mémoires*, 188–190.
128. Schneersohn to Simon Segal, May 25, 1949, ACDJC, box 9, French; Joseph Billig to Schneersohn, March 4, 1948, ACDJC, box 28, French.
129. In a letter to Schneersohn, Billig mentioned that forty boxes of documents, weighing seventy-five kilograms each, had been sent to Paris (see Billig to Schneersohn, January 22, 1949, ACDJC, box 35, French). A later statement mentions five tons of materials, probably including the films, whereas Billig had only referred to documents. Cf. "Note on the Project to Erect the Tomb of the Unknown Jewish Martyr," undated pamphlet [1951/1952], ACDJC, box 8.
130. Schneersohn to the Direction des Relations Culturelles Paris, December 2, 1948, CDJC, box 20, French; list of films received from the American tribunal, assembled by Billig, no date, ACDJC, box 20, French; Memorandum by Office of the Chief Counsel for War Crimes (APO 696 A), April 1949, ACDJC, box 35.
131. On the presence of the Holocaust but the absence of its victims at the Nuremberg trials, see, for example, Marrus, "The Holocaust at Nuremberg," 5–41, Bloxham, "Jewish Witnesses in War Crimes Trials," 539–553, and Bloxham, *Genocide on Trial*, esp. chap. 2.
132. Billig to Schneersohn, March 18, 1949, ACDJC, box 35, French.
133. Billig wished to stay in Germany to collect archival material and observe public opinion there. See his letter to Schneersohn, March 18, 1949, and Schneersohn to Billig, March 23, 1949, ACDJC, box 35, French.
134. CDJC, *The Jewish Contemporary Documentation Center*, 6.
135. Cf. Schneersohn to Arthur D. Greenleigh, November 20, 1945, ACDJC, box 9, English.
136. Schneersohn to Greenleigh, November 29, 1945, ACDJC, box 9, English.
137. Protocol, Press Commission, February 26, 1945, p. 6.
138. Schneersohn, preface to Sarraute and Tager, *Les juifs sous l'occupation*.
139. Protocol, Camp Commission, February 22, 1945, p. 7.
140. Schneersohn, preface to Weill, *Contribution à l'histoire des camps d'internement*, 5.
141. Schneersohn, preface to Sarraute and Tager, *Les juifs sous l'occupation*.
142. Protocol, Camp Commission, February 22, 1945, p. 7.
143. "Procès-verbal de la Séance consacrée au Bulletin du Centre de Documentation," March 22, 1945, ACDJC, box 10, p. 2.
144. Ibid.
145. Isaac Schneersohn, "Pâque de la Libération," *Bulletin du Centre de Documentation Juive Contemporaine* 1 (April 1945): 1.
146. Ibid.
147. Isaac Schneersohn, "Notre tâche," *Le Monde Juif* 1 (August 1946): 1.
148. Sarraute and Rabinovitch, *Examen succinct de la situation juridique actuelle des Juifs*; Lubetzki, *La Condition des Juifs en France sous l'Occupation allemande*; and Sarraute and Tager, *Les Juifs sous l'occupation*.
149. Protocol, Press Commission, February 26, 1945, p. 3.
150. Polonski, *La presse, la propagande et l'opinion publique*; Weill, *Contribution à l'histoire des camps d'internement*; Wellers, *De Drancy à Auschwitz*.

151. Isaac Schneersohn, preface to Knout, *Contribution à l'histoire de la Résistance juive*, 5.
152. Ibid.
153. CDJC, *Activité des organisations juives*; Knout, *Contribution à l'histoire de la Résistance juive*; Lazarus, *Juifs au combat*.
154. Yehuda Bauer pioneered in calling for a more inclusive understanding of resistance that would not focus solely on armed struggle but would also include "any group action consciously taken in opposition to known or surmised laws, actions or intentions directed against the Jews by the Nazis and their supporters." See Bauer, *A History of the Holocaust*, 246, as well as Bauer, *Rethinking the Holocaust*, 119–166.
155. Meiss's speech, April 26, 1947, p. 4.
156. CDJC, *La bataille du ghetto Varsovie*; Poliakov, *La condition des Juifs en France*; Poliakov, *L'étoile jaune*.
157. Board of Directors Meeting, June 5, 1947, p. 2.
158. Cassou, *Le pillage par les Allemands*; Monneray, *La persécution des Juifs en France*; Monneray, *La persécution des Juifs dans les pays de l'Est*.
159. CDJC, *Les Juifs en Europe*; Ansky, *Les Juifs en Algérie*; and Billig, *Allemagne et le genocide*.
160. Poliakov, *La bréviaire de la haine*; three years later it appeared in English as *Harvest of Hate*. For further discussion of this book, see the conclusion.
161. Poliakov, *Mémoires*, 199–200.
162. Poznanski, "Vichy et les Juifs," 59.
163. Annette Wieviorka attributed non-Jewish historians' lack of interest in the CDJC's early studies to the Jacobin traditions of French academia, which viewed the Jews solely as French citizens. She also cited postwar French historiography's orientation toward the Annales School, which focused on the study of political, economic, and social history over a long span of time rather than on the recent past. This prevented the development of a separate field of "contemporary history" in France. See Wieviorka, *Déportation et génocide*, 430ff. On the separate spheres that characterized the historiography on Jews and non-Jews in wartime France until the 1970s, see Poznanski, *Jews in France*, 475, and Jackson, *France*, 15.
164. Poznanski, *Propagandes et persécutions*, 590, 592.
165. Protocol, Board of Directors, March 15, 1945, p. 2.
166. CDJC Report, January 1946, p. 1; Board of Directors Meeting, June 5, 1947, p. 4.
167. Eric Conan and Henry Rousso claimed that survivors preferred to be part of an all-inclusive category of victims rather than being singled out; see Conan and Rousso, *Vichy*, 19–20, 51–52.
168. Meiss's speech, April 26, 1947, p. 7.
169. Board of Directors Meeting, June 5, 1947, p. 5.
170. Ibid.
171. "Procès-verbal de la réunion," June 9, 1947, ACDJC, box 10, p. 2.
172. Board of Directors Meeting, June 5, 1947, p. 5ff.
173. Ibid., 5.
174. This was true for French Jewish organizations in general in the early postwar years. In 1947, 82 percent of the funds on which Jewish organizations depended came from abroad, mostly the United States. See Mandel, *In the Aftermath of Genocide*, 170.
175. Protocol, Press Commission, February 26, 1945, p. 2; Schneersohn to Greenleigh, June 6, 1946, ACDJC, box 9, French.
176. For a discussion of the role of American Jewish philanthropic organizations in the material reconstruction of the Jewish community in France, see Mandel, *In the Aftermath of Genocide*, 167–169, and Mandel, "Philanthropy or Cultural Imperialism?," 54. For a general overview of AJDC activities in postwar Europe and its aid to survivors, see Bauer, *Out of the Ashes*, xviii, 237–245, and Hobson Faure, "Performing a Healing Role."
177. See Protocol, Board of Directors, March 15, 1945, p. 2; Board of Directors Meeting, June 5, 1947, p. 4; Moses Beckelman to Justin Godart, January 22, 1948, ACDJC, box 9, English; Schneersohn to Beckelman, January 28, 1948, ACDJC, box 9, French; Joseph Schwartz to Justin Godart, May 23, 1949, ACDJC, box 9, French.

178. Laura Margolis to Isaac Schneersohn, November 28, 1946, ACDJC, box 9, French; Schneersohn to Beckelman, December 13, 1946, ACDJC, box 9, French; Beckelman to Schneersohn, May 17, 1947, ACDJC, box 9, English.
179. Schneersohn to Beckelman, February 8, 1950, ACDJC, box 9, French; Schneersohn to Moses A. Leavitt, January 4, 1952, ACDJC, box 9; Schneersohn to Beckelman, February 6, 1952, ACDJC, box 9, French.
180. Schneersohn to Marcel Livian, October 14, 1952, ACDJC, box 21, French.
181. Schneersohn to Simon Segal, March 11, 1947, ACDJC, box 3, French. See also Isaac Schneersohn to Max Weinreich, October 21, 1947, ACDJC, box 31, French; statute of the Comité des Amis du Centre de Documentation Juive Contemporaine, esp. article 2, no date, ACDJC, box 24.
182. Cf. Schneersohn, "Mes chers Amis," April 25, 1947, ACDJC, box 19, pp. 1–7; Schneersohn to Zalman Shneour, May 7, 1949, ACDJC, box 26, French; Schneersohn to Philip Friedman, October 21, 1949, ACDJC, box 26, French; "Dr. Shafran's Return to France; Sought Funds in US for Publication of Documents," *JTA News*, November 27, 1949, 6.
183. Godart reported back to Paris that his mission was proving difficult because of American Jewish leaders' stronger commitment to humanitarian relief; see Godart to Schneersohn, June 24, 1948, ACDJC, box 16, French. Moreover, Philip Friedman (see chapter 3), who by then had settled in New York, surmised that the lack of English and Yiddish publications limited the center's appeal to a Jewish audience in the United States; see Friedman to Schneersohn, November 28, 1949, ACDJC, box 27, Yiddish. Nathan Chanin of the Workmen's Circle in New York informed Schneersohn that American Jews were more inclined to donate what they could spare of their limited financial resources to the nascent Jewish state, rather than to a documentation center in Paris; see Chanin to Schneersohn, October 31, 1949, ACDJC, box 27, Yiddish.
184. Isaac Schneersohn to Maurice Bisgyer, September 27, 1949, ACDJC, box 26, French.
185. Justin Godart to Henry Morgenthau Jr., October 17, 1949, ACDJC, box 35, English.
186. Schneersohn to Bisgyer, October 13, [1950], ACDJC, box 26, English.
187. Schneersohn to Bisgyer, September 27, 1949, ACDJC, box 26, French.
188. The AJC made the largest contributions: $7,500 in March 1947, an additional 250,000 francs in November, and finally 1,869,715 francs in August 1948. Despite Schneersohn's repeated requests, this was the AJC's last payment, due to its own budgetary difficulties and a growing focus on the Middle East. See John Slawson to Schneersohn, March 18, 1947, ACDJC, box 18, French; Joel D. Wolfsohn to Schneersohn, November 25, 1947, ACDJC, box 9, French; Godart to Schneersohn, June 24, 1948, ACDJC, box 16, French; Wolfsohn to Schneersohn, August 17 1948, ACDJC, box 3, French; Schwartz to Schneersohn, August 23, 1948, ACDJC, box 9, English; AJDC to Godart, December 18, 1948, ACDJC, box 9, French; Schneersohn to Wolfsohn, May 20, 1949, ACDJC, box 3, English; Zachariah Shuster to Schneersohn, July 7, 1949, ACDJC, box 27, English; Slawson to Godart, July 8, 1949, ACDJC, box 3, French; Slawson to Meiss, December 13, 1949, ACDJC, box 9, English; Simon Segal to Meiss, February 20, 1950, ACDJC, box 3, French; Slawson to Schneersohn, June 2, 1952, ACDJC, box 9, English.
189. HIAS provided 100,000 francs; see Schneersohn to L. Neikrug, July 27, 1948, ACDJC, box 33.
190. The ACDJC received 700,000 francs; see Schneersohn to Wolfsohn, May 20, 1949, ACDJC, box 3, English.
191. The Circle donated $750; see Schneersohn to Chanin, May 30, 1950, ACDJC, box 3, Yiddish.
192. Schneersohn to Leftwich, June 9, 1948, ACDJC, box 34, English; September 20, 1948, ACDJC, box 34, French; Schneersohn to Jacques Bloch, December 19, 1949, ACDJC, box 6, French; Léon Czertok to Pierre Bigar, July 16, 1951, ACDJC, box 23, French.
193. The hint that the center needed to widen its scope to be attractive to Jews in Britain came from Leftwich in a letter to Schneersohn, April 23, 1948, ACDJC, box 34, English.
194. In early May 1948, Leftwich and Machover advised Schneersohn to postpone the campaign until events in the Middle East had calmed down. But Schneersohn forged ahead. See Leftwich

and Machover to Schneersohn, May 11, 1948, and Schneersohn to Leftwich, June 9, 1948, both in ACDJC, box 34, English.
195. Leftwich to Schneersohn, March 16, 1950, ACDJC, box 34, English; Schneersohn to Machover, April 28, 1950, ACDJC, box 34, French; Schneersohn to Paul Philipson, August 29, 1950, ACDJC, box 35, French; Schneersohn to Machover May 5, 1950, ACDJC, box 34, French.
196. Schneersohn to René Mayer, January 27, 1951, ACDJC, box 26, French; Léon Czertok to Pierre Bigar, July 16, 1951, ACDJC, box 23, French.
197. Justin Godart to Joseph Schwartz, May 4, 1949, ACDJC, box 9, French; Schneersohn to Wolfssohn, May 20, 1949, ACDJC, box 3, French.
198. The AJDC responded with a payment of 1.85 million francs to cover part of the debts; see Moses Beckelman to Schneersohn, May 5, 1952, and Schneersohn to Beckelman, May 6, 1952, and May 17, 1952, all in ACDJC, box 9, French.
199. Schneersohn to Beckelman, May 6, 1952, ACDJC, box 9.
200. Schneersohn to Shneour, January 29, 1951, ACDJC, box 26, French.
201. Schneersohn to Adolph Held, October 13, 1949, ACDJC, box 35, French.
202. These commemorative projects had begun with pilgrimages to the Drancy camp, starting in September 1944. The site's return to commercial use preempted any memorial there. A memorial plaque in the synagogue at the rue de la Victoire in Paris, dedicated in February 1949, was the first central memorial in Paris. See Wieviorka, *Déportation et genocide*, 391–411. Other memorials likely to have inspired Schneersohn were the Warsaw Ghetto Memorial, dedicated in April 1948, as well as the failed but much-debated American Jewish initiative to build an American Memorial to Six Million Jews of Europe in New York City in the years 1947–1950. See Diner, *We Remember With Reverence and Love*, 24–25.
203. "Procès-verbal de la Réunion du Comité Directeur," November 8, 1950, ACDJC, box 10, p. 2 (hereafter Protocol, Board of Directors, November 8, 1950).
204. Ibid.
205. Ibid., 2ff. The idea to use ashes from the death camps in eastern Europe in memorials was not new to France. In 1947 Jewish communists had facilitated the transfer of ashes from Auschwitz-Birkenau with the help of the French Ministry of Foreign Affairs and the Consistoire Central, and over twenty urns had been distributed among Jewish communities and societies of deportees in October 1947. See Wieviorka, *Déportation et genocide*, 396ff.
206. Protocol, Board of Directors, November 8, 1950, p. 3.
207. Ibid.
208. "Note on the Project to Erect the Tomb of the Unknown Jewish Martyr."
209. On that tradition, see Bartov, "Fields of Glory"; Becker, "From Death to Memory." Henri Rousso discusses the post-1945 popularity of memorials for the Unknown Soldier, established after the First World War, in *The Vichy Syndrome*, 17–22.
210. Announcement of the decision by the Second Commission of the Prefect de la Seine and the Conseil Municipal de Paris, July 12, 1951, ACDJC, box 34; "Note pour mémoire," February 21, 1952, ACDJC, box 18 (hereafter memorandum, February 21, 1952). See also "Bulletin Municipal Officiel" of the City of Paris (no. 80).
211. "Note on the Project to Erect the Tomb of the Unknown Jewish Martyr," English, emphasis in original.
212. Schneersohn and Godart to Mrs. Moise S. Cahn, May 5, 1953, ACDJC, box 27, French.
213. "Note on the Project to Erect the Tomb of the Unknown Jewish Martyr."
214. Memorandum, February 21, 1952.
215. Undated note on the memorial project, ACDJC, box 18, French.
216. Schneersohn to Nachum Goldmann, September 9, 1953, ACDJC, box 27, French.
217. Schneersohn to Robert Schuman, May 15, 1951, ACDJC, box 8, French.
218. Memorandum, February 21, 1952.
219. Schneersohn to Schuman, May 15, 1951, ACDJC, box 8, French.
220. Schneersohn to Benjamin Nathan Michelson, April 27, 1951, ACDJC, box 34.
221. Schneersohn to Joshua Shindler, February 18, 1953, ACDJC, box 34.

222. "Note on the Project to Erect the Tomb of the Unknown Jewish Martyr." The idea was to send copies of the memorial book to institutions in Israel and the United States.
223. Schneersohn to Jacob Kaplan, November 2, 1950, ACDJC, box 8.
224. On the antimemorial agitation, which was made public in 1951, see Bernard Kessler, "Nous n'oublierons jamais notre passé," in *La Terre retrouvée*, August 3, 1951, and other articles from the Jewish press in France (mainly *L'Élan Nouveau, Undzer Vort, Undzer Shtime*) collected in 1956 in Rudy, *Emes vegn sheker*. Opponents in the Jewish press argued that the memorial broke with halakhic traditions of burial and mourning and that the project was too expensive. Some claimed that the money should instead benefit France's Jewish community; others wanted to support Israel. See also Wieviorka, "Un lieu de mémoire," 83ff, and Wieviorka, "Du Centre de documentation juive contemporaine au Mémorial de la Shoah," 26–28.
225. See "Memorandum," May 8, 1951, AJDCJ, GI/5A1/43.052.
226. Laura Margolis Jarblum to Moses Beckelman, January 16, 1952, AJDCJ, GI/5A1/43.052. Several key AJDC members continued to oppose the monument, even though its chairman, Eduard Warburg, agreed to be a patron. The AJDC itself did not contribute financially to the memorial; see Moses Beckelman to Moses Leavitt, July 28, 1953, and Leavitt to Beckelman, August 27, 1953, AJDCNY, AR 45/54, file 296.
227. Schneersohn to John Machover, July 29, 1952, ACDJC, box 34, French.
228. Schneersohn to Machover, December 9, 1952, ACDJC, box 34.
229. In January 1950 it received 250,000 francs from CNRS (see Georges Jamati to Godart, January 7, 1950, ACDJC, box 8, French), and in November 1951 it received one million francs from the municipal council of Paris; see Wieviorka, "Un lieu de mémoire," 85.
230. Undated note on the memorial project, ACDJC, box 18, French.
231. Memorandum, February 21, 1952. In North Africa, the Résidence Générale de Tunis, the Gouvernement Général d'Algérie, and the Conseil Municipal d'Algers along with six other municipalities allocated financial support for the memorial (the city of Algiers gave 150,000 francs). By July 1951, the CDJC had raised 500,000 francs in the Netherlands and 350,000 francs in Belgium. Committees planned for South Africa and Australia never became a reality. See Schneersohn to Louis Questle, April 29, 1952, ACDJC, box 34, English; CDJC to A. Stuczynski, April 2, 1951, ACDJC, box 2, French. On the idea of a friends society in Sydney to publish the CDJC's books in English, see memorandum, February 21, 1952, and "Note on the Project to Erect the Tomb of the Unknown Jewish Martyr." See also Schneersohn to Questle, April 29, 1952, ACDJC, box 34, English; Léon Czertok to Pierre Bigar, July 16, 1951, ACDJC, box 23, French.
232. Schneersohn to Jacob Blaustein, December 20, 1952, ACDJC, box 27, English; Schneersohn to Herbert Lehman, December 23, 1952, ACDJC, box 27, English.
233. Godart and Marius Moutet to Senator Lehman, June 2, 1953, ACDJC, box 27, English.
234. Ibid. See also "Note on the Ceremony of Laying the Foundation Stone of the Memorial to the Unknown Jewish Martyr to Take Place on April 19, on the Site Presented by the Paris Municipality Located at the Corner of rue Geoffroy-l'Asnier and Grenier-sur-l'Eau," AJDCNY, AR 45/54, file 296.
235. Schneersohn to André Mayer, May 23, 1953, ACDJC, box 27, French. The "March of the Ghetto Partisans" referred either to the Yiddish-language partisan song "Zog nit keynmol az du geyst dem letstn veg," by Hirsh Glik, or Szmerke Kaczerginski's "Partizaner marsh," both composed in 1943 in the Vilna ghetto; see Gilbert, *Music in the Holocaust*, 68–74. The "Chant à mort" (also known as "Sonnerie aux morts") was composed by Pierre Dupont, head of the Republican Guard, and adopted in 1932 for official ceremonies honoring France's dead. The children throwing flowers also recalled post-1918 republican ceremonies.
236. Godart and Moutet to Senator Lehman, June 2, 1953, ACDJC, box 27, English. According to another report, the public recited the Kaddish with the orphan. Schneersohn to André Mayer, May 23, 1953, ACDJC, box 27, French.
237. Wieviorka, "Du CDJC au Mémorial de la Shoah," 30–31; Wieviorka, *Il y a 50 ans*, 20.
238. CDJC to Salomon Dingol, May 18, 1953, ACDJC, box 27, English.
239. Schneersohn to André Mayer, May 23, 1953, ACDJC, box 27, French.

240. The ashes were moved from the Père Lachaise Cemetery, where they had been deposited on June 30, 1946. Wieviorka, *Déportation et génocide*, 136ff. On the further history of the memorial and its architecture, see Perego, "Histoire, justice, mémoire."
241. Zweig, *German Reparations and the Jewish World*, 158–159.
242. See Wieviorka, "Un lieu de mémoire," 89–91, and Stauber, *The Holocaust in Israeli Public Debate*, 50.

Chapter 3

1. Some 30,000–40,000 Polish Jews liberated from German and Austrian camps did not return to Poland, nor did 50,000 of those who survived in the Soviet Union. Most of the Soviet group returned in accordance with the Polish-Soviet repatriation agreements of September 1944 and July 1945. For demographics, see Benz, *Dimension des Völkermords*, 411–497; Engel, *Ben shihrur li-verihah*, 154–155n7; Engel, "Poland since 1939," 1406–1407; Gutman, "Poland," 1174–1175.
2. Gross, *Fear*, 31–80.
3. See Engel, "Poland since 1939," 1407. Cf. Lucjan Dobroszycki, who estimates that there were 275,000 Jews in Poland during the period from summer 1944 to spring 1947. Dobroszycki, *Survivors of the Holocaust*, 25.
4. Gross, *Neighbors*, 6–7. Also see Okey, *Eastern Europe*, 191.
5. Gross, *Neighbors*, 6.
6. Immediately after the war, the Polish government estimated its loss of citizens at 6 million, with Jews and non-Jews equal in number. Although this figure is still often quoted, most scholars now estimate non-Jewish deaths at no more than 1.5–2 million; cf. Gross, *Fear*, 4, and Finder, introduction, 5.
7. National minorities made up one-third of the population of interwar Poland (Jews constituting one-third of the minorities and ten percent of the total population). See Mendelsohn, *The Jews of East Central Europe*, 14.
8. Rothschild and Wingfield, *Return to Diversity*, 79–80. Territories lost to the USSR included western Ukraine, western Byelorussia, and eastern Lithuania.
9. On the Polish underground see Gross, *Polish Society under German Occupation*, and on the Polish government-in-exile see Engel, *In the Shadow of Auschwitz* and *Facing a Holocaust*.
10. See Gross, *Fear*, 3–30, esp. 5–7, and Polonsky and Drukier, *The Beginnings of Communist Rule*, 1–139.
11. Judt, *Postwar*, 135–136; Steinlauf, "Poland," 108–109; Steinlauf, *Bondage to the Dead*, 44–45; Davies, *God's Playground*, 2:539–555.
12. Davies, *God's Playground*, 2:556–577, and Kersten, *The Establishment of Communist Rule*.
13. See Gutman, *Ha-yehudim be-Polin*, 1–14, 19; and Dobroszycki, *Survivors of the Holocaust*, 4. On the beginnings of the Jewish community in Lublin, see Blatman, "The Encounter between Jews and Poles."
14. The Liberation of Poland occurred in three stages: in January and February 1944 the Red Army took control of Poland's eastern borderlands, western Byelorussia and western Ukraine; in July it liberated the territories east of the Vistula River; in January and February 1945 it liberated the territories west of the Vistula River.
15. On the CKŻP, see Engel, "The Reconstruction of Jewish Communal Institutions," and Shlomi, "Reshit ha-hitargenut shel yehude Polin."
16. On the Jewish Writers' Union, see Nathan Cohen, "The Renewed Association of Yiddish Writers and Journalists"; on other cultural activities, see Aleksiun, "Rescuing a Memory," and Grözinger and Ruta, *Under the Red Banner*.
17. Jews provided an insignificant percentage of the new administration's personnel, although some Jewish communists filled prominent positions at the top of the regime and in its security apparatus, thus lending credence to the stereotype that the regime was in fact in "Jewish hands"; see Gutman and Krakowski, *Unequal Victims*, 369.
18. Aleksiun, "The Vicious Circle," 163–164. By early 1947 financial support for Jewish institutions was entirely in the hands of American Jewish organizations, mainly the AJDC.

19. David Engel cautiously estimates 500–600 Jewish victims between 1944 and 1947; Jan Gross cites 1,500 for the same period; while Joanna Michlic speaks of 2,000. Cf. Engel, "Patterns of Anti-Jewish Violence"; Gross, *Fear*, 35; Michlic, "Anti-Jewish Violence," 39. Michael Fleming has argued that the communist government consciously used ethnic violence against Jews and other minorities in its quest to establish communist rule, aware that the ethnic Polish population largely opposed communism and that Soviet dominance could be won by directing social unrest against minorities (rather than Polish communists and their Soviet allies) and by fulfilling longstanding nationalist aspirations of creating an ethnically homogeneous Polish nation state. See Fleming, "Minorities, Violence and the Establishment of Communist Rule in Poland."
20. Gross, *Fear*, 192–243. On the concept of Żydokomuna, see also Engel, *Facing a Holocaust*, 47–78; Michlic, "Żydokomuna"; and Michlic, *Poland's Threatening Other*, chap. 6.
21. See Gross, *Fear*, 245–261; similarly, Steinlauf, *Bondage to the Dead*, 53–60.
22. On this distinction, see, for example, Bauer, *Rethinking the Holocaust*, 56–57. See also Niewyk and Nicosia, *The Columbia Guide to the Holocaust*, 49–50. For the view that ethnic Poles did suffer a Holocaust, see Lukas, *Forgotten Holocaust*.
23. Polish-Jewish relations during the war are a highly complex and debated issue; see, for example, Błoński, "The Poor Poles Look at the Ghetto"; Dreifuss, *Anu yehude Polin?*; Grabowski, *Rescue for Money*; Gutman and Krakowski, *Unequal Victims*, esp. chaps. 4 and 7; Polonsky, "Beyond Condemnation"; and Zimmerman, *Contested Memories*.
24. The term is used in Finder, introduction, 5. A similar separation characterizes some historiography on World War II in Poland; see Gross, "A Tangled Web," 91–92, and Gross, *Neighbors*, 7–13. See also Dawidowicz, *The Holocaust and the Historians*, 88–124; Tomaszewski, "Polish History on the Holocaust," 111–135; Aleksiun, "Polish Historiography of the Holocaust," 406–432.
25. Steinlauf, *Bondage to the Dead*, 49. See also Young, *Writing and Rewriting the Holocaust*, 176–180.
26. Aleksiun, "The Vicious Circle," 158.
27. Irena Hurwic-Nowakowska's sociological study of the Polish Jewish community in the years 1945–1950 provides evidence that a large majority of Polish Jews (73.9 percent of the 817 respondents) saw themselves as members of a Jewish nation and believed that rebuilding their distinct national culture was possible in the new democratic Poland. Only 38.4 percent viewed Palestine/Israel as their homeland (p. 52). At the same time, 76.1 percent of 653 respondents strongly opposed giving up their distinct Jewish cultural identity in order to assimilate further into Polish society, as against the 23.9 percent who claimed that assimilation was necessary and inevitable (p. 108). For some this stance resulted from wartime trauma, fear of anti-Jewish assaults, or the hope for better living and working conditions; others simply saw the advantages of socialism. In general, the survey reveals that the respondents' relations to Poland and the Poles were highly ambivalent; many feared that maintaining a distinct national Jewish culture and identity would not be possible in the long run due to catastrophic losses of Poland's Jewish community, possible shifts in the political system, anti-Semitism, and emigration. See Hurwic-Nowakowska, *A Social Analysis*, esp. 51–85, 108–124.
28. A number of recent articles on Jewish history writing in postwar Poland have provided a valuable basis for this chapter; none, however, has placed survivors' activity in the wider context of Jewish Holocaust documentation in Europe. See Aleksiun, "The Central Jewish Historical Commission"; Aleksiun, "Polish Historiography of the Holocaust"; Horn, "Visnshaftlekhe un editorishe tetikeyt fun tsentraler yidisher historisher komisye"; Horn, "Żydowski Instytut Historyczny w Polsce w latach 1944–1949"; Stach, "Geschichtsschreibung und politische Vereinnahmungen"; Stach, "Das Jüdische Historische Institut"; Stach, "Praktische Geschichte"; Szurek, "Être témoin sous le stalinisme"; Tych, "The Emergence of Holocaust Research"; Wein, "The Jewish Historical Institute."
29. Protocols of the historical commission in Lublin, August 29, 1944, AŻIH/CŻKH/303/XX, folder 10, p. 1, Yiddish.

30. Ibid., 2–3. The first preserved testimony from a witness known only by the name Gertner, on the liquidations of the Sandomierz and Staszów ghettos, was collected on August 20, 1944, in Lublin. On the day before the founding meeting of the historical commission, Ada Lichtman wrote down the testimony of the twenty-one-year-old tailor Perec Szapiro, who related his experiences in the Gniewoszów and Zwoleń ghettos and the Dęblin and Stawy forced labor camps and described murders of Jews by the local Polish population; in the days following the commission's founding, Lichtman, Marek Asz, and others continued their task with greater vigor; see Żydowski Instytut Historyczny, *Holocaust Survivor Testimonies Catalogue*, 1:11–17.
31. New members were Szabse Klugman, an activist in the Writers' Union; Paweł Zelicki, a communist PPR member who, like Bitter, was also active in the local Jewish committee; Cwi Epstein, a.k.a. Ben-Efraim; Leon Szczekacz; and Dawid Kupferberg.
32. AŻIH/CŻKH/303/XX, folder 10, p. 12.
33. Ibid., 13–14.
34. Ibid., 5–8.
35. Ibid., 8, 12; 16; 19.
36. Ibid., 5–7; 8–10, 12–15; 16.
37. On Friedman's early collection in Lvov, see Kahane, *Ahare ha-mabul*, 17; Friedman, *Roads to Extinction*, 316–318; and Stauber, *Laying the Foundations*, 12–13.
38. Grüss, *Rok pracy*, 7. After Vilna's liberation on July 13, 1944, Kovner and the poets Szmerke Kaczerginski and Abraham Sutzkever began to collect the remnants of the YIVO Institute's archives, which they had hidden and buried during the war, along with other documents and artifacts they found in deserted Jewish houses. They also helped found a short-lived Jewish museum in August 1944, even though the Soviet authorities opposed a separate Jewish museum and recognized the initiative only as a "committee for the collection of documents." See Arad, "Ha-arkhiyon ha-mehtarti shel geto Vilna," 151–160, 157–159; and Porat, *Me-'ever le-gishmi*, 206–209. Other coworkers present at the founding meeting included Menachem Marek Asz, Szabse Klugman, Dawid Kupferberg, Leon Szczekacz, and Marek Bitter.
39. "Vegn der tsentraler yidisher historisher komisye," in *YPO Buletin* 6, no. 16 January 19, 1945, p. 3.
40. "Antshteyung fun tsentraler yidisher historisher komisye in Poyln," December 1944, AŻIH/CKŻP/KH, folder 1, p. 11; "One Year's Work of the Central Jewish Historical Committee in Poland," (hereafter "One Year's Work") [December 1945], AYIVO RG 1258, box 11, folder 474, p. 1.
41. On Lodz in the years 1945–1950, see Redlich, *Life in Transit*, esp. chaps. 2 and 3.
42. Dobroszycki, "Re-emergence and Decline," 13–14.
43. District commission leaders included: Michał Borwicz (director), Dr. Nella Rost (vice-director), and Joseph Wulf (secretary) in Krakow; Hersh Wasser (director) and Dr. Adolph Berman (secretary) in Warsaw; Mendel Turek (director) and Szymon Datner (secretary) in Bialystok; Dr. Rita Sobol-Masłowska (director) and Franciszka Modrzew (secretary) in Katowice; and Leon Lekowiecki (director) and Erwin Fuchs (secretary) in Wrocław. See Grüss, *Rok Pracy*, 10–13. Many of the commissions lacked suitable offices and adequate personnel. For example, the Bialystok commission was unable to establish a network of local commissions or correspondents because of Jewish out-migration. Report by Kh. Fabrycki from Bialystok, April 23, 1945, AŻIH/CŻKH/303/XX, folder 32, Yiddish. The Warsaw branch lacked even a suitable office to store its collections, and it could only afford to employ three people. Protocol, Second scholarly meeting of CŻKH, September 19–20, 1945, AŻIH/CKŻP/KH330, folder 29, p. 21, Yiddish.
44. The local sites were Będzin, Bielsko, Bydgoszcz, Bytom, Chorzów, Częstochowa, Dzierżniów, Gdańsk, Gliwice, Kielce, Kutno, Lublin, Parczew, Piotrków, Pietrolesie, Przemyśl, Radom, Sosnowiec, Tarnów, Toruń, and Włocławek. Work report, April 30, 1945, AŻIH/CKŻP/KH330, folder 27, p. 10, Polish; list of the local commissions, no date, AŻIH/CŻKH, folder 12, p. 7.

45. Work report, May 10, 1945, AŻIH/CKŻP/KH, folder 27, p. 10, Polish; Grüss, *Rok pracy*, 10. As discussed below, this goal would first become a reality in October 1947, with the founding of the Jewish Historical Institute in Warsaw.
46. "One Year's Work," 1; CŻKH to Jewish organizations abroad [Spring 1945], AŻIH/CKŻP/KH, 303/XX, folder 37, p. 40, English; protocol, Scholarly Council, November 30, 1945, AŻIH/CKŻP/KH, folder 16, p. 24, Polish.
47. Philip Friedman and Leon Bauminger for the CŻKH; Feldschuh and Bitter for the Central Committee; and the actor Jonas Turkow and writers Jehoshua Szlajen and Jehuda Elberg for the Union of Jewish Writers, Journalists, and Artists. See Grüss, *Rok pracy*, 7.
48. See the protocols of the committee's presidium for the regular granting of funds for the historical commission, AŻIH/CKŻP Pryzidium, 303 I/1-27.
49. Examples of monthly CŻKH payments in April 1947 included: accountant Esfira Jochwed, 9,200 zloty; researcher Leon Szeftel, 8,400 zloty; clerk Róża Dobrecka, 5,250 zloty; and canteen cook Regina Sołęlinka, 4,875 zloty. See AŻIH/CKŻP/KH, folder 45, pp. 55-60.
50. Philip Friedman and Noe Grüss to Raphael Mahler, November 2 [1945], AŻIH/CKŻP/KH, folder 85, p. 88, Yiddish. In total there were about eighty workers, forty-five of whom were women. That December, Friedman wrote of eighty employees, 70 percent (i.e., fifty-six) of them women; see Friedman to Alfred (Abraham) Silberschein, December 12, 1945, YVA, M20, folder 187, p. 32. This is all the more remarkable because fewer Jewish women had survived than men. For example, the Jewish population in Lodz in 1945 included 96 Jewish women for every 100 Jewish men (that is, 48.5 percent female and 51.5 percent male). In contrast, the Polish government census of February 1946 counted 118.5 women for every 100 men (or 54.2 percent women and 45.8 percent men) in the general population. Before the Holocaust, in 1931, the Jewish population showed a surplus of women: 108.7 Jewish women for every 100 Jewish men (or 52 percent women and 48 percent men). See Dobroszycki, "Re-emergence and Decline," 12. Possible factors explaining the prominence of women among commission workers include the large number of female *zamlers* working in and around YIVO before the war, Jewish women's strong position in prewar social and communal activism, and the disruption of traditional gender roles as a consequence of the war, which made it easier for women to become active in newly established and provisional institutional contexts.
51. CŻKH to the Union of Jewish Writers, Artists, and Scholars in New York (hereafter Writers' Union), April 24, 1945, AŻIH/CKŻP/KH, folder 118, pp. 2-3, Yiddish.
52. Grüss, *Rok pracy*, 10.
53. Philip Friedman and Noe Grüss to Raphael Mahler, November 2 [1945]. See also CŻKH to Jewish organizations abroad [Spring 1945], 39.
54. Philip Friedman, "Der tsushtand un di oyfgabe fun undzer historiografye in itstikn moment," September 19, 1945, AŻIH/CKŻP/KH, folder 29, p. 4.
55. "Vegn der tsentraler yidisher historisher komisye," p. 3.
56. On the notion that Nazis targeted Jewish culture as well as Jews, see CŻKH to Writers' Union, April 24, 1945, pp. 2-3.
57. CŻKH, *Metodologishe onvayzungen*, 1.
58. Friedman, "Der tsushtand un di oyfgabe fun undzer historiografye in itstikn moment," 5-6.
59. Philip Friedman, "Undzere historishe oyfgabe" [April 1945], AŻIH/CKŻP/KH, folder 7, p. 35.
60. Friedman, "Der tsushtand un di oyfgabe fun undzer historiografye in itstikn moment," 6.
61. CŻKH to Writer's Union, April 24, 1945, pp. 2-3.
62. Ibid.; Friedman, "Undzere historishe oyfgabe," 35.
63. Grüss, *Rok pracy*, 9ff.
64. Protocol of Friends Society inauguration, September 10, 1945, p. 2.
65. CŻKH press conference, March 21, 1945, AŻIH/CKŻP/KH, folder 15, p. 2, Polish.
66. Friedman, "Der tsushtand un di oyfgabe fun undzer historiografye in itstikn moment," p. 4.
67. Grüss, "Der yidisher historisher institut in Poyln," no date, AŻIH/CKŻP/KH, folder 7, p. 41.
68. Grüss, "Dokumenty wrodzonej szlachetności," no date, AŻIH/CKŻP/KH, folder 7, pp. 44-45.

69. Friedman, "Undzere historishe oyfgabe," 35.
70. Rost, "Verfolgungsvorgang," ZAH, B.2/1, Zg. 00/03, no. 73.
71. Nella Rost, "Badanie zbrodni, która nigdy nie przeminie," no date, ZAH, B.2/1.C, no. 527, p. 3.
72. Philip Friedman, "Die grundsätzlichen Probleme unserer Churbnforschung," ACDJC, box 13, p. 1.
73. Philip Friedman, "Die Probleme der wissenschaftlichen Erforschung unserer letzten Katastrophe," ACDJC, box 13, p. 1, and protocol, Friends Society inauguration, September 10, 1945, p. 2. See also Noe Grüss, "Der yidisher historisher institut in Poyln," 39.
74. Friedman, "Die Probleme der wissenschaftlichen Erforschung unserer letzten Katastrophe," 8ff.
75. CŻKH, *Metodologishe onvayzungen*, 2.
76. Kermisz, *Instrukcje dla zbierania materiałów historycznych*, and CŻKH, *Metodologishe onvayzungen*, 8–17; Rachel Auerbach, Nachman Blumental, Noe Grüss, Philip Friedman, and Ada Eber also worked on the questionnaire. For an earlier version, see "Fregboygn far di gvies eydes," AŻIH/CŻKH 303/XX, folder 577. Those working on the questionnaires were familiar with the work of historian, sociologist, and YIVO cofounder Jacob Lestschinsky, who had left Poland for the United States in 1938. In 1944, under the aegis of the Institute of Jewish Affairs in New York, he published a methodological essay and questionnaire as a guideline to researching the European catastrophe. Apparently the CŻKH workers generally appreciated Lestschinsky's work but saw the fact that he had not experienced the Holocaust himself as a limitation. See Lestschinsky, *Di yidishe katastrofe*.
77. CŻKH, *Metodologishe onvayzungen*, sections 1 and 2, p. 8.
78. Ibid., sections 4 and 5, pp. 9–10, and section 6, p. 10, 12.
79. Ibid., section 5, pp. 9–10, and section 6, pp. 12–13.
80. Ibid., section 7, pp. 10–11.
81. Ibid., section 8, p. 11.
82. Ibid., sections 8 and 9, pp. 13–15.
83. Ibid., section 7, p.13.
84. Ibid., section 9, p. 11.
85. Ibid., section 3, p. 9; section 10, pp. 15–16; and section 11, p. 16.
86. Ibid., sections 13, 14, and 15, p. 17.
87. These experiences also corresponded with those of the 38,171 Jews registered in Lodz in December 1945, of whom 18,188 had survived in camps, 6,479 on the "Aryan side," 1,055 in forests, 1,440 in partisan units, 740 in the Red Army, and 10,220 in the Soviet Union. See Dobroszycki, "Re-emergence and Decline," 14.
88. Grüss and Silkes, *Instrukcje dla badania przeżyć dzieci żydowskich*.
89. CŻKH, *Metodologishe onvayzungen*, 40–46.
90. Shandler, *Awakening Lives*, xi–xlii, and Kirshenblatt-Gimblett, "Coming of Age in the Thirties," 86–88, 95–97.
91. On Jewish children in postwar Poland see Michlic, *Jewish Children in Nazi-Occupied Poland*, and Michlic, "Who Am I?"
92. According to Dobroszycki, 2,858 Jewish infants and children up to fourteen years of age were registered in Lodz in 1945; 422 had survived in camps, 861 on the "Aryan side" of ghettos, 158 in forests, 83 in partisan units, and 1,306 in the Soviet Union. He estimates a total of some five thousand child survivors for all of Poland. See Dobroszycki, "Re-emergence and Decline," 17.
93. Protocol, second scholarly meeting of CŻKH, September 19–20, 1945, AŻIH/CKŻP/KH, folder 29, p. 8–9.
94. CŻKH, ed., *Metodologishe onvayzungen*, 31.
95. Ibid., 35 and 31.
96. Ibid., 31–33.
97. Blumental, *Instrukcje dla zbierania materiałów etnograficznych*.
98. Grüss, "Der yidisher historisher institut in Poyln," 39.
99. Protocol, second scholarly meeting of CŻKH, September 19–20, 1945, p. 14.

100. CŻKH, ed., *Metodologishe onvayzungen*, 18–30. See also the draft of this questionnaire, "Kwestionariusz dla użytku zbierających materiał etnograficzny," AŻIH/CŻKH/303/XX, folder 606.
101. CŻKH, ed., *Metodologshe onvayzungen*, 2–4.
102. Ibid., 4.
103. Ibid.
104. Of all testimonies, 92 percent were written in Polish, 7 percent in Yiddish, and 1 percent in Hebrew, German, or French; see Feliks Tych, "The Emergence of Holocaust Research," 232.
105. CŻKH to Jewish organizations abroad, [Spring 1945], 40. See also Kermisz, "Trois années d'activité," in CDJC, *Les Juifs en Europe*, 141–142.
106. Speech by Philip Friedman, [April 1945], AŻIH/CKŻP/KH, folder 7, p. 48, Yiddish.
107. CŻKH to Jewish organizations abroad, [Spring 1945], 40.
108. "One Year's Work," 4.
109. Ibid., 2, and Joseph Kermisz, "Vegn der loyfndiker arbet baym arkhiv fun der tsentraler historisher komisye," [Fall 1946], AŻIH/CKŻP/KH, folder 30, pp. 1–3.
110. "One Year's Work," 8.
111. Protocol, CŻKH Executive Board meeting, May 1, 1946, AŻIH/CKŻP/KH, folder 17, p. 12, Polish; protocol, CŻKH Secretariat, May 18, 1946, AŻIH/CKŻP/KH, folder 17, pp. 55–56.
112. An agreement signed in late July 1946 committed YIVO to carry 25 percent of the total costs of the Ringelblum project, to be paid when the archives were unearthed. CŻKH would retain possession of any material found, but YIVO would pay an estimated 500,000 zloty for copies. Subsequently, YIVO requested a revision that did not include the retrieval costs. CŻKH signed the revision only after the dig's completion in late November. YIVO did pay for reproductions. Apparently, funds from the JLC and the Central Committee proved sufficient. See YIVO to CŻKH, July 31, 1946, AŻIH/CŻKH/303/XX, folder 35, Yiddish; Nachman Blumental and Joseph Kermisz to the Central Committee of Polish Jews, November 22, 1946; and Hersh Wasser and Józef Sak to YIVO, with the revised agreement, no date, Yiddish. (I thank Professor David Engel for making these documents available from his personal archives.) According to Jacob Pat, the original estimate for the excavation was one million zloty, of which the JLC provided 250,000 zloty; see Pat, *Ash un fayer*, 81ff.
113. For a short report on the excavation, see Kermisz, "Trois années d'activité" 141–142. See also Kassow, *Who Will Write Our History?*, 2, 150, 205–206, 216, and 445n20. A second cache, kept in milk jars that had better preserved the documents, was found in October 1950; the third is still missing.
114. Kermisz, "Trois années d'activité," 142. Collection of the Rumkowski archive began on November 17, 1940, under the leadership of Henryk Neftalin. Shortly before the liquidation of the ghetto in August 1944, archive workers hid the material in different places in and outside of the ghetto. The Germans found and destroyed some materials, but Zonabend, one of a few hundred Jews left behind to clean up the ghetto and collect Jewish property, gathered and hid all records he found in emptied apartments and in the offices of the Jewish council. See Unger, "Ha-ti'ud ha-yehudi mi-geto Lodz," 146. See also *Dos Naye Lebn* 45 (November 28, 1946) and 52 (December 23, 1946). The CŻKH received the chronicle in 1945; see "One Year's Work," 2–3.
115. See Klibanski, "The Underground Archives of the Bialystok Ghetto," 295, 302–303. See also Bender, "Arkhiyon ha-mahteret be-Bialistok."
116. "One Year's Work," 4. See also CŻKH to Jewish organizations abroad [Spring 1945], 41.
117. Rost, "Badanie zbrodni, która nigdy nie przeminie," 1–3. Although Holocaust scholars currently view the production of soap from the remains of Jewish victims as a myth, the story was widespread among survivors. The commission workers were cautious but not entirely convinced that it had not occurred. See Hilberg, *The Destruction of the European Jews*, 2:547, 779, 785–786; 3:1032–1033 and 1203.
118. CŻKH to Jewish organizations abroad, [Spring 1945], 40.

119. Kermisz, "Trois années d'activité," 142. Jacob Pat describes his visit to the CŻKH's Lodz archives in February 1946 in Pat, *Ash un fayer*, 78–80.
120. Protocol, meeting of CŻKH representatives with the Municipality of Lodz, February 5, 1947, AŻIH/CKŻP/KH, folder 24, pp. 3–4, Polish.
121. According to Kermisz, in 1947 the plan had been to gather artifacts for a separate state-sponsored museum of Jewish culture. Kermisz, "Trois années d'activité," 142; see also Sieramska, "The Jewish Historical Institute Museum."
122. Protocol, second scholarly meeting of CŻKH, September 19–20, 1945, p. 25; see also "Vegn der tsentraler yidisher historisher komisye," 3, and undated resolution by the Central Committee and the Writers' Union on the foundation of the Central Jewish Historical Commission, AŻIH/CŻKH, folder 1, p. 1, Polish.
123. The CŻKH's extensive use of Polish drew criticism from those who believed that Yiddish publications would reach a larger domestic and foreign audience. See the letter by physician Mark Dworzecki to CŻKH, August 19, 1947, AŻIH/CKŻP/KH, folder 75, p. 74. Historian Maurycy Horn attributed the predominance of Polish publications to the scarcity of printing presses with the Hebrew type required for Yiddish: "Visnshaftlekhe un editorishe tetikeyt fun der tsentraler yidisher historisher komisye," 146. The commission might also have hoped that the use of Polish would assuage public hostility to the use of Yiddish. Jonas Turkow reported that the Yiddish-language radio program of the Central Committee and the Writers' Union prompted regular bomb threats to the station; no one was hurt in the one actual bombing. Because of harassment, the radio journalists had to be escorted home by military personnel. The broadcasters ultimately decided to use only Polish, except for one program: "Zukh-vinkl fun kroyvim," which helped survivors find relatives and friends in and outside Poland. In this case, it was feared that a program accessible to anti-Semites would endanger Jews who retained the Polish names they had adopted during the occupation. See Turkow, *Nokh der bafrayung*, 36–42.
124. See AŻIH/CKŻH/303/XX, folders 117 and 118, for the correspondence with the AJDC representatives in Poland on the funding of CŻKH's publications from 1945 through 1947.
125. See this chapter's section "*Khurbn-Forshung* Revisited: Survivor Historians Research the Holocaust."
126. By September 1945, the CŻKH had compiled a list of the camps in the Generalgouvernement and was collecting materials for monographs on specific camps. Protocol, second scholarly meeting of CŻKH, September 19–20, 1945, p. 19. As members of government delegations, commission workers visited the death camps at Bełżec, Sobibór, and Majdanek and wrote expert reports on the fate of the Jews in these camps.
127. Friedman, *To jest Oświęcim!*, published in English as *This was Oswiecim*; Borwicz, *Uniwersytet zbirów*; Reder, *Bełżec*; Auerbach, *Oyf di felder fun Treblinke*.
128. Local studies were Szternfinkel, *Zagłada Żydów Sosnowca*; Taffet, *Zagłada ŻydówŻółkiewskich*; Bałberyszski, *Likwidacja getta Wileńskiego*; and Melezin, *Przyczynek do znajomości stosunków*.
129. Friedman, *Zagłada Żydów Lwowskich*, also published in Friedman, *Roads to Extinction*, 244–321; Kermisz, *Powstanie w getcie Warszawskim*; Rudnicki, *Martyrologia i zagłada Żydów Warszawskich*. On Bialystok, see Datner, *Walka i zagłada Białostockiego ghetta*.
130. Borwicz, Thon-Rost, and Wulf, *Dokumenty zbrodni i męczeństwa*; Ajzensztajn, *Ruch podziemny w ghettach i obozach*; the three volumes of annotated documents, *Dokumenty i materiały*, are vol. 1, Blumental, *Obozy*, on camps; vol. 2, Kermisz, *Akcje i wysiedlenia*, on *Aktionen* and deportations; and vol. 3, Eisenbach, *Getto Łódzkie*, on the Lodz ghetto.
131. Bauminger, *Przy piktynie i trotylu*; Weliczker, *Brygada śmierci*; Szac-Wajnkranc, *Przeminęło z ogniem*; Dawidsohn-Draenger, *Pamiętnik Justyny*; Hescheles, *Oczyma 12-letniej dziewczyny*.
132. Hochberg-Mariańska and Grüss, *Dzieci oskarżają*; published in English as *The Children Accuse*.
133. Gebirtig, *Es brent*; Borwicz, *Literatura w obozie*; Borwicz, *Pieśń ujdzie cało*; Szajewicz, *Lekh lekho*; Blumental, *Słowa niewinne*.
134. Taffet, *Zagłada Żydostwa Polskiego*.

135. Friedman, *Roads to Extinction*, 238, originally published as: "Zagłada Żydów Polskich 1939–1945."
136. For example, CŻKH did not assign a price to the one hundred copies of the photo album sent to the journal *Eynikeyt* in New York because of unfamiliarity with the American book market and what price would ensure that the work would find readers. See Friedman and Kermisz to *Eynikeyt*, October 3, 1946, AŻIH/CKŻP/KH, folder 105, p. 7. When a group of survivors in a Davos hospital requested several CŻKH publications because of their interest in the "memory of Jewish martyrdom," but admitted that they could not pay, the commission sent the books without charge; anonymous letter to CŻKH, August 1947, AŻIH/CKŻP/KH, folder 75, p. 67.
137. For example, Leon Weliczker, whose wartime diary (*Brygada śmierci*) on the Janowska camp and the Sonderkommando 1005 (which had the task of eliminating the traces of Jewish mass graves in eastern Galicia) was published by CŻKH in March 1946, received letters from readers in the United States, the Soviet Union, and Palestine inquiring about their relatives and friends. See Wells, *The Janowska Road*, 317–319.
138. The photo album was the most popular publication for Jews abroad. See for example the postcard by Shlomo Joachimsohn, a student in Jerusalem, October 31, 1946, AŻIH/CKŻP/KH, folder 95, pp. 133–134; Jack Tannenblat, Brooklyn, to CŻKH, November 1946, folder 79, p. 19; CŻKH's reply to Stanley Zigman of Chicago, April 30, 1947, folder 109, p. 125; request by Józef Kuperschmidt, a survivor in an AJDC hospital in Rome, August 1947, folder 76, pp. 40–41.
139. Rost, "Badanie zbrodni, która nigdy nie przeminie," 1–3. For a similar description, see Pat, *Ash un fayer*, 77, 191.
140. In Lublin, commission workers had initially considered ways to make testifying obligatory for every Jew who registered with the local Jewish Committee. The issue of sanctions against commission workers who did not take their work seriously also repeatedly arose; however, it appears that sanctions were never used. See Protocol, October 10, 1944, AŻIH/CKŻP/KH, folder 11, pp. 16–17, and protocol, second meeting of the CŻKH Friends Society, November 29, 1945, folder 13, p. 11.
141. "Zokhoyr es asher oso lekho Amoleyk!'" October 30, 1946, AŻIH/CKŻP/KH, folder 28, p. 17, Yiddish, emphasis in original.
142. "Komunikat fun tsentraler yidisher historisher komisye," [probably 1945], AŻIH/CKŻP/KH 330, folder 28, p. 33.
143. "Yizker-leksikon," [1946], AŻIH/CŻKH/303/XX, folder 195, pp. 11–13.
144. "Tsu ale yidn in Poyln!," no date, AŻIH/CŻKH/303/XX, folder 406, pp. 23–24.
145. "Yizker-leksikon," 11–13.
146. Ibid.
147. "Tsu ale yidn in Poyln!," 23–24.
148. Kermisz, Blumental, and Grüss participated in a commission on school curricula within the Central Committee's School and Education Department. Cf. Turkow, *Nokh der bafrayung*, 220, and AŻIH/CŻKH/303/XX, folder 42. On essay contests, see "Preisausschreiben!," August 15, 1945, Regional Historical Commission in Wrocław in collaboration with the CŻKH in Lodz, AŻIH/CŻKH/303/XX, folder 590. On working with teachers, see "A kolektiver oysflug fun di lerer in der Ts. Y. H. K.," November 2 [1945], folder 36.
149. For example, Szymon Datner, "Koniec warszawkiego ghetta: W drugą rocznicę powstania" (April 20, 1945), Noe Grüss, "Polacy w obronie dzieci żydowskich podczas okupacji"; Joseph Kermisz, "Kat Żydów łódzkich: Hans Biebow"; Kermisz, "W 3–cią rocznicę wybuchu powstania getta warszawkiego"; and others, all in CŻKH/303/XX, folder 304. The audience for these programs is unclear. Most likely they were broadcast on the Jewish radio program of the Central Committee and the Writers' Union in Lublin and later Lodz, which focused on reading German documents in translation to encourage listeners to engage in writing and collecting. See Turkow, *Nokh der bafrayung*, 38–41.
150. I. Tomska-Osatowa, radio program, May 23, 1945, AŻIH/CŻKP/KH, folder 7, pp. 46–47, Polish.

151. The official name was Towarzystwo Przyjaciół Centralnej Żydowskiej Komisji Historycznej (in Yiddish, Gezelshaft fraynd fun der tsentraler yidisher historisher komisye). Local societies had been established several weeks earlier in Krakow and Katowice. See Noe Grüss's report, July 12, 1945, AŻIH/CKŻP/KH, folder 31, p. 2, Polish; and Protocol, inauguration meeting of the Friends Society, September 10, 1945, AŻIH/CŻKH/303/XX, folder 405, pp. 7–8.
152. Protocol, inauguration meeting, 5–7.
153. Statute of the Friends Society in Lodz, AŻIH/CKŻP/KH, folder 4, pp. 6–18. The CŻKH closed this branch in early 1947 because it was deemed expensive and inefficient. See protocol, meeting of workers, February 5, 1947, AŻIH/CKŻP/KH, folder 24, p. 2. In London, local Jews of Polish origin gave financial support to CŻKH as early as August 1945. A formal group was established in early 1946; see correspondence between CŻKH and I. A. Lisky in AŻIH/CŻKH/303/XX, folders 410 and 411. In Paris, an "Association d'Amis de la Commission Historique Juive de Pologne," directed by Miriam Novitch (Nowicz), began in July–August 1946; folder 411. On the founding of societies in Prague and Paris, see the work report for June and July 1946, AŻIH/CKŻP/KH, folder 94, p. 84ff, Polish.
154. Sh. Ayges to CŻKH, May 22, 1946, AŻIH/CKŻP/KH, folder 93, p. 170, Yiddish.
155. Nachman Blumental and Joseph Kermisz to Mr. Gotlieb, February 17, 1947, AŻIH/CKŻP/KH, folder 108, pp. 76 and 81, Yiddish.
156. Cf. "Vu es lign yidn, korbones fun daytshn fashism," *Dos Naye Lebn* 16, no. 41 (June 24, 1946).
157. Gesja Grynwald to CŻKH, July 1, 1946, AŻIH/CKŻP/KH, folder 93, pp. 167–168.
158. Ibid., 168. Among other survivors who responded to this article, Israel Bekerman offered to show the CŻKH the graves of Jews killed in mass executions in his home town of Kamina Podlaska; June 24, 1946, AŻIH/CKŻP/KH, folder 93, p. 76.
159. Zelig Pacanowski to CŻKH, May 30, 1946, AŻIH/CKŻP/KH, folder 93, pp. 67–68, Yiddish.
160. Zelig Pacanowski to CŻKH, June 4, 1946, AŻIH/CKŻP/KH, folder 93, pp. 73, 82, and 93.
161. Friedman and Kermisz to an anonymous *zamler*, July 1946, AŻIH/CKŻP/KH, folder 101, p. 43, Yiddish. See also Nachman Blumental and Pola Hirsz to Mr. Y. Shapiro in Parczew, January 4, 1946, folder 83, p. 75, Yiddish.
162. For example one *zamler*, in return for testimonies collected, requested a photograph of a tsaddik, a righteous person and leader of Hasidic Judaism. Friedman and Kermisz to an anonymous *zamler*, June 17, 1946, AŻIH/CKŻP/KH, folder 101, p. 42, Yiddish.
163. AŻIH/CKŻP/KH, folder 75, pp. 43–44, Yiddish. Similar requests: Sonia Frisch to CŻHK, January 2, 1947, folder 75, p. 81, Yiddish; Fela Fuks to CŻKH, May 15, 1947, folder 75, p. 99, Yiddish; Ewelina Mass to CŻKH, May 16, 1947, folder 77, p. 35, German.
164. H. Besler to CŻKH, August 6, 1947, AŻIH/CKŻP/KH, folder 75, pp. 25–26, Yiddish.
165. Isaac Bondar to CŻKH, November 2, 1946, AŻIH/CKŻP/KH, folder 75, p. 39, Yiddish.
166. Efraim Grünbaum to CŻKH, December 29, 1946, AŻIH/CKŻP/KH, folder 75, pp. 155–156, Yiddish.
167. A. Sz. Ejdelman to ŻIH, November 30, 1947, AŻIH/CKŻP/KH, folder 75, p. 75, Yiddish. As discussed later in this chapter, the CŻKH became the ŻIH in September 1947.
168. All documents in AŻIH/CKŻP/KH. On employment records, see Boruch Fidler, Bergen-Belsen, to CŻKH, January 20, 1947, folder 75, p. 106, Yiddish; and Szmuel Felman, Türkheim, Bavaria (U.S. Zone) to ŻIH, Warsaw, November 13, 1947, folder 75, p. 103, Yiddish. On the back of the letter Felman confirms the receipt of his work permit. On diplomas, see Sara Wajl-Grossman, Fulda (U.S. Zone), to CŻKH, Lodz, no date, folder 79, p. 57, Yiddish. On marriage certificates, see Ber Teuer (U.S. Zone) to CŻKH, Lodz, December 8, 1946, folder 79, p. 14–15, Yiddish.
169. United Dubienker Relief Committee to CŻKH, May 14, 1947, AŻIH/CKŻP/KH, folder 115, p. 5, Yiddish.
170. Jewish community of Montevideo to CŻKH, June 6, 1947, AŻIH/CKŻP/KH, folder 111, p. 30, Yiddish.
171. Press conference protocol, March 21, 1945, AŻIH/CKŻP/KH, folder 15, pp. 1–2, Polish. Present at the conference were the Polpress agency, *Robotnik* and *Rzeczpospolita* (large-circulation

dailies), and the local Lodz dailies *Tygodnik Łódzki* and *Głos Ludu*, as well as the Union of Journalists (*Związek Dziennikarzy*).
172. Ibid. Similarly, Noe Grüss praised historical materialism as "the only suitable scholarly method" in "Der yidisher historisher institut in Poyln," 41.
173. Engel, *In the Shadow of Auschwitz*, 60–61, 168–169.
174. CŻKH to Writers' Union, April 24, 1945, p. 2–3; also CŻKH to Jewish organizations abroad [Spring 1945], 39.
175. Report on the inaugural meeting of the Society of the Friends of CŻKH, September 10, 1945, AŻIH/CŻKH/303/XX, folder 405, p. 8.
176. See, for example, the discussion between Betti Ajzensztajn and Mejlech Bakalczuk regarding research on Jewish resistance: Protocol, second scholarly meeting of CŻKH, September 19–20, 1945, pp. 17–18.
177. Friedman, "Der tsushtand un di oyfgabe fun undzer historiografye in itstikn moment," 4. In February 1946 Friedman told Jacob Pat that this had been the motivation to begin documenting; see Pat, *Ash un fayer*, 77.
178. Protocol of Friends Society, September 10, 1945, p. 2–4.
179. Grüss, *Rok pracy*, 10.
180. On the delegation to Auschwitz, see Grüss, *Rok pracy*, 20; on the Chełmno delegation, see documents in AŻIH/CŻKH/303/XX: "Skład Komisji dla badania zbrodni hitlerowskich w Chełmnie," May 26, 1945, folder 33, p. 8; Nachman Blumental's Yiddish report "Khelmno," no date, folder 293, pp. 1–5; and "Sprawozdanie komisji dla badań zbrodni niemieckich w Polsce zpierwszego wyjazdu na teren obozu straceń w Chełmnie," folder 33. See also Turkow, *Nokh der bafrayung*, 222–224. On other camp delegations, see Nachman Blumental, "Obóz śmierci: Sobibór," folder 293, and Jehoshua Szlajen, "Majdanek: Notatki z sali sądowej," folder 293. Rachel Auerbach's *Oyf di felder fun Treblinke* describes a delegation to Treblinka on November 7, 1945.
181. Kermisz, "Trois années d'activité," 143; Grüss, *Rok pracy*, 21ff. The manuscript of the affidavit is in CŻKH 303/XX, folder 272. See also Aleksiun, "The Central Jewish Historical Commission," 82–84.
182. CŻKH involvement began when Michał Borwicz and Nachman Blumental served as expert witness in the trial against Amon Goeth, commander of the Płaszów concentration camp, held August 28–September 5, 1946, in Krakow. In 1947 the commission published the transcript of the trial, *Proces ludobójcy Amona Goetha*. See Gawron, "Amon Goeth's Trial in Cracow," 290–294. See also Prussin, "Poland's Nuremberg"; Stach, "'Praktische Geschichte,'" 249–251; and Borodziej, "Hitleristische Verbrechen."
183. This debate not only anticipated the later debate between functionalist and intentionalist historians, but its positions also correspond with more recent research findings on the policies of the German ghetto administration in Lodz; see Browning, *The Path to Genocide*, 28–56.
184. Protocol, meeting of CŻKH workers, March 17, 1947, AŻIH/CKŻP/KH, folder 20, p. 5, Polish.
185. Ibid., 3.
186. Ibid., 2.
187. Ibid., 3.
188. Ibid., 1.
189. Ibid., 2.
190. Ibid., 1.
191. Ibid., 5.
192. Ibid., 4.
193. Ibid., 2.
194. At the conclusion of the seven-day trial on April 30, 1947, Hans Biebow was sentenced to death and was executed on June 23 of that year.
195. Protocol, meeting of CŻKH workers, March 21, 1947, AŻIH/CKŻP/KH, folder 20, p. 12, Polish.
196. Ibid., 12–14.

197. Ibid., 14.
198. Ibid., 17.
199. Ibid., 18–19.
200. Ibid., 16.
201. Ibid., 18.
202. Ibid., 19.
203. Ibid., 20, and AŻIH/CKŻP/Protocols/Prezydium 303 I/6b, "protocol 19," February 10, 1947, p. 124, Polish.
204. Stach, "Praktische Geschichte," 250.
205. Protocol, second CŻKH scholarly meeting, September 19–20, 1945, pp. 9–12, 24–25, and Protocol no. 108, Presidium of the Central Committee, December 19, 1946, AŻIH/CKŻP/Prezydium 303 I/4, p. 100, Polish.
206. See the protocols of the CKŻP presidium on continuation of funding for the historical commission, usually 200,000 to 300,000 zloty as the fixed monthly budget plus additional payments for publications,:AŻIH/CKŻP/Prezydium, 303 I/1–27. See also CŻKH's work report, April 30, 1945, AŻIH/CKŻP/KH, folder 27, p. 10, Polish.
207. On this conflict, see Friedman's letters to Jacob Pat (secretary of the JLC in New York), April 20, 1946, AŻIH/CKŻP/KH, folder 113, p. 23, and no date, p. 24, Yiddish.
208. Tych, "The Emergence of Holocaust Research," 235.
209. As will be discussed in chapter 4, rather than returning from a four-month trip to France and Germany, Friedman accepted the AJDC's offer to head its Education and Culture Department in the U.S. Zone; two years later, he moved to the United States; see Salo W. Baron's introduction to Friedman, *Roads to Extinction*, 1–8, 4–5.
210. The provisional Polish government's commitment to hold free elections, a concession to the British and the Americans at the Potsdam Conference in August 1945, was finally carried out after several postponements as the communists consolidated their position. Over one million voters were disenfranchised on allegations of wartime collaboration, fraudulent ballot counting, and a campaign of terror against opponents of the new regime. The "Democratic Block" won 80.1 percent of the votes versus 10.3 percent for the Peasant Party. See Rothschild and Wingfield, *Return to Diversity*, 80–85.
211. Stach, "Geschichtsschreibung und politische Vereinnahmungen," 407–410.
212. Of those remaining—in Lodz, Krakow, Wrocław, Katowice, Bialystok, Szczecin, and Wałbrzych—all but the first two were closed down by January 1949, and those in Krakow and Lodz were reduced in size.
213. See, for example, Blumental and Kermisz to Citizen Modrzewski in Lublin, September 23, 1947, informing him that as of September 2, the CŻKH had become the ŻIH: AŻIH/CKŻP/KH, folder 10, p. 2, Polish.
214. Initially the Soviet Union had supported the foundation of the State of Israel, mainly for strategic considerations to end British hegemony in the Middle East and cultivate a possible ally in the region. Towards the end of 1948 it began to side with Israel's neighbors, which promised a greater chance of Soviet influence in the region. At the same time Stalin prepared a campaign against Soviet Jews. Polish policies toward the Jewish community in Poland directly followed the Soviet dictate. See Pinkus, *The Soviet Government and the Jews*, 232–235; Ro'i, "Soviet Policies and Attitudes toward Israel"; and Szaynok, "The Anti-Jewish Policy."
215. Aleksiun, "Zionists and Anti-Zionists in the Central Committee," and Shlomi, "The Communist Caucus in the Central Committee."
216. Bauer, *Out of the Ashes*, xviii, 168–169. By 1947 the Central Committee received 95 percent of its budget from funds from abroad; see Dobroszycki, "Restoring Jewish Life," 65.
217. On the postwar history of the Bund in Poland, see Blatman, *For Our Freedom and Yours*, 165–192, 211–218. See also Szaynok, "The Bund and the Jewish Fraction."
218. In Moscow, Mark had been active in the Union of Polish Patriots and the Jewish Anti-Fascist Committee. On the history of the ŻIH, see, "Das Jüdische Historische Institut," 42–114, and Stach, "Geschichtsschreibung und politische Vereinnahmungen," 410–431.

219. Hurwic-Nowakowska, *A Social Analysis*, 49–50; Aleksiun, "The Vicious Circle," 165; and Weinryb, "Poland," 299–307.
220. On this institution see Cała, "An Attempt to Recover Its Voice," and Kichelewski, "A Community under Pressure."
221. This was the message of Artur Eisenbach's *Hitlerowska polityka eksterminacji Żydów*.
222. See Aleksiun, "Polish Historiography of the Holocaust," 420–422, and Stach, "Geschichtsschreibung und politische Vereinnahmungen," 410–414.
223. Fox, "The Holocaust under Communism."
224. On the broader scope of research, see Kermisz, "Trois années d'activité," 144. On the institute's "self-ghettoization" and official toleration, see Tych, "The Legacy of Emanuel Ringelblum," 186, and Tych, "The Emergence of Holocaust Research," 237–238.
225. These numbers follow Engel, "Poland since 1939," 1407–1408.

Chapter 4

1. Proudfoot, *European Refugees*, 115 and 149.
2. Statistical data on the total number of Jews in the three countries are highly imprecise; see Grossmann, *Jews, Germans, and Allies*, 131–132, 316–317n11. Scholars dealing with Austria claim similar numbers; for example, Susanne Rolinek speaks of 250,000–300,000 Jews passing through Austria in the years 1945–1955. Rolinek, *Jüdische Lebenswelten*, 33.
3. The first comprehensive work on the death marches is Blatman, *The Death Marches*.
4. Estimates of how many Jews were liberated on Reich territory vary widely; cf. Jacobmeyer, "Jüdische Überlebende als 'Displaced Persons'," 421n; Lavsky, *New Beginnings*, 28; Marrus, *The Unwanted*, 296–345; Oertel, *Juden auf der Flucht*, 25; Rolinek, *Jüdische Lebenswelten*, 29.
5. For a general overview on the history of Jewish and non-Jewish DPs in postwar Europe, see Wyman, *DPs*. For an overview of Allied DP policies and the problem of repatriation, see Kochavi, *Post-Holocaust Politics*, 13–31.
6. Königseder and Wetzel, *Waiting for Hope*, 15; Geller, *Jews in Post-Holocaust Germany*, 21.
7. The Soviets followed a policy of forced repatriation and thus did not maintain DP camps after the end of 1945. To avoid repatriation some Jews left for the western zones; many DPs who were repatriated to eastern Europe subsequently returned to Germany's western zones. See Mertens, "Schwieriger Neubeginn," and Geller, "Representing Jewry in East Germany," 195–214.
8. Grossmann, *Jews, Germans, and Allies*, 132.
9. Harrison Report quoted in Dinnerstein, *America and the Survivors*, 300–301.
10. Ibid., 295.
11. On the significance of the Harrison Report, see, for example, Dan Diner, "Elemente der Subjektwerdung," 229–248.
12. Dinnerstein, *America and the Survivors*, 39–71; Lavsky, "The Experience of the Displaced Persons," 230.
13. Königseder and Wetzel, *Waiting for Hope*, 215–255.
14. Rolinek, *Jüdische Lebenswelten*, 201–203.
15. Bauer, *Out of the Ashes*, 246–251; Abraham S. Hyman, "Displaced Persons," 317; Kokkonen, "Jewish Displaced Persons" and Kokkonen, "The Jewish Refugees in Postwar Italy," 20. Researchers disagree on the number of DP camps in Italy; Bauer counts 9, Hyman 8, and the more recent work by Kokkonen gives 17.
16. Grossmann, *Jews, Germans, and Allies*, 159–162.
17. U.S. zonal borders remained open for "infiltrees" until April 1947, while the British closed their borders to the refugees as of the end of 1945. See Kochavi, "British Policy," 63–76. On the Brichah see Bauer, *Flight and Rescue*; Alberich, *Flucht nach Eretz Israel*; Alberich, *Exodus durch Österreich*; and Alberich and Zweig, *Escape through Austria*.
18. Proudfoot, *European Refugees*, 339 and 341; see David Engel, *Ben shihrur li-verihah*, 155n7, for the numbers of Jews emigrating from Poland.
19. Alberich, "Zionisten wider Willen," 36.

20. Pfanzelter, "Zwischen Brenner und Bari," 233, 246.
21. See, for example, Fulbrook, *The Divided Nation*, 129–167.
22. In 1933 the Jewish population in Germany numbered 499,700 (0.77 percent). Between 1933 and 1941, some 270,000–300,000 Jews emigrated; 160,000 German Jews were murdered; 18,000–20,000 Jews survived in Germany (15,000 due to their marriages with non-Jews; 3,000–5,000 in hiding); 9,000 Jews survived in camps outside Germany and returned after the liberation. See Arndt and Boberach, "Deutsches Reich," 65; Lavsky, *New Beginnings*, 29; Meyer, *German-Jewish History in Modern Times*, 4: 32, 234; Niewyk and Nicosia, *The Columbia Guide to the Holocaust*, 419, 421.
23. See Jelavich, *Modern Austria*, 245–268.
24. Of the 185,000 Jews in Austria in 1938, 128,500 emigrated, 65,459 were murdered, 2,142 survived the camps, some 7,000 survived in Austria (6,200 in marriages with non-Jews, 700 in hiding), and 12,000–15,000 Jews returned to Austria in the postwar years. See Pauley, "Austria," 491–493. Helga Embacher writes of there being less than 5,000 Austrian Jews in Austria in December 1945. See Embacher, *Neubeginn ohne Illusionen*, 21 and 44.
25. U.S. and British troops landed in Sicily on July 25, 1943, followed by an armistice with a provisional government on September 8; Italian partisans and Anglo-American troops finally drove the Wehrmacht from all of Italy on April 25, 1945. After December 1945 the only occupied provinces were Venetia Giulia and Friuli in the north. See, for example, Duggan, *A Concise History of Italy*, 240–255; Mammarella, *Italy after Fascism*, 159–160; Warner, "Italy and the Powers."
26. In the fall of 1943, there were 37,241 Jewish citizens living in Italy; through February 1945, 8,500 of them were murdered. See Pavan, *Persecution, Indifference, and Amnesia*, 8 and 16.
27. Markovizky, "The Italian Government's Response." Jews constituted approximately 90 percent of Italy's postwar refugee population—16,779 out of 17,985 in June 1947. This was an exceptionally high percentage compared to Germany and Austria (both under 25 percent); see Woodbridge, *UNRRA*, 2:498.
28. Markovizky, "The Italian Government's Response," 23.
29. Although these laws opened immigration to 500,000 DPs, non-Jews more easily met the eligibility criteria; only 80,000 Jewish DPs entered the United States; see Dinnerstein, *America and the Survivors*, chaps. 7–9.
30. Grossmann, *Jews, Germans, and Allies*, 254 and 260.
31. Rolinek, *Jüdische Lebenswelten*, 31; Kokkonen, "Jewish Displaced Persons," 93.
32. On the lack of understanding among army personnel and relief workers, see Grossman, *Jews, Germans, and Allies*, 142, 148–153.
33. Mankowitz, *Life between Memory and Hope*, 39–40, 102–103; Grossman, *Jews, Germans, and Allies*, 142–147; Moore, *GI Jews*, 200–247; Grobman, *Rekindling the Flame*; Rolinek, *Jüdische Lebenswelten*, 39–41.
34. Bauer, *Out of the Ashes*, xviii, 45–70, 193–236; see also Grossman, *Jews, Germans, and Allies*, 153–159; Königseder and Wetzel, *Waiting for Hope*, 55–77; and Webser, "American Relief and Jews in Germany."
35. On Bavaria, Hessen, and Wurttemberg see Brenner, "East European and German Jews," 49–50; Eder, "Jüdische Displaced Persons im deutschen Alltag"; and Eder, *Flüchtige Heimat*, 1–22.
36. On the criminalization of Jewish DPs, see Berkowitz, *The Crime of My Very Existence*, 145–219; Feinstein, *Holocaust Survivors in Postwar Germany*, 33–43, 46–57; and Stern, *Whitewashing the Yellow Badge*, 53–157. On Austria, see Oertel, *Juden auf der Flucht*, 123–136; Ramp, "Die DP bezahlen alle Preise"; and Rolinek, *Jüdische Lebenswelten*, 71–76.
37. See, for example, Herf, *Divided Memory*, 201–266; Moeller, *War Stories*; and Schissler, *The Miracle Years*.
38. See Uhl, "From Victim Myth to Co-Responsibility Thesis."
39. Grossmann, *Jews, Germans, and Allies*, 208–235. The birth rate among Jewish DPs was 50.2 per thousand in the fall of 1947, a rate among the highest in the world at that time. See Abraham S. Hyman, "Displaced Persons," 317.

40. See Kokkonen, *The Jewish Refugees in Postwar Italy*, 276–282, and Bauer, *Out of the Ashes*, 249, on the lack of anti-Semitism in Italy. Claudio Fogu critically notes an idealized self-perception as *italiani brava gente* (good Italians), an image also adopted by Allied liberators and Jewish refugees. See Fogu, "Italiani brava gente," and also Guri Schwarz, "On Myth Making and Nation Building." See also Kokkonen, "The Jewish Refugees in Postwar Italy," 110–123.
41. Fogu, "Italiani brava gente," 149.
42. Ibid., 169.
43. Lavsky, *New Beginnings*, 63–77, and Lavsky, "The Experience of the Displaced Persons," 236–241.
44. Bauer, "The Initial Organization of the Holocaust Survivors"; Mankowitz, "The Formation of the She'erit Hapleta"; and Mankowitz, *Life between Memory and Hope*, 101–130.
45. Rolinek, *Jüdische Lebenswelten*, 37 and 94; Oertl, *Juden auf der Flucht*, 117–118.
46. AYIVO, Series 1, Central Committee of the Organization of Jewish Refugees in Italy, JM 10.517, folder 2, roll 1, frame 4.
47. Brenner, *After the Holocaust*, 41–51; Brenner, "East European and German Jews"; Bauer, *Out of the Ashes*, 246.
48. On the efforts of German, Austrian, and Italian Jewish citizens to rebuild their communities, see Gay, *Safe among the Germans*; Geller, *Jews in Post-Holocaust Germany*; Geis, *Übrig sein*; Adunka, *Die vierte Gemeinde*; Embacher, *Neubeginn ohne Illusionen*; and Rolinek, *Jüdische Lebenswelten*, 138–140. See also Toscano, "The Abrogation of Racial Laws"; Consonni, *Rezistentsa o Shoah*; and Guri Schwarz, "The Reconstruction of Jewish Life in Italy after World War II."
49. Grossmann, *Jews, Germans, and Allies*, 178–182.
50. Debate continues on whether DPs' commitment to Zionism was a "logical conclusion" from their experiences or the result of outside influences. Israeli historians taking the latter position include Zertal, *From Catastrophe to Power*, 1–2, 11, and 271–274, and Grodzinsky, *In the Shadow of the Holocaust*. For a nuanced discussion of Zionism's attractions to the survivors, see Mankowitz, *Life between Memory and Hope*, 51–100, which speaks of an "intuitive" turn to Zionism. In a study of DP youth, Avinoam Patt speaks of "functional Zionism" in terms of its productive, therapeutic, and redemptive effect on the lives of young survivors; see Patt, *Finding Home and Homeland*, 9.
51. On these cultural facilities, see, for example, Eder, "Kultur und Kulturveranstaltungen in den jüdischen DP-Lagern"; Giere, "Wir sind unterwegs, aber nicht in der Wüste"; Lewinsky, "Kultur im Transit"; and Rolinek, *Jüdische Lebenswelten*, 107–113.
52. On the police and camp courts, see Eder, *Flüchtige Heimat*, 168–172; Feinstein, *Holocaust Survivors in Postwar Germany*, 238–248; Königseder and Wetzel, *Waiting for Hope*, 134–141, 199–201; Rolinek, *Jüdische Lebenswelten*, 103–107.
53. On the Yiddish press and publishing, see Kuper-Margaliot, "Yiddish Periodicals"; Lewinsky, *Displaced Poets*; and Lewinsky, "Dangling Roots?"
54. Pinson, "Jewish Life in Liberated Germany," 108–109.
55. The first historians to address the Jewish historical commissions in the DP camps in separate articles and chapters were Krakowski, "Memorial Projects and Memorial Institutions Initiated by She'erit Hapletah," and Mankowitz, *Life between Memory and Hope*, 192–225. Recent articles and chapters include: Boaz Cohen, "Representing the Experiences of Children"; Jockusch, "Jüdische Geschichtsforschung im Lande Amaleks"; Jockusch, "A Folk Monument"; Schein, "Everyone Can Hold a Pen."
56. Niger and Shatzky, *Leksikon fun der nayer yidisher literatur*, 8:94, and Dawidowicz, *From that Place and Time*, 304–305. See also Israel Kaplan's recollections of the Riga Ghetto, "Gever in Riger geto," *Fun Letstn Khurbn* 1 (August 1946): 4–6; on the death march, see "Marsh fun di Kaufering lagern," *Fun Letstn Khurbn* 5 (May 1947): 7–28; see also the autobiography of Kaplan's son Shalom Eilati, *Crossing the River*.
57. Feigenbaum, *Podlyashe in umkum*; Leo W. Schwarz, *The Root and the Bough*, 142–154; Niger and Shatzky, *Leksikon fun der nayer yidisher literatur*, 7:342.

58. Leo W. Schwarz, *The Root and the Bough*, 228; Shmuel Glube, "Di din toyre," *Fun Letstn Khurbn* 6 (August 1947): 44–47.
59. Protocol, November 28, 1945, YVA M1P, folder 2, p. 9, Yiddish.
60. Protocols of December 1 and 3, 1945, YVA M1P, folder 2, pp. 12–14.
61. "Di Centrale historisze komisje," September 3, 1946, YVA M1P, folder 7I, p. 6.
62. Work report for 1946, AYIVO DPG, reel 13, frame 0190–0191; list of historical commissions in the U.S. Zone, February 21, 1947, AYIVO RG 294.1, reel 35, frame 990; work report, May 12, 1947, AYIVO DPG, reel 13, frame 0154; work report, July 16, 1947, YVA M1P, folder 7I, p. 54.
63. *Fun Letstn Khurbn* 10 (December 1948): 163, 169. Similarly, Kaplan, *In der tog-teglekher historisher arbet*, 20.
64. Ajzensztajn, *Ruch podziemny w gettach i obozach*, and Weliczker, *Brygada śmierci*. See also Weliczker's later memoir, Wells, *The Janowska Road*, 278, 311–315, 327.
65. *Fun Letstn Khurbn* 5 (May 1947): 102.
66. As in Poland, the activity of female survivors in the documentation work is particularly remarkable because they constituted a minority among the Jewish DPs. In July 1945, women made up 47 percent of the Jewish DPs. See Warhaftig, *The Uprooted*, 53.
67. Feigenbaum, "Tetitkeytsbarikht," March 15, 1948, ACDJC, box 5, p. 1.
68. Call to the public, no date, YVA M1P, folder 789, Yiddish.
69. Conference report, May 11–12, 1947, YVA M1P, folder 38, p. 11, Yiddish.
70. Feigenbaum, "Tsu vos historishe komisyes?," *Fun Letstn Khurbn* 1 (August 1946): 2.
71. "Vendung num. 1," May 12, 1948, YVA M1P, folder 6, p. 25, Yiddish.
72. Work report, May 12, 1947, AYIVO DPG, reel 13, frame 0155.
73. Ibid, frame 0154.
74. "Tetikajts baricht fun der regionaler historiszer komisje. Fun der cajt fun oktober 1946 biz februar 1947," AYIVO DPG, reel 116, frame 1225.
75. *Fun Letstn Khurbn* 10 (December 1948): 162.
76. Feigenbaum, "Tetitkeytsbarikht," March 15, 1948, ACDJC, box 5, p. 1, Yiddish.
77. Israel Kaplan, "Zamlen un fartseykhenen!," *Undzer Veg* 3 (October 26, 1945), 5 (November 9, 1945), 9 (November 30, 1945) and 12 (December 21, 1945).
78. Instructions for new historical commissions, Regional Historical Commission Frankfurt, no date, YVA O37, folder 8, Yiddish. See also Kaplan, *In der tog-teglekher historisher arbet*, 10–14.
79. TsHK to all regional and local historical commissions in the U.S. Zone, no date, YVA M1P, folder 10II, p. 37, Yiddish.
80. Instructions for historical commissions, January 27, 1947, YVA M1P, folder 6II, p. 15, Yiddish.
81. TsHK to all regional and local historical commissions in the U.S. Zone, no date, YVA M1P, folder 10II, p. 37.
82. See YVA M1S for some six thousand completed "statistical questionnaires."
83. Work report, April 27, 1947, YVA M1P, folder 7I, p. 48.
84. "Historisher fregboygn," AYIVO DPG, reel 13, frames 0217 to 0226. See YVA M1Q for 667 completed "historical questionnaires."
85. Kaplan, *In der tog-teglekher historisher arbet*, 18.
86. "Fregboygn," AYIVO DPG, reel 13, frames 0236 and 0227 to 0229.
87. Questionnaire for German Landräte and Oberbürgermeister, AYIVO DPG, reel 13, frame 0241, German. YVA M1L contains 542 completed questionnaires.
88. *Fun Letstn Khurbn* 10 (December 1948): 164–165.
89. Protocol, December 3, 1945, YVA M1P, folder 2, p. 14, Yiddish.
90. *Fun Letstn Khurbn* 10 (December 1948): 164–166; Kaplan, *In der tog-teglekher historisher arbet*, 7; work report for July 1948, YVA M1P, folder 7I, pp. 101–102.
91. For example, YVA M1L folders 3 and 18.
92. For example, YVA M1L, folder 10.
93. For example, YVA M1L, folders 9, 10, 15, 18.
94. YVA M1L, folders 3, 5, 6, 9, 15, 18.

95. YVA M1L, folder 10, German.
96. YVA M1L, folder 7.
97. Protocol, November 28, 1945, YVA M1P, file 2, p. 9.
98. *Fun Letstn Khurbn* 10 (December 1948): 166.
99. Work report, March 3, 1948, YVA M1P, file 7I, p. 92. YVA M1P, folder 5, contains some four hundred completed questionnaires.
100. For example, one questionnaire reported on a group of armed German men who entered the camp in Feldafing but were overwhelmed by the camp police. Another reported that a piece of land cultivated by Jews near Traunstein in Upper Bavaria had been plundered and destroyed by the local population, and also that local former Hitler youth had made anti-Semitic threats: YVA M1P, folder 5, pp. 403–405; 417–419.
101. TsHK to regional and local historical commissions and Jewish committees in the U.S. Zone, May 1947, YVA M1P, folder 10II, p. 59; work report, June 3, 1947, YVA M1P, folder 7I, p. 52.
102. Questionnaire for drama groups, AYIVO DPG, reel 13, frame 0232 and YVA M1P, folder 4, pp. 4–5 and 23–24.
103. Questionnaire for Jewish front fighters, YVA M1P, folder 3, pp. 5–6.
104. Work report for September 1–October 15, 1946, YVA M1P, file 7I, p. 19; TsHK to regional and local historical commissions, and Jewish committees, September 1946, YVA M1P, folder 10II, p. 18.
105. TsHK to regional and local historical commissions and Jewish committees in the U.S. Zone, May 1947, YVA M1P, folder 10II, p. 59; work report, June 3, 1947, YVA M1P, folder 7I, p. 52.
106. See the letter by Lucy Schildkret, AJHS P-675, box 55, folder 3, November 19, 1946; Feigenbaum to Philip Friedman, October 12, 1950, AYIVO RG 1258, box 2, folder 63.
107. Friedman's comments on Kaplan's *In der tog-teglekher historisher arbet* (AYIVO RG 1258, box 11, 474), indicate his disapproval of Kaplan's idea that the testimonies themselves were historical works, rather than the raw material for more analytical studies. In a later article in the New York-based *Di Tsukunft* on the writing, research, and publication activities of the She'erit Hapletah, Friedman severely criticized the TsHK for not having treated the rich material it had collected in a scholarly way and for not having made greater efforts to recruit professional historians or to provide better training for its workers. See Friedman, "Dos gedrukte vort bay der sheyres-hapleyte in daytshland," *Di Tsukunft* 54, no. 3 (March 1949): 151–152.
108. Conference report, May 11–12, 1947, YVA M1P, folder 38, pp. 2, 4–5.
109. Ibid., 8.
110. Ibid., 6, Yiddish.
111. Ibid., 2–3, Yiddish.
112. Feigenbaum, "Tetitkeytsbarikht," March 15, 1948, ACDJC, box 5, p. 1, Yiddish.
113. Protocol, November 28, 1945, YVA M1P, folder 2, p. 9.
114. Work report for December 3–31, 1945, YVA M1P, folder 7I, p. 1. It remains unclear whether this appeal elicited any responses.
115. Work report, May 12, 1947, YIVO DPG, reel 13, frame 0161; see also Grossman, *Jews, Germans, and Allies*, 156.
116. Report on the use of the municipal archives in Munich, January 11, 1946, YVA M1P, folder 7I, p. 3.
117. "Vu es vert gezamlt," *Undzer Veg* 57 (December 6, 1946); work reports of March 3, 1948, and May 5, 1948, YVA M1P, folder 7I, pp. 92, 96.
118. "Di Centrale historisze komisje," September 3, 1946 YVA M1P, folder 7I, p. 6; work reports of May 23, 1946, and May 27, 1947, YVA M1P, folder 7I, pp. 12, 50.
119. Instructions for newly founded historical commissions, Regional Historical Commission Frankfurt, no date, YVA O37, folder 8.
120. "A yor tsentrale historishe komisye," January 1, 1947, AYIVO DPG, reel 13, frame 0190.
121. Feigenbaum, "Tetitkeytsbarikht," March 15, 1948, ACDJC, box 5, p. 3.
122. *Fun Letstn Khurbn* 10 (December 1948): 164–165.
123. Work report, May 23, 1946, YVA M1P, folder 7I, p. 13.

124. "Di Centrale Historisze komisje bajm Central Komitet fun di bafrajte Jidn in der amerikanischen cone in München," *DP Express* 2–1/23–24 (June 15, 1946). See also TsHK to all regional and local historical commissions in the U.S. Zone, no date, YVA M1P, folder 10II, p. 37, asking to send singers with knowledge of ghetto and camp songs.
125. The Yad Vashem sound archives contain some of the TsHK recordings from the years 1946–1948. See also Gilbert, "Buried Monuments," and "We Long for a Home."
126. Feigenbaum, "Tetitkeytsbarikht," March 15, 1948, ACDJC, box 5; work report, May 12, 1947, AYIVO DPG, reel 13, frame 0156.
127. "Di Centrale historisze komisje," September 3, 1946, YVA M1P, 7I, pp. 6–8.
128. Feigenbaum, "Tetitkeytsbarikht," March 15, 1948, ACDJC, box 5.
129. *Fun Letstn Khurbn* 2 (September 1946): 101.
130. Work report for February 17–March 3 1946, YVA M1P, folder 7I, p. 5. Apart from *Fun Letstn Khurbn*, the commission in Munich published a few small monographs: Kaplan, *In der togteglekher historisher arbet*; Vaysbrod, *Es shtarbt a shtetl*; Feigenbaum, *Podolye in umkum*; Kaplan, *Dos folks-moyl in natsi klem*. The commission also prepared an album with photographs from the Lodz ghetto and two almanacs, one prepared by Leon Weliczker on the camps of East Galicia, and the other on camps in the Baltic countries and the Eastern Kresy—none of which saw publication due to difficulties in securing paper supplies.
131. According to Lucy Schildkret, until the summer of 1946, the only set of Yiddish linotype matrices in the Munich region had been donated from the United States. See Dawidowicz, *From that Place and Time*, 290.
132. Work reports for January 12–26, 1947, and March 1–26, 1947, YVA M1P, folder 7I, pp. 41, 46.
133. Work report, April 13, 1947, YVA M1P, file 7I, p. 47. Schildkret also purchased four sets of Yiddish linotype matrices from a type foundry in Frankfurt for 2,000 marks or "22 packs of cigarettes black," which the commission began to use in July 1947. See Schildkret's letters, AJHS P-675, box 55, folder 3, Munich, February 22, 1947, p. 3, and folder 4, Belsen, July 24, 1947.
134. Dawidowicz, *From that Place and Time*, 289–290.
135. As we have seen in chapter 3, this concern with children's testimonies was a general characteristic of the Jewish documentation projects. However, Kaplan's biographical circumstances make this case especially interesting. In March 1946, Kaplan was reunited with his thirteen year-old son, Shalom, who had survived because his mother had arranged his escape from the Kovno ghetto and a Lithuanian widow had taken care of him. Just three weeks after reuniting with his son in Munich, Kaplan sent Shalom to live with an aunt in Palestine. Busy with the historical commission and his journalistic activities in the DP press, Kaplan would only join Shalom two and a half years later. In his memoir (Eilati, *Crossing the River*), written decades later, Shalom admitted feeling estranged and abandoned and hurt that while in Munich his father had never asked about his son's survival nor addressed the deaths of his mother and younger sister. As reported by historian Boaz Cohen, in the following year Kaplan beseeched his son to write down his experiences in several letters, which, however, remained unanswered. See Boaz Cohen, "Representing the Experiences of Children in the Holocaust," 87–90, and Eilati, *Crossing the River*, 250–258.
136. Kaplan, *In der tog-teglekher historisher arbet*, 23; see also "Vu es vert gezamlt . . . ," *Undzer Veg* 57 (December 6, 1946).
137. Schein, "Everyone Can Hold a Pen," 126. The journal's collective focus also meant that it rarely reported on individual personalities such as communal leaders and rabbis, nor did it raise controversial issues such as the official Jewish leadership in the ghettos. The only notable exceptions were an article in the first issue on Rabbi Jacob Melamed of the Bialystok ghetto (Rabbi Aviezer Burstein, "Der Bialistoker kodesh Yankev Melamed z"l," *Fun Letstn Khurbn* 1 [July 1946]: 7) and one on the Jewish council of the Kovno ghetto (Yankev Goldberg, "Bletlekh fun Kovner eltestnrat biz nokh der groyser aktsye," *Fun Letstn Khurbn* 7 [May 1948]: 30–56).
138. Kaplan, *In der tog-teglekher historisher arbet*, 6, 9; Lewinsky, *Displaced Poets*, 110–117.

139. Schein, "Everyone Can Hold a Pen," 126–128.
140. Kaplan, *In der tog-teglekher historisher arbet*, 8–9.
141. Friedman, "Dos gedrukte vort bay der sheyris-hapleyte," 151. See also Boaz Cohen, "Representing the Experiences of Children," 85–86.
142. Conference report, May 11–12, 1947, YVA M1P, folder 38, p. 7, Yiddish.
143. Dawidowicz, *From that Place and Time*, 303–304.
144. Work report, Historical Commission Leipheim [1947], YVA M1P, folder 1, p. 8, Yiddish.
145. Cf. CDJC, *Les Juifs en Europe*, 175.
146. *Fun Letstn Khurbn* 10 (December 1948): 163.
147. Kaplan, *In der tog-teglekher historisher arbet*, 8.
148. Instructions for historical commissions, January 27, 1947, YVA M1P, folder 6II, p. 17, Yiddish.
149. Protocol, December 3, 1945, YVA M1P, folder 2, p. 14; work report, January 3, 1946, folder 7I, p. 2.
150. See the protocols of November 28 and December 3, 1945, YVA M1P, folder 2, pp. 10 and 14; "A yor tsentrale historishe komisye in der amerikaner zone, daytshland," January 1, 1947, AYIVO DPG, reel 13, frame 0189; and *Landsberger Lager Cajtung* 12 (April 2, 1946): 7.
151. "Di Centrale historisze komisje," September 3, 1946, YVA M1P, folder 7I, p. 8; and the work reports in YVA M1P, folder 7I: May 5, 1948, p. 96, and June 3, 1948, p. 102.
152. Kaplan, *In der tog-teglekher historisher arbet*, 16–17. He noted that some teachers opposed confronting children with their traumatic experiences. Kaplan himself deemed children's recollections less valuable as historical documents than those of adults, but they had particular psychological and pedagogic value for explaining how children coped with persecution. See work report, August 27, 1946, YVA M1P, folder 7I, p. 15; TsHK to vocational training schools, June 1946, AYIVO DPG, reel 13, frame 0211; "Tsu ale kibutzim in der amerikaner zone," YVA M1P, folder 10II, p. 15; "Kibuts bne-midbar," September 17 [1947], YVA M1P, folder 9, p. 3; instructions for newly established historical commissions, no date, YVA O37, folder 8, no page.
153. Contest announcement, February 1947, AYIVO DPG, reel 69, frame 1366, Yiddish.
154. "A yor tsentrale historishe komisye in der amerikaner zone, daytshland," January 1947, AYIVO DPG, reel 13, frame 0192. From local publication: *Undzer Hofenung* (Eschwege): "Ojfruf fun der Centr. Historiszer Komisje," June 14, 1946, 2, and "Fun der Centraler Historiszer Komisje," September 13, 1946, 7; *Dos Fraye Vort* (Feldafing): "Cu ale judn," February 15, 1946, 2, and "Fun der centr. hist. jidiszer komisje," September 6, 1946, 6; *A Heym* (Leipheim): "Fun nontn owar (Materjaln far der historiszer komisje)," March 14, 1946, 12, and "Mer ojfmerkzamkajt der 'Centraler jidiszer historiszer komisje,'" March 21, 1946, 7; "Wendung fun Centr. Historiszer Komisje," August 23, 1946, 7; *Landsberger Lager Cajtung*: "Ojfruf cu der szejres-hapleto in amerik. Zone," January 18, 1946, 14, "Grindung fun a historisze komisje in Landsberg," March 24, 1946, 7, "Fun der historiszer komisje in Landsberg," May 17, 1946, 8, and "Tetikajt fun der jidisz-historiszer komisje in Ansbach," November 29, 1946, 8; *Oyf der Fray* (Stuttgart): "Grindung fun der 'historisher komisye,'" January 1946, 57, "Historishe komisye," "Di historishe komisye in Stuttgart," and "Tsu der yidisher bafelkerung!" (1946/1947), 18; *Undzer Veg* (Munich): "Zamlen un fartseykhenen!," November 9, 1945, 3. "Oyfruf," December 7, 1945, 8, and "Tsentrale historishe komisye," April 20, 1948, 3; *Der Morgn* (Bad Reichenhall): "Far di, wos hobn szoin fargesn!,"(January 1947, 10; *Undzer Shtime* (Bergen-Belsen): "Historishe Komisye," September 15, 1946, 12.
155. "Cu der landsberger jidiszer bafelkerung!," *Landsberger Lager Cajtung* 12, no. 24 (April 2, 1946): 7.
156. For example the calls to the public from various camps: YVA M1P, folder 2, p. 33; folder 3, pp. 42, 44, 45; and folder 9, p. 11.
157. YVA digital image M1P/789.
158. "Vendung" (Leipheim), no date, YVA M1P, folder 9, pp. 4, 6, 7, Yiddish. See also "Yid!," no date, folder 6I, p. 27.
159. "Vendung num. 1," May 12 1948, YVA M1P, folder 6, p. 25.

160. "Protokol," June 4, 1947, YVA M1P, folder 2, p. 32, Yiddish.
161. YVA M1P, folder 2, p. 36. The depiction of the dead Katsetler is based on a photograph taken by Mendel Grossman in the Lodz ghetto; see Shaar, "Mendel Grossman," 134.
162. As discussed in chapter 1, Nathan Nata Hannover, a seventeenth-century preacher, rabbi, Kabbalist, lexicographer, and chronicler witnessed the Chmielnicki pogroms and the Cossack and peasant uprisings in Poland and the Ukraine in 1648–1649. Other pairings included the destruction of the First Temple with the book of Lamentations and the Jews' expulsion from Spain in 1492 with Joseph Ha-Kohen's *Emek ha-Bakhah* (The valley of tears), which chronicled the hardships of the Jewish Diaspora, especially the expulsions from Spain and Portugal. The parents of the author, a sixteenth-century Italian historian, physician, and philologist, witnessed the expulsions.
163. YVA M1P, folder 2, p. 37.
164. "A yor tsentrale historishe komisye in der amerikaner zone, daytshland," January 1947, AYIVO DPG, reel 13, frame 0193.
165. By November 1947, the TsHK had received about six thousand statistical questionnaires and 345 historical questionnaires.
166. Protocol, fifth day of the conference of Jewish historical commissions in Paris, December 7, 1947, afternoon session, ACDJC, box 4, p. 3.
167. See Dinnerstein, *America and the Survivors*, 279; Proudfoot, *European Refugees*, 340; Warhaftig, *The Uprooted*, 50.
168. Mankowitz, *Life between Memory and Hope*, 19, 291.
169. By the end of 1949, some 190,000 of the roughly 250,000 Jewish DPs in German, Austrian, and Italian camps in the summer of 1947 had left. See Proudfoot, *European Refugees*, 341 and 362.
170. Work report, May 12, 1947, AYIVO DPG, reel 13, frame 0153–0154; letters by Feigenbaum and Kaplan to the Central Committee (October 27, 1946) and to the Neu-Freimann Camp Committee (November 3, 1946), AYIVO DPG, reel 13, frames 0118 and 0120.
171. "Vu es vert gezamlt . . . ," *Undzer Veg* 57 (December 6, 1946). See also work report, July 16, 1947, YV M1P, folder 7I, p. 55.
172. Work report, January 3, 1946, YVA M1P, folder 7I, p. 2, Yiddish.
173. On conflicts over funding and supplies, see the work reports in YVA M1P, folder 7I: April 27, 1947, p. 48; May 13, 1947, p. 49; June 3, 1947, p. 53; November 1, 1947, p. 39; February 12, 1948, p. 89; April 12, 1948, p. 94; and Feigenbaum, "Tetitkeytsbarikht," March 15, 1948, ACDJC, box 5.
174. Conference report, May 11–12, 1947, YVA M1P, folder 38, p. 2–3, Yiddish.
175. Resolutions of the Third Congress of the *She'erit Hapletah*, Bad Reichenhall, March 30–April 2, 1948, YVA M1B, folder 7b.
176. The idea of Yad Vashem, a central secular memorial to the destruction and heroism of European Jews, originated in September 1942 with Mordechai Shenhavi, a member of Ha-Shomer Hatsa'ir Kibbutz Mishmar Ha-Emek who had suggested the Jewish National Fund to build a "Memorial (*Yad Vashem*) to the Destroyed Diaspora" (the name is taken from Isaiah 56:5). Since Palestine found itself under the threat of German occupation at the time, nothing became of his idea until August 1945, when a conference of the Zionist movement in London approved the project in principle. As a result, the Jewish National Council in Palestine established an executive committee in charge of planning the memorial. Headed by National Council chairman David Remez, it included, in addition to Shenhavi, prominent figures such as the Zionist leader Baruch Zuckerman and Zorah Warhaftig for the World Jewish Congress, sociologist Arie Tartakower of the Hebrew University, and Shlomo Zalman Shragai of the Jewish Agency for Palestine. See Brog, "In Blessed Memory of a Dream," and Ofer, "The Strength of Remembrance," 32–38.
177. For more on the Jerusalem conference, see chapter 5 of this book.
178. *Fun Letstn Khurbn* 9 (September 1948): 107. Some of the archive had already been shipped in July and August 1948. See also work reports in YVA M1P, folder 7I: August 2, 1948, p. 105, and August 12, 1948, p. 109.

179. YVA M1P, folder 7I, pp. 117 and 120. See also Feigenbaum, "Peulot shel ha-va'adah ha-historit be-minkhen," 107–108.
180. Brenner, *After the Holocaust*, 40; Proudfoot, *European Refugees*, 362. Some 72,000–100,000 Jewish DPs went to the United States, and 100,000–142,000 to Palestine/Israel, according to Grossmann, *Jews, Germans, and Allies*, 251–252.
181. See YVA M1P, folder 7I, pp. 102, 117, 118, and 119.
182. See the conclusion for an extended discussion on Yad Vashem's attitude toward survivor historians.
183. Feigenbaum to Isaac Schneersohn, May 17, 1949, and Schneersohn to Feigenbaum, June 20, 1949, ACDJC, box 35, Yiddish.
184. Feigenbaum to Isaac Schneersohn, September 9, 1949, ACDJC, box 35, Yiddish.
185. On the beginnings of Yad Vashem, see Boaz Cohen, "The Birth Pangs of the Holocaust Research," and Boaz Cohen, "Ha-mehkar ha-histori ha-israeli."
186. Lavsky, "The Experience of the Displaced Persons in Bergen-Belsen," 230.
187. Report of the cultural office of the Central Committee of Liberated Jews in the British Zone, June 1946, YVA O70, folder 30, p. 19, Yiddish. Further collaborators included Sami Feder, a Polish-born actor, and the Orthodox Rabbi Yehuda Leib Gerst.
188. Note on the foundation of an archive, November 1, 1945, AYIVO DPG, reel 114, frames 0353–0354, Yiddish.
189. Ibid., frame 0353.
190. Note from the cultural office, June 11, 1947, YVA O70, folder 3.
191. "Tsu der yidisher bafelkerung in Belzn!," July 1947, AYIVO DPG, reel 114, folder 1581, frame 0350.
192. Invitation to the exhibition in German and Yiddish, AYIVO DPG, reel 114, frames 0037–0038.
193. "Undzer veg in der frayheyt: Barikht fun der oysshtelung," *Undzer Shtime* 22 (August 22, 1947): 3–6. On the postwar reconstruction of the small Jewish community in Göttingen, see Tollmien, "Nach 1945."
194. Dr. Fahlbusch to Oberstadtdirektor Schmidt, July 17, 1947, and municipal museum to Belsen commission, July 17, 1947, MAG CO, no. 475.
195. Municipal museum to Belsen commission, July 27, 1947, MAG CO, no. 475, p. 11.
196. Horowic to Stadtdirektor Kuss, September 1, 1947, MAG CO, no. 475, German.
197. Municipality to Göttingen commission, July 8, 1947; Horowic to Stadtdirektor Kuss, August 7, 1947; Stadtdirektor Kuss to Kulturdezernent Pfauter, September 3, 1947, German; all in MAG CO, no. 475.
198. Memorandum "Zur Frage der Jüdischen Hist. Kommission für Niedersachsen in Göttingen," no date, MAG CO, no. 475, German.
199. Stadtdirektor Kuss to Cwi Horowic, September 2, 1947; Stadtdirektor Kuss to Kulturdezernent Pfauter, September 3, 1947; and "Notiz für Amtsgerichtsrat Arndt," September 3, 1947; all in MAG CO, no. 475.
200. Ernst Engwicht to Oberstadtdirektor Schmidt, May 23, 1947; Oberstadtdirektor Schmidt to Göttingen commission, June 4, 1947; municipal archives to Oberstadtdirektor Schmidt, June 26, 1947; Cwi Horowic to Stadtdirektor Kuss, August 28, 1947; all in MAG CO, no. 475.
201. Municipal construction office to Kulturdezernent Pfauter, September 25, 1947, MAG CO, no. 475, German. In addition to issues of title, the bunker had to be removed so landscaping and construction could begin, and all available workers were needed for a river regulation project.
202. Horowic to Stadtdirektor Kuss, December 10, 1947; note from the construction office, December 16, 1947; Kulturdezernent Pfauter to JHK, December 17, 1947; Kulturdezernent Pfauter to Göttingen commission, January 30, 1948; all in MAG CO, no. 475.
203. JHK to press office of the city of Göttingen, November 29, 1947; Horowic to Oberstadtdirektor Schmidt, December 30, 1947; cultural office to Fahlbusch, January 28, 1948; Horowic to cultural office, March 8, 1948; all in MAG CO, no. 475.

204. See Feder, *Zamlung fun katset un geto lider*; Olevsky, Trepman, and Rosental, *Undzer khurbn in bild*; Jüdische Historische Kommission in Göttingen, *Unser Weg in die Freiheit*; Jüdische Historische Kommission in Göttingen, *Jüdische Professoren und Dozenten*; Horowic, *Die Wacholders*.
205. "Arkhiv fun der oysrotungs tkufe funem eyropeyishn yidntum baym yidishn tsentral komitet in Bergn-Belzn," November 1, 1945, AYIVO DPG, reel 114, frame 0354.
206. This was the policy as of June 1946. Central Committee of Liberated Jews, ed., *Zentral-Komitee der befreiten Juden in der Britischen Zone 1945–1947*, ZAH B.8, 296.052 CENT, 33; report of the cultural office of the Central Committee in the British Zone, June 1946, YVA O70, folder 30, p. 19.
207. John, "Zwischenstation Oberösterreich," 75.
208. Central Committee protocols, July 26, August 5 and 28, 1946, YVA M9, folder 16, pp. 15, 20, 24. On Wiesenthal's work as an interrogator for the Counter Intelligence Corps and the Office of Strategic Services until the end of 1945, see Segev, *Simon Wiesenthal*, 66–67; see chaps. 2 and 3 for a detailed description of Wiesenthal's survival.
209. JHD Statutes, January 14, 1947, YVA M9, folder 36, p. 1, German, signed by Simon Wiesenthal, Dr. Michal Reizes, Dr. Sofie Preisman, and Herszel Jägermann.
210. Simon Wiesenthal, "Die Rolle der Jüdischen Historischen Dokumentation bei der Verfolgung und Bestrafung der Kriegsverbrecher (Beispiel Österreich)," November 25, 1947, AYIVO DPA, reel 4, frames 0962–0963.
211. See Frydman's autobiography, *The Hunter*, and Niger and Shatzky, *Leksikon*, 7:476.
212. Work report, May 16, 1947, YVA O5, folder 2. See also the JHD statutes approved by the Sicherheitsdirektion Wien, July 24, 1947, published in Frydman, *Die Dokumentation in Wien*, no page numbers.
213. Frydman, *The Hunter*, esp. 68–122.
214. See Stach, "Praktische Geschichte," 253. On "Arthur" see Ben-Natan and Urban, *Die Bricha*.
215. Adunka, *Die Vierte Gemeinde*, 59, 119–137; Rolinek, *Jüdische Lebenswelten*, 109. Twenty stateless Jewish students provided the initiative for the association, officially founded in February 1947. They asked for material support and stipends from the AJDC in June 1946.
216. Wiesenthal, "Die Rolle der Jüdischen Historischen Dokumentation," frame 0962.
217. Ibid.
218. Ibid.
219. Segev, *Simon Wiesenthal*, 32–38.
220. Simon Wiesenthal, "Zeitzünder Hitlers," no date, YVA M9, folder 41.
221. Wiesenthal "L'importance de la Documentation Historique Juive," [November 1947], YVA M9, folder 49, p. 472. In fact, the Nazi party had 688,000 Austrian members (8.2 percent of the Austrian population); over one million Austrian men served in the Wehrmacht; and 13–14 percent of all SS personnel were Austrian nationals, although Austrians made up only 8 percent of the population of Greater Germany. See Pauley, "Austria," 491; Perz, "Österreich," 151; and Uhl, "From Victim Myth to Co-Responsibility Thesis," 47.
222. "Rapport de M. Tobie Frydman," [November 1947], YVA O5, folder 10, p. 1. After Frydman moved to Israel he revised his estimate to "500,000 Nazis of Austrian descent ... of whom 10,000 served in the SD, 32,000 in the SS, 1,600 in the Gestapo, and 7,000 in the Security Police, who actively participated in the extermination of Europe's Jews." He identified Austria as the native land of Hitler, Arthur Seyss-Inquart, Odilo Globocnik, and (wrongly) Adolf Eichmann, in addition to many lower-ranking Nazi officials who had played a central role in the Jewish catastrophe. See Frydman, *Die Tragödie des österreichischen Judentums*, 50–53.
223. Undated manuscript of a speech by Simon Wiesenthal to an Austrian Jewish audience, YVA M9, folder 41, German.
224. Wiesenthal, "Pressekonferenz zur Lage der jüdischen DPs und der Weltlage des Judentums," [Summer/Fall 1946], AYIVO DPA, reel 22, folder 582, frames 1191–1195.
225. Wiesenthal to League for Human Rights in Vienna, October 23, 1952, YVA M9, folder 31, pp. 226–227.

226. AYIVO, DPA, reel 5, frame 0799, German. See also "Achtung ehem. KZ-Häftlinge aus KZ Monowice-Buna!," YVA M9, folder 50, p. 116; "Achtung! Gewesene Häftlinge vom Zwangsarbeitslager der Firma 'HASAG' in Skarzyszko-Kamienna, Czenstochow und Kielce," YVA M9, folder 53, p. 222; "Wir suchen Zeugen!," YVA M9, folder 42, p. 405; "Achtung ehem. Häftlinge aus dem KZ Dachau!!," YVA M9, folder 42, p. 438; "Achtung! Juden aus Czenstochau!," April 12, 1948, YVA O5, folder 2; "Achtung Juden aus Lemberg!," March 2, 1948, YVA O5, folder 2.
227. Wiesenthal, "Die Rolle der Jüdischen Historischen Dokumentation," frame 0964.
228. Helen Fuchsman to Simon Wiesenthal, February 17, 1948, AYIVO DPA, reel 5, frame 1000, German.
229. Fuchsman to Wiesenthal, January 27, 1948, YVA M9, folder 49, pp. 80–81, and February 17, 1948, AYIVO, DPA, reel 5, frame 1000.
230. See, for example, JHD Vienna to Benjamin Schreiber, January 18, 1948, YVA O5, folder 2.
231. Towia Frydman to AJDC Vienna, September 30, 1947, YVA O5, folder 2, German; see also: Frydman to AJDC worker Ms. Linden, June 28, 1948, and to the AJDC in Vienna, June 28, 1948, both in YVA O5, folder 2.
232. Appeal to the public, U.S. Zone Austria, no date, AYIVO DPA, reel 5, folder 151, frame 0968, Yiddish, emphasis in original. See also: "Vendung fun der Yidisher historisher dokumentatsye tsu der sheyres-hapleyte in Estraykh," August 1948, YVA M9, folder 50, p. 494; "Meldung," *Ojfgang* 1–2 (March 8, 1946): 6; "Di jidisze historisze komisje in Linc," *Ojfgang* 3–4 (April 15, 1946): 6; "Gewezene K-Cetler!" *Ojfgang* 48 (April 29, 1948): 3.
233. "Bestätigung Jüdische Historische Dokumentation in Linz," YVA M9, folder 18, p. 130, German; and Wiesenthal to Frydman, September 25, 1947, YVA M9 folder 42, p. 535.
234. Wiesenthal, "Die Rolle der Jüdischen Historischen Dokumentation," frame 0964.
235. Work report, December 30, 1947, YVA O5, folder 98, pp. 1–5.
236. Towia Frydman, interview with author, Haifa, August 11, 2005.
237. Wiesenthal, "Die Rolle der Jüdischen Historischen Dokumentation," frame 0965, which mentions the roles of Eichmann's staff (eleven of whom had been arrested), his "relations to the Grand Mufti [of Jerusalem]," and the presence of his family in Vienna.
238. Murer's crimes in the Vilna ghetto first received public attention at the trial of the major war criminals at the International Military Tribunal at Nuremberg through the testimony of the Jewish poet and partisan Abraham Sutzkever, one of the three Jewish witnesses who testified at the IMT. For his testimony on the sixty-ninth day of the tribunal, see IMT, *Trial of the Major War Criminals*, 8:301–308.
239. Letter by the British Allied Commission for Austria, dated August 25, 1947, concerning the Murer case, which suggests that he had already been arrested, YVA M9, folder 36, p. 272, English. Cf. Wiesenthal, *The Murderers Are Amongst Us*, 67, which claims that survivors discovered Murer one week before the Yom Kippur holiday (September 24, 1947).
240. JHD Linz to Dr. Levit, November 10, 1947, YVA M9, folder 48, p. 99. The delay was due to jurisdictional uncertainty between the British Allied Commission for Austria and the American War Crimes Commission in Linz; see note on Murer, Allied Commission for Austria (British Element) to JHD Linz, August 25, 1947, YVA M9, folder 36, p. 272. Cf. YVA M9, folder 42, p. 548. By the end of September, the Linz commission had provided the U.S. War Crimes Commission (then in charge of the case) with over thirty testimonies on Murer's crimes.
241. See Wiesenthal to Max Weinreich, September 28, 1947, YVA M9, folder 42, p. 548.
242. JHD Linz to Dr. Levit, September 10, 1947, YVA M9, folder 48, p. 99. In July the plan had still been to hand him over to the Polish authorities; see Wiesenthal to Farband fun Vilner Yidn in the U.S. Zone of Germany, July 23, 1947, YVA M9 folder 42, p. 381.
243. Murer returned to his farming in Austria. In 1961 his case was reopened but ended in an acquittal. See, for example, Segev, *Simon Wiesenthal*, 172–173.
244. Wiesenthal, "Die Rolle der Jüdischen Historischen Dokumentation," frame 0965.
245. Frydman, *Die Tragödie des österreichischen Judentums*, 54–55; Stach, "Praktische Geschichte," 255.

246. Wiesenthal, "Die Rolle der Jüdischen Historischen Dokumentation," frame 0964.
247. Work report, December 30, 1947, YVA O5, folder 98, p. 2. These numbers seem more realistic than Wiesenthal's. Evelyn Adunka speaks of thirty to fifty arrests that resulted from testimonies collected by Frydman in Vienna; see Adunka, *Die vierte Gemeinde*, 58–59.
248. Work report, December 30, 1947, YVA O5, folder 98, p. 3.
249. Wiesenthal, "Die Rolle der Jüdischen Historischen Dokumentation," frame 0965.
250. The government initiated investigations on 136,820 suspected war criminals, but only 28,148 were brought to trial; 13,607 were found guilty; forty-three received a death penalty (of whom thirty were executed); 9,870 were acquitted. Pauley, "Austria," 497; Perz, "Österreich," 152–153; Weinke, "'Alliierter Angriff auf die nationale Souveränität'?," 68.
251. "Rapport de M. Tobie Frydman (Vienne)," YVA O5, folder 10, p. 1.
252. Wiesenthal, "Die Rolle der Jüdischen Historischen Dokumentation," frame 0966.
253. Ibid., frame 0965.
254. Towia Frydman to CDJC in Paris, April 11, 1948, YVA O5, folder 9, German; Frydman and Otto Suschny to Union of Jewish Students, September 9, 1949, YVA O5, folder 2, German. Frydman outlined the book in a letter to the CDJC, October 27, 1948, YVA O5, folder 9, and in "Geschichte der Juden Österreichs 1938–1945: Kurze Inhaltsangabe," YVA O5, folder 144. See also the complete manuscript in YVA O5, folder 144. In 1952 the JHD in Vienna published a call to the Jews of Austria to donate material for the work. Adunka, *Die Vierte Gemeinde*, 59–60.
255. Frydman to Max Zenner, February 8, 1948, YVA O5, folder 2. The monographs he edited, as Tobias Friedmann, were published in 1957 with the help of landsmanshaftn from these places in Israel as *Schupo- Kriegsverbrecher in Kolomea*; *Schupo-Kriegsverbrecher in Stryj*; and *Schupo-und Gestapo-Kriegsverbrecher von Stanislau*.
256. Frydman, *Die Tragödie des österreichischen Judentums*.
257. Wiesenthal, "Die Rolle der Jüdischen Historischen Dokumentation," frames 0962–0963.
258. On Frydman's bitter struggle for his documentation center and his frustration at not being able to make a living from collecting evidence against Nazi war criminals, see Frydman, *The Hunter*, 211–239.
259. Segev, *Simon Wiesenthal*, 85, 117–127. In 1977 another documentation center was opened in Wiesenthal's name in Los Angeles. Until his death in 2005, he and Frydman maintained a lifelong love-hate relationship dominated by envy and competitiveness as well as cooperation. While Wiesenthal often disparaged Frydman as incompetent and of minor intelligence, he envied him for being fourteen years younger. Frydman, meanwhile, envied Wiesenthal for his international fame, while his own documentation center remained a oneman orchestra that hardly received public recognition beyond Israel.
260. In a separate effort, Italian Jews collected material on their coreligionists deported from Italy. In September 1944 the Union of Jewish Communities established the Committee for the Search of Jewish Deportees (Comitato Ricerche Deportati Ebrei; CRDE) under the leadership of Massimo-Adolpho Vitale in Rome. For more on Vitale, see chapter 5.

The committee's aim was less historical research than information gathering on the fate of the deportees, in the hope that they could be found, released, and repatriated, and providing support to their families. In April 1955 the committee was replaced by the Center of Contemporary Jewish Documentation (Centro di Documentazione Ebraica Contemporanea; CDEC) in Milan, whose broader agenda included documenting the fate of Italian Jews under Fascism and their contribution to the anti-Fascist resistance. These Italian Jewish initiatives had no connection to the historical commissions of the Jewish DPs in Italy. See Nidam-Orvieto, "Fighting Oblivion."
261. F. Falk, "Tsvey yor Pakhakh," *Farn Folk* 20 (November 30, 1947): 4. On Pakhakh see Bauer, *Brichah*, 24–25; Engel, *Ben shihrur li-verihah*, 198–199n152; Zuckerman, *A Surplus of Memory*, 571, 585, 607–610, 637–640.
262. Yitskhok Kvintman, "Tsvey yor tetikeyt fun der historisher komisye bay Pakhakh," *Farn Folk* 20 (November 30, 1947): 18.
263. "Khaveyrim partizaner!," no date, AYIVO DPI, reel 26, frame 0504; Mankowitz, *Life Between Memory and Hope*, 158–160.

264. "Informatsye Buletin," no. 1 (November 25, 1945), AYIVO DPI, reel 26, frame 0467.
265. "Fun der historisher komisye," *Farn Folk* 3 (September 5, 1946): 12.
266. The partisans' actual collection work began even earlier in 1945 at the places where they paused on their way southwest, especially Romania and Austria, where Kaganovitch began to collect testimonies. See Yitskhok Kvintman, "A denkmol dem umbakantn yidishn partizan un geto-kemfer," *Farn Folk* 27 (October 12, 1948). Pakhakh's historical commission in Linz had no connection with that city's JHD, and the two organizations do not seem to have collaborated.
267. Kvintman, "A denkmol," 10; see also "Khaveyrim partizaner!," no date, AYIVO DPI, reel 26, frame 0504. Kvintman, "A denkmol," 10.
268. Ibid. See also "Khaveyrim partizaner!," no date, AYIVO DPI, reel 26, frame 0504; "Fun der historisher komisye tsu ale partizaner!," July 20, 1947, YVA AM1, frame 0554; and "Di Centrale Historisze Komisje Bajm Farband P.Ch.Ch. in Italje: Cu ale jidisze partizaner!" *Ojfgang* 33–34 (September 3, 1947): 7.
269. Kvintman, "Tsvey yor tetikeyt," 18.
270. "Shikt tsu fotografyes!," *Farn Folk* 7 (January 5, 1947): 12.
271. "Khaveyrim partizaner!," no date, AYIVO DPI, reel 26, frame 0504.
272. Ibid.
273. "Fregboygn (tsu der oysgabe fun 'partizaner-almanakh')," no date, AYIVO DPI, reel 26, frame 0503.
274. "Khaveyrim partizaner!," AYIVO DPI, reel 26, frame 0504, and "Tsu ale yidishe partizaner!" *Farn Folk* 14 (August 8, 1947), 11.
275. "Fregboygn (tsu der oysgabe fun 'partizaner-almanakh')," no date, AYIVO DPI, reel 26, frame 0503.
276. Kvintman, "Tsvey yor tetikeyt," 8.
277. Kvintman, "A denkmol," 10.
278. "In der historisher opteylung," *Farn Folk* 1 (July 1, 1946): 10.
279. *Farn Folk* 8 (February 10, 1947): 5.
280. Kvintman, "Tsvey yor tetikeyt," 18; Kaganovitch, *Der yidisher onteyl in der partizaner bavegung*; Kaganovitch, *Di milkhome fun di yidishe partizaner*.
281. Kvintman, "A denkmol"; Kvintman, "Tsvey yor tetikeyt," 18.

Chapter 5

1. Philip Friedman, "Die Formen der wissenschaftlichen Erforschung unserer letzten Katastrophe" [October 1947], ACDJC, box 13, p. 4.
2. CŻKH to YKUF (Yidisher Kultur Farband), New York, May 8, 1945, AYIVO RG 701, box 26, folder 497, and to the Hebrew University and the Jewish National Council in Palestine, May 7, 1945, AŻIH/ CKŻP/KH, folder 118, p. 80; Memorandum for Jewish organizations abroad, AŻIH/CKŻP/KH, folder 98, pp. 41–42, no date.
3. Tych, "The Emergence of Holocaust Research," 234–235.
4. Protocol, first meeting of historical commissions in the U.S. Zone, May 10–11, 1947, YVA M1P, folder 38; May 1947 report on the Education and Culture Department, AYIVO RG 294.1, reel 35, frame 0020.
5. On the visa issue, see Moshe Yosef Feigenbaum to Isaac Schneersohn, June 12, 1947, ACDJC box 6. On the conference, see Philip Friedman to Herbert Katzki, May 11, 1947AJDCJ GI, 7 A1/C-47.801, pp. 1–2. In a memorandum to the AJDC, May 11, 1947, ACDJC, box 21, Friedman suggested delegates from Poland, Slovakia, Romania, Hungary, Switzerland, the U.S. Zone of Germany, Great Britain, and France, as well as the United States and Palestine.
6. See chapter 2.
7. Max Weinreich to Isaac Schneersohn, April 30, 1947, ACDJC, box 3, Yiddish.
8. Memorandum by Zorah Warhaftig to Schneersohn, March 17, 1947, p. 1, ACDJC, box 11, pp.1–2. The National Council in Palestine established the planning committee for the

memorial in August 1945. In addition to Warhaftig (who settled in Palestine in 1947), its members included National Council chairman David Remez, the Zionist leader Baruch Zuckerman, sociologist Arie Tartakower of the Hebrew University, Shlomo Zalman Shragai of the Jewish Agency, and Mordechai Shenhavi, an activist in Palestine since 1919 who himself had already proposed a memorial in 1942. See Kenan, *Between Memory and History*, 43–47; Ofer, "The Strength of Remembrance," 32–38; and Stauber, *The Holocaust in Israeli Public Debate*, 49–50.

9. Moshe Mark Prager, "The State of Research Activity on the Destruction of Israel in Europe and the Program of Concentrating the Documentation in the General Archives of Yad Vashem (Report on My Trip and Research in Europe, January–May 1947)," June 17, 1947, YVA AM1, folder 527, frame 191, Hebrew. Prager (1908–1984) had escaped to Palestine in 1940 after a brief time in the Warsaw ghetto, where he had collected statistical data on the situation of Polish Jews under the German occupation. In 1941 he published *Yeven metsulah ha-hadash: Yahadut Polanya be-tsipurne ha-Natsim*.

10. See Boaz Cohen, "Ha-ve'ida ha-olamit le-heker ha-sho'ah," 99–108.

11. On the Jerusalem conference, see Boaz Cohen, "Ha-mehkar ha-histori ha-israeli," chap. 6, and Boaz Cohen, *Ha-dorot ha-ba'im*, chap. 5.

12. See YVA AM1, folder 97, frames 0116–0110. See also Boaz Cohen, *Ha-dorot ha-ba'im*, 106–107.

13. "Resolution of the Conference for Investigation of the Devastation and Heroism of Our Epoch Convened by Yad Vashem and the Institute of Jewish Sciences of the Hebrew University, held on 13–14 July, 1947," YVA AM1, folder 28, frame 0794.

14. YVA AM1, folder 237.

15. Warhaftig to Schneersohn, November 3, 1947, YVA AM1, folder 420V, frame 0424; Warhaftig to Moshe Sneh (Jewish Agency Executive in Paris), November 21, 1947, YVA AM1, frames 0621–0623.

16. Schneersohn's invitation to the conference in Paris, May 25, 1947, ACDJC, box 11, pp. 1–2, English.

17. "Séance du Comité Direction," June 5, 1947, ACDJC, box 10 (hereafter Board of Directors meeting), p. 4.

18. "Procès-verbal de la réunion du 22 juillet 1947," ACDJC, box 11 (hereafter Protocol, meeting of July 22, 1947), p. 1.

19. Ibid.

20. Ibid., 2.

21. Ibid., 1.

22. Undated memorandum for conference participants and "Procès-verbal de la réunion de la commission préparatoire de la Conférence Européenne," October 29, 1947, p. 1, both in ACDJC, box 11 (hereafter Protocol, planning meeting, October 29, 1947) Ibid.

23. Board of Directors meeting, June 5, 1947, ACDJC, box 10, p. 4. At this same meeting, he indicated that Yad Vashem was indeed the only competition: "Even in the United States it is understood that all of Europe cannot just come to New York, and that France must take its place in Europe."

24. "Procès-verbal de la réunion de Mardi 15 juillet 1947, de la commission pour la préparation de la conférence des représantants des centres de documentation des pays d'Europe anciennement occupés par les Allemands," ACDJC, box 11 (hereafter Protocol, planning meeting, July 15, 1947), p. 2.

25. Ibid.

26. Protocol, planning meeting, July 22, 1947, ACDJC, box 11, p. 1. See also protocol, planning meeting, July 15, 1947, p. 3, and "Conference of European Centers of Jewish Documentation," undated first overview of the responses and ideas received from delegates invited [June/July 1947], p. 2, both in ACDJC, box 11.

27. "Procès-verbal de la réunion préparatoire du 'Congrès des Centres de Documentation Juive'," September 18, 1947, ACDJC, box 11, p. 2.

28. Ibid.

29. Protocol, planning meeting, October 29, 1947, ACDJC, box 11, p. 1.
30. Borwicz's center, which operated in Paris between 1947 and 1952, left no known archives. However, it aimed to study the history of Polish Jews from sociological, psychological, and historical perspectives, primarily during the German occupation, but including Polish Jewish history in general. The center was affiliated with the Association of Polish Jews in France (Association des Juifs Polonais en France). Borwicz and Joseph Wulf, the center's main activists, frequently published on historical topics in the Paris-based Yiddish press.
31. Borwicz certainly meant the works published by the CŻKH, which at that time had already published a dozen works dealing with ghettos.
32. Michał Borwicz to Isaac Schneersohn, November 3, 1947, ACDJC, box 11, French.
33. For the list of participants, see CDJC, *Les Juifs en Europe*, 247–248.
34. Similar organizations were the Central Consistory of the Jews of Bulgaria, the Council of Jewish Communities of Greece, the Federation of Jewish Societies in Algeria, and the Board of Deputies of British Jews.
35. Yad Vashem had asked to give two lectures, one on its program and memorial project and the other on issues of documentation. See Zorah Warhaftig to Jacques Fink, October 15, 1947, YVA AM1, folder 420V, frame 365; Warhaftig to Schneersohn, November 3, 1947, YVA AM1, folder 420V, frame 0424. Of the two intended delegates, Arie Tartakower had an aircraft problem; the reasons for Shlomo Zalman Shragai's absence are unexplained. The telegram was signed by David Remez, Mordechai Shenhavi, Tartakower, and Warhaftig.
36. Protocol, fourth day, December 4, 1947, morning session, ACDJC, box 4, pp. 6–7, French; telegram of December 3, 1947, YVA AM1, folder 420VI, frame 570.
37. See the list of invitees to a luncheon in honor of foreign delegates on December 5, 1947, in the Palais d'Orsay in Paris, ACDJC, box 11.
38. Protocol, first day, Monday, December 1, 1947, morning session, ACDJC, box 15, folder "1ere journée."
39. The conference protocols contain no information on the content of this ceremony or the text of Rabbi Schwartz' sermon.
40. Protocol, first day, December 1, 1947, morning session, ACDJC, box 4, p. 2, French.
41. See Protocol, first day, December 1, 1947, afternoon session, ACDJC, box 4, p. 9, French; see also CDJC, *Les Juifs en Europe*, 40–43.
42. Protocol, second day, December 2, 1947, morning session, ACDJC, box 4, pp. 3–5.
43. Protocol, seventh day, December 9, 1947, morning session, ACDJC, box 4, pp. 6–7. In fact it took the Romanian government from December 1944 until May 1947 to enact comprehensive legislation to restore full civic rights for Jews, and the law for the return of property was stage dressing with little practical value for Jews. It is likely that political pressures at home influenced Halevy's idealized picture. See Ancel, "The New Jewish Invasion," and Volovici, "Romanian Jewry," 182–184; see also Sylvain, "Romania," 518–519. Bulgarian delegate David Jeroham concurred with Halevy: Protocol, seventh day, December 9, 1947, morning session, p. 7.
44. Collected as *Les Juifs en Europe*, the reports included: Joseph Lubetzki, "Spoliation des biens juifs en France," 84–88; Fayvel Schrager, "Le rôle des volontaires juifs dans l'armée française pendant la campagne 1939–1940," 107–109; David Knout, "La Résistance juive en France," 116–118; M. A. Akerberg, "Historique du Mouvement des Eclaireurs Israélites de France," 118–122; Maurice Moch, "La recherche des disparus (l'exemple du SER)," 133–135, and Samy Lattès, "L'attitude de l'Eglise en France à l'égard des Juifs pendant la persécution," 166–170.
45. Fred Herz, "Allocution," in CDJC, *Les Juifs en Europe*, 32–33.
46. Eugène Minkowski, "L'enfance victime du nazisme," in ibid., 89–93; Léon Kurland, "La medicine allemande au service de l'extermination des Juifs," in ibid., 96–101.
47. Jósef Kermisz, "Le Musée Juif à Auschwitz," in ibid., 164–165.
48. Schneersohn, opening address, in ibid., 24.
49. Georges Garel, "L'O.S.E. face à l'ennemi," in ibid., 109–115; Walter Beckelman, "L'activité de l'American Joint Distribution Committee pendant l'occupation," in ibid., 151–154; Joel Wolfsohn, "L'activité de l'American Jewish Committee contre l'antisémitisme," in ibid., 154–160;

Isaïe Klimoff, "L'activité de l'Agence Juive pendant la guerre en faveur des Juifs des pays occupés," in ibid., 135–137.
50. Henri Hertz, "Historique du CDJC," in ibid., 58–62; Edmond-Maurice Lévy, "La conservation et l'exploitation des matériaux d'archives au Centre de Documentation Juive Contemporaine," in ibid., 25–28.
51. Maurice Moch, "Exploitation de la documentation (exemple: Centre Israélite d'Information)," on a 1945 collection effort by the CRIF, in ibid., 34–36; Maurice Vanikoff, "Origines et activités du Centre de Documentation Politique," on a documentation project supported by the Alliance Israélite Universelle since 1944, in ibid., 144–148; Léon Meiss, "Activités et archives du Consistoire Central de France sous l'occupation," in ibid., 103–107.
52. Joseph Kermisz, "Trois années d'activité de la Commission Centrale Historique Juive et de l'Institut Historique Juif auprès du Comité Central des Juifs en Pologne," in ibid., 140–144; Moshe Yosef Feigenbaum, "L'activité de la Commission Centrale Historique auprès du Comité Central des Juifs libérés," in ibid., 149–151; Simon Wiesenthal, "L'importance de la documentation historique juive pour la recherche et le châtiment des criminels de guerre (exemple autricien)," in ibid., 37–40; Nella Rost, "La Commission Historique de Stockholm," in ibid., 57–58; Alfred Wiener, "L'histoire et les buts du Jewish Central Information Office (Wiener Library)," in ibid., 125–128.
53. Mayer Halevy, "Pour une lexicographie du 'Churban,'" in ibid., 161–164; Léon Poliakov, "Technique et buts de la recherche historique," ACDJC DCCXIV 714, 1.
54. Philip Friedman, "Les problèmes de recherche scientifique sur notre dernière catastrophe," CDJC, *Les Juifs en Europe*, 72–80, quotation on 73.
55. Ibid., 75.
56. Michał Borwicz, "Les tâches de la nouvelle historiographie juive," in ibid., 93–96; Protocol, third day, December 3, 1947, morning session, ACDJC, box 4, p. 11.
57. Friedman, "Les problèmes," 75.
58. Poliakov, "Technique et buts," 1.
59. Ibid., 3.
60. Friedman, "Les problèmes," 74–75.
61. Feigenbaum's speech, December 8, 1947, YVA AM1, folder 128, frame 0641.
62. Poliakov, "Technique et buts," 1.
63. Ibid., 2–3.
64. Borwicz, "Les tâches," 94.
65. Poliakov, "Technique et buts," 3.
66. Borwicz, "Les tâches," 95.
67. Protocol, sixth day, December 8, 1947, morning session, ACDJC, box 4, p. 3, French; Feigenbaum's speech, YVA AM1, folder 128, frames 0640–0642, Yiddish.
68. Friedman, "Les problèmes," 75.
69. Poliakov, "Technique et buts," 4.
70. Protocol, sixth day, December 8, 1947, morning session, ACDJC, box 4, p. 2, French.
71. Friedman, "Les problèmes," 77.
72. Ibid., 78.
73. Ibid., 79.
74. Ibid., 78–79.
75. Ibid., 75–76.
76. Ibid., 74. He referred to Germany's national unification into an empire after its victory over France in the Franco-Prussian war of 1870–1871. It was accompanied by aggressive nationalism and the rise of anti-Semitic parties and publications.
77. Ibid., 73–74, 76.
78. Ibid., 74–75.
79. Poliakov, "Technique et buts," 1.
80. Friedman, "Les problèmes," 79–80; protocol, sixth day, December 8, 1947, morning session, pp. 2 and 4; Borwicz, "Les tâches de la nouvelle historiographie juive," 95–96.
81. CDJC, *Les Juifs en Europe*, 175.
82. Protocol, sixth day, December 8, 1947, morning session, p. 3, ACDJC, box 4, French.

83. Ibid., 4–5.
84. Protocol, fourth day, December 7, 1947, morning session, p. 7, ACDJC, box 4, French. By using the term *Memorbuch* (memorial book) Halevy referred to an Ashkenazi tradition going back to the Middle Ages in which Jewish communities commemorated their dead through creating memorial books registering memorial prayers, necrologies of names, places, and stories of those who died for their faith.
85. Protocol, fourth day, December 7, 1947, morning session, ACDJC, box 4, pp. 7–8, French.
86. Ibid., 6.
87. Halevy, "Pour une lexicographie du 'Churban,'" 163.
88. Protocol, fourth day, December 7, 1947, morning session, ACDJC, box 4, pp. 7–8, French.
89. Protocol, third day, December 3, 1947, morning session, ACDJC, box 4, p. 11, French.
90. Friedman, "Les problèmes," 79–80.
91. Poliakov, "Technique et buts," 5.
92. Friedman, "Les problèmes," 80.
93. Protocol, sixth day, December 8, 1947, morning session, ACDJC, box 4, p. 2, French.
94. CDJC, *Les Juifs en Europe*, 174.
95. Henri Monneray in Protocol, sixth day, December 8, 1947, morning session, ACDJC, box 4, p. 5, French.
96. CDJC, *Les Juifs en Europe*, 23.
97. Protocol, first day, December 1, 1947, morning session, ACDJC, box 4, p. 2, French.
98. Poliakov, "Technique et buts," 5.
99. Protocol, first day, December 1, 1947, morning session, ACDJC, box 4, p. 2, French.
100. CDJC, *Les Juifs en Europe*, 23.
101. The conference volume published the manuscript of his lecture, but because it was not delivered during the conference, it was not discussed there. See Blumental, "Aperçu sur les ghettos de Pologne sous l'occupation allemande," in CDJC, *Les Juifs en Europe*, 199–204.
102. Protocol, sixth day, December 8, 1947, morning session, ACDJC, box 4, p. 3, French.
103. Protocol, third day, December 3, 1947, morning session, ACDJC, box 4, p. 11.
104. Protocol, fourth day, December 4, 1947, afternoon session, ACDJC, box 4, p. 13.
105. Protocol, sixth day, December 8, 1947, morning session, ACDJC, box 4, pp. 2–3, French; CDJC, *Les Juifs en Europe*, 174ff.
106. CDJC, *Les Juifs en Europe*, 177.
107. Protocol, sixth day, December 8, 1947, morning session, ACDJC, box 4, p. 7, French.
108. CDJC, *Les Juifs en Europe*, 32.
109. Protocol, third day, December 3, 1947, morning session, ACDJC, box 4, pp. 11–12, French.
110. CDJC, *Les Juifs en Europe*, 51–53.
111. Protocol, fifth day, December 7, 1947, morning session, ACDJC, box 4, p. 9, French.
112. CDJC, *Les Juifs en Europe*, 174; Protocol, sixth day, December 8, 1947, morning session, ACDJC, box 4, p. 2, French.
113. Ibid., 10.
114. Protocol, first day, December 1, 1947, morning session, ACDJC, box 4, p. 4, French.
115. Protocol, fifth day, December 7, 1947, morning session, ACDJC, box 4, p. 12, French.
116. Protocol, sixth day, December 8, 1947, morning session, ACDJC, box 4, p. 7, French.
117. Protocol, seventh day, December 9, 1947, morning session, ACDJC, box 4, p. 5, French.
118. Protocol, third day, December 3, 1947, evening session, ACDJC, box 4, pp. 18–19, French.
119. CDJC, *Les Juifs en Europe*, 118.
120. Protocol, third day, December 3, 1947, evening session, ACDJC, box 4, p. 17, French. See also Vitale's report on the prominent role of Italian Jews in the *resistenza* and Moissis' report on Jews in the Greek resistance: CDJC, *Les Juifs en Europe*, 45, 53.
121. CDJC, *Les Juifs en Europe*, 173.
122. Protocol, sixth day, December 8, 1947, morning session, ACDJC, box 4, p. 16, French.
123. CDJC, *Les Juifs en Europe*, 173.
124. Protocol, seventh day, December 9, 1947, morning session, ACDJC, box 4, p. 17, French.
125. CDJC, *Les Juifs en Europe*, 165.

126. Ibid., 28–31, 80–84.
127. Ibid., 82.
128. An adherent of the *Action Française* movement, Xavier Vallat (1891–1972) was a militarist, nationalist, Catholic right-wing parliamentarian in the 1930s. As head of the Vichy Commissariat Général aux Questions Juives, he shaped the concept of *antisémitisme d'état*, which portrayed French anti-Semitic policies as a matter of national interest rather than German orders. The Germans forced him out of office in May 1942. Vallat served only two years of his sentence. See Marrus and Paxton, *Vichy France and the Jews*, 75–119, 179, 344, 347.
129. Protocol, third day, December 3, 1947, morning session, ACDJC, box 4, p. 12.
130. Protocol, fourth day, December 4, 1947, afternoon session, ACDJC, box 4, p. 12; Protocol, fifth day, December 7, 1947, morning session, ACDJC, box 4, pp. 10ff.
131. Ibid., 14.
132. Ibid., 13.
133. Ibid., 10–11; Protocol, fourth day, December 4, 1947, afternoon session, ACDJC, box 4, pp. 12–13.
134. Protocol, fifth day, December 7, 1947, morning session, ACDJC, box 4, p. 9.
135. CDJC, *Les Juifs en Europe*, 88.
136. Protocol, fifth day, December 7, 1947, morning session, ACDJC, box 4, p. 9. Wiesenthal agreed that, as "the political center of Europe," Paris offered access for researchers. CDJC, *Les Juifs en Europe*, 176ff.
137. Protocol, sixth day, December 8, 1947, morning session, ACDJC, box 4, p. 6, French; CDJC, *Les Juifs en Europe*, 32–33, 176.
138. CDJC, *Les Juifs en Europe*, 82; Protocol, sixth day, December 8, 1947, morning session, ACDJC, box 4, p. 6.
139. Feigenbaum's speech of December 8, 1947, YVA AM1, folder 128, frame 0642, Yiddish. Kermisz dismissed these concerns, arguing that both the Polish government and people were committed to protecting the memorial. He also invoked the symbolism of Auschwitz and the Warsaw ghetto. Nonetheless, he promised that the ŻIH would support a European center in Paris. Protocol, sixth day, December 8, 1947, morning session, ACDJC, box 4, p. 8.
140. Protocol, sixth day, December 8, 1947, morning session, ACDJC, box 4, p. 3; Feigenbaum's speech of December 8, 1947, YVA AM1, folder 128, frame 0642, Yiddish.
141. Protocol, sixth day, December 8, 1947, morning session, ACDJC, box 4, p. 7.
142. Ibid., 5, and Protocol, third day, December 3, 1947, morning session, ACDJC, box 4, pp. 11–12.
143. CDJC, *Les Juifs en Europe*, 175; Protocol, sixth day, December 8, 1947, morning session, ACDJC, box 4, pp. 4–5.
144. Protocol, sixth day, December 8, 1947, morning session, ACDJC, box 4, p. 4, French.
145. Ibid., 5.
146. CDJC, *Les Juifs en Europe*, 171–172.
147. Protocol, sixth day, December 8, 1947, morning session, ACDJC box 4, p. 13, French.
148. Ibid., 16–17.
149. Protocol, sixth day, December 8, 1947, morning session, ACDJC, box 4, p. 17, French.
150. The commission consisted of one representative each from Germany, Bulgaria, Austria, Greece, Italy, and Sweden, as well as Fred Herz for the American Military Tribunal at Nuremberg, plus eleven delegates based in France. See Protocol, first day, December 1, 1947, afternoon session, ACDJC, box 4, pp. 9–10, and CDJC, *Les Juifs en Europe*, 46; Protocol, fourth day, December 4, 1947, afternoon session, ACDJC, box 4, p. 13.
151. CDJC, *Les Juifs en Europe*, 173; protocol, seventh day, December 9, 1947, morning session, ACDJC, box 4, p. 5.
152. Protocol, seventh day, December 9, 1947, morning session, ACDJC, box 4, p. 4, French.
153. CDJC, *Les Juifs en Europe*, 185–186.
154. Ibid., 186–187.
155. Ibid., 188.
156. Ibid., 189.

157. Protocol, sixth day, December 8, 1947, morning session, ACDJC, box 4, p. 9. Countries eligible but not represented included Hungary, Yugoslavia, Czechoslovakia, the Soviet Union, Belgium, and the Netherlands.
158. Protocol, seventh day, December 9, 1947, morning session, ACDJC, box 4, pp. 12, 5–6.
159. Ibid., 11. Borwicz, whose Polish center was such an organization, took this position. As a compromise, Friedman suggested that France's additional delegates should represent different organizations. Ibid., 12.
160. Ibid., 13–14; CDJC, *Les juifs en Europe*, 187.
161. As will be discussed in the conclusion, Friedman had been seeking a visa since the spring of 1947. He and his wife arrived in Paris at the beginning of 1948. They worked with the CDJC until October of that year, when they immigrated to the United States, after Salo Baron offered Friedman a teaching position at Columbia University. See Stauber, *Laying the Foundations*, 29–30, and Orenstein, *Dos lebn un shafn fun Dr. Filip Fridman*, 16.
162. France's fourth representative was Eugène Weill. Other country representatives were Elie Echkenazy (Bulgaria), Asher Moissis (Greece), Massimo-Adolfo Vitale (Italy), and Mayer Halevy (Romania). Hungary, Switzerland, and Czechoslovakia were each invited to designate a representative. The Council of Directors began its work December 10, 1947, in Schneersohn's apartment. Protocol, first meeting, Conseil d'Administration, December 10, 1947, YVA M9, folder 49, pp. 182–183; Protocol, second meeting, December 12, 1947, ibid., 180–181; Protocol, third meeting, December 15, 1947, ibid., 178–179.
163. CDJC, *Les juifs en Europe*, 243.
164. Kermisz stressed the importance of a Scholarly Committee to international cooperation. Protocol, sixth day, December 8, 1947, morning session, p. 8, ACDJC, box 4, and CDJC, *Les Juifs en Europe*, 177.
165. Protocol, seventh day, December 9, 1947, morning session, ACDJC, box 4, p. 18, French. See Henri Monneray's objections, ibid., 16.
166. Ibid. Thus France was represented by five members; Romania, Poland, and Great Britain each had one.
167. "Procès-verbal de la séance du 9 Decembre 1947," YVA M9, folder 49, pp. 176–177.
168. Protocol, first meeting, "Conseil Scientifique," December 11, 1945, YVA O5, folder 10, p. 2. Among the scholars whom the council hoped to involve in its work were Liebman Hersh (Geneva), Cecil Roth (Oxford), and Israel Kaplan (Munich), as well as others from Paris, including some not affiliated with the documentation effort, such as Prof. Edmond Vermeil, a specialist in German history, and Prof. Robert Anchel, an expert on Jews during the Napoleonic period.
169. Schneersohn to the Jewish Historical Documentation in Vienna, October 11, 1948, YVA O5, folder 10.
170. Formal letter by Schneersohn regarding the exhibition, June 25, 1948, AYIVO RG 1258, box 51, folder 893, English.
171. Ibid. See also a detailed plan for the exhibition, December 1948, "Schema du plan de l'exposition internationale 'Du Cataclysme à la Vie Nouvelle,'" AYIVO RG 1258, box 51, folder 893; the memorandum "'Du cataclysme à la vie nouvelle': Destruction et Reconstruction; Grande Exposition Internationale organisée par le Centre de Documentation Juive Contemporaine avec le concours des Commissions Historiques et des Grandes Organisations Juives," [April 2, 1949], ACDJC box 20; and "Destruction, Résistance et Reconstruction," ACDJC, box 20. The plan for the exhibition was drawn up in a series of meetings by a committee that included Friedman, Borwicz, Schneersohn, Henri Hertz, Eugène Weill, Georges Wellers, Léon Czertok, Maurice Moch, Jacques Polonski, Philippe Hosiasson, and Michel Mazor; see the protocols of that commission for April 15, 1948, April 29, 1948, and May 3, 1948, ACDJC, box 20.
172. Protocol, second meeting, "Conseil d'Administration," December 12, 1947, YVA M9, folder 49, pp. 180–181. In a letter to Koppel S. Pinson (December 15, 1947), Friedman was confident that the new institutions would have great potential if only their means of financial support were secured. AYIVO RG 1258, box 4, folder 182, English.

173. For example, Schneersohn to Friedman, February 17, 1948, AYIVO RG 1258, box 6, folder 296.
174. Michał Borwicz and Joseph Wulf to the ECC, December 16, 1947, ACDJC, box 31, French and Yiddish.
175. Léon Czertok, "Note," December 31, 1947, ACDJC, box 31, French. Borwicz was a fierce critic of the conference's choice to organize documentation material by country rather than by issue or subject; see protocols, "Compte rendu de la réunion de la commission technique de l'exposition," for April 15 and April 29, 1948, ACDJC, box 20.
176. See chapter 2.

Conclusion

1. These myths largely ignored the fact that most anti-Nazi resistance arose late in the war and was often carried out by groups such as communists, not motivated by nationalist impulses and hardly representing the entire nation. On the emergence of "resistance myths" as well as the complex reasons for the misrepresentations of the past in postwar memory throughout Europe, see Judt, "The Past Is Another Country."
2. Judt, *Postwar*, 829, emphasis in original.
3. On the transformation in European understanding of the Second World War and the Holocaust over the past sixty years, see Tony Judt's epilogue to his *Postwar*, 803–831; and the essays in the following edited volumes: Bankier, *The Jews are Coming Back*; Bessel and Schumann, *Life after Death*; Biess and Moeller, *Histories of the Aftermath*; Knigge and Frei, *Verbrechen erinnern*; Lebow, Kansteiner, and Fogu, *The Politics of Memory in Postwar Europe*; Müller, *Memory and Power in Post-War Europe*; and Wyman, *The World Reacts to the Holocaust*.
4. Bartov, "The Holocaust as the Leitmotif of the Twentieth Century," 3–25. Looking at the process of European unification since 1945 and especially since 1989, Tony Judt observed that genocide became a unifying factor for member states; "Holocaust recognition is our contemporary European entry ticket." Postwar, 803. Similarly, Daniel Levy and Natan Sznaider argued that at the end of the twentieth century, under the impact of globalization and postmodernism, the Holocaust became the universal yardstick of evil; see Levy and Sznaider, *The Holocaust and Memory in the Global Age*.
5. See for example, Friedman, "Research and Literature on the Recent Jewish Tragedy," 25–26.
6. Friedman, "American Jewish Research and Literature on the Jewish Catastrophe," *Jewish Social Studies* 13 (1951): 235–250, also published in Friedman, *Roads to Extinction*, 525–538, quotation at 525.
7. Liberles, *Salo Wittmayer Baron*, 322–337; Yablonka, *The State of Israel vs. Adolf Eichmann*, 100–106, and Baron, "European Jewry Before and After Hitler," 3–53.
8. On this organization, founded in New York in 1947, see Gallas, "Gedächtnisspuren," chaps. 1 and 3; Herman, "Hashavat Avedah"; Sznaider, *Gedächtnisraum Europa*.
9. Engel, *On Studying Jewish History*, 9. See also Engel, *Historians of the Jews and the Holocaust*, chap. 1, esp. 68–69. As Engel points out, although the Holocaust deeply affected Baron as a human being, it nevertheless did not prompt him to rethink his adherence to an antilachrymose historiography that focused primarily on long-term creative forces and social dynamics, rather than on the Jewish people's history of suffering. Baron remembered Friedman in a 1960 obituary, "Philip Friedman," 1–7, and in his introduction to Friedman, *Roads to Extinction*, 1–8. On Baron's views on the Holocaust see Engel, *Historians of the Jews and the Holocaust*, 42–71.
10. Baron, introduction to Friedman, *Roads to Extinction*, 1.
11. Baron, foreword to Friedman and Robinson, *Guide to Jewish History under Nazi Impact*, xix. The bibliography was published jointly by Yad Vashem and YIVO.
12. Ibid., xix–xx. Baron had taken a similar stance ten years earlier at a scholarly conference convened by the Conference on Jewish Relations in collaboration with the YIVO Institute held at the New School for Social Research in April 1949 in New York marking the tenth anniversary of *Jewish Social Studies*. Baron, Hannah Arendt, Max Weinreich, Samuel

Gringauz, and Joshua Starr and among others discussed "Problems of Research in the Study of the Jewish Catastrophe 1939–1945." In his preface to the publication of the conference papers in *Jewish Social Studies* a year later, Baron forcefully pleaded:

> In taking the initiative of assembling the present conference, we have felt that the time has come to subject the harrowing experiences of the great Catastrophe to rigorous scientific scrutiny. We are, to be sure, still too close to the events and, despite the great transformations of the last half a decade, do not yet possess the broad historic perspectives. Few, if any of us, can divorce ourselves completely from the emotional strain under which we have lived for so many years. Nevertheless, we must not only intensify our efforts in salvaging from imminent oblivion the vast source materials still extant, but also begin at least with the preliminary investigation and the blocking out of the ramified and complex research problems confronting the students of the Nazi onslaught.
> —Baron, "Opening Remarks," 14.

13. Dawidowicz, *The Holocaust and the Historians*, 129.
14. Ibid., 130.
15. Among Wulf's most significant publication were three volumes which he published together with Léon Poliakov in the 1950s: Poliakov and Wulf, *Das Dritte Reich und die Juden*; Poliakov and Wulf, *Das Dritte Reich und seine Diener*; and Poliakov and Wulf, *Das Dritte Reich und seine Denker*.
16. Berg, "Joseph Wulf," 190.
17. Hans-Guenther Seraphim, "Das Dritte Reich und die Juden," in *Das Historisch Politische Buch* 4 (1956): 215, quoted in ibid., 188.
18. Berg, "Joseph Wulf," 187–188. See also Berg, *Der Holocaust und die westdeutschen Historiker*, 343–345, and Berg, *The Invention of "Functionalism,"* 14–36.
19. Dinur became a lecturer of Jewish history at the Hebrew University of Jerusalem in 1936 and a minister of education in 1951. See Boaz Cohen, "The Birth Pangs of the Holocaust Research in Israel," 204–205; Engel, *Historians of the Jews and the Holocaust*, chap. 2; Kenan, *Between Memory and History*, 3–17; and Stauber, *The Holocaust in Israeli Public Debate*, 60–65 and 133–148.
20. Boaz Cohen, "The Birth Pangs of the Holocaust Research in Israel, 208. On Dinur's intellectual and ideological background, see Myers, *Re-Inventing the Jewish Past*, 129–150; Myers, "History as Ideology"; and Myers, "A New Scholarly Colony in Jerusalem."
21. On the history of Yad Vashem's Testimony Division and Auerbach's work, see Boaz Cohen, "Rachel Auerbach," 199–203, and on Dinur's criticism of Auerbach, see Kenan, *Between Memory and History*, 59.
22. Engel, *Historians of the Jews*, 126–133.
23. On this confrontation see Boaz Cohen, "Rachel Auerbach," 203–213, and Kenan, *Between Memory and History*, 56–62. On the general agenda of Holocaust research in Israel until the 1960s, see Boaz Cohen, "Setting the Agenda of Holocaust Research."
24. On the general development of Holocaust research in Israel in the 1960s and 1970s, see Boaz Cohen, "Ha-mehkar ha-histori ha-israeli," 241–328, and *Ha-dorot ha-baim*, chaps. 15 and 16.
25. Michman, "Is There an 'Israeli School' of Holocaust Research?," 64.
26. These developments included a growing public concern with personal stories of Holocaust survivors in the wake of the Eichmann trial, as well as a general interest in oral history less connected with the Holocaust per se than with the history of Jewish immigrants in Palestine/Israel. For the trial's impact on Israeli society, see Yablonka, *The State of Israel vs. Adolf Eichmann*, and Lipstadt, *The Eichmann Trial*, esp. 188–203.
27. Hilberg, "The Development of Holocaust Research," 29.
28. This was the bias of the Nuremberg trials, whose perpetrator-centered approach reflected the tribunal's aim to bring the individuals at the center of the Nazi regime to justice on the basis of their own evidence, rather than to focus on the stories of the regime's individual victims.

29. Neumann, *Behemoth*.
30. Yad Vashem turned it down precisely because Hilberg ignored the Jewish perspective and also because of its generalizations regarding the victims' culpability for their deaths; publishers in the United States feared that the work would not sell; see Engel, *Historians of the Jews*, 134–145.
31. Hilberg, *The Politics of Memory*, 70.
32. Ibid., 109.
33. Born in Prague in 1932, Friedländer, who lost his family in the Holocaust, survived in a Catholic boarding school in occupied France. See his memoir, *When Memory Comes*.
34. In essence, the conflict pitted victims' sources (the realm of memory) against perpetrators' sources (the stuff of history). The two historians carried on the debate in 1987 in an exchange of letters, published as "Martin Broszat/Saul Friedländer: A Controversy about the Historicization of National Socialism."
35. Friedländer, *Nazi Germany and the Jews*, 1:1–2. Friedländer also spoke of an "integrated history" of the Holocaust; see Friedländer, *Den Holocaust beschreiben*, 7–27. See also David Cesarani's review of *Nazi Germany and the Jews*: Cesarani, "Integrative and Integrated History."
36. Friedländer, *Nazi Germany and the Jews*, 2:xv.
37. Poznanski, *Jews in France during World War II*, esp. xv–xviii; the French original of her book appeared in 1997, the same year as Friedländer's study; Kaplan, *Between Dignity and Despair*, esp. 4–5. An early example of a work integrating both perpetrator and victim sources is Lucy Dawidowicz, *The War Against the Jews*, first published in 1975.
38. See, for example, the recent volumes Roseman and Matthäus, *Jewish Responses to Persecution*; Roseman, *A Past in Hiding*; and Nicosia and Scrase, *Jewish Life in Nazi Germany*.
39. As an example, see Browning, *Collected Memories*, esp. 37–59; Browning, *Remembering Survival*, 1–12; and Browning, Hollander, and Tec, *Every Day Lasts a Year*. See also Bartov, *Erased*, and Bartov, "Wartime Lies and Other Testimonies." Hilberg's later monographs gave considerably more room to victims and their sources, such as his 1992 *Perpetrators, Victims, Bystanders*. Indeed, his 2001 *Sources of Holocaust Research* takes a nuanced and sensitive inclusive approach to the great variety of documentation relevant for researching the Jewish catastrophe, duly crediting Jewish wartime and postwar sources.
40. See the interview with Gross at the Princeton University website: http://www.princeton.edu/history/people/display_person.xml?netid=jtgross&;interview=yes. Testimony collected by the Central Jewish Historical Commission also played a central role in his book *Fear*, on the Kielce pogrom in 1946.
41. Bartov, "Wartime Lies and Other Testimonies," 487, 489–490.
42. See O'Toole and Cox, *Understanding Archives and Manuscripts*, 100–121.
43. Hilberg, *Sources of Holocaust Research*, 48.
44. On the Nazi plans to determine how the world would remember—or forget—the extinct Jews of Europe, see Rupnow, *Vernichten und Erinnern*.

Appendix

1. The following works served as the main basis for these biographical sketches: Gutman, *Encyclopedia of the Holocaust*; Hundert, *The YIVO Encyclopedia of Jews in Eastern Europe*; Kagan, *Leksikon fun yidish-shraybers*; Niger and Shatsky, *Leksikon*; Roth, *Encyclopaedia Judaica*; Shrayer, *An Anthology of Jewish-Russian Literature*; Skolnik, *Encyclopaedia Judaica* (2nd ed.); and Szajkowski, *Analytical Franco-Jewish Gazetteer, 1939–1945*; as well as *Who's Who in World Jewry* (for the years 1955–1965) and *Who's Who in Israel* (for the years 1955–1965).

BIBLIOGRAPHY

Archival Collections

ALLIANCE ISRAÉLITE UNIVERSELLE, PARIS
Archives of the Consistoire Central during World War II (Maurice Moch Collection)

AMERICAN JEWISH HISTORICAL SOCIETY, NEW YORK
P 675: Lucy Dawidowicz Papers

AMERICAN JEWISH JOINT DISTRIBUTION COMMITTEE ARCHIVES, JERUSALEM
Geneva Collection, G I and G II

AMERICAN JEWISH JOINT DISTRIBUTION COMMITTEE ARCHIVES, NEW YORK
AR 45/54: Poland and France

BIALIK HOUSE, TEL AVIV
Bialik's Notebooks from Kishinev, 1903
Correspondence between Chaim Nachman Bialik and Simon Dubnow

CENTRE DE DOCUMENTATION JUIVE CONTEMPORAINE (CDJC), PARIS
Administrative Archives of the CDJC (not cataloged)
DCCXIV (European Conference, December 1947)

JEWISH HISTORICAL INSTITUTE (ŻIH), WARSAW
Centralny Komitet Żydow Polskich, Komisja Historyczna
Centralny Komitet Żydow Polskich, Presydium
Centralna Żydowska Komisja Historyczna

NATIONAL AND UNIVERSITY LIBRARY, JERUSALEM
AR 4° 1795: Israel Kaplan Papers

STADTARCHIV GÖTTINGEN, GERMANY
Records of the Cultural Office, No. 475
Sammlung No. 16

YAD VASHEM, JERUSALEM

AM1: Yad Vashem Administrative Archives
M1: Central Historical Commission in Munich
M9: Simon Wiesenthal Collection
M20: Alfred (Abraham) Silberschein (Relico) Archives
O5: Towia Frydman Collection
O37: Displaced Persons (She'erit Hapletah) Collection
O70: Rosensaft Bergen-Belsen Collection

YIVO ARCHIVES, NEW YORK

RG 80: Elias Tcherikower Collection
RG 294.1: Leo W. Schwarz Papers
RG 294.2: Displaced Persons Camps and Centers in Germany
RG 294.3: Displaced Persons Camps and Centers in Italy
RG 294.4: Displaced Persons Camps and Centers in Austria
RG 1258: Philip Friedman Papers
RG 701: Yiddish Writers' Union

ZENTRALARCHIV ZUR ERFORSCHUNG DER GESCHICHTE DER JUDEN IN DEUTSCHLAND, HEIDELBERG

B.2/1.C: Joseph Wulf Papers

Periodicals

PREWAR

Der Moment (Warsaw)
Der Tog (Vilna)

POSTWAR

A Heym (Leipheim)
American Jewish Year Book (New York)
Biuletyn ŻIH (Warsaw)
Bleter far Geshikhte (Warsaw)
Bulletin du Centre de Documentation Juive Contemporaine (Paris)
Der Morgn (Bad Reichenhall)
Di Tsukunft (New York)
Dos Fraye Vort (Feldafing)
Dos Naye Lebn (Lodz)
DP Express
Farn Folk/Per il Popolo (Rome)
Frayer Kemfer: Tsentralorgan fun P.Kh.Kh. in Lints (Linz)
Fun Letstn Khurbn (Munich)
Jewish Social Studies (New York)
Jüdisches Gemeindeblatt für die Britische Zone
Kiyoum (Paris)
Landsberger Lager Cajtung (Landsberg)
Le Monde Juif (Paris)
Ojfgang (Linz)
Oyf der Fray (Stuttgart)
Undzer Hofenung (Eschwege)
Undzer Shtime (Belsen)
Undzer Veg (Munich)
YIVO Bleter (New York)

PUBLICATIONS OF THE JEWISH HISTORICAL COMMISSIONS AND DOCUMENTATION CENTERS

Austria

Wiesenthal, Simon. *Grossmufti—Grossagent der Achse*. Salzburg, Austria: Ried-Verlag, 1947.
———. *KZ Mauthausen*. Linz, Austria: Ibid-Verlag, 1946.

France

Ansky, Michel. *Les Juifs en Algérie, du décret Crémieux à la libération*. Preface by Henri Aboulker; epilogues by Pierre Paraf and André Philip. Paris: Éditions du Centre, 1950.
Billig, Joseph. *L'Allemagne et le génocide: Plans et réalisations nazis*. Preface by François de Menthon. Paris: Éditions du Centre, 1950.
———. *Le Commissariat general aux questions juives, 1941–1944*. Preface by Edmond Vermeil. 3 vols. Paris: Editions du Centre, 1955–1960.
Cassou, Jean. *Le pillage par les Allemands des œuvres d'art et des bibliothèques appartenant à des Juifs en France, recueil des documents*. Introduction by Jacques Sabille. Paris: Éditions du Centre, 1947.
CDJC, ed. *Activité des organisations juives de France sous l'occupation*. Paris: Éditions du Centre, 1947.
———, ed. *The Jewish Contemporary Documentation Center*. Paris: Éditions du Centre, 1949.
———, ed. *La bataille du ghetto Varsovie: Vue et rencontée par les Allemands*. Paris: Éditions du Centre, 1946.
———, ed. *Les Juifs en Europe (1939–1945): Rapports*. Paris: Éditions du Centre, 1949.
Knout, David. *Contribution à l'histoire de la Résistance juive en France, 1940–1944*. Paris: Éditions du Centre, 1947.
Lazarus, Jacques. *Juifs au combat: Témoignage sur l'activité d'un mouvement de résistance*. Preface by Henri Hertz. Paris: Éditions du Centre, 1947.
Lubetzki, Joseph. *La Condition des Juifs en France sous l'Occupation allemande, 1940–1944: La législation raciale*. Preface by Justin Godart. Paris: Éditions du Centre, 1945.
Monneray, Henri, ed. *La persécution des Juifs dans les pays de l'Est presentée à Nuremberg*. Preface by Telford Taylor; introduction by René Cassin. Paris: Éditions du Centre, 1949.
———, ed. *La persécution des Juifs en France et dans les autres pays de l'Ouest presentée par la France à Nuremberg*. Preface by René Cassin; introduction by Edgar Faure. Paris: Éditions du Centre, 1947.
Poliakov, Léon. *La bréviaire de la haine*. Paris: Calmann-Lévy, 1951. Published in English as *Harvest of Hate: The Nazi Program for the Destruction of the Jews of Europe* (Syracuse, NY: Syracuse University Press, 1954).
———. *La condition des Juifs en France sous l'occupation italienne*. Preface by Justin Godart. Paris: Éditions du Centre, 1946. Published in Yiddish as *Yidn unter italyenisher okupatsye* (Paris: Éditions du Centre, 1952) and English as *French Jews under the Italian Occupation* (Paris: Éditions du Centre, 1954).
———. *L'étoile jaune*. Paris: Éditions du Centre, 1949. Published in Yiddish as *Di gele late* (Paris: Éditions du Centre, 1952).
Polonski, Jacques. *La presse, la propagande et l'opinion publique*. Paris: Éditions du Centre, 1946.
Sarraute, Raymond, and Jacques Rabinovitch, eds. *Examen succinct de la situation juridique actuelle des Juifs*. Paris: Éditions du Centre, 1945.
Sarraute, Raymond, and Paul Tager. *Les Juifs sous l'occupation: Recueil de textes français et allemands*. Preface by Isaac Schneersohn. Paris: Éditions du Centre, 1945.
Weill, Joseph. *Contribution à l'histoire des camps d'internement dans l'Anti-France*. Paris: Éditions du Centre, 1946.
Wellers, Georges. *De Drancy à Auschwitz*. Paris: Éditions du Centre, 1946.

Germany

Feder, Sami. *Zamlung fun katset un geto lider*. Bergen-Belsen, Germany: Tsentral Komitet fun di Bafrayte Yidn in der Britisher Zone, 1946.

Feigenbaum, Moshe Yosef. *Podlyashe in umkum: Notitsn fun khurbn*. Munich: Tsentrale Historishe Komisye, 1948.
Horowic, Cwi, *Die Wacholders: Eine jüdische Familiengeschichte*. Göttingen, Germany: Jüva-Verlag, [1947].
Jüdische Historische Kommission in Göttingen, ed. *Unser Weg in die Freiheit*. July 20, 1947.
———. *Jüdische Professoren und Dozenten der Georg-August Universität zu Göttingen*. August 20, 1947.
Kaplan, Israel. *Dos folks-moyl in natsi-klem: Reydenishn in geto un katset*. Munich: Tsentrale Historishe Komisye, 1949.
———. *In der tog-teglekher historisher arbet*. Munich: Tsentrale Historishe Komisye, 1947.
Olewski, Rafael, Paul Trepman, and Dovid Rosental, eds. *Undzer khurbn in bild*. Bergen-Belsen, Germany: Undzer Shtime, 1946.
Tsentrale Historishe Komisye. *Fregboygns far zamler fun historishe materyaln*. Munich: Tsentrale Historishe Komisye, 1947.
———. *Ta'arukhah me-ha-hurban ha-aharon/Oysshtelung fun letstn khurbn*. Munich: Tsentrale Historishe Komisye, 1947.
Vaysbrod, Avrom. *Es shtarbt a shtetl: Megiles Skalat*. Munich: Tsentrale Historishe Komisye, 1948.

Italy

Kaganovitch, Moshe. *Der yidisher onteyl in der partizaner bavegung fun Soviet Rusland*. Rome: Tsionistisher Arbeter Komitet far Hilf un Oyfboy, 1948.
———. *Di milkhome fun di yidishe partizaner in misrekh-eyrope*. Buenos Aires: Farband fun poylishe yidn in Argentine, 1956.

Poland

Ajzensztajn, Betti, ed. *Ruch podziemny w gettach i obozach: Materiały i dokumenty*. Warsaw: CŻKH, 1946.
Auerbach, Rachel. *Oyf di felder fun Treblinke: Reportazh*. Warsaw: CŻKH, 1947.
Bałberyszski, Mendel. *Likwidacja getta Wileńskiego*. Warsaw: CŻKH, 1946.
Bauminger, Róża. *Przy piktynie i trotylu: Obóz pracy przymusowej w Skarżysku-Kamiennej*. Krakow: Centralny Komitet Żydów Polskich, 1946.
Blumental, Nachman, ed. *Dokumenty i materiały do dziejów okupacji niemieckiej w Polsce*. Vol. 1, *Obozy*. Lodz: CŻKH, 1946.
———, ed. *Instrukcje dla zbierania materiałów etnograficznych w okresie okupacji niemieckiej*. Lodz: CŻKH, 1945.
———. *Słowa niewinne*. Krakow: CŻKH, 1947.
Borwicz, Michał. *Literatura w obozie*. Krakow: CŻKH, 1946.
———, ed. *Pieśń ujdzie cało: Antologia wierszy o Żydach pod okupacją niemiecką*. Warsaw: CŻKH, 1947.
———. *Proces ludobójcy Amona Goetha (stenogram z procesu)*. Lodz, CŻKH, 1947.
———. *Uniwersytet zbirów*. Krakow: CŻKH, 1946.
Borwicz, Michał, Nella Thon-Rost, and Józef Wulf, eds. *Dokumenty zbrodni i męczeństwa: Antologia*. Krakow: Centralny Komitet Żydów Polskich, 1945.
———, eds. *W 3-cia rocznicę zagłady ghetta w Krakowie: 13. III 1943–13.III 1946*. Krakow: Centralny Komitet Żydów Polskich, 1946.
CŻKH, ed. *Metodologishe onvayzungen tsum oysforshn dem khurbn fun poylishn yidntum*. Lodz: CŻKH, 1945.
Datner, Szymon. *Walka i zagłada Białostockiego ghetta*. Lodz: CŻKH, 1946.
Dawidsohn-Draenger, Gusta. *Pamiętnik Justyny*. Krakow: CŻKH, 1946. Published in English as *Justyna's Narrative* (Amherst: University of Massachusetts Press, 1996).
Eisenbach, Artur. *Di Hitleristishe politik fun yidn-farnikhtung in di yorn 1939–1945 vi an oysdruk fun daytshishn imperializm*. Warsaw: Yidish Bukh, 1955.
———, ed. *Dokumenty i materiały do dziejów okupacji niemieckiej w Polsce*. Vol. 3, *Getto Łódzkie*. Krakow: CŻKH, 1946.
———. *Hitlerowska polityka eksterminacji Żydów w latach 1939–1945 jako jeden z przejawów imperializmu niemieckiego*. Warsaw: ŻIH, 1953.

Friedman, Philip. *To jest Oświęcim!* Warsaw: Panstwowe Wydawn, Literatury Politycznej, 1945. Published in English as *This Was Oswiecim: The Story of a Murder Camp* (London: United Jewish Relief Appeal, 1946).

———. *Zagłada Żydów Lwowskich*. Lodz: CŻKH, 1945. English translation in Friedman, *Roads to Extinction*, 244–321.

———. "Zagłada Żydów Polskich 1939–1945." *Biuletyn Głównej Komisji Badania Zbrodni Hitlerowskich w Polsce* 1 (1946): 163–208. English translation in Friedman, *Roads to Extinction*, 211–243.

Gebirtig, Mordechai. *Es brent*. Edited by Joseph Wulf. Krakow: WŻKH, 1946.

Grüss, Noe. *Rok pracy Centralnej Żydowskiej Komisji Historycznej*. Lodz: CŻKH, 1946.

Grüss, Noe, and Genia Silkes, eds. *Instrukcje dla badania przeżyć dzieci żydowskich w okresie okupacji niemieckiej*. Lodz: CŻKH, 1945.

Hescheles, Janka. *Oczyma 12-letniej dziewczyny*. Introduction by Maria Hochberg-Mariańska. Krakow: CKŻP, 1946.

Hochberg-Mariańska, Maria, and Noe Grüss, eds. *Dzieci oskarżają*. Krakow: CŻKH, 1947. Published in English as *The Children Accuse* (London: Vallentine Mitchell, 1996).

Kermisz, Joseph, ed. *Dokumenty i materiały do dziejów okupacji niemieckiej w Polsce*. Vol. 2: *Akcje i wysiedlenia*. Warsaw: CŻKH, 1946.

———, ed. *Instrukcje dla zbierania materiałów historycznych w okresie okupacji niemieckiej*. Lodz: CŻKH, 1945.

———. *Powstanie w getcie Warszawskim 19 kwietnia–16 maja 1943*. Lodz: CŻKH, 1946.

Mark, Ber. *Ruch oporu w getcie Białostockim*. Warsaw: CŻKH, 1946. Published in Yiddish as *Der oyfshtand fun bialistoker geto* (Warsaw: ŻIH, 1950).

Melezin, Abraham. *Przyczynek do znajomości stosunków demograficznych wśród ludności żydowskiej w Łodzi, Krakowie i Lublinie podczas okupacji niemieckiej*. Lodz: CŻKH, 1946.

Otwinowski, Stefan. *Wielkanoc*. Krakow: Centralny Komitet Żydów Polskich, 1946.

Reder, Rudolf. *Bełżec*. Introduction by Nella Rost. Krakow: CŻKH, 1946. English translation in *Polin* 13 (2000): 268–289.

Rudnicki, Henryk. *Martyrologia i zagłada Żydów Warszawskich*. Lodz: Łodzki Instytut Wydawniczy, 1946.

Ryczywól, Ber. *Vi azoy ikh hob iberlebt di daytshn*. Warsaw: CŻKH, 1946.

Szac-Wajnkranc, Noemi. *Przeminęło z ogniem: Pamiętnik pisany w Warszawie w okresie od założenia ghetta do jego likwidacji*. Warsaw: CŻKH, 1947.

Szajewicz, Simcha. *Lekh lekho*. Lodz: CŻKH, 1946.

Szternfinkel, Natan. *Zagłada Żydów Sosnowca*. Katowice: CŻKH, 1946.

Taffet, Gerszon, ed. *Zagłada Żydostwa Polskiego: Album zdjęć fotograficznych*. Lodz: CŻKH, 1946.

———. *Zagłada Żydów Żółkiewskich*. Lodz: CŻKH, 1946.

Weliczker, Leon. *Brygada śmierci*. Introduction by Rachel Auerbach. Lodz: CŻKH, 1946.

Theses and Unpublished Manuscripts

Aleksiun, Natalia. "Ammunition in the Struggle for National Rights: Jewish Historians in Poland between the Two World Wars." Ph.D. diss., New York University, 2010.

Brenner, Michael. "Vergessene Historiker: Ein Kapitel deutsch-jüdischer Geschichtsschreibung der fünfziger und sechziger Jahre." Unpublished manuscript.

Cohen, Boaz. "Ha-mehkar ha-histori ha-israeli shel ha-shoah, 1945–1980: Meafyenim, megamot ve-kivunim." Ph.D. diss., Bar Ilan University, 2004.

Gallas, Elisabeth. "Gedächtnisspuren: Vom Offenbacher Depot zum jüdischen Geschichtsverständnis nach 1945." Ph.D. diss., University of Leipzig, 2011.

Giere, Jacqueline Dewell. "'Wir sind unterwegs, aber nicht in der Wüste': Erziehung und Kultur in den jüdischen Displaced Persons-Lagern der amerikanischen Zone im Nachkriegsdeutschland, 1945–1949." Ph.D. diss., Goethe University Frankfurt am Main, 1993.

Herman, Dana. 'Hashavat Avedah': A History of Jewish Cultural Reconstruction, Inc. Ph.D. diss., McGill University, 2008.

Kokkonen, Susanna. "The Jewish Refugees in Postwar Italy, 1945–1951." Ph.D. diss., Hebrew University, Jerusalem, 2003.

Kuper-Margaliot, Ayelet. "Yiddish Periodicals Published by Displaced Persons." Ph.D. diss., Oxford University, 1997.
Kuznitz, Cecile. "The Origins of Yiddish Scholarship and the YIVO Institute for Jewish Research." Ph.D. diss., Stanford University, 2000.
Lamm, Hans. "Über die innere und äußere Entwicklung des deutschen Judentums im Dritten Reich." Ph.D. diss., University of Erlangen, 1951.
Maor, Harry. "Über den Wiederaufbau der jüdischen Gemeinden in Deutschland seit 1945." Ph.D. diss., University of Mainz, 1961.
Perego, Simon. "Histoire, justice, mémoire: Le Centre de Documentation Juive Contemporaine et le Mémorial du Martyr juif inconnu 1956–1969." MA thesis, École Doctorale de Sciences Po, 2007.
Stach, Stephan. "Das Jüdische Historische Institut in Warschau, 1947–1968." MA thesis, University of Leipzig, 2008.

Published Sources

Abramson, Henry. *A Prayer for the Government: Ukrainians and Jews in Revolutionary Times, 1917–1920*. Cambridge, MA: Harvard University Press, 1999.
Adler, H. G. *Der verwaltete Mensch: Studien zur Deportation der Juden aus Deutschland*. Tübingen, Germany: Mohr, 1974.
———, ed. *Die verheimlichte Wahrheit: Theresienstädter Dokumente*. Tübingen, Germany: Mohr, 1958.
———. *Theresienstadt 1941–1945: Das Antlitz einer Zwangsgemeinschaft*. Göttingen, Germany: Wallstein, 2005. First published 1955.
Adler, Jacques. *The Jews of Paris and the Final Solution: Communal Response and Internal Conflicts, 1940–1944*. New York: Oxford University Press, 1987.
Adunka, Evelyn. *Die Vierte Gemeinde: Die Wiener Juden in der Zeit von 1945 bis heute*. Berlin: Philo, 2000.
Alberich, Thomas. *Exodus durch Österreich: Die jüdischen Flüchtlinge 1945–1948*. Innsbruck, Austria: Haymon Verlag, 1987.
———, ed. *Flucht nach Eretz Israel: Die Bricha und der jüdische Exodus durch Österreich nach 1945*. Vienna: Studien Verlag, 1998.
———. "Zionisten wider Willen: Hintergründe und Ablauf des Exodus aus Osteuropa." In Alberich, *Flucht nach Eretz Israel*, 13–48.
Alberich, Thomas, and Ronald Zweig, eds. *Escape through Austria: Jewish Refugees and the Austrian Route to Palestine*. London: Frank Cass, 2001.
Aleksiun, Natalia. "The Central Jewish Historical Commission in Poland, 1944–1947." In Finder et al., "Making Holocaust Memory," 74–97.
———. "Polish Historiography of the Holocaust: Between Silence and Public Debate." *German History* 22, no. 3 (2004): 406–432.
———. "Polish Jewish Historians before 1918: Configuring the Liberal East European Jewish Intelligentsia." *East European Jewish Affairs* 34, no. 2 (2004): 41–54.
———. "Rescuing a Memory and Constructing a History of Polish Jewry: Jews in Poland, 1944–1950." *Jews in Russia and Eastern Europe* 1–2 (2005): 5–27.
———. "Setting the Record Straight: Polish Jewish Historians and Local History in Interwar Poland." *Simon Dubnow Institute Yearbook* 7 (2008): 127–141.
———. "The Vicious Circle: Jews in Communist Poland, 1944–1956." *Studies in Contemporary Jewry* 19 (2003): 157–180.
———. "Zionists and Anti-Zionists in the Central Committee of the Jews in Poland: Cooperation and Political Struggle, 1944–1950." *Jews in Eastern Europe* 2 (Fall 1997): 33–50.
Alishan, Leonardo P. "Crucifixion without 'The Cross': The Impact of the Genocide on Armenian Literature." *Armenian Review* 38, no. 1 (1985): 27–50.
Ancel, Jean. "'The New Jewish Invasion': The Return of the Survivors from Transnistria." In Bankier, *The Jews Are Coming Back*, 231–256.
An-ski, S. *The Enemy at His Pleasure: A Journey through the Jewish Pale of Settlement during World War I*. Edited and translated by Joachim Neugroschel. New York: Metropolitan Books, 2002.

———. *Khurbn Galitsye*. 3 vols. Gezamlte Shriftn 4–6. Vilnius: S. Šreberk, 1921.
Arad, Yitzhak "Ha-arkhiyon ha-mehtarti shel geto Vilna." In Gutman, *Mi-genizah le-tsiyune derekh historiyim*, 151–160.
Armborst, Kerstin. "Wegbereiter der Geschichtsforschung: Über den Vorstand der Jüdisch Historisch-Ethnographischen Gesellschaft in St. Petersburg." *Simon Dubnow Institute Yearbook* 6 (2007): 411–440.
Arndt, Ino, and Heinz Boberach, "Deutsches Reich." In Benz, *Dimension des Völkermords*, 23–65.
Asch, Sholem. *Dos bukh fun tsar*. Gezamlte Shriftn 6. 2nd ed. New York: Sholem Ash Komite, 1923.
Assmann, Aleida. *Der lange Schatten der Vergangenheit: Erinnerungskultur und Geschichtspolitik*. Munich: C. H. Beck, 2006.
Auerhahn, Nanette, and Dori Laub. "Holocaust Testimony." *Holocaust and Genocide Studies* 5, no. 4 (Winter 1990): 447–462.
Ballinger, Pamela. "The Culture of Survivors: Post-Traumatic Stress Disorder and Traumatic Memory." *History and Memory* 10, no. 1 (1998): 99–132.
Bankier, David, ed. *The Jews Are Coming Back: The Return of the Jews to Their Countries of Origin after WWII*. Jerusalem: Yad Vashem, 2005.
Bankier, David, and Dan Michman, eds. *Holocaust Historiography in Context: Emergence, Challenges, Polemics and Achievements*. Jerusalem: Yad Vashem, 2009.
Bardgett, Suzanne, David Cesarani, Jessica Reinisch, and Johannes-Dieter Steinert, eds. *Survivors of Nazi Persecution in Europe after the Second World War*. Vol. 1 of *Landscapes after Battle*. London: Vallentine Mitchell, 2010.
———. *Justice, Politics and Memory in Europe after the Second World War*. Vol. 2 of *Landscapes after Battle*. London: Vallentine Mitchell, 2011.
Barkai, Avraham. *"Wehr dich!": Der Centralverein deutscher Staatsbürger jüdischen Glaubens (C.V.) 1893–1938*. Munich: C. H. Beck, 2002.
Barkow, Ben. *Alfred Wiener and the Making of the Holocaust Library*. London: Vallentine Mitchell, 1997.
Barkow, Ben, Raphael Gross, and Michael Lenarz, eds. *Novemberpogrom 1938: Die Augenzeugenberichte der Wiener Library London*. Frankfurt: Jüdischer Verlag im Suhrkamp Verlag, 2008.
Barnouw, David, and Gerold van der Stroom, eds. *The Diary of Anne Frank: The Critical Edition*. Translated by Arnold J. Pomerans and B. M. Mooyaart-Doubleday. New York: Viking Penguin, 1989.
Baron, Salo W. "European Jewry Before and After Hitler." *American Jewish Yearbook* 63 (1962): 3–53
———. Foreword to Friedman and Robinson, *Guide to Jewish History under Nazi Impact*, xix–xx.
———. Introduction to Friedman, *Roads to Extinction*, 1–8.
———. "Opening Remarks." *Jewish Social Studies* 12 (1950): 13–16.
———. *The Russian Jew under Tsar and Soviets*. New York: Macmillan, 1964.
Bartov, Omer. *Erased: Vanishing Traces of Jewish Galicia in Present-Day Ukraine*. Princeton, NJ: Princeton University Press, 2007.
———. "'Fields of Glory': War, Genocide, and the Glorification of Violence." In Postone and Santner, *Catastrophe and Meaning*, 117–135.
———. "The Holocaust as the Leitmotif of the Twentieth Century." In *Lessons and Legacies*, vol. 7, *The Holocaust in International Research*, ed. Dagmar Herzog, 3–25. Evanston, IL: Northwestern University Press, 2006.
———. "Intellectuals on Auschwitz: Memory, History and Truth." *History and Memory* 5 (1996): 87–129.
———. *Murder in Our Midst: The Holocaust, Industrial Killing, and Representation*. New York: Oxford University Press, 1996.
———. "Wartime Lies and Other Testimonies: Jewish-Christian Relations in Buczacz, 1939–1944." *East European Politics and Societies* 25 (2011): 486–511.
Bauer, Yehuda. *A History of the Holocaust*. New York: F. Watts, 1982.
———. *Flight and Rescue: Brichah*. New York: Random House, 1970.
———. "The Initial Organization of the Holocaust Survivors in Bavaria." *Yad Vashem Studies* 8 (1970): 127–157.

———. *Out of the Ashes: The Impact of American Jews on Post-Holocaust European Jewry*. Oxford: Pergamon, 1988.

———. *Rethinking the Holocaust*. New Haven, CT: Yale University Press, 2001.

———. "Teguvotehen shel kibutsim yehudiyim la-mediniyut ha-natsit be-'et ha-shoah lenokhah moreshotehen ha-meyuhadot: Mabat kolel u-mashve." In *Ha-shoah ba-historiyah ha-yehudit: Historiografiyah, toda'ah ve-parshanut*, ed. Dan Michman, 109–128. Jerusalem: Yad Vashem, 2005.

Becker, Annette. "From Death to Memory: The National Ossuaries in France after the Great War." *History and Memory* 5, no. 2 (Fall–Winter 1993): 32–49.

Bein, Alex, ed. *Sefer Motzkin: Ktavim u-neumim, biografiyah ve-divre ha'arakhah*. Jerusalem: World Zionist Organization and World Jewish Congress, 1939.

Beledian, Krikor. "Die Erfahrung der Katastrophe in der Literatur der Armenier." In *Generation und Gedächtnis: Erinnerungen und kollektive Identitäten*, ed. Kristin Platt and Mihran Dabag, 186–254. Opladen, Germany: Leske & Budrich, 1995.

Benbassa, Esther. *The Jews of France: A History from Antiquity to the Present*. Princeton, NJ: Princeton University Press, 1999.

Bender, Sarah. "Arkhiyon ha-mahteret be-Bialistok." In Gutman, *Mi-genizah le-tsiyune derekh historiyim*, 121–131.

Ben-Natan, Asher, and Susanne Urban. *Die Bricha: Aus dem Terror nach Eretz Israel; Ein Fluchthelfer erinnert sich*. Düsseldorf, Germany: Droste, 2005.

Bensoussan, Georges. "The Jewish Contemporary Documentation Center (CDJC) and Holocaust Research in France, 1945–1970." In Bankier and Michman, *Holocaust Historiography*, 245–254.

Benz, Wolfgang, ed. *Dimension des Völkermords: Die Zahl der jüdischen Opfer des Nationalsozialismus*. Munich: Deutscher Taschenbuch Verlag, 1996.

Berenstein, Tatiana. "Documents in the Archives of Poland: A Basis for Historical Research Concerning the Jewish Population during the Nazi Occupation." *Yad Vashem Studies* 3 (1959): 67–78.

Berg, Nicolas. *Der Holocaust und die westdeutschen Historiker: Erforschung und Erinnerung*. Göttingen, Germany: Wallstein, 2003.

———. "Ein Aussenseiter der Holocaustforschung: Joseph Wulf (1912–1974) im Historikerdiskurs der Bundesrepublik." *Leipziger Beiträge für jüdische Geschichte und Kultur* 1 (2003): 311–346.

———. *The Invention of "Functionalism": Josef Wulf, Martin Broszat, and the Institute for Contemporary History (Munich) in the 1960s*. Jerusalem: Yad Vashem, 2003.

———. "Joseph Wulf: A Forgotten Outsider among Holocaust Scholars." In Bankier and Michman, *Holocaust Historiography*, 167–206.

Berg, Nicolas, and Anke Hilbrenner. "Der Tod Simon Dubnows in Riga 1941: Quellen, Zeugnisse, Erinnerungen." *Simon Dubnow Institute Yearbook* 1 (2002): 457–471.

Berkovitz, Jay R. *The Shaping of Jewish Identity in Nineteenth-Century France*. Detroit: Wayne State University Press, 1989.

Berkowitz, Michael. *The Crime of My Very Existence: Nazism and the Myth of Jewish Criminality*. Berkeley: University of California Press, 2007.

Bessel, Richard, and Dirk Schumann, eds. *Life after Death: Approaches to a Cultural and Social History of Europe during the 1940s and 1950s*. Cambridge, UK: Cambridge University Press, 2003.

Bialik, Chaim Nachman. *Shire H. N. Bialik 5659–5694*. Edited by Dan Miron. Tel Aviv: Devir, 1990.

Biess, Frank and Robert G. Moeller, eds. *Histories of the Aftermath: The Legacies of the Second World War in Europe*. New York: Berghahn Books, 2010.

Birnbaum, Pierre. "Beween Social and Political Assimilation: Remarks on the History of Jews in France." In *Paths of Emancipation: Jews, States, and Citizenship*, ed. Pierre Birnbaum and Ira Katznelson, 94–127. Princeton, NJ: Princeton University Press, 1995.

———. *Jewish Destinies: Citizenship, State, and Community in Modern France*. New York: Hill & Wang, 2000.

———. *The Jews of the Republic: A Political History of State Jews in France from Gambetta to Vichy*. Stanford, CA: Stanford University Press, 1996.

Blatman, Daniel. *The Death Marches: The Final Phase of Nazi Genocide*. Translated by Chaya Galai. Cambridge, MA: Belknap Press of Harvard University Press, 2011.

———. "The Encounter between Jews and Poles in Lublin District after Liberation, 1944–1945." *East European Politics and Societies* 20, no. 4 (2006): 1–24.

———. *For Our Freedom and Yours: The Jewish Labor Bund in Poland, 1939–1949*. Portland, OR: Vallentine Mitchell, 2003.

Blonski, Jan. "The Poor Poles Look at the Ghetto: Polish-Jewish Relations during the Second World War." In *My Brother's Keeper? Recent Polish Debates on the Holocaust*, ed. Antony Polosky, 34–52. London: Routledge, 1990.

Bloxham, Donald. *Genocide on Trial: War Crimes Trials and the Formation of Holocaust History and Memory*. New York: Oxford University Press, 2001.

———. *The Great Game of Genocide: Imperialism, Nationalism, and the Destruction of the Ottoman Armenians*. Oxford: Oxford University Press, 2005.

———. "Jewish Witnesses in War Crimes Trials of the Postwar Era." In Bankier and Michman, *Holocaust Historiography*, 539–553.

Borodziej, Włodzimierz. "'Hitleristische Verbrechen': Die Ahndung deutscher Kriegs- und Besatzungsverbrechen in Polen." In Frei, *Transnationale Vergangenheitspolitik*, 399–437.

Brenner, Michael. *After the Holocaust: Rebuilding Jewish Lives in Postwar Germany*. Princeton, NJ: Princeton University Press, 1995.

———. "East European and German Jews in Postwar Germany, 1945–1950." In *Jews, Germans, Memory: Reconstruction of Jewish Life in Germany*, ed. Y. Michal Bodemann, 49–63. Ann Arbor: University of Michigan Press, 1996.

———. *Propheten des Vergangenen: Jüdische Geschichtsschreibung im 19. und 20. Jahrhundert*. Munich: C. H. Beck, 2006.

Brog, Mooli. "In Blessed Memory of a Dream: Mordechai Shenhavi and Initial Holocaust Commemoration Ideas in Palestine, 1942–1945." *Yad Vashem Studies* 30 (2002): 297–336.

Browning, Christopher. *Collected Memories: Holocaust Memory and Postwar Testimony*, Madison: University of Wisconsin Press, 2003.

———. *The Origins of the Final Solution: The Evolution of Nazi Jewish Policy, September 1939–March 1942*. Lincoln: University of Nebraska Press, 2004.

———. *The Path to Genocide: Essays on Launching the Final Solution*. Cambridge, UK: Cambridge University Press, 1992.

———. *Remembering Survival: Inside a Nazi Slave-Labor Camp*. New York: W. W. Norton, 2010.

Browning, Christopher, Richard S. Hollander, and Nechama Tec, eds. *Every Day Lasts a Year: A Jewish Family's Correspondence from Poland*. New York: Cambridge University Press, 2007.

Burds, Jeffrey. *The Early Cold War in Soviet West Ukraine, 1944–1948*. Pittsburgh, PA: Russian and East European Studies Program, University of Pittsburgh, 2001.

Cade, John B. "Out of the Mouths of Ex-Slaves." *Journal of Negro History* 20 (July 1935): 294–337.

Cała, Alina. "An Attempt to Recover Its Voice: The Towarzystwo Społeczno-Kulturalne Żydów w Polsce, the Jewish Community, and the Polish State, 1956–1960." *Polin* 19 (2007): 557–568.

Caron, Vicki. *Uneasy Asylum: France and the Jewish Refugee Crisis, 1933–1942*. Stanford, CA: Stanford University Press, 1999.

Carpi, Daniel. *Between Mussolini and Hitler: The Jews and the Italian Authorities in France and Tunisia*. Hanover, NH: University Press of New England, 1994.

Caruth, Cathy, ed., *Trauma: Explorations in Memory*, Baltimore: Johns Hopkins University Press, 1995.

Cesarani, David. "'Integrative and Integrated History': A Sweeping History of the Shoah Rooted in Everyday Life—and Death." *Yad Vashem Studies* 36, no. 1 (2008): 271–277.

Cesarani, David, and Eric J. Sundquist, eds. *After the Holocaust: Challenging the Myth of Silence*. London: Routledge, 2012.

Cohen, Boaz. "'And I was only a child': Children's Testimonies, Bergen Belsen 1945." *Holocaust Studies* 12, nos. 1–2 (2006): 153–169.

———. "The Birth Pangs of the Holocaust Research in Israel." *Yad Vashem Studies* 33 (2005): 203–243.

———. *Ha-dorot ha-ba'im—ekhakha yed'u? Ledato ve-hitpathuto shel heker ha-sho'ah ha-yisraeli*. Jerusalem: Yad Vashem, 2010.

———. "Ha-ve'ida ha-olamit le-heker ha-sho'ah ve-ha-gvura shel tekufatenu, yerushalayim 1947." *Cathedra* 125 (2007): 99–108.

———. "Rachel Auerbach, Vad Vashem, and Israeli History." In Finder et al., "Making Holocaust Memory," 197–221.

———. "Representing the Experiences of Children in the Holocaust: Children's Survivor Testimonies Published in *Fun Letsten Hurbn*, Munich, 1946–49." In Patt and Berkowitz, *We Are Here*, 74–97.

———. "Setting the Agenda of Holocaust Research: Discord at Yad Vashem in the 1950s." In Bankier and Michman, *Holocaust Historiography*, 255–292.

———. "The Children's Voice: Postwar Collection of Testimonies from Child Survivors of the Holocaust." *Holocaust and Genocide Studies* 21, no. 1 (2007): 73–95.

Cohen, Nathan. "The Diaries of the Sonderkommando in Auschwitz: Coping with Fate and Reality." *Yad Vashem Studies* 20 (1990): 273–312.

———. "The Renewed Association of Yiddish Writers and Journalists in Poland, 1945–48." In *Yiddish after the Holocaust*, ed. Joseph Sherman, 15–36. Oxford: Boulevard, 2004.

Cohen, Raya. "Emmanuel Ringelblum: Between Historiographical Tradition and Unprecedented History." *Gal Ed* 15–16 (1997): 105–117.

Cohen, Richard. *The Burden of Conscience: French Jewry's Response to the Holocaust*. Bloomington: Indiana University Press, 1987.

Comité des Délégations Juives, ed. *Les pogromes en Ukraine sous les gouvernements ukrainiens (1917–1920)*. Paris: L. Beresniak, 1927.

Conan, Éric, and Henry Rousso, *Vichy: An Ever-Present Past*. Translated by Nathan Bracher. Hanover, NH: University Press of New England, 1998.

Consonni, Manuela. *Rezistentsa o Shoah: Zikaron ha-gerush ve-ha-hashmada be-Italia, 1945–1985*. Jerusalem: Magnes, 2010.

Dabag, Mihran. "Der Genozid an den Armeniern im Osmanischen Reich." In Knigge and Frei, *Verbrechen erinnern*, 33–55.

Dahl, Izabela. "'. . . this is material arousing interest in common history': Zygmunt Łakociński and Polish Survivors' Protocols." *Jewish History Quarterly* 3 (2007): 319–338.

Davies, Norman. *God's Playground: A History of Poland*. Oxford: Clarendon, 1981.

Dawidowicz, Lucy S. *From that Place and Time: A Memoir, 1938–1947*. New York: Bantam Books, 1991.

———. *The Holocaust and the Historians*. Cambridge, MA: Harvard University Press, 1981.

———. "Khronikes fun khurbn: Di tsentrale historishe komisye in minkhn." *Di Tsukunft* 55 (1950): 156–159.

———. *The War against the Jews, 1933–1945*. New York: Holt, Rinehart & Winston, 1975.

Deák, István, Jan T. Gross, and Tony Judt, eds. *The Politics of Retribution in Europe: World War II and Its Aftermath*. Princeton, NJ: Princeton University Press, 2000.

De Haan, Ido. "The Paradoxes of Dutch History: Historiography of the Holocaust in the Netherlands." In Bankier and Michman, *Holocaust Historiography*, 355–376.

———. "Paths of Normalization after the Persecution of the Jews: The Netherlands, France, and West Germany in the 1950s." In Bessel and Schumann, *Life After Death*, 65–92.

De Jong, Loe. *Het Koninkrijk der Nederlanden in de Tweede Wereloorlog*. 14 vols. The Hague: Staatsdrukkerij- en Uitgeverijbedrijf, 1969–1989.

Dekel-Chen, Jonathan, David Gaunt, Natan M. Meir, and Israel Bartal, eds. *Anti-Jewish Violence: Rethinking the Pogrom in East European Jewish History*. Bloomington: Indiana University Press, 2011.

Demir, Ljatif. "Literarische Antworten auf den Roma-Holocaust in Osteuropa." In Fischer von Weikersthal et al., *Der nationalsozialistische Genozid an den Roma*, 169–184.

Des Pres, Terrence. *The Survivor: An Anatomy of Life in the Death Camps*. New York: Oxford University Press, 1976.

Diner, Dan. "Elemente der Subjektwerdung." In Fritz Bauer Institut, *Überlebt und unterwegs*, 229–248.

Diner, Hasia R. "Post-World-War-II American Jewry and the Confrontation with Catastrophe." *American Jewish History* 91, nos. 3–4 (2003): 439–467.

———. *We Remember with Reverence and Love: American Jews and the Myth of Silence after the Holocaust, 1945–1962*. New York: New York University Press, 2009.
Dinnerstein, Leonard. *America and the Survivors of the Holocaust*. New York: Columbia University Press, 1982.
Dobroszycki, Lucjan. *The Chronicle of the Lodz Ghetto*, New Haven, CT: Yale University Press, 1984.
———. "Re-emergence and Decline of a Community: The Numerical Size of the Jewish Population in Poland, 1944–47." *YIVO Annual* 21 (1993): 3–32.
———. "Restoring Jewish Life in Post-War Poland." *Soviet Jewish Affairs* 3, no. 3 (1973): 58–72.
———. *Survivors of the Holocaust in Poland: A Portrait Based on Jewish Community Records, 1944–1947*. Armonk, NY: M. E. Sharpe, 1994.
———. "YIVO in Interwar Poland: Work in the Historical Sciences." In *The Jews of Poland Between Two World Wars*, ed. Yisrael Gutman, Ezra Mendelsohn, Jehuda Reinharz, and Chone Shmeruk, 494–518. Hanover, NH: University Press of New England, 1989.
Donat, Aleksander. *The Holocaust Kingdom: A Memoir*. New York: Holt, Rinehart & Winston, 1965.
Douglas, Lawrence. *The Memory of Judgment: Making Law and History in the Trials of the Holocaust*. New Haven, CT.: Yale University Press, 2001.
Douzou, Laurent. *La Résistance française: Une historie périlleuse*. Paris: Éditions du Seuil, 2005.
Dreifuss (Ben-Sasson), Havi. *"Anu yehude Polin?" Ha-yahas ben yehudim le-polanim bitkufat ha-shoah min ha-hebet ha-yehudi*. Jerusalem: Yad Vashem, 2009.
Dubnov-Erlich, Sophie. *The Life and Work of S. M. Dubnov: Diaspora Nationalism and Jewish History*. Translated by Judith Vowles; edited by Jeffrey Shandler. Bloomington: Indiana University Press, 1991.
Dubnow, Simon. *Buch des Lebens: Erinnerungen und Gedanken; Materialien zur Geschichte meiner Zeit*. Translated by Vera Bischitzky. 3 vols. Göttingen, Germany: Vandenhoeck & Ruprecht, 2004–2005.
———. *Dos bukh fun mayn lebn*. 3 vols. Buenos Aires: Alveltlekher Yidisher Kultur-Kongres, 1963.
———. "Iz izucheniia istorii russkikh evreev i uchrezhdenii istoricheskogo obshchestva." *Voskhod* 4–9 (April–September 1891): 1–91.
———. *Mein Leben*. Edited by Elias Hurwicz. Berlin: Jüdische Buchvereinigung, 1937.
———. "Nahpesa ve-nahkora: Kol kore et ha-nevonim ba-'am ha-mitnadvim le'esof homer le-binyan toldot bene Israel be-Polin ve-Rusiya." *Ha-Pardes* 1 (1892): 221–242.
———. *Ob izuchenii istorii ruskikh evreev i ob uchrezhdenii russko-evreiskogo istoricheskogo obshchestva*. St. Petersburg: A. E. Landau, 1891.
Dubnow, Simon, and G. I. Krasnyi-Admoni, eds. *Materialy dlia istorii antievreiskikh pogromov v Rossii*. Vol. 1. St. Petersburg: n.p., 1919.
Duggan, Christopher. *A Concise History of Italy*. New York: Cambridge, UK: Cambridge University Press, 1984.
Eder, Angelika. *Flüchtige Heimat: Jüdische Displaced Persons in Landsberg am Lech, 1945 bis 1950*. Munich: Kommissionsverlag, 1998.
———. "Jüdische Displaced Persons im deutschen Alltag: Eine Regionalstudie, 1945–1950." In Fritz Bauer Institut, *Überlebt und unterwegs*, 163–187.
———. "Kultur und Kulturveranstaltungen in den jüdischen DP-Lagern." In *Leben in Land der Täter: Juden im Nachkriegsdeutschland (1945–1952)*, ed. Julius H. Schoeps, 63–77. Berlin: JVB, 2001.
Eder-Jordan, Beate. "Die nationalsozialistische Rassen- und Vernichtungspolitik im Spiegel der Literatur der Roma und Sinti." In Fischer von Weikersthal et al., *Der nationalsozialistische Genozid an den Roma*, 115–167.
Egypt, Ophelia Settle, ed. *Unwritten History of Slavery: Autobiographical Accounts of Negro Ex-Slaves*. Nashville, TN: Social Science Institute, Fisk University, 1945.
Eilati, Shalom. *Crossing the River*. Translated by Vern Lenz. Tuscaloosa: University of Alabama Press, 2008.
Eisenbach, Artur. "Jewish Historiography in Interwar Poland." In *The Jews of Poland Between Two World Wars*, ed. Yisrael Gutman, Ezra Mendelsohn, Jehuda Reinharz, and Chone Shmeruk, 453–493. Hanover, NH: University Press of New England, 1989.
Embacher, Helga. *Neubeginn ohne Illusionen: Juden in Österreich*. Vienna: Picus Verlag, 1995.

Engel, David. "Being Lawful in a Lawless World: The Trial of Scholem Schwarzbard and the Defense of East European Jews." *Simon Dubnow Institute Yearbook* 5 (2006): 83–97.

———. *Ben shihrur li-verihah: Nitsule ha-shoah be-Polin ve-ha-ma'avak 'al hanhagatam, 1944–1946.* Tel Aviv: 'Am 'Oved, 1996.

———. *Facing a Holocaust: The Polish Government-in-Exile and the Jews, 1943–1945.* Chapel Hill: University of North Carolina Press, 1993.

———. *Historians of the Jews and the Holocaust.* Stanford, CA: Stanford University Press, 2010.

———. *In the Shadow of Auschwitz: The Polish Government-in-Exile and the Jews, 1939–1942.* Chapel Hill: University of North Carolina Press, 1987.

———. *On Studying Jewish History in the Light of the Holocaust.* Washington, DC: United States Holocaust Memorial Museum, 2003.

———. "Patterns of Anti-Jewish Violence in Poland, 1944–1946." *Yad Vashem Studies* 26 (1998): 43–85.

———. "Poland since 1939." In Hundert, *The YIVO Encyclopedia of Jews in Eastern Europe*, 2:1404–1411.

———. "The Reconstruction of Jewish Communal Institutions in Postwar Poland: The Origins of the Central Committee of Polish Jews, 1944–1945." *East European Politics and Societies* 10, no. 1 (1996): 85–107.

———. "World War I." In Hundert, *The YIVO Encyclopedia of Jews in Eastern Europe*, 2:2032–2037.

———. "Writing History as a National Mission: The Jews of Poland and Their Historiographic Traditions." In Gutman, *Emanuel Ringelblum*, 117–140.

Estraikh, Gennady. "Vilna on the Spree: Yiddish in Weimar Berlin." *Aschkenas* 16, no. 1 (2006): 103–127.

Ezrahi, Sidra DeKoven. *By Words Alone: The Holocaust in Literature.* Chicago: University of Chicago Press, 1980.

Fabréguet, Michel. "Frankreichs Historiker und der Völkermord an den europäischen Juden, 1945–1993." In *Der Umgang mit dem Holocaust: Europa—USA—Israel*, ed. Rolf Steininger, 317–328. Vienna: Böhlau, 1994.

Faure, Edgar. *Mémoires.* Vol. 2, *Si tel doit être mon destin ce soir . . .* Paris: Plon, 1984.

Feigenbaum, Moshe Yosef. "Peulot shel ha-va'adah ha-historit be-minkhen." *Dapim le-heker ha-sho'ah ve-ha-mered* 1 (1951): 107–110.

Feinstein, Margarete Myers. *Holocaust Survivors in Postwar Germany, 1945–1957.* New York: Cambridge University Press, 2010.

Felman, Shoshana, and Dori Laub. *Testimony: Crises of Witnessing in Literature, Psychoanalysis, and History.* New York, Routlegde, 1992.

Finder, Gabriel N. Introduction to Finder et al., "Making Holocaust Memory," 3–54.

Finder, Gabriel N., Natalia Aleksiun, Antony Polonsky, and Jan Schwarz, eds. "Making Holocaust Memory." Special issue, *Polin* 20 (2008).

Fischer von Weikersthal, Felicitas, Christoph Garstka, Urs Heftrich, and Heinz-Dietrich Löwe, eds. *Der nationalsozialistische Genozid an den Roma Osteuropas: Geschichte und künstlerische Verarbeitung.* Cologne: Böhlau, 2008.

Fishman, David E. *The Rise of Modern Yiddish Culture.* Pittsburgh, PA: University of Pittsburgh Press, 2005.

Fleming, Michael. "Minorities, Violence, and the Establishment of Communist Rule in Poland." In Bardgett et al., *Survivors of Nazi Persecution in Europe after the Second World War*, 71–90.

Fogu, Claudio. "Italiani brava gente: The Legacy of Fascist Historical Culture on Italian Politics of Memory." In Lebow, Kansteiner, and Fogu, *The Politics of Memory in Postwar Europe*, 147–176.

Fox, Thomas C. "The Holocaust under Communism." In *The Historiography of the Holocaust*, ed. Dan Stone, 420–439. London: Palgrave Macmillan, 2004.

Frankel, Jonathan. "The Crisis of 1881–82 as a Turning Point in Modern Jewish History." In *The Legacy of Jewish Migration: 1881 and Its Impact*, ed. David Berger, 9–22. New York: Brooklyn College Press, 1983.

Fredj, Jacques. "Le Centre de Documentation Juive Contemporaine (CDJC)." In *Storia e memoria della deportazione: Modelli di ricerca e di communicazione in Italia e in Francia*, ed. Paolo Momigliano Levi, 151–164. Florence: Giuntina, 1996.

Freeden, Herbert. *Jüdisches Theater in Nazideutschland*. Tübingen, Germany: Mohr, 1964.

Frei, Norbert, ed. *Transnationale Vergangenheitspolitik: Der Umgang mit deutschen Kriegsverbrechern in Europa nach dem Zweiten Weltkrieg*. Göttingen, Germany: Wallstein Verlag, 2006.

Friedländer, Saul. *Den Holocaust beschreiben: Auf dem Weg zu einer integrierten Geschichte*. Göttingen, Germany: Wallstein Verlag, 2007.

———. *Memory, History, and the Extermination of the Jews of Europe*. Bloomington: Indiana University Press, 1993.

———. *Nazi Germany and the Jews*. 2 vols. New York: HarperCollins, 1997–2007.

———, ed. *Probing the Limits of Representation: Nazism and the "Final Solution."* Cambridge, MA: Harvard University Press, 1992.

———. "Trauma, Transference and 'Working Through' in Writing the History of the Shoah." *History and Memory* 4 (1992): 39–59.

———. *When Memory Comes*. New York: Farrar, Straus & Giroux, 1979.

Friedländer, Saul, and Martin Broszat. "Martin Broszat/Saul Friedländer: A Controversy about the Historicization of National Socialism." *Yad Vashem Studies* 19 (1988): 1–47.

Friedman, Philip. "A fertl-yorhundert khurbn-literatur." *Di Tsukunft* 9 (September 1959): 358–362.

———. "American Jewish Research and Literature on the Jewish Catastrophe of 1939–1945." *Jewish Social Studies* 13 (1951): 235–250.

———. *Bibliografyah shel ha-sefarim ha-ivriyim 'al ha-Shoah ve-'al ha-gevurah*. Jerusalem: Yad Vashem, 1960.

———. "Dos gedrukte vort bay der sheyres-hapleyte in daytshland." *Di Tsukunft* 54, no. 3 (March 1949): 151–155.

———. "The European Jewish Research on the Recent Jewish Catastrophe in 1939–1945." *Proceedings of the American Academy for Jewish Research* 18 (1948–1949): 179–211.

———. "Holocaust Research and Literature in America." *Dapim le-heker ha-shoah ve-ha-mered* 1 (1951): 51–68.

———. "Polish Jewish Historiography between the Two Wars (1918–1939)." *Jewish Social Studies* 9, no. 4 (October 1949): 373–408.

———. "Preliminary and Methodological Problems of the Research on the Jewish Catastrophe in the Nazi Period." *Yad Vashem Studies* 2 (1958): 95–131.

———. "Problems of Research on the Jewish Catastrophe." *Yad Vashem Studies* 3 (1959): 25–39.

———. "Research and Literature on the Recent Jewish Tragedy." *Jewish Social Studies* 12, no. 1 (1950): 17–26.

———. *Roads to Extinction: Essays on the Holocaust*. Edited by Ada June Friedman. Philadelphia: Jewish Publication Society of America, 1980.

Friedman, Philip, and Joseph Gar. *Bibliografye fun yidishe bikher vegn khurbn un gvure*. New York: YIVO, 1962.

———. *Bibliography of Yiddish Books on the Catastrophe and Heroism*. New York: YIVO Institute for Jewish Research, 1962.

Friedman, Philip, and Jacob Robinson. *Guide to Jewish History under Nazi Impact*. New York: YIVO Institute for Jewish Research, 1960.

———. *Guide to Research in Jewish History, 1933–1945: Its Background and Aftermath*. New York: YIVO, 1958.

Fritz Bauer Institut, ed. *Opfer als Akteure: Interventionen ehemaliger NS-Verfolgter in der Nachkriegszeit*. Frankfurt: Campus Verlag, 2008.

———, ed. *Überlebt und unterwegs: Jüdische Displaced Persons im Nachkriegsdeutschland*. Frankfurt: Campus, 1997.

Frydman, Towia [T. Friedman]. *Die Dokumentation in Wien in den Jahren 1946–1952*. Haifa: Institute of Documentation in Israel, 2000.

——— [Tobias Friedmann], ed. *Die Tragödie des österreichischen Judentums: Bericht und Dokumentensammlung*. Haifa: WJC, 1958.

——— [Tuviah Friedman]. *The Hunter*. Edited and translated by David C. Gross. London: Gibbs & Phillips, 1961.
——— [Tobias Friedmann], ed. *Schupo- Kriegsverbrecher in Kolomea vor dem Wiener Volksgericht*. Haifa: Verband der Ehemaligen Einwohner von Kolomea in Israel, 1957.
——— [Tobias Friedmann], ed. *Schupo-Kriegsverbrecher in Stryj vor dem Wiener Volksgericht*. Haifa: Verband der Ehemaligen Einwohner von Stryj in Israel, 1957.
——— [Tobias Friedmann], ed. *Schupo-und Gestapo-Kriegsverbrecher von Stanislau vor dem Wiener Volksgericht*. Haifa: Historisches Institut für Erforschung der Nazikriegsverbrechen, 1957.
Fulbrook, Mary. *The Divided Nation: A History of Germany, 1918-1990*. New York: Oxford University Press, 1992.
———, ed. *Europe since 1945*. Oxford: Oxford University Press, 2001.
Gar, Joseph. *Bibliografye fun artiklen vegn khurbn un gvure in yidishe periodike*. 2 vols. New York: YIVO, 1966-1969.
Garbarini, Alexandra. *Numbered Days: Diaries and the Holocaust*. New Haven, CT: Yale University Press, 2006.
Gawron, Edyta. "Amon Goeth's Trial in Cracow: Its Impact on Holocaust Awareness in Poland." In *Holocaust and Justice: Representation and Historiography of the Holocaust in Post-War Trials*, ed. David Bankier and Dan Michman, 281-298. Jerusalem: Yad Vashem, 2010.
Gay, Ruth. *Safe among the Germans: Liberated Jews after World War II*. New Haven, CT: Yale University Press, 2002.
Geis, Jael. *Übrig sein: Leben "danach"; Juden deutscher Herkunft in der britischen und amerikanischen Zone Deutschlands 1945-1949*. Berlin: Philo, 2000.
Geller, Jay Howard. *Jews in Post-Holocaust Germany, 1945-1953*. Cambridge, UK: Cambridge University Press, 2005.
———. "Representing Jewry in East Germany, 1945-1953: Between Advocacy and Accommodation." *Leo Baeck Institute Yearbook* 47 (2002): 195-214.
Gilbert, Shirli. "Buried Monuments: Yiddish Songs and Holocaust Memory." *History Workshop Journal* 66 (2008): 107-128.
———. *Music in the Holocaust: Confronting Life in the Nazi Ghettos and Camps*. New York: Oxford University Press, 2005
———. "'We Long for a Home': Songs and Survival among Jewish Displaced Persons." In Patt and Berkowitz, *We Are Here*, 289-307.
Goren, Ya'akov. *'Eduyot nifge'e Kishinov 1903 kefi she-nigbe'u al-yede Kh. N. Bialik ve-haverav*. Ramat Efal, Israel: Yad Tabenkin, 1991.
Goslan, Richard J. "The Legacy of World War II in France: Mapping the Discourses of Memory." In Lebow, Kansteiner, and Fogu, *The Politics of Memory in Postwar Europe*, 72-101.
Gottesman, Itzik Nakhmen. *Defining the Yiddish Nation: The Jewish Folklorists of Poland*. Detroit: Wayne State University Press, 2003.
Grabowski, Jan. *Rescue for Money: "Paid Helpers" in Poland, 1939-1945*. Jerusalem: Yad Vashem, 2008.
Graf, Philipp. *Die Bernheim-Petition 1933: Jüdische Politik in der Zwischenkriegszeit*. Göttingen, Germany: Vandenhoeck & Ruprecht, 2008.
Graif, Gid'on. *We Wept without Tears: Testimonies of the Jewish Sonderkommando from Auschwitz*. New Haven, CT: Yale University Press, 2005.
Graupe, Heinz Mosche. *Die Entstehung des modernen Judentums: Geistesgeschichte der deutschen Juden, 1650-1942*. Hamburg: Leibnitz Verlag, 1961.
Greenspan, Henry. *The Awakening of Memory: Survivor Testimony in the first Years after the Holocaust, and Today*. Washington, DC: United States Holocaust Memorial Museum, 2001.
———. *On Listening to Holocaust Survivors: Recounting and Life History*. Westport, CT: Praeger, 1998.
Grobman, Alex. *Rekindling the Flame: American Jewish Chaplains and the Survivors of European Jewry, 1944-1948*. Detroit: Wayne State University Press, 1993.
Grodzinsky, Yosef. *In the Shadow of the Holocaust: The Struggle between Jews and Zionists in the Aftermath of World War II*. Monroe, ME: Common Courage, 2004.

Gross, Jan T. *Fear: Antisemitism in Poland after Auschwitz; An Essay in Historical Interpretation*. New York: Random House, 2006.

———. *Neighbors: The Destruction of the Jewish Community in Jedwabne, Poland*. Princeton, NJ: Princeton University Press, 2001.

———. *Polish Society under German Occupation: Generalgouvernement, 1939–1944*. Princeton, NJ: Princeton University Press, 1979.

———. "A Tangled Web: Confronting Stereotypes Concerning Relations between Poles, Germans, Jews and Communists." In Deák et al., *The Politics of Retribution*, 74–129.

Grossmann, Atina. *Jews, Germans, and Allies: Close Encounters in Occupied Germany*. Princeton, NJ: Princeton University Press, 2007.

Grözinger, Elvira, and Magdalena Ruta, eds. *Under the Red Banner: Yiddish Culture in the Communist Countries in the Postwar Era*. Wiesbaden, Germany: Harrassowitz, 2008.

Grynberg, Anne. "Après la tourmente." In *Les Juifs de France de la Révolution française à nos jours*, ed. Jean Jacques Becker and Annette Wieviorka, 249–286. Paris: Editions Liana Levi, 1998.

Gutman, Israel, ed. *Emanuel Ringelblum: The Man and the Historian*. Jerusalem: Yad Vashem, 2010.

———, ed. *Encyclopedia of the Holocaust*. 4 vols. New York: Macmillan, 1990.

———, ed. *Mi-genizah le-tsiyune derekh historiyim: Arkhiyonim yehudiyim mi-tekufat ha-milkhamah ve-ha-sho'ah*. Jerusalem: Yad Vashem, 1997.

———. *Ha-yehudim be-Polin ahare milhemet 'olam ha-shniyah*. Jerusalem: Zalman Shazar Center for Jewish History, 1985.

———. "Poland." In Gutman, *Encyclopedia of the Holocaust*, 3:1151–1176.

Gutman, Israel, and Gideon Greif, eds. *The Historiography of the Holocaust Period*. Jerusalem: Yad Vashem, 1988.

Gutman, Israel, and Shmuel Krakowski. *Unequal Victims: Poles and Jews during World War Two*. New York: Holocaust Library, 1986.

Gutman, Israel, and Avital Saf, eds. *She'erit Hapletah, 1944–1948: Rehabilitation and Political Struggle*. Jerusalem: Yad Vashem, 1990.

Hancock, Ian. "Responses to the Porrajmos: The Romani Holocaust." In *Is the Holocaust Unique? Perspectives on Comparative Genocide*, ed. Alan S. Rosenbaum, 39–64. Boulder, CO: Westview, 1996.

Hartman, Geoffrey H. *The Longest Shadow: In the Aftermath of the Holocaust*. Bloomington: Indiana University Press, 1996.

———, ed. *Holocaust Remembrance: The Shapes of Memory*. Oxford: Blackwell, 1994.

Herf, Jeffrey. *Divided Memory: The Nazi Past in the Two Germanys*. Cambridge, MA: Harvard University Press, 1997.

Herzberg, Abel. *Amor Fati: Zeven opstellen over Bergen-Belsen*. Amsterdam: Moussault, 1946.

———. *Kroniek der Jodenvervolging, 1940–1945*. Arnhem, the Netherlands: Van Loghum Slaterus, 1956.

———. *Tweestromenland: Dagboek uit Bergen-Belsen*. Arnhem, the Netherlands: Van Loghum Slaterus, 1950.

Hilberg, Raul. *The Destruction of the European Jews*. 3rd ed. 3 vols. New Haven, CT: Yale University Press, 2003.

———. "The Development of Holocaust Research: A Personal Overview." In Bankier and Michman, *Holocaust Historiography*, 25–36.

———. "I Was Not There." In *Writing and the Holocaust*, ed. Berel Lang, 7–25. New York: Holmes & Meier, 1988

———. *Perpetrators, Victims, Bystanders: The Jewish Catastrophe, 1933–1945*. New York: HarperCollins, 1992.

———. *The Politics of Memory: The Journey of a Holocaust Historian*. Chicago: Ivan R. Dee, 1996.

———. *Sources of Holocaust Research: An Analysis*. Chicago: Ivan R. Dee, 2001.

Hilbrenner, Anke. *Diaspora-Nationalismus: Zur Geschichtskonstruktion Simon Dubnows*. Göttingen, Germany: Vandenhoeck & Ruprecht, 2007.

———. "Simon Dubnow als eine Art intellektueller Pate: Das YIVO in Wilna und Dubnows Aufruf zur Arbeit am nationalen Gedächtnis." In *Jüdische Kultur(en) im Neuen Europa: Wilna*

1918–1939, ed. Marina Dmitrieva and Heidemarie Petersen, 147–162. Wiesbaden, Germany: Harrassowitz, 2004.

Hitchcock, William I. *Liberation: The Bitter Road to Freedom; Europe, 1944–1945*. London: Faber & Faber, 2008.

Hobson Faure, Laura. "'Performing a Healing Role': American Jewish Communal Workers and the American Jewish Joint Distribution Committee in Post-World War II France." *Parcours Judaïques* 10 (2006): 139–156.

Hocheneder, Franz. *H. G. Adler (1910–1988): Privatgelehrter und freier Schriftsteller*. Vienna: Böhlau, 2009.

Hoffmann, Christhard, ed. *Preserving the Legacy of German Jewry: A History of the Leo Baeck Institute, 1955–2005*. Tübingen, Germany: Mohr Siebeck, 2005.

Hoffmann, Christhard, Werner Bergmann, and Helmut Walser Smith eds. *Exclusionary Violence: Antisemitic Riots in Modern German History*. Ann Arbor: University of Michigan Press, 2002.

Holian, Anna. *Between National Socialism and Soviet Communism: Displaced Persons in Postwar Germany*. Ann Arbor: University of Michigan Press, 2011.

Holquist, Peter. "The Role of Personality in the First (1914–1915) Russian Occupation of Galicia and Bukovina." In Dekel-Chen et al., *Anti-Jewish Violence*, 52–73.

Honigmann, Peter. "Das Projekt von Rabbiner Dr. Bernhard Brilling zur Errichtung eines jüdischen Zentralarchivs im Nachkriegsdeutschland." In *Historisches Bewusstsein im jüdischen Kontext: Strategien—Aspekte—Diskurse*, ed. Klaus Hödl, 223–241. Innsbruck, Austria: Studien Verlag, 2004.

Horn, Mauricy. "Visnshaftlekhe un editorishe tetikeyt fun tsentraler yidisher historisher komisye baym Ts. K. Y. P. un funem Yidishn Historishn Institut in Poyln in di yorn 1945–1950." *Bleter far Geshikhte* 24 (1986): 143–159.

———. "Żydowski Instytut Historyczny w Polsce w latach 1944–1949." *Biuletyn Żydowskiego Instytutu Historycznego* 109 (1979): 3–15.

Horváth, Rita. "'A Jewish Historical Commission in Budapest': The Place of the National Relief Committee for Deportees in Hungary [DEGOB] Among the Other Large-Scale Historical-Memorial Projects of *She'erit Hapletah* after the Holocaust (1945–1948)." In Bankier and Michman, *Holocaust Historiography*, 475–496.

———. "Jews in Hungary after the Holocaust: The National Relief Committee for Deportees, 1945–1950." *Journal of Israeli History* 19, no. 2 (Summer 1998): 69–91.

Hundert, Gershon D., ed. *The YIVO Encyclopedia of Jews in Eastern Europe*. 2 vols. New Haven, CT: Yale University Press, 2008.

Hurwic-Nowakowska, Irena. *A Social Analysis of Postwar Polish Jewry*. Jerusalem: Zalman Shazar Center for Jewish History, 1986.

Hyman, Abraham S. "Displaced Persons." *American Jewish Yearbook* 51 (1950): 315–324.

Hyman, Paula. *From Dreyfus to Vichy: The Remaking of French Jewry, 1906–1939*. New York: Columbia University Press, 1979.

———. *The Jews of Modern France*. Berkeley: University of California Press, 1998.

International Military Tribunal, ed. *Trial of the Major War Criminals before the International Military Tribunal, Nuremberg 14 November 1945–1 October 1946*. 22 vols. Nuremberg, Germany: International Military Tribunal, 1947.

Jackson, Julian. *France: The Dark Years, 1940–1944*. New York: Oxford University Press, 2001.

Jacobmeyer, Wolfgang. "Jüdische Überlebende als 'Displaced Persons': Untersuchungen zur Besatzungspolitik in den deutschen Westzonen und zur Zuwanderung osteuropäischer Juden, 1945–1947." *Geschichte und Gesellschaft* 9, no. 3 (1983): 421–452.

Jacobson, Kenneth. *Embattled Selves: An Investigation into the Nature of Identity through Oral Histories of Holocaust Survivors*. New York: Atlantic Monthly Press, 1994.

Jelavich, Barbara. *Modern Austria: Empire and Republic, 1815–1986*. New York: Cambridge University Press, 1987.

Jewish Central Information Office, ed. *The Jewish Central Information Office—The Wiener Library: A New Type of Research Institution; Its History and Activities, 1934–1945*. London: William Lea, 1946.

Jockusch, Laura. "A Folk Monument to Our Destruction and Heroism: Jewish Historical Commissions in the Displaced Persons Camps of Germany, Austria, and Italy." In Patt and Berkowitz, *We Are Here*, 31–73.

———. "Introductory Remarks on Simon Dubnow's 'Let Us Seek and Investigate.'" *Simon Dubnow Institute Yearbook* 7 (2008): 343–353.

———. "Jüdische Geschichtsforschung im Lande Amaleks: Jüdische Historische Kommissionen in Deutschland, 1945–1949." In *Zwischen Erinnerung und Neubeginn: Zur deutsch-jüdischen Geschichte nach 1945*, ed. Susanne Schönborn, 20–41. Munich: Maidenbauer Verlag, 2006.

———. "*Khurbn-Forshung*: Jewish Historical Commissions in Europe, 1943–1949." *Simon Dubnow Institute Yearbook* 6 (2007): 441–473.

John, Michael. "Zwischenstation Oberösterreich: Die Auffanglager und Wohnsiedlungen für jüdische DPs und Transitflüchtlinge." In Albrich, *Flucht nach Eretz Israel*, 67–92.

Judge, Edward H. *Easter in Kishinev: Anatomy of a Pogrom*. New York: New York University Press, 1992.

Judt, Tony. "The Past Is Another Country: Myth and Memory in Postwar Europe." In Müller, *Memory and Power in Post-War Europe*, 157–183.

———. *Postwar: A History of Europe since 1945*. New York: Penguin, 2005.

Kagan, Berl. *Leksikon fun yidish-shraybers: Mit hoysofes un tikunim tsum leksikon fun der nayer yidisher literatur un 5,800 psevdonimen*. New York: R. Iman-Kohen, 1986.

Kahan, Anne. "The Diary of Anne Kahan, Siedlce, Poland, 1914–1916." *YIVO Annual* 18 (1983): 141–371.

Kahane, David. *Ahare ha-mabul: Nisayon lehehayot et ha-kehilot ha-datiyot be-Folin she lehar milhemet 'olam ha-shniyah (1944–1949)*. Jerusalem: Hotsa'ah Mosad Ha-rav Kuk, 1981.

Kaplan, Marion A. *Between Dignity and Despair: Jewish Life in Nazi Germany*. New York: Oxford University Press, 1998.

Kapralski, Slawomir. "The Voices of a Mute Memory: The Holocaust and the Identity of the Eastern European Romanies." In Fischer von Weikersthal et al., *Der nationalsozialistische Genozid an den Roma*, 93–111.

Karlip, Joshua. "Between Martyrology and Historiography: Elias Tcherikower and the Making of a Pogrom Historian." *East European Jewish Affairs* 38, no. 3 (2008): 257–280.

Kaspi, André. *Les Juifs pendant l'Occupation*. Paris: Éditions du Seuil, 1997.

Kassow, Samuel. *Who Will Write Our History? Emanuel Ringelblum, the Warsaw Ghetto, and the Oyneg Shabes Archive*. Bloomington: Indiana University Press, 2007.

Kaelble, Hartmut. *Der historische Vergleich: Eine Einführung zum 19. und 20. Jahrhundert*. Frankfurt: Campus, 1999.

Kenan, Orna. *Between Memory and History: The Evolution of Israeli Historiography of the Holocaust, 1945–1961*. New York: Peter Lang, 2003.

Kenez, Peter, "Pogroms and White Ideology." In Klier and Lambroza, *Pogroms*, 293–313.

Kenkmann, Alfons, and Elisabeth Kohlhaas. "'Die Hitlerzeit hat die Seele des jüdischen Kindes zutiefst verändert': Interviews der Zentralen Jüdischen Historischen Kommission mit jüdischen Kindern nach dem Holocaust, 1944–1948." *Simon Dubnow Institute Yearbook* 7 (2008): 385–400.

Kermish, Joseph. "La-matsav ba-heker ha-sho'ah." *Yedi'ot Yad Vashem* 1 (1954): 8–10.

———, ed. *To Live with Honor and Die with Honor! Selected Documents from the Warsaw Ghetto Underground Archives "O.S."* Jerusalem: Yad Vashem, 1986.

Kersten, Krystyna. *The Establishment of Communist Rule in Poland, 1943–1948*. Berkeley: University of California Press, 1991.

Kichelewski, Audrey. "A Community under Pressure: Jews in Poland, 1957–1967." *Polin* 21 (2009): 159–186.

Kirshenblatt-Gimblett, Barbara. "Coming of Age in the Thirties: Max Weinrich, Edward Sapir, and Jewish Social Science." *YIVO Annual* 23 (1996): 1–103.

Klarsfeld, Serge. *Le Mémorial de la Déportation des Juifs de France*. Paris: B. & S. Klarsfeld, 1977.

———. *Vichy-Auschwitz: Le rôle de Vichy dans la solution finale de la question Juive, 1943–1944*. 2 vols. Paris: Fayard, 1983.

Klibanski, Bronia. "The Underground Archives of the Bialystok Ghetto Founded by Mersik and Tennenbaum." *Yad Vashem Studies* 2 (1958): 295–329.

Klier, John D., and Shlomo Lambroza, eds. *Pogroms: Anti-Jewish Violence in Modern Russian History.* Cambridge, UK: Cambridge University Press, 1992.

Knigge, Volkhard, and Norbert Frei, eds. *Verbrechen erinnern: Die Auseinandersetzung mit Holocaust und Völkermord.* Munich: C. H. Beck, 2002.

Kochavi, Arieh J. "British Policy toward East European Reguees in Germany and Austria, 1945–1947." *Simon Wiesenthal Center Annual* 7 (1990): 63–76.

———. *Post-Holocaust Politics: Britain, the United States, and Jewish Refugees, 1945–1948.* Chapel Hill: University of North Carolina Press, 2001.

Kocka, Jürgen. "Comparative Historical Research: German Examples." *International Review of Social History* 38 (1993): 369–379.

———. *Geschichte und Aufklärung: Aufsätze.* Göttingen, Germany: Vandenhoeck & Ruprecht, 1989.

Kokkonen, Susanna. "Jewish Displaced Persons in Postwar Italy, 1945–1951." *Jewish Political Studies Review* 20, nos. 1–2 (Spring 2008): 91–106.

Königseder, Angelika, and Juliane Wetzel. *Waiting for Hope: Jewish Displaced Persons in Post–World War II Germany.* Evanston, IL: Northwestern University Press, 2001.

Krakowski, Shmuel. "Memorial Projects and Memorial Institutions Initiated by She'erit Hapletah." In Gutman and Saf, *She'erit Hapletah, 1944–1948*, 388–398.

Krakowski, Shmuel, and Ilya Altman. "The Testament of the Last Prisoners of the Chelmno Death Camp." *Yad Vashem Studies* 21 (1991): 105–123.

Krasnyi-Admoni, G. I., ed. *Materialy dlia istorii antievreiskikh pogromov v Rossii.* Vol. 2. St. Petersburg: n.p., 1923.

Kristel, Conny. "Survivors and Historians: Abel Herzberg, Jacques Presser and Loe de Jong on the Nazi Persecution of the Jews in the Netherlands." In Bankier and Michman, *Holocaust Historiography*, 207–224.

Kugelmass, Jack, and Jonathan Boyarin, eds. and trans. *From a Ruined Garden: The Memorial Books of Polish Jewry.* 2nd ed. Bloomington: Indiana University Press, 1998.

Kushner, Tony. *The Holocaust and the Liberal Imagination: A Social and Cultural History.* Oxford: Blackwell, 1994.

Kuznitz, Cecile E. "An-sky's Legacy: The Vilna Historic-Ethnographic Society and the Shaping of Modern Jewish Culture." In *The Worlds of S. An-sky: A Russian Jewish Intellectual at the Turn of the Century*, ed. Gabriella Safran and Steven J. Zipperstein, 320–345. Stanford, CA: Stanford University Press, 2006.

LaCapra, Dominick. *History and Memory after Auschwitz.* Ithaca, NY: Cornell University Press, 1998.

———. "Holocaust Testimonies: Attending to the Victim's Voice." In Postone and Santner, *Catastrophe and Meaning*, 209–231.

———. *Writing History, Writing Trauma.* Baltimore: Johns Hopkins University Press, 2001.

Lachower, Fishel, ed. *Igrot Hayim Nahman Bialik.* Tel Aviv: Devir, 1937.

Lagrou, Pieter. *The Legacy of Nazi Occupation: Patriotic Memory and National Recovery in Western Europe, 1945–1965.* Cambridge, UK: Cambridge University Press, 2000.

———. "Victims of Genocide and National Memory: Belgium, France and the Netherlands, 1945–1965." *Past and Present* 154 (February 1997): 181–222.

Lambert, Raymond-Raoul. *Carnet d'un témoin, 1940–1943.* Edited by Richard Cohen. Paris: Fayard, 1985.

Lambroza, Shlomo. "The Pogroms of 1903–1906." In Klier and Lambroza, *Pogroms*, 195–247.

Lang, Berel. *Post-Holocaust: Interpretation, Misinterpretation, and the Claims of History.* Bloomington: Indiana University Press, 2005.

Langer, Lawrence L. *Holocaust Testimonies: The Ruins of Memory.* New Haven, CT: Yale University Press, 1991.

Lappin, Eleonore. "Zwischen den Fronten: Das Wiener Jüdische Archiv; Mitteilungen des Komitees 'Jüdisches Kriegsarchiv' 1915–1918." In *Die jüdische Presse im europäischen Kontext, 1686–1990*, ed. Susanne Marten-Finnis and Markus Winkler, 209–222. Bremen, Germany: Edition Lumière 2006.

Lavsky, Hagit. "The Experience of the Displaced Persons in Bergen-Belsen: Unique or Typical Case?" In Patt and Berkowitz, *We Are Here*, 227–256.

———. *New Beginnings: Holocaust Survivors in Bergen-Belsen and the British Zone in Germany, 1945–1950*. Detroit: Wayne State University Press, 2002.

Lebow, Richard Ned, Wulf Kansteiner, and Claudio Fogu, eds. *The Politics of Memory in Postwar Europe*. Durham, NC: Duke University Press, 2006.

Leff, Lisa Moses. *Sacred Bonds of Solidarity: The Rise of Jewish Internationalism in Nineteenth-Century France*. Stanford, CA: Stanford University Press, 2006.

Lestschinsky, Jacob. *Di yidishe katastrofe: Di metodes fun ir forshung*. New York: Institute for Jewish Affairs, 1944.

Levine, Mark. "Frontiers of Genocide: Jews in the Eastern War Zones, 1914–1920 and 1941." In *Minorities in Wartime: National and Racial Groupings in Europe, North America and Australia during the Two World Wars*, ed. Panikos Panayi, 83–117. Oxford: Berg, 1993.

Levy, Carl, and Mark Roseman, eds. *Three Post-War Eras in Comparison: Western Europe, 1918–1945–1989*. New York: Palgrave, 2001.

Levy, Daniel, and Natan Sznaider. *The Holocaust and Memory in the Global Age*. Philadelphia: Temple University Press, 2006.

Lewinsky, Tamar. "Dangling Roots?: Yiddish Language and Culture in the German Diaspora." In Patt and Berkowitz, *We Are Here*, 308–334.

———. *Displaced Poets: Jiddische Schriftsteller im Nachkriegsdeutschand, 1945–1951*. Göttingen, Germany: Vandenhoeck & Ruprecht, 2008.

———. "Kultur im Transit: Osteuropäisch-jüdische Displaced Persons." *Osteuropa* 8–10 (2008): 265–277.

Lewy, Guenther. *The Nazi Persecution of the Gypsies*. New York: Oxford University Press, 2000.

Liberles, Robert. *Salo Wittmayer Baron: Architect of Jewish History*. New York: New York University Press, 1995.

Lipstadt, Deborah E. *The Eichmann Trial*. New York: Schocken, 2011.

Lohr, Eric. "1915 and the War Pogrom Paradigm in the Russian Empire." In Dekel-Chen et al., *Anti-Jewish Violence*, 41–51.

Lukas, Richard C. *Forgotten Holocaust: The Poles under German Occupation, 1939–1944*. New York: Hippocrene Books, 2001.

Lunsky, Khaykel. "Di yidishe historish-etnografishe gezelshaft." In *Pinkes far der geshikhte fun Vilne in di yorn fun milkhome un okupatsye: Aroysgegebn fun der historish-etnografisher gezelshaft oyfn nomen fun S. An-Ski, z"l*, ed. Zalman Rayzen, 855–864. Vilnius: B. Tsienson, 1922.

———. "Di yidishe historish-etnografishe gezelshaft in Vilne." In *Unzer tog—Vilne: Spetsyele oysgabe far Amerike*, 45–47. Vilnius: n.p., 1921.

Malinovich, Nadia. *French and Jewish: Culture and the Politics of Identity in Early Twentieth-Century France*. Oxford: Littman Library of Jewish Civilization, 2008.

Mammarella, Giuseppe. *Italy after Fascism: A Political History, 1943–1949*. Notre Dame, IN: University of Notre Dame Press, 1966.

Mandel, Maud S. *In the Aftermath of Genocide: Armenians and Jews in Twentieth-Century France*. Durham, NC: Duke University Press, 2003.

———. "Philanthropy or Cultural Imperialism? The Impact of American Jewish Aid in Post-Holocaust France." *Jewish Social Studies* 9, no. 1 (Fall 2002): 53–94.

Mankowitz, Zeev W. "The Formation of the She'erit Hapleta: November 1944–July 1945." *Yad Vashem Studies* 20 (1990): 337–370.

———. *Life between Memory and Hope: The Survivors of the Holocaust in Occupied Germany*. Cambridge, UK: Cambridge University Press, 2002.

Markovizky, Jacob. "The Italian Government's Response to the Problem of Jewish Refugees, 1945–1948." *Journal of Israeli History* 19, no. 1 (Spring 1998): 23–39.

Marrus, Michael R. "The Holocaust at Nuremberg." *Yad Vashem Studies* 26 (1998): 5–41.

———. *The Holocaust in History*. Hanover, NH: Published for Brandeis University Press by University Press of New England, 1987.

———. *The Unwanted: European Refugees in the Twentieth Century*. New York: Oxford University Press, 1985.
Marrus, Michael R., and Robert Paxton. *Vichy France and the Jews*. Stanford, CA: Stanford University Press, 1981.
Mazower, Mark, Jessica Reinisch, and David Feldman, eds. "Post-War Reconstruction in Europe: International Perspectives, 1945–1949." *Past and Present* supplement 6 (2011).
Meisel, Yosef "Ha-va'ada ha-historit le-toldot ha-yehudim be-germania." *Tzion* 19 (1954): 171–172.
Mendelsohn, Ezra. *The Jews of East Central Europe between the World Wars*. Bloomington: Indiana University Press, 1987.
Mertens, Lothar. "Schwieriger Neubeginn: Die jüdischen Gemeinden in der SBZ/DDR bis 1952/1953." In *Leben im Land der Täter: Juden im Nachkriegsdeutschland (1945–1952)*, ed. Julius H. Schoeps, 171–188. Berlin: JVB, 2001.
Meyer, Michael A., ed., *German-Jewish History in Modern Times*. 4 vols. New York: Columbia University Press, 1996–1998.
Michlic, Joanna B. "Anti-Jewish Violence in Poland, 1918–1939 and 1945–1947." *Polin* 13 (2000): 34–61.
———. *Jewish Children in Nazi-Occupied Poland: Survival and Polish-Jewish Relations during the Holocaust as Reflected in Early Postwar Recollections*. Jerusalem: Yad Vashem, 2008.
———. *Poland's Threatening Other: The Image of the Jew from 1880 to the Present*. Lincoln: University of Nebraska Press, 2006.
———. "The Raw Memory of War: Early Postwar Testimonies of Children in Dom Dziecka in Otwock." *Yad Vashem Studies* 37, no. 1 (2009): 11–52.
———. "Who Am I? Jewish Children's Search for Identity in Post-War Poland, 1945–1949." In Finder et al., "Making Holocaust Memory," 98–121.
———. "Żydokomuna: Anti-Jewish Images and Political Tropes in Modern Poland." *Simon Dubnow Institute Yearbook* 4 (2005): 303–329.
Michman, Dan. *Holocaust Historiography: A Jewish Perspective; Conceptualizations, Terminology, Approaches and Fundamental Issues*. London: Vallentine Mitchell, 2003.
———. "Is There an 'Israeli School' of Holocaust Research?" In Bankier and Michman, *Holocaust Historiography*, 37–65.
Miller, Donald, and Lorna Touryan Miller. *Survivors: An Oral History of the Armenian Genocide*. Berkeley: University of California Press, 1993.
Mintz, Alan. *Hurban: Responses to Catastrophe in Hebrew Literature*. New York: Columbia University Press, 1984.
Miron, Guy. "The Leo Baeck Institute and German-Jewish Historiography on the Holocaust." In Bankier and Michman, *Holocaust Historiography*, 305–323.
———. *The Waning of Emancipation: Jewish History, Memory, and the Rise of Fascism in Germany, France, and Hungary*. Detroit: Wayne State University Press, 2011.
Moeller, Robert G. *War Stories: The Search for a Usable Past in the Federal Republic of Germany*. Berkeley: University of California Press, 2001.
Moisel, Claudia. "Résistance und Repressalien: Die Kriegsverbrecherprozesse in der französischen Zone und in Frankreich." In Frei, *Transnationale Vergangenheitspolitik*, 247–282.
Möller, Horst, and Udo Wengst, eds. *50 Jahre Institut für Zeitgeschichte: Eine Bilanz*. Munich: Oldenbourg, 1999.
Moore, Deborah Dash. *GI Jews: How World War II Changed a Generation*. Cambridge, MA: Harvard University Press, 2004.
Motzkin, Leo ["A. Linden"], ed. *Die Judenpogrome in Russland: Großes Sammelwerk der zur Erforschung eingesetzten Kommission*. 2 vols. Cologne: Jüdischer Verlag, 1910.
Müller, Jan-Werner, ed. *Memory and Power in Post-War Europe: Studies in the Presence of the Past*. Cambridge, UK: Cambridge University Press, 2002.
Myers, David N. "History as Ideology: The Case of Ben Zion Dinur, Zionist Historian 'Par Excellence.'" *Modern Judaism* 8, no. 2 (1988): 167–193.
———. "A New Scholarly Colony in Jerusalem: The Early History of Jewish Studies at the Hebrew University." *Judaism* 45, no. 2 (1996): 142–159.

———. *Re-Inventing the Jewish Past: European Jewish Intellectuals and the Zionist Return to History.* New York: Oxford University Press, 1995.
Nathans, Benjamin. "On Russian Jewish Historiography." In *Historiography of Imperial Russia: The Profession and Writing of History in a Multinational State*, ed. Thomas Sanders, 397–432. Armonk, NY: M. E. Sharpe, 1999.
Nattermann, Ruth. *Deutsch-jüdische Geschichtsschreibung nach der Schoah: Die Gründungs- und Frühgeschicht des Leo Baeck Institute.* Essen, Germany: Klartext Verlag, 2004.
Neumann, Franz. *Behemoth: The Structure and Practice of National Socialism, 1933–1944.* London: Gollancz, 1942.
Niborski, Yitskhok, and Bernard Vaisbrot. *Dictionnaire Yiddish-Français.* Paris: Bibliothèque Medem, 2002.
Nicosia, Francis R., and David Scrase, eds. *Jewish Life in Nazi Germany: Dilemma and Responses.* New York: Berghahn Books, 2010.
Nidam-Orvieto, Iael. "Fighting Oblivion: The CDEC and Its Impact on Italian Holocaust Historiography." In Bankier and Michman, *Holocaust Historiography*, 293–304.
Niewyk, Donald L., ed. *Fresh Wounds: Early Narratives of Holocaust Survival.* Chapel Hill: University of North Carolina Press, 1998.
Niewyk, Donald L., and Francis Nicosia. *The Columbia Guide to the Holocaust.* New York: Columbia University Press, 2000.
Niger, Samuel, and Jacob Shatsky, eds., *Leksikon fun der nayer yidisher literatur.* 8 vols. New York: Congress for Jewish Culture, 1956–1981.
Nora, Pierre. *Rethinking France: The Lieux de Memoire.* Translated by Mary Trouille. 4 vols. Chicago: University of Chicago Press, 2001–2010.
Novick, Peter. *The Holocaust in American Life.* Boston: Houghton Mifflin, 1999.
Oertel, Christiane. *Juden auf der Flucht durch Austria: Jüdische Displaced Persons in der US-Besatzungszone Österreichs.* Vienna: Werner Eichbauer Verlag, 1999.
Ofer, Dalia. "The Community and the Individual: The Different Narratives of Early and Late Testimonies and Their Significance for Historians." In Bankier and Michman, *Holocaust Historiography*, 519–535.
———. "Israel." In Wyman, *The World Responds to the Holocaust*, 836–924.
———. "The Strength of Remembrance: Commemorating the Holocaust during the First Decade of Israel." *Jewish Social Studies*, n.s., 6, no. 2 (Winter 2000): 24–55.
Okey, Robin. *Eastern Europe, 1740–1985: Feudalism to Communism.* Minneapolis: University of Minnesota Press, 1999.
Orenstein, Benjamin. *Dos lebn un shafn fun Dr. Filip Fridman: Kurtser bio-bibliografisher iberblik.* Montreal: Jewish Culture Club, 1962.
O'Toole, James M., and Richard J. Cox. *Understanding Archives and Manuscripts.* Chicago: Society of American Archivists, 2006.
Pat, Jacob. *Ash un fayer: Iber di khurves fun Poyln.* New York: CYCO Bikher-Farlag, 1946.
Patt, Avinoam J. *Finding Home and Homeland: Jewish DP Youth and Zionism in the Aftermath of the Holocaust.* Detroit: Wayne State University Press, 2009.
Patt, Avinoam J., and Michael Berkowitz, eds. *"We Are Here": New Approaches to Jewish Displaced Persons in Postwar Germany.* Detroit: Wayne State University Press, 2010.
Pauley, Bruce. "Austria." In Wyman, *The World Responds to the Holocaust*, 473–513.
Pavan, Ilaria. *Persecution, Indifference, and Amnesia: The Restoration of Jewish Rights in Postwar Italy.* Jerusalem: Yad Vashem, 2006.
Pawliczek, Aleksandra. "Zwischen Anerkennung und Ressentiment: Der jüdische Mediävist Harry Bresslau (1848–1926)." *Simon Dubnow Institute Yearbook* 6 (2007): 389–410.
Paxton, Robert O. *Vichy France: Old Guard New Order, 1940–1944.* New York: A. Knopf, 1972.
Perz, Bertrand. "Österreich." In Knigge and Frei, *Verbrechen erinnern*, 150–162.
Pfanzelter, Eva. "Zwischen Brenner und Bari: Jüdische Flüchtlinge in Italien 1945 bis 1948." In Alberich, *Flucht nach Eretz Israel*, 225–252.
Pinkus, Benjamin. *The Soviet Government and the Jews, 1948–1967: A Documentary Study.* New York: Cambridge University Press, 1984.

Pinson, Koppel S. "Jewish Life in Liberated Germany." *Jewish Social Studies* 9, no. 2 (April 1947): 101–126.

———. "Simon Dubnow: Historian and Political Philosopher." Introduction to *Nationalism and History: Essays on Old and New Judaism*, by Simon Dubnow, 3–65. Philadelphia: Jewish Publication Society, 1958.

Poliakov, Léon. "Le Centre de Documentation Juive, ses archives ses publications." *Cahiers d'Histoire de la Guerre* 2 (1949): 39–44.

———. *Mémoires*. Paris: Jacques Grancher Éditeur, 1999.

Poliakov, Léon, and Joseph Wulf, eds. *Das Dritte Reich und die Juden: Dokumente und Aufsätze*. Berlin: Arani, 1955.

———, eds. *Das Dritte Reich und seine Diener: Dokumente*. Berlin: Arani, 1956.

———, eds. *Das Dritte Reich und seine Denker: Dokumente*. Berlin: Arani, 1959.

Polonsky, Antony. "Beyond Condemnation, Apologetics, and Apologies: On the Complexity of Polish Behavior toward the Jews during the Second World War." *Studies in Contemporary Jewry* 13 (1997): 190–224.

Polonsky, Antony, and Bolesław Drukier. *The Beginnings of Communist Rule in Poland, December 1943–June 1945*. London: Routledge, 1980.

Porat, Dina. *Me-'ever le-gishmi: Parashat hayav shel Aba Kovner*. Tel Aviv: 'Am 'Oved, 2000.

Postone, Moishe, and Eric Santner, eds. *Catastrophe and Meaning: The Holocaust and the Twentieth Century*. Chicago: University of Chicago Press, 2003.

Pougatch, Isaac. *Figures Juives de Théodore Herzl à Ida Nudel*. Paris: Ramsay, 1984.

Poznanski, Renée. "French Apprehensions, Jewish Expectations: From a Social Imaginary to a Political Practice." In Bankier, *The Jews Are Coming Back*, 25–57.

———. "Hakamat ha-merkaz le-ti'ud yahadut zmanenu be-tsarfat: Mitos u-metsiyut." In Gutman, *Mi-genizah le-tsiyune derekh historiyim*, 161–180.

———. *The Jews in France during World War II*. Translated by Nathan Bracher. Hanover, NH: University Press of New England, 2001.

———. "La création du Centre de Documentation Juive Contemporaine en France (Avril 1943)." *Vingtième Siècle* 63 (July–September 1999): 51–64.

———. *Les Juifs en France pendant la Seconde Guerre mondiale*. Paris: Hachette Littératures, 1997.

———. *Propagandes et persécutions: La Résistance et le "problème juif," 1940–1944*. Paris: Fayard, 2008.

———. "Vichy et les Juifs: Des marges de l'histoire au coeur de son écriture." In *Vichy et les Français*, ed. Jean-Pierre Azéma and François Bédarida, 57–68. Paris: Fayard, 1992.

Prager, Moshe Mark. *Yeven metsulah ha-hadash: Yahadut Polanya be-tsipurne ha-Natsim*. Tel Aviv: Mosad Bialik, 1941.

Presser, Jacques. *Ondergang: De vervolging en verdelging van het Nederlandse jodendom, 1940–1945*. 2 vols. The Hague: Staatsuitgeverij, 1965.

Proudfoot, Malcolm. *European Refugees, 1939–1952: A Study in Forced Population Movement*. London: Faber & Faber, 1957.

Prussin, Alexander V. "Poland's Nuremberg: The Seven Court Cases of the Supreme National Tribunal, 1946–1948." *Holocaust and Genocide Studies* 24, no. 1 (Spring 2010): 1–25.

Rabinbach, Anson. "The Challenge of the Unprecedented: Raphael Lemkin and the Concept of Genocide." *Simon Dubnow Institute Yearbook* 4 (2005): 397–420.

Ramp, Norbert. "'Die DP bezahlen alle Preise . . .': Vorurteile und Konklikte zwischen Einheimischen und jüdischen DPs in Salzburg und Oberösterreich." In Alberich, *Flucht nach Eretz Israel*, 137–160.

Rawick, George P., ed. *The American Slave: A Composite Autobiography*. 41 vols. Westport, CT: Greenwood, 1972–1979.

Rayski, Adam. *The Choice of the Jews under Vichy: Between Submission and Resistance*. Notre Dame, IN: University of Notre Dame Press, 2005.

Redlich, Shimon. *Life in Transit: Jews in Postwar Lodz, 1945–1950*. Boston: Academic Studies Press, 2010.

Ringelblum, Emanuel. *Ksovim fun geto*. Warsaw: Yidish Bukh, 1963.

Roemer, Niels. *Jewish Scholarship and Culture in Nineteenth-Century Germany: Between History and Faith*. Madison: University of Wisconsin Press, 2005.

Rohrbacher, Stefan. *Gewalt im Biedermeier: Antijüdische Ausschreitungen in Vormärz un Revolution*. Frankfurt: Campus Verlag, 1993.

Ro'i, Yaacov. "Soviet Policies and Attitudes toward Israel, 1948–1978: An Overview." *Soviet Jewish Affairs* 8, no. 1 (1978): 35–45.

Rolinek, Susanne. *Jüdische Lebenswelten 1945–1955: Flüchtlinge in der amerikanischen Zone Österreichs*. Vienna: Studienverlag, 2007.

Roseman, Mark. *A Past in Hiding: Memory and Survival in Nazi Germany*. New York: Metropolitan Books, 2001.

Roseman, Mark, and Jürgen Matthäus. *Jewish Responses to Persecution*. Lanham, MD: AltaMira, 2010.

Rosen, Alan. "Evidence of Trauma: David Boder and Writing the History of Holocaust Testimony." In Bankier and Michman, *Holocaust Historiography*, 497–518.

———. *The Wonder of Their Voices: The 1946 Holocaust Interviews of David Boder*. New York: Oxford University Press, 2010.

Rosenfeld, Alvin. *A Double Dying: Reflections on Holocaust Literature*. Bloomington: Indiana University Press, 1980.

Roskies, David G. *Against the Apocalypse: Responses to Catastrophe in Modern Jewish Culture*. Cambridge, MA: Harvard University Press, 1984.

———. *The Jewish Search for a Usable Past*. Bloomington: Indiana University Press, 1999.

———, ed. *The Literature of Destruction: Jewish Responses to Catastrophe*. Philadelphia: Jewish Publication Society of America, 1989.

Rosman, Moshe. "Jewish History across Borders." In *Rethinking European Jewish History*, ed. Jeremy Cohen and Moshe Rosman, 15–29. Oxford: Littman Library of Jewish Civilization, 2009.

Roth, Cecil, ed. *Encyclopaedia Judaica*. 16 vols. Israel: Keter, 1971–1972.

Rothberg, Michael. *Traumatic Realism: The Demands of Holocaust Representation*. Minneapolis: University of Minnesota Press, 2000.

Rothschild, Joseph, and Nancy M. Wingfield. *Return to Diversity: A Political History of East Central Europe since World War II*. 3rd ed. New York: Oxford University Press, 2000.

Rousso, Henri. *The Haunting Past: History, Memory, and Justice in Contemporary France*. Translated by Ralph Schoolcraft. Philadelphia: University of Pennsylvania Press, 2002.

———. *The Vichy Syndrome: History and Memory in France since 1944*. Translated by Arthur Goldhammer. Cambridge, MA: Harvard University Press, 1991.

Rudy, Abraham. *Emes vegn sheker*. Paris: Imprimérie Moderne de la Presse, 1956.

Rupnow, Dirk. *Vernichten und Erinnern: Spuren nationalistischer Gedächnispolitik*. Göttingen, Germany: Wallstein, 2005.

Sakowska, Ruta. "Two Forms of Resistance in the Warsaw Ghetto: Two Functions of the Ringelblum Archives." *Yad Vashem Studies* 21 (1991): 189–219.

Sartre, Jean-Paul. *Anti-Semite and Jew: An Exploration of the Etiology of Hate*. New York: Schocken Books, 1995.

Schechtman, Joseph. *Pogromy dobrovolcheskoi armii na Ukraine*. Berlin: Ostjüdisches Historisches Archiv, 1932.

———. *Ver iz farantvortlekh far di pogromen in Ukraine? Loyt naye nitfarefentlekhte dokumentn*. Paris: Imprimérie Scientifique Commercielle, 1927.

Schneersohn, Isaac. "Der yidisher dokumentatsye-tsenter in Frankraykh." *YIVO Bleter* 30, no. 2 (Winter 1947): 249–257.

———. *Lebn un kamf in tsaristishn rusland: Zikhroynes*. Paris: Éditions Poliglottes, 1968.

Schwarz, Guri. "On Myth Making and Nation Building: The Genesis of the 'Myth of the Good Italian,' 1943–1947." *Yad Vashem Studies* 36, no. 1 (2008): 111–143.

———. "The Reconstruction of Jewish Life in Italy after World War II." *Journal of Modern Jewish Studies* 8, no. 3 (2009): 360–377.

Schwarz, Leo W. *The Root and the Bough: The Epic of an Enduring People*. New York: Rinehart, 1949.

Schein, Ada. "'Everyone can hold a pen': The Documentation Project in the DP Camps in Germany." In Bankier and Michman, *Holocaust Historiography*, 103–134.

Schissler, Hanna. *The Miracle Years: A Cultural History of Germany*. Princeton, NJ: Princeton University Press, 2001.

Schorsch, Ismar. *From Text to Context: The Turn to History in Modern Judaism*. Hanover, NH: University Press of New England, 1994.

———. *Jewish Reactions to German Anti-Semitism, 1870–1914*. New York: Columbia University Press, 1972.

Segev, Tom. *Simon Wiesenthal*. London: Jonathan Cape, 2010.

Shaar, Pinchas. "Mendel Grossman: Photographic Bard of the Lodz Ghetto." In Shapiro, *Holocaust Chronicles*, 125–140.

Shabad, Zemach, and Moshe Shalit, eds. *Vilner zamlbukh*. 2 vols. Vilnius: n.p., 1916–1918.

Shandler, Jeffrey, ed. *Awakening Lives: Autobiographies of Jewish Youth in Poland before the Holocaust*. New Haven, CT: Yale University Press, 2002.

Shapiro, Robert Moses, ed. *Holocaust Chronicles: Individualizing the Holocaust through Diaries and Other Contemporaneous Personal Accounts*. Hoboken, NJ: KTAV, 1999.

Shatsky, Jacob. "Idishe memuarn literatur." *Di Tsukunft* 30 (1925): 483–486.

Shephard, Ben. *The Long Road Home: The Aftermath of the Second World War*. London: Bodley Head, 2010.

Shlomi, Hana. "The Communist Caucus in the Central Committee of Jews in Poland, November 1944–February 1947." *Gal Ed* 13 (1993): 81–100.

———. "Reshit ha-hitargenut shel yehude Polin be-shilhe milhemet-olam ha-shniyah." *Gal Ed* 2 (1975): 287–331.

Shrayer, Maxim D., ed. *An Anthology of Jewish-Russian Literaure: Two Centuries of Dual Identity and Poetry*. 2 vols. Armonk, NY: M. E. Sharpe, 2007.

Shtif, Nokhem. *Pogromen in Ukraine: Di tsayt fun der frayviliger armey*. Berlin: Farlag Vostok, 1923.

Sieramska, Magdalena. "The Jewish Historical Institute Museum." In *The Jewish Historical Institute: The First Fifty Years, 1947–1997*, ed. Eleonora Bergman, 55–61. Warsaw: Jewish Historical Institute, 1996.

Simon, Ernst. *Aufbau und Untergang: Jüdische Erwachsenenbildung im nationalsozialistischen Deutschland als geistiger Widerstand*. Tübingen, Germany: Mohr, 1959.

Sinkoff, Nancy. "*Yidishkayt* and the Making of Lucy S. Dawidowicz." Introduction to *From That Place and Time: A Memoir, 1938–1947* by Lucy S. Dawidowicz, xiii–xl. Rev. ed. New Brunswick, NJ: Rutgers University Press, 2008.

Skolnik, Fred, ed. *Encyclopaedia Judaica*. 2nd. ed. 22 vols. Detroit: Macmillan Reference, 2007.

Stach, Stephan. "Geschichtsschreibung und politische Vereinnahmungen: Das Jüdische Historische Institut in Warschau, 1947–1968." *Simon Dubnow Institute Yearbook* 7 (2008): 401–431.

———. "'Praktische Geschichte': Der Beitrag jüdischer Organisationen zur Verfolgung von NS-Verbrechen in Polen und Österreich in den späten 40er Jahren." In Fritz Bauer Institut, *Opfer als Akteure*, 242–262.

Stafford, David. *Endgame 1945: Victory, Retribution, Liberation*. London: Little, Brown, 2007.

Stauber, Roni. *The Holocaust in Israeli Public Debate in the 1950s*. London: Vallentine Mitchell, 2007.

———. *Laying the Foundations for Holocaust Research: The Impact of the Historian Philip Friedman*. Jerusalem: Yad Vashem, 2009.

———. "Philip Friedman and the Beginning of Holocaust Studies." In Bankier and Michman, *Holocaust Historiography*, 83–102.

Steinlauf, Michael. *Bondage to the Dead: Poland and the Memory of the Holocaust*. Syracuse, NY: Syracuse University Press, 1997.

———. "Poland." In Wyman, *The World Responds to the Holocaust*, 81–155.

Stern, Frank. *Whitewashing the Yellow Badge: Antisemitism and Philosemitism in Postwar Germany*. Oxford: Pergamon, 1992.

Sternhell, Zeev. "The Roots of Popular Anti-Semitism in the Third Republic." In *The Jews in Modern France*, ed. Frances Malino and Bernard Wasserstein, 103–134. Hanover, NH: University Press of New England, 1985.

Sylvain, Nicolas. "Romania." In *The Jews in the Soviet Satellites*, ed. Peter Meyer, Bernard D. Weinryb, Eugene Duschinsky, and Nicolas Sylvain, 493–556. Syracuse, NY: Syracuse University Press, 1953.

Szajkowski, Zosa. *Analytical Franco-Jewish Gazetteer, 1939–1945*. New York: American Academy for Jewish Research, 1966.

———. "Di geshikhte fun dem itstikn bukh." In Tcherikower, *Di Ukrainer pogromen in yor 1919*, 333–349.

Szaynok, Bożena. "The Anti-Jewish Policy of the USSR in the Last Decade of Stalin's Rule and Its Impact on the East European Countries with Special Reference to Poland." *Russian History* 29, nos. 2–4 (2002): 301–315.

———. "The Bund and the Jewish Fraction of the Polish Workers' Party in Poland after 1945." *Polin* 13 (2000): 206–223.

Sznaider, Natan. *Gedächtnisraum Europa: Die Visionen des europäischen Kosmopolitismus; Eine jüdische Perspektive*. Bielefeld, Germany: Transcript Verlag, 2008.

Szurek, Jean-Charles. "Être témoin sous le stalinisme: Les premières anneés de l'Institut Historique Juif de Varsovie." In *Ecriture de l'Historie et Identité Juive: l'Europe ashkénaze XIXe–XXe siècle*, ed. Delphine Bechtel et al., 51–82. Paris: Les Belles Lettres 2003.

Tal, Uriel. "Holocaust." In Gutman, *Encyclopedia of the Holocaust*, 2:681.

Tcherikower, Elias. *Antisemitizm i pogromy na Ukrainie, 1917–1918 gg.: K istorii ukrainsko-evreiskikh otnoshenii*. Berlin: Ostjüdisches Historisches Archiv, 1923.

———. *Antisemitizm un pogromen in Ukraine: Di tkufe fun der tsentraler Rada un Hetman, 1917–1918*. Berlin: Ostjüdisches Historisches Archiv, 1923.

———. *Di Ukrainer pogromen in yor 1919*. New York: YIVO, 1965.

———, ed. *In der tkufe fun revolutsye: Memuarn, materialn, dokumentn; Zamlbikher*. Vol. 1. Berlin: Idisher Literarisher Farlag, 1924.

Tollmien, Cordula. "Nach 1945: Organisation des Überlebens und die Entstehung einer neuen jüdischen Gemeinde." In *Göttingen: Geschichte einer Universitätsstadt*, vol. 3, *Von der preussischen Mittelstadt zur südniedersächsischen Grossstadt 1866–1989*, ed. Rudolf von Thadden and Marc-Dietrich Ohse, 733–760. Göttingen, Germany: Vandenhoeck & Ruprecht, 1999.

Tomaszewski, Jerzy. "Polish History on the Holocaust." In *Nazi Europe and the Final Solution*, ed. David Bankier and Israel Gutman, 111–135. Jerusalem: Yad Vashem 2003.

Torrès, Henri. *Le procès des pogromes*. Paris: Les Éditions de France, 1928.

Toscano, Mario. "The Abrogation of Racial Laws and the Reintegration of Jews in Italian Society (1943–1948)." In Bankier, *The Jews Are Coming Back*, 148–168.

Toynbee, Arnold J., ed. *The Treatment of Armenians in the Ottoman Empire 1915–1916: Documents Presented to Viscount Grey of Fallodon, Secretary of State for Foreign Affairs by Viscount Bryce*. London: His Majesty's Stationery Office, 1916.

Turkow, Jonas. *Nokh der bafrayung*. Buenos Aires: Tsentral Farband fun Poylishe Yidn in Argentine, 1959.

Tych, Feliks. "The Emergence of Holocaust research in Poland: The Jewish Historical Commission and the Jewish Historical Institute (ZIH), 1944–1989." In Bankier and Michman, *Holocaust Historiography*, 227–244.

———. "The Legacy of Emanuel Ringelblum and the Historical Awareness of the Holocaust." In Gutman, *Emanuel Ringelblum*, 179–188

Tych, Feliks, Alfons Kenkmann, Elisabeth Kohlhaas, and Andreas Eberhardt, eds. *Kinder über den Holocaust: Frühe Zeugnisse, 1944–1947; Interviewprotokolle der Zentralen Jüdischen Historischen Kommission in Polen*. Berlin: Metropol, 2008.

Uhl, Heidemarie. "From Victim Myth to Co-Responsibility Thesis: Nazi Rule, World War II, and the Holocaust in Austrian Memory." In Lebow, Kansteiner, and Fogu, *The Politics of Memory in Postwar Europe*, 40–72.

Unger, Michal. "Ha-ti'ud ha-yehudi mi-geto Lodz." In Gutman, *Mi-genizah le-tsiyune derekh historiyim*, 141–150.

United States Holocaust Memorial Museum, ed. *In Pursuit of Justice: Examining the Evidence of the Holocaust*. Washington, DC: United States Holocaust Memorial Museum, [2006].

Volkov, Shulamit. "Jewish History: The Nationalism of Transnationalism." In *Transnationale Geschichte: Themen, Tendenzen und Theorien*, ed. Gunilla Budde, Sebastian Conrad, and Oliver Janz, 190–201. Göttingen, Germany: Vandenhoeck & Ruprecht, 2006.

Volovici, Leon. "Romanian Jewry under Rabbi Moses Rosen during the Ceausescu Regime." *Studies in Contemporary Jewry* 19 (2003): 181–192.

Warhaftig, Zorah. *The Uprooted: Jewish Refugees and Displaced Persons after Liberation*. New York: Institute for Jewish Affairs of the American Jewish Congress and World Jewish Congress, 1946.

Warner, G. "Italy and the Powers, 1943–49." In *The Rebirth of Italy, 1943–50*, ed. Stuart Joseph Woolf, 30–56. New York: Humanities Press, 1972.

Waxman, Zoë Vania. *Writing the Holocaust: Identity, Testimony, Representation*. Oxford: Oxford University Press, 2006.

Web, Marek. "Dubnov and Jewish Archives: An Introduction to His Papers at the YIVO Institute." In *A Missionary for History: Essays in Honor of Simon Dubnov*, ed. Kristi Groberg and Avraham Greenbaum, 87–92. Minneapolis: University of Minnesota Press, 1998.

Webser, Ronald. "American Relief and Jews in Germany, 1945–1950." *Leo Baeck Institute Yearbook* 38 (1993): 293–321.

Wegs, J. Robert, and Robert Ladrech. *Europe Since 1945: A Concise History*. 5th ed. Basingstoke, UK: Palgrave Macmillan, 2006.

Wein, Abraham. "The Jewish Historical Institute in Warsaw." *Yad Vashem Studies* 8 (1970): 203–213.

Weinberg, David. "Between America and Israel: The Quest for a Distinct European Jewish Identity in the Postwar Era." *Jewish Culture and History* 5, no. 1 (Summer 2002): 91–120.

———. *A Community on Trial: The Jews of Paris in the 1930s*. Chicago: University of Chicago Press, 1977.

———. "France." In Wyman, *The World Responds to the Holocaust*, 3–44.

———. "The Reconstruction of the French Jewish Community after World War II." In Gutman and Saf, *She'erit Hapletah, 1944–1948*, 168–186.

Weinke, Annette. "'Alliierter Angriff auf die nationale Souveränität'?: Die Strafverfolgung von Kriegs- und NS-Verbrechen in der Bundesrepublik, der DDR und Österreich." In Frei, *Transnationale Vergangenheitspolitik*, 37–93.

Weinryb, Bernard. "Poland." In *The Jews in the Soviet Satellites*, ed. Peter Meyer, 205–326. Syracuse, NY: Syracuse University Press, 1953.

Weissman, Gary. *Fantasies of Witnessing: Postwar Efforts to Experience the Holocaust*. Ithaca, NY: Cornell University Press, 2004.

Wells, Leon Weliczker. *The Janowska Road*. Washington, DC: United States Holocaust Memorial Museum, 1999.

Wieviorka, Annette. *Déportation et génocide: Entre la mémoire et l'oubli*. Paris: Plon, 1992.

———. "Du CDJC au Mémorial de la Shoah." *La Revue d'Histoire de la Shoah* 181, no. 2 (2004): 11–36.

———. *The Era of the Witness*. Translated by Jared Stark. Ithaca, NY: Cornell University Press, 2006.

———. "From Survivor to Witness: Voices from the Shoah." In *War and Remembrance in the Twentieth Century*, ed. Jay Winter and Emmanuel Sivan, 125–141. Cambridge, UK: Cambridge University Press, 1999.

———. *Il y a 50 ans: Aux origines du Mémorial de la Shoah*. Paris: CDJC, 2006.

———. "Le Combat de Justin Godart pour l'érection du 'tombeau du martyr juif inconnu.'" In *Justin Godart: Un home dans son siècle (1871–1956)*, ed. Annette Wieviorka, 125–135. Paris: CNRS Éditions 2005.

———. "Un lieu de mémoire et d'histoire: Le Mémorial du Martyr juif inconnu." *Pardès* 2 (1985): 80–98.

Wiesenthal, Simon. *The Murderers Are Amongst Us*. Edited by Joseph Wechsberg. New York: McGraw-Hill, 1967.

Winter, Jay. *Remembering War: The Great War between Memory and History in the Twentieth Century*. New Haven, CT: Yale University Press, 2006.

Woodbridge, George. *UNRRA: The History of the United Nations Relief and Rehabilitation Administration*. 3 vols. New York: Columbia University Press, 1950.

Wróbel, Piotr. "The Kaddish Years: Anti-Jewish Violence in East Central Europe, 1918–1921." *Simon Dubnow Institute Yearbook* 4 (2005): 211–236.
Wyman, David, ed. *The World Reacts to the Holocaust.* Baltimore: Johns Hopkins University Press, 1996.
Wyman, Mark. *DPs: Europe's Displaced Persons, 1945–1951.* Ithaca, NY: Cornell University Press, 1998.
Yablonka, Hanna. "The Myth of Holocaust Survivors' Silence: The Case of the Israeli Artists." In *The Holocaust: History and Memory: Essays Presented in Honor of Israel Gutman,* ed. Shmuel Almog, Daniel Blatman, David Bankier, and Dalia Ofer, 207–235. Jerusalem: Yad Vashem 2001.
———. *The State of Israel vs. Adolf Eichmann.* New York: Schocken Books, 2004.
Yerushalmi, Yosef Hayim. *Zakhor: Jewish History and Jewish Memory.* Seattle: University of Washington Press, 1996.
Yetman, Norman R. "The Background of the Slave Narrative Collection." *American Quarterly* 19, no. 3 (Fall 1967): 534–553.
———. "Ex-Slave Interviews and the Historiography of Slavery." *American Quarterly* 36, no. 2 (Summer 1984): 181–219.
Young, James E. "Between History and Memory: The Uncanny Voices of Historian and Survivor." *History and Memory* 9, nos. 1–2 (Fall 1997): 47–58.
———. *The Texture of Memory: Holocaust Memorials and Meaning.* New Haven, CT: Yale University Press, 1993.
———. *Writing and Rewriting the Holocaust: Narrative and the Consequences of Interpretation.* Bloomington: Indiana University Press, 1988.
Zapruder, Alexandra, ed. *Salvaged Pages: Young Writers' Diaries of the Holocaust.* New Haven, CT: Yale University Press, 2004.
Zertal, Idith. *From Catastrophe to Power: Holocaust Survivors and the Emergence of Israel.* Berkeley: University of California Press, 1998.
Zerubavel, Yael. *Recovered Roots: Collective Memory and the Making of Israeli National Tradition.* Chicago: University of Chicago Press, 1995.
Zimmerman, Joshua D., ed. *Contested Memories: Poles and Jews during the Holocaust and Its Aftermath.* New Brunswick, NJ: Rutgers University Press, 2003.
Zuccotti, Susan. *The Holocaust, the French, and the Jews,* New York: Basic Books, 1993.
Zuckerman, Itzkhak, *A Surplus of Memory: Chronicle of the Warsaw Ghetto Uprising.* Translated and edited by Barbara Harshav. Berkeley: University of California Press, 1993.
Zweig, Ronald. *German Reparations and the Jewish World: A History of the Claims Conference.* 2d ed. London: Frank Cass, 2001.
Żydowski Instytut Historyczny, ed. *Holocaust Survivors Testimony Catalogue.* 6 vols. Warsaw: ŻIH, 1998–2009.

INDEX

Abetz, Otto, 63
Abramovich, Sholem Yankev, 19
accidental selection, documents, 170, 203
activists
    connecting history and memory, 186–187
    influencing future historians, 131
The Activity of Jewish Organizations in Occupied France, 68
Adler, H. G., 41–42
African Americans, slavery, 229n6
AJDC (American Jewish Joint Distribution Committee), 5, 7, 13, 16, 29, 65, 92, 122
    Displaced Persons camps, 125
    financial assistance to CŻKH, 102
    investment in France, 72
Ajzersztajn, Betti, 130
Aleksiun, Natalia, 31
Alexander II (Tsar), 20
Alitzka, S., 130
Alliance Israélite Universelle (AIU), 7, 55, 166
Alltagsgeschichte avant la lettre, 10, 199, 201
Alperin, Aron, 72
Amalek
    future Holocaust research, 146–147
    poster of historical commission, 143
    remembering and not forgetting, 144
American Jewish Committee, 72, 73, 168, 244n188
American Jewish Labor Committee, 72, 73, 99, 109
American Joint Distribution Committee (AJDC/Joint), *see* AJDC
American Military Tribunal, Nuremberg, 7, 45, 64, 166, 175
American War Crimes Commission, 268n240
Aminado, Don, 55, 66, 207
Anglo-American Allied Control Council, 124
An-ski, S., 25, 26, 30, 32, 37
Ansky, Michel, 70
anti-Nazi resistance, 277n1
anti-Semitism, 8, 9

American Jewish Committee, 168
Austria, 125, 151
    Christian, 151
    contamination of research, 173
    documentation, 175, 182, 203
    French, 47, 49, 57–58
    Germany, 125
    Italy, 125–126
    Nazism, 167
    Poland, 111, 112, 114
    Russian, 232n60
    stereotypes, 124–125, 192
Armée Juive, Jewish resistance, 61–62, 69
Armenianians, Turkish genocide, 229n6
Armia Krajowa (AK), 85
Aryanization
    Jewish property, 135, 138, 163, 167
    racial laws and policies, 236n6
Aryanization policies, 48, 49, 51
Aryan papers, survival on, 104, 108
Association for the Defense against Antisemitism, 234n109
Association of Foreign Jewish Volunteers, Second World War, 176
Association of Polish Jews in France, 272n30
Asz, Menachem Marek, 6, 89, 130, 207
Auerbach, Pesach, 23
Auerbach, Rachel, 91, 95, 102, 120, 130, 194, 197–198, 207–208
Aufbau, 72
Auriol, Vincent, 78, 166
Auschwitz-Birkenau
    Birkenau extermination camp, 108
    Blumental's accounting of deaths, 115–116
    death camp, 48, 114
    exhibition, 168
    Friedman's history of, 102
    resistance, 177
    Sonderkommando, 33
    symbolizing crime against humanity, 119–120, 193

Austria
  anti-Semitism, 125, 151
  British Zone of DPs in, 121, 123
  differences among commissions, 188–189
  interzonal cooperation, 126–127
  Jewish Displaced Persons (DP) population, 123, 124
  Jewish documentation centers in, 149–156
  Jewish population, 259n24
  Lesser Incrimination Amnesty, 154
  political and social conditions, 124
  refugees, 236n1
  war criminals, 269n250

Baeck, Leo, 78
Bakalczuk, Mejlech, 91, 150, 208
Bakalczuk, Neche, 150, 208
Balaban, Majer, 31
Bankier, David, 14
Baron, Salo W., 194, 195, 200, 277n9, 277–278n12
Bartov, Omer, 193, 201–202
Bass, Joseph, 61
The Battle of the Warsaw Ghetto from the Perspective of the Germans, Stroop, 69
Bauer, André, 208–209
Bauer, Yehuda, 39, 243n154
Bauminger, Leon, 91, 209
bearers of history, 10
Beckelman, Moses, 77
Ben-Gurion, David, 78
Ben-Natan, Asher, 150
Berg, Nicolas, 196
Berlin Document Center, 45
Berman, Joseph, 73
Bernheim, Léonce, 52, 53, 54, 209
Bialik, Chaim Nachman, 19–20, 23, 30
Biebow, Hans, 106, 113, 114
Billig, Joseph, 55, 64–65, 70, 194, 209
Bitter, Marek, 89, 90, 309
Blaustein, Jacob, 78
Bloch, Jacques, 73
blockade of silence, French, 57
Blum, Léon, 47, 166
Blumental, Nachman, 91, 92, 97, 103, 113, 114, 115, 116, 117–118, 120, 174, 194, 197–198, 209, 256n182
B'nai B'rith, 72
Boder, David, 14
Bondar, Isaac, 109
Bonnet, Georges, 61
Borusztajn, Róžka, 109
Borwicz, Michal, 6, 38, 91, 102, 103, 120, 165, 169–170, 173, 174–175, 179, 182–184, 209–210, 256n182, 272n30
Boyarin, Jonathan, 4–5, 224n6
breaking the silence, French, 56–63
Brenner, Michael, 235n118
Brichah, Zionist organization, 123, 150

British Zone of Austria, 121, 123, 149–156
British Zone of Germany, 121, 123, 147–149
British Zone of Italy, 121, 123, 156–158
Broszat, Martin, 197, 200
Browning, Christopher, 201
Bulletin du Centre de Documentation Juive Contemporaine, Knout, 67
Burds, Jeffrey, 13

campography, 169
campology, 169
Cassin, René, 69, 78
Cassou, Jean, 69
catastrophe
  chronicling, during Second World War, 33–36
  conference about Jewish, 160–162
  documentation of, 30
  greatest national, for Jewish people, 93–94
Center for Israelite Information (Centre d'Information Israélite), 166
Center for Political Information (Centre d'Information Politique), 166
Center for the Study of the History of Polish Jews (Centre d'Étude d'Histoire des Juifs Polonais), 165, 166, 169
Center of Contemporary Jewish Documentation (Centre de Documentation Juive Contemporaine, CDJC), 3, 50, 51, 53, 188
  core of Holocaust research, 202
  Holocaust memorial, 74–81
  Paris, 54–56, 63–66, 161
Central Association of German Citizens of the Jewish Faith (Centralverein deutscher Staatsbürger jüdischen Glaubens, CV), 6, 40
Central Board of Hungarian Jews, 7
Central Committee for the Relief of Pogrom Victims, 27
Central Committee in British Zone, 148
Central Committee of Liberated Jews, 144, 147
Central Committee of Liberated Jews in Bavaria, 126
Central Committee of Liberated Jews in the British Zone, 126
Central Committee of Polish Jews (Centralny Komitet Zydow Polskich, CKŽP), 86, 161
Central Consistory of the Jews in France, 166
Central Historical Commission (Tsentrale Historishe Komisye, TsHK), 6, 130
  collections and publications in DP camps, 137–141
  communication with camp populations, 142–145
  establishment, 128–132
  Munich, 7
  posters, 143, 145
  research methods, 132–137
Central Jewish Consistory, 7

Index

Central Jewish Historical Commission (Centralna Żydowska Komisja Historyczna CŻKH), 5, 37, 38, 92
   collecting archives in Lodz, 99–102
   collective history writing, 104–110
   documentation work, 91–93
   founding meeting, 90–91
   friends society, 107–108
   history vs. politics in Poland, 117–119
   idea for conference, 160–162
   Kaplan, Glube and Feigenbaum, 128–130
   publication activities, 102–104
   researching Holocaust, 94–98, 188
   women in, 92, 93, 250n50
Centre de Documentation Juive Contemporaine. *See* Center of Contemporary Jewish Documentation (CDJC)
Cesarani, David, 14
Chelmno extermination camp, 33, 112
children
   memoirs, 103
   recollections of experiences, 264n152
   survivors, 251n92
   wartime experiences, 97, 106
Children's Relief Agency (OSE), 55, 56, 73, 168, 238n41
Chmielnicki pogroms, 19, 231n25, 265n162
Christian anti-Semitism, 151
Churchill, Winston, 78
cloak of oblivion, 151
Cohen, Boaz, 14
Cohen, David, 40
Collection Commission for Jewish History Lublin, 90
collective notebook, prisoners, 33
Commissariat Général aux Questions Juives, 163. *See also* General Commissariat for Jewish Questions
Committee for Relief of Pogrom Victims, 230–231n25
Committee for Research on the Jewish Deportees in Rome, 165
Committee for the Finding of Jewish Deportees, 269n259
Committee of Liberated Jews, 126
Conseil représentatif des Israélites de France (CRIF), 55, 71–72, 238n41
Contribution to the History of Jewish Resistance in France, 1940–1944, Knout, 68
Council of Jewish Communities of Greece, 6–7
Crusade chronicles, 19
Czechoslovakia, 236n1
Czertok, Léon, 180, 182

Dachau concentration camp, 138, 139
DANA, German General News Agency, 138
Dannecker, Theodor, 59, 63
Das Dritte Reich und die Juden, Poliakov and Wulf, 196
Dawidowicz, Lucy S., 13, 139, 196, 226n38

death brigade, 103
deep memory, 10
de Gaulle, Charles, 56
de Jong, Louis, 42
Denikin, Anton, 29
Der Moment, 25, 29
Der Stürmer, 151
Der Tog, 72, 109
The Destruction of the European Jews, Hilberg, 199
destruction research. *See* khurbn-forshung
Diaspora Jewry, 32, 146, 178, 197, 205
Die Judenpogrome in Russland, 24
Die Neue Zeitung, 139
Diner, Hasia R., 14
Dinesohn, Jacob, 25
Dinur, Ben-Zion, 81, 147, 162, 197, 278n19
Displaced Persons (DPs), 16
   archival collections and publications in DP camps, 137–141
   category by Allies, 121–122
   Jewish, camps, 121, 188–190
   Jewish, in Austria, 123, 124
   Jewish, in Germany, 123–124
   Jewish, in Italy, 123, 124
   materials from DP camps, 164–165
   politicalization, 127–128
   refugees, 236n1
   survivors documenting their past, 141–145
   Zionism, 260n50
District Jewish Historical Commissions, 91
Dizengoff, Meir, 20
documentation
   accidental selection, 170
   artifacts, 203–204
   Central Jewish Historical Commission in Lublin, 89–94
   collecting evidence of crime in France, 63–66
   delegates at European conference 1947, 165–168
   European Holocaust conference, planning, 163–165
   European Jewish, center in Paris, 177–179
   European understanding of Holocaust, 204–206
   French Jewish, 50–54
   immediate aftermath of Holocaust, 36–43
   Jewish Holocaust, 10–15
   methodology, 169–173
   Oyneg Shabes, 34–36
   Paris conference, 8–10
   personal recollections, 21–22
   postwar Jewish Holocaust, 191–192
   practical value, 30
   protecting collections, 28–29
   recording atrocities during war, 33–36
   research methodology, 169–173
   survivor documentarians journey to recognition, 193–202
   U.S. Zone of Germany, 128–132

Documentation Center for Nazi War Criminals in Haifa, 155
documentation centers. *See also* historical commissions
  Austria, 149–156
  comparative history, 15–17
Documents of Crime and Martyrdom, CŻKH, 103
Donat, Aleksander, 33
Dos Naye Lebn (New Life), 87
Drancy camp, 48, 68, 216, 241n97, 245n202
Dubnow, Simon, 19, 21–23, 27, 29, 30, 32, 33, 37, 156, 170
Dutch Jewish Holocaust, research and publication, 42

Eastern Jewish Historical Archive, 29
Eber, Ada, 5, 36, 92, 120, 210
Echkenazy, Elie, 7, 167, 175
Eden, Anthony, 78
Eichmann, Adolf, 59, 153, 156, 195, 198, 278n26
Einstein, Albert, 78
Eisenbach, Artur, 31, 100, 113, 114, 118, 194, 210
Ejdelman, Abraham Szmuel, 109
Elberg, Jehuda, 89, 210
elections, 257n210
Eliashev, Isidor Yisroel, 27
emancipation, 76
  Age of, 41
  belief in legal systems, 39
Engel, David, 36, 84, 248n19
era of the witness, 10
Eretz Yisrael, 162
Ethnographic Historical Commission, 22
ethnographic materials, collectors of, 97–98, 134, see also folklore, Jewish
Europe, Holocaust research, 160–162
European Coordination Committee (ECC), 181–183
European Jewish Holocaust conference
  Coordination Committee, 181
  Council of Directors, 181–182
  European Coordination Committee (ECC), 181–183
  European documentation center in Paris, 177–179
  first, 3, 4
  Paris, December 1947, 165–168
  planning, 163–165
  Resolution Commission, 180
European Jews, 39–40, 84, 189, 203, 234n108

Fabritz, Shoshana, 130
Fareynikte party, 27
Farn Folk, 157, 158
Faure, Edgar, 69
Fédération des Sociétés Juives de France (FSJF). *See* Federation of Jewish Societies in France (FSJF)

Febvre, Lucien, 56
Federation of Jewish Relief Organisations, 73
Federation of Jewish Relief Organisations to Assist Jewish Victims of War and Persecution, 73
Federation of Jewish Societies in France (FSJF), 51, 55, 56, 63
Feigenbaum, Moshe Yosef, 6, 38, 128–132, 133, 136–137, 139–140, 144, 146–147, 162, 168, 182, 183, 210–211
  memorial at Auschwitz, 179
  research methodology, 169–172
Feinstein, Margarete Myers, 14
Feldschuh-Safrin, Ruven, 91, 211
film footage, German occupation, 101
Final Solution, 9, 18, 48, 151
Fink, Jacques, 182, 211
First World War, 24, 53
Fishman, David, 32
folk culture, preserving Jewish, 25
folklore, Jewish, collection of, 10, 27, 43, 90, 103, 138
Fortunoff Video Archive, Yale University, 10, 11, 12
Forverts, 72
Foyer Amicale, 54
France
  Centre de Documentation Juive Contemporaine (CDJC), 54–56
  collecting evidence of crime, 63–66
  differences among commissions, 188–189
  documentation activity, 204–205
  Grenoble 1943, 50–54
  Holocaust and French Jewry, 46–50
  Holocaust historiography publication, 66–71
  Holocaust memorial, 74–81
  Jewish population, 46, 239n59
  Jewish tragedy's place in, 56–63
  mass arrests and roundups, 237n7
  mobilization of resources and awareness, 71–74
  Résistance, 56, 61–62, 176, 189
  representatives, 276n162
  survivors in liberated, 48–49
Frank, Anne, 42
Frankfurter, David, 40
French Jews, 46–50, 174, 189, 190
French Jews under Italian Occupation, Poliakov, 69
Friedländer, Saul, 12, 201
Friedman, Philip, 5, 7, 11, 12, 31, 36, 90, 91, 92, 93–94, 102–104, 109, 116, 117, 120, 137, 200, 203
  AJDC's Education and Culture Department, 137
  archives, 107
  Auschwitz-Birkenau history, 102–103
  biography, 211–212
  CŻKH's goal, 111
  "The Destruction of Polish Jewry, 1939–1945," 103–104
  European conference, 160–162, 179, 182–183

Fun Letstn Khurbn, 140
  Holocaust memory, 94–95
  objectivity, 194–195
  Poland's Jewish community, 112
  research methodology, 169–173, 176
From Drancy to Auschwitz, Wellers, 68
From the Cataclysm to a New Life, 182
Frydman, Towia, 6, 150, 151, 153, 155, 162, 168, 194, 212
Fuchsman, Helen, 152, 212
fundraising, for documentation work
  France, 71
  Great Britain, 73, 184
  Poland, 117
  United States, 72
Fundraising for Paris memorial, 78
Fun Letstn Khurbn (From the Latest Destruction), 130–131, 139–140, 144, 146

Gamzon, Robert, 56
Gar, Joseph, 12
Garbarini, Alexandra, 33
Garel, Georges, 168
General Commissariat for Jewish Questions (Commissariat Général aux Questions Juives), 48, 53, 63
Genocide, term, 223–224n2
Gerber, Rafal, 118
German/Austro-Hungarian alliance, 24
German fascism, theory and practice, 94
German General News Agency, DANA, 138
German occupiers
  Lodz, 99
  Poland, 111–112
The German Pillage of Works of Art and Libraries in the Possession of French Jews, Cassou, 69
Germany
  anti-Jewish violence, 234n108
  anti-Semitism, 125
  British Zone of DPs in, 121, 123
  differences among commissions, 188–189
  Jewish Displaced Persons (DP) population, 123–124
  Jewish historical commissions in British Zone of, 147–149
  Jewish population, 259n22
  looting Poland, 85
  political and social conditions, 123–124
  refugees, 236n1
Germany and the Genocide: Nazi Plans and Implementations, Billig, 70
Gestapo, 135
Giett, Josef, 152
Ginsberg, Asher, 19
Glaeser, Léo, 52, 54, 212
Glube, Shmuel, 128–130, 212
Godart, Justin, 63, 72, 79, 166, 167, 174, 176, 213, 244n183

Goeth, Amon, 256n182
Gottfarstein, Joseph, 178, 182, 213
Graber, David, 35
Graysdorf, Dovid, 137
Great Britain, fundraising, 73
Grenoble, French Jewish documentation, 50–54, 238n28
Grinberg, Ruven, 51, 52, 55, 56, 62, 75, 213
Gross, Jan T., 13, 85, 87, 201, 279n40
Grossmann, Atina, 14, 125, 127
Grünbaum, Efraim, 109
Grüss, Noe, 91, 92, 94, 97, 103, 112, 120, 213
Grynwald, Gesja, 108
Gustloff, Wilhelm, 40
Gypsies, Nazi genocide, 229n6

Ha'apalah (illegal immigration to Palestine), 157
hachsharot (agricultural training farms), 123
Haidamak massacre, 232n60
Halevy, Mayer, 7, 167, 173, 177, 182
Handelsman, Marceli, 31
Hannover, Nathan Nata, 19, 29, 265n162
Harrison, Earl G., 122–123, 127
Hartman, Geoffrey, 11, 12
Harvest of Hate, Poliakov, 70, 199
Ha-Yesod, Keren, 52
Haynt, 25
Hebrew Immigrant Aid Society, 73
Hebrew University, 162, 198, 278n19
Held, Adolph, 74
Hermann, Nahum, 52, 54, 213
Hersch, Liebmann, 73
Hertz, Henri, 7, 52, 54, 55, 60, 62, 69, 168, 176, 214
Herz, Fred, 167, 175, 178
Herzberg, Abel, 42
HICEM, Jewish emigration society, 55, 238n41
High Commission for the Investigation of German Crimes in Poland (Glowna Komisja Badania Zbrodni Niemieckich w Polsce), 104, 112, 235n124
Hilberg, Raul, 12, 199–201, 236n127, 279n30
Hillgruber, Andreas, 197
Hirschler, René, 51, 54, 213–214
Hirsz, Pola, 108
historical commissions
  British Zone of Germany, 147–149
  commission leaders, 249n43
  differences, 187–191
  documentation initiatives, 186–190
  generalizing and individualizing comparisons, 228n57
  historians addressing, in DP camps, 260n55
  history, 15–17
  individuals, 227–228n52
  Italy, 156–158
  transnational perspective, 228n56
  workers, 224–225n15

Historical Ethnographic Society, 26
historical research, Poland, 117–119
historical scholarship, documentation, 8–9
Historical Society of Israel, 162
historiography
  classical, 72
  contemporary, 173
  Holocaust, 170
  Holocaust, publication in France, 66–71
  Jewish Holocaust documentation, 10–15
  Jewish scholarship and, in Germany, 40, 41
  Polish Jewish, 31–32
  postwar French, 243n163
  surviving remnant, 13
  trauma, 19
  victim-focused Holocaust, 9–10
Historiska Kommissionen, 165
History and Memory, 11
history writing, Holocaust research among survivors, 104–110
Hitler, Adolf, 36, 151, 267n222
Hitlerism, 129, 192
Höss, Rudolf, 114
Hochberg-Mariańska, Maria, 103, 214
Holocaust, 3
  comparing Amalekites' smiting Jewish people, 144
  CŻKH, 188
  disunity in documentation, 174–177
  documentation in immediate aftermath, 36–43, 191–193
  documentation initiatives, 4, 8–10, 186–190, 204–206
  European conference of, documentation, 163–165
  French and English words, 223n2
  French Jewry, 46–50
  from Amalek to Land of Israel, 146–147
  historiographical documentation, 10–15
  myth of silence, 191–193
  research methodology, 169–173
  survivor documentarians' journey, 193–202
  survivor historians researching, 94–98
  suspension of collaboration, 179–184
  Yiddish terms for, 223n2
The Holocaust and the Historians, Dawidowicz, 13, 196, 226n38
Holocaust Historiography in Context, 14
The Holocaust in History, Marrus, 12
Holocaust Martyrs' and Heroes' Remembrance Authority, see also Yad Vashem, 16, 81, 147
Holocaust memory
  Friedman, 94–95
  Rost, 95
Holocaust research, 226n37
  Europe or Palestine as center, 160–162
  promotion among survivors in and outside Poland, 104–110
  purpose, 174–177
  questionnaires, 96–98
  survivor historians and, 94–98
  survivor legacy, 202–206
Home Army, Poland, 85
honte refoulée, repressed shame, 57
Horowic, Cwi, 148–149, 214
Hosiasson, Philippe, 55, 69, 182, 214
humiliation markings, 89

Institute for Contemporary History (Institut für Zeitgeschichte), 196
Institute for Jewish Affairs, 161
Institute for Jewish Studies in Warsaw, 31
International Committee for Jewish Concentration Camp Inmates and Refugees in Transit (Internationales Komitee für durchreisende jüdische KZler und Flüchtlinge), 127
International Military Tribunal (IMT), Nuremberg, 3, 44, 64, 138, 176, 192, 199–200
interviews. *See also* questionnaires; testimonies
  instructions for, 98, 133
  quality of testimonies, 98
  twenty-question survey, 157
Israeli parliament, 16
Italy
  anti-Semitism, 125–126
  British Zone of DPs in, 121, 123
  differences among commissions, 188–189
  Italian Jews, 269n259
  Jewish Displaced Persons (DP) population, 123, 124
  Jewish historical commissions in, 156–158
  Jewish population, 259n25, 259n26
  political and social conditions, 124

Jarblum, Laura Margolis, 77
Jarblum, Marc, 56
Jasinski, Tadek, 150
Jasny, Abraham Wolf, 114
Jerusalem, future Holocaust research, 146–147
Jewish Affairs, Eichmann, 59
Jewish Agency for Palestine, 7, 123, 127, 129, 146, 150, 162, 166, 168, 265
Jewish Brigade, 123
Jewish cataclysm, history of Poland, 93
Jewish Central Committee, 145
Jewish Central Information Office (JCIO), 6, 40–41, 165, 168
Jewish Colonization Association, 73
Jewish Committee for the Relief of War Victims, 26
Jewish Cultural Reconstruction Inc., 195
Jewish cultural treasures
  documents for Nuremberg, 69–70
  in questionnaires, 96, 134
  preserving culture, 25
  TsHK's collection, 139

Index

Jewish Documentation Action, 7
Jewish Ethnographic Historical Society, 25
Jewish experience, Jewish Voice in Polish chorus, 110–116
Jewish Historical Commission (Jüdische Kommission), 150
Jewish Historical Documentation (Jüdische Historische Dokumentation, JHD), 6, 150, 153, 165
Jewish Historical Ethnographic Society, 26
Jewish Historical Institute (Żydowski Instytut Historyczny, ŻIH), 5, 101–102, 118, 119, 203
Jewish National Council, 27, 29
Jewish nationalism, ideology, 21
Jewish News, 41
Jewish Press Agency, 91
Jewish property, Aryanization, 135, 138, 163, 167
Jewish resistance, 182–184, 198
   France, 61–62, 176, 189
   Poland, 111–112, 177
Jewish Scientific Institute of Sofia, 7, 166
Jewish Social Studies, 195
Jewish state in Palestine, 122, 126, 127, 146, 189, 197, 257n214
Jewish suffering
   Poland, 110–116
   specificity, 115
The Jews in Algeria, Ansky, 70
Jews in Combat: Testimony on the Activity of a Resistance Movement, Lazarus, 68–69
Jews of Galicia, 155
Judt, Tony, 13, 49, 192, 277n3, 277n4

Kaczerginski, Shmerke, 139
Kagan, Chaim, 129
Kaganovitch, Moshe, 156, 158, 214, 270n266
Kahan, Anne, 25, 231n38
Kahn, Gaston, 55, 60, 75, 178, 214–215, 241n97
Kaplan, Israel, 7, 128–129, 133, 134, 146–147, 162, 188
   biography, 215, 263n135
   testimonies, 136–140, 262n107
Kaplan, Jacob, 77
Kaplan, Marion, 201
Kassow, Samuel, 31
Katzki, Herbert, 77
Kenan, Orna, 14
Kermisz, Joseph, 5, 8, 31, 37, 91, 92, 100, 103, 109, 113, 114, 116, 117–118, 120, 168, 177, 182, 183, 194, 197–198, 215
khurbn (destruction), 3, 74, 111, 172, 173, 187, 223n2
khurbn-forshers, 171, 173
khurbn-forshung
   destruction research, 19–33, 82, 95, 120, 169–173, 187
   focus, 37–40
   indifference, 146

non-Jewish initiatives, 228–229n6
practices of, 43
survivor historians researching Holocaust, 94–98
Kishinev pogrom, 19–23
Klimoff, Isaïe, 168
Knesset, 16
Knochen, Helmut, 63
Knout, David, 55, 58, 60–62, 67, 68, 176, 215
Kowarsky, Alexandre, 60
Krakow University, 91
Kristallnacht, 41, 149
Kristel, Conny, 42
Kugelmass, Jack, 4, 224n6
Kurland, Léon, 168
Kurowski, Stefan, 112
Kvintman, Yitskhok, 156, 157

LaCapra, Dominick, 11, 225n16
Lagrou, Pieter, 13
Lambert, Raymond-Raoul, 51, 54, 216
Lamentations, 19
Lamm, Hans, 42
Landsberger Lager Cajtung, 142
landsmanshaftn, 110, 140, 162, 198
Langer, Lawrence L., 10
language, disunity at conference, 174–175
Lattès, Samy, 54, 164
Laval, Pierre, 48
Lazarus, Jacques, 68–69
League of Nations, 53
Lebensraum, 114, 116
Left Poale Zion, 31
Leftwich, Joseph, 73
Lehman, Herbert, 78
Leibowitz, Joseph, 129
Le Monde Juif, 68
Leo Baeck Institute (LBI), 41, 235n115
Les Juifs en Europe (1939–1945), 182
Lesser Incrimination Amnesty, 154
Lestschinsky, Jacob, 32
Levitas, Mina, 130
Lévy, Edmond-Maurice, 168
lexicographic bibliography, 173
Lichtman, Ada, 89, 216
Life Between Memory and Hope, Mankowitz, 14
literature of destruction, 19
Livian, Marcel, 7, 55, 58, 61, 62, 71, 164, 176, 177, 179–180, 182, 216
Lodz, archives of destruction, 99–102
Lodz Jewish council, 99–102
Lubavitch Hasidic dynasty, 50
Lubetzki, Joseph, 178
Lublin, Central Jewish Historical Commission, 89–94
Lublin, Poland, liberation by Soviet Army, 84–86
Lvov, destruction of Jews, 103

Machover, John, 73
Mahler, Raphael, 31
Mandatory Palestine, 124
Mankowitz, Zeev, 14
mantel of silence, 151
Marrus, Michael R., 12
medical experiments, 96, 133
Mein Kampf, 116
Meiss, Léon, 7, 51, 52, 55, 56, 71, 176, 178, 182, 216
memorials
   antimemorial agitation, 246n224
   Eretz Yisrael for Holocaust, 162
   Holocaust, in France, 74–81
   memory books, 274n84
   use of ashes from death camps, 245n205
Mersik, Tsvi, 101
Meyer, René, 166
Michel, Henri, 56
Michman, Dan, 14, 198, 227n42
Milbauer, Joseph, 54, 216
Milner, Joseph, 55, 56, 58, 61, 216–217
Minkowski, Eugène, 168
Miron, Guy, 41
missing gravestone syndrome, 4–5, 224n6
Moch, Jules, 166
Modrzew, Franciszka, 93
Moissis, Asher, 6, 167
Monneray, Henri, 69, 176, 181, 217, 242n126
Morgenthau, Henry, Jr., 78
Motzkin, Leo, 23–24, 30, 37
Murer, Franz, 153–154, 268n238–239
Muselman, 103
myth of silence, postwar Jewish Holocaust, 14, 191–192, 227n44

National Center for Scientific Research (CNRS), 78
National Council for the Homeland, Poland, 85
National Socialism, 40
Nazi genocide, Gypsies, 229n6
Nazi Germany
   Final Solution, 9, 18, 48
   genocidal scheme, 9
   Poland as extermination site, 84
Nazi ghetto administration, Lodz, 99–102
Nazi Party, responsibility, 135
The Nazis at War, 41
Neighbors, Gross, 201
Netherlands, Dutch Jewish Holocaust, 42
Netherlands Institute for War Documentation (NIOD), 42, 194
Neumann, Franz, 199
Nîmes Committee, 60
Nomberg, Hersh Dovid, 29
Nuremberg
   Nuremberg Military Tribunal, 7, 45, 64, 175
   documentation of Jewish cultural treasures, 69–70
   International Military Tribunal (IMT), 3, 44, 138, 176, 192, 199–200
   postwar justice, 106, 278n28
   trials, 153–154, 190
   U.S. Military Tribunal, 166, 167

Olewski, Rafael, 147, 217
On the History of Interment Camps in Anti-France, Weill, 68
oral sources, collection, 21–22
Organisation–Reconstruction–Travail (ORT), 55, 56, 63, 238n41
Organization of Jewish Refugees in Italy (Irgun ha-Plitim be-Italia), 127
ORT. *See* Organisation–Reconstruction–Travail (ORT)
OSE. *See* Children's Relief Agency
Ottoman Empire, Armenians, 229n6
Oyneg Shabes (joy of Sabbath), 34–36, 37, 38, 91, 95

Pacanowski, Zelig, 108
Pakhakh movement, Poland, 156–157, 270n266
Pakhakh's Central Historical Commission (Tsentrale Historishe Komisye bay Pakhakh), 156
Pale of Settlement, 22, 25
Palestine
   entry visas to, 122
   Holocaust research, 160–162
   illegal immigration to Mandatory, 124
   Jewish state, 122, 126, 127, 146, 159, 189, 197, 257n214
Paraf, Pierre, 55, 217
Paris. *See also* France
   European conference December 1947, 165–168
   European Jewish documentation center, 177–179
   Jewish memorial, 75–76, 79, 80
partizaner almanakh, 157
Passover Haggadah, 144
Pétain, Marshal Philippe, 47
Peretz, Isaac Leib, 25
persecution, Jewish responses, 96
The Persecution of the Jews in France and other Western Countries as presented by France at Nuremberg, Monneray, 69
The Persecution of the Jews in the Countries of the East as Presented at Nuremberg, Monneray, 69
personal recollections, 21–22, 27–28
photographs
   documentation, 20, 28, 204
   German occupation, 101
   Jewish life and death, 139
   photo album for Jews abroad, 104, 254n138
Piernikarz, Arthur, 150, 153
Pinson, Koppel S., 37, 128
pogroms, 18, 144
   Central Relief Committee for Pogrom Victims, 232n54

Index

Chmielnicki, 19
documentation initiatives, 27
Kielce, 161
Kishinev, 19–23
Poland
  archives of destruction in Lodz, 99–102
  Central Jewish Historical Commission (CŻKH), 89–94
  collective writing of history, 104–110
  cost of looting, 85
  differences among commissions, 188–189
  documentation activity, 204–205
  estimate of deaths, 247n6
  extermination site, 84
  historical research and political agendas, 117–119
  historiography of Polish Jews, 31–32
  Jewish history writing in postwar, 248n28
  journalist's report, 106–107
  liberation by Soviet Army, 84–86, 247n14
  Pakhakh movement, 156–157
  Polish Jewish historical commission, 88–89
  postwar government, 86–88
  publication activity of CZKH, 102–104
  publications, 253n123
  quest for Jewish voice, 110–116
  survivor historians researching Holocaust, 94–98
  testimonies of citizens, 44
Poliakov, Léon, 7, 12, 63–65, 69, 70, 169–171, 173, 174, 188, 194, 196, 199, 200, 217, 239n57
Polish Committee of National Liberation (Polski Komitet Wyzwolenia Narodnego, PKWN), 85–86, 87
Polish Communist Party, 85
Polish Jews, 174, 189
Polish Ministry of Public Security in Danzig, 150
Polish Mission in Augsburg, 138
Polish National Library in Warsaw, 100
Polish Peasant Party, 86, 117
Polish Supreme National Tribunal (Najwyższy Trybunał Narodowy, NTN), 112–113
Polish United Workers' Party (Polska Zjednoczona Partia Robotnicza, PZPR), 118
Polish Worker's Party (PPR), 85, 117
political agendas, Poland, 117–119
politicalization, Jewish Displaced Persons (DPs), 127–128
Polonski, Jacques, 61, 68, 240n89
Polski Komitet Wyzwolenia Narodowego (PKWN). *See* Polish Committee of National Liberation (PKWN)
Posters, Central Historical Commission, 143, 145
postwar
  Jewish Holocaust documentation, 191–193
  justice at Nuremberg trials, 106, 278n28
  reconstruction, 13

Postwar, Judt, 13, 277n3
Potsdam Conference, 257n210
Poznanski, Renée, 14, 49, 201, 239–240n64, 279n37
Prager, Moshe Mark, 146, 161
Pregel, Boris, 72
Press, Propaganda, and Public Opinion in Occupied France, Polonski, 68
Presser, Jacques de, 42
Prince Jean of Luxembourg, 78
Princess Wilhelmina of Holland, 78
printed matter, occupation period, 101
Professional Retraining and Reorientation Organization. *See* Organisation-Reconstruction-Travail (ORT)
protection
  documentation, 28–29
  western European Jews before Nazis, 39–40
Provisional Central Committee of Polish Jews, 86
psychosis of publicity, 170
publication
  Central Jewish Historical Commission (CŻKH), 102–104
  Holocaust historiography in France, 66–71
  Yiddish, 253n123
Pucyz, Marian, 129

Quaker American Friends Service Committee, 60
Queen Elisabeth of Belgium, 78
questionnaires
  Central Historical Commission (TsHK), 133–137
  Holocaust research, 96–98
  Lestschinsky, 251n76
  report on armed German men, 262n100
  zamlers, 108–109

Rabinovitch, Jacques, 59
racist ideology, 229n6
Rajak, Michal, 115
Rapaport, Nathan, 88
Rapoport, Shloyme Zaynvl, 25
Ratner, Jacques, 55, 56–59
Ratner, Yitzkhok, 129
Résistance, French, 56, 61–62, 176, 189, 239n64, 241n113
Rechtsstaat (state of laws), 39–40
Red Army, 99
relief work, Jewish war victims, 26
Representations, 11
Ringelblum, Emanuel, 31, 32, 34, 35, 37, 38, 90, 91, 95, 99, 171, 234n96, 252n112
Robinson, Jacob, 195
Roosevelt, Eleanor, 78
Rosen, Alan, 14
Rosenberg, Alfred, 63
Rosental, Dovid, 147, 217–218
Roskies, David, 19

Rost, Nella, 5, 91, 92, 95, 103, 104, 120, 168, 182, 218
Roth, Cecil, 78
Rothschild, Guy de, 78
Rousso, Henry, 13, 49
Rozenberg, Abraham, 116
Rumkowski archive, 252n114
Russian Empire
  anti-Jewish violence, 24–25
  pogrom in Kishinev, 19–23
Russian Jewish Historical Society, 21
Russian Revolution, 27, 231n34

Sabile, Jacques, 69
Safran, Alexandre, 72
Schah, Eugène, 55
Schah, Wladimir, 55, 56, 218
Schechtman, Joseph, 29
Scheid-Haas, Lucienne, 59
Schildkret, Lucy, 13, 139
Schiper, Ignacy, 31, 33
Schneersohn, Isaac, 4, 7, 50–54, 146
  biography, 218
  CDJC, 54–56, 58, 66, 70, 72, 74
  European conference, 161, 163–164, 174, 177–178, 179, 182–183
  Holocaust memorial, 74–78, 80, 81
  Jewish resistance, 62, 63
  "The Passover of Liberation," 67
Schneour, Zalman, 74
Scholarly Committee, 182, 276n164, 276n168
Schorr, Moses, 31
Schrager, Fayvel, 176
Schuman, Robert, 78, 166
Schwartz, Isaïe, 75, 78, 167
Schwartzbard, Sholem, 30
Second World War, 33–36, 43, 176, 192–193, 194
Sefer Kishiniov, 23
Seraphim, Hans-Guenther, 196
Sforim, Mendele Moykher, 19
Shabad, Zemach, 26
Shalit, Moyshe, 26, 27
Shapiro, Judah J., 77
She'erit Hapletah, 13, 15, 16, 37, 38, 126, 130–132, 137, 141, 147–148, 162, 194, 204
Shoah, 223n2
Shoah Visual History Foundation, 10, 12
Shtif, Nokhem, 28, 32
Shuldenreyn, P., 144
Shvarts, Pinkhes, 143
silence, 191–193, 227n44
Silkes, Genia, 97, 120, 218–219
Sobol-Masłowska, Rita, 93
Social and Cultural Association of Jews in Poland (Towarzystwo Społeczno-Kulturalne Zydów w Polsce, TSKŻ), 118
Social Democrats, 136
Society for Jewish Studies in Romania, 166

Society for the Promotion of Culture among the Jews of Russia (OPE), 22–23
Society for the Study of Romanian Jewry, 7
Society of Jewish Historical Studies, 7
Sonderkommando, Auschwitz-Birkenau, 33
Soviet Army, liberation of Lublin, 84–86, 247n14
Soviet Union, 257n214, 258n7
Spielberg, Steven, 11
Spire, André, 62
State Institute for War Documentation, 42
Statut des Juifs, Vichy regime, 47–48
Storey, Robert, 45
Stroop, Jürgen, 69
Stroop Report, 69
substitute gravestones, term, 4–5, 224n6
suffering
  gathering evidence of, 24–25
  impetus for recording Jewish, 30–31
  Jews in France, 56–63
  specificity of Jewish, 115
Sundquist, Eric, 14
surviving remnant, historiography, 13
survivors, 223n1
  activists' frustration with apathy of, 152–153
  Aryan papers, 104, 108
  children, 251n92
  collective history writing, 104–110
  committing to document their past, 141–145
  documentation by female, 92, 130, 250n50, 261n66
  documentation initiatives, 8–10
  duty to dead and generations to come, 130–132, 142–143, 186
  historical commissions and documentation, 186–190
  historical recognition, 193–202
  humiliation markings, 89
  Jewish history writing in postwar Poland, 248n28
  liberated France, 48–49
  marginalization, 191
  memory and history, 186–187
  myth of silence, 191–193, 227n44
  objectivity of researchers, 171–172
  questionnaires for, 133–137
  recording atrocities, 33–34
  researching Holocaust, 94–98
  testimonies, 104–106, 139–140
  timidity complex, 141
Suschny, Otto, 155
Swedish Wars, Poland, 101
Syngalowski, Aron, 51, 73, 219
Szeftel, Jacques, 55, 56, 61, 75, 219
Szeftel, Leon, 114, 116, 219
Szpecht, Mieczysław, 89

Tabachowicz, Neche, 150, 208
Taylor, Telford, 64, 70, 167

Index

Tcherikower, Elias, 27–30, 32, 37
Tcherikower, Rivka, 28
Tennenbaum, Mordechai, 101
testimonies
   Anders Collection in Hoover Institution Archives, 235n123
   artifacts, 203–204
   Bartov's use of, 201–202
   commissions in Linz and Vienna, 154
   common terms, 226n29
   Farn Folk, 157, 158
   Fun Letstn Khurbn, 139–140
   Hilberg, 225–226n29
   historical commission recording, 134
   history, memory and trauma, 225n25
   Holocaust research, 198–200
   Kaplan's, 262n107
   quality, 98
   questionnaires, 133–137
   Romania and Austria, 270n266
   survivor, 104–106
Theresienstadt 1941–1945, Adler, 42
Third Reich, 3, 18, 41, 197, 198
This is Auschwitz, Friedman, 102
Todesraum (death space), 116
Tombeau du Martyr Juif Inconnu (tomb of unknown Jewish Martyr), 75, 79, 80, 185, 246n222
Torrès, Henri, 30
Toynebee, Arnold J., 194
Tracing Bureau, 236n125
transnational phenomenon, 15
Treaty of Versailles, 176
Treblinka, 6, 90, 102, 111–112, 139, 208, 211
Trepman, Paul, 147, 219
Truman, Harry S, 122–123
Trunk, Isaiah, 31, 113, 118, 120, 194, 203, 219–220
Turek, Menachem, 101
Turkish genocide, Armenians, 229n6

Ukrainian Jews, 27, 28
Ukrainian Soviet Socialist Republic, 27
Undzer Shtime, 147
Union Général des Israélites de France (UGIF), 48, 51, 53, 54, 59, 163, 240–241n95
Union of Jewish Intellectuals of France, 166
Union of Jewish Students of Austria (Verband Jüdischer Hochschüler Österreichs), 150
Union of Jewish Writers, Journalists, and Artists, 86, 250n51
United Dubienker Relief Committee, 110
United Nations Relief and Rehabilitation Administration (UNRRA), 121, 125
United Nations' Universal Declaration of Human Rights, 70
United States Holocaust Memorial Museum, 11
U.S. Military Tribunal, Nuremberg, 166, 167
U.S. War Crimes Commission, 268n240
U.S. Zone of Germany, 121, 123, 128–147
   Central Historical Commission in Munich, 128–132
   recording Jewish tragedy, 128–132

Vallat, Xavier, 48, 61, 178, 275n128
Vanikoff, Maurice, 182
Verlag, Jüdischer, 24
Vichy regime
   anti-Jewish legislation, 47–48
   anti-Semitism, 47, 49
   cooperation with, 240–241n95
   crimes, 49–50
Vichy syndrome, 49–50, 237n18
Vinaver, Maxim, 22
vision
   Holocaust research, 160–162
   lost Jewish world, 202–206
Vitale, Massimo-Adolfo, 6, 164, 175, 178
Völkischer Beobachter, 139
Vogelsang, Thilo, 197
Volkov, Shulamit, 15
Voskhod, 21
voters, 257n210

Warburg, Edward, 78
Warhaftig, Zorah, 161, 270–271n8
Warsaw ghetto, 106, 176–177, 275n139
Warsaw University, 31, 91
Wasser, Hersh, 91, 95, 99, 120, 220
Waxman, Zoë Vania, 14
Wehrmacht, responsibility, 135
Weigel, Kurt, 155
Weil, Eugène, 7
Weill, André, 52
Weill, Joseph, 68
Weinberg, David, 46, 241n104
Weinreich, Max, 32, 161
Weismann, Chaim, 78
Weliczker, Leon, 130, 220
Wellers, George, 68
Wiener, Alfred, 6, 40–41, 168, 182, 184, 194, 220
Wiener Library, 6, 40–41, 73, 203
Wiesenthal, Simon, 6, 150, 151, 153, 159, 162, 168, 175, 182, 183, 194, 220–221
Wieviorka, Annette, 10, 14, 243n163
Wischnitzer, Mark, 32
Wissenscraft des Judentums, 22, 197
Women, 130, 136, 186, 250n50, 261n66
The Wonder of Their Voices, Rosen, 14
Workers of Zion, 31
Workmen's Circle, 72, 73, 74
World Committee to Erect a Tomb for the Unknown Jewish Martyr, 78
World Documentation Center, Jerusalem, 162

World Jewish Congress, 5, 72
World Zionist Organization (WZO), 23–24
Wulf, Joseph, 6, 91, 103, 120, 183–184, 194, 196–197, 221

Yablonka, Hanna, 14
Yad Vashem, see also Holocaust Martyrs' and Heroes' Remembrance Authority, 7, 11, 12, 13, 16, 81, 147, 155, 162, 179, 197, 199, 203, 265n176, 272n35
Yale University, Fortunoff Video Archive, 10
The Yellow Star, Poliakov, 69
Yeven Metsulah, Hannover, 19
Yishuv, 127, 145, 146, 227n42
YIVO Institute for Jewish Research, 12, 16, 32, 34, 90, 95, 97, 99, 117, 249n38, 277–278n12
yizker-bukh, 140, 157
Yizker-leksikon project, 105–106
Young, James E., 224n5

Young Historians Circle (Yunger Historiker Krayz), 31, 32, 91, 95

Zachariasz, Szymon, 117
zaml-arbet (collection work), 189–190
zamlers (voluntary collectors), 26, 33, 37, 90, 97–98, 102, 104, 108, 109, 133, 136–137
Zeitschel, Carl-Theodor, 63
Zilberfarb, Moyshe, 27
Zionism
    Displaced Persons (DPs), 260n50
    motivation for documentation, 159
    utopia and political agenda, 127
Zionist Federation of Great Britain and Ireland, 73
Zionist Relief Fund, 24
Zionist resistance, France, 61–62
Zonabend, Nachman, 100
Zuckerman, Baruch, 29
Żydokomuna (Judeobolshevism), 87, 120

www.ingramcontent.com/pod-product-compliance
Ingram Content Group UK Ltd.
Pitfield, Milton Keynes, MK11 3LW, UK
UKHW022241230426
12048UKWH00018BA/1404